1,001
Komputer
Answers

FROM KIM KOMANDO

Here's what Kim Komando's fans have to say...

Novices and power users alike have learned something from Kim Komando's "Komputer Klinic" on America Online. Kim uses simple language and everyday metaphors to help you navigate the often murky waters of the computing world. Her clear and entertaining explanations are a soothing balm for those nagging, irritating terms that flare up again and again like a bad skin condition. Kim and her staff also sift through shareware and demo files — so you don't have to — and offer the best in the Komando area on AOL.

— Julia Wilkinson
Manager,
Media Production
America Online, Inc.

Dear Kim!

I enjoy your terrific radio show, reading your weekly newspaper column, and keeping up-to-date on your menu on America Online, and just about everything you touch seems to be exactly what I need! I ordered your training tapes and I am really looking forward to them! Another one of your loyal fans!

— Tony Monte

Kim,

Can't believe your system really works! I'll be looking forward to hearing abut any more tapes you do in the future. Thanks for making a program that really does what it advertises. It's a rarity these days.

— Pam DeKoeyer

Hi Kim,

It's not often I write someone who sells a product I like; normally I write only to complain. Gotta tell you, you present yourself so professionally and knowledgeably in your tapes. I'm a doctor and learned a lot from your "bedside manner." I didn't tell anyone in my office I bought your tapes until after I watched them; then I went into my office and said, "How come we don't have our patients in a database program?" You should have seen the look on their faces, Kim! I set your tapes up in our waiting room so the patients can watch them, too! Keep up the great work, Kim! You should be proud of yourself!

— Dr. Berger

Kim,

I love your tapes and I've tried others, but yours are the best! Thanks for making computers easy to understand.

— Matt

Kim,

You offer an invaluable service, and I'm sure I speak for others when I say thanks. It's nice to have a computer wizard who can translate the arcane patois of the PC world into plain English.

— Minister B.

Your advice always hits the spot, and I will continue to seek it. Thanks again for past and future help.

— James S. Kaplan

Kimmie K,

I tape your radio show every week and listen to it again while I'm driving. I'm a truck driver and use a notebook computer. I have learned so much from you and really like the way you don't talk down to anyone.

— Larry

Thanks again for your very timely and helpful advice regarding a frustrating "challenge." I enjoy paging through your area on AOL and wish you good luck in the future.

— Randy Buckwalter

I greatly appreciate the assistance Kim Komando has given me with my computer questions. When I get hung up on a hardware or software problem, Kim has been a gold mine of assistance. Her answers are direct, concise, understandable, and often with a twist of humor. Her approach is a welcome relief from the cryptic "techno-jargon" so prevalent in the computer industry.

Kim Komando has saved me hours of wading through dry technical manuals and has gotten me back on track quickly.

— Jack Drake

I asked a question of Komando via e-mail about upgrading my computer. Her answer was prompt and accurate. Komando saved me money and grief by cautioning me that the expensive add-on I was thinking of buying would not have worked with my setup.

— Len Saari

Thanks to your help, I am much more confident that I can learn to handle whatever comes along and much less hesitant to tackle new challenges. In other words, you have taken the fear out of learning computers!

While most "computer experts" try to impress you with how much they know (usually leaving us novices hopelessly buried in technical jargon), you actually take the time to explain things in terms even the beginner can understand. It is a great feeling to know there really is someone to turn to for good advice and real answers.

— Frank Baxter

I would like to commend you not only on your vast knowledge of computers, software, and procedures; but also on your excellent ability to communicate complex topics and procedures in a way that novices can comprehend and follow.

Talking with someone through the operation of a computer is very similar to an air controller talking a novice pilot through his or her first solo landing of a Boeing 747, and *you've prevented many a crash landing!* Many thanks.

— Jim Maas

A voice from cyberspace that really cares. Kim responded to my questions immediately, simply, and most important, effectively. Understandable answers in ordinary non-computer language. It's almost a pleasure to have trouble when you know Kim is there to help.

— Richard Goldwater

1,001
Komputer
Answers

FROM KIM KOMANDO

---

by Kim Komando

**Foreword
by Sarah Purcell**

IDG
BOOKS

IDG Books Worldwide, Inc.
An International Data Group Company

Foster City, CA ◆ Chicago, IL ◆ Indianapolis, IN ◆ Braintree, MA ◆ Dallas, TX

1,001 Komputer Answers from Kim Komando

Published by
IDG Books Worldwide, Inc.
An International Data Group Company
919 E. Hillsdale Blvd.
Suite 400
Foster City, CA 94404

Library of Congress Catalog Card No.: 94-73285

ISBN: 1-56884-460-3

Printed in the United States of America

10 9 8 7 6 5 4 3 2 1

1D/SX/QS/ZV

Distributed in the United States by IDG Books Worldwide, Inc.

Distributed by Macmillan Canada for Canada; by Computer and Technical Books for the Caribbean Basin; by Contemporantea de Ediciones for Venezuela; by Distribuidora Cuspide for Argentina; by CITFC for Brazil; by Ediciones ZETA S.C.R. Ltda. for Peru; by Editorial Limusa SA for Mexico; by Transworld Publishers Limited in the United Kingdom and Europe; by Al-Maiman Publishers & Distributors for Suadi Arabia; by Simron Pty. Ltd. for South Africa; by IDC Communications (IIK) Ltd. for Hong Kong; by Toppan Company Ltd. for Japan; by Addison Wesley Publishing Company for Korea; by Longman Singapore Publisher Ltd. for Singapore, Malaysia, Thailand and Indonesia; by Unalis Corporation for Taiwan; by WS Computer Publishing Company, Inc. for the Philippines; by WoodsLane Enterprises Ltd. for New Zealand.

For general information on IDG Books in the U.S., including information on discounts and premiums, contact IDG Books at 800-434-3422 or 415-655-3000.

For information on where to purchase IDG Books outside the U.S., contact IDG Books International at 415-655-3021 or fax 415-655-3295.

For information on translations, contact Marc Jeffrey Mikulich, Director, Foreign & Subsidiary Rights, at IDG Books Worldwide, 415-655-3018 or fax 415-655-3295.

For sales inquiries and special prices for bulk quantities, write to the address above or call IDG Books Worldwide at 415-655-3000.

For information on using IDG Books in the classroom, or for ordering examination copies, contact Jim Kelly at 800-434-2086.

 is a registered trademark of International Data Group

About the Author

Kim Komando

Kim Komando sat down in front of a computer for the first time at age 9. She hasn't taken much time off since.

Kim is President and CEO of The Komando Corporation, a company devoted to making technology easier to understand. Kim also hosts the Komputer Klinic forum on America Online, where she regularly solves the computer-related problems put to her by many of AOL's 1.5 million subscribers. In addition, she routinely hosts a talk radio show, Fox television computer segments, and airline in-flight video programs.

Called "a one-person industry" by *Information Week*, Kim has written an all-purpose business communications book, *401 Great Letters*. She also has developed and marketed several software programs, including 401 Great Letters, 101 Great Sales Letters, 101 Great Professional Letters, 101 Great Complaint Letters, and 101 Great Love Letters. Kim is into numbers, obviously, and resides in sunny Scottsdale, Arizona, home of The Komando Corporation.

Welcome to the world of IDG Books Worldwide.

IDG Books Worldwide, Inc., is a subsidiary of International Data Group, the world's largest publisher of computer-related information and the leading global provider of information services on information technology. IDG was founded more than 25 years ago and now employs more than 7,200 people worldwide. IDG publishes more than 233 computer publications in 65 countries (see listing below). More than sixty million people read one or more IDG publications each month.

Launched in 1990, IDG Books Worldwide is today the #1 publisher of best-selling computer books in the United States. We are proud to have received 3 awards from the Computer Press Association in recognition of editorial excellence, and our best-selling *...For Dummies*™ series has more than 12 million copies in print with translations in 25 languages. IDG Books, through a recent joint venture with IDG's Hi-Tech Beijing, became the first U.S. publisher to publish a computer book in the People's Republic of China. In record time, IDG Books has become the first choice for millions of readers around the world who want to learn how to better manage their businesses.

Our mission is simple: Every IDG book is designed to bring extra value and skill-building instructions to the reader. Our books are written by experts who understand and care about our readers. The knowledge base of our editorial staff comes from years of experience in publishing, education, and journalism — experience which we use to produce books for the '90s. In short, we care about books, so we attract the best people. We devote special attention to details such as audience, interior design, use of icons, and illustrations. And because we use an efficient process of authoring, editing, and desktop publishing our books electronically, we can spend more time ensuring superior content and spend less time on the technicalities of making books.

You can count on our commitment to deliver high-quality books at competitive prices on topics consumers want to read about. At IDG, we value quality, and we have been delivering quality for more than 25 years. You'll find no better book on a subject than an IDG book.

John Kilcullen
President and CEO
IDG Books Worldwide, Inc.

Dedication

To my mother, Virginia, and my late father, Richard, whose answers to my questions made me all that I am.

Acknowledgments

For this book, I waded through piles of letters and miles of America Online messages from frustrated computer users so that I could pick the most commonly asked questions. (Whew, what a challenge: I sometimes receive thousands of questions in a single day.) This book would not have been possible without you, the everyday folks who don't want to earn an engineering degree to use their personal computers. I thank every person who has trusted me with their problems.

I would be remiss if I didn't acknowledge America Online for giving my corporation a chance and allowing us to be part of a progressive service. America Online's staff proved instrumental in making the Komputer Klinic a happening place.

I also want to thank my brother, Rich, for handling the company's business affairs while I was chained to my computer; Bruce Boyle for understanding that programming is an art; Michelle Frenkel for shielding me from interruptions; Carolyn Heineken for working long hours; Dino Landis for making me laugh; Ray Moore for helping me pull everything together; and Barry Young for pointing the way back toward sanity.

And then, of course, there is my mother, who convinced members of my staff to take, word for word, her telephone messages that said, "I love you. Eat, you're too skinny. You don't have to call me back. I have nothing to say, really."

I also want to thank David Solomon, Karen Bluestein, Erik Dafforn, Melissa Duffy, Shawn MacLaren, Beth Slick, and the others at IDG; their assistance was invaluable. I guess IDGers are into pain: they are already talking about the next book.

Keep those questions coming,

Kim Komando

Scottsdale, Arizona

(The Publisher would like to give special thanks to Patrick J. McGovern, without whom this book would not have been possible.)

Credits

Publisher
Karen Bluestein

Acquisitions Manager
Gregory Croy

Brand Manager
Melisa M. Duffy

Editorial Director
Mary Bednarek

Editorial Managers
Mary C. Corder
Andy Cummings

**Editorial
Executive Assistant**
Jodi Lynn Semling-Thorn

Editorial Assistant
Nate Holdread

Production Director
Beth Jenkins

**Supervisor of
Project Coordination**
Cindy L. Phipps

Project Coordinator
Valery Bourke

Pre-Press Coordinators
Steve Peake
Tony Augsburger

Project Editor
Erik Dafforn

Editors
Shawn MacLaren
Patricia Seiler
Susan Christophersen
Pat O'Brien
N. Jeannie Smith

Technical Reviewer
Beth Slick

Production Staff
Paul Belcastro
J. Tyler Connor
Drew Moore
Dwight Ramsey
Patricia R. Reynolds
Theresa Sánchez-Baker

Proofreaders
Betty Kish
Charles A. Hutchinson

Indexer
Sharon Hilgenberg

Cover Design
Kavish+Kavish

Cover Photo
Don Giannatti

Contents at a Glance

Table of Contents

Chapter 3:

Buying a Computer 71

Table of Contents

Chapter 6:

Chapter 7:

Desktop Publishing 241

Chapter 8:

DOS 279

Table of Contents

Chapter 10:

Graphics 375

Chapter 11:

Hardware 407

Chapter 12:

The Internet 473

Table of Contents

Chapter 13:

Macs and PCs — Working Together to Build a Better World 505

Chapter 14:

Music and Sound 525

Chapter 15:

OS/2 559

Chapter 16:

Printers 583

Basics 583

Chapter 17:

Shareware and Other On-line Stuff 607

Chapter 20:

Windows 719

Foreword

These days, most people can play a compact disc in their stereo and pick a political candidate with little trouble. But when it comes to home computers — with their RAM and ROM, hard drives and floppies, SVGA and MHz — we're all lost.

We have a computer in our home, and I always hoped for a computer-savvy friend — other than my 6-year-old son Colin — who could answer my questions, fix my problems, and not confuse me with "computer nerd talk." Let me tell you, it's an awkward position to be in when your kids know more than you!

I had seen Kim Komando on television (who hasn't?) but did not actually meet her until I was hosting ABC's "Home Show" when she was a guest. I was amazed at Kim's ability to translate all the techno-jargon into everyday words that made sense. So was the audience.

Kim and I struck a lasting friendship. I have to confess, however, that even though I often called her "just to chat," along the way I would just happen to work in a computer question, or two, or maybe even three. She always gave me an answer that suddenly made perfect sense of the entire situation. Kim cuts to the bottom line so you don't have to read those confusing computer manuals or waste your time trying to figure out how to fix a problem.

This book is just like having Kim's personal telephone number and her knowledge to help you any time you need her! At last, the answers we all need — without all the "computerese" — are within reach.

And here's something you won't find anywhere else in this book. It's my thanks to her — not just for answers to my questions. Kim's help has gone far beyond getting a mouse to work and making Windows appear on-screen. Kim has also shared her knowledge with a wonderful organization that is dear to me, The Big Sisters of Los Angeles. Kim took the time to research and select their new office computer system and she arranged for more than $40,000 in computer hardware to be donated by Hewlett-Packard!

And so I give her my thanks for all her personal help when I was stuck with a rebellious computer, and for helping The Big Sisters of Los Angeles, who owe our increased efficiency and productivity to her. Thank you, Kim!

Now, for those of you (like me) who are in eternal need of computer help, start turning those pages! Help is here.

Sarah Purcell

Los Angeles, California

February 1995

Introduction Q&A

Problems with computers are as inevitable as death and taxes. Heck, even I run into one from time to time. For this book, I culled the questions asked most often

> ➤ On my Komputer Klinic on America Online
> ➤ Through standard mail
> ➤ Through e-mail (via the Internet, CompuServe, or Prodigy)
> ➤ By callers to my talk radio show
> ➤ By readers of my syndicated computer column
> ➤ By people who have seen my weekly appearances on the Phoenix Fox television affiliate (KSAZ, Channel 10) and major airline in-flight video programming

The book is organized by subjects. Each chapter contains questions and answers about a particular area of computing. Some answers define nagging techno-mumbo-jumbo computer terms. Many of the answers, however, help solve a specific problem.

Oftentimes, it's difficult to diagnose the source of a problem. Say that you are not hearing sounds in Windows. Is the sound card malfunctioning? Is Windows doing something to cause the silence? Or has someone turned off the sounds because a colleague was tired of hearing the "Star Trek" theme each time you turned on your computer?

When you're trying to figure out the source of a problem that just appears seemingly out of nowhere, the first question to ask is, "What has changed since the problem appeared?" The answer will point you in the right direction. The second question is, "Can you help me, Kim?"

The first rule of computing: Always keep a backup of the most important information on your computer, including your AUTOEXEC.BAT and CONFIG.SYS files. If you use Windows, you also should back up all files with the .INI and .GRP file extensions.

The second rule: You should keep an emergency start-up disk within reach, because this disk often will let you get to the information on your hard disk when the computer appears to deny you such access.

Third: Any time you pop open the computer's case, practice safe computing: ground yourself and turn off all power going to the unit.

Don't worry. I cover all these points elsewhere in the book.

In the back of the book is an index. Refer to it if you need help finding an answer. Appendix A, meanwhile, contains sales and technical support telephone numbers for the most popular computer companies. And Appendix B details how to set up the CD-ROM version of this book *and* how to get a month's free trial to America Online (home of the Komputer Klinic).

By the way, once you set up the CD-ROM that's enclosed with this book, you can search easily and quickly through all of the book's questions and answers. In other words, you are in for a good time if you own a CD-ROM drive — assuming, of course, that your question isn't, "Why doesn't my CD-ROM drive work?"

Top Ten Things to Remember While Using This Book

10. "$E = MC^2$," said Albert Einstein. "$E = PC^2$," says Kim Komando.

9. You can flirt on the Internet in your underwear.

8. Contrary to what you've heard, computers are smart and we are dumb.

7. Your computer is your best friend because it has all your money.

6. Throwing your computer out of a window solves your problem only temporarily.

5. No matter what software you have, you need to upgrade.

4. You're always just ten minutes away from solving any computer problem.

3. No matter what hardware you have, you need to upgrade.

2. While you were reading this list, Bill Gates made another million dollars.

1. Relax, in the end, it's only computers.

Chapter 1

And She Said, "Let There Be Light"

 Computer uses

I recently walked out of a computer store $3,900 poorer. Now that I have a computer, what can I do with it?

Psssst, let me tell you about a moneymaking breakthrough that can make you $100,000 — in a bad month. Not interested, you say? That's OK: if I knew how to rake in that kind of dough, do you really think I'd be burning the midnight oil writing this book?

Most people have some idea of how they'll use a computer before they write the check or hand over the plastic. For example, you can use your computer to write the next great unauthorized biography that lands you on *The New York Times* bestseller list and "Lifestyles of the Rich and Famous." You can manage your checkbook and plan your financial future. You can trace your family roots, learn a foreign language, keep tabs on your weight, schedule appointments, maintain an electronic Rolodex, make friends in faraway places, design your home, see what you'll look like when you are 100 years old, and, most important, play games.

With a computer, you can tap into that whole big world out there; the ultimate adventure is within reach. Not convinced? Go to a few software stores; the shelves are lined with different software programs. I'm sure you'll find at least ten ways to use your computer.

Another way to find out what you and your computer can do is to talk to other people who use computers. In many towns, nonprofit organizations called *user groups* are multiplying faster than rabbits. These groups usually hold monthly meetings where you can see demonstrations of computer programs and accessories. Friendly computer geeks normally run the groups, and they're assisted by volunteers who are more than happy to help those new to computers.

Also look for *special interest groups*, or SIGs. Typical SIGs cover specific computer topics, such as accounting, communications, databases, desktop publishing, Windows, and more. SIGs are especially useful when you have a particular problem with a software program.

Many user groups offer other services for their members, such as *electronic bulletin board systems*, or BBSs (you connect your computer to the group's computer over telephone lines), computer classes, and discounts from companies that sell computer products.

Call the User Group Locator line (914-876-6678), sponsored by the Association of Personal Computer User Groups, to find the user group nearest you. After you punch in your area code, ZIP code, or state, you hear a list of groups in your area.

Computer ergonomics

What's the best way to sit in front of a computer? My back is killing me.

It's easy to lose track of time while you are working on a computer. At least that's what I tell the IRS when they ask me why my tax returns are late every year. *Note:* Don't use this excuse. It doesn't work.

You're not alone with your aches and pains. Many people get so wrapped up with using their computers that they forget to take breaks. Or they are so concerned about buying the best hardware and software that they forget about themselves.

The techie term for the science concerned with designing a healthy and friendly environment is *ergonomics*. Unfortunately, if you want to buy a so-called ergonomic chair, desk, or foot rest, you can bid your money adieu; while a normal office chair can cost $100, an ergonomic chair can cost as much as $1,000.

You don't need ergonomic furniture, however, to practice healthy computing. Sit with your thighs and arms parallel to the floor; slinking down in your chair and leaning over the keyboard may seem comfortable now, but you'll pay in the long run. There should be a 90-degree angle from your elbow to the keyboard. Padded arm rests on the chair save strain on your shoulders.

Neck pains often result from sitting too high, too low, or too far from the monitor: the center of the screen should be level with your chin, and there should be 20 inches between you and the monitor.

Adjust your chair so that your feet rest on the floor. If this isn't possible, buy a foot rest. A good rule of thumb is: For every hour you're using a computer, take a ten-minute break. If you tend to forget, set an alarm.

Q: What's the best way to sit in front of a computer?

A: Facing the screen.

Peripherals

Monitors

 Radiation

I'm afraid that if I use my computer too much, I'll start glowing. Is it true that computer monitors emit bad, harmful radiation?

Although I am not a nuclear scientist, I don't think there's such a thing as *good* radiation. But, yes, monitors do emit some radiation. The radiation levels aren't high enough, though, to make you start glowing in the dark.

Monitors emit ELF (extremely *low frequency*) and VLF (*very low frequency*). Most radiation comes from the back and sides of a monitor. Special antiradiation shields, which you can find at office-supply stores, really aren't worth the money because they only block the area where the potential threat is the lowest — the front of a monitor.

Initially, the folks in Sweden were more aware of potential monitor radiation than people anywhere else in the world. In fact, the Swedish government came up with the MPR I standard (detailing ELF and VLF restrictions) in 1987; the MPR II standard replaced MPR I in 1990. Although no one has uncovered conclusive proof that display transmissions are harmful, you should purchase a monitor that boasts it complies with the MPR II standard.

In 1992, the TCO standard tightened the MPR II standard: TCO standard-compliant monitors must meet power-saving requirements as well as emission limits. Nanao is one of the few manufacturers currently offering monitors that meet the TCO standard.

The Bottom Line

All things considered, a computer poses little radiation danger. So forget going to the neighborhood army-surplus store and buying one of those stylish nuclear fallout suits.

Adjustments

What's the best way to adjust a monitor so I can see the characters on-screen better? I've had little luck playing with my monitor's knobs.

Almost every monitor has buttons or knobs. The two used most often are those that change brightness and contrast. To adjust your monitor, fill the screen with text, turn the brightness up as far as it can go, then adjust the contrast button. The characters should be clear; reading a block of text should feel comfortable to your eyes.

Squinting strains your eyes and produces wrinkles around your eyes, so avoid glare from overhead lighting or sunlight.

You should also center the monitor so the center of the screen is even with your chin. Some luxury-model monitors have a swivel base that allows you to get real comfy by moving the monitor up, down, left, and right, matching how you're sitting. If your monitor isn't as high-tech, most office-supply stores sell swivel stands. I use a monitor arm that attaches to my desk: the monitor sits on the arm, which I can move up, down, left, and right, depending on my mood and my position, relative to my desk.

 *Flicker*

My monitor has always had this annoying little flicker. How do I fix my monitor so it doesn't flicker?

I know the old monitor works fine and you don't want to spend money foolishly. (Forget about all the software you bought and didn't use more than five times.) But aren't your eyes worth it? Screen flicker, which causes eye fatigue, is pretty common with older monitors or monitors that have 60Hz or lower refresh rates.

Yikes! I know that I used some techie terms there, but I'll explain them in a second.

Monitors redraw the image on-screen trillions of times per second. (OK, maybe not trillions but a lot — 60 to 75 times or higher per second.) This continual screen redraw, which happens so fast that you don't see it, occurs one horizontal line at a time from top to bottom. The horizontal frequency (or *scan rate*), measured in kilohertz (kHz), is the number of lines the monitor draws per second. The vertical scan rate (or *refresh rate*), measured in hertz (Hz), is the number of complete screens drawn per second. Today's standard is a *noninterlaced* monitor that has a 70Hz to 75Hz refresh rate. (*Interlaced* monitors draw every other line; non-interlaced monitors draw the lines one by one, which reduces screen flicker.)

If your monitor's refresh rate is near today's standard, check the lighting: fluorescent lights can interfere with monitors. In addition, radios, TVs, and even other computer components — such as another monitor or a laser printer — can make your monitor flicker. Move the offending item(s) farther from the monitor.

Also, the information coming from the video card may be at too high a frequency for the monitor to handle. Compare the specifications for the monitor with the specifications for the video card and see whether they match. And, while you're in this mode, try running the monitor at a lower resolution.

Finally, hook up a friend's monitor to your computer and see whether the flicker still exists. If it does, there's something else going on with your computer (perhaps a bad plug or a bad outlet). If the problem goes away, your monitor is probably to blame.

Of course, something more serious may be wrong with the monitor; it may be time to buy a new one.

Centering images on-screen

Windows displays too far to the right and DOS too far to the left. What gives?

Stop dancing in your chair, and I'm sure that the problem will go away. If it doesn't, the DOS programs are probably to blame.

DOS programs leave the computer in *text mode*: everything you see on-screen is made up of letters, numbers, and special line-drawing characters. Windows, on the other hand, puts the monitor into *graphics mode*: everything you see on-screen, including letters, is actually part of a big picture.

When monitors switch between modes, the image displayed on-screen is often pushed to one side or the other. Some video cards come with a utility program — often called Center — that automatically centers the image in the middle of the monitor. Check the disks that came with your video card for this handy utility. Then change the AUTOEXEC.BAT file to make the centering utility run every time the computer starts up. There is more information about editing the AUTOEXEC.BAT file in the DOS chapter of this book.

Almost all monitors have buttons or knobs that allow you to adjust the image's placement and size on-screen. Just so you know, you may have no other choice than fiddling with the screen image's position manually after changing video modes.

Monitor display quality

My software asks me which type of monitor I have. The sales receipt is no help; it simply says *One Monitor*. Which monitor setting should I choose: EGA, VGA, or SVGA?

IMHO (*in my humble opinion*), I think computer people like to use acronyms to keep folks who don't know much about computers in the dark.

It's hard to hear the Rolling Stones's newest CD blaring from your stereo without speakers. Similarly, you need a monitor to show you what's going on inside a computer. A video card inside the computer tells the monitor how to show you the information.

EGA, VGA, and SVGA relate to different monitor display qualities. EGA (*E*nhanced *G*raphics *A*dapter), which was introduced in 1985 with the IBM AT computer, was replaced in 1987 by VGA (*V*ideo *G*raphics *A*rray). SVGA (*S*uper *V*ideo *G*raphics *A*rray) displays even more colors and with better quality. Most computers sold in the last few years have SVGA video cards and monitors, so pick SVGA. If you don't believe me, and you have to know the ins and outs of everything, read on.

Komando Klues

You can find out which video type is inside your computer by using the Microsoft Diagnostics program (MSD), which comes free with DOS 5.0 or above. At the DOS prompt, type **MSD** and press Enter. Press V for video; the type of monitor being used is named on-screen. To exit MSD, press the F3 key.

OK, say you're sorry for not believing me. Say it louder.

Color capabilities

The monitor box says I have 256 colors on my monitor. I don't see anywhere near that many colors. How do I find them?

Did you connect the monitor to the computer? Just kidding. You did, *didn't you*? Remember that the software itself must support 256 colors. Check the software program's hardware requirements; they're normally listed on the box or in the software manual.

If you look through a magnifying glass at a newspaper photo, you'll see that the picture is made up of dots. The same is true with the picture shown on a computer monitor (the dots are called *pixels*).

The VGA standard for computer video is 640 × 480 pixels. VGA calls for 16 different colors shown on-screen at once. To see more colors, say 256-colors, you need to add memory to the video card that drives the monitor, not the computer. You need 512K of video memory to see 256 colors with VGA.

The SVGA standard displays 16 or 256 colors when the display size, or *resolution*, is 800 × 600 pixels. The 16-color option requires 256K of video memory; the 256-color option requires 512K of video memory. But, like most rules that relate to computer memory, the more memory you have, the better the performance. The typical amount of memory installed on video cards sold in the last few years is 1MB.

Hold on. I'm not done yet. I need to tell you about *video drivers*, or the software that stands between the video card and the monitor, telling the monitor what to do. Most video drivers let you change the monitor to different resolutions and numbers of colors displayed. In fact, many video drivers can display more than 256 colors at one time — up to 16 million colors! Here's the catch: If the video card doesn't have the memory to handle the extra colors, they won't be displayed; worse, your software may not work at all.

You can change the video settings in the Windows Setup program that's found in the Main program window. Some video cards have their own little windows where you can set the resolution and colors, too.

Komando Klues

Remember that when the computer shows you 256 colors, it has a lot of information to track. Unless you really need 256 colors, or have a souped-up video card with over 1MB of memory, you're probably better off sticking with 16 colors.

Disks

Floppy disk capacity

High-density, low-density, 3¹/₂-inch, 5¹/₄-inch! How can I tell which floppy disk type I need?

The short answer: You should buy floppy disks that hold the largest amount of data and whose size and type fit your computer's floppy disk drives.

Most computers sold since 1985 have high-density floppy disk drives; some disks are 3¹/₂ inches and some are 5¹/₄ inches wide. Although high-density drives can read, write, and format both high-density and low-density floppy disks, you should use high-density disks, because they hold more information. The only reason to use a low-density disk is when you have to give the disk to someone who has a computer with low-density floppy disk drives.

You can tell a computer's floppy disk drive type a few ways, including

> ➤ When started, many computers display a brief inventory of their components. Read fast. This list is shown on-screen only for a second or two.

➤ If you have Microsoft DOS 6.0 or above, run the Microsoft Diagnostics program (MSD). To do so, go to the DOS prompt, type **MSD**, and press Enter. Press D to see information about all the computer's drives. Press the F3 key to exit.

A high-density $3^1/_2$-inch floppy disk can hold up to 1.44MB of information; a low-density $3^1/_2$-inch floppy can hold only 720K of information. A high-density $5^1/_4$-inch floppy disk can hold up to 1.2MB of information; a low-density $5^1/_4$-inch disk can hold only 360K of information. The easiest way to check which kind of disk you're using is to look at the disk. High-density disks have the letters *HD* printed on them. Or use the DOS command CHKDSK on the floppy and look at the disk capacity.

Handling and storing floppy disks

I keep floppy disks handy — right on top of the computer. Is this bad?

A recent caller to my radio show told me that he had used a magnet to hold a disk on his refrigerator. I questioned his taste in decor. He then asked, "Can a magnet damage a floppy disk?"

Yes, a magnet can scramble information on the disk, making it unreadable. Disks use magnetism to record information. As a result, electrical devices that have magnetic fields, such as televisions, computer monitors, and even telephones, can damage the information on your floppy disk. It's a good idea to keep diskettes at least three to five feet away from electrical devices.

Here are more tips for handling floppy disks:

Komando Klues

➤ Do not bend, fold, staple, or otherwise mutilate diskettes.

➤ Always use a felt-tipped marker when writing on a disk label that's already on a disk. If you use a ball-point pen and press too hard, you can damage the information on the disk.

➤ Dust and dirt can cause disk failure. A $3^1/_2$-inch floppy disk is housed in a plastic case; it has a metal shutter that slides, revealing the magnetized disk inside. A $5^1/_4$-inch floppy disk doesn't have a shutter — you can just reach out and touch the magnetized disk. But don't. Getting dust, smoke, or even the oil from your fingers on the magnetized disk may make the diskette unusable.

➤ Heat is another floppy disk danger. Plastic warps when left in a hot place, such as your car in summer or near a heater in winter.

By practicing a little common sense, floppy disks can be used for a long, long time. Still, just as the picture and sound quality of videotapes decreases after many plays, so does the quality of a diskette. Keep a spare box of new floppy disks handy. You'll always use them.

Floppy disk formats

Do I have to format all floppy disks? What's a volume label? The computer asks me for one after it's done formatting.

Think of floppy disks as ordinary filing cabinets. Formatting a floppy disk is like setting up a filing cabinet before you put information in it. You can buy preformatted floppy disks and avoid the hassle; these disks are a little more expensive, however, than their unformatted cousins.

Formatting is easy, especially in Microsoft Windows. Go to File Manager (usually found in the Main program group) and select Disk⇨Format Disk. In the small window that appears on-screen, you have to make some choices: Select the letter of the drive — A or B — that contains the floppy disk to be formatted. Next, select the capacity of the floppy disk, where 1.44MB is high density and 720K is low density. Don't click OK yet.

If you're formatting a disk to start your computer, select the Make System Disk option. The Quick Format option formats the floppy disk quickly if the floppy disk has been formatted at least once. The *volume label* is an electronic name (such as *Books94* or *MyMoney*) for the floppy disk. It's visible when you use the DIR command at the DOS prompt and when you're looking at what's on the disk in Windows File Manager. This name can be up to 11 characters long. In addition, the volume label usually cannot include spaces; use dashes or underscores instead. (The exception is if you're using DOS 6.20 or higher.)

Now click OK. After the disk is formatted, you're asked whether you want to format another floppy with the same options. It's a good idea to format a whole box of floppy disks at once. That way, in the future, you don't have to waste time formatting a disk before you can use it.

Formatting a floppy disk with DOS 5.0 or above at the DOS prompt is almost as easy. At the DOS prompt, type **FORMAT A:** (or **FORMAT B:** if you are working with drive B) and press Enter.

Notice the command structure: you type the DOS command, the drive where the floppy disk is located, and the formatting options. You can use as many options as you want. To use the quick format option, for example, type **FORMAT A: /Q** and press Enter. To make the floppy disk a *system* or *boot* disk, add **/S**. To put a volume label on the floppy, add **/V**.

DOS saves the existing information on the floppy disk, just in case you formatted the disk accidentally. If this happens, use the UNFORMAT command to get the information back. If you're absolutely sure that you'll never want to unformat the floppy, you can add the /U option, or the unconditional format option.

If you forget the options for the DOS FORMAT command, type **FORMAT /?** at the DOS prompt and press Enter. You'll see a brief explanation of all the options. With all these options available to format a disk in DOS, you can see why it's easier to do things in Windows. Besides, talking about DOS commands can put anyone to sleep.

Always remember that when you format a disk, you erase *everything* on the disk.

Floppy disk fundamentals

How is information saved on floppy disks? My kids will think I'm smart if I tell them.

Why is the sky blue? How can fish breathe under water? Why is noise coming from your bedroom at night? How does a computer disk hold information? Kids ask the damnedest things.

Whether you work with $3^1/_2$- or $5^1/_4$-inch floppies, the plastic disk inside the plastic envelope looks and works very similarly to a phonograph record, cassette tape, or videotape. Where a record, cassette tape, or videotape saves music, a floppy disk stores information, or data.

Special material found on floppy disks magnetizes the information. Because magnets have north and south ends, information stored on a floppy disk is magnetized north or south. In other words, information is basically saved on disks in coordinates, like coordinates on a globe.

So information on a disk is stored as tiny spots that are magnetized alternately north and south. The floppy disk drive holds the floppy disk in place and translates the north or south spots into either on or off — computers work with on/off switches (like light switches). The drive works like a phonograph record player, spinning the diskette at a certain speed. Where a record player has an arm that moves and gets information from the record, the floppy disk drive has a *read/write head* that moves to get, or read, information from the diskette. Unlike the record player arm, though, the read/write head never actually touches the diskette. Instead, it magnetizes those little spots in a special way on the disk's surface.

A hard disk drive works much the same. Sealed in a special box inside the computer, a hard disk drive spins metal disks around like a floppy disk drive spins your little plastic disks — but much faster. Which is why accessing information or using a program saved on a hard disk drive takes less time than if that same information or program is saved on a floppy disk.

Have you ever put a magnet near a compass? When you do, the compass needle doesn't point north; rather, it points toward the magnet. Put a magnet near a disk you don't care about, and the little magnetized spots on the disk will get all confused. Next time you try to use that diskette, you may not be able to use its information or save more information.

Mice

 ## Two-button mice

Did I miss the boat? I've mastered the left mouse button's action, but nowhere in the manual is there any mention of the right mouse button. Why is there a right button on my mouse?

As the radical 1960s (psychedelic colors and folk songs) exited stage left, the moderate 1970s (polyester and disco) took center stage: hippies became computer designers and engineers. The marches may have ended, but flashing the peace sign was still habit. Needing some place to rest their middle finger, the erstwhile left wingers designed the right mouse button. Well, not really.

The right mouse button is used a few ways. Windows, OS/2, and other operating systems and programs let you orient the mouse for your dominant hand. Left-handed people, for example, can switch the mouse orientation so that the right mouse button works like the right-handed user's left mouse button.

Why doesn't Windows use a one-button mouse like the Macintosh? Pressing the right mouse button in many Windows programs displays shortcuts (of course, these commands are also available through the drop-down menu bar). For example, put the cursor anywhere on a page in a Windows word processor and then click the right mouse button. Commands (such as cut, copy, paste, and so on) pop out right there for you to use. Press the right mouse button in a drawing program and you can work with the graphic on-screen.

Programs that use the right mouse button bring the most common commands to you with one click. The commands change, depending on what you right-click.

By the way, clicking the right mouse button is practically a Windows 95 requirement.

Mice for DOS and Windows

My mouse works in Windows programs but not in DOS programs. Do I need a special type of mouse that works in both DOS and Windows programs?

The Bottom Line

It points. It clicks. It makes life easy. Just one mouse (plugged in) is all you need to work in DOS and in Windows. But make sure that your DOS programs can use a mouse, because not all DOS programs do. Check the setup for your DOS program and see whether you need to tell the program that you want to use a mouse.

If you can use a mouse with a DOS program (and want to), you need to tell DOS that a mouse is hooked up to the computer; you need a program called a *mouse driver.* (Can't you just picture a little mouse, fitted with a tiny racing helmet, whiskers flapping in the breeze?) Without installing this program, DOS doesn't know that a mouse is attached to the computer. So much for the folks who call computers "electronic brains."

The mouse driver, usually called something like MOUSE.EXE or MOUSE.COM, ships with the mouse; check the disk that was included inside the mouse's box. Put this mouse disk in drive A and type **A:INSTALL** at the C:> prompt; usually, your AUTOEXEC.BAT file is updated automatically.

If not, you can add the line the mouse needs to the AUTOEXEC.BAT file: For example, assume that you have a file called MOUSE.EXE in a subdirectory called MOUSE on drive C. You need to add the following line to AUTOEXEC.BAT:

```
C:\MOUSE\MOUSE.EXE
```

Be sure to save the AUTOEXEC.BAT file and reboot the computer before trying the mouse out in the DOS program.

Mice versions

I'm left-handed and thought I could just walk casually into the store and purchase a mouse. Was I naive! Rodents come in all shapes and sizes. How do I know which kind to buy?

Do you see what happens when we leave the engineers in the labs too long? The mice are breeding like rabbits!

Actually, choices in mice are a good thing. Just like one car model doesn't satisfy everyone's needs, one mouse can't make everyone happy. Only you can know what feels right for you.

Today's top software programs require a mouse. You'll see different resolutions, measured in dots per inch (dpi), when looking at mice. The higher the resolution, the finer the control of mouse movements on-screen.

A resolution between 200 and 400 dpi is good. Unless you're into some heavy-duty graphics, anything above 400 dpi is a waste of money and computer resources. Inside the mouse packaging is usually a disk that has various utilities and drivers.

Mice come in left- and right-handed models. Some mice are specifically tailored (that is, shaped) for lefties. Depending on the mouse's installation routine, you may not need to tell the mouse this information. But if you buy a rightie and you are a leftie, the mouse utilities let you customize the mouse for left- or right-handed use. Open the Control Panel in Windows and click on Mouse. Besides telling your computer's mouse that you are left- or right-handed, you can adjust the tracking and clicking speed, too.

If you are the clutter king or queen, consider a cordless mouse. Logitech's MouseMan Cordless is a radio-based mouse that works up to six feet away and gives or receives commands through a stack of papers. If many radio-controlled mice are in your work area, you may encounter some problems.

Standard mice cost between $20 and $120; infrared or radio-controlled mice are near the $150 range.

An alternative to the mouse is the trackball, which is basically a standard mouse flipped over. Trackballs save space, so they're ideal for portable computer users. Instead of moving a mouse around a desk, you move the ball with your thumb. Pay attention to this ball's size: the bigger the ball, the easier it is the move around and control. The left and right mouse buttons should also be comfortable to reach while your hand is resting on the trackball: you shouldn't have to lift your hand from the trackball to click a button.

Other

 Function keys

I keep accidentally hitting these "extra" keys that are on my computer keyboard but not on a typewriter. What is their purpose in life?

Because you can do so much with a computer, a regular old typewriter keyboard isn't good enough. A computer keyboard looks like a typewriter but has additional keys along the top and sides. In addition, computer designers devised ways to turn one set of keys into three or four keyboards.

The *Enter* keys are marked Enter on some computers and Return on others. Whether the key says Enter or Return, pressing it does the same thing: tells the computer to do something.

Like Enter (or Return), the *Ctrl* and *Alt* keys are on most keyboards twice for convenience. By pressing Ctrl or Alt and a letter key at the same time, you can do something other than type that letter. (Computer manuals specify this action by showing the key and letter separated by a hyphen or a plus sign, such as *Ctrl-A* or *Ctrl+A*. The proper way to carry out this action is to hold down Ctrl and press the letter key A. If the manual says *Alt-A*, press Alt and then A.)

Other special keys, called *function keys*, are situated along the top or left side of computer keyboards — they have the letter F and a number. Most computer keyboards have at least 10 function keys, and some have 12. If your computer only has 10, don't feel left out; most users hardly use the

17

11th and 12th keys anyway. Probably the most important function key is F1, which is often the help key. Whenever you're stuck while using a computer, and need a hand to point you in the right direction, try pressing F1.

The *Caps Lock* key works like the shift lock key on a typewriter. When the caps lock key is on, every letter you type is an uppercase, or capital, letter. To turn the caps lock on or off, press the caps lock key once. By the way, the caps lock key only works with alphabetic letters, not numbers or punctuation. Also, if you have the caps lock key on and use the Shift key, you get lowercase letters.

I want you to forget that the *Scroll Lock* key even exists. Very few software programs use it.

On the right side of every keyboard is a numeric keypad. When the *Num Lock* key is on, this part of a computer keyboard turns into a numeric keypad. It's great when you need to type a bunch of numbers. The numeric pad also has some other keys along the top and sides that are specifically for mathematical formulas. The slash key is used for division. The asterisk key is used in multiplication. The minus key is used in subtraction and the plus key is for addition. The enter key on the numeric keypad is the same as the keyboard's other Enter key. When the num lock key is off, you don't get numbers; the numeric keys turn into arrow and shortcut keys for moving around quickly in your documents.

They say that the *SYSREQ* key will be used someday, but I've been hearing that for years and I've almost given up hope. *Pause* works like the hold button on a telephone, except it only works in certain situations. *Break* tells a computer to stop acting like a dog chasing its tail; to use the Break key, hold down the Ctrl key and then press Break.

The *Esc* key normally gets you back to a place in a software program that looks strangely familiar. *Backspace* erases one character at a time to the left of the cursor. *Delete* erases one character at a time to the right of the cursor.

Sounds like a new dance step: OK, folks, make a circle and backspace to the left. Delete to the right, do-si-do, and swing your partner.

Adding game controllers

I bought some computer games, but using the keyboard and mouse to play them stinks. Can I add a joystick to my computer?

It depends. Not all computers were created equal, although all have slots inside where you can insert different *expansion cards*, which allow you to add extra goodies, such as a joystick, to your computer. Today's computers have at least three or four empty slots.

Many newer computers have a game port built in, so you don't need a special card. You can tell whether your computer has a game port by looking at the back of the computer and seeing whether anything is labeled *Game*. If so, that is where you plug in your joystick, much like you connect a mouse.

If your computer does not have a game port already, don't fret. You simply need to buy a card that goes in an empty expansion slot; the joystick plugs into it. Expansion cards come in long, tall, short, and wide sizes, so check which size you need before shopping.

If you are one of those unlucky users without an empty slot, get a *combination expansion card*. Typically, this card type has a serial port, a parallel port, and a joystick port. These combination cards are a little more difficult to install, however, because you have to make sure that there aren't any conflicts. Expansion cards have small switches and jumpers that you may have to change to get the game port to work. If it's any consolation, I can install a game port and get it working without breaking a nail.

Laptop computers don't have expansion slots for adding accessories. You need an adapter that plugs the joystick into the laptop's serial port. No big deal.

If you're using a laptop on an airplane, though, avoid playing Flight Simulator: you may be inclined to scream, "We've lost power, I can't find the airport, and we're falling at 7,000 feet a minute!"

Start-up disks

I went to install a new modem and the instructions say to make a start-up disk. What is a start-up disk?

A *start-up disk* is a floppy disk that has the special files on it that a computer needs to start itself. These files are located on the computer's hard disk, which is where the computer normally finds them. But, as a safety measure, you should store those special files on a floppy disk. This way, if, for some strange reason, the computer cannot find the files it needs on the hard disk, you're not out of luck. You normally can still get to the information on your computer's hard disk by starting the computer with the start-up disk in drive A.

To create a start-up disk with the necessary files, format a floppy disk (either a new one or one that can be erased) in drive A. Select the option for making it bootable.

Komando Klues

I suggest putting other important files on the start-up disk: EDIT.COM, AUTOEXEC.BAT, CONFIG.SYS, SYSTEM.INI, and WIN.INI. The easiest way to find these files is to use the File Search feature in Windows File Manager and use the Copy command. Once you copy all the important files onto one start-up disk, be sure to put that disk in a safe place. A start-up disk is like insurance: you may not need it, but if you do, you're sure glad you have it.

Software

Apps

Software development

Just when I have a program figured out, a new version hits the streets. Am I alone?

Isn't it amazing how software companies know the precise moment you finally learn a program? They must have a special clock in their corporate headquarters.

Believe it or not, software companies actually improve their programs with each release. Although they used to simply add additional features, now they also focus on making their programs easier to use.

The big software companies have *usability labs*, where engineers watch (through hidden cameras and two-way mirrors) computer users actually working with their programs; they watch which keys are pressed, where the mouse is moved, and even the users' facial expressions! The companies analyze this information to help decide how the programs should be made better. This type of monitoring has brought toolbars with useful buttons, pop-up help messages about what the buttons do, right-mouse-button menus of options, and more.

Many software companies figure on an 18-month application life cycle. A few companies even work with a 9- to 12-month life cycle. The reasoning is that users will get the new version within the first few months of its release. The user takes a few months to learn all the program's enhancements and then has a year of bliss and increased productivity. This may happen in a perfect world; in ours, it rarely does. There are bound to be a few problems, affectionately called *bugs*, in any new program. Luckily, these usually are corrected quickly.

You play the odds if you stick to using old, old versions, much like you'd have problems finding parts for a 1961 Corvette. Try to find support; without it, you may not be able to use the information created with the older software in newer programs.

The Bottom Line

As a rule of thumb, I don't let a program that I use once in a while get more than two revisions old. I make sure that I have the most recent version of something I use every day. The good news is that registered users of software programs almost always can get substantial discounts on new versions.

21

Software updates and upgrades

I'm confused by the stuff software companies mail me. Is a software update and a software upgrade the same thing?

A software update is not a software upgrade. An *update* is nothing other than a bug fix (leave it to marketing folks to find a better way of saying so). An *upgrade* is a new and improved version of software, not merely files to fix common problems.

When a company upgrades software, the program's version number changes (for example, Microsoft Word for Windows 2.0 became Microsoft Word for Windows 6.0). Updates are usually designated by letters. So when you see a letter after a program's version number (as in Microsoft Word for Windows 6.0a), it is the update, or *bug fix*. Most of the WinWord 6.0a revisions, for example, are cosmetic; the menus and features are the same. The only difference: after you install the update, you encounter fewer errors.

Software bugs

Why do software publishers sell products that do not work? I bought a new program and the darn thing keeps messing my computer up. Do software publishers test their products, or do they leave that job up to consumers? I think the government should become involved.

Lighten up. Frankly, any new technology is full of potholes. And when products are rushed to market, real testing is possible far too often only after the product is in the consumers' hands. It's unrealistic to expect that testing done within a company's research and development departments finds every kink. There are just too many variables.

Of course, software companies don't just package disks and manuals without testing products. On the contrary, a software program may undergo years of testing before reaching store shelves. Software programs are typically *beta-tested*. The company prereleases the programs to a group of users outside the publishing company; these users find and report problems or bugs. Most of the time, these testers are existing customers of the software publisher or members of a computer user group. As compensation for their work, these users receive the polished software for free, or for a reduced price.

Unfortunately, despite the beta-testing, problems often pop up only after the program hits the streets. Hence, you hear about quick fixes that are called *bug fixes*, *maintenance releases*, *patches*, and *updates*. These revised versions promise to correct the troubles that plague users. You usually find out about updates directly from the publisher or when you call the company's technical support hot line. If you register your software (to do so, send in the software registration card included with the program), you are eligible for technical support and you get update notices in the mail.

If you encounter any bugs, don't bother calling your lawyer; the license agreement protects the software company from litigation when you face problems caused by bugs.

How can you even suggest that the government become involved with software development? Politicians can't even balance the budget.

 READMEfiles

What are README.TXT files?

README.TXT files are a computer software maker's way of saying, "Oh, by the way, we forgot to mention something in the manual." The files contain last-minute information not included in the user's manuals.

Often, the information in the README.TXT file was discovered after printing the manuals. Software companies save some money by informing you about any changes or gotchas in the README.TXT file rather than reprinting the manuals.

It's always a good idea to read the README.TXT files. A few minutes spent reading this information can save lots of frustration later. To read them, use the Windows Notepad, which is usually found in the Windows Accessories program group. Select File from Notepad's menu bar; then choose Open and highlight the directory where the README.TXT file is located. Click OK and the file appears on-screen. You'll be amazed at the hints and tips found in a README.TXT file.

Software compatibility

I went to a software store and was overwhelmed by the number of programs available. How can I tell whether a piece of software works with my computer?

Inside clothes are tags that list their size. Similarly, computer software boxes list requirements, telling you whether the software works on your computer. You need to know a little about your computer to read the software's requirements.

First, check whether the software works on an IBM-compatible or an Apple Macintosh. If IBM-compatible, make sure that you have the appropriate type of computer processor (386, 486, or Pentium). Next, check the amount of RAM and DOS version needed (DOS 3.1 or above, for example, means that you can use DOS 3.1, 4, 5, or 6). The requirements list also tells you how much hard disk space is needed and whether the program comes on 5 1/4-inch or 3 1/2-inch disks. Sometimes, software boxes contain disks of both size. If you don't know any of this information about your system, use Microsoft Diagnostics (MSD) for the lowdown. Type the following at the DOS prompt and press Enter:

```
MSD
```

All kinds of information will appear about your computer, including the details you need to know. Select File⇨Print to get a hard-copy report of your computer's innards. To exit MSD, press the F3 key.

Komando Klues Whenever you see *Optional* on the box, know that you should have it. For example, a mouse may be optional because you don't need a mouse to run the program, but a mouse makes the program easier to use.

To make sure you buy the right software for your computer, go software shopping with your computer's purchase receipt. Just match the hardware on the receipt to the software requirements.

Rating computer games

Are ratings for computer games available? How do I tell whether a computer game has too much violence or sexual content for children?

We have had ratings on movies for years, but ratings for entertainment and game software are just now beginning to appear on software boxes. Look on boxes for thermometers, which indicate the rating set by the nonprofit Recreational Software Advisory Council (RSAC). To design the rating system, the RSAC worked with Donald Roberts, chairman of Stanford University's communications department, who has researched media's effects on children for almost 30 years.

Not all games are rated, though. Software companies have to volunteer to have the RSAC rate their games. The RSAC ratings, which cover three categories (violence, nudity and sex, and language), provide five levels: "Suitable for all audiences" and four numerical levels. Think of 1 as a PG-rated movie and a 4 as an R- or X-rated movie. Unfortunately, the RSAC's ratings do not include age appropriateness; you must determine that yourself. But at least you can tell something about the game's temperature and content just by looking at a thermometer on the software box.

Physically challenged computer users

My daughter is visually impaired and has some movement disabilities. Does Microsoft offer special Windows products for the handicapped?

How easy it is to take life for granted. There are numerous resources available for physically-challenged computer users. For example, Access Pack for Windows, available free of charge from Microsoft, provides better access to Windows for people who have movement or hearing disabilities. For example, if your daughter types with one finger, a mouthstick, or a wand, she will have easier control of Shift, Ctrl, and Alt key combinations. Plus, there are settings for disregarding accidental key presses, avoiding extra characters on-screen if a key is pressed more than once, controlling the mouse with the keyboard, using another type of input device, getting visual rather than aural cues from the computer, and more. For more information or to obtain a copy of Access Pack for Windows, call Microsoft's Product Support Services at 206-637-7098.

In addition, Recording for the Blind distributes many Microsoft product manuals and books from Microsoft Press on audio cassettes. You can choose from more than 80,000 titles. For more information, call Recording for the Blind at 800-221-4792.

I also recommend that you take a trip to your local library and browse the Resource Book from the University of Wisconsin's Trace Research and Development Center. It contains nearly 500 pages and 2,000 photographs of product aids. The CD-ROM that comes with the book has a database of more than 12,000 products for people with disabilities. You can reach the Trace Research and Development Center at 608-263-2309. Or your daughter can use a text phone and call 608-263-5408. There are screen readers that can actually read aloud, in plain language, any stuff shown on-screen. Various agencies that specialize in specific disabilities can be very useful in this regard.

Komando Klues

As you're looking at various computer products, stay away from DOS utilities; they won't help your daughter because Windows uses its own drivers, which override DOS utilities.

The computer is a wonderful tool for your daughter to explore the world. It can help her feel connected and not alone.

Operating systems

Windows

OK, I know this is going to sound really, really stupid, but what is Windows?

If you've ever been to an expensive French restaurant, odds are you couldn't pronounce what you saw on the menu. But you didn't go home without eating: to order your meal, you pointed. (Have you ever noticed that the servings at a French restaurant are small but the prices are high?)

Windows is somewhat like that French menu: the computerized Windows menu lists all the things that you can do using your computer. To choose an action, you point at a picture on-screen, called an *icon*. But pointing with your finger doesn't do anything; you must point at the icon in Windows with a mouse. When you move your mouse, an arrow-shaped pointer moves on-screen. When the arrow is hovering over the correct icon, you push down, or *click*, the left mouse button; this action tells Windows that you want the action represented by the icon. In other words, to get Windows to work, you don't have to memorize a bunch of commands.

Forget the French restaurant for a moment, and imagine that you're sitting at your desk. You can talk on the phone, open mail, and yell at your kids, seamlessly moving from one responsibility to another. In Windows, you can switch easily from one program to another, the same way that you switch your attention from one job to another at your desk. This is called *multitasking*.

Almost all computers sold nowadays include Windows. The newest version is called Windows 95, because that's how many floppy disks the program comes on.

Come back! I just wanted to see whether you were paying attention.

 OS/2

I got OS/2 for Windows free with my computer. Just one little question. What is it?

OS/2 is IBM's challenger to Microsoft Windows. Like Windows, OS/2 is a *graphical user interface* — it has windows and icons. It's slightly different technically, however, and information is processed differently. OS/2 can run Windows, DOS, and special programs designed just for OS/2.

OS/2 for Windows is a special version of OS/2 that's good for people who already have Windows on their computers. Rather than supplying the files required to run Windows and paying Microsoft a fee, IBM designed OS/2 for Windows to use the copy of Windows already installed on your computer. Pretty smart move by IBM, if you ask me.

OS/2 for Windows saves you disk space and money. Because OS/2 for Windows uses the copy of Windows already installed on your computer, you need only one copy of Windows taking up space on the hard disk drive. And because IBM doesn't include Windows in the package, it doesn't have to pay Microsoft. As a result, OS/2 for Windows costs less than regular OS/2.

OS/2 has a new name: OS/2 Version 3.0 with Win-OS/2, or *Warp* for short.

Dependence of Windows on DOS

I swear DOS was designed by a conspiracy of pocket-protected computer nerds. Can I do the big DOS delete and just get rid of the darn thing?

All computers need software to make them work. The IBM-type computer is designed like a multistory building. The foundation is good ol' DOS. On top of DOS are one or more floors, or software programs. Windows, for example, is a floor that rests on DOS. From Windows, you can run programs, such as Microsoft Word for Windows, or games, such as Solitaire. If you pull out the DOS foundation, the whole building will come tumbling down around you; the result will be worse than a trip to the county jail on a Saturday night. If you delete DOS, your computer won't start up.

The next version of Windows, called Windows 95, won't need the DOS layer. It will be built in. But until you get Windows 95, be good and don't touch the merchandise.

DOS names

Are PC-DOS, MS-DOS, and DOS the same thing? How can I tell which I have?

PC-DOS, MS-DOS, and DOS are like different brands of vanilla ice cream.

PC-DOS is IBM's customized version of the disk operating system developed by Microsoft; PC-DOS supports IBM PCs' special features. Generally, PC-DOS and *MS-DOS* work virtually identically. In fact, IBM has included utilities in PC-DOS to accomplish the same tasks provided by MS-DOS utilities. Because PC-DOS and MS-DOS are so similar, the term *DOS* is used.

A third type of DOS, called *DR-DOS* (or *D*igital *R*esearch *DOS*), did basically the same things as MS-DOS, but it didn't have all the same engine parts as MS-DOS. Some of DR-DOS's enhancements sometimes caused minor incompatibilities with certain programs. Eventually, DR-DOS was removed from life as we know it.

To find out the exact version and brand of DOS you have, type **VER** and press Enter at the DOS prompt.

DOS version numbers

I have DOS 6.22 and my friend has DOS 5.0. What do the different numbers mean?

Those numbers just tell you the age of the program. It's very much like comparing model years for cars. With software, the higher the number, the more recent the model. The more recent the model, the more features.

By now, DOS 5.0 and below should be in retirement. These versions are a lot like 1969 Dodge Darts. They just can't do all that the newer models can do. MS-DOS 6.2 and above are the most recent versions.

Komando Klues

To find out which version of DOS is running, type **VER** at the DOS prompt and press Enter.

DOS instruction books

Where can I get a new DOS manual? I hate it but I need it. (My dog made a mess on the original. I guess he hated seeing his owner cry over it all the time.)

It makes you want to believe that dogs really do have extra senses. Don't worry; you're not in the doghouse. If you remembered to send in the registration card for DOS, Microsoft will gladly send you a new manual. For a price.

I have a better plan — one that may end your crying days. Who do you think writes computer manuals for computer companies? That's right, most manuals are written by the same people who wrote the programs. That's why you can't understand the books. Computer books written by someone other than the company that made the software are generally better than the manuals that come with the program. So go to your local bookstore and browse the computer section. You'll find an unbelievable selection of books on almost every computer subject, including DOS. *Note:* It's important to read the first chapter or two to get a feel for whether the book is written for beginners or pros.

One of the best books is *DOS For Dummies* by Dan Gookin, published by IDG Books. Microsoft even includes this book in special versions of DOS 6.2.

On-screen DOS help

Whenever I need help using DOS, I pick up the manual. But I remember hearing that DOS has help available at the prompt. How do I get to it?

I'd rather have my teeth drilled than work at the DOS prompt and rely on DOS's on-screen help. But, sometimes, a little help is all you need.

Starting with DOS 5.0, you can bring up a brief description (up to a screenful) about a command by typing the name of the command followed by a slash (/).

My favorite help message is the one you get by typing **CLS /?**. You're told that this command *Clears the screen.* Boy, that was helpful.

Usually, you see the command options, a brief explanation, and the *syntax*, or the correct usage, of the command. DOS 5.0 and above gives more in-depth help when you type **HELP** and press Enter. DOS 6.0 and above includes examples and notes; it's more like having the bona fide manual available on-screen.

Komando Klues

Here's a tip for using the HELP command: Type the topic for which you want help right after the word *help*. For example, type **HELP COPY** and press Enter to find out more about the COPY command.

Damaging computers with erroneous instructions

I'm afraid of typing something horrible at the DOS prompt and destroying my computer. Am I paranoid?

Are people suddenly giving you strange looks? Do you double- and triple-check whether you locked your front door before leaving home? Is the world out to get you? If you answer "Yes" to any of these questions, you should think about seeking professional help.

Granted, DOS isn't the friendliest thing around. C> or C:\> is DOS's way of saying, "Tell me what you want me to do." Unlike some people, DOS won't finish a sentence, or command, for you. With DOS, you must follow precise syntax rules or you get those nasty error messages.

The Bottom Line

Luckily, you can't do much damage to DOS if you pay attention. DOS is smart enough to double-check potentially devastating commands before an accident may occur. During these times, you receive the chance to say, "Yes, go ahead" or "No, you saved my day, and I'll love you forever."

Komando Klues

Nonetheless, think twice before you give the machine the go-ahead to erase any file. And stay away from using the `FORMAT C:` and `FDISK` commands: when you use them, you lose everything on your hard disk.

One last thing: Remember that just because you're not paranoid doesn't mean they're not out to get you.

Maintenance

Q&A Leaving computers running all the time

When I am not using my computer, should I turn it off? I hear that turning the computer on and off once a day damages it.

This debate has been raging on again off again for years. The two sides remain, ahem, polarized on the issue.

The leave-the-computer-on-all-the-time-people claim that the power surge that happens when you turn on your computer causes more damage than just leaving it powered up. All in all, I don't buy this argument (rumor has it that these folks also own considerable stock in the public utilities). Don't forget, a computer is a machine; leaving it turned on all the time causes components, like the hard drive, to wear out sooner. Even if you're not using the computer, the hard drive spins on bearings, and bearings can only last so long. Ask your car mechanic if you don't believe me. In addition, turning the computer off when you're not using it is better for the environment. (By the way, the Environmental Protection Agency has created a power-consumption standard for computers and peripherals — the Energy Star program.)

Komando Klues

Here's what I do: If I know that I'm going to be away from the computer for more than an hour, I shut it off. When I do have to leave the computer on for a long period of time (like overnight when I'm backing up the hard drive), I turn the monitor off, saving wear and tear.

Smoking and computers

I think my husband loves his computer more than me. For years, I tried to get him to quit smoking. Finally, I told him that smoke is bad for the computer. Now he won't smoke around the computer, and I feel guilty. Is smoke, in fact, harmful to a computer?

Keep your mouth shut; don't confess anything. You didn't lie.

Smoking near your computer takes its toll. Yellowish-brown stains appear on the monitor, keyboard, and other components; with a little scrubbing, they can be removed. Worse, where there's smoke, there are ashes — and little particles can ruin floppy disks, backup tapes, floppy disk drives, and tape drives.

Most disk drives have a door to keep out stray particles, preventing possible damage. But if ashes, dust, and other microscopic particles get on a floppy disk or backup tape, they can make information inaccessible. The parts of the drive that actually read information from a diskette or tape, called *heads*, sit just a fraction of an inch above the disk or tape. Particles that rest between the disk or tape and a head obstruct contact, resulting in disk error messages and marginal performance. Over time, ashes can build up in the keyboard or get stuck inside the mouse. They gum up the works, too.

You may want to invest in a computer cleaning kit, which usually includes a floppy disk drive cleaning solution and disk, a can of compressed air, a bottle of isopropyl alcohol, a soft cloth, and some cotton swabs.

With your guilt gone, you can stop being extra nice to your husband now. He's probably starting to wonder what's going on.

Cleaning computers

I just had to replace the power supply on my computer because it was clogged with dust and dirt. Do you have any tips to stop this problem from occurring?

Clean your house. Afterward, pick up a can of compressed air, available at computer-supply stores, to clean the power supply. With the computer turned off, make several short blasts of air into the back of the computer, where the power supply is located (it's the part that looks like the back of a fan). You'll be surprised at all the dust bunnies that are hiding in the computer!

If your power supply is extremely dusty, remove the computer's case and give it a real good cleaning. Be careful; don't use the can of compressed air like a blow torch. The power supply is the dirtiest area inside the computer. As you clean off the power supply, dust will get invariably on the components. Using short bursts of compressed air, dust off the insides.

Most cans of compressed air come with a plastic straw that you can insert into the spray nozzle. Put this straw on the nozzle to get into nooks and crannies. The floppy disk drives are bound to build up dust, too, especially if you're blowing the dust out from the power supply. Gently put the straw into the floppy disk drive, where you would insert the diskette itself. Just a couple of sprays should do the trick.

Your computer needs good ventilation and should be located in as dust-free an environment as you can find. If your computer is on the floor, put it on a table. It's also helpful to keep pets away, and remember not to eat or drink over the computer, too.

Inspecting portable computers

I travel a lot, and security guards from New York to Los Angeles give me dirty looks when I ask them to scan my laptop by hand. All I hear is, "Lady, it's not necessary." Can airport X-ray machines ruin floppy disks and hard disks?

So you're the person who insists on holding up the entire line so you can lecture the security guards and the 50 people behind you on the dangers of computers and X-rays? Trust me, I don't want any of my bytes going into the intergalactic bit bucket, but I usually place my laptop computer on the conveyer belt, and I have never had a problem.

The Bottom Line

X-rays, similar to light but on a much higher frequency, are not a risk to your computer; they are not strong enough to harm your laptop's circuits or hard disk drive. The magnetic field generated by the X-ray machine's conveyor belt motor isn't strong enough to harm anything, either.

If you're still a bit wary, you can insist on a hand inspection. To make your trip through security easier (and your fellow passengers happier), follow these tips:

Komando Klues

> ➤ Be sure the computer's batteries are fully charged, but have the power cords handy, in case the battery fades out unexpectedly. If your computer has a sleep mode, use it. This will help you avoid a long boot-up process when you are asked to turn the computer on to prove that it's not a bomb.

> ➤ Back up your most important files to floppy disks and keep these disks in your pocket. Hand the disks to the security guard for a hand inspection, too.

Your concerns have some justification. During the Gulf War, X-ray machines were cranked up to high. And airport X-ray machines in other countries are usually older and more powerful than those in the U.S., too. These larger-than-normal magnetic fields can endanger floppy and hard disks.

Q&A Selling computers

I need to find someone who will take some computer equipment off of my hands. I have display terminals that are a decade old, look like washing machines, and are completely useless to me in my molecular modeling work. Is there a company that takes old computer equipment and either scraps it for the materials or sells off the components? P.S. It doesn't even matter whether I get money.

Wow, a molecular modeler asking little ol' me a computer question. I am flattered. Do I get an honorary degree — a Ph.D. in computer engineering would look good on my wall — for this answer?

Old computer monitors don't die, they just fade. There are a few companies that will take the junk off your hands. The East-West Education Development Foundation (Boston, Massachusetts; 617-542-1234) and the Computer Recycling Center (Mountain View, California; 408-734-5030) are companies that collect old, outdated computer systems and donate them to various organizations. Usually, the groups accept nonfunctioning equipment and recycle it properly if they find it nonrepairable.

And NACOMEX, a Manhattan-based company, purchases used computer equipment. I don't think they want the stuff you have, but it's worth a phone call. Call 800-NACOMEX for more information.

Internal

Directories and subdirectories

What are directories and subdirectories? Can they keep me from forgetting where I save files?

To better organize your computer files, you can create a storage hierarchy à la a filing cabinet. In this storage hierarchy, the hard disk corresponds to the cabinet, each drawer is a directory, and folders are nested within. You can even put folders inside folders — just as you can group manila folders within a hanging file.

Well-organized drawers and directories contain specific information relating to one or two things. For example, I put my word processing program and documents in one directory, a budgeting program in another, a graphics program in another, and so on. Keeping related information in one directory, or drawer, makes finding things quicker. In fact, you can boost the computer's performance by grouping documents and applications into folders — you reduce the number of files the computer has to scan to find the file you want.

To find a file in a cabinet, you need to open the right drawer. In computers, you need to change to the right directory. File management programs make directories easier to work with. File Manager in Windows, for example, displays directories in a picture. Moving between directories and moving files between directories becomes less confusing when you can see what you're doing.

One last thing: The terms *directory* and *subdirectory* are often used interchangeably. The *sub* means that the subdirectory is underneath, or *subordinate* to, a directory. In fact, all directories are subordinate to the special directory found on every type of disk: the *root directory*.

Copying from hard disk to floppy disk

I need to copy a file for a friend who lives in another state. How do I take files off my hard disk and put them on a floppy disk? I use Windows.

Some computer things make total sense. Would you believe that File Manager in Windows helps when you need to work with files? Incredible. The engineers must have been out sick that day.

Find the File Manager icon in the main window: it looks like a two-drawer filing cabinet. Double-click on the filing cabinet; the contents of your computer's filing cabinet, the hard disk, appear on-screen. On the left side of the screen are the file folders. On the right side are the names of files inside the folders.

Scroll through the list of folders, and click on the folder that holds the file you want. On the right side of the screen, select the file you want to copy. Underneath the File Manager menu, at the left side of the screen, are pictures representing the different disk drives in your computer.

Say that you want to copy the file to a diskette in drive A. Drag the file you want to copy from the hard disk to the floppy disk. (A *drag,* in computer terms, means using the mouse to click on, then move, the selected object.) In other words, move the mouse pointer on top of the file you want to copy; then press and hold down the left mouse button and move the mouse to the drive A icon. See how the mouse pointer changes shape and becomes an arrow with a piece of paper? When the mouse pointer is over the icon for drive A, let the left mouse button go. The file is copied to the floppy disk.

Komando Klues

When it's time to mail the disk to your friend, it's a good idea to send it in a special disk-mailing envelope. Disk mailers are sturdy and protect the disk in transit. You can find disk mailers at most office-supply stores.

Fonts

What's a font? I have 16 of them.

I love fonts the way that I love my friends: the stranger they are, the better.

A *font* is a high-tech typeface that is a lot more flexible than the "hot type" lead letters typesetters once used. Fonts seem to have their own personalities. Some scream at you, and others are a little demure, like the fine print in a contract.

My fonts are scalable "on the fly" — I can make them any size I want, when I want. A *scalable font* is a file of information that contains the outlines of a font. The printer or your computer's operating system takes those outlines, which are actually based on mathematical formulas, and fills them in (usually in black, but you choose the color in your software). Don't worry; the computer does the math for you.

The most popular scalable fonts are PostScript and TrueType (Windows 3.1 ships with 16 TrueType fonts). Although TrueType font fans claim that their font format gives you slightly better quality on low-resolution laser printers, in practice PostScript and TrueType fonts look about the same.

Motherboards

What's a motherboard?

You know that women rule the world. A *motherboard* is the main circuit board of the computer. It invariably has the main processor chip, or the brain, of the computer on it. Often, the computer's memory is located on the motherboard, too.

The other important cards, such as the hard disk controller and the video card, plug into the motherboard and, in a way, "nurse" from it. As the computer is working, information in the form of electrical pulses circulates through the motherboard and the cards. Ultimately, the information lands on the monitor for you to see.

CMOS

My computer is lost in a time warp: it has stopped keeping track of the date and time.

Computers made after 1987 keep the important information about what's inside the computer in a place called the CMOS (*C*omplementary *M*etal-*O*xide *S*emiconductor, pronounced "sea moss"). Stored in the CMOS are a computer's vital statistics, such as the amount of memory, the hard disk drive type, the floppy drive sizes and types, the current date and time, and more. (If humans had a CMOS, the settings would include height, weight, shoe size, real eye and hair color, and social security number.)

Like a digital watch, which stops keeping the date and time when the battery runs out, a computer stops keeping date and time when the battery runs out in the CMOS. You replace your computer's CMOS battery as you do a watch battery. That is, you take out the old one and put in a new one.

Before you replace the battery, or the battery wears out, make sure that you have a printout of your computer's CMOS settings. You may find them in the paperwork that came with your computer when you bought it. If you can't find the CMOS settings, turn on your computer and watch the screen for something like *Press F1 for setup*. Some computers ask you to press the Del key or Esc rather than F1. After you press the appropriate key, you are in the CMOS zone.

Toto, I don't think we're in DOS anymore. The CMOS zone looks a little scary at first; it's no pretty software program. With your printer turned on, hold down Shift and press the Print Screen key. This action sends a copy of what's shown on-screen, the CMOS settings, to your printer. Keep this printout in a safe place; it's important.

A quick peek in your computer manual will tell you where your computer's CMOS battery is physically located. You should take the battery out of the computer and take it with you to the store to make sure you get the right kind. This usually requires no special tools. But if the battery is soldered in place, unless you're a real electronics pro with lots of experience working on computer circuit boards (most people are not), take the computer to a repair shop. A battery will cost you anywhere from $30 to $50.

Komando Klues

Before opening your computer's case, turn off the power to the computer. Take off all jewelry from your hands and wrists. Remember to *always* ground yourself by continually touching the computer chassis to discharge static electricity. Do this before, and while, your hands are near any of the circuit boards. The power cord, being plugged into the wall, will carry the static electricity to ground. Static electricity, even though it may seem harmless in everyday life, can do great harm to your computer and its attachments. Also, try to do this work in an uncarpeted area, if possible.

Some CMOS batteries are mounted right on the motherboard. These batteries usually look like a tiny barrel or a large watch battery, and they're a little tricky to change. Other computers have a battery that attaches to the motherboard with two wires. When this type of battery dies, disconnect the wires from the motherboard and take the old battery out of the case. If the battery doesn't have the voltage information printed on it, be sure to check the computer manual. Once you put the new battery in your computer, you need to update the date and time information in your CMOS settings.

Restoring CMOS settings

When my computer starts, it says *Press F1 for setup*. I did, and now it's all messed up. How do I get the original CMOS settings back?

A computer's start-up message should really say *Press F1 for setup if you know what you're doing. Otherwise, do yourself a favor and stay out!*

The CMOS setup program that you entered when you pressed F1 is a dangerous place for new computer users. A computer's vital statistics are stored in the CMOS. Most CMOS settings can usually be set back to the original settings, sometimes called *factory settings*, by selecting the default option from the setup program. Keep in mind that these factory default settings may not be the optimal settings for your computer. You should call the company that made the computer, or the store where you bought it, and verify the CMOS settings.

If your computer won't boot, you messed up the hard disk drive portion of CMOS. Changing these settings back can be tricky, so you need some help. Call the computer's manufacturer or the store where you bought the computer and confess your sins. Then ask for help. If you don't feel comfortable doing so, seek the professional help of a trained pocket-protected computer technician.

Komando Klues

If you ever find yourself in the CMOS setup, look for the option to exit without saving changes.

Computer security

How do I keep my curious kids out of my important computer files?

I have a few ideas. How about taking the computer with you? You could put the kids on a leash. Lock the door to the room where the computer is located. Cut the electricity to the house when you're gone. Well, there are some less extreme methods of protecting the information on your computer.

The best method for securing information away from prying eyes — kids or industrial spies — is to take any sensitive information out of the computer. Saving important information on floppy disks works, but floppies don't hold much information. Removable hard disk drives are more practical solutions for storing large amounts of data. This method probably offers more protection than you need with your kids.

39

The Bottom Line

I'd opt for installing a password-protection program: the user must type a special password before a program will start. Security programs, such as PC Dynamics Inc.'s MenuWorks Total Security, let you customize security and software access. You can protect data, disk drive access, files, and software programs. For Brink's-type PC security, Micah Development Corp.'s Full Armor is used by banks to protect funds-transfer information.

Komando Klues

Pick a password that is at least five characters and includes letters and numbers. Be sure to memorize the password (don't write it on a sticky note and then post that note on the side of your monitor).

Many computers are equipped with a built-in lock that requires a key to start the computer. If you use this method, though, the kids probably will sit in front of the television and not the computer when you're not around.

Computer memory

What's the difference between memory and hard disk space? How can I tell whether I need more of either?

Put a gallon of water in your gas tank, rather than a gallon of gas, and you do some serious damage. True, it's hard to confuse water for gasoline, but the two liquids use the same unit of measurement: the gallon.

The unit of measurement for computer memory is the *byte*. A byte represents one character, such as a letter, a number, or a space. Kilobyte, abbreviated as K, is used to describe 1,000 bytes. (The tech heads will complain unless I mention that a kilobyte is actually 1,024 bytes.) One million bytes is one megabyte (MB).

If you see any number greater than 32MB, rest assured that it has to do with hard disk space. If the number is between 640K and 32MB, odds are it has to do with computer memory (or RAM). Hard drives are typically 40, 100, 200, 400, 500, or even more MB. It's not uncommon to see hard drives that are a gigabyte (GB), where 1GB equals 1,000MB. Typical RAM sizes are 1, 2, 4, 8, 16, and 32MB.

One difference between hard disk and memory is that information on the hard disk is kept when the power to the computer is turned off. Information in a computer's memory is lost when power is turned off. A hard disk drive is invariably much larger than the amount of memory in a computer.

To tell which type of space your computer needs, take a closer look at the messages that appear on the monitor. A message about needing more memory sometimes appears when you're trying to run a program. A message about needing more hard disk space usually appears when you're installing a program or when you try to save something to the hard disk while the program is running.

I don't know about you, but after all this excitement, I'm ready for a little nap.

Partitioning hard drives

My friend came over and told me that I should partition the hard disk because it makes things easier to use. Is a partitioned hard disk really better?

Marty the Magician knew he was in love with his assistant when the crowd gave them a standing ovation the first time he performed the electric chainsaw trick. He gleamed as he announced the news to his parents, "Mom and Dad, I'd like you to meet my new fiancé, Sheila Haser-Parzentoo."

Partitioning is a lot like magic. It's a way of splitting a hard disk with an invisible wall to make the computer think that there are two hard disk drives in the computer, not just one. Depending on the hard drive's size, one or more partitions can be set up. Each partition looks like another hard drive to the computer. The total capacity of all partitions cannot exceed the total size of the hard drive.

Most times, you set up two partitions: a drive C and a drive D. Then, you can put all your applications on one drive, and all the information you create with the applications on the other drive. This method makes backups more manageable, because you really only have to back up one drive. (You can always put the software back on the computer from the original distribution disks. But if the hard disk takes a nosedive, it's hard to recreate those reports, letters, tax files, game scores, and other information that you store.)

A program may run faster if all its data is in one partition and it's the only program running, because the drive won't have to work as hard. Partitions are more useful when working with a hard drive that can hold 200MB or more.

Remember, when you partition a hard drive, you must start from scratch and reformat the entire drive. That means backing up everything and reinstalling all your programs. So ask this question: "Is what I need the partition for worth all the time, energy, and possible problems I may have?" There's an old saying that I think you should remember: If it ain't broke, don't fix it!

Recovering a deleted hard drive

My friend, who just bought a computer, tried to delete a file, using the old `DEL *.*` **entry (at the C prompt, of course). She erased everything. My friend does not have a boot or backup disk. And my boot disk won't work because it's a 3¹/₂-inch disk, while her floppy drive is 5¹/₄-inches. How can I recover the deleted files to get my friend going again?**

A funny thing happens with mistakes of this magnitude: you only have to make them once to learn a lesson. First, get a 5¹/₄-inch boot disk. Call the store where your friend bought the computer and ask for help. I bet they'll give you a boot disk. *Note:* The version of DOS on the start-up disk must exactly match the version of DOS that's installed on your friend's computer.

After you boot up the computer with the start-up disk, copy the file COMMAND.COM to the root directory of your friend's computer. (Three files are required to start up a computer, but you only need to replace this one, because the other two are hidden and haven't been deleted.) To do so, keep the boot disk in drive A, type

```
COPY COMMAND.COM C:\
```

and press Enter. Restart the computer. You should see the C prompt.

The good news is that DOS 5.0 includes an undelete utility. You have a very good chance of recovering lost files if you use this utility right after the files were erased. All you have to do is type **UNDELETE** at the C prompt and see whether it works. Pay close attention, looking for the AUTOEXEC.BAT and CONFIG.SYS files. You must re-create these files from scratch if they can't be undeleted.

If `UNDELETE` doesn't undelete anything, don't give up hope. Pick up a copy of Norton Utilities, which has a program called Unerase. Often, Unerase works better than `UNDELETE`.

Do yourself and your friend a favor. After the computer is back up and running, make a start-up disk and put it in a safe place. Unless, of course, you like playing the knight in shining armor racing to your friend's rescue!

"Will the real computer stand up?"

My computer guru sold me a computer, installed software, and then took off for college. If my guru supposedly sold me a 486/33 SVGA (with 4MB of RAM), why does DOS diagnostics state that I have a 386 and a VGA monitor? Has my guru sold me a bill of goods?

I wouldn't call your college-bound buddy a "guru." All the gurus I know are pretty up-front about what they sell.

I bet that you have a 486 SLC-33 chip inside your computer. The Cyrix Texas Instruments SLC line is a 486 Intel clone that straddles the range somewhere between 386 and 486 performance. So you really have a souped-up 386 in disguise. A 486 SLC33 shows up as a 386 when you run Microsoft Diagnostics (MSD), the diagnostics program that comes with DOS.

If you look at the description that MSD gives for your video board, it probably says something like *VGA mode 3*, which is the standard mode that DOS uses when a VGA or SVGA monitor is attached. It does not mean that the board in your machine is not capable of SVGA; it's just that at the moment, DOS is using a VGA mode. Next time you turn on your computer, watch the screen. As soon as the beeps start, you'll see the video card's manufacturer, amount of video memory, and, sometimes, additional information about the video card.

Using a computer while traveling

I need to use my computer when I'm on the road, but hotels seem way behind the times. Can you offer some tips for mobile computer users who try to stay connected on the road?

Many hotel staffers don't know the difference between a laptop and a lapdog. But a growing number of hotels stock rooms with personalized voice mail, PC-ready telephones, ergonomic furniture, and so on. And, if you're willing to pay the piper, some hotels offer full-blown business suites.

Regardless, it's not uncommon to find in-hotel business centers, complete with computers, fax machines, copiers, and printers. Because many hotels cater to tourists, however, these business traveler-oriented services are still fairly new. You cannot assume that all hotels in a chain are created equally. Your best bet is to call ahead and ask specific questions, such as

> ➤ "Is the phone in the room dual-line, and can I hook a modem up to it easily?"

> ➤ "How far is the desk in the room from the nearest electrical outlet and phone jack?"

> ➤ "Does your hotel have a business center guests can use? When is it open?"

> ➤ "What types of computers, printers, and software are in the business center? What versions of the software are available?"

> ➤ "Do you rent notebook computers, fax machines, and cellular phones?"

Komando Klues

If you're traveling on a tight budget, confirm prices on more than the room. Ask about fax charges and outgoing call charges, especially: some hotels charge as much as $15 per page for faxes, while local and long-distance telephone charges add up quickly. If you're using an on-line service, be sure to get the local access number for your destination before you leave home. In-hotel business centers cost money sometimes, too. Rentals are often cheaper at a nearby independent company or business center.

Call a travel agent who knows your needs and can recommend computer-friendly hotels, which are the much-needed bridges that keep you in touch with the rest of the world.

Q&A *Pronouncing DOS*

How do you pronounce the word "DOS"?

You say *tom-ate-toe*, I say *tom-ott-toe*! Oddly enough, *DOS* rhymes with the last syllable in *chaos*.

Chapter 2

Backing Up Isn't Hard to Do

Basics

How often should I back up?

I know that it's a good idea to make backups, but how often should I back up my system?

What would you do if you turned on your computer and didn't hear any welcoming beeps? The monitor remained pitch dark? The computer was as lifeless as the stench behind a seafood restaurant in the middle of summer? Would you belt out your best Frank Sinatra impersonation of "That's Life," or would you assume the fetal position?

Your answers tell you how often you need to make a backup. Here's the backup rule of thumb: Whenever the possible loss of information is greater than the time, effort, and energy you spent creating it, you need to make a backup. If you're working on an important file, copy that file from the hard disk to a floppy disk every half hour. Some people who suffer from a slight case of paranoia back up their computers twice daily.

Most computer users should make backups weekly or monthly. Then again, some folks never make backups, and they learn the backup lesson the hard way. I hear that data loss is one reason for the increase in childhood regression therapy.

The Bottom Line

Computers are machines, and you cannot predict when they will go to the great hardware cosmic bit bucket. You should make a full backup monthly and incremental backups every day or week. Backups are like insurance policies. You may not always need them, but when and if you do, you are sure glad you have them lying around.

What kind of backup should I make?

My backup software asked me what kind of backup I'd like. What's the difference between the full, full/copy, incremental, and differential backup options?

Think of backup options as different types of insurance policies. The policy that you need depends on how much risk you are willing to take for a lower premium. To understand the different backup options, you need to know a little bit about how computers keep track of files.

When you leave mail in your mailbox for the letter carrier to pick up, you raise the little red flag. The carrier lowers the flag to indicate that your mail has been picked up and the day's delivery is in the box. You thus can tell from the flag's position whether the mail has arrived. Every computer file has four *flags*. The flag used for backups is called the *archive* flag. Each time you save a file on the hard disk or a floppy disk, the archive flag is raised. After a backup program copies the file to a floppy disk or a backup tape, it puts the archive flag down.

The different backup options tell the computer what to do relative to the flags. The options determine which files are copied to a backup tape or disk and what the computer does with the flags when the backup concludes. Being able to choose from these backup options gives you more control:

> ➤ A *full backup* copies every file whether the archive flag is up or down. Afterward, the archive flags for all the files are put down. You should make a full backup the first time you use the backup software.

> ➤ Like a full backup, the *full/copy option* also copies every file regardless of archive flag position. But full/copy doesn't change any archive flag positions. Use the full/copy option only after you have made a full backup.

> ➤ The *incremental backup* copies only those files that you have changed or added since the last time you made a backup. The computer looks for archive flags that are raised and puts them down when it's done. If you're making only one backup copy of the files that have changed, use the incremental backup option.

> ➤ The *differential backup* copies only those files where the archive flag is up, but the computer doesn't put the flags down when it's done. Use a differential backup when you want to make more than one backup copy.

Keep in mind that you don't have to back up everything. Just back up the information that you created by using software programs. You have the original software that you loaded on the computer, so you don't need to back up software program directories. If you need the software program again, you can reinstall the software. You save tons of time and many floppy disks or backup tapes this way.

Komando Klues

My suggestion is to make a full backup periodically — say once a month — and an incremental backup more regularly — at the end of the day or weekly. Rotate the floppy disks or backup tapes once a year because they don't last forever.

How many blank disks will the backup take?

I'm backing up my hard drive for the first time, and I have about 150MB of used space. Will I need something like 100 blank floppy disks to make a backup?

Not only will you need 100 (or more) floppy disks, but you'll also need a great deal of free time. You'll be sitting there for hours and hours backing up that 150MB hard drive.

To figure out the number of floppy disks required for a backup, divide the disk space that the files require by the floppy disk's storage capacity. Or in mathematical terms,

```
Number of Floppy Disks = Disk Space You Want to Back Up
                          One Floppy Disk's Capacity
```

The formula, however, does not consider a huge variable — most backup software programs shrink, or *compress,* files. Although graphics and program files do not compress very well, document and data files do. Therefore, by selecting the maximum compression ratio in your backup software, you effectively can fit twice as much, or more, information on a floppy disk or backup tape. By the way, compression has little effect on the backup speed.

Komando Klues Consider investing in a tape backup system. After you use one, you'll never go back to taking floppies in and out of the computer for hours again. With a tape backup system, you select the files, insert the backup tape, walk away, and let the computer do all the work. What more could you ask? I know, a hard disk that never fails would be nice.

Q&A Transferring large files via backups

I want to transfer a huge file to disks. First I tried to the use the COPY command, and then I tried to use a compression program. All I get is some error message about the disk being full. How can I get one 10MB file onto 3½-inch floppy disks?

My Rubik's Cube silently mocked me for months. I tried meditation to visualize getting all the colored squares lined up ("Be the Cube, Kim"). No luck. I finally decided not to let a puzzle get the best of me. I put Rubik back to the way it was when I got it as a gift.

The moral: Even if you can visualize getting that huge file on some floppy disks, you need some backup software. The program will put as much of one file as it can squeeze on every disk, no matter the size of the original file. When one disk is full, you'll be asked to insert the next disk, and the next disk, and so on, until the 10MB file is broken up into little pieces on the floppy disks.

Backup software uses compression techniques to shrink the file, so it uses fewer floppy disks than the COPY command uses. To put the file back on the computer, use the RESTORE command. DOS 6.0 and higher includes a backup program and a restore program so you don't have to buy any special backup software.

Komando Klues Make sure you number the disks in the order that you put them in the computer when you make the backup. Otherwise, you'll have a heck of time restoring that file later. Oh, and I have a confession to make — I bought *The Rubik's Cube Insider's How-to Book.*

Remind me to back up

I love all this supposed "automation." I still forget to make backups, and I'm a Mensa member. How can I make my computer automatically back itself up, say every Friday at 5 p.m.? It seems to me that the engineers should have thought of this feature.

The high-tech hoopla does get to you after awhile. I mean, if they can make whizbang computers and send people to the moon, why can't anyone invent panty hose that don't run or snag? I'm always peeling nail polish off my legs.

First, you need a tape backup system. If you don't have one, you'll be feeding your computer floppy disks while your friends meet for drinks and solve Mensa brainteasers.

If your backup software has a scheduling feature, you usually set the day of week and the time of day for backups when you put the backup software on your computer. During the software installation, lines are added to the AUTOEXEC.BAT file. These lines start the backup scheduling program whenever you turn on the computer. I don't mean to insult someone of your intelligence, but remember that the scheduling program can't do anything unless the computer is running.

When the designated backup day and time arrives, the backup scheduling program checks whether you are running another program. If you are, the scheduling program pops up a notice telling you to stop what you are doing. After all, it is Friday at 5 p.m. When no other program is running, the scheduling program takes over and starts up the tape backup program. The backup is made without your help, and you're free to have some fun.

Resting the monitor during backups

Sometimes my backups take 12 or 14 hours to complete. Can I turn off my monitor to prevent screen burn-in during this long process?

Sure. But screen burn-in isn't the computer issue of the hour anymore. Back in the good old days of computing, when we had those hideous green or orange monochrome displays, burn-in was a real threat.

Today's VGA and SVGA monitors aren't subject to burn-in, but you may still want to turn them off. A monitor, like any other electronic device, uses electricity when it's on. Saving every little bit of energy not only keeps your utility bills down, it also helps save the environment. Energy-saving *Energy Star* and *green* monitors are now available for the politically correct. When such a monitor is not in use, it "goes to sleep" and uses little or no energy. A special video card works with a green monitor.

Komando Klues Don't be fooled if someone tries to sell you a screen blanker. It doesn't save any energy because the monitor is still on even though no picture is on-screen.

Restoring just one file

OK, Komando, are you ready for this one? I made backups by using the DOS BACKUP command. Can I restore just one file from my backup and not the entire thing?

My, my, my, a challenge. I really don't like challenges. When I was about 8 years old, I was playing with Kenny Sikes, and he dared me to swing higher than he could. I won. I went over the bar, and the swing hit me in the mouth and knocked out one of my front teeth.

DOS 6.0 and later include a backup program from Microsoft, called MSBACKUP. You'll like the graphical representation of the information stored on the floppies and the hard drive. You simply look at the screen and pick where the file is, drive A, and then where you want the file to go, drive C. Prior to DOS 6.0, it isn't so simple. Separate backup and restore programs are included, but they're not all that pretty. Because you didn't mention MSBACKUP, I guess that you're using the good old BACKUP command in DOS 5.0 or lower.

If, for example, you want to restore a file called MYLETTER.DOC to a subdirectory called C:\LETTERS and the floppy disk that you're using is in drive A, you use the following command at the DOS prompt:

```
RESTORE A: C:\LETTERS\MYLETTER.DOC
```

RESTORE is the command that you use to get the file back. The A: is the floppy disk drive where the information you want to restore is located. C:\LETTERS tells the restore command what drive and subdirectory you want the file MYLETTER.DOC to be restored to. That's it. Is your name Kenny? Just wondering. . . .

Troubleshooting

MSBACKUP *gave my drive an F*

I really want to use MSBACKUP, **but my drive failed the compatibility test. Does this mean that the drive doesn't like my computer?**

Have you noticed that the one who loves the least controls the relationship? Doggone it, your computer needs you to make it fall in love with your backup floppies once and for all. Be patient. There is no such thing as a quick fix, and bad habits don't disappear overnight.

You need to look at the incompatibility issue as a symptom of the big problem. The *compatibility test* makes sure that the information backed up to floppies is a good copy of the information contained on the hard drive. If you're lucky, you may simply be trying to make backups on a bad floppy disk. Try using another disk or two. If the drive still fails the test, you're going to have to go to step two: serious counseling.

I'm going to run through some more realistic problems and solutions. They have to do with DOS itself, and you'll find more information about the DOS commands in the DOS chapter (Chapter 8). If you have DOS 6.2 or later, run the SCANDISK program at the DOS prompt by typing the following and pressing Enter:

```
SCANDISK
```

Follow the instructions on-screen to have SCANDISK check out the hard drive and fix the errors it finds. So you know, the errors fixed by SCANDISK involve files that have not been saved on the hard disk properly. These problems creep up when you turn off the computer without exiting programs; then again, they can show up without any help from you. Try the compatibility test again.

Another possible problem — oops, I mean *symptom* — is that the CONFIG.SYS file isn't set up properly. Make sure that the CONFIG.SYS file contains the following lines:

```
FILES=30
BUFFERS=30
STACKS=9,256
```

If the files and buffers are less than 30, increase them to 30. Save the CONFIG.SYS file and reboot the computer.

When the message *Starting MS-DOS* appears on-screen, press F8. You get to answer yes or no to the lines in the AUTOEXEC.BAT and CONFIG.SYS files when the computer starts. Answer yes to only the three lines that precede this paragraph, and then try the compatibility test again.

Playing a game of doom and gloom, what if the disk fails the compatibility test again? You're probably a little frustrated by now, so take a ten-minute break. When you come back, check the amount of free space on the hard disk. A hard disk that is full to the rim doesn't leave enough room for MSBACKUP to create the temporary files it needs during the backup process. Make sure that you're giving the computer enough space to work; about 5MB is good enough. Try the compatibility test again.

Here's another thought about the incompatibility issue. Maybe you and your computer have simply grown too far apart after all these years. If the computer is older, the floppy controller card may not support a feature called *DMA,* or *direct memory access.* A newer floppy controller card should solve this problem.

I hope that by the time you have read this far, you are compatible again. If not, the cable connecting the floppy drive to the floppy controller card, or the floppy drive itself, could be bad. These problems aren't serious enough to cause a breakup. An authorized computer repair center can fix them in a jiffy, and you can live happily ever after.

Increasing DMA buffer size

I tried to use `MSBACKUP` **for DOS, but it says my DMA buffer size is too small. How do I make the DMA buffer bigger, whatever this is? My wife is nagging me.**

The size of your buffer doesn't matter. It's how you use it that really counts. DMA, which stands for *direct memory access,* is a way for the computer to transfer information quickly from a device that's connected to the computer, such as the tape backup, without using the computer's CPU (*Central Processing Unit*).

When a program tells you that the DMA buffer size is too small, you can increase it easily if you're using a computer that has an 80386 or greater CPU chip. But if you're using an 80286-based or an 80886-based computer, you're out of luck, buddy. You won't be able to increase the buffer size, so you'll need to get another backup software program.

To increase the DMA buffer size, you need to tap into EMM386.EXE, the memory manager that's included with DOS 5.0 and above. You should have a line near the top of the CONFIG.SYS file that mentions EMM386.EXE. Because you're going to change CONFIG.SYS, copy this file to a floppy disk just in case something goes wrong and you need the original CONFIG.SYS file again. To change CONFIG.SYS, go to the DOS prompt, type the following, and press Enter:

```
EDIT CONFIG.SYS
```

Near the top of the CONFIG.SYS file, you should see a line that says `DEVICE=C:\DOS\EMM386.EXE`. At the end of this line, type **D=64**. The line should look like this when you're done:

```
DEVICE=C:\DOS\EMM386.EXE D=64
```

This addition tells EMM386.EXE to increase the DMA buffer size to 64K of memory. Save your work by using the File⇨Save command. Exit the Edit program by using File⇨Exit. Reboot the computer and try running the backup program again. You should be all set.

DOS upgrade creates backup error

I upgraded from DOS 5 to DOS 6.22. Everything works except that I get a message that says that I have an incorrect version installed when I try to use the BACKUP **command. How can this be?**

Sounds like you've got your back up against the wall. Starting with DOS 6.0, Microsoft put in a real backup program called MSBACKUP. MSBACKUP is a special version of Symantec's Norton Backup program.

You'll like it. MSBACKUP is more powerful, faster, and easier to use than the old DOS BACKUP command. When you installed DOS 6, you had the option of installing a version of MSBACKUP that's designed to be used with Windows. In fact, an antivirus program and an undelete program (for both DOS and Windows) come free with DOS 6 and higher too.

If you didn't install any of these optional utilities, you can install them now. Exit Windows, put DOS disk #1 in the floppy drive, change the prompt to the drive where the disk is located, type **SETUP /E**, and press Enter. After you install the extra utilities, use MSBACKUP, and all will be well.

Backup program won't read backup tape

My computer nags me to back up every time I start it, so I do. I tried to restore data from the backup, but the software won't recognize it! It says something about the tape being invalid. What did I do wrong? I'm losing sleep over this one.

If it's any consolation, you're not losing sleep over nothing. You've described a fairly common trap that computer users fall into and have trouble getting out of. Backing up information is only one step. For complete data security and peace of mind, you need to verify or compare the data after the backup is complete.

When you run a backup program, it copies, or attempts to copy, the information from the hard drive to a backup tape or floppy disks. If there is a problem with the tape or disks, the backup program *may* not know how to handle it. Some backup programs just ignore errors and keep right on working, never letting the computer user know that something could be wrong.

The verification process compares the information on the backup tape or floppy disks with the information on the hard disk drive, character by character. Some backup programs call this the *Compare* option. The comparison happens after the backup is done or simultaneously during the backup.

Unfortunately, comparing the data takes almost as long as backing it up, so many folks skip the compare process because they wrongly think that it's a waste of time. I can think of other time wasters that are much worse, such as staying for the weekend in some awful place to get a cheaper air fare.

The Bottom Line

Invest the time to verify your backups, and you'll sleep better at night.

Saving Norton Backup configuration

I used Norton Backup for Windows and set up the program. It took me about an hour to configure the darn thing. But now every time I use the program, I still have to configure the software. Why does Norton keep asking me to configure the software when I already did it?

Well, the .INI file that contains the Norton configuration information is hosed. How's that for a technical answer?

The way to fix this problem is to edit the NDW.INI file that is in the WINDOWS directory. You can use Windows Write or Notepad for this job. As a safety measure, use the Windows File Manager to make a copy of the file to a floppy disk before you start messing around with the file's innards.

Using Write or Notepad, open the NDW.INI file just as you would open any other file. When it's on-screen, remove the [NBACKUP] section and the other areas after this section that refer to the tape drive. Save the file with the changes intact and exit the program. Start Norton Backup for Windows and configure the software the way you want it. Next time you use Norton Backup for Windows, the configuration should be there.

Tape Backups

Do I need extra software?

If I buy a tape backup system, will I also need to purchase software, or will the DOS backup program work?

It's a royal bummer, but the DOS backup utility is missing the part that enables you to back up to a tape. DOS backs up the information only to floppy disks, so you need a different backup software program that works with a tape backup drive. Before buying backup software, however, check the tape backup system's box for any disks. Most manufacturers include the backup software with the drive.

Even if the backup program that came with the tape backup system works, it may not be the best software for you to use. I like Norton Backup from Symantec because it's easy to use and very fast. Norton Backup works with a wide range of tape backup systems and is available in a version for DOS and a version for Windows. Unfortunately, this software is rarely included with tape backup drives.

Try the software that came with the tape backup system because you may find that it's all you need to get the job done. If not, look for backup software that includes such features as automatic scheduling, unattended backups, automatic configurations, compression ratio options, and a user interface that allows you to point and click on the files, the directories, or the drives to back up. Before you trash the back up software that came with the tape drive, make sure that you have another backup software program that supports your tape backup drive. Make a quick call to the tape backup system's manufacturer for a list of such programs.

How do I use a tape backup?

I got tired of messing with floppy disks, so I bought a tape backup drive. I hooked it up to the computer, but I have one little problem. How do I use it?

Maybe you haven't heard this, but most computer goodies come with a handy-dandy book that's full of very interesting information. Would you believe it's called a *user's manual,* of all things? It's OK that you asked this question because many people can't understand the manual anyway. Buying the tape backup system is the place to start, but you need something else to make it work: backup software.

Most tape backup drives include software that you need to make the drive work. I'm surprised that you didn't mention that a software program was included in the drive's box. No? Are you sure? Look in the box again. If software wasn't included, take a trip to a software store and pick up a program. Central Point Backup and Norton Backup are good choices that are often faster and easier to use than the software programs that come with the drives.

Backup software enables you to use the tape backup drive. First you need to configure the drive. Then look for the software feature that searches for a tape backup drive that's hooked up to the computer. Before you can click on Start Backup, you need to select a compression ratio, pick the files to back up, and do a few more things. After you set up the software, you're ready to use the tape backup drive. Unfortunately, the fact that you figured out how to connect the tape backup drive to your computer doesn't mean that the computer is smart enough to know that you want to use it.

How much data fits on a tape?

I need to make a full backup of my computer. I have about 200MB to back up, so I bought two 125MB cartridges. How much information can I put on one backup tape?

A lot. Next question, please. Seriously, some tape backup systems are designed to back up 40MB to 250MB. Other tape backup systems go way above 250MB and up into the stratospheric gigabyte range. Backup software uses data compression and can squeeze, say, 200MB on a tape cartridge that's designed to store only 125MB. So you need only one backup tape for this backup.

Here's what happens: You select the files to be backed up and the backup software program estimates how many backup tapes it needs. To fit more information on one tape, use the program's maximum compression option. Text-only files compress much better than program files ending with .EXE and graphics files.

The backup software program may lie to you about the estimated length of time and number of tapes needed because of the different file formats. Oftentimes, the estimates are higher than the actual time needed and the number of backup tapes required. In other words, your mileage may vary.

Can I reuse tapes?

Backup tapes are pretty expensive. Can I just keep using the same tape every time I back up my system?

You can, but it may be like pouring curdled milk into your coffee. You really want to use at least four different tapes and alternate their use from backup to backup. This method provides two advantages:

➤ *Longer tape life:* Four tapes will last longer than one because you aren't using the tapes as often as you'd use just one tape.

➤ *Greater protection:* Because you have more than one tape, you have more than one source of backup data.

If you play a cassette tape over and over again, the sound quality suffers. Along the same lines, a backup tape loses quality when you use it repeatedly. Using more than one tape spreads the wear and tear over several tapes. Use tape one for the first week of the month, tape two for the second week, and so on. In case the hard drive has a problem and you need to restore information, you're no more than a week out of date.

What if your one and only backup tape was damaged somehow? What if your bungee cord was too long? Using multiple tapes provides an extra margin of safety. Most backup software have options such as data verification (information is read off the backup after writing and then compared to information on the hard disk), error correction code (special codes are added to a backup to increase the chances of recovery if the backup floppy or tape is damaged), and compare (information is read off the backup, compared to the hard disk, and verified as identical).

Komando Klues
For reliable backups, you must properly care for your backup tapes and store the tapes at room temperature. You should replace backup tapes at least once a year.

Backup program says new tapes are bad

I bought a new package of backup tapes. The tape drive said that the tapes were bad, so I took the tapes back to the store and exchanged them. I tried the new tapes, and my tape drive said these tapes were bad, too. One more exchange later, I still get the same error message. Do you think that the drive is bad or that this store may have received a box of defective tapes?

Backup tapes are similar to floppy disks and dates: all have to be formatted before you can use them the first time.

You can buy preformatted or unformatted tapes. Buying preformatted tapes costs a little more money, but you don't have to waste time formatting them. Be sure to buy the right backup tapes for your tape drive. Check the owner's manual for the tape drive to find out the exact type that you need.

Backup software has an option for formatting tapes. Try formatting one of the new tapes in your tape drive and backing up. If the format doesn't work, make sure that the tape drive is installed properly. One of the most common errors is putting the cable to the tape drive in the wrong way. Finally, if you've been using the tape drive for a while, the heads may be dirty. You can clean them by using a cotton swab and rubbing alcohol. Or take the easy way out and buy a tape backup drive cleaning kit. The cleaning kits are especially useful for people like me who break fragile objects just by looking at them.

What's the difference between DC and QIC tapes?

I noticed while shopping for a backup drive that some drives take DC tapes and other drives take QIC tapes. What's the difference? I think I bought the wrong type, and the store won't let me return them because I opened the box.

Backup tapes make terrible coasters. You can take the tape out, however, and use it for party streamers. The tapes are heavy enough to be a good paperweight. Then again, so is your computer.

The important thing is to buy the kind of backup tape that works with your tape backup system. DC and QIC are two types of backup tapes. DC stands for *data cartridge,* and a number of different DC 1/4-inch magnetic tapes are available. The DC tapes differ in length, which is what determines how much information you can store on the tape.

But this is where the DC standard stops being logical. (It always seems to happen somewhere in the computer products food chain.) DC 600, DC 1000, DC 2000, DC 2000XL, and DC 6000 are some of the tape cartridge standards. If you think that DC 600 means that the cartridge has 600 feet of tape and that DC 1000 means that the cartridge has 1,000 feet of tape, you're wrong. DC 600 has 600 feet of tape in the cartridge, but DC 1000 has 185 feet of tape in the cartridge. Don't ask me why, this is just the way it is sometimes with "standards."

Another backup tape standard is QIC. QIC stands for *quarter-inch cartridge.* The standards are the QIC-40, QIC-80, and QIC-1350. The QIC-80 is today's choice. It improves on the QIC-40 by doubling capacity. It also provides complete compatibility among tape drives that follow this standard. As a result, you can use one company's drive to format a QIC-80 tape and back up information on it and then use the tape in another manufacturer's drive. This feature is helpful if your computer dies and all you have left is the tape backup. You don't have to sweat because a QIC-80 tape backup can be restored on another system unless you made the tape on a system that uses custom compression and only that system's drives can read the format.

The safest ways to make sure that you are getting the correct tapes for your tape backup system are to check the tape drive's user's manual or to call the manufacturer's tech support line. If your tape backup drive calls for QIC tapes, use QIC tapes. Only use DC tapes in tape backup systems that call for DC tapes.

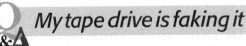

My tape drive is faking it

I installed my new IDE tape drive, and it looks like it works. The lights go on and all. After I made a backup, I checked the tape. The software told me that the tape was blank. What could be wrong?

The lights and gadgets on "Star Trek: The Next Generation" always amaze me, but I can't believe that in such an advanced, high-tech world they haven't figured out a way to give Picard hair. What's the point? There isn't any.

Perhaps the backup tape that you used wasn't formatted properly. The tape backup software has an option to format the tape before a backup is made. You may want to format the tape during lunch or at the end of the day because the process typically takes an hour. Try the backup again after the tape has been formatted.

Another possibility is that the cable that's plugged into the tape drive is in backwards. The flat, gray ribbon cable that goes from the hard drive to the tape drive has a stripe (usually red) on one edge. Look for a special mark or the words *Pin 1* on the cable's connector near the red stripe. Make sure that the cable is in the right way. If you're not sure, most tape drive manuals have a picture that shows how the cable should be connected and what it should be connected to inside the computer.

After you've checked out the cables, reinstall the backup software program. Sometimes files that are needed to make a program work get messed up, and a reinstall of the software is the quickest way to fix them. If none of these changes solves the problem, you may have a bad tape drive. Contact the tech support department of the company that made the tape drive and describe the situation. Check the warranty and ask for a replacement unit or instructions on how to get your tape drive serviced.

Backing up with no DOS

My adult children worked on my computer. I use the term *adult* loosely, by the way. They left, and then my hard drive died, and I now have no DOS, no Windows, no anything on the hard drive. Where do I even start to use my backup tapes?

Call one of those personal-injury attorneys. On second thought, this is a bad idea. I've never seen a customer testimonial about the justice that parents received after their children mutilated a hard disk. Nonetheless, you start restoring the information on the hard disk at the very beginning — that is, with DOS.

Assuming that the hard drive is working properly, you need to install DOS. Next, install the tape backup software. Put the backup tape in the tape backup drive and select Restore in the backup software. This option copies the information from the tape to the hard disk drive. Select the option to overwrite all files so that important files, including the AUTOEXEC.BAT and CONFIG.SYS files that were put on the computer when you installed DOS, are replaced with the files you had before the kids stopped by.

Now, reboot the computer so it uses the files you restored. Try some DOS programs to check that the computer is working properly. Start Windows — but be forewarned, you may get an error message that says something about your permanent swap file being corrupt. You get this error because the swap file is not there! Don't worry about it. Click OK so that Windows can get up and going. After you get inside Windows, you need to recreate the permanent swap file. If you're not sure how to make a permanent swap file, look in the Windows chapter of this book.

If after all this you're thinking seriously about taking some action against your children, I can't say that I would really blame you.

Will SmartDrive speed up my tape drive?

I use SmartDrive to speed up my computer. Can I use SmartDrive to speed up my tape drive, too?

Just because they call it *Smart*Drive doesn't mean that it's *that* smart. SmartDrive doesn't know how to work with tape drives. Some, but not all, tape backup drives work with tape backup accelerator cards. Check the tape backup manual to see whether your drive will support such a card. Aside from that, other types of tape backup drives, such as DAT (digital audio tape), are much quicker, but they're also much more expensive.

Komando
Klues

One thing that many people don't know is that the SmartDrive program included with DOS 6.2 and later can speed up the CD-ROM drive. All you need to do is make sure that the MSCDEX.EXE line appears before the SMARTDRV line in the AUTOEXEC.BAT file.

Getting the fastest backup

I went from floppies to tape for backups, but the backup process still isn't fast enough for me. I want speed-demon backups. Do you think magneto-optical should be my next move?

I bet you make obscene gestures at blue-haired ladies who drive big white cars in the fast lane. And people who signal left 20 miles before they turn and women who apply mascara while driving 55 miles per hour must really put you over the edge.

Magneto-optical (MO) is like a good wine that you shouldn't drink before its time. One MO disk can hold more than one gigabyte and lasts more than 20 years. They're great for portable storage because they're almost resistant to damage from extreme temperatures, magnetic fields, and X-rays. But MO is expensive, and its relatively slow access time makes it better for storage purposes than for daily jobs. Computer speed freaks should use DAT tapes.

DAT technology basically is the same type of technology that's used in DAT video and audio tapes. DAT drives typically store one gigabyte or more of information, and any file can be retrieved within about 20 seconds. Most DAT drives back up .5MB per second, but the Conner Peripherals MS4000 DAT backs up about 1.2MB per second. Plus, DAT tapes do not have to be formatted.

DAT drives use the DDS and DDS-2 standards. Pick the DDS-2 format because it holds more information, works faster, and is more reliable than DDS tapes. Although DAT is more expensive than conventional QIC tape backups, it's much less expensive than MO. DAT tapes are commonly used for backing up large computer networks. As DAT backups are getting more popular, their price is coming down.

The Bottom Line

I recommend that you forget about the MO right now. Get a DAT backup system, and you'll be happy.

Putting a tape drive in the floppy drive bay

I looked on the front of my computer, and there's a piece of plastic where you can put in another disk drive. Instead of another disk drive, which I don't need, can I get a tape drive to fit in the 3¹/₂-inch slot?

I am as confident that you can add a tape drive to your computer as I am that I'll be stepping on sharp Christmas tree needles that are stuck in the carpet until July. Most of the major tape drive manufacturers, including Conner, Iomega, and Summit, make 3¹/₂-inch backup drives. These drives are designed to fit right into that 3¹/₂-inch floppy disk drive space. All the holes line up and everything. It's incredible. Most companies also include a step-by-step chart showing you how to install the new tape backup drive. It's not hard to do. In fact, installing a tape backup is probably easier than vacuuming up dead pine needles.

So many drives, so little room

Desk space is at a premium, so I really want an internal tape backup drive. The problem is that most drives seem to connect to the floppy controller. I already have two floppy drives. Will I have to remove one?

It's bound to happen: The day you take out one of the floppy drives, you'll get a disk of that size in the mail, and the disk will contain moneymaking secrets. You'll never be rich. You'll be destined to live a life of mediocrity and shop for blue-light specials.

The Bottom Line

Keep the two drives because there is no reason to take one of the drives out. Companies that make tape backups realize that many computer users have two floppy disk drives already, and they've come up with a clever way of saving your computer from surgery.

The tape backup kit includes a special type of cable that plugs into the floppy controller port. The cable also has a connector to plug into the cable that goes to the floppy disk drives. It's not hard to install at all. I put one in my computer, and I'm a blonde. P.S. And it worked.

Tape drive screws up sound card

During boot up, my computer says no *SCSI host adapter* (Pro Audio Studio card) *is found, driver aborted.* I've tried sending back the sound card for a new one, moving the sound card to different 16-bit slot, and so on. No dice. The CD-ROM worked perfectly before I added a Colorado Jumbo 250. The technician at Media Vision said that the tape drive's DMA/IRQ configuration is messing up with CD-ROM, so the sound card is not recognized. I have never heard of such a thing happening. Can tape drives really mess up CD-ROM drivers?

Don't you hate it when the doctor that you go to for a second opinion directly contradicts what the first doctor told you? You're in luck because my answer is, "Yes, such conditions exist." Please pay on your way out.

DMA (*d*irect *m*emory *a*ccess) is a method that enables the CPU (the *c*entral *p*rocessing *u*nit) to talk directly to a device such as the tape backup drive or the sound card. IRQs (*i*nterrupt *req*uests) can be thought of as little flags that a device uses to get the CPU's attention. When a device such as the tape backup uses the same DMA or IRQ as another device, the computer gets confused.

The Bottom Line

So which group of settings should you change? Many sound cards expect to use certain settings to emulate or pretend that they're another type of sound card. Trying to change the settings for the tape backup is probably easier. You need to use what is called the *Columbus method*: do some exploring.

Usually, the tape backup software gives you several options for changing settings. Make a note of what the current settings are and try different combinations of settings. Just to make life harder, you have to reboot the computer each time that you change the settings. After rebooting, try running the tape backup software to see whether you can actually back something up. When you find a setting that enables you to back up, try running a test program for your sound card.

You'll need to do a little bit of work, but you should be able to find the settings that will let both the tape backup and the sound card work. Aren't computers fun?

My tape drive won't quit spinning

When the computer starts, my Jumbo 120 tape drive starts spinning and never stops. It doesn't matter whether there is a tape in it or not. How do I make it stop?

"Jane, stop this crazy thing!" Remember how cartoon character George Jetson screamed out this phrase as he was running and running on a treadmill? I think you should call your tape backup drive George.

Open up the computer case and make sure that the cable is connected tightly to George. A loose cable can cause all kinds of grief. If you don't feel comfortable working on the computer's insides, have a more experienced friend help you or take the computer to a repair facility.

Another thing: Old George could be dirty from use. Computer-supply companies make cleaning kits, but a bottle of rubbing alcohol and a package of cotton swabs can do the trick. Dip the swab in the alcohol and gently rub George's insides. He'll like this special treatment.

If neither of these tips helps, it may be time to set George out to pasture and get a new tape backup drive.

Parallel port tape drives

There is no room at my computer's inn. Do they make tape drives that hook to the parallel port?

These engineers think of everything, including zero-fat ice cream and tape backup systems that connect to the parallel, or printer, port of the computer. Colorado Memory Systems and Iomega make such animals.

Parallel port tape backup drives aren't the fastest models around. But they're still a lot better than trying to back up to floppy disks. And, if it's easier to do, chances are that you'll back up more often. A parallel port tape backup is portable and can be used easily on two or more computers. The bad news is that parallel port tape backup drives are a little more expensive than the kind that fits inside the computer. You knew this, though. Anytime you need something special, it costs a little more.

Central Point doesn't recognize tape drive

I use Central Point Backup. When it came time to configure my tape backup drive, I used the Search option. It searched and searched but could not find the tape backup drive. I tried to use the Manual Configuration option, and it asked me for an address of something. Where can I find this address?

I had this problem, too. Don't you feel better knowing that another person in this universe suffered frustration at the hands of the electronic beast? Some computer manufacturers use nonstandard addresses for certain devices. Here's how you can find out where the parallel port is located.

DOS 5.0 and above include a utility called *MSD*, which stands for *Microsoft Diagnostics*. This program enables you to take a peek at what's going on inside the computer. At the DOS prompt, and not through Windows, type **MSD** and press Enter. You'll see an option for LPT ports. Press L to see a description of a parallel port.

A computer can have up to three parallel ports, numbered LPT1 through LPT3. LPT stands for *line printer.* On-screen, find the column that says *port address.* The funny-looking number underneath is written in hexadecimal. No, the number is not cursed. *Hexadecimal* is a computer's numbering system. The standard address for LPT1 is 0378. The little *H* that you see at the end of the port address reminds you that it's in hexadecimal. Write down this number because you'll use it in the tape backup program's setup.

Run the tape backup program, and when it asks you to search for the tape backup, be brave. Tell the software that you want to put the information in all by yourself, that is, select the Manual Configuration option. Type the hexadecimal number you found in MSD and save the configuration in your backup software. All the other information should be OK. Continue running the setup and try the compatibility test. The tape backup drive should run just fine.

I think I should have verified

I admit it, I was stupid! To save time, I haven't been using the verify option when I make backups. You guessed it. Now, just when I need my tapes, I found out that they are no good! I use a Colorado drive.

You said it, not me. Not turning on the verify or compare option is a common mistake that many tape backup users make. Most tape backup programs have an option to verify that the information on the tape backup matches the information on the hard disk. Some programs perform this step while the backup is being made, and other programs verify the information after the backup is completed. Although comparing the data takes almost as long as backing it up, the time is well invested. It's like taking a moment to unplug your electric guitar before you play it while taking a bath.

You need to consult the professionals to find out whether anything can be done. One option is to send the tape to Colorado Memory Systems. They have utilities that are not available to the public, plus full-time technicians who work at retrieving data. Call the tech support number and explain the situation. They'll tell you what to do and how much the service will cost. Or look in the computer section of the Yellow Pages for a local company that specializes in data recovery. Be sure to check the company's track record and experience. If the data is important and you don't have any other copies of it or would have a rough time duplicating it, one wrong move by a data recovery technician will ruin your day.

Is anything easier than Central Point 7.22?

Is there any better software to support a 250 tape backup external port drive other than Central Point 7.22? It's pretty difficult to use.

You can count on working until May 10 every year to pay your taxes, and you can count on there always being some computer product that is better than the one you have. I know. It stinks, but that's the way of the world.

You may just need to get with the program. Central Point is up to Version 8.0 of PC Tools for DOS and Windows. The updated backup program is available only as part of the new PC Tools product. It has some enhancements, including the Format Tape option. With Version 7.22, you had to select a file to back up and turn on the Format Always option. Perhaps the Central Point upgrade is the cure you need. This option is less expensive than the alternative — buying another backup software program.

Another option, depending on the make and model of the external tape backup drive, is to use Norton Backup. Norton Backup comes in versions for DOS and Windows, and it is easier to use than Central Point's backup program. But save yourself some possible headaches over incompatibility. Before you rush out to buy Norton Backup, call the technical support department of the company that made the tape backup drive. Ask for the names of backup software programs that work with your tape backup drive. Norton is a popular program, so it's probably on the list. If you have to get another program, make sure that it's automated so that you can set it to run overnight, and make sure that you can schedule both full and incremental backups.

Komando Klues Because I already know that you're not the type to see how many extra days you can get out of a razor, find out about return policies wherever you buy the Norton program in case you don't like it. Some stores let you return software within 30 days, and other stores will never take an opened or unopened software box back.

Magneto-optical drive cross-compatibility

I'm looking to buy a magneto-optical rewriteable 5¹/₄-inch drive. I would like it to be compatible with someone else's magneto-optical drive. Are all 5¹/₄-inch magneto-optical drives compatible with each other? I can't use DAT tapes.

Unfortunately, the current state of affairs with most MO drives is worse than with foreign trade policies. Not only are the MO drives incompatible with other MO drives, there are incompatibilities within manufacturer's product lines too. Bummer.

Rather than MO, CD-R (*C*ompact *D*isc *R*ecordable) is a better choice that uses CD-ROMs. The MO cost per megabyte is about 15 cents; CD-R costs less than 4 cents per megabyte. Plus, CD-ROMs are extremely durable, have low failure rates, and are write-once protected, which means that you can't erase the data on a CD-ROM. Because there aren't any compatibility issues and there are so many CD-ROM drives now, using the CD-ROM backup on another computer isn't a problem.

CD-Rs cost about $15,000 when the units first hit the streets. I expect them to drop in price to about $1,000 in 1995. You can choose between a double-speed or single-speed CD-R drive. Double-speed is double the speed, so it's the one to get. Some other things to compare among CD-R drives include compatibility, recording speed, features, and software quality. The drives usually include software, and you have to buy the CD-ROMs separately.

The Bottom Line

The bottom line is to go with the times and with CD-R. You can thank me later.

Chapter 3

Buying a Computer

Do I even need one?

I think I want to buy a computer, but I'm not sure. And the people at computer stores won't even talk to me. What can I do with a computer? How can I tell whether I need a computer?

The salespeople won't talk to you? I can't get them to stay away from me. Tell them you have $2,000 to spend. I promise that they'll talk to you.

You can use a computer to work with words, numbers, information, and graphics. You also can use a computer for fun.

When you use a computer to work with words, you can use a word processing program to write letters, articles, and books. Word processing is a lot like using a typewriter — but better. For example, most word processing programs check your grammar and spelling. (Did you hear about the blonde who couldn't erase her typos in letters written on a computer? She used White-Out on the monitor. Hey, I'm a blonde, I can get away with it).

When you use a computer to work with numbers, you can use an electronic accountant's pad or a spreadsheet program to

➤ Manage personal and business finances.

➤ Track investments, savings, and retirement funds.

When you use a computer to work with information, you can

- ➤ Manage projects and identify goals.
- ➤ Organize personal and business schedules.
- ➤ Impress clients with whizbang presentations.
- ➤ Keep personal and business contact names and addresses in one place.
- ➤ Make mailing labels.
- ➤ Send and receive faxes.

When you use a computer to work with graphics, you can

- ➤ Create custom artwork, including logos.
- ➤ Draw architectural plans.
- ➤ Design brochures, fliers, newsletters, greeting cards, invitations, and stationery.
- ➤ Place photographs inside your publications.

When you use a computer for fun and learning, you can

- ➤ Connect to the Library of Congress.
- ➤ Get the latest sports scores, weather reports, stock quotes, and so on.
- ➤ Make travel arrangements.
- ➤ Learn a foreign language.
- ➤ Compose and play music.
- ➤ Play games.

You can do all this stuff at home or in the office. *Note:* Bosses don't understand the importance of toning up your video game skills on the job.

Many people buy the wrong computer because they forget one rule: The only reason to buy a computer is because it will help you do something. Almost anything you can imagine happens easier and quicker on a computer.

If you're like most people, you make some kind of list before heading out the door to shop. This list reminds you what you need when you get to the store. (I have lists for my lists, but that's another story.) If you make a list, buying a computer is as easy as picking up groceries at the supermarket. (Heck, it's even easier if you routinely jump behind someone in the express checkout line who has 152 items and then writes a check.) When you go to the computer market, your shopping list needn't be full of techno mumbo jumbo. It should simply list ways that you plan to use a computer.

**Komando
Klues**

So put the computer magazines away. Forget the newspaper ads. To draw up your shopping list, you need only stretch your imagination. What do you envision doing in front of the computer? (Crying isn't an option here.) It's OK to be selfish, but also think how your family or colleagues may use the computer. As you try to figure out how a computer can make your life easier or more enjoyable, don't look beyond the next year. Technology moves too fast.

If your list contains just one or two items, forget about the computer and get a dog. You'll have an easier time housebreaking a dog than justifying the money wasted on a big paperweight.

How much money do I need?

I want to tap into the global computer explosion. Is $2,000 enough money for a computer or should I save some more money before shopping?

For the sake of my other readers, please try not to use the words *computer* and *explosion* in the same sentence.

You can see the world and, at the same time, keep your life savings in an interest-bearing bank account. How? Join the Navy. Think about it. You get three good meals a day, clean clothes, some money, an education, and lots of free haircuts.

Buying a computer is like buying a car: Computers come in many different makes and models. You need to avoid fast-talking salespeople. You can choose among tons of options. You can even choose from different financing plans. And depreciation starts the moment you drive off the lot.

Do you want a mode of transportation, or do you want a status symbol? If you just want to keep up with the Joneses, save some money and aspirin and install an underground pool instead.

**Komando
Klues**

When buying a computer, first pick the software you plan to use and then pick the hardware you need to use the software. You also need to ask yourself the following questions:

> ➤ Do you need a printer?
> ➤ Do you want to send and receive faxes from your computer?
> ➤ Do you like CDs, multimedia, games, and sound?
> ➤ Do you plan to create high-end graphics, such as animation?
> ➤ Do you need to find the on-ramp to the information superhighway?
> ➤ Do you want to hook your computer up to your home entertainment center?

The bad news is that you have some homework to do before you go shopping. The good news is that for $2,000, you'll be well on your way to cruising down that information superhighway!

IBM or compatible?

Is an IBM computer better than an IBM clone?

Back when I was a kid picking coal up off the railroad tracks, um, I mean selling computers for IBM, *clone* computers carried a stigma. Worse, in those golden days of yore — remember the green and amber monitors — some software made for IBM computers wouldn't run on clones. But clone manufacturers eventually figured out how to make their computers 100 percent compatible. Plus, software companies learned to test their programs to make sure that they worked on both IBMs and clones. As a result, IBM lost its hold on the PC market, and clone computer makers raked in the profits. When clone manufacturers became more "respectable," they decided that they wanted to be called *IBM-compatible* computer makers.

IBM always has had a reputation for providing high-quality merchandise and customer support. Despite the influx of low-cost compatibles, IBM won't close its doors any time soon. And IBM-compatible manufacturers should be able to keep at least their windows open for awhile. That's good news for consumers: you don't want to buy a computer with a three-year warranty if the company will go out of business a year after you pay off your bill.

The Bottom Line

A computer not stamped with IBM logo is not inherently inferior. Top-notch IBM-compatible computer companies include AST, Compaq, Dell, Epson, Gateway, Hewlett-Packard, and Packard Bell. But folks who grew up with IBM typewriters seem to feel an extra sense of security when they work on an IBM computer. If you know this feeling, buy an IBM; otherwise, you'll kick yourself if the clone breaks. I bet you'll find that an IBM computer costs about the same as a similarly equipped and warrantied clone.

Which configuration?

How do I decide which computer configuration is right for me? I want an IBM or compatible.

Whatever computer setup you buy, you'll regret the decision in about six months. Why? A bigger better (or smaller better) computer will hit the streets, and you'll want it.

The shock is usually easier to take if you know ahead of time that your computer will seem obsolete in half a year. Or you can just wait the six months and buy the computer you *really* want.

All in all, you want power, a low price, and the most bang for your buck. Forget about the confusing chip numbers and computer slang. Focus instead on the jobs you want to do with your computer. The buying processor (ahem, *process*) is as easy as buying a T-shirt or a soft drink: small, medium, or large computer.

> ➤ A *small* IBM-compatible configuration — a good home office, student, or small office computer — will let you do light desktop publishing and word processing at a fairly good speed. Look for a 486SX 33MHz with 4MB of RAM. (You can work with 4MB of RAM, but 8MB makes life easier, especially if you plan on using more than one Windows program simultaneously.) The hard disk should hold more than 200MB of information. A CD-ROM drive is optional — you can add a CD-ROM drive later, just like you can add a CD player to your car. You also need a $3^1/_2$-inch floppy drive, a Windows accelerator local bus video card with at least 1MB of video RAM, and a 14-inch SVGA noninterlaced color monitor with a .28mm dot pitch. To send or receive faxes on your computer and connect to the Internet, an on-line service, or an electronic BBS, get a 14,400 bits per second data/fax modem. Of course, you need DOS, Windows (or Windows for Workgroups), a keyboard, and a mouse, too.

> ➤ For a little extra money, a *medium* configuration is good for the busier home office and business user. Try a 486DX2 66MHz with 8MB of RAM with a 256K RAM cache. (*Cache* is a memory trick that speeds up the computer.) The hard disk should hold more than 300MB of information. In addition, add a double-speed CD-ROM drive, a 16-bit sound board, a pair of stereo speakers, a 14,400 bits per second data/fax modem, a $3^1/_2$-inch floppy drive, a Windows accelerator local bus video card with 2MB of video RAM, and a 15-inch SVGA noninterlaced color monitor with a .28mm dot pitch. Of course, you also need DOS, Windows (or Windows for Workgroups), a keyboard, and a mouse.

> ➤ For those who win the lottery or simply want the best, get a *large* configuration: a Pentium-based computer that cruises at 60MHz or higher; 16MB of RAM with a 256K or 512K RAM cache; 500MB hard disk; a quadruple-speed CD-ROM drive; a 16-bit sound board; a pair of stereo speakers; a 28,800 bits per second data/fax modem; a $3^1/_2$-inch floppy drive; a Windows accelerator local bus video card with 4MB of RAM; a 17-inch SVGA noninterlaced color monitor with a .28mm dot pitch. Of course, you also need DOS, Windows for Workgroups, a programmable keyboard, and a mouse.

Don't worry about what all this stuff means, just know that you need to get it. While you're shopping, look at tape backup systems. A tape backup system makes it easy to ensure that you have an extra copy of the information in your computer. A tape backup system copies the information on your computer to a special tape; it works a lot like a cassette tape machine.

If you're new to computers, find a local retail store that's open on Saturdays. Look for a computer that comes with a one- to three-year warranty and a 30-day money-back guarantee. And ask about the computer hardware and software toll-free customer service numbers, their hours of operation, product warranty information, and return policies.

Note: You want free technical support. It's a good idea to call the technical support phone number before you buy the computer so that you'll know firsthand what to expect when you call for help.

Keep me upgradable!

I'm ready to have a nervous breakdown, thanks to confusing advertisements and salespeople. How can I keep from buying myself into a nonupgradable corner?

Relax — nervous breakdowns show you care. When there's nothing left to break, that's when you should worry.

Painting yourself into a nonupgradable corner happens all too easily. To help prevent this, check whether the computer you want claims to be upgradable or a computer manufacturer could "socket" to you.

Almost all Intel 486-based computers have an extra socket in the motherboard, in which you can insert a Pentium OverDrive chip — a special version of Intel's Pentium. Internally, the OverDrive chip works like a Pentium, but the rest of the computer thinks that it's still a 486 chip. The Intel OverDrive chip produces substantial across-the-board improvements. As a result, you get a faster computer and some next-generation processor advantages without buying a new computer.

You have to be careful because the vacant socket in your PC may accept only upgrade chips that have a certain number of pins: for example, 169, 237, 238, or 273. Soon, you should see 235-pin and 320-pin sockets, too. So look for a computer that has a 238-pin socket on the motherboard; this socket can handle just about any OverDrive chip.

By the way, computers that meet Intel's upgrade standards carry the *Intel Verified* logo.

Komando Klues

No matter what you buy today, something better will be available tomorrow. The trick is to buy as much computer as you can afford now. That way, you get the most out of your investment.

If you buy older technology, you won't be happy. You'll wind up looking at that old computer and feeling the same way people do when they look at wedding pictures after a divorce.

Upgrade or start over?

I have a 486SX 25MHz with 4MB of RAM and a 135MB hard drive. I recently installed a multimedia kit, a new floppy disk drive, and an internal fax modem (14.4). I do not need a new monitor or printer, but I want to upgrade my RAM by at least 4MB, and I really need a new hard drive. A friend suggested that I can get a new computer for as low as $1,100. What do you recommend?

First, check what it will cost to buy a new computer that has all the features you want (I believe $1,100 will net you a computer almost identical to what you have now). If you can use another computer, you may want to keep the first one and just buy a new one. If not, you can upgrade your current computer, but you usually end up with some components (such as the hard drive) collecting dust on your shelf.

Many 80486-based computers sold in the last few years have a Pentium OverDrive socket in it, where you can plug in an OverDrive chip. You can think of this chip as halfway between a 486 and a Pentium. It speeds up the operation of the computer without forcing you to replace any other components.

If you want to make the jump to the next level of computer performance and buy a Pentium, you really can't simply upgrade. To get the full Pentium experience, the motherboard must be designed to work with the Pentium. A faster computer brain goes to waste if the other components, such as the video card and the hard drive controller, operate at a slow speed. So if you're going to invest in a Pentium computer, you can't go halfway. You have to buy a completely new computer.

What's my old computer worth?

I want to sell a 33MHz 386DX computer with a 150MB hard drive, Sound Blaster (8 bit, no stereo), and without the monitor. How much should I ask for it?

This question is tough to answer because the market is constantly changing. A common mistake that people make when selling their computers is to ignore the going prices. For example, if your computer cost you over $3,000, you may think that $1,200 is a fair price, but you probably won't get more than $600.

Your best bet is to look at your local newspaper's classified section and check out prices on similar systems. If you have access to America Online, you can surf the NACOMEX listing of used-computer prices (updated monthly) in our Komputer Klinic menu — gain access by using the keyword *KOMANDO*. NACOMEX is a company that tracks and brokers used-computer equipment; you can reach it by calling 1-800-NACOMEX.

You'd better hurry. The price of your computer just dropped $30 in the time it took you to write me.

Are mail-order companies any good?

I'm leery about buying something I have never seen, but mail-order prices are great. Do a lot of people get ripped by computer mail-order companies?

Be careful. When you want to order a computer by mail order, first contact the Better Business Bureau in the city where the mail-order company is based. See whether other people have complained about the service from these companies.

Komando Klues
Another good idea is to pay for the computer system with your credit card; you have a bit more control. If the computer you ordered isn't shipped, is damaged, or isn't what you've ordered, you can dispute the charge with your credit card company. You will not be charged for the computer until you are satisfied with your purchase. Also, many credit card companies offer extended warranties on purchases made with the credit card.

If you can, use your ex's credit card. Doing so minimizes almost all the risk.

Warranty or service contract?

What's the difference between a computer warranty contract and a computer service contract?

Computer warranties and service contracts are the high-tech equivalent of the Maytag repair people. Computers are like any other electrical appliances; they are machines, subject to breakdowns, which often occur at the most inopportune times. Think of warranties and service contracts as insurance: you may never need it, but if you do, you're sure glad you have it.

Warranties are offered by the manufacturer generally as an incentive to buy from it and not the competition. With warranties, manufacturers say "Our product is so good, we stand behind it." Warranties, which usually cover a specific time period (such as 30 days, 90 days, or a year), assure users that the product will be fixed at no, or a reduced, charge should the product fail during the proscribed time period because of a defect.

Service contracts extend the warranty period. But watch out: Service costs an average of $1\frac{1}{2}$ percent of the original purchase price per month, so you wind up paying for the system twice over in five years. Service organizations divide the type of service they offer into two categories:

➤ *On-site service* means that the equipment is serviced at your home or office. You place a call and a qualified technician arrives within a given time (this is response time, not repair time), as stated in the contract.

➤ *Carry-in service* is generally less expensive because you haul the unit in for repair. Some service companies offer loaner units, but you usually have to ask for one. It's a good idea to negotiate getting loaner units before signing the service contract.

It's a good idea to negotiate a service contract when you're buying the computer system. This way you're not limited to reading the fine print, you can help write it, too. So make sure you don't pay for service on warranted items. And make sure the equipment listed in the service contract matches the equipment on the purchase order.

You can always let your cousin work on your computer; remember, he had the same problem a year ago with his. Of course, he fixed it by dropping it a half inch from the table.

Burn-in period

I ordered a new computer, but they won't let me take it home until they do a 72-hour burn-in. What's a burn-in?

Sounds like you're buying a custom-built computer. Reputable computer manufacturers typically run a computer for a few days — a *burn-in* period — to make sure that all the components work together properly.

A burn-in is necessary when setting up a computer system, period. If an electronic component is going to go bad, it will go bad within the first couple of days. (If only we could find out so quickly in our personal relationships.) If you're buying a computer off the shelf, the burn-in has already been done. A 72-hour burn-in period is well worth the wait.

Upgrade — now or later?

I'd like to buy a cheap system and upgrade later. Is this a good idea?

Wake up and smell the coffee, buddy. Unless you're buying the best of the best, you are ready to upgrade as soon as you buy. I bet you're driving a Pinto with headers and chrome all over it.

Computer technology moves so fast that there's always something better. If you buy a cheap system now with hopes of upgrading later, you'll inevitably end up with a cash cow.

New technology enters the market relatively high-priced; the price reduction (more like a price landslide) occurs in about six months, or when newer, faster technology is introduced. For example, say you buy a low-end VGA card for $100, but in a year you want to sell that video card and get a faster one; that $100 video card will be worth less than $40. You will have lost $60 seemingly overnight. More important, the latest games and programs for your computer will look pretty bad on the VGA, too.

Komando Klues As a rule of thumb, buy as much computer as you can afford when handing the credit card over to the retailer.

Upgrade it or replace it?

I keep buying new parts for my old computer. How can you tell when you've reached the end of the upgrade road and it's time to take the plunge with a new system?

You know you've reached the end of the upgrade road when the money spent on upgrades nearly equals the price of a new system. Is it worth buying a new transmission for an old car when the motor sounds like it has smoker's hack? I recently spent $500 just to get new speakers to block out the awful noise in my engine.

Most people start adding bigger and better computer parts innocently — maybe some more memory, a larger hard disk, a new video card, and a better monitor. But they would have been better off financially buying a new computer from the start. Some components can actually keep a new computer from working at peak performance levels. For example, a VGA card that you've been using since 1989 works in the latest Pentium-based computer, but it works *very slowly*.

The Bottom Line

My advice is sell the old computer, donate it for a tax deduction, or give it to a young relative. Then buy a new computer.

Building a computer

I want to build my own computer. Where can I find kits, manuals, and reasonably priced parts?

I bet you like hunting for your own food although you live near a supermarket.

My recommendation: Forget about it. Get another hobby. It's cheaper to just buy the prebuilt system. Besides, you're asking for trouble: it's tough getting pieces and parts from different companies to work together.

If you're committed, drop by a bookstore or library and check out the books on building your own PC. In particular, *Build Your Own Multimedia PC* by Aubrey Pilgrim (Windcrest/McGraw-Hill) is a gold mine of information. And techs far and wide boast about a publication called *Processor* (1-800-334-7443).

Memory

A friend told me that I should stay away from buying a big-name computer, such as one made by IBM or Compaq. He said that the memory upgrades were almost four times the price of these computers. Is this true?

I think you're hanging out with the wrong crowd. Don't let your friend impose his fears on you.

Many big, brand-name computers are, brace yourself for a five-syllable word, *proprietary*. In other words, the CEOs of the companies who make these computers flunked sharing in kindergarten. Some of a proprietary — go ahead, say it, it won't bite — computer's components, including memory, may work in only that type of computer.

While the type of memory in (repeat after me) proprietary computers is often different from the type used by clone computers, even the biggest computer companies don't design and manufacture their own memory chips. And because the big-name computer companies sell a lot of computers, other companies have made fortunes from selling parts, such as memory upgrades, that work on proprietary computers. Buying memory and parts from these other companies, called *third-party manufacturers*, is like buying car parts made by a company other than the company that made the car. Third-party memory upgrades usually are less expensive than the computer maker's upgrades. Capitalism breeds competition, especially in the computer industry.

Check the back pages of any computer magazine and look for advertisements from companies that sell memory. Make sure you have your exact computer make and model number handy; you need this information to buy the right memory upgrade kit for your computer. Be sure to ask the third-party company and the computer's manufacturer if installing a third-party upgrade kit will void any warranties. If you don't feel comfortable doing the job yourself, any reputable computer repair center should be able to sell and also install an upgrade kit.

The Bottom Line

The bottom line: Don't worry about memory upgrade prices if you're contemplating buying a big-name computer.

What is RAM, anyway?

I am considering purchasing a computer that comes with 2MB of RAM. What's RAM? Is 2MB enough for Windows programs?

I daresay you'll be sorry if you answer a personal ad in *Soldier of Fortune* magazine. But you may be even sorrier if you buy a computer that has only 2MB of RAM.

RAM, or *random access memory*, is the holding area where the computer keeps information that it's working on. That is, RAM is temporary memory (the permanent place you save information on your computer is *hard disk space*). The more RAM you get, the better off you are.

You can start Windows with 2MB of RAM, but it's not enough to do any real work, unless you consider playing the card game Solitaire work; you need at least 4MB of RAM. If you have 4MB but constantly see the Windows hourglass, you probably need even more RAM. So if you can afford it, get 8MB; in fact, the biggest Windows performance boost you can see corresponds to an increase from 4MB to 8MB RAM.

Sophisticated Windows-based programs — such as high-end graphics, desktop publishing, or large database programs — may need 16MB of RAM or more.

Processors

Model numbers

386, 486, DX, SX, DX2, SX2, DX4, Pentium. Yikes! How can I buy a computer when I can't read the ads? What do these numbers mean?

The higher the number, the more dollars you're going to fork over.

Want to impress your friends, dazzle your teachers, and amaze your dates? Tell 'em that there are more CPU (central *processing unit*) chip models than there are players in a basketball game. And like a number on a basketball player's jersey, each model number merely identifies the chip. Some microprocessor chips are better at layups (word processing), while others are better at dunks (more demanding graphic-, video-, and calculation-intensive applications).

In a computer, the microprocessor controls all the components inside your computer — such as memory, screen displays, video cards, disk drives, printers, software programs, and more. So although it's about the size of a postage stamp, the main CPU chip is the star player on a computer court.

Since the 8088 CPU chip used in the original IBM PC, a variety of better and faster chips has hit the marketplace — 80286, 80386, 80486, and the Pentium. The Pentium is Intel's latest microprocessor (Intel would have called it the 586 had it been able to avoid a trademark war). By the way, Intel is the company that designed the original version of all these CPU chips, and it is the leading computer chip maker in the world.

Forget about the 386 if you want a new computer; the 486- and Pentium-based computers are today's first-stringers. To understand, you have to experience the difference for yourself: CD-ROM and multimedia applications chug along on a 386-based computer.

The 486SX is the 486DX's little brother. The biggest difference: The math coprocessor has been disabled on the SX. The 486SX2 50, meanwhile, has the clock-doubling technology, which means it's faster than the plain SX chip. In fact, the 50MHz SX2 averages 30 percent better performance than the 25MHz SX.

The 486DX is virtually extinct, thanks to Intel's positioning of the 486DX2, which is a 486DX 25MHz or 33MHz chip with one add-on — a neato feature, called an OverDrive chip, that doubles the CPU's speed. In other words, with the OverDrive chip, a 25MHz chip cruises at 50MHz and a 33MHz screams along at 66MHz. You don't have to pay a lot more money for the extra speed.

The DX4 chip uses the OverDrive technology, too, but don't be fooled by the *4* in DX4. This chip works two to three times as fast, not four times as fast, as a vanilla DX chip. The DX4 CPUs, however, have an internal 16K cache (a memory trick to speed up the computer), twice as large as the cache in DX- and DX2-family processors. The DX4 also boasts 3.3-volt circuitry and built-in power management. This means that it runs cooler than 5-volt circuitry and uses less battery power in portable computers. But the Pentium processor, Intel's latest technological feat, is the future. A 66MHz Pentium is almost twice as fast as a 486DX2 running at 66MHz.

DX4 computers are a value choice, and Pentium computers are a performance choice. Buying a DX4 is a good decision if you want a fast processor but you need to save money. Of course, when the 90 and 100MHz Pentium becomes preeminent, prices of 60 and 66MHz Pentium PCs will drop.

Intel engineers are like Santa's little elves: they keep working on faster CPUs year-round. The newest Pentium successor, code-named P6, is expected to be three times as powerful as the 60MHz Pentium. The Pentium chip is the most powerful processor currently available for IBM-compatible computers. There are other chips, like the DEC Alpha, that are more powerful. But the Pentium is only made by Intel. Other chip makers are working on "Pentium-class performance" Intel-compatible processors.

Here's the important thing to remember: The higher the number chip, the newer the chip, the more powerful the computer, and the more expensive the computer.

Math coprocessor

I want a 486 computer. The guy at the computer store said that everyone needs a math coprocessor. Is he right?

Look into the salesperson's eyes. Do you see dollar signs where the pupils should be?

A math coprocessor is a special type of CPU chip that only does mathematical calculations. It's natural to think, "Hey, I need a math coprocessor." But not all software takes advantage of a math coprocessor. If your software doesn't look specifically for a math coprocessor, the math coprocessor just sits there and does nothing — much like the salesman after you leave the store. Most spreadsheet programs, heavy-duty computer-aided design programs, and graphics programs use a math coprocessor. Word processors and desktop publishing programs do not.

Komando Klues

If you're not going to be using software that needs a math coprocessor, why pay for it? You're better off putting that money in extra RAM or cool software.

Note: DX- and DX2-based computers have math coprocessors. The 486SX and SX2 models do not, but the 50MHz SX2 is 30 percent faster than the 25MHz SX. So by buying the SX2, you can save a couple of hundred dollars while getting pretty fast performance.

Megahertz (MHz)

What's the MHz rating?

Mega-hurts is slamming your thumb with a hammer. It's going outside in the freezing cold. It's buying a 386SX in a Pentium world.

Actually, *MHz* (or megahertz) is the number of times per second in millions that a CPU does its thing. Yeah, right.

The Bottom Line

In other words, think of the difference in MHz ratings (also called *clock speed*) as the difference between cruising down the freeway at 55 mph versus crawling through a school zone at 15 mph. The harder you press a car's accelerator, the more gas it takes and the quicker you arrive at your destination. The higher a CPU's MHz rating, the faster the chip processes information and the faster you get the information from the computer.

Point at a computer in a computer store and ask a salesperson what kind of computer it is. You'll hear something like, "This power horse is a 486DX4 100MHz." The first number is the processor; the second number is the clock speed.

Ultimately, the MHz rating is just one piece of the computer's speed puzzle. You also need to take into account the amount of RAM, the CPU model number, and other nitty-gritty details.

Different processor brands

I see that computer processors are made by Intel, AMD, Cyrix, and others. Are all brands created equal? It seems the computers with Intel processors cost more than the other brands.

Go back "Intel" your mom that you are going to need more money for your new computer. But tell her it's worth it.

I hired an interior designer who keeps telling me that the high-priced couch in the family room is a Chesterfield because it's designed by someone with a fancy name. Couch or Chesterfield, what's the diff? No matter what you call it or who made it, it's still something that guests ruin and the cat uses to sharpen its claws.

Same deal with computer processors — almost. Intel, AMD, Cyrix, NexGen Microsystems, and so on are companies that make computer chips. Intel is the king of computer processors and sells most of the chips in PCs. The other manufacturers make almost-Intel computer chips.

Who can sell which chip design has been the subject of several lawsuits; it's pretty dry stuff, so I won't go into detail. But for the most part, the compatible CPUs work like the Intel processors. A few software programs, however, may have trouble using a non-Intel chip. This problem isn't as big as before because mainstream popular programs are tested today on the most commonly sold computer chips.

Sometimes, compatible chip makers try to differentiate their product by improving Intel's design. For example, they may increase the size of the cache inside the chip. Intel's Pentium 100MHz chip currently outperforms all other chips, but who knows what the future will bring? Although the Intel chips cost a little bit more, they are the standard for IBM-compatible computers.

Drives

 *MTBF*

I'm sick of all these acronyms! What is MTBF?

Not much. *MTBF*, or *mean time between failure*, means the average time (usually measured in hours of operation) that a device will work before it goes to the great computer graveyard in the sky. Hard disk drives are usually advertised with an MTBF number after them.

Although hard disks are very reliable, they can fail. Some hard disk manufacturers *claim* an MTBF rate of five years, but there is no standard for determining MTBF rates. Thus, the calculation is left more or less to the manufacturers. In other words, MTBF claims are like the phrases *works like a charm* or *so easy, a 2-year-old can do it*.

Even the most dependable hard disks can die before their time, like Thunderbird wine. If the hard disk sounds like a cat (mine did once), or if a saved file magically changes into strange symbols when retrieved, be aware that danger is approaching.

Hard disk problems are not confined to the unit. Often, a loose cable connection or bad hard disk controller card can cause problems.

Because it's hard to say precisely when a hard disk will fail, keeping regular backups is essential. If you experience hard disk failure, the pain will be eased if you know you have a copy of the information on the hard disk outside the computer.

Hard drive size

How much hard drive space is enough?

You can never be too rich, too thin, or have too much hard drive space.

If you're buying a computer, you should get at least a 200MB hard drive. In fact, many computers are now sold with 300MB or larger hard drives.

The problem: Programs are getting bigger. Windows by itself consumes about 9MB of hard drive space. DOS 6.22, with all the components installed, takes almost 5MB. Microsoft Word for Windows 6 uses almost 14MB of space, and CorelDRAW! 5 when fully installed eats up almost 50MB of hard drive space.

As your hard disk fills, you have to start erasing programs to make room for new programs. That's a bummer, especially if you have to choose between Flight Simulator and your contact management program.

Stac Electronics developed a program to help solve the hard drive space problem. Stacker is an "on-the-fly" disk compression program. When the computer wants to save something to the hard disk, Stacker jumps in and says, "Let me put that away for you." While Stacker puts the file away, Stacker crunches the file to take the least possible amount of space. When the computer wants to read a file, Stacker says, "Let me get that for you." While Stacker gets the file, it unpacks the file, which returns to its original size.

Microsoft included a disk compression program called DoubleSpace with MS-DOS 6.0. In MS-DOS 6.2 DoubleSpace was replaced by a program called DriveSpace. These disk compression programs do a good job, but I don't consider them a long-term solution for more hard drive space.

Buy as much hard drive as you can afford. Believe me, you will fill it up quicker than the time it takes Christmas to pack up and leave town.

$3^1/_2$- or $5^1/_4$-inch floppy drive?

Hardly any good software comes on $5^1/_4$-inch disks anymore. Is it a good idea to save a little money and buy just the $3^1/_2$-inch drive? Or will $5^1/_4$-inch disk drives come back in style?

Much like ugly polyester leisure suits, $5^1/_4$-inch disks are dead.

Why? You need fewer $3^1/_2$-inch disks than $5^1/_4$-inch disks to store the same amount of information. A $5^1/_4$-inch floppy disk can hold a maximum of 1.2MB of information. A high-density $3^1/_2$-inch disk can hold 1.44MB of information. An extra high-density $3^1/_2$-inch disk holds 2.88MB of data.

Plus, $3^1/_2$-inch disks are encased in a hard plastic case and are more durable. And the metal sliding door on the $3^1/_2$-inch disk helps keep dust and fingerprints off the disk itself.

Save those $5^1/_4$-inch floppy disks, though: they make great high-tech drink coasters.

Preinstalled Software

Software registration cards

My new computer came with preinstalled copies of DOS 6.2 and Window 3.1. The manuals were printed by the manufacturer under the Microsoft copyright. My problem: There were no individual software registration cards.

Relax, a real problem is when you receive a registration card and no software.

You have what is known as an *OEM package* of DOS and Windows, which typically comes with a system from a large computer manufacturer.

OEM stands for *original equipment manufacturer*. Microsoft often licenses its products to various computer manufacturers and vendors, who *bundle*, or include, software with their hardware. Most of the time, OEM software from Microsoft isn't registered with Mr. Bill and his gang. Rather, OEM software is registered with the company that sold you the software; that vendor then provides all support and upgrade services.

So call your vendor. By all means, however, check for a Microsoft support number in the manuals. You may be the exception to the OEM rule.

Preinstalled software — no disks!

I just bought a laptop. DOS and Windows were already installed, and I don't have any program disks. What happens if I need to put DOS and Windows back on the computer?

Computer companies save money by not including the program disks. When you buy a computer that has DOS and Windows preinstalled, you need to create your own DOS and Windows installation disks. The information you need is located on the computer's hard drive.

Look for a program icon called DiskImage (or something like that) in Program Manager. Double-clicking on the icon starts a program that allows you to make DOS and Windows disks. Once the copies are made, the program usually removes from the hard drive the information it copied, freeing up a lot of hard drive space.

Komando Klues

Make the program disks today. The five minutes it takes now can save you heartache (or in some cases, a heart attack) later if you need for some reason to put DOS and Windows back on your computer. After you finish making the DOS and Windows disks, make a "bootable" emergency disk. Start by putting a blank formatted disk in the computer's floppy disk drive. From the DOS prompt, type **SYS A:** and press Enter. Now, copy two important files your computer needs to run: the AUTOEXEC.BAT and CONFIG.SYS files. Finally, copy all the files that have the .INI file extension in your WINDOWS directory: these are important for Windows to run.

Monitors

If I get an SVGA monitor, do I need a special video card?

Probably. SVGA (or *Super Video Graphics Array*) is better than plain old VGA like Superman is better than an ordinary man.

VGA, which hit the world in 1987 when IBM debuted the IBM PS/2 computer, was better than the previous video standard, EGA, because it could display more tiny dots, known as *picture elements* or *pixels* (but not pixies). EGA displays 640×350 pixels; VGA, on the other hand, displays 640×480 pixels; while SVGA displays 800×600 pixels. The more pixels you have, the better the picture looks on-screen.

SVGA also can display 256 colors on-screen at once. It makes for some strange pictures.

The number of pixels and colors you see depends on the *driver* installed, another piece of the monitor puzzle. The video driver lets a program such as Windows talk to the video card. A new SVGA monitor works on a plain old VGA card, but chances are you have an SVGA card and don't even know it. The drivers, provided with the video card, are the key to taking advantage of all that an SVGA monitor gives you.

The Bottom Line

The bottom line: Your current card will probably work, but you may need to get new video drivers that are available from the video card's manufacturer.

Video drivers get updated all the time but not everyone knows it. You normally have to call the company that made the video card to find out whether a new driver exists. The new drivers typically solve problems, or *bugs*, that occur with certain programs. Oftentimes, the new video drivers work faster than the old drivers, too.

Boy, after reading this answer, you probably are glad you didn't ask me what time it is for fear that I may tell you how a watch works.

Video accelerator cards

The computer store told me that Windows runs faster with an accelerator card. Is this true? The salesperson wants to sell me one that has 2MB of RAM.

A *video accelerator card* has special built-in circuitry that speeds up the screen display in Windows. The card is tailored for Windows because everything in Windows (including words, menus, and buttons) is a graphic or a picture. Working with Windows is a lot like ordering food at Denny's; everything on the menu is shown with a picture. A computer takes longer to draw a picture on-screen in Windows than it does to display text on-screen in DOS.

The 2MB of RAM on the accelerator card speeds up the video display. With the extra RAM, you can increase the number of colors that appear on-screen at once and adjust the size of the video display (VGA mode: 640 × 480 pixels or SVGA mode: 800 × 600 pixels). Some cards help draw fonts on-screen, too.

The standard Windows VGA display shows 16 colors, and enhanced Windows modes let you see over 24 million colors. But colors take juice: the more colors, the slower the screen display. Unless you're doing high-end graphics work, a 256-color display should suit you just fine and won't slow down the system very much.

The 14- or 15-inch monitors that are sold with computer systems have a screen size of 800 × 600 pixels. Although the video card can display 1,024 × 786 pixels, the size of icons and text on-screen is so small that it's not practical for most people to use. You need a magnifying glass to see anything.

Color – active or passive?

I want to buy a laptop. What's the difference between active color and passive color?

Usually, a couple of thousand dollars. Next question, please.

Active matrix LCDs (*l*iquid *c*rystal *d*isplays) may cost more money than their passive matrix cousins, but they look a lot better. Just ask anyone in Los Angeles; they'll tell you that your image is, like, well, you know, everything.

A picture appears on-screen as *transistors* turn pixels on and off. *Passive* matrix screens use one transistor for each row of pixels. Each pixel in a row, therefore, must share a transistor. *Active* matrix screens have a transistor for each pixel. In an active matrix screen, pixels never have to wait for a transistor; they are turned on or off without delay. As a result, you see images on-screen faster.

The difference between displays is not too problematic for people with geriatric mouse movements. But passive matrix screens are often too slow for users who move their mouse pointer quickly; the mouse pointer is lost until the mouse stops and the screen can catch up with the user's movements. The active matrix screen is fast enough to keep up with mouse movements, animation, and more.

Komando Klues

Know also that the color on passive matrix screens tends to be washed out when compared to active matrix screens.

You have to pay the price for active matrix screens, though. They say a picture is worth a thousand words; in the world of computers, it's also worth a thousand dollars. Part of the price tag is tied directly to current manufacturing technology results: almost 80 percent of active matrix LCD screens are rejected due to transistor problems. As soon as manufacturing obtains higher yields, active matrix screens will be much less expensive. In turn, they will be found on more desktops. They may even invade other screen domains, such as television.

Printers

Q&A *Is dot matrix outdated?*

I don't have a lot to spend but I need a printer. Is a dot matrix printer a good printer for cheapos like me?

Congratulations. The first step on the road to recovery is admitting that you're a cheapo.

How you look on paper is as important as how you look in person. I know that money may be tight, but your image is important. You have to consider what you'll be printing and who will see it. Dot matrix printers, which drive a lot of little dots on the page to form words and images, are the least expensive printers; they get the job done and produce acceptable printouts. On the flip side, they don't provide the best output possible; in addition, they're noisy. Dot matrix printers cost a few hundred dollars and are good to use at home or college. If you're in business, don't even consider buying a dot matrix printer unless you're printing a multipart form or lots of mailing labels.

If you do decide to purchase a dot matrix printer, get a 24-pin printer. Older 9-pin printers are cheaper, but they spit out lousy results. Besides, if you do any printing at 2 a.m., everyone will know because 9-pin printers sound like jackhammers. Nearly all 24-pin dot matrix printers, meanwhile, offer something called *near letter quality*. Each letter is printed twice at a slight offset, so the printout looks a little better.

Dot matrix printers come in two sizes: narrow and wide. The narrow type uses $8^1/_2$ x 11-inch paper. The wider printer accepts paper 14 inches wide; you can easily print accounting sheets and wide spreadsheets. Epson, Okidata, Panasonic, Star, and IBM or Lexmark sell the most dot matrix printers.

Komando Klues

Before you get a dot matrix printer, look at inkjet printers, which squirt tiny beads of ink at the paper. These ink droplets are so fine there can be as many as 90,000 dots in a square inch of paper. Incredible. An inkjet printer may cost almost the same as a high-end dot matrix printer, but it's a better choice. Inkjet printers produce a higher-quality output than dot matrix printers, and some produce the same resolution as low-end laser printers. You can even find color inkjet printers for a little more money than vanilla inkjet printers.

So check out inkjet printers. They are cheap and your image on paper won't suffer.

Cheap, good, and in color?

I can't afford a laser printer, but print quality is important. Does someone make a really good printer that I can afford? Oh yeah, I need color, too.

I hope you didn't spend too much on the computer. Every computer buyer should leave something for a printer.

Inkjet printers, the cheapest way to get desktop publishing and graphics on paper, are popular with people who don't want to spend the extra money for a laser printer. You may see inkjet printers advertised as laser quality because they produce almost the same resolution as low-res laser printers. But an inkjet is not a laser printer. You can see the difference in printouts. If you get an inkjet printer, pick one that prints both normally ($8^1/_2 \times 11$ inch or *portrait mode*) and sideways ($11 \times 8^1/_2$ or *landscape mode*).

Inkjets, which spray-paint tiny drops of ink onto a page, are fairly quiet printers; I like them. Instead of using a ribbon like dot matrix printers, inkjet printers use a plug-in cartridge. How long the cartridge lasts depends on whether you're printing all text, text and graphics, or just graphics. You can expect about 300 double-spaced pages of text per cartridge. Hewlett-Packard, Canon, and Epson are the leading manufacturers of inkjet printers. The printers cost around $300.

Color inkjet printers are becoming very popular. Their ink cartridge actually contains four different colors, from which all the other colors are made. When you're not printing a color picture, you can snap the usual black ink cartridge in place of the color ink cartridge. Color inkjet printers run a couple of hundred dollars more expensive than black-and-white inkjet printers.

 ## *Is laser worth the cost?*

Laser printers are supposed to be the best, but do I really need one?

Laser printers are better than inkjet printers and work twice as fast. Unfortunately, laser printers are more expensive than inkjet printers.

Many companies are now making personal laser printers. These models aren't quite as fast as their professional relatives, but they cost only about $500. Personal laser printers usually print out at a lower resolution than the professional models. Don't worry, though, 300 dpi (*dots per inch*) was the standard for the professional laser printers for many years. For most work, 300 dpi is just fine.

Serial and parallel printers

What's the difference between serial and parallel printers?

Printers connect to computers at ports. Parallel printers connect at parallel ports; serial printers connect at serial ports.

IBM computers invariably use parallel printers, while most Macintosh computers use serial printers. Serial ports can take only one bit of information at a time; parallel printers take eight bits of information at a time, so parallel printers work faster than serial printers. Some laser printers can connect to both serial and parallel ports.

If a salesperson doesn't know the difference, run, do not walk, from the store.

PCL and PostScript printers

What is the difference between PCL, PostScript, and regular laser printers?

The difference is money — a few hundred dollars to be exact.

Laser printers actually have their own computer brains (also known as processing units), memory, and languages. PCL, or *P*rinter *C*ommand *L*anguage, is the language used by Hewlett-Packard laser printers. PostScript is a language developed by Adobe Systems. If a laser printer is not PostScript-compatible, it is invariably PCL-compatible.

In many ways, PostScript laser printers are more sophisticated than PCL laser printers. You often see them at better parties, and they don't get so drunk that you can't talk to them. No, really, PostScript is a page-description language. Every item that a PostScript printer prints on a page was put there by a programming statement. Although this approach makes PostScript laser printers very powerful, it also makes them a bit slower and more expensive than PCL laser printers.

Komando
Klues

For IBM-compatible computer users, PCL printers are the standard. PostScript laser printers are the standard for Macintosh computers. However, anyone who is serious about desktop publishing (IBM or Mac) uses a PostScript printer. In fact, virtually all commercial printing, including this book, is printed on high-res PostScript imagesetters, which typically print at 1,200 or 2,400 dpi. This resolution is much better than the 300 or 600 dpi found on the typical computer laser printer. You can find imagesetters at service bureaus or companies that specialize in creating high-quality images for use in the publishing industry.

CD-ROMs

 Preinstall now or upgrade later?

I know I will want a CD-ROM drive eventually. Should I wait and get an upgrade kit later or should I buy one preinstalled?

That depends on whether you're the type of person who pulls up to the self-serve pump at the gas station or if you have someone "fill-er-up" for you.

Computer CDs are really, really cool. You can see video clips, hear music, and get tons of information on one CD. The drive that runs CDs in a computer is called a CD-ROM drive.

If you can't afford a computer with a CD-ROM drive, you can add one later. If you do so, always buy it as part of a *multimedia upgrade kit*: you get a sound board, a CD-ROM drive, and everything else needed to make a PC a multimedia PC. (You typically get some free CDs in upgrade kits, too.) If you try to piece together multimedia components from different manufacturers, odds are you're going to have trouble getting the PC to work.

Users with some experience may be able to install a multimedia upgrade kit, but the process is often a source of frustration for many people. The era of *plug and play* computing isn't here, yet. When installing a multimedia kit, you have to deal with IRQs, DMAs, memory addresses, device drivers, and more. If this doesn't sound like fun to you, buy a computer with the CD-ROM drive and sound card already installed. That way, you can spend your time using the CD-ROM drive and software and not configuring the thing.

Internal or external?

What's the difference between internal and external CD-ROM drives?

Tough question. Let me put on my thinking cap and turn over my crystal ball. Hmmmmmm, the answer is . . . an internal CD-ROM sits inside the computer and an external CD-ROM sits outside the computer.

The real differences are cost, space, installation ease, and flexibility. There is no real performance difference, for internal and external CD-ROMs work the same way. Performance is based on access speed, spin rating, and how the drive sends the data from the CD-ROM to the computer.

Installing the CD-ROM drive vertically

I'm considering upgrading my system with a CD-ROM and sound card, but the drive will have to be in the vertical position. Is this OK?

Why does the drive have to be in a vertical position? You're not sacrificing decent living space for that CD-ROM and sound card, are you?

Some CD-ROM drives can be mounted vertically, but not all work in this position. You have to check with each CD-ROM drive's manufacturer. If the manufacturer says not to run the CD-ROM drive on its side, listen. The drive may work now, but you may wind up damaging the drive itself and/or your CDs. You also void your warranty.

Komando Klues

You're better off sticking to the traditional horizontal position. It's really hard to juggle CDs when the drive is vertical, and you don't want fingerprints or scratches on your CDs. Get an external CD-ROM instead. You get more flexibility without jeopardizing the CDs' life span and the CD-ROM drive's use or warranty.

Spin speed

Picking out the best CD-ROM drive is driving me bonkers. If I plan to use the CD-ROM drive for games and encyclopedias, which speed should I buy?

If you drive a Pinto, you may not be qualified to drive an Indy car. But if you can drive an Indy car, you certainly can handle the clutch in a Pinto. Encyclopedias and games usually have rather different minimum requirements. If the CD-ROM setup can handle a fast-paced, action-packed, and video-rich game, it can certainly deal with an encyclopedia.

The more complex and vivid the pictures, the greater the demands placed on the system. The more rich, complete, and intricate the music, the greater the demands placed on the system. And the more digitized speech and sounds that are used, the greater the demands placed on the system.

For encyclopedias and reference, double speed is fine. For games, especially the newer software, double speed works but triple speed and quadruple speed are better. (At this time, not all software can take advantage of faster-speed CD-ROM drives, but all software will work with faster drives.)

Drive speed is just one buying consideration because a fast drive doesn't guarantee smooth playbacks if the buffer is small. The drive's *buffer* is dedicated memory that lets the drive send information to the computer's processor piece by piece rather than all at once. This process frees up the CPU to work on getting the information you asked for on-screen so that it looks and sounds the best it can. The perfect CD-ROM drive has at least a 256K buffer. Quadruple-speed CD-ROM drives may have up to a 1MB buffer.

The *access time* determines how fast the CD-ROM can find a piece of information. Hard disks have access times around 10 to 15 milliseconds. A good CD-ROM drive has an access time 300 milliseconds or less, which is a lot slower than a hard drive. See why you need a big buffer? You should also look for a SCSI drive that is also multisession PhotoCD capable and XA Ready.

The Bottom Line Games can be some of the most demanding programs, so spend the extra money and get a CD-ROM drive that is triple-speed and meets the specifications above. It's really what you need. And heck, you work hard, so splurge on yourself!

Portable CD-ROM drives

Can I hook a portable CD-ROM drive to my laptop computer?

Yes. There are CD-ROM drives that connect externally in various ways. You can do so via a docking station, a PCMCIA-slot SCSI adapter, or a parallel port. CD-ROM drives are lightweight; most weigh in under two pounds with attachments. And they are usually $2 \times 5^1/_2 \times 10^1/_2$ inches (HWD). Some newer laptops come with a CD-ROM drive built in.

CD-ROM drives take a lot of power, so always carry your laptop's power supply. Generally speaking, you need eight nickel cadmium batteries (four when used only for audio CDs) that last two hours with constant access. Some portable CD-ROM drives use their own batteries, so they don't draw from your laptop's power supply.

Most folks opt for the parallel CD-ROM connection because it's the best deal now. Don't expect the world, though, because performance is hampered by the slow throughput of a parallel connection.

Go shopping with your laptop computer and CD-ROM catalog disc so that you can test different portable setups and find out what works, what it takes to get it going, and the differences among makes and models.

The ideal upgrade kit

What should I look for when buying a CD-ROM upgrade kit? I have a 486DX2 66MHz with 8MB of RAM.

First, make sure there's no dust on the CD-ROM upgrade kit's box. Dust means it's an old kit.

Because you have a powerful computer, you should get a double-speed CD-ROM drive. *Note:* Triple- and quadruple-speed CD-ROM drives are available now; they're more expensive than double-speed drives, but they're getting cheaper every day.

You may want to consider getting a multimedia upgrade kit, which provides a sound card and a CD-ROM drive that work together. It's always better to buy a kit than to buy individual pieces and try to make them work together. Also, make sure that the price you see includes everything needed to install the drive and not just the drive itself. If you don't want to install an add-in card, you can use a model that attaches through your computer's parallel port. You can take these slower drives with you on the road and plug them into your portable.

What about future compatibility with not only all of today's ISO 9660 discs, but tomorrow's even more interactive and animated CD-ROM software? Look for CD-ROM XA, where *XA* stands for Extended Architecture, a specification created by Sony, Philips, and Microsoft that governs audio compression and allows interleaving of audio and computer data. Not many discs take advantage of XA yet, but those that do are closer to true multimedia.

IBM has been an early backer of CD-ROM XA, supporting the specification as part of its Ultimedia product line. Other drive makers have either recently released XA-ready drives or announced XA upgrade strategies (some costly makeovers, some simple ROM chip replacements). Today's most important XA application is Kodak's PhotoCD technology, which lets users store photographic images on CD-ROM.

Finally, check out how a CD gets loaded into the CD drive. Some load like an audio CD: you put them in a tray. Others require that the CD first be put into a *caddie*, which protects the disc and the drive. But cumbersome caddies are awkward to use, especially if you use many different CDs. Your best choice is to find a CD player with an extra set of doors or a seal that keeps out dust and protects the drive. Most new CD-ROM drives use SCSI controller cards, although a few still use proprietary interfaces. Avoid proprietary drives because they limit you to the manufacturer's technology (and prices) and are typically slower than SCSI drives. Check whether the controller is included; if not, watch your total cost balloon by a couple hundred dollars.

Multimedia

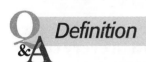 *Definition*

What does it mean if a computer can give a multimedia presentation?

Someone asks whether you want to see pictures of their family. Before you can say "Some other time," out comes a jam-packed wallet of photos of the children, grandchildren, cats, dogs, and last five family reunions. Have you noticed that looking at the photos isn't half as bad as listening to the life histories that accompany the photos? This is a low-tech multimedia presentation.

Bored? Wait until you see pictures of that family on their computer. Or worse, your computer.

Multimedia is, essentially, the integration of many media (for example, audio, video, text, and graphics) to present information. Soon, multimedia will incorporate fax and telephone technologies, too. Some of the earliest multimedia applications were encyclopedias, which were mostly text with a few pictures and sound bites thrown in. Today's applications, ranging from encyclopedias to games to interactive training systems, take full advantage of full-motion video and rich, vibrant sound.

A *multimedia PC* is a computer that's equipped to handle sound, pictures, and mass storage. For a PC to be called a multimedia computer, it must comply with certain specifications (called the MPC standards) put out by an industry consortium — the Multimedia Marketing Council. The specifications spell out what the computer has to have, including the amount of memory, the processor type and speed, CD-ROM speed, sound board, and so on. The latest specification is MPC 2, but rest assured that MPC 3 is gaining momentum. Although MPC standards are relatively new, virtually all computer manufacturers follow them. Computer companies slap little MPC stickers on computers that adhere to the Council's minimum multimedia specifications.

If your computer is not yet multimedia equipped, get a multimedia upgrade kit. This kit can be added to most 386-based and higher computers and usually includes a CD-ROM drive and a sound board. If you're in the market for a new computer, buy a computer that has the MPC sticker.

Otherwise, you'll end up wishing for a different-size computer — remember when you bought clothes a little tight because you just knew that you'd lose weight?

What is MPC?

What does that cute little MPC logo signify? I see it on just about every computer and in every computer advertisement. Is this a little marketing game the computer manufacturers are playing to charge more for their computers or what?

MPC stands for *Multimedia Personal Computer*. The distinctive MPC and MPC 2 logos certify compliance with the corresponding MPC specification — that is, products bearing these marks have passed tests to ensure that they meet bottom-line multimedia standards. Compliance with an MPC specification guarantees compatibility with multimedia PC software.

You see, the whole technology race would get out of hand if someone, or some group, didn't grab the industry's developers and engineers by the collar and say, "Hey, do us a favor. Make sure whatever you sell works within these parameters."

These specifications help the consumer. You don't have to worry too much whether what you buy works with what you have on or underneath your desk.

I said, what is MPC?

I went computer shopping and now I am really confused. What's the difference between a regular old personal computer and a multimedia personal computer?

I've always found that the more you know, the more you realize you don't know. Get ready to find out how much you don't yet know.

In a nutshell, the difference is power and cost. A multimedia PC (MPC) is a souped-up PC: it has a CD-ROM drive, a sound board, Windows 3.1 or Windows 3.0 with Multimedia Extensions 1.0, and a set of speakers (or headphones).

The minimum PC configuration for a multimedia PC is a machine with a 386SX processor and 2MB of RAM, a 30MB hard disk, and a VGA or SVGA display. Virtually all multimedia PCs produced today exceed these minimum specifications; just try running a multimedia application on one of these configurations and you'll know why in a heartbeat.

Adding a CD-ROM drive to this base gives the multimedia PC tremendous information-retrieval capabilities and the ability to do multimedia. Adding a sound board and speakers (or headphones) lets the multimedia PC play and manipulate speech, music, and other sounds.

Multimedia PCs that meet or exceed the following specifications are known as Level 2 MPCs:

486SX processor

4MB of RAM

160MB hard disk

Double-speed CD-ROM drive

A monitor that can display 65,536 colors at 640×480 resolution

Any machine with the preceding standards is hot, but it's a good idea to bump up the RAM to 8MB and double the hard disk size. A multimedia PC that meets some but not all of the Level 2 specifications is considered a Level 1 MPC. Do yourself a favor: If you're in the market for a multimedia PC, make sure it's a Level 2.

You may purchase a multimedia PC as a preconfigured system. On the other hand, if your current PC meets either MPC 1 or 2 specifications, it's a snap to jump on the multimedia bandwagon with an upgrade kit. Prices for full MPC systems start at under $1,100, and upgrade kits are available for about $300.

Most CD-ROM drives sold these days are *double-speed* drives (they can transfer information from the CD-ROM to the computer twice as fast as a standard CD-ROM drive), but there are even triple- and quadruple-speed CD-ROM drives. These faster CD-ROM drives help make the multimedia experience better because the video and sound come out faster — less choppiness.

MPC – Level 1 or Level 2?

What do I really get, beyond a better computer and enhanced performance, if I go with a Level 2 MPC rather than a Level 1?

Hey, what more do you need than a better computer and enhanced performance? Isn't it better to have an office with a view from the top floor?

Buying a Level 2 MPC offers you more in the way of applications:

➤ Most applications run faster on Level 2s.

➤ Software-based video performs better on Level 2s.

➤ PhotoCD applications, not supported by Level 1s, perform well on Level 2s.

The Bottom Line

Although Level 2s provide better overall performance, Level 1s are viable multimedia machines. (Most of the Level 1s sold today meet a number of the Level 2 requirements.) The bottom line: Higher-end applications need to go up to Level 2.

By the way, as if two levels of MPC standards weren't enough, there's talk about a Level 3.

Expansion slot requirements

How many extra expansion slots do I need to put in a multimedia upgrade kit?

Twelve. Just kidding.

An expansion slot is a connector on the main circuit board of the computer (the motherboard) that lets you *expand* your computer by plugging in different types of cards. You usually only need one expansion slot because one card contains the sound card and a connection for the CD-ROM drive. But a multimedia PC upgrade kit may take two slots, depending on the type and number of cards in the kit.

If you're pressed for computer real estate, check how many slots the multimedia upgrade kit you want occupies. That way, you won't be disappointed after you get home and you haul the kit out only to find out that there's no room at the inn.

Upgrade kit or separate pieces?

I built my computer from scratch. I want to add a CD-ROM and sound card. Is it better to buy a multimedia upgrade kit or get separate parts to make the computer multimedia?

Just like you never want to go to your hairdresser and say, "Surprise me," you never want to piece together components to make a multimedia computer.

When you buy a kit, you know the parts will work together. OK, you lose some flexibility and freedom (someone else is picking the pieces for you), but your sanity is worth it. Plus, the cost of a kit is lower than what you pay if you go out and buy separate parts. Besides, many kits come with all sorts of nifty CD-ROMs.

Kits come in a variety of flavors and usually contain a double-speed CD-ROM drive, 16-bit sound card, a pair of stereo speakers, installation software, and some CD-ROMs. *Note:* Get a kit that complies with the MPC 2 standard.

Creative Labs, Media Vision, Procomm Technology, and Turtle Beach Systems market good upgrade kits. You can find the kits at computer dealers, superstores, and mail-order houses.

Do I need an expert?

It took me a week to figure out how to plug in my computer. Do you think I can install an internal multimedia upgrade kit by myself?

Yes, but it may take you six years.

If you are comfortable and know how to work safely inside your computer, you should have smooth sailing. But let me tell you a little about the upgrade installation, and then you decide whether you can handle it.

Upgrade installation requires turning off your computer, grounding yourself by touching the frame of the computer, opening your PC, and inserting a sound board into one of the PC's expansion slots. Then you need to put in the internal CD-ROM drive and connect it to the sound board. Afterwards, load the necessary CD-ROM drivers and software.

Follow the instructions; don't try any custom installations if you can avoid it. Remember that not all upgrade kits or manufacturers are created equal and neither are their instructions. In fact, before you buy an upgrade kit, take a peek at its manual. If you can't quickly get a clear understanding of what is required for installation, call the deal off!

If I were you, I'd bribe a friend who wears a pocket protector to swing by for a quick bite and a quicker installation. If you insist on doing the work yourself, stay away from coffee or other possible irritants.

Other

Surge protectors

What is a surge, and why should it be protected? Do I really need a surge protector?

Yes. A surge protector, which looks like a regular multiplug outlet, is a simple way to turn one wall outlet into enough plugs for a computer. But a surge protector costs a few dollars more than a plain multiplug strip because it controls the flow of power from the electric company to your computer. Surges can occur when more-than-expected voltage comes through the electrical lines; surge protectors prevent this extra voltage from reaching the computer and causing damage. All kinds of things can cause power surges — storms, wind, even other appliances. A surge protector is a valuable insurance policy for your computer.

However, a surge protector only solves one potential electrical problem. Ever experience this phenomenon? The refrigerator cranks up to maintain a certain temperature; about the same time, the kitchen lights dim for a split second. Brownouts occur when the voltage dips below the required level. Insufficient voltage can be as damaging as too much voltage.

Rural areas and heavy industrial areas usually have power problems that require a step up in protection — an *uninterruptable power supply*, or UPS. The UPS, which sits between the computer and the electrical outlet, filters almost every type of power problem because the computer is never connected directly to the electrical outlet; rather, the UPS is plugged into an electrical outlet and has a battery that constantly charges itself. A UPS, which is more expensive than a surge protector, can supply a few extra minutes of power if the electricity is shut off accidentally, such as during a storm. These few minutes leave you enough time to save what you're doing and shut the computer down normally.

And remember, kids, even with a surge protector, it's not a good idea to work on that term paper while your mother is ironing and your father is in the garage using the electric saw during an electrical storm.

Modem dilemma

I can save money by not getting a modem. Am I hurting myself?

What, exactly, are you planning to do to yourself with a modem?

A modem isn't necessary, but I think everyone should have one. Hey, they're really cool.

In real life, a modem is good for a lot of things. For example, Mary, an accountant, uses the modem in her home to send work back to her office computer — *telecommuting*. William's family uses their modem to connect to the on-line service America Online; they can send mail, read the latest news and sports scores, peruse AOL's electronic encyclopedia, and more. Barry is on a tight budget and can't afford a full-blown fax machine, so he put a fax modem inside his computer to make his computer work like a fax machine.

Basically, a modem lets your computer talk to another computer over ordinary phone lines. You can use a modem to connect to an on-line service or electronic bulletin board system (BBS). You can send or receive files from computer to computer and more.

A *fax modem* is different from a regular ol' modem. A fax modem is a modem that also sends and receives faxes. A fax modem works like a regular fax machine, sending information over phone lines. It can send any document directly from your computer to either a real fax machine or a fax modem in another computer. The challenge (thanks to corporate America, I've learned to call problems challenges) is when you want to send something outside your computer. Then you need another piece of gear — a *scanner*. It puts a picture of what is outside your computer — a photo or contract, for example — inside your computer.

The slowest modem that you should buy today is a 14,400 bps (*bits per second*) modem. You can think of bps, or *baud* rate, as a modem's speedometer: the higher the baud, the faster the information flows to and from your computer.

- ➤ 2,400 baud modems are cheap but behind the times.
- ➤ 14,400 baud modems start at under $100.
- ➤ The fastest modems offering good price and performance ratios are 28,800 baud.

Modems come in two varieties. *Internal* modems, which go inside the computer, are a little less expensive than *external* modems, but they don't have the little lights on them like external modems, which sit outside the computer. External high-speed modems require a high-speed chip, called a 16550A UART, in the serial port circuitry of the computer. Without this high-speed chip, you won't get reliable high-speed communications. Internal high-speed modems have the right UART included.

With all the buzz over the information superhighway, buying a computer without a modem may be a mistake in the long run. The increasingly popular Internet is the precursor to what the information superhighway promises to bring in the future.

Tape backup systems

Is it worth the extra money to buy a system with a tape backup drive?

Yes! Backups are like insurance policies: you may never need it, but if you do, you're sure glad you have it.

A backup is a copy of the information inside the computer. You can use a tape backup drive to put this copy on a special tape (you also can back up to floppy disks). The tape backup can be installed in the computer or you can get an external tape backup system that sits outside the computer.

A tape backup system, a good addition to any computer, costs a couple of hundred dollars. Normally, the tape backup systems store up to 250MB of information on one cartridge. An internal tape backup costs about $100 and stores 120MB of information; for 50 more dollars, you can store 250MB.

By running special software, you automatically back up the hard disk at preset times; you can start the backup and go off and do something else.

Motherboards

I wish I had a computer to tell me what computer to buy. Is one motherboard manufacturer better than another?

If you had a computer to tell you which computer to buy, it would undoubtedly choose itself. But that question has more to do with artificial intelligence (or artificial ignorance, perhaps).

Car engines may look and work pretty much the same, but a car's performance varies by make and model number. Like cars, computers are made of a bunch of different pieces. Nowadays, it's pretty common for a computer part inside different computers to be from the same company. Still, all computers are not created equal.

A computer's motherboard is an important piece of the computer. It's the main circuit board that all the other circuit boards, the memory, and the computer's brain or CPU chip plug into. Some motherboards include or integrate more components on them than other motherboards. For example, you can save some money if the motherboard includes the video card (you don't have to buy a separate video card for the computer). Unfortunately, upgrading the video card later can cause headaches.

You should pay attention to the stuff on the motherboard and not the board itself. After all, the CPU chip brand/type is more significant than the motherboard manufacturer. The motherboard simply holds all the stuff that makes the computer work; the stuff makes or breaks a computer's performance.

VESA and PCI

What's the difference between VESA and PCI? Which is better to buy today?

VESA and PCI are different buses.

Let me first explain a *bus*. Picture a highway: exits, speeding cars, and perhaps a traffic jam or two. The highway inside our computer has exits, traffic, and jams, too. A computer's highway exits correspond to the different parts of the processor, memory, hard disk drive, floppy disk drive, printer, modem, sound board, and so on. These are different connections to the system unit. If all goes well, the path is as clear as an interstate at 3 a.m.; you see what you asked for on-screen instantaneously. Traffic jams happen when you ask for too much information to travel along the highway.

For example, when you issue the command that starts your communications software and resets your modem, everything needed to get the job done (that is, the communications software, the modem initialization commands, the dialing directory, and so on) gets on a bus and cruises down the highway. The bus holding the information gets on and off the exits necessary, picking up details and instructions. Presto, you're connected to the world of electronic information.

VESA local bus (commonly referred to as a *VL bus*) and PCI describe different bus designs, or architecture. A VL bus is an extension of the 486 local bus, where information goes straight from the CPU to the peripheral connected to the CPU. It's a 32-bit highway.

PCI puts the CPU peripheral connections on an *accelerator chip*, or a booster-powered bus full of high-octane gas. The PCI bus travels separately from the CPU and thus can support more exits or peripherals connected to the computer. The PCI bus is a 62-bit highway.

Since early 1993, VL buses were standard in most 486-based computers. VL bus systems and components often can deliver tremendous performance gains over their ISA counterparts. The upsurge of graphics, true colors, full-motion video, made the ISA bus choke far too often.

Intel then brought forth the PCI bus, claiming that it was bigger, better, and faster than the VL bus. Although PCI has been endorsed by such heavyweights as IBM, Compaq, Dell, and NEC, you should know that the PCI doesn't enhance performance that much for traditional applications; a recent report cited only a 2 percent increase. Hard-core graphics and videos users reap the most benefits.

One of PCI's biggest advantages is automatic peripheral connections. In other words, users no longer have to worry whether a mouse can cause a conflict with a modem because add-on boards look past IRQ levels, DMA channels, and memory addresses. Given the number of calls to my radio show from people who faced conflicts, I suspect that the PCI seemed like a slam dunk. In addition, the PCI's low electrical requirements and design is a natural for running more than six peripherals from one CPU.

The PCI bus is typically used on motherboards with the Pentium processor chip. Because the Pentium works faster than the 486 chip, it needs to send and receive information more quickly. That little bit of extra speed found in the PCI bus can help you get the most performance out of a Pentium-based computer.

The PCI may be tomorrow's computer, but the current price is high and add-ons are sparse — as is customary until technology gains market acceptance. Meanwhile, a new VL standard, 2.0, may bridge the gap between VL and PCI systems, but it's too soon to tell.

Buying a Mac

Why are there no Mac clones?

I'd like to buy a Macintosh, but Macs are more expensive than IBM compatibles. Why hasn't some company made a Mac clone?

Until very recently, Apple forbade cloning and was willing to spend fortunes defending its patents in court. It was easier to clone a real apple than the Apple computer.

Nonetheless, some companies tried to duplicate Apples — most notably, the portable Macs — and failed. The problem: The clones required genuine Apple ROMs, but Apple doesn't sell ROMs separately. And you can't have a computer without ROM.

One company that tried to produce a Mac-compatible ROM thought it had struck the mother lode by proving that its clone chips didn't infringe any Apple patents. Unfortunately, the company could neither assure 100-percent compatibility nor offer great cost savings. No sales means no revenue: a case of one bad apple ruining the potential for everyone.

Apple, though, is intent on offering competitive prices and gaining market share. As a result, permitting Mac clones now makes sense for the company, ever mindful that IBM and its compatibles are trying to take over the world.

In fact, Apple has licensed portions of its ROM for the production of third-party chips based on the PowerPC chips (which Apple and IBM are using in their jointly developed line of computers). Plus, Apple announced licensing agreements for Mac clones outside the U.S. and other English-language markets. It's only a matter of time before you see true Mac compatibles in America — possibly even from IBM!

The Bottom Line

True, Macs still cost a little more than similarly equipped IBM-compatible computers. (Even without clones, however, Macs will not remain more expensive than their PC counterparts forever.) But choosing a computer isn't just about price. You must consider which type of computer you will be more productive using. Yes, you can always find a Mom-and-Pop clone that costs significantly less than a Mac, but you tend to get what you pay for when cutting corners on hardware.

Computer in college

Should we buy our college-bound daughter another Mac or let her graduate to Windows?

Wow, she's ready to graduate to Windows. Seems like just yesterday she went off to school. Mac aficionados will tell you that Windows isn't a graduation as much as it is a demotion.

Because your daughter already knows the Mac, why rock the boat? She doubtless will work more efficiently on a platform with which she's comfortable. On the other hand, Windows dominates the marketplace, so a familiarity with it may help her in the long run.

What's a mother to do? I say get your daughter a new Power Macintosh: it can pretend that it's running, or *emulate,* Windows, either via software emulation or a NuBus card. Then she'll have the best of both worlds. If that's too expensive, check with the new school and see whether its courses and computer labs strongly favor one platform.

Finally, but most important, ask your daughter what she wants. She's the one who'll have to work with the computer practically every day until she graduates, if not beyond.

Computer for kids

Where can I pick up a used Mac for my 7-year-old daughter? I want her off my Pentium!

Many used-Mac dealers advertise in Mac magazines and local newspapers. The better dealers offer warranties that are arguably worth the premium you have to pay to buy from them. The better dealers also accept credit cards, affording you better protection against a lemon or nondelivery.

You can find lower prices by looking through the local classifieds or online (America Online, for example, has a large folder teeming with ads for used Macs). Although your local paper may have fewer ads, you at least get to see the computer and meet the seller before you buy. Shopping for used equipment on-line entails more risks: not only don't you meet the dealer, but also you can't be certain of the computer's condition until it arrives. However, if you get references from satisfied buyers and stay away from people who insist on cash up front or anything similarly suspicious, you can find some truly wonderful bargains.

Finally, you can attend an auction where Apple inventory is cleared out. Just make sure that you know how much these systems are worth on the used market so that you don't end up overbidding.

Windows for the Mac

I am interested in purchasing some Mac hardware. After listening to a few salespeople, I'm more confused than ever. I will be eternally grateful if you tell me which Mac hardware can run MS Windows software.

That's the nature of salespeople. They confuse you and then go in for the strike. Here, let me unconfuse you.

You can run Windows on a Mac with either

> ➤ Software emulation
> ➤ Hardware add-on with a real 80 x 86 chip

SoftWindows now runs only on Power Macs (models 6100, 7100, and 8100) with at least 16MB of RAM. *Note:* SoftPC 3.1 technically allows you to run Windows on top of it on other Macs, but only a masochist would run Windows that way.

Apple's first DOS card, which officially only worked in the Quadra 610, has been discontinued; the second card has yet to ship.

The Orange Micro cards work in any Macintosh with a 12-inch NuBus slot:

➤ Any Mac from the II series except the IIsi (including the Mac II, IIx, IIcx, IIci, IIfx, IIvx, IIvi)

➤ Performa 600

➤ Centris 650

➤ Quadra 650, 700, 800, 840AV, 900, 950

➤ Workgroup Server 80, 8150, 9150

➤ Power Mac 7100, 8100

You cannot run Windows on

➤ Any compact Mac, including the 128K, 512K, Plus, SE, SE/30, Classic, Classic II, or Color Classic

➤ Centris 610

➤ Quadra 605, 610, 630

➤ Any LC, PowerBook, or Performa other than the 600. The most recent PowerBooks are designed to be upgradable to PowerPC, at which point they can run SoftWindows. However, such upgrades have yet to arrive.

You also can run Windows on a Mac with Farallon's Timbuktu Pro, which will run on nearly any Mac and perform reasonably well on any '040 Mac. What's the catch? It's essentially a *terminal emulator*. That is, to use Timbuktu Pro, you must be connected on a network to a PC running Windows, then you must "take over" the PC with the Mac and Timbuktu. This solution is great if you have an extra high-speed PC lying around, but most individuals and small businesses don't.

Chapter 4

CD-ROMs

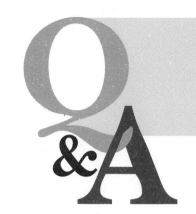

What Is a CD-ROM?

 Definition

Everyone I know says CD-ROMs are the best thing since sliced bread. What is a CD-ROM, and what makes it so great?

Do you want to make friends and influence people? You really should expand your vocabulary and avoid using cliches like the plague. A CD-ROM can help you do that like a charm.

A CD-ROM looks a lot like an audio CD, but it works in your computer. Of course, your computer has to have a CD-ROM drive to use the CD-ROMs.

Can CD-ROMs change history? No, but they can store it! Imagine, four CD-ROMs are equivalent to 1,000,000 pages of text.

On one CD-ROM disc, for example, you can squeeze 660MB worth of text, pictures, and sound. In fact, you can get an entire set of encyclopedias on a CD-ROM. (No more hauling those heavy, dusty, outdated volumes year after year to your neighbor's annual spring-cleaning garage sale; good thing, no one ever bites.) Another CD-ROM, meanwhile, can hold an entire art museum, including discussions and artist profiles. And because CD-ROMs contain so much information, installing big software programs such as Microsoft Office from a CD-ROM takes a quarter of the time needed when installing the same programs from dozens of $3^{1}/_{2}$-inch disks.

By the way, a CD-ROM's information is *read-only*, which means you can't write over data on the disc; you can copy information from the disc to your computer's hard drive, but not vice versa. Perhaps, instead of calling the technology *C*ompact *D*isc *R*ead *O*nly *M*emory, they should have called it *C*ompact *D*isc *R*ead *O*nly *D*isc. Er, on second thought, CD-ROD would sound more like some kind of shifty guy rather than high-tech computer stuff.

Hardware requirements for video

I have a 25MHz 386 computer. Is it good enough to capture and play video?

It's as good as growing lima beans as a cash crop.

Capturing and playing full-motion video is one of the most data-intensive tasks you can do with a computer. You see, to produce real-time video, a PC must refresh the screen image at least 16 frames per second, the rate at which the human eye stops seeing individual pictures and starts seeing a movie (television shows run at 30 frames per second). A 386 25MHz computer just doesn't have the horsepower to handle video well. Playback is possible if you have a fast hard drive — but not at full screen or high resolution.

Because full-screen, full-motion video converts to about $1\frac{1}{2}$ gigabytes of information per minute of video, hard disk real estate is vital. A gigabyte is 1,000 megabytes. You can reduce the amount of hard disk space needed by making the image smaller, reducing the frames per second, and using video-compression techniques. But I bet you really won't want to do any of those things after you see the resulting choppy video.

The Bottom Line

The larger your screen and the higher the resolution, the greater the demands for hard disk space, speed, and raw power. The bottom line: Full-motion desktop video really requires a Pentium-based computer with a data transfer rate of at least 18MB/second (megabytes per second); this computer also must have a lot of memory (16 or 32MB of RAM) and a video-capture card.

Komando Klues

Of course, adding a high-priced video-capture card to a 386 25MHz is overkill because the card offers high resolution at a high frame rate. So save your money. (If you want to see full-motion, high-res video, splurge and spend 25 cents in the arcade at the mall.)

In the meantime, go to a few computer stores and see video capturing and playback in action. Pay close attention to the video-capture card, but also get a rundown on all the hardware. And ask for a demonstration of Microsoft Video for Windows, which has become the de facto standard for desktop video.

CD audio cable

My CD-ROM drive has a ribbon cable and a four-wire connector that plugs into a board on my computer. Does this four-wire connector carry sound? If so, will the drive function without the four-wire cable connected?

Leave the four-wire connector alone. It didn't do anything to you.

Let me ask you a question: Does a big Saturday night include wine, cheese, and using tweezers to take the legs off a dead roach? Gross.

The Bottom Line

The four-wire connector lets the CD audio signal play through the sound card. If the four-wire connector isn't plugged in, you won't hear regular music CDs through your computer. In addition, you will miss out with any games and applications that incorporate CD audio.

I'm keeping this answer short because I have some shopping to do for the weekend. You know, just the basics: wine, cheese, and a Roach Motel.

Intermediate

XA Ready

What does XA Ready mean?

XA is computerese for *extended architecture*. CD-ROM XA is a standard for interleaving audio and video on a CD. Instead of having a video file in one huge chunk and an audio file in another huge chunk, the files are broken into smaller bite-size pieces and mixed together, so they're easier for the computer to grab. You know, like trail mix at a cocktail party.

117

Komando Klues

If you are buying a multimedia computer or multimedia upgrade kit, look for the *MPC 2* multimedia computer specification, which assures you that the latest and greatest CD-ROMs will work. The MPC 2 spec calls for a CD-ROM drive that is XA Ready and *dual-speed reading* (that is, 150kps for audio and 300kps for data).

The XA feature allows for multiple sessions of a writable CD drive and some CDs, namely the Kodak PhotoCD. If you want to take full advantage of PhotoCD technology, however, you need a multisession drive as well. Regular CD-ROM drives can read only those CDs that were made at one sitting (or single-session). If you didn't have enough information to fill up the CD, well, the storage space just went to waste. *Multisession* means that you can fill up that unused space at a later time. If the CD-ROM drive isn't made for the XA standard, it doesn't know how to read the rest of the information from the CD-ROM.

Beware, some stores do not accept returns of CD-ROMs, so do some homework before buying any CD-ROMs that list XA Ready as a requirement. Get out the CD-ROM drive's manual and check the drive's specifications. Or better yet, pick up the phone and call the drive's manufacturer's sales line and ask whether the model number of your CD-ROM drive is XA Ready.

FILES.BBS

As I understand it, to use files on a bulletin board system's CD-ROM drive, I must have something called FILES.BBS. What exactly is a FILES.BBS? Can I get one? How?

Live your dreams. You can get anything you want, even FILES.BBS.

FILES.BBS contains a list of files on the electronic bulletin board system's CD-ROM. That is, the FILES.BBS file is an index that people can use to find a file on the CD-ROM.

Ah, but not all software programs that run and manage BBSs use FILES.BBS. Check the BBS software's documentation to see whether FILES.BBS is part of the program.

If the BBS software doesn't use the FILES.BBS file, you'll need to make a file with descriptions of all the files on the CD-ROM. Either way, there remains a healthy number of maintenance tasks: you have to mark the CD-ROM's files for access and then write a description for each file.

SCSI expansion

What does it mean if a CD-ROM is SCSI?

SCSI (*S*mall *C*omputer *S*ystem *I*nterface standard, pronounced *scuzzy*) is a type of expansion card; so a CD-ROM can't be SCSI, but the connection from the CD-ROM drive to your computer can be.

From one SCSI expansion card you can chain together CD-ROM drives, hard drives, scanners, tape backup units, printers, and more. The attached devices are assigned a number from 0 to 7. You can place more than one SCSI host adapter in a PC, each with a maximum of seven things hooked up to it.

In theory, connecting SCSI devices to your computer is as easy as giving the device a number. But you and I both know that theory is one thing, and the way the *real world* works is something else; it takes a little more work in the real world. On the other hand, if you have few expansion cards in your computer, a SCSI card is a quick cure.

SCSI, which has a high data-transfer rate, is perfect for high-end multimedia applications. A friend of mine is into this stuff big time. Because he uses SCSI devices, my friend can hook his gigabyte hard drive to the scanner, to the CD-ROM drive, and more without eating up every expansion slot.

SCSI-2 is the latest specification, but SCSI-3 should arrive shortly. Naturally, SCSI-3 will work better at mixing and matching devices.

In addition, SCSI-3 proposes the *SCSI Configured Auto-Magically* (SCAM), which will enable you to add things to your computer and get them to work immediately. Right. Dream on.

CD-ROM buffer

My CD-ROM drive has a 256K buffer. What does the buffer do?

The CD-ROM buffer is like the holding pattern at a busy airport. Before the information you asked for from the CD-ROM lands on-screen, it goes to a special area called the *buffer*. The CD-ROM's buffer is special, dedicated memory that the computer uses to hold the information you asked for from the CD-ROM. The bigger the holding area, the more information it can hold.

The buffer allows the computer to receive information from the CD-ROM in part rather than the whole enchilada at once. Because this process frees up the computer to do other things, such as work with the video card, you see what you requested on-screen quicker.

You can see (and hear) the buffer in action when you use a CD-ROM program that contains a great deal of information — for example, the nation's phone book. Suppose that you search for all the people named *Smith* in Arizona; a listing pops up on-screen. As you scroll down the listing, though, you hear the CD-ROM spin. Only the top of the listing is available to you instantly: that's the part held in the buffer. To get to the bottom of the listing, more information must be added to the buffer.

DMA/IRQ

 DMA and IRQ settings

Every time I put something new in the computer, my wife yells at me, because nothing ever works the first time. Do I need to worry about DMA and IRQ lines? Does the software that comes with the CD-ROM take care of them? I've heard that these problems are horrible to fix, and I'm afraid I won't be able to handle them (or her).

I think you may need to upgrade your wife.

Time for a little tech talk. *DMA* (*d*irect *m*emory *a*ccess) and IRQ (*i*nterrupt *req*uest) lines refer to particular hardware settings on the controller board. If the settings are wrong, the CD-ROM drive won't work.

Think of DMA as a train track, where information travels between parts of the computer's memory without using the computer's processor (or CPU chip). DMA thus offers a fast way to get information off a CD-ROM drive and frees up the CPU to do other things. Unfortunately, the average 386, 486, or Pentium computer has no more than eight DMA channels. To make matters more difficult, many DMA channels are reserved and used by the computer itself. Trying to let more than one device use the same DMA channel in a computer is usually risky business. DMA channels must be set so that only one adapter board, such as the CD-ROM controller board, uses it.

IRQs are flags that some devices, such as a CD-ROM drive, use to get the CPU's attention. That is, an IRQ is when your CD-ROM controller (or other board) signals the computer when it has information to deliver. Most PCs have no more than 13 IRQ lines. Like DMA channels, many IRQ lines are reserved.

Note: The DMA and IRQ settings are set usually by jumpers or DIP switches on the CD-ROM controller card.

Problems can happen in a couple of places:

> ➤ Just as you can't have two trains rolling down the same track in opposite directions, you can't have two devices using the same DMA channel to transfer information. On *some* computer systems, you can, however, share DMA channels. Check your user manual to see whether your computer can share DMA channels.

> ➤ If two devices use the same IRQ, the CPU gets confused. In fact, the computer does nothing because it doesn't know which flag it's supposed to pay attention to. Hence, the CD-ROM drive and/or sound card and/or mouse and/or modem and/or scanner may not work.

Here's the good news: Almost all CD-ROM drive installation software determines which DMA and IRQ channels are being used and untangles DMA or IRQ conflicts. Moreover, the installation software picks and tests the settings for you.

After the CD-ROM is working, start the Microsoft Diagnostics (MSD) program (type **MSD** at the DOS prompt and press Enter). MSD will tell you more than you care to know about your computer's innards on-screen and in a report sent to your printer. Keep this printout in a safe place; you may need the gory details later.

The CD-ROM installation process is a lot harder than it should be. And from the sounds of it, it's an adventure you should undertake when your wife is out of town. Think of the points you'll earn for your technical prowess when she returns, especially when you point out that getting a CD-ROM drive to work is like moving a piano up four flights of stairs.

Standard IRQ settings

My CD-ROM drive has an IRQ conflict with the sound board. Can you give me a list of typical IRQ port uses?

Too many roommates and you spend all your time fighting over the phone line. Add enough hardware goodies to your computer and they fight over who gets to use the IRQ line.

Sometimes, you can share an IRQ line, but it's not easy. You have to make sure that one hardware device isn't using an IRQ that another device wants at the same time.

To determine the ins and outs of IRQ settings, I use WinSleuth Gold Plus by Dariana Software (800-892-9950), which is a bit more user-friendly than Microsoft Diagnostics.

As requested, here is a list of standard IRQ settings. Happy hunting!

IRQ	Device
0	System timer
1	Keyboard
2	Reserved for system use
3	COM 2, COM 4, network adapters, CD-ROM adapters, and sound boards
4	COM 1 and COM 3
5	LPT2 parallel port
6	Floppy disk controller
7	LPT1
8	Real-time clock
9	Reserved for system use
10	Available
11	Available
12	Available
13	Math coprocessor
14	Hard disk controller
15	Available

Generally, IRQ 5 works for most sound cards. A standard 16-bit sound card can use IRQ 10, 11, 12, and 15, but you must make sure that the sound board doesn't need a specific IRQ setting.

IRQs with Pro Audio card

I want to make sure that my Pro Audio sound card is loading IRQs properly. What do I look for inside my AUTOEXEC.BAT and CONFIG.SYS files to see which DMA and IRQ settings are being used?

It's nice to see someone using their time wisely. Whenever life affords me an extra minute, I also like to make sure that my IRQs are being loaded properly.

However, you should check the IRQ and DMA settings after you boot up — not in the computer's boot-up files. To do so, start Microsoft Diagnostics (type **MSD** at the DOS prompt); all kinds of boring technical stuff pops up on-screen. Although lines in the AUTOEXEC.BAT or CONFIG.SYS files tell the computer which settings to use, you may get error messages and not even know. Using MSD (or other software such as PC Tools, Norton Utilities, or WinSleuth Gold Plus) is a better way to determine which DMA and IRQ settings the computer is using.

Most add-on hardware goodies tell the computer which IRQ and DMA settings to use with a DEVICE= line. For example, your sound card's reference may look like the following in your CONFIG.SYS file:

```
DEVICE=C:\PROAUDIO\MVSOUND.SYS D:3 Q:7
```

So the computer wants the sound card set at DMA 3 and IRQ 7. If you need to change these settings, look in the Pro Audio manual. You probably need to change the jumper settings to change the DMA channels. *Jumpers* are tiny rectangular metal-lined plastic caps that slide over tiny metal "prongs" sticking out of the CD-ROM controller card.

Trial and error isn't much fun, but sometimes it's the only way to figure out how to set the darn computer so that it works. With MS-DOS 6 or higher, if the system locks up when you start it, you can press F8 when you see the message *Starting MS-DOS.* You then can say yes or no to each line in your CONFIG.SYS and AUTOEXEC.BAT files. By doing so, you can skip the root of the problem and at least get to a place where you can start fixing it.

If you don't have MS-DOS 6 or higher, you'll have to edit the AUTOEXEC.BAT and CONFIG.SYS files one line at a time, saving the files and rebooting between each edit. If you thought trial and error wasn't much fun, this is trial by torture. The ability to choose which lines to load while starting a computer is just one of many, many reasons to upgrade to the latest version of MS-DOS.

Komando Klues

Word to the wise: Once you figure out all these nasty DMAs and IRQs, write them down and keep them in a safe place. You just never know when you may need them again.

Advanced

Q&A   *Making CD-ROMs*

I roll my own cigarettes and I want to roll my own CD-ROMs. Is this possible?

Yes, but don't smoke your CD-ROMs.

You are going to need a lot of money, time, and patience. The recordable CD-ROM (or *CD-R*) technology is just now leaving the hands of engineers and entering mainstream consciousness. Technology suffers incredible growing pains. CD-R is expensive and doesn't always work the way engineers and marketing folks claim.

CD-R packages usually come as bundled hardware-software combination plates. (At least, you know that the products will work together.) The faster the drive (single-, double-, and quadruple-speed CD-R drives are available), the more money and computer power you need. Beyond a CD-R drive, plan on getting a gigabyte hard drive or two, some top-of-the-line SCSI cards, and a high-end Pentium.

The Bottom Line

My advice: Unless you want to suffer at the hands of technology still in puberty, forget buying your own CD-R setup. An easier way is to check the back of computer magazines or in your local Yellow Pages for companies who will master CD-ROMs for you. Some companies will duplicate the CDs, too. Plus, you don't have to shell out all that money or lose your hair trying to make the equipment work.

Troubleshooting

Basic

Q&A | *Protecting CD-ROMs*

My music CDs seem pretty durable. Do I need to take any extra precautions when handling CD-ROMs?

I learned the hard way that you should keep CD-ROMs away from drooling children: I still wince when I remember how little Adolf used my favorite CD-ROM game as a pacifier. The cherub's mom thought it was cute, but that particular CD-ROM never worked again. It only contained information about animal cookies and spit.

Although I've never baby-tested an audio CD, CD-ROMs aren't as durable. If you leave your fingerprint on an audio CD, you probably won't hear the difference. But if a fingerprint gets on the part of an executable file stored on a CD-ROM, the program probably won't run at all. So hold a CD-ROM by its edges. Or put your finger through the CD-ROM's donut hole and pretend that it's an oversized ring.

To protect the discs, manufacturers of CD-ROM players have replaced the disc tray used in audio CD players with a *caddy*, which has a sliding metal door that looks and works much like the door over a 3^1/$_2$-inch disk drive. You place the CD-ROM in the caddy and then place the entire caddy in the player.

Komando Klues

You can use one caddy for all your CD-ROMs, carefully loading and unloading them as you need them (remember: by the edges). But it is much wiser to buy a separate caddy (mail-order price: $3.99 each and up) for each disc that you use frequently, eliminating the need to handle your favorite CDs. Keep an extra caddie for infrequently used CD-ROMs and audio CDs. Extra caddies make great storage containers. When you want to use the CD-ROM, just pop it into the drive; no muss, no fuss, and no damaged CDs.

If you have many CD-ROMs, you may want to invest in a drive that holds 6 to 18 CD-ROMs simultaneously. Better CD-ROM drives have anti-Messy Marvin features, such as automatic lens cleaning, dust protection doors, and emergency eject buttons.

I recommend explaining the CD-ROM dos and don'ts to anyone in your family using discs. In addition to taking the precautions outlined in the previous graphs,

- ➤ Don't put labels on CD-ROMs.
- ➤ Don't write on CD-ROMs.
- ➤ Store discs out of direct sunlight.
- ➤ Don't place a warped disc into a CD-ROM drive.
- ➤ Don't touch the bottom of the disc, where the laser reads the information.

Fixing scratches

I scratched my favorite CD-ROM, and now it doesn't work. How can I get rid of the scratch?

Have you ever noticed that scratches never appear on CD-ROMs you hate?

Stereo stores sell petroleum-based products that can repair scratches on audio CDs. These handy-dandy solutions restore unreadable files on CD-ROMs, too.

I use CD-Repair, which costs around $20. The solution comes in a kit along with a workstation cloth, cotton balls, an extra bottle of the goo, and instructions.

Keep in mind that the solution doesn't work on human skin. Only a kiss from mom can do that.

Komando Klues

Make sure the disc is completely dry before putting it in the CD-ROM drive. If the CD-ROM still won't work, contact the CD-ROM's publisher. Many publishers have a replacement policy where you ship them your damaged CD-ROM and, for a small fee, they ship you a replacement CD-ROM.

Old CD-ROM drive, new CD-ROM

A computer book that I bought came with a CD-ROM, but the disc won't play properly on my CD-ROM drive, which I've owned for a couple of years.

Many older CD-ROM drives can read only the first 550MB of information on a disc, but today's CD-ROMs hold 660MB. This is not good. The old drive just doesn't know how to read the new disc.

Check your drive's documentation and see whether the drive is limited to 550MB. If it is, and if the disc in question contains more than 550MB, you need a new CD-ROM drive.

 Some dealers still sell CD-ROM drives with this 550MB limit. Check the drive's hardware features sheet carefully for full compliance with the MPC 2 specification.

CRC error

All but one of my CD-ROMs run just fine. When I try to run the problem CD-ROM, however, I get a *CRC Error* and my computer just stops. What's wrong?

CRC is a cyclical redundancy check, which a computer uses to verify disc sectors. In other words, a CRC is how a computer makes sure that a disc is okeydokey. A CRC error usually means there are lost bits and bytes on the disc. You need to get a replacement CD-ROM from either the manufacturer or the store where you bought the CD-ROM.

Assigning your CD-ROM drive a letter

I just installed a CD-ROM drive from a kit. All I have left to do is give the drive a letter. Why do I need to do that, and how do I do that?

Putting the CD-ROM drive in the computer isn't enough to make the drive work. You need to tell the computer that the CD-ROM drive exists. The installation or setup program on the disks provided by the CD-ROM drive's manufacturer takes care of this step for you.

In particular, the CD-ROM drive installation software installs a CD-ROM device driver in your CONFIG.SYS file and Microsoft's CD Extensions (MSCDEX.EXE) in your AUTOEXEC.BAT file. MSCDEX.EXE controls the letter assigned to your CD-ROM drive.

Picking the drive letter is a no-brainer. The CD-ROM drive installation software automatically selects the next available drive letter (usually D or E) for the CD-ROM drive.

Testing your new CD-ROM drive

I just installed a CD-ROM drive. Is there a quick way to test the drive to see whether it works?

Some CD-ROM drives come with a testing feature, but those of us in the know take a shortcut: after your computer boots, request a directory of the CD that's in the CD-ROM drive. (Your computer treats a CD-ROM like a floppy disk in a disk drive.) If you get an error message rather than a directory listing, the CD-ROM drive isn't working.

Note: Ordinary DOS commands or Windows File Manager commands also work on the CD-ROM in the CD-ROM drive, but don't try the COPY command because you can't write or save any information on a CD-ROM.

Komando Klues

A good way to check the CD-ROM drive's hardware, software, and connections is to play a regular music CD in the CD-ROM drive. (But by all means, try to stay away from disco CDs.) Some CD-ROM upgrade kits include a multimedia or CD player. If not, use the MediaPlayer included with Windows.

Newer CD-ROM hardware, by the way, is not compatible with bad music. You'll get an error message.

Lights, but no action

When I put a disc in my CD-ROM drive, the lights go on and I hear a whirring, but the drive doesn't seem to be reading the disc. Do you think the drive is going bad?

You know a drive has gone bad when it holds you up. Get it? Holds you up . . . wow, tough crowd.

If the problem happens with just one CD, most likely the disc is dirty, scratched, or otherwise damaged. Or the CD-ROM drive's lens reader may have dust on it. If the CD-ROM is new, exchange it. Otherwise, buy a CD repair kit at an electronics or stereo store. If the problem happens with *every* CD you put in the drive, your CD-ROM player may be heading for that big recycling bin in the sky. Take the system to a computer repair facility.

Data cable

The CD driver loads, but the CD-ROM doesn't work. When I use a test program that came with the CD's software, it says that I should check the data cable. What's a data cable? And what the heck is wrong with it?

Know how to get ahead in multimedia show business? Data cable. They're long on info, but short on connections.

The *data cable* is a wide, flat cable that connects the CD-ROM drive to the controller card. This cable is the "highway" that information, or data, travels from the CD-ROM drive to the computer.

For your CD-ROM drive to work, the data cable must be connected to the CD-ROM drive and the controller card in a precise way: Most CD-ROM cables have 50 little holes in their connector ends. If you look very, very closely at the sockets, you'll see a mark or a tiny number *1* next to a hole. Most data cables have a red stripe on one edge, to mark pin number 1. This particular hole corresponds with a pin on the CD-ROM and a pin on the controller card. If these holes and pins are not aligned correctly, the cable will not transfer data or acknowledge the device drivers at start-up.

Note: Before you bust open your computer, unplug it. Then ground yourself, by touching the metal chassis of the computer before touching any cards in the computer, to prevent any static charges.

If the data cable is attached properly, give both ends a little nudge to ensure that the connection is not loose. If your CD-ROM drive still doesn't work, try replacing the data cable. The wires in data cables sometimes break when a cable is bent too much or handled too roughly.

If all else fails, haul the computer in for service and let the professionals do what they do best. Tell them to check dat cable right over der.

New DOS kills CD-ROM drive

My CD-ROM drive worked fine when I was running DOS 5. But when I upgraded to DOS 6.2, the drive dropped dead. What's the problem? P.S. I tried reinstalling the software.

Many programs expect certain DOS versions. When the current DOS version does not match expectations, even well-oiled machines may grind to a halt.

In your case, the *driver* (that is, a program that helps make your CD-ROM drive work) called MSCDEX was perfectly happy under DOS 5. DOS 6 and above has a new version of MSCDEX. It can be loaded into high memory, which leaves you with more regular memory, and used with the DOS disk caching program called SmartDrive.

Chances are that the line in your AUTOEXEC.BAT file that loaded MSCDEX was pointing to the old version of the driver, not the new one that came with DOS 6.2. First, make a copy of the AUTOEXEC.BAT file to a floppy disk or another directory. Next, open up the AUTOEXEC.BAT file with a text editor like the DOS EDIT command. Look for the line that has the word MSCDEX.EXE in it. You want to make sure that the line starts out as follows:

```
C:\DOS\MSCDEX.EXE ...
```

Don't change any of the information at the end of the line.

Save the AUTOEXEC.BAT file, restart the computer, and try using that CD-ROM drive again. Alas, you're rescued from the crypt.

Intermediate

Can I blame ISA?

My CD-ROM drive works terribly. Is this because I have an ISA system? Do I need a VESA local bus machine?

A dog is a dog is a dog. If your CD-ROM drive is a dog, it will bark on any kind of computer.

VESA local bus (VLB) systems may enhance performance a bit, but a CD-ROM drive is limited by its features. If the drive is a single-spin model with poor performance throughput, you can expect the same poor performance on a VLB computer as on an ISA (*Industry Standard Architecture*) computer. If the CD-ROM drive is blazingly fast, like a quadruple-spin drive, and has a fast interface board, a quality ISA machine will keep up with anything your CD-ROM can throw at it. Well, anything but high-resolution video and lots of sound.

Strange CD-ROM sounds

My CD-ROM sounds like it's revving up when I turn on my computer. Is this normal?

My aunt sleeps in the clothing that she wants to wear to work the next day. Is that normal? It is to her. Don't worry about this sound unless it's something new.

Like most hard drives, CD-ROM drives spin constantly so that you don't have to wait for the hardware whenever you or a program asks for more information. If the information is ready to go as soon as it's requested, you see it on-screen quicker.

Note: Newer hard drives retrieve information as much as 20 times faster than CD-ROM drives.

CD-ROM drives automatically begin looking for information as soon as they're powered up and find a CD-ROM. In fact, some drives look for info even if you haven't inserted a disc yet — during a mini self-test.

Don't confuse normal operation hum for something more sinister, however. If the CD-ROM drive hasn't always sounded as it does today, be careful. You should investigate any unusual or unexplained changes. For example, a dust ball may be lurking inside the drive. Pick up a CD-ROM drive cleaning kit and see whether a little scrubbing quiets things down.

If you're still concerned, give the drive's manufacturer tech support line a call, put the phone near the drive, and let the representative hear the strange sounds. If the representative says something like, "Hmmm, never heard anything like that before," you should ask, "Where do I send my drive to get it fixed for free while it's under warranty?"

Killing time while the drivers load

How can I shorten the painfully long wait at start-up while the CD drivers load?

Hey, how are you when you first wake up? I bet you need a minute or two to get reoriented. Imagine if you had to wake up at work.

When you start your computer, a lot happens:

> ➤ Your computer looks for and then communicates with different adapter boards — hard drive controller, video board, and CD-ROM controller.

> ➤ The controllers oftentimes must communicate with their devices. That is, the hard drive controller checks in with the hard drive, the video board finds out what kind of monitor is attached, and the CD-ROM controller tries to determine how many drives are attached and whether they have discs (data or audio) inside.

All this electronic chatter takes time. Time enough to get another cup of coffee so that you are up and running when your computer is ready.

Invalid Drive Specification *message*

I get this funky error message — something about *Invalid Drive Specification* — when I try to turn on my computer. What should I do?

So you say your computer is moody when you try to turn it on. Are you really talking about computers here? If so, haven't you spent a few too many hours in front of old faithful?

My guess: The little DOS driver MSCDEX, which makes the CD-ROM drive work, has taken a leave of absence. To test whether MSCDEX is loading properly, go to the directory that contains the CD-ROM drive files. The directory usually is called BIN, CDROM, or the model number of the CD-ROM drive (for example, SONY31A). To change to the CD-ROM drive's directory from the DOS prompt, type

```
CD directory name
```

and press Enter. Then type **MSCDEX** and press Enter. If MSCDEX is in fact working, you'll see a message that mentions the version number of MSCDEX. If MSCDEX is not working, you'll see a different message: *Usage...*

Either way, run the setup or installation program that came with the CD-ROM drive. (The program should be on the disks that came with your computer or multimedia upgrade kit.) After the CD-ROM setup is done, make sure that the MSCDEX command line in the AUTOEXEC.BAT file is placed before any menu program but before a line that starts Windows. Restart your computer.

MSCDEX line in AUTOEXEC.BAT

Windows won't recognize my CD-ROM drive unless DOS jogs its memory. When I boot up, Windows refuses to recognize my drive. If I exit Windows and then go back in, the CD-ROM drive works great. What should I do?

Don't feel bad. My grandfather doesn't recognize my grandmother unless you jog his memory a little. Lately he's even exiting the house via windows. Strange man.

You have to enter the AUTOEXEC.BAT zone. Using the DOS text editor EDIT, check the position of the line that loads the MSCDEX driver in the AUTOEXEC.BAT file. The MSCDEX driver, which sets up the CD-ROM drive parameters, must load before the line that starts Windows. Normally, the line in the AUTOEXEC.BAT file that starts Windows looks like

```
WIN
```

or

```
C:\WINDOWS\WIN
```

or something similar.

If the MSCDEX driver is loaded after Windows, then Windows starts without loading this driver; hence, the CD-ROM won't work in Windows. But because the CD-ROM driver loads after you exit Windows, everything is OK the next time you enter Windows.

Komando Klues

A quick fix is to move the MSCDEX line in the AUTOEXEC.BAT file so that it's after the sound card drivers, SmartDrive, and whatever else but before the line that starts Windows. Save the change and reboot.

Remember, never make any changes in the AUTOEXEC.BAT file without first making a backup of the file to a floppy disk.

More information about using the EDIT command is in the DOS chapter.

PC won't recognize CD-ROM drive

My PC (with CD-ROM and sound card) worked fine for months. When I came home after a weekend away, my system no longer recognized the CD-ROM drive. I reinstalled all my drivers and restored the CONFIG.SYS and AUTOEXEC.BAT files, but nothing helped. How do I get the drive to show up again?

Do you believe in the screwdriver fairy?

First check whether the cable going to your CD-ROM drive is loose.

If the connection is snug, check that the CD-ROM cable is firmly attached to the sound board. *Note:* Only open the computer's case with the power off.

If the computer doesn't find the CD-ROM drive after rebooting, run some antivirus software like Microsoft AntiVirus (MSAV), which comes with MS-DOS 6.0 and above. (Remember, your computer has "been" with every other computer that your software has contacted.) Some *boot sector viruses*, which show up when you restart your computer, trick the computer into thinking that you haven't installed a CD-ROM drive.

Of course, the CD-ROM drive or controller card may be bad. If you own diagnostic tools and know how a CD-ROM drive should be hooked up, you can test the components yourself. But you still may not be able to pinpoint some problems (perhaps a power surge zapped the computer's insides, or maybe the power supply on the drive's laser lens reader is dead). If you can't identify the problem, it's time to haul the computer in to an authorized computer repair center.

Video crashes the computer

I finally bought a CD-ROM title that uses video, and now my computer keeps crashing. What's going on?

You have old video drivers. Video challenges your video card's performance, and most video card manufacturers have released updated drivers to incorporate changes needed to handle the video data effectively. Contact the manufacturer of your video card and get the latest version of the video drivers. If an update is not available, it's probably time to update to a newer video card, which you can buy for less than $100.

Advanced

Sector buffer adjustments

It seems that whenever I give the parameter of my CD-ROM drive more than M:1, the CD-ROM locks up. The only thing I can do is set it to M:0, which causes a choppy playback. How do I fix this?

The M: parameter (part of the MSCDEX.EXE line in your AUTOEXEC.BAT file) refers to the number of sector buffers (what a techie term, eh?). *Sector buffers* are chunks (how's that for a nontechie term?) of CD information that is read into memory. As the number of chunks goes up, more information goes from the CD to a special place in the computer's memory: a buffer. Because the information is in memory and not on the CD, you can access it quicker. When the M: parameter is greater than 0 or 1, more information off the CD is put in memory.

Some drivers require that the M: parameter be set to only certain values — 6, 8, and 20 are common favorites. If you can't find any reference to the M: parameter in the CD-ROM drive's documentation, try eliminating this parameter altogether.

To get rid of the M: parameter, you need to edit the AUTOEXEC.BAT file:

1. Make a backup of the AUTOEXEC.BAT file.

2. Use the DOS EDIT command to erase the M: parameter and its respective number. Don't erase the entire MSCDEX line — only the part after MSCDEX with the M: and a number.

If an M: parameter is not indicated, an automatic default setting often automatically kicks in when the CD-ROM driver loads. In my experience, this default is better than anything you guesstimate manually.

If you're using MS-DOS 6.2 or above, SmartDrive, the disk caching program that comes with DOS, will also help speed up reading information from a CD-ROM drive. Edit your AUTOEXEC.BAT file (taking the cautions mentioned above) and make sure that the line with MSCDEX.EXE appears *before* the line with the SMARTDRV command.

Mixing a Sony drive with a Pro Audio card

I have a Sony CDU-31a and a Pro Audio 16 with SCSI port. Is there a way to make the two work together?

Sorry. The Sony has a proprietary interface and requires a special AT bus interface card. Even a special AT bus pass won't help. Your Pro Audio card, meanwhile, has a SCSI port.

The Pro Audio card works wonderfully, however, with a drive that uses a SCSI interface and a 50-pin connector. In my humble opinion, ditch the Sony, which is a single-speed drive and hopelessly out of date.

Komando Klues

When you get a double-, triple-, or even quadruple-speed drive, be sure to check the drive's interface before cracking open the computer's case to install the drive. With so many CD-ROM drives, makes, and models on the market, it's easy to buy the wrong type.

Missing drivers

My friend gave me a CD-ROM drive. Unfortunately, he didn't have the device drivers disk anymore. Is there a way to use DOS commands to tell my computer that I have a CD-ROM drive?

DOS commands aren't the answer; you need the CD-ROM driver disk. Before you start yelling at your friend, though, remember that he gave you a free CD-ROM drive.

First, call the drive's manufacturer. Even if it no longer makes the drive, your drivers may be hanging out in some technician's cubicle.

If you strike out, call the local PC user group. (You can find more information about this kind of nonprofit organization in Chapter 1.) Better, go to a meeting and beg for help. Or, if you're shy, ask the person running the meeting to ask for you or post your request on the group's BBS.

As a last resort, if the CD-ROM has a SCSI interface, you can buy a Universal SCSI Adapter, such as CorelSCSI. It's a bundle of drivers and utilities for most SCSI peripherals, including CD-ROM drives.

Note: I wouldn't tell your friend if you track down the driver. This may be why he gave the CD-ROM drive to you in the first place.

 Static

Every time I exit Windows to work in DOS, I get such terrible static from my CD-ROM that I have to reboot. This static not only wastes my time, but it also keeps me from listening to my audio CDs while doing boring bookkeeping! Any suggestions?

Sounds like your computer hates bookkeeping as much as you do. It also sounds like Windows is finding its way into some memory that your sound board or the CD-ROM controller is trying to use — probably in an area called *upper memory blocks* (UMBs).

Sometimes this space is occupied by video boards, hard drive controllers, CD-ROM controllers, and sound boards; each claims its own little piece of UMB real estate. Trouble is, some of these little buggers are hard for the memory manager in Windows to see, so it mistakenly tries to use memory that's already busy. To maximize the use of memory, try running your memory manager, the DOS MEMMAKER command, or some third-party memory management software.

Of course, static also can be caused by a DMA or IRQ conflict (that is, when two boards try to use the same connection to the main computer at the same time) or a port address conflict. The *port address* is the memory location where the data is actually transferred. If the port address selected by the sound board or CD-ROM controller is already occupied by another device, you can expect some type of strange behavior.

137

If you are routing the CD sound through an audio cable to the sound card, the static may come from the sound card rather than the CD-ROM. If this is the case (you can check by listening through the CD-ROM's headphone jack), you most likely have a driver conflict or a channel conflict. Some versions of sound drivers are buggy and may not set the card up properly upon start-up. New driver versions are routinely available; they usually come with an installation program that makes modifications for you in the AUTOEXEC.BAT and CONFIG.SYS files.

Finally, check the setup program for the sound card. Most Media Vision sound cards are software controlled and can choose among several choices for port and IRQ channels. Try some different channels and check the results.

Komando Klues

Note: In rare cases, to make sound and video cards work well together, you must add the following line to the section of the Windows SYSTEM.INI file that has your Media Vision settings:

```
dmabuf=4
```

You can edit the SYSTEM.INI file through any text editor, such as Windows Notepad. Save the changes and exit Windows. Changes made to the SYSTEM.INI file don't take effect until you restart Windows.

Will SCANDISK evaluate my CD-ROM drive?

Can I use the DOS command SCANDISK to maintain my CD-ROM drive?

Good thought, but no, SCANDISK doesn't work on CD-ROM drives, network drives, or phantom drives. SCANDISK works on hard disks, floppy disks, and RAM disks.

The *RO* in CD-ROM stands for *read-only* — you can't save any information on a CD-ROM. Because you can't save any information on a CD-ROM, you can't change the information on the CD-ROM. Hence, the files remain intact and don't require any help from you to remain that way.

Audio

 No sound from audio CDs

When I put an audio CD in my CD-ROM drive, nothing comes out of the speakers. My game and program CD-ROMs work.

At least, it's easier to fix your problem than it is to stop expensive tropical fish from spending all their time behind an aquarium's seaweed. But enough about that.

The not-so-sweet sounds of silence can be caused by a few things. Before you get the Maalox out, here is a simple test:

1. Plug in a pair of headphones into the headphone jack on the front of your CD-ROM drive. Some multimedia upgrade kits and multimedia computers include headphones. If yours didn't, an ordinary pair of headphones normally fits into a CD-ROM's headphone outlet.

2. Put in the audio CD.

3. Select the Multimedia Player icon in the Accessories group.

4. Click Device and a handy-dandy drop-down menu appears.

5. Select Audio CD from the list. If you don't see Audio CD on the list, you are missing a driver and you need to install the sound board drivers. (Hold on. I'll tell you how to install the drivers in a minute.)

   Notice that the Multimedia Player has little arrows that look very much like an audio CD player's controls. The play button is a single arrow pointing to the right. Fast forward is two arrows pointing to the right. Reverse is two arrows pointing to the left. Stop is the square.

6. Press the play button.

If you hear sounds through the headphones, the CD-ROM drive is set up properly.

If you don't hear anything, the audio cable that plugs into the back of the CD-ROM drive and runs to the sound card probably is not connected or is connected incorrectly. (You see, even if the cable is connected incorrectly, you can still hear sounds from your game or program CDs because the computer's operating system routes game or software CD sounds directly to the sound card.) If you feel comfortable opening up the computer, verify that the speakers are connected to the *output* jack, not input jack, of the sound board. Then look for a thin three- or four-wired cable going from the back of the CD-ROM to the sound board. Now, make sure that the power, data, and audio cables are seated properly and that the data cable between the sound card and CD-ROM drive is seated with pin 1 aligned between the cable and the two connectors. (Pin 1 is usually marked by a red stripe on one side of the cable and marked by an arrow or 1 on the board and the drive.)

If you weren't able to pick Audio CD from the Multimedia Player, you need to check that the sound board drivers are loaded:

1. Open the Windows Main group and double-click Control Panel.

2. Double-click the Drivers icon (the icon that looks like a piano keyboard with a CD and a speaker).

If you don't see your sound board's multimedia drivers installed, you need to put the drivers on your computer:

1. Put an audio CD into the CD-ROM drive. (This step is crucial for the CD Audio driver to install properly.)

2. Click the Add button and select CD Audio. When Windows asks, insert the installation disk that contains MCICDA.DRV; Windows will tell you exactly which disk to insert.

3. Exit and restart Windows, so the new driver changes are recognized.

 No sound at all

Even with the speakers at full volume, I can't hear sounds coming from my CD-ROM. The programs work fine.

Could you repeat the question? Speak up, I can't hear you.

Sound cards come with *mixer utilities*, which let you adjust the volume. Sound Blaster Pro 16, for example, includes the Creative Mixer application, which is normally installed when you put the sound board drivers software on your computer. Then again, what is normal in computers isn't always the case in real life. Check your manual for instructions about how to access your mixer utility.

If you don't know whether you have mixer utilities, do a little searching on your Windows desktop. Often, Sound Mixer Utility is a separate window somewhere in Program Manager's view.

When you find the Creative Mixer window, double-click it to open it; then double-click on the Creative Mixer program icon. Find the control labeled *Volume* and move it up slowly. This control allows you to set the master level for the sound board as well as individual levels for different input devices and files, including MIDI, CD-ROMs, audio CDs, and .WAV files.

If you still don't hear anything, check your external speakers and the back of the Sound Blaster Pro 16 card for a volume control knob. Pump up the volume. Soon you'll be following the bouncing cursor and whistling while you work.

Headphones work, speakers don't

When I try to play music CDs, I can hear them only by using headphones. How can I hear the new Pearl Jam CD through my Yamaha YST-M10 speakers?

Be careful. Your Mozart-loving computer-literate neighbors may have crept into your house late at night and disabled your speakers.

Let's play connect the dots. You have a left speaker and a right speaker. On the back of the right speaker are three plugs, marked *stereo input*, *output to L*, and *DC power*. Make sure that the cable from the back of the computer's sound board is plugged into the right speaker's stereo input plug. Then make sure that the left speaker is plugged into the back of the right speaker where it says *output to L*. And, finally, check that power is flowing to the right speaker's DC power plug.

If you are absolutely, positively sure that all is connected properly, go to Plan B. The fact that you can hear something through the headphones is a good sign. You simply may need to pump up the volume:

1. The sound card's mixer utilities have their own special window, visible from Program Manager. Find the master control volume and turn it up.

2. Then find the volume controls for the speakers (marked *volume* on the right speaker). Don't fool with the *presence* button. Doing so won't raise the volume.

Now put an audio CD in the CD-ROM drive and click Media Player, which is in your Accessories group. Click Device and a handy-dandy drop-down menu appears. Select Audio CD from the list.

If you aren't able to pick Audio CD from the Media Player, you need to check that the sound board drivers are loaded:

1. Open the Windows Main group and double-click Control Panel.

2. Double-click the Drivers icon (the icon that looks like a piano keyboard with a CD and a speaker).

If you don't see your sound board's multimedia drivers installed, you need to put the drivers on your computer:

1. Put an audio CD into the CD-ROM drive. (This step is crucial for the CD Audio driver to install properly.)

2. Click the Add button and select CD Audio. When Windows asks, insert the installation disk that contains MCICDA.DRV; Windows will tell you exactly which disk to insert.

3. Exit and restart Windows, so the new driver changes are recognized. You should be jammin' in no time!

Right speaker, wrong sound

When I play music CDs, the sounds that should come out of the left speaker come out of the right speaker and vice versa.

Do not embark on any of these adventures until you've read this complete answer. Otherwise, you may mess up your system up totally.

If your sound board has separate plugs for each speaker, try switching the cables running from the card to the speakers. That is, take the cable going to the left speaker and connect it to the right speaker and vice versa. If your speakers connect to the sound board through an external amplifier, reverse the two input jack plugs on the amplifier. The jacks are usually labeled something like *AUX left* (or *right*) *input*. If neither setup sounds familiar (for example, perhaps your speakers plug into the sound board directly via a single *stereo mini* jack) or neither solution works, it's time for a little surgery.

Ground yourself by touching the metal chassis of the computer and then unplug the computer. Inside the computer's case is a three- or four-wire cable leading from the CD-ROM drive to a jack on the sound board. This wire carries the audio from your CD to the sound board.

Call the sound board manufacturer's technical support line and ask whether reversing the order of the cables to your speakers will damage your system.

If the sound board's manufacturer gives you the green light, unplug one end of the three- or four-conductor wire leading from the CD-ROM drive to a jack on the sound board. Turn the plug over (or 180 degrees around) and plug it in again. Some connectors are *keyed*, however, and will not fit on backwards. If so, try reversing the other end instead.

Wow, this procedure reminds me of that old game Operation. Remember, if you weren't careful when taking out a bone, the fat man's nose started buzzing.

No CD plug on the sound card

My sound card doesn't have a plug for a direct CD connection. What can I do?

Some sound cards have a *line in* jack rather than a plug. You need to run a *Y-cable* from the CD-ROM card's output jacks to the sound card's line in jack. *Note:* The output jacks of CD-ROM cards are normally RCA stereo type, so you will need a male miniplug to attach to the sound card's line in jack.

If there is no separate output CD-ROM card, you can run an audio cable from the headphone jack at the front of the CD-ROM to the sound card's line in jack.

External CD-ROM drives need a cable to run from its output jack or headphone jack to the sound card's line in jack. So many Jacks and no Jills.

Once you connect your CD-ROM drive to the sound card, the CD Audio will be mixed and output with whatever other sounds are being used by the sound card. Be sure that the volume levels are set, the drivers installed, and the speakers plugged in.

Playing audio CDs through Media Player

I've played music CDs before by using the Media Player in Windows. Now the Device menu doesn't list CD Audio as an option. How do I get it back?

Your computer probably just doesn't like your taste in music. After all, computers only like industrial-techno music. Don't sweat it, though. You can get the CD Audio option back.

Just so you know, the device often vanishes from the list when you install a new CD-ROM title. Some CD-ROM installation routines change certain Windows system files — without informing you. Yes, it's rude, but some computer programs don't know any better. In addition, the CD Audio option sometimes goes away when you install other sound drivers.

Audio drivers that allow you to play music CDs are controlled by a special file in the Windows Control Panel. The Media Player is controlled by the special MPLAYER.INI file, which is in your WINDOWS\SYSTEM subdirectory. To get the CD Audio option back, you need to examine the insides of this file. To do so, use any text editor program. I suggest using the Notepad program found in the Accessories group; it comes free with Windows and is easy to use.

1. Open the MPLAYER.INI file in Notepad as you do any other file. That is, use the File⇨Open option.

2. Look for the CD Audio=0 line in the [Devices] section. (If the line reads CD Audio=17, skip to the graph following the numbered list.)

3. Change the 0 to a 17. 17 is the magic number for audio CDs.

4. Save your changes and exit Notepad.

5. Put an audio CD in the drive and restart the Media Player. The CD Audio device should reappear in the Device menu.

If the line in the [Devices] section reads `CD Audio=17`, go to the Control Panel in Windows and double-click the Drivers icon. Click on the Add button and select CD Audio. When Windows asks, insert the installation disk that contains MCICDA.DRV. Now when you go back to the Media Player, CD Audio should be back in action under Devices.

If none of the above works, perhaps the MSCDEX driver needs to be reinstalled. Or maybe the speakers, the sound card, or the CD-ROM drive is on the blink.

 Drive won't play audio CDs

My friend can play music CDs on his new computer. But when I try to play the same CDs, my computer tells me that there are *no MCI drivers* or something like that. I have the drivers. Does it matter than my CD-ROM drive is older than his?

Remember when you had the new computer and your friend would come over just to look at it? Not the big guy on the block anymore, are you?

Some early-generation CD-ROM drives can't play audio CDs. It's a little deceiving if you check the normal places for the CD-ROM drivers because Windows installs the MCI CD Audio device driver regardless of whether the CD-ROM drive can play an audio CD.

If your CD-ROM drive can play audio CDs, you need to call the CD-ROM drive's manufacturer for an updated drivers disk. After you get the disk and install the new drivers, double-check that all is well:

1. Open the Control Panel window and double-click Drivers.

2. From the list of drivers, highlight MCI CD Audio driver.

3. Click the Setup button. A message should pop up on-screen saying, *One CD-ROM drive was detected. Installation is complete.*

Now try to play the music CD. I bet you'll be humming along quite nicely.

Komando Klues

Still, it's time to upgrade. Your older CD-ROM drive may not be able to handle the newer and cooler CD-ROMs even with the newest drivers.

Sounds skip in Encarta

When using my Encarta CD-ROM, the sound effects skip. My other CD-ROMs work fine. Did I pick a wrong option somewhere? I'm ready to pull out my trusty old World Book encyclopedias.

Perish the thought. If you think the sound effects are bad now, what kind of sound can you expect from a book?

When installing a program on your computer, you're often given two options: complete or minimal installation. In Encarta's case, the full installation takes almost 8MB of hard disk space and the minimal installation takes 2.5MB of hard disk space. I bet you opted for the minimal installation.

The full installation enhances performance; some goodies aren't included in the minimal installation. As a result, it's common to hear skips if you choose the minimal installation. (It seems that this phenomenon occurs more as the computer opens pictures or animations from the CD-ROM.)

The Bottom Line

The solution: Reinstall Encarta, choosing the full installation option. If that doesn't work, call the CD-ROM drive's manufacturer and request the most current drivers. Follow the instructions that come with the driver disk and try Encarta again. And, don't throw out those old encyclopedias. They come in handle to hold up any off-balance table or refrigerator.

Commercial CD-ROMs

Games

Do I have to install the whole thing?

When I used the install command, my new CD game took up a lot of hard disk space. I was surprised that the game doesn't just run off the CD. Do CD games always require you to install massive amounts of information on the hard drive?

Most CD-ROM games and other applications put certain files on the hard disk. Because a CD-ROM is read-only, the program can't write any information, such as current scores, on the CD. So the program has to save this information on the hard disk. There's no way around this sad fact. Worse, it's hard to tell without installing whether a program will hog up your hard disk — although sometimes you can find the hard disk requirements on the CD-ROM's box. Of course, you also can call the CD-ROM publisher's sales line and ask how much space the game requires.

Komando Klues If hard disk space is at a premium, buy a second hard disk or replace the current disk with a bigger one. Gee, suddenly that game became a lot more expensive.

Allocating memory for games

I can't find enough memory for my CD games! They just freeze up. How can I free up some memory to play my games?

Here's a rule of thumb: The cooler the game, the more memory it needs. But games are picky and won't accept just any kind of memory. And remember, the games are fighting with other goodies in your computer for that precious memory.

When your computer starts, CD-ROM drivers, sound drivers, mouse drivers, and so on are loaded into the computer's memory. This way, the drivers that are necessary to make the CD-ROM drive, sound board, mouse, and so on work are all ready to go.

But DOS has this aggravating little problem called *conventional memory*. No matter how much total memory your system has, you only have 640K of conventional memory. Where are most drivers loaded? You got it, conventional memory. Which type of memory do your games want? You got it again, conventional memory.

As a result, to play games, you need to squeeze more conventional memory out of your computer. Although many have written books about memory management, you can try a few simple approaches.

If you have MS-DOS 6 or higher, try running MEMMAKER by typing **MEMMAKER** and pressing Enter at the DOS prompt. Check whether the game needs EMS memory (it should be listed on the side of the game's box). If it does, tell MEMMAKER that you need EMS memory by answering yes to the question *Do any of your applications require EMS memory?* MEMMAKER will reboot the computer a couple of times. When the process is done, give the game another shot.

147

If you still don't have enough free conventional memory, you have to load some device drivers. Reboot; then press F8 when the computer says *Starting MS-DOS*. This action enables you to process the individual lines in your configuration files; that is, you are prompted to respond yes or no to each line. Make sure you say yes to the statements referring to the CD-ROM drive and any other statements that contain MSCDEX. Say no to any TSRs, such as virus protection or fax management programs. Say yes to any line necessary for running the CD-ROM program, including sound drivers, HIMEM.SYS, EMM386, mouse driver, CD-ROM drivers, and so on.

Because your CD-ROM's drivers load when your system boots, you may find that the driver constrains your system's conventional memory. If so, it's time to call in the cavalry: QEMM and NetRoom are third-party memory management programs that can wring the very last byte of usable conventional memory out of your system.

Transferring games from CD to disk

How do I transfer CD-ROM games to a hard or floppy disk?

In very rare cases, you can transfer a program from a CD-ROM to your hard disk. But unless the game's documentation explicitly says that the game will work from the hard disk, don't count on it! The games are simply too big.

Meanwhile, a CD-ROM disc can hold in excess of 600MB of information; a high-density 3½-inch floppy disk holds only 1.44MB. So you need 417 floppies to hold the info contained on one CD-ROM disk. You'll die of disk swapping.

Speeding up Critical Path

I just bought a new CD-ROM game, Critical Path. The video lags behind the sound, and both skip. How can I speed up my CD-ROM drive?

Playing high-intensity games such as Critical Path without the right equipment is like sitting in the drive-thru lane at a fast-food restaurant behind an indecisive family of six.

Here are some rules of thumb:

Komando Klues

➤ Maximize your free memory by using the DOS MEMMAKER command. Type **MEMMAKER** at the DOS prompt and press Enter. When you are asked to choose express or custom setup, get on board the express train.

➤ Check the box that Critical Path came in. If it says you need a certain amount of expanded memory, say yes to EMS memory when MEMMAKER asks you.

➤ If you're using MS-DOS 6.2 or above, know that the SmartDrive program (DOS and Windows's disk caching program) helps speed up CD-ROM drives, too.

SmartDrive improves drive performance by getting the information together from the CD-ROM that you'll probably be using next. *Note:* Make sure that the SMARTDRV line is placed before the MSCDEX line in your AUTOEXEC.BAT file; otherwise, the cache may not recognize your CD-ROM drive. MSCDEX lets the computer see the CD-ROM drive. By the way, use the Windows version (not the DOS version) of SmartDrive. If you need to change your AUTOEXEC.BAT file, save a copy of your AUTOEXEC.BAT file to a floppy disk or another directory on your computer. At the DOS prompt, type **EDIT** and press Enter. Make sure the line with MSCDEX comes *before* the line with SMARTDRIV. Also, be sure that the statement with SmartDrive is being loaded from the WINDOWS directory.

➤ Many high-demand games have settings that allow you to select trade-offs in performance versus video detail, screen size, sound amount, sound type, and sound complexity.

Configuration options are a resource balancing act. Decide what's most important and crank up the detail in those areas. Of course, if you want a great-looking screen, you may see fewer colors. (Generally, the more colors displayed on-screen, the slower the screen refresh rate and other video idiosyncrasies, like the lag you mentioned. In fact, I suggest changing your video driver to use fewer colors in the CD's settings.)

Sound and video skipping on 7th Guest

My CD-ROM drive's specifications say that it works at 146K per second. Why does the sound and video skip on 7th Guest?

7th Guest is an exciting but demanding game. I have a few ideas:

➤ The folks at Virgin Games, the makers of 7th Guest, recommend using at least a double-speed CD-ROM drive for best results; it sounds as though you have a single-speed drive.

➤ Make sure that you have the most recent CD-ROM drivers.

➤ Several products *cache* the data coming from your CD-ROM drive. Cache is a memory trick that speeds up the transfer of information inside a computer. CD Speedway, Lightening CD, and MS-DOS 6.2 or above have utilities that can speed up your drive's performance. By caching, or *buffering*, the information to and from the CD-ROM, these products let the CD-ROM drive move more information in a shorter period of time.

Problems with the video palette

When I put in a game CD, I got an error message — something about a video palette. I didn't know that a video had a palette. What's wrong with this picture?

You really should leave the comedy writing for the professionals.

Usually, a video driver or video palette error message means you need a 256-color video driver. Most video boards sold today have 256-color video drivers, but older boards have measly 16-color video drivers.

To check your computer's video card driver and number of colors, double-click on Windows Setup (in the Windows Main group). Then look under Display. I bet it says 16 colors. So pick 256 colors and follow the instructions on-screen. *Note:* Keep your Windows disks or the video card driver disks handy; you'll need them to change the video card settings.

Komando Klues

If you haven't received any upgraded video driver disks from the video card's manufacturer in the last six months, call the manufacturer and request an updated driver's disk.

MS Golf working below par

My Microsoft Golf CD-ROM doesn't work when I do a flyby stroke. Instead, I see a message about an undetectable error and driver. What can I do to leave the driving range?

You know you're a bad athlete when your golf and bowling scores resemble each other. Actually, you know you're a bad athlete if you only golf and bowl.

Luckily, undetectable errors are detectable if you know where to look. The word *driver* in your error message indicates that something is wrong with the video driver Microsoft Golf needs for the flyby stroke to appear on-screen.

To fix your problem, follow these steps:

1. Save and close all documents and files. (You're going to restart Windows after making a few driver fixes; I don't want you to lose any information you haven't saved.)

2. From the Main group in Windows, double-click the Control Panel and choose the Drivers icon (which looks like a piano keyboard with a CD and a speaker).

3. From the list box (which shows the drivers installed on your computer), highlight [MCI] Microsoft Videos for Windows.

4. Click the Remove button and select yes to remove the driver.

5. Don't panic.

6. Click Restart Now, closing down and then restarting Windows.

7. Reinstall the game from the original Microsoft Golf CD-ROM.

8. When you're asked during the installation whether you want to install Video for Windows, say yes.

Now when you use Golf, the only error you'll see is your slice.

Double vision in A Hard Day's Night

I see a double image when I open up my Voyager's A Hard Day's Night CD-ROM. This double image includes a blown-up version of the image that covers the screen with bars. Any ideas?

Sounds like you've been "working like a dog" on this one. Stop beatle-ing yourself over the head.

Your software is using the wrong video driver for your monitor, or the program's resolution is higher than your monitor and video board supports. This kooky-looking display happens when the timing of the video card and the game is off. Select the next lower resolution display type in the game's program setup and restart.

Other

Creating a sharper image

Can I do anything to improve the quality of the pictures on the Animals CD-ROM that came bundled with my drive?

Video cards have different settings and resolutions — the number of colors and the quality of images shown on-screen. Many programs that display photographic quality images work best in at least 256-color mode. Of course, if your video card has higher settings, use them instead to get better-quality pictures.

You can check the video card settings in the Windows program settings. To do so:

1. Open the Main window and double-click on the Windows Settings icon.

2. Look under Display Type and make a note of what driver you're currently using. Make sure your card is set for 256 colors.

3. To change the setting in Windows Settings, click Options and select Change System Settings.

4. From the pull-down list, pick SVGA 256 colors, 640 × 480 mode. Your computer may ask you for the Windows disks or video card drivers disk.

5. Restart Windows and try your program again.

You may not have enough memory on your video card (you usually need 1MB) to work in 256-color mode. If so, you won't be able to see the screen in Windows. You can change the video card settings back to what they were originally. From the DOS prompt,

1. Change to the WINDOWS directory (usually by typing **CD \WINDOWS**).

2. Type **SETUP** and press Enter.

3. Move the cursor to the Display Type field and press Enter.

4. Pick out the old video driver from the list.

Exit Setup, type **WIN**, and press Enter. Your screen should be back to using the old video drivers.

Komando Klues

It's a good idea to get in touch with the video card's manufacturer and make sure that you have the latest drivers for the video card. Manufacturers update video card drivers constantly. But you often need to call the manufacturer to find out about the updates.

CD-ROMs that teach Japanese

In a Berlitz Japanese class, I picked up a brochure about a CD-ROM that teaches Japanese. But I accidentally threw away the brochure. Can you help?

You're talking about Berlitz for Business Japanese by Bright Star Technology. This CD-ROM is based on the Berlitz immersion method, where you eat and breathe a new language. The CD-ROM's audio, video, and text beats the pants off any Windows language program. (Heck, it even has a Samurai instructor who holds your hand throughout the lessons.) After you finish the lessons, you can take a trip on the Tokyo Subway to test what you just learned. For more information, call Bright Star Technology at 206-562-6050.

CDs for travel

Which travel-oriented CD-ROMs do you recommend?

Modern-day Marco Polos use their computer to help them journey from place to place, find a good meal, take in the sights, and get some rest. A travel-oriented CD-ROM is a live-in travel agent armed with the latest books, 35-mm slides, and video tapes. Reviews, pictures, maps, trivia, and video clips help chart your course, whether your purpose is business or pleasure. Today's software is so good, in fact, you won't have to leave the house.

➤ Compton's New Media (800-862-2206) — With Compton's New Media electronic book version, gone are the days of frantic index searching and dog-earing pages. Type your destination and a jam-packed presentation pops up on-screen. *Let's Go* CD-ROMs are known for their practical tips, written especially for the traveler on a simple budget. For example, did you know that there are 12 hotels or hostels in Los Angeles priced under $19 a night? (Of course, you're going to want to sleep holding on to your laptop.) And did you know that you get half-price admission to both the Heard Museum and the Art Museum if you get a *Valley Pass* from the Phoenix Visitor's Bureau?

➤ Multicom Publishing (800-245-4525) — Visiting our nation's national parks should be mandatory for citizenship. *The National Parks of America* CD-ROM from Multicom Publishing is a multimedia journey through 230 parks. The more popular sights are shown on 20 narrated full-motion videos. The 950 pictures by award-winning photographer David Meunch on the CD-ROM were originally published in a coffee-table book. You can search easily and quickly for parks by region, state, monument, photos, or videos. General information about each park includes camping, hiking, lakes, lodging, monuments, and the park's address and phone number.

➤ Mindscape (415-883-3000) — Next time you're ready to pick up an atlas, choose *US Atlas 4* from Mindscape (formerly The Software Toolworks). This high-tech CD-ROM textbook and travel guide has 11 major categories divided among national, state, and county levels covering social, geographic, and economic information in more than 400 subtopics. The 150 full-motion video clips taken from the America by Air series by Douglas Kahan are incredible. Like a traditional atlas, the CD-ROM version also has highway and topographic maps covering regional, state, county, and city levels. Plus, you can see 1,000 scenic and historic spot photos and hear each state's anthem as well as a pronunciation guide.

This is such a hot area for CD-ROM publishers that many other companies are getting into the business, too. Even the American Auto Association (AAA) has its own travel CD.

Updating your CD-ROM information

I have some fact-filled CD-ROMs that include travel guides, phone books, databases, and other business information. How do I make sure I have the latest information?

Top five ways to determine whether your fact-filled CD-ROM travel guide is old:

5. It gives directions to the Berlin Wall.

4. It says, "President Nixon vacationed here last year."

3. It describes Los Angeles as "sprawling with uncluttered freeways."

2. Its version of Mount Rushmore has only three heads.

1. It tells you where to buy unleaded fuel.

Although CD-ROMs hold incredible amounts of stuff, they must be updated regularly, especially when the information is date sensitive. If you purchase a fact-filled CD-ROM, be sure to send in the registration card. Registered users typically receive updates at substantial discounts. More important, the publisher contacts registered users when updates are available.

If you're not sure whether you have the latest version, call the publisher. Companies are usually more than happy to help you determine whether you need to spend more money.

Chapter 5

Communications

 Basics

I'm new at this, so feel sorry for me. What's a modem?

I only feel sorry for people who owe me money.

A *modem* (stands for *mo*dulator *dem*odulator) is a gadget that enables your computer to talk to, or exchange information with, another computer through ordinary phone lines. When a modem modulates, it sends information. When it demodulates, it receives information.

Note: An *internal* modem sits inside your computer; an *external* modem sits outside your computer.

After your computer is connected by telephone line and modem to another computer, all kinds of neat things are possible. Simply by making a phone call, you can connect to a computer on the other side of town (or, for that matter, on the other side of the planet). When you establish a connection, the information on the other computer is available to you. If you connect to the right computer, all sorts of stuff — news, the latest sports scores, stock and weather reports, romance chat areas, and re-search libraries — are literally at your fingertips.

Most new computers include a modem; if yours doesn't, you can buy one. You tell the computer when you want to use the modem by using a communications program. After you identify the target computer, your communications software dials the number and translates the computers' conversation for you. By the way, a conversation between computers is made up of information — bits and bytes, to be exact.

The modem's talk speed is called the *baud rate* (often referred to as *bits per second* or *bps*), which is nothing more than the speed at which information travels from computer to computer. Baud rate works much like the speedometer on a car: the higher the baud rate, the faster the information moves between computers. Speeds usually range from 300 to 28,800 bps. Most people today travel the electronic corridors at 9600 bps.

Definition of bps and cps

Is bps the same thing as cps? I want to communicate, but I don't even know where the heck to start. (Why can't you computer people speak in English?)

You start by softening that tone, mister.

Let me start with the ABCs. The entire computer alphabet is made up of only two numbers: 0 and 1. That's all a computer can understand!

This computer alphabet is called *binary* (meaning two, get it?). Old-timers call the alphabet's "letters" *binary digits*; the modern term is *bits*.

Bits travel between computers at different speeds. How fast depends on

- ➤ Type of modem
- ➤ The communications speed that the computer you connect to can accept
- ➤ The quality of the telephone connection between computers

The speed that bits travel is measured in *bits per second* (*bps*), or *baud rate*. Modem speeds are defined by bps (a 9600 bps modem, for example, moves 9600 bits per second). The higher the bps, the faster the information moves between computers.

A group of eight bits is called a *character*. In other words, a computer needs a combination of eight 1s and 0s to form each character of the human alphabet. For example, one character looks like this:

```
10011100
```

You guessed it, the speed that characters travel is measured in *characters per second* or *cps*.

Why do we have both bps and cps? Because computer engineers (who never see sunlight) invented this whole deal. And who knows how they think?

Actually, when you send files to your friends by modem, it's easier to track a file transfer in cps because files are made up of characters.

See why computer geeks have a hard time getting a date? And when they do, they only go out with ones and zeros. Ha Ha Ha.

Phone line needed

Do I need a special type of phone line to use a modem?

No. Any regular phone line works — as long as you've paid your phone bill.

Be careful, though, if the phone line is connected to a PBX (a typical phone system in a larger office); you have to tell the communications software to dial 9 to get an outside line.

Getting to know on-line services

All my friends are meeting via an on-line service. I think they're talking about me. What software do I need to join them?

Well, you know what they say: Worry when they stop talking about you.

Major on-line services and larger BBSs (*bulletin board system*) usually give you their own software to connect to their service.

When you join an on-line service or BBS, you become a *member*. The service sends you a membership kit comprising instructions, communications software, and the information you need to sign on (namely, user ID and password). Most services give you the software free of charge.

To use an on-line service, however, you usually need a credit card or checking account (you type the appropriate information in when you first sign on to the service). Usually, on-line services automatically charge a monthly membership fee; sometimes, they levy hourly charges and other fees.

Smaller on-line services and BBSs, meanwhile, typically require a bare-bones communications program.

159

Microsoft Windows includes a basic communications program called Terminal, but you can find more sophisticated communications software programs at major computer software stores. As usual, the more you spend, the more features you get. You can even program some software to connect to a service from a single keystroke.

Understanding modem lights

I suppose that the markings and lights on my external modem tell me what my modem is doing. Am I right? If so, what does it all mean?

My "right" light just flashed.

Some software programs simulate external modem lights, too. Here is a list of lights commonly found on external modems and within communications software programs:

Modem Marking	What It Means	Description
CD	Carrier detect	Tells you whether the computer (that is, the modem) that you are trying to connect to has answered.
AA	Automatic answer	Lets you know whether the modem has been configured to answer incoming calls automatically.
HS	High speed	Stays on during those connections that the modem considers to be high speed. (Of course, *high speed* is a relative term. Just ask anyone who made the jump from a 2400 to a 9600 baud modem.)
OH	Off hook	No light means no connection.
SD	Send	Indicates that the modem is sending information.
TX	Send	Some modems use TX rather than SD.
RS	Request to send	Lights up when your computer asks your modem if everything is cool to send information.
CS	Clear to send	Lights up when your modem says to your computer, "Go ahead and send me the goods."
RD	Receive	Indicates that the modem is receiving information.

Modem Marking	What It Means	Description
EC	Error correction	Flashes when the modem is sending a fax. Stays lit when the modem is working in error correction mode. (Contrary to popular belief, EC lights on a modem aren't the same as lights used by highway workers.)
SQ	Signal quality	Flashes when the connection is poor.
MR	Modem ready	Flashes when the modem is testing itself.
LB	Low battery	Lights up when the charge of the portable modem is almost gone.
HDJ	He's dead, Jim	(Optional) Tells you that the modem isn't working. Just kidding.

What's file transfer protocol?

What's a file transfer protocol?

File transfer protocols help correct bad phone connections and verify that what was sent is received.

If you make a telephone call and the connection is noisy, you can call the party back. Or if you're like my impoverished nephew, you place the call, make noises in the telephone, and then say, "Can't hear you. Call me back." I don't mind: I do the same thing when he asks me for money.

When you're sending a file over a phone line, your communications software and your modem try to correct phone line troubles that could disrupt the transfer. You don't need to have the same communications software running on both the sending and receiving computers; in fact, the computers can have different operating systems. But the sending party and receiving party do need to use the same file transfer protocol.

Putting a file transfer protocol into practice isn't hard. Suppose, for example, that you want to send a friend the latest office-football-pool statistics. You send the file, or *upload* it, to your friend, and your friend sets up his communications software to accept, or *downloads*, the file. Beforehand, you and your friend must agree to use a certain file transfer protocol. Your choice of protocol depends on many things; most important is the quality of the phone line.

Komando Klues

Generally, use the protocol ZMODEM or XMODEM.

To decipher the file transfer mumbo jumbo and pick the right protocol, follow these guidelines:

Phone Line Quality	Recommended FTP
Good	Use HS-Link, ZMODEM, YMODEM-G, or IMODEM in that order. If you can, use HS-Link (a new protocol supported by high-speed modems) because it allows you to upload and download files at the same time. ZMODEM is the fastest and best of the rest, particularly because it can restart a file transfer that stopped unexpectedly right where it left off.
Fair	Use XMODEM, YMODEM, and YMODEM Batch in that order. Although XMODEM is real popular, it fails when it encounters time delays. (By the way, XMODEM was invented by Ward Christensen, the designer and programmer of the first BBS.)
Bad	XMODEM-CRC, which provides error checking, is tops. Kermit is another possibility, but it has so many options that it's hard to get the sending and receiving protocols to match.

Basic troubleshooting

Sometimes my software asks for the name of my internal 2400 baud modem. I can't answer because I don't know.

Well, give your modem a name. I've always liked *Michelle*. But I warn you, if you introduce your software to the modem, you may as well let them date. Otherwise, you may wake up someday to an empty house. Elopement is very common among modems.

Don't worry, the make and model number isn't all that important, especially when you're talking about a low-speed modem. Almost all 2400 bps modems, for example, follow the same standards when sending a file, receiving a file, or connecting to an on-line service.

As a result, when your communications program prompts, you can't go wrong picking the Hayes or Hayes compatible standard. It's a one-size-fits-all selection. Your modem should perform just fine.

Note: The Hayes modem standard is a set of rules that modems use to communicate with each other. These rules are generally referred to as *AT commands*.

If you won't sleep unless you know the exact make and model number, look in the manual that came with your computer. Or call the manufacturer. Or open the computer's case and look at the modem.

Turning off call waiting

Call waiting, teenagers, and trying to use a BBS spells disaster. When someone calls, call waiting kicks in and disconnects me from the BBS. Why can't my computer just ignore the incoming call? Can I turn off call waiting?

With call waiting, a beep sounds to let you know that you have another incoming call. This signal also sounds if you're connected with your modem; the tone blocks the modem from hearing the other modem just long enough for them to disconnect.

Most Bell companies provide a way for you to temporarily turn off call waiting. The most common way is to dial *70 before dialing the number you want to call. Incoming callers then will hear a busy signal until that particular call ends.

Note: The actual command required to turn off call waiting varies by telephone carrier. Contact your phone company and ask for the correct dialing sequence.

To disable call waiting on a call-by-call basis when you're using your modem, just add *70 to the phone number of the board you want to call (if the *70 sequence doesn't work, call your local phone company for the correct sequence). For example, if the BBS has a phone number of 555-1234, make sure that the communications software dials

```
*70,555-1234
```

It's also easy to make your modem ignore the call waiting altogether. If you always want to disable call waiting when using your modem, look in your communications software under Setup. Change the command string ATDT so that it reads as follows:

```
ATDT*70,
```

where ATDT tells the modem, "Hey, get me a dial tone," and *70 temporarily turns off call waiting (if the *70 sequence doesn't work, call your local phone company for the correct sequence). The comma makes the modem pause for two seconds — while call waiting is disabled. Now, any number dialed by your communications software won't be bothered by calls from your children's friends.

Just for the record, have you ever faked call waiting just to get off the phone? If not, look for that chicanery (and more) in my next book, *10,001 Ways to Get Off the Phone and Back on the Computer.*

Communications software help

I bought a Practical Peripherals 14,400 modem at a computer store going-out-of-business sale. It was a demonstration unit and had no manual. What do I do?

Strike three, you're out. Now pinch hitting, Kim Komando-o-o-o (Echo on).

Some modems, including the PPI 14,400 modem, have help available from within your communications software. To see the help, type **AT$H** from within your communications software and press Enter.

Several pages of help should appear on-screen, including AT commands. If you can't find what you need, call PPI at 800-442-4774 (keep your credit card handy, a new manual costs about $10).

Komando Klues

To see information about your current, or most recent, connection, type **ATI6** from within your communications software and press Enter.

Modem security

I'm concerned about leaving my computer turned on and connected to a phone line. Can hackers get into my computer through my modem?

Gee, buy one modem, and suddenly you're Mr. Top Secret.

The answer is no. The combination of computer, modem, and phone line isn't enough to let someone actually inside your computer — unless you set your modem or your communications software into an auto-answer mode. Even then, you can set up user IDs and passwords to limit access.

Muffling your modem

My modem's sound is real annoying. How can I turn the volume off?

Use an AT command: start your communications software, type **ATM0**, and press Enter.

You should get an OK on-screen. Save your new setting in your communications software. Look in your software manual under *save settings* for more information.

You didn't ask, but here are some more popular AT commands that relate to the speaker:

Komando Klues

AT Command	Description
ATM1	Turns the speaker on until the connection is made (or, in techie talk, until a carrier is detected).
ATM2	Turns the speaker on.
ATM3	Except while dialing, turns the speaker on.
ATL0, ATL1	Sets the speaker volume to low.
ATL2	Sets the speaker volume to medium.
ATL3	Sets the speaker volume to loud.
ATBOZO	Turns down the volume of a neighbor's stereo. (Wouldn't that be great?)

Q&A *Turning off auto-answer*

Whenever I plug a phone line into the modem, my computer answers the phone and I get the dreaded squelch sound. What can I do to prevent this?

Either your communications software or your modem believes that it should answer all incoming calls. To silence the squelch, you need to turn off the auto-answer feature.

Komando Klues

After you disable this feature in your communications software, remember to save your settings.

If you cannot find the auto-answer feature in the program, it's time to get radical, I mean technical. (Don't worry, it's not that technical.) Type **ATS0=0** (those are zeros, not ohs) in your communications software and press Enter. You should get an OK from the communications software. If you do not, make sure that you are typing the command in all capital letters (some modems require AT commands to be entered in all caps).

To make this setting permanent, use the save settings feature in your communications software. Or type **AT&W** in your communications software and press Enter. This command writes the new settings into the modem's memory.

Everything should be swell now. But if the computer continues to answer the phone, check your modem manual under auto-answer: you may need to change the dip switches (no, *dip* isn't an insult) on the modem to turn off auto-answer.

Taking your office on the road

When I'm on the road, I want to transfer files from my laptop to my office. Do I need an e-mail program?

A number of communications programs can do what you need. With them, there are basically two ways to set up your system:

> ➤ Before you leave, set up your machine at work to run in *host* mode. In essence, host mode sets up your computer as a mini-BBS. When you call from the road, the host answers the phone and allows you to connect to your computer. You then can upload a file from your laptop to your computer at work, download a file to your laptop, find files, and even copy a file from one location of your drive at work to another location. Most high-end communications programs have this option built in.

> ➤ The better option, however, is to use a program specifically made for what you need to do: *remote control software* puts everything on your office computer on your laptop computer. You can run software programs, transfer files, and more with a modem and a phone line. When your office machine receives a call from your laptop, your laptop is your office machine. It's as though you are actually in your office — only you don't have to deal with the constant flirting every time you walk in the copyroom.

Using Microsoft Diagnostics

How do I find out whether I have a UART 16550 chip in my internal modem? I use Windows 3.1.

You don't even need to open the computer's case. Snooping around inside your computer is easy with Microsoft Diagnostics (MSD), a great program that you probably didn't know you had.

To use MSD, exit Windows. At the DOS prompt, type **MSD** and press Enter. Press C (as in Com Ports); at the bottom of the screen you can see the model numbers of the UART chips installed in your computer.

Komando Klues

The 16550 comes in different flavors: 16550A, 16550AF, and 16550AFN. The 16550AFN is the best of the three.

Of course, if you're into adventures, you also can

➤ Check your computer's manual

➤ Call your vendor

➤ Fish around the motherboard (near the back of your PC) to find the chip; it will have *8250* or *16450* or *16550* on it

Using the Hayes standard setup

My Telepath modem isn't listed in the pull-down list for modems in my software setup. I selected Hayes compatible. Is a better selection available?

If the generic Hayes driver is working, you don't have a problem. Hayes is the de facto standard and will work with just about any modem on the market. If you like to tinker, though, call the technical support number for your communications software to see whether anyone can suggest a better match.

Defining transfer rate

I have a 14,400 baud modem. When I select a speed in any communications application, the list jumps from 9600 to 19-something-or-other. Where's 14,400?

It's confusing, so read this answer at 2400 bps.

The *transfer rate* in your communications program is not the speed of your modem. Rather, it's the speed that you want your computer and modem to exchange information. And with data compression, your 14,400 bps modem can transfer more than 14,400 bps.

However, the speed set in your communications software is the speed at which the modem works, even if the modem in fact can work at a higher speed. For example, if you choose the 9600 bps option in your communications software, your modem won't cruise at anything higher.

Meanwhile, thanks to its built-in compression technology, the effective speed of a 14,400 bps modem can be considerably higher than 14,400 bps. Of course, a lot depends on the type of file you're sending. If you're sending a precompressed file, such as a .ZIP file, your modem can't make it any smaller. But if you're sending text files, the modem can shrink them, send them, and then, on the other end, decompress them. (Modems also can compress some graphics file formats and other fluff files.) As a result, speeds above 14,400 bps are definitely possible. (Still, if you tell your computer and modem to talk to each other at 14,400 bps, your modem is limited to that speed.)

The Bottom Line

Go ahead and select 19,200 in your communications program. But remember, your modem will communicate only at the highest speed you *and* the other end can communicate.

Checking modem settings

The modem used to work. But I got bored and played with the modem's settings. Now the modem doesn't work at all. What can I do?

Wait until you're bored again and then fix it. (The quickest way, yawn, is to crack open the user manual.)

I know a family secret, passed from generation to generation, and can magically restore your modem to its youthful glow overnight. (I think I've been watching too many infomercials.) But before I simply hand over the key to everlasting happiness, you may as well learn something from this experience, right?

All modems come with a factory default setting. The manufacturer set up your modem to meet most people's needs. These settings control everything, from the speed that the modem dials to the type of error correction. If you know which settings control which area of your modem's performance, you can customize the way the modem works.

You can adjust all these setting with commands that begin with the prefix AT. For most modems, the commands are not case sensitive, but a few modems will accept commands entered in uppercase letters only. One AT command is ATM0, which turns off your modem's speaker when dialing. Another is ATS0=1, which tells your modem to go into auto-answer mode and connect to the modem of the calling party.

As you found out (the hard way), some incorrect settings can paralyze your modem. Whenever you don't know what you did, set the modem back to the factory settings.

The Bottom Line

168

To do so (this is the magic potion), start your communications software program (or the Windows Terminal program). Then type **AT&F** and press Enter. To save the new (that is, old) settings, type **AT&W** and press Enter.

Tracking phone line noise

I was having trouble connecting to BBSs, so I bought an error correcting modem. But I'm still encountering line noise. Please don't tell me that I need to rewire my house. My husband gripes when I ask him to take the trash out.

Remember: Trash in, trash out.

Luckily, line noise isn't necessarily caused by bad wiring. To try and isolate the origin of the line noise, do the following:

➤ Cross your fingers and check whether it's related to the wiring in your house (if so, don't shoot the messenger). Of course, checking the wiring in your house may be next to impossible. Nonetheless, first disconnect any portable phones and all other extensions. If doing so doesn't clear up the problem, go ask your neighbors whether they hear any static when they're talking on the phone. If so, you know that your whole neighborhood has wiring problems.

➤ Contact your phone company and, through the static, see whether anyone can check the wiring that runs to your house. (*Tip:* For quicker service, crinkle some plastic wrap while you're talking to them.) It's easy for the phone company to check a line at the main substation or outside your home in a connection box. Static on the line means that the problem lies in the phone wiring from your house to the telephone pole or beyond.

When contacting the phone company, make sure that you explain that the line's quality is important for modem communications. Unfortunately, you may find that the wiring in your area is not up to speed for use by a modem. In this case, the phone company may offer to install a data line. This solution may cost a little more than your standard line, but for the extra money, you get a noise-free line into the telephone's network.

➤ Find out whether the system you're calling has bad wiring. To test this theory, try calling another BBS in your area. (In fact, try calling one that's a good distance away from your original target in case that whole area is prone to bad service.)

With a little legwork, you should be able to identify where the problem most likely lies. In the end, you may find that the noise is not on your end. Whew.

Now take that trash out. Phew. It's beginning to smell.

169

BBSs vs. on-line services

What's the difference between a BBS and an on-line service?

Millions of dollars and thousands of people.

What are BBSs (*b*ulletin *b*oard *s*ystems)?

➤ Usually operated by one or two people.

➤ Often just a hobby to its owner/operator(s).

➤ Cater to as many as a few thousand local users.

➤ Have up to 30,000 files for downloading.

➤ Limited e-mail capability.

➤ Supported by one home PC; larger BBSs may require two or three home PCs.

➤ One phone number.

➤ Users need standard communications software, such as CrossTalk, Procomm, Qmodem, Windows Terminal, and more.

➤ Hundreds of thousands are in operation across the country.

What are on-line services?

➤ Can easily need thousands of people to run it.

➤ Operated for profit. In fact, some large U.S. on-line services are publicly held corporations whose stock is traded on the major exchanges; in short, they are big business.

➤ Allow hundreds of thousands of users (maybe even worldwide) on-line simultaneously.

➤ Have a few hundred thousand files available for downloading. On-line services have the latest worldwide news, stocks, sports, weather, and special-interest groups. You also can find the latest editions of major magazines, newspapers, newsletters, and more.

➤ Wide-ranging e-mail capability — with access to the Internet.

➤ Operated by one or more large mainframe industrial computer systems.

➤ Local access numbers in most cities.

➤ You are provided, free of charge, special communications software designed for use solely with that service. (The exception is CompuServe, which still allows you to use a standard communications program. However, CompuServe also will sell you specially tailored software that makes using the service a snap.)

> ➤ In the U.S., major on-line services operating 24 hours a day include America Online, CompuServe, Delphi, GEnie, InterChange, ImagiNation, and Prodigy.

On-line services are not a fad

How do you know that all these on-line services aren't just a flash in the pan?

How do you know that compact discs aren't a flash in the pan? How about microwave ovens? How about flashes in the pan? Face it. All these things are here to stay. Deep down, you know so. That's why you bought this book.

Love 'em or hate 'em, computers aren't the wave of the future. They're the present. It's called progress — faster, cheaper, stronger.

Just as billions are being spent every day on home computers, billions are being spent to make on-line services better. No wonder Bill Gates, founder of Microsoft (the world's largest software company), is now one of the richest individuals in the world. He's worth over six billion dollars. That's

```
$6,000,000,000.00
```

Gulp. When you last blinked, he made a few thousand dollars. Just think, before computers, he was a pencil-neck geek with a pocket protector. (After Gates earned his first billion, his marketing and public relations staff told him to lose the pocket protector. He did.)

Besides, all this may end tomorrow. You have to live every day like it's your last. And you may as well spend your last day on an on-line service.

Speaking of living life to the fullest, my Uncle Norman lives every day as if it were his last. No such luck. He runs around all day every day screaming, "I'm gonna die. I'm gonna die." I wish he'd stop already.

Choosing a BBS or on-line service

My local computer newspaper devoted two pages to listing different BBSs. Why are there so many different BBSs? It bothers me.

Really? Choice bothers you? How about relief, convenience, and enjoyment? Do they bother you, too?

Most BBSs are aimed at users with specialized interests. In most cities and towns, you can find local BBSs that specialize in computing as a hobby, photography, ham radio, SCUBA, horses, cooking, genealogy, pets, outdoors and camping, flying, programming, Scouts, and so on.

In fact, if you can think of a topic for which there is no BBS in your town, you should start your own BBS. If you build it, they will come.

Picking an on-line service

My wife and I can afford only one on-line service. We have been arguing about which is the best for the past month? What do you say?

Gee, I hate to think that a marriage is riding on my decision. (OK, it actually thrills me.)

My question to you is, what do you want to do on the on-line service? Because I can't hear you, here's an overview of the three most popular on-line services in the U.S.:

➤ The biggest is CompuServe Information Service (800-848-8199), owned by H&R Block. One of the oldest services, CompuServe has the most members, provides international access, and has the largest number of files for downloading and searching (in fact, it offers more than 1,700 databases and more special-interest groups than any other service). The downside: CompuServe can be difficult to learn. Worse, it doesn't offer Kim Komando's Komputer Klinic as a menu option.

➤ The most popular service for new users is Prodigy (800-822-6922), a joint venture by IBM and Sears. Prodigy is colorful and fun, and it helps users get acquainted with on-line services. But most new users grow out of it eventually. Although Prodigy's mail facilities are fairly good, there is a limit to the length of message you can send and you cannot attach files with e-mail notes. And some folks find the constant advertisements (they take up one-fourth of each screen) rather annoying. Worse, Prodigy doesn't offer Kim Komando's Komputer Klinic as a menu option.

➤ America Online (800-827-6364) is the fastest growing on-line service in the U.S. AOL, which has a good file library, has been praised for its easy access to the Internet and its e-mail capabilities (especially how it allows you to easily attach files to your e-mail). Moreover, AOL is becoming known as *the* service for magazines and newspapers on-line. And the real-time chat areas in the People Connection entertain a steady stream of folks. The downside: AOL is growing — fast. Some users get busy signals when connecting. Nonetheless, AOL is the service to watch for innovation. Besides, it's home to Kim Komando's Komputer Klinic (accessible by using the keyword *KOMANDO*). If you call the America Online 800 number listed here, use my name or promotion code 7973 and get a month's free trial membership, including software and ten free hours of usage.

Hmmm, I didn't pick one. It's still up to you.

BBS troubleshooting

I am in the midst of a full-scale modem mystery. When I sign on to services such as America Online or Prodigy, my modem works fine. When I use a local BBS, the modem connects but starts spewing random ASCII characters across the screen until I am automatically disconnected. How can I solve the mystery before I murder my modem?

Elementary, friend. You just told me whodunnit.

Make sure that your communications software settings match the BBS's settings. Normally, the settings are in the communications software *phone book* (also known as a *dialing directory*) — the same place where you tell the software what number to call. The most common settings for a BBS are 8-N-1. If you're not sure that these are the BBS's settings, call the BBS's *system operator*, or *sysop* (the person who runs the BBS). Usually, sysops are a friendly bunch who love to help you enjoy the fruits of their labor.

Another possible cause: If your communications program automatically sets the modem to the speed you choose, make sure that it matches the BBS modem's speed. And be sure your modem works at the speed you picked in your communications software. For example, a 2400 baud modem will not work if you set the speed to 9600 baud in the communications program.

Note: From time to time, you may run into a BBS that just won't work with your modem and communications program because your settings and their settings can't match up.

Defining ANSI and emulation

When accessing BBSs from the Terminal program in Windows, I can't see any graphics. All I see is a bunch of characters grouped as some shape (I think that it's either a rabbit or a nude woman on a motorcycle).

I think you just failed a Rorschach test.

Bad news: The strange-looking shapes appear because Windows Terminal can't handle ANSI (*A*merican *N*ational *S*tandards *I*nstitute) graphics.

By the way, this process of interpreting certain kinds of characters and converting them to graphics is called *emulation*.

Most terminal programs can mimic the display features offered by many types of computer terminals. But Windows Terminal emulates only DEC (Digital Equipment Corp.) VT52 or VT 100 terminals. Here's the kicker: The VT 100 terminal understands basic ANSI but not the ANSI graphics characters. To see the graphics, you need to do two things:

> ➤ Get a good communications software program.
> ➤ When connecting to a BBS with your new software, select ANSI graphics before you sign on.

Some BBSs can figure out whether you're running ANSI graphics automatically; that makes your life easier.

Of course, if you really don't care about graphics, and you're happy with Windows Terminal, just choose non-ANSI terminal emulation when connecting.

Dealing with busy signals

I found this popular BBS, but it's always busy. Can I set the modem so that it automatically hangs up when it gets a busy signal?

Not all modems know that "eee-eee-eee" means that the line is busy. I hope your modem does. But before reading more about what you can do, check your user's manual or call the modem manufacturer to get the particulars about busy signals and your modem; fact is, your particular modem may not ever recognize a busy signal.

If it can recognize a busy signal, look in your communications software program for a handy feature called automatic-redial. With this feature enabled, your communications software will automatically redial a BBS until a connection is made.

Note: If you use the Windows Terminal program, you will see the word *BUSY* on-screen, but you can't set up an automatic redial in the program. You may need to spring for a better communications program.

Communications software use attention-getting commands, called AT commands, with the modem. Oftentimes, you can tell your modem to automatically hang up with an AT command even if the feature isn't in your program of choice. For more information, look in the modem's manual under *AT commands, show busy signal* and see what you drum up. Or call the modem's technical support folks and tell 'em Kim Komando sent you.

Start your communications software, type the AT command, and press Enter. You should get an OK on-screen. Then save your changes in the software; look in the communications software manual for the exact steps.

Note: For most modems, AT commands are not case sensitive, but a few modems will only accept commands entered in uppercase letters.

Komando Klues

ATV1X4 is a popular AT command that makes a modem recognize a busy signal.

Of course, you can always just call during the early morning hours.

Establishing file transfer protocol

Help. I signed on to a BBS but couldn't download anything. My protocol didn't match.

Yeah, you certainly can't go to a party with mismatching protocol.

In most communications software, you set the file transfer protocol you're using. And it must match the file protocol supported by the BBS. When you sign on to the BBS, look for a menu option for View User Settings; there you can learn which file transfer protocol you need to use.

The Bottom Line

XMODEM is supported by nearly all BBSs. If the BBS you're calling supports the ZMODEM protocol, however, you should use it. ZMODEM is faster and simpler than XMODEM. XMODEM requires that you start the file transfer by giving it a download command. With ZMODEM, you tell the BBS to send the file; your computer figures this out and receives the file automatically.

Most BBSs normally allow you to download a file as soon as it is selected *or* at the end of a session (called a Download Batch). *Tip:* Try downloading a file immediately to make sure that you have the steps down.

When you download, you should see a pop-up window with the

➤ Name of the file you're downloading

➤ File's original size

➤ Bits received (this number increases during the download until it equals the file's original size)

➤ Time elapsed

➤ Time remaining for the transfer to complete

When the file transfer is complete, you can use other areas on the BBS or sign off.

Komando Klues

Most BBSs have a file that lists all the available files. This file is normally a text file that you can view in any word processing program. By looking at this list before you sign on, you can save valuable on-line time.

Handling a BBS callback

When a local BBS calls back, I see the word *RING* on-screen. How do I answer the call with my modem?

After you hang up, turn on the auto-answer or modem-answer feature in your communications software. When the BBS calls back, the modem answers the incoming call and connects to the BBS.

If there isn't enough time between the time you hang up and the time the BBS calls back and you see *RING RING* on-screen, type **ATA** in your communications software and press Enter.

Selecting communications software

I recently bought an IBM with a built-in modem. I know how to connect to America Online, but how do I call BBSs? I hate DOS, so tell me how to do it from Windows.

I won't have you speak of DOS that way. DOS put me through school.

The coolest thing about on-line services is that they give you the software. Then all you have to do is

➤ Complete some basic setup procedures.

➤ Make sure that everything is hooked up correctly.

➤ Pay your phone bill.

➤ Establish a billable account.

Bingo, you're connected to the world of information.

The same basic steps hold true for using other services, such as BBSs. First, you need some communications software, which allows your computer to talk to — that is, exchange information with — other computers, including those that run the BBSs you've heard about.

Communications software come in DOS or Windows flavors. You can pick the program you like most, but the Windows ones are normally easier to use because they shield you from DOS commands.

With a Windows communications program, you get a dialing directory (also known as a phone book), where you type in the phone number of the service and some basic parameters — start bits, stop bits, parity, and baud rates. Don't worry too much about these weird words. The standard settings are 8-N-1 and work 99 percent of the time. For that 1 percent, call the BBS's voice telephone line and ask for the settings.

Windows ships with the Terminal program; you may as well start your BBSing adventures using it. If you get hooked, check out CrossTalk, Procomm Plus, or Qmodem. Or try one of the good shareware communications programs, such as Telix or Unicom. No matter which communications program you choose, you type the BBS name and phone number in a phone book (or dialing directory).

Komando Klues
I suggest starting with a local BBS until you get up to speed to save some money. For example, find the name/phone number of a local computer user group's BBS. You may want to ask the sysop to walk you through the process the first time.

What are you waiting for? Go reach out and touch something, like a computer.

Scripting

Is there a way for the computer to do certain things every time I sign on to a BBS? For example, I want the computer to enter my user ID and password.

You need a script. (Places everybody, this is a take. Check for speed. Five, four, three, two. And action.) *Scripts* automate repetitive tasks, such as logging on to a BBS and giving your password.

Every communications program has its own script language, however, so I can't give you a universal script lesson. But many communications programs have *auto-learn scripts*: the software watches what you do and then writes a script for you.

Komando Klues

If security is an issue, rethink whether you want to use scripts. Otherwise, anyone who has access to your computer can sign on as you with just a keystroke or two. What will you do when you find out that "you" have been flirting with an ex-con named Bubba and he's flying out for a visit?

Using a calling card

I want to use my calling card with BBSs. But I can't figure out for the life of me how to have my modem wait for a line to pick up, enter my code, and call the BBS.

Ah, that's a very *comma* problem. What do I mean? Read on.

The challenge you face is also typical

> ➤ In offices where you must dial a certain number to get an outside line
> ➤ If you want to use your modem to call out of the country
> ➤ If your preferred phone service requires you to dial a special phone number first

Fortunately, your modem knows how to handle the job.

When you use your modem to dial out, it usually just dials as fast as it can. But sometimes it's necessary to have the modem dial a few numbers, *pause*, and then continue to dial. You can insert a two-second pause between numbers by entering a comma where you want the modem to pause.

For example, suppose that you add the following phone number in the dialing directory (or phone book) of your communications software:

```
1-800-555-5555,123412341234,1-619-123-1234
```

Your modem interprets the preceding group of numbers as a command to

1. Dial 1-800-555-5555 (your phone service's special phone number).

2. Pause for two seconds (giving your phone service time to connect and prompt you for a calling card number).

3. Dial 123412341234 (your calling card number).

4. Pause for two seconds.

5. Dial 1-619-123-1234 (the actual phone number you're trying to reach).

Note: If the pauses are not long enough, you can use multiple commas. Two commas equal a four-second pause, three commas are a six-second pause, and so on.

If you work in an office setting and need to dial some digit to access an outside line, use the following syntax:

```
9,1-619-123-1234
```

Your modem dials 9, pauses for two seconds, and then finishes dialing.

Komando Klues

Some communications software let you tell the modem to always dial some prefix before the actual phone number. By setting the prefixes as defaults in the communications software, you then don't have to include the calling card information in every phone record.

Chatting on-line

Several friends and I can't for the life of us figure out how to send messages back and forth on a modem. We have looked in books and wracked our brains.

Hey, when did using the telephone become old-fashioned? Oh, sorry, I got old for a second there.

What you're trying to do is really pretty easy. In fact, you can talk to others via a modem by chatting "live" or leaving messages.

To chat with each other, both of you must have some basic communications package, such as CrossTalk, Procomm, Qmodem, Quick Link, or Telix. (Any of these programs give you the option to leave a message, upload a file, download a file, or chat.) The communications settings also must be the same on both computers. Use 8-N-1.

When two people want to chat, one acts as the caller; the other is the callee — that is, the person who receives the call, or the *host*. (The caller logs on to the host's computer.) Follow these steps:

1. The callee sets the host modem to answer the incoming call by placing the computer in auto-answer mode. (To do so, type **ATS0=1** in the communications software and press Enter.)

2. The caller places the call by entering the host's phone number in the communications software.

3. The callee will see *RING* on-screen and hear tones as the two modems connect.

The caller and callee now can type back and forth to each other.

Komando Klues If you can't see what you're typing, your echo is probably disabled. Check for settings in the software to enable half- or full-duplex switching (also known as Echo on and Echo off).

Saving money on file transfers

My brother lives in Australia. I'm spending a fortune sending files to him. We both work in the wee hours, use Procomm Plus, and have 28.8 baud modems. Sometimes, though, we have to dial each other a few times because of lost connections.

I'd opt for using a good file compression utility and then joining a commercial on-line service with international access, such as CompuServe. Or better yet, tap into the Internet, the network of networks. By moving away from a communications file transfer program such as Procomm Plus, you'll gain greater flexibility in sending or receiving files.

With a good file compression utility, you can avoid some time charges (smaller files take less time to transfer). PKZip from PKWare, the most popular compression utility, can shrink text files by as much as 70 percent.

Although using CompuServe to exchange files overseas isn't cheap, you won't incur any more long-distance charges because most towns throughout the world now have a local CompuServe dial-up number. Moreover, if you do lose a connection, you just redial a local number.

With CompuServe, you send a file domestically or internationally by composing mail and attaching the file to the mail. It's quite simple. But be aware that CompuServe typically adds surcharges (beyond the normal monthly membership fee and hourly rates) to larger files. It's called a CompuSurcharge.

The Bottom Line

Using the Internet is probably more cost-effective than using CompuServe. As a result, I encourage you and your brother to find Internet providers in your respective areas. The main drawback in using the Internet to exchange files is the Internet: it can be kind of cryptic to use. Be prepared to spend time on it before it's easy.

If you're considering the Internet route as a possible alternative, make sure that you read the Internet chapter in this book. I cover many aspects of your question, including different types of Internet accounts and getting around on the Net.

Starting a BBS

I'd like to start a BBS to make some extra money. What software and hardware do I need?

Before you select the software and hardware, you must decide on the type of services you plan to offer. What do you want your BBS to be? A place where users gather to transfer files? A place for people to socialize? A place for on-line games? All of the above? You also need to decide

> ➤ Whether you want the BBS to be a free or a pay system
> ➤ The number of incoming phone lines
> ➤ How big you expect the BBS to become

Two basic types of software packages are on the market:

> ➤ Single-line — one telephone for one computer
> ➤ Multiline — multiple telephone lines for one or more computers

Single-line programs are usually the easiest to start and the least expensive (in fact, some very good shareware packages are available). Multiline software, however, enable you to use one computer to control multiple telephone lines and multiple modems on one machine; some packages can handle as many as 255 phone lines at once. By the way, you probably will find a chat feature, which allows everyone that's logged on to go into one area of the system and talk in a real-time mode, in a multiline software package only. *Note:* Users love to chat.

Komando Klues

Check out other BBSs and match the features that you want for your board. For example, a chat or dating service BBS must make sure that it can handle real-time chats, photograph file uploads and downloads, and a good mail system. When you find a BBS that you like, ask the sysop for the name of the board's system software. PC Board and Wildcat! are two popular programs.

Once you have decided on a software package, you need the right hardware:

> ➤ For single-line systems, you need a modem and a computer with enough hard drive space to support the type of service you want to offer. If you want to provide files, you need a large drive, ranging from 200 megabytes to a gigabyte — a CD drive may be worthwhile. In fact, a CD-ROM changer can come in handy; then you can place files on multiple CDs.

> ➤ For multiline BBSs, specialized hardware is needed. Software packages that allow multiple lines on a single computer usually require multiport hardware. These multiport cards can allow 4, 8, 16, or even 32 25-pin RS-232 ports. (One of the most popular multiport cards is made by DigiBoard.) You even can have multiple cards in one machine, allowing you to support many modems per machine. If you go this route, it's important that you confirm that the hardware will work with your software before you buy it; the software is usually designed to support a specific type of multiport hardware.

Running a BBS can be a lot of fun whether you're operating it as a hobby or for profit. Although the preceding information may seem daunting, taking the time to make the right decisions can save you many headaches. So take your time, expect to learn a great deal, and have fun.

Managing a BBS

I'm a future BBS operator. How many hours a week should I expect to spend running the thing? Can you offer any tips and secrets for a wannabe sysop?

The type of BBS you run dictates how much time you spend maintaining it. Another factor is how much you want to customize it to attract users. Keep in mind that the time spent running a BBS directly affects the quality of your BBS.

BBSs that specialize in one area are usually the easiest to maintain. For example, if the key feature of your bulletin board system is its file area, you can expect to spend as little as one to two hours per week or as much as five to ten hours per week. On the other hand, if you want a large file area, a large message area, multiple lines, on-line games, and so on, you can expect to spend anywhere from five hours to 168 hours per week. But when would you sleep? So get some help. (And not just psychological, although you can soon lose your mind if you're running a complex BBS.) You will find users who will be more than happy to help you maintain your BBS in exchange for either higher access privileges or free access. These people are called *cosysops* and usually do things such as maintain the file area, manage some or all of your message areas, and call new users to validate their accounts.

But be careful. Giving someone access to maintain features means giving them the power to cause great harm to your system. In fact, it's a good idea to give cosysops access only to those commands needed for them to perform whatever jobs that you ask.

Defining e-mail

The newspapers act like we all know what e-mail is. Am I the only one who doesn't know what e-mail is?

E-mail is computer jargon for *electronic mail*. You can send an electronic letter or message to almost anyone that has an electronic account, or *address*. Sending e-mail is a lot like sending a letter through the U.S. Postal Service, only you know your electronic message won't get burned under some Chicago bridge.

E-mail works pretty simply: You compose a message and send it. The message arrives at your friend's electronic mailbox within seconds (or minutes). There the message stays until your friend signs on to the service. Upon signing on, your friend is notified that e-mail is waiting. Sounds good, especially given the frequency of postal rate increases, right?

Besides, most on-line services are now linked via the Internet, an e-mail bridge among the different services. So if you're a Prodigy member, you can send a message to a friend on America Online, for example.

But e-mail has certain drawbacks. First, you won't get to lick Elvis anymore. More important, the security and confidentiality of your message can't be guaranteed unless you encrypt your message. (The courts have not yet determined whether it's illegal for a nonrecipient to read your message.) In short, e-mail is great for quick and nonsecret messages, but it's a long way from replacing snail mail.

Komando Klues about e-mail:

Komando Klues

➤ Don't type in all capital letters. It means that you're SCREAMING at the recipient.

➤ Use ** before and after a word to show emphasis. For example,

```
I **love** this book.
```

➤ Watch humor and your language carefully. One person's joke is another person's grounds for a lawsuit.

➤ If you're responding to an e-mail that requests an answer from you, include portions of the note you received and then underneath provide your answer. For example, suppose that a friend sent a note asking what you think about this book. The >> means a quote was taken from the previous exchange of e-mail. Your response could be

```
>>Christine, I've been hearing about Kim Komando's
book. That it contains help for just about any
computer problem. Have you bought it yet? Frank

Sure did, Frank, and one for every member of my
family so that they will stop bugging me with their
computer problems. It's been a real sanity saver. ;>
```

Sending e-mail to different services

I have a CompuServe and an Internet account, but all my friends are on America Online. Is it possible to send e-mail between CompuServe or the Internet and America Online, or do I need to get new friends?

There's nothing like new friends, but you don't need to delete the old ones.

When you call your out-of-state friends, you don't have to have the same long-distance carrier. In the same fashion, you can send e-mail to friends who don't belong to the same on-line service. The Internet serves as the go-between. Let me show you what I mean with the following examples:

➤ *From CompuServe or the Internet to America Online:* If you're sending mail from CompuServe or from within the Internet, type the recipient's America Online screen name and America Online's Internet address (that's `@aol.com`) in the address box. For example, to send me mail from CompuServe or from within the Internet, address the message as follows:

```
komando@aol.com
```

➤ *From America Online to the Internet:* To send mail from America Online to a friend with an Internet address, put your friend's complete Internet address in the To: box. For example, to send me mail from America Online, address the message as follows:

```
komando@komando.com
```

➤ *From America Online or the Internet to CompuServe:* From America Online, you address the mail by using your friend's CompuServe ID number and CompuServe's Internet address (that's `@compuserve.com`). Note that you change the comma in the CompuServe ID to a period. For example, to send me mail from America Online or from an Internet account, address the message as follows:

```
71062.1071@compuserve.com
```

➤ *From CompuServe to America Online:* For example, to send me mail at America Online from CompuServe, address the message as follows:

```
INTERNET:komando@aol.com
```

➤ *From CompuServe to the Internet:* To send mail from CompuServe to someone with an Internet account, type **INTERNET:** *recipient's Internet address* in the To: box. For example, to send me mail at my Internet address, address the message as follows:

```
INTERNET:komando@komando.com
```

As you can see, you aren't limited; just use the Internet addresses. In addition, be sure to check with your on-line service regularly: e-mail capabilities are growing daily.

Komando Klues

If you send me e-mail, please use my America Online account. My Internet server, `komando.com`, is under construction and won't be up and running until mid-1995.

Discovering magazines and newspapers on-line

How do they get magazines and newspapers on the on-line service?

How do they get the pimento in the olive?

The magazines and newspapers that had the foresight to go on-line have a special division dedicated to creating the on-line editions. Most editions include the full text of the magazines — but without any direct mail cards, ads, or perfumed inserts.

With these editions, by the way, you usually have *text search capability*. That is, you can type in a word or phrase and the on-line service tells you where to find that word or phrase in the magazine you're reading.

But wait! There's more. You also get your magazine a few days on-line before it arrives at the newsstand. What about pictures? You betcha! In most cases, all the pictures you find in the publication are also on-line. In fact, more and more of these services are moving to full multimedia, complete with sight and sound, on-line!

Paying bills on-line

I heard that I can soon pay my bills on-line. When will this be available?

How about now? Really!

You can pay most of your bills on-line right now by using simple, low-cost software. The funds are electronically transferred and legally treated as a check. Appropriate software is now included with most of the popular financial programs, including Quicken and Microsoft Money. Check with your local bank about electronic bill paying services, too.

The system is as safe and as foolproof as the banking system. The law governing this system has been fully hammered out by the courts and banks.

A close friend has been paying his bills electronically for several years and swears by it — not at it. He buys fewer checks from his bank and owes virtually no postage fees!

This system also appeals to those who like to wait till the last minute to pay. Now you can wait till the very last second.

Faxing with your modem

I noticed on my computer's purchase receipt that I got a fax modem. Is a fax modem the same thing as a fax machine? Can I use my fax modem to connect to an on-line service?

You found that information on your receipt? You'd better take another look to see what other goodies you're missing.

The Bottom Line

A *fax modem* is a modem that also sends and receives faxes. You can use your fax modem to connect to an on-line service or a BBS.

A fax modem transfers and receives information over phone lines, just as a regular fax machine does. A fax modem can send any document directly from your computer to either a fax machine or another fax modem.

If you want to send a document that you did not create with your computer, say a handwritten list, you need another piece of gear called a *scanner*. A scanner, which works much like a copy machine, takes a picture of something and saves it inside your computer as a file, which you then can send with your fax modem.

Explaining the fax modem process

I received a bonus at work, so I'm considering buying a fax modem. But I'm not clear about what files a fax modem can send. Does it depend on the hardware and software I use? I refuse to buy a fax modem until I know exactly what it can do.

No wonder you got your bonus: you want all the details before plunking down the cash. You must work in accounting.

Fax modems, like regular modems, send and receive information between your computer and another computer over telephone lines. Your fax software tells the fax modem whether to be a fax or a regular modem.

When you want to send a fax, the fax program can change a document, worksheet, or picture that's in your computer into a format that fax machines and fax modems understand. When someone sends you a fax, the software saves the incoming document as a computer file — no more dealing with hard-to-handle fax thermal paper. (You then can print the received fax on your regular printer.)

187

For example, suppose that you want to fax a report. If you don't have a fax modem, you must print out the report, walk over to a real fax machine, put the report in the machine, dial the number, and then stand there until the transmission ends. With a fax modem, you simply print the document. But instead of selecting your printer, you select the fax modem. In a flash, your fax software pops up on-screen; you then select (ah, don't you love point-and-click technology) the recipient from the phone book that's in the fax program. The software automatically makes a cover sheet, dials the number, and sends the fax. *Note:* If the recipient's phone line is busy, most fax software programs will try three times before giving up.

When someone sends you a fax, meanwhile, the fax modem in your computer automatically answers the phone, receives the fax, and stores it on your computer's hard disk. The fax software allows you to read the fax on-screen or print it out. The downside: Multiple faxes eat up a lot of hard disk space.

Almost all the different types of fax software on the market send and receive faxes. A basic, inexpensive fax program works with text files only. If you spend more money (and if you do much faxing, you should), you can send faxes directly from within your applications. You even can schedule a fax to be sent automatically in the wee hours of the morning, when telephone charges are lower.

Komando Klues

Look for a fax software package with optical character recognition (OCR). A fax is a facsimile of an original (it's a picture), but OCR actually reads the characters in the document and converts the picture into a usable, editable text document.

Q&A *Upgrading with the UART chip*

Do I need a 486 or better computer to use the new 14,400 fax modems? I have a 286, and the folks at work told me that it wouldn't work because I need a UART chip.

Your coworkers had better get their fax straight. You don't have to replace your entire 286 to get reliable performance out of a 14,400 bps fax modem, but you will need to upgrade your serial card to one that supports the newer UART chips. Or purchase an internal 14,400 bps fax modem that comes with the new UART chip right on the modem card.

As you may gather, the key is the UART chip, which provides reliable information transfers. That becomes real important on an older, slower machine where the computer itself is not able to handle the incoming data quickly enough. The UART chip has a small amount of internal memory that it can use to temporarily hold this data. Without the UART chip, most problems occur during the transfer of data (that is, up- and downloading files).

Komando Klues

If you just need a new UART chip for your computer, buy a new input/output (I/O) card that has a 16550AFN on it.

Choosing fax modem software

We just bought a fax modem. Will the software that came with it be sufficient? (My boss doesn't want to spend money on more software. He says that the programs are all too expensive and we can make do with what we already own.)

I hope your boss isn't as stingy when it comes to raises.

I recommend getting another fax software program if you plan to use your fax modem regularly. The software included with a fax modem usually is sufficient only for the essentials: sending and receiving faxes. Programs with extra features increase your modem's flexibility and functionality.

Komando Klues

> ➤ For example, software with optical character recognition (OCR) capabilities enable you to take text from incoming faxes and convert it from a graphics format to a text format. Suppose that someone faxes you a letter, and in your return letter, you want to quote something from the original. If your fax software supports OCR, you can import the fax you received as a text file and then use the copy command to put portions of the original in your return letter.

> ➤ Another handy feature allows you to select your fax modem as a printer. Then you can send practically any kind of document, picture, or more to a fax machine instead of your printer.

> ➤ What happens when you are out of town and your computer receives a fax? Better fax software programs will forward the fax received by your computer to another computer or facsimile machine.

> ➤ You also may want a program that lets you receive faxes with your fax modem without interrupting your work. In other words, receiving a fax becomes a background operation.

➤ If you have multiple phone books in your computer, it's convenient if the fax software can use an existing phone book.

➤ With some programs, you can create custom fax cover sheets — complete with company logo — and jazz up your transmissions.

➤ To reduce phone charges, you need a feature that allows you to schedule faxes in the wee morning hours.

As you can see, the software you use for your fax modem can make all the difference in how useful (and cost-efficient!) it actually is. Check out Delrina's WinFax Pro. Although it takes about 10MB of hard drive space, I think it's the best fax management software around.

Selecting fax modem resolution

FaxSTF 3.0 has two resolutions for sending faxes: 203 × 196 or 203 × 98. Is the 203 vertical or horizontal resolution?

Speaking of resolution, have you made your New Year's resolutions? How about your Jewish New Year's resolutions? OK, Chinese New Year's resolutions?

When talking about resolution, the first number is the number of pixels (that is, dots) horizontally. The second number is the number of pixels vertically. High resolution is referred to as *fine mode* and is usually 200 × 200 dpi (*dots per inch*); low resolution is *standard mode* and is usually 200 × 100 dpi.

Komando Klues

As a general rule of thumb, select fine mode when the fax's quality is important and select standard mode when the transmission cost is more important than the quality.

Determining fax modem speed

How long does it take to send a one-page fax with your computer?

About as long as it takes Bill Gates to make another million dollars.

The length of time depends on many things. Primarily, it is related to the speed of your fax modem and the amount of graphics and text on the page. For example, a one-page business letter (logo at the top of the page, text in the middle, and scanned signature on the bottom) faxed in fine mode at 9600 bps should take about one minute total connect time, give or take 20 seconds.

Note: Normally, it takes about 15 seconds longer to receive a fax than to send a fax.

Komando Klues

If you send or receive in standard mode, you can shave about 30 seconds off the total transmission time.

Tracking faxes

I work for a lawyer who's a real stickler about details. How do you tell whether a fax has completely gone through?

Most fax machines print a transaction log automatically after every transmission or after a certain number of faxes have been sent or received. By looking at these reports, you know whether a fax was completely sent. How often you get a report depends on the machine.

Your fax software — which works like a fax machine, only a lot better — keeps a log of all faxes sent and received. The log also lists faxes that were incomplete. With a few clicks of a mouse, you can ask your computer to resend the entire fax or only the missing pages.

You also can save the faxes in your computer — no more looking through files for a fax sent weeks ago. The downside: Those saved faxes take up hard disk space. But, hell, it's Mr. Stickler's hard disk; let him worry about something else for a change. Nonetheless, you can tell your fax software to automatically delete faxes sent after a certain number of days.

My transaction log, for example, automatically deletes attachments, but not the events, every 30 days. (*Attachments* are the actual fax; *events* describe who sent or received the fax, including the date, time, and number of pages.) Most fax logs can be printed; as a result, you can stash hard copies of the logs in a file for safekeeping.

With most fax programs, you can type a description of the fax in a subject area, as well as keywords (which you can use later in searches). This feature is especially helpful when you swear that you sent someone a fax but they deny receiving it: simply open up your fax log, enter a few search phrases, and you can confirm that you indeed sent the fax on that day and at that time. Even better, if you saved the fax, there's no need to recreate the fax from scratch, so you can magnanimously offer to resend the fax.

A

The better (and more expensive) fax programs offer greater control and enhanced paper trails. Unfortunately, these programs aren't included with most modems. You normally get a scaled-down program that's just enough to wet your whistle.

Q: How many lawyers does it take to change a light bulb?

A: One, but he'll bill you for three.

Classes of modems

What's the difference between a Class 1 and a Class 2 fax modem?

Karl Marx just turned over in his grave. Even hardware is having class struggles.

Class 2 fax modems are better than Class 1 modems because they offer better error correction routines and compression techniques. In addition, background operations happen smoother with a Class 2 modem because they happen in the hardware rather than the software.

Class 2 modems are still relatively new, so they are a little difficult to find and more expensive than Class 1 modems. And almost any fax software you want to use will work with a Class 1 modem. The newer fax software support Class 2 fax modems, too.

Fax troubleshooting

I always pick up the phone when I'm not supposed to. My teenage daughter yells at me; my computer beeps at me. Is there a way to set up my computer so that it knows whether the incoming call is for the fax modem?

Some phone carriers offer you the opportunity to request a distinctive ring for certain incoming calls. If you pay for this option, you can have voice calls ring differently than data calls. (Basically, you have two phone numbers on one phone line.) Then visit your local office-supply store and buy a gadget that routes the calls to the right place.

Of course, it may be cheaper and less of a hassle to simply install another phone line in your home dedicated for use only by the fax modem. (Many phone carriers offer substantial discounts for second lines used by teenagers.)

You also can consider purchasing a special electronic receptionist for your computer. One such product is the $349 Envoy from Spectrum Signal Processing (call 800-667-0018), which is just a fancy 14,400 bps fax modem that distinguishes fax calls from voice calls. Envoy routes fax calls to the fax modem. If the call is a voice call, a button bar pops up on-screen. If you're in do-not-disturb mode, you can send the voice call to Envoy's message box on your hard drive. The downside to Envoy is that you need at least 8MB of RAM (for background processing) and about 20MB of free hard disk space (voice messages devour hard disk space).

 ## Resolving modem conflicts

I'm having problems with WinFax. I can send one fax OK, but then I can't send another. I have a Packard Bell 486 computer, which came with a 2400 baud fax modem, and an external 14,400 fax modem. What's wrong?

That's a baudy question.

WinFax is a great piece of software, but it's getting confused by your two fax modems. You need to remove or disable that 2400 baud fax modem.

Most internal fax modems are installed like any other card. Taking this card out is easy:

1. Exit all programs and turn the power off.

2. Remove the cover from the computer.

3. Ground yourself by touching the metal frame of the computer.

4. Find the modem card and remove the screw that's holding it in place.

5. Gently rock the card back and forth to loosen it.

6. Remove the modem card.

Some fax modem cards, however, are designed to fit in a special location in the computer and aren't installed (or removed) like a regular card. In these cases, you usually need to tell the computer to forget that the fax modem is installed. To change the way the computer hardware is set up, you need to get into the CMOS (pronounced "sea moss") settings. CMOS isn't a green plant that lives in the ocean; it's where the computer stores information about the type and size of hard drive and other things.

To get a Packard Bell's CMOS settings, press F2 when you're starting the computer up. After in CMOS setup,

1. Press the left-arrow key. This action gets you into advanced setup.

2. The Packard Bell computer shows you that the fax modem is at COM B (in other words, the second communications port). Press the plus (+) key until the setting for COM B reads *disabled*.

3. Press Esc twice to get back to the main CMOS menu.

4. With the cursor on the Save changes & exit option, press Enter.

When the computer restarts, it will completely ignore the 2400 baud fax modem.

Note: You may need to reinstall WinFax.

Configuring software for new hardware

Even though I have a 14,400 modem with a 16550 UART, WinFax Pro 4 only sends faxes at 9600 bps in Windows 3.1. Do I need to upgrade my fax software to send faxes at the higher speed?

So you automatically assume that you must upgrade your software to keep pace with new hardware, eh? Apparently, you've been around computers for some time. Most times, you're right, but put away your credit card. On second thought, use it to take me to dinner; I'm about to save you some bucks.

You can fix things without a software or hardware upgrade. Before you start, though, make sure that you have a backup copy of your computer's SYSTEM.INI file and the WINFAX.INI file. Both files are located in your C:\WINDOWS directory.

From Program Manager, open the Accessories window and then double-click the Windows Notepad icon. Select File⇨Open and select the SYSTEM.INI file in your C:\WINDOWS directory. In the [Boot] section of the file, change the line

```
COMM.DRV=COMM.DRV
```

to

```
COMM.DRV=WFXCOMM.DRV
```

Select File⇨Save and then close the SYSTEM.INI file — but don't exit Notepad.

 Windows for Workgroups 3.1 users should not make the preceding change because WFXCOMM.DRV isn't compatible with Windows for Workgroups. Use the COMM.DRV that comes with Windows for Workgroups.

Select File⇨Open. This time, open the WINFAX.INI file in your C:\WINDOWS directory. In the [General] section of the file, change

```
ModemMaxRate=9600
```

to

```
ModemMaxRate=14400
```

Save your changes to the WINFAX.INI file and exit Notepad. Exit Windows and restart Windows for your changes to take effect. Your faxes should be sent at 14,400 bps from here on out.

I expect a faxed invitation to dinner.

 ## Deleting extra fax headers

I have an Intel Satisfaxtion modem. For some reason, the faxes that I send have two headers. I checked my WinFax setup; it looks OK. Where did I go wrong?

Sing it, "I can't get no . . . Satisfaxtion."

Your modem is a Communications Application Specification (or CAS-type) modem. (CAS is Intel's standard for fax modem communications.) CAS modems typically make their own headers, and because you told WinFax also to add a header, your sent faxes have two headers. I know what you're thinking: "Wow, she can add, too."

Remove the headers in WinFax and let the CAS headers be. To do so, open WinFax and select Program. Erase the information that appears in the Left, Center, and Right header fields. Click OK.

195

Resolving software conflicts

My WinFax software worked fine until I installed the AfterDark screen saver. Now, WinFax doesn't always receive faxes and I get error messages when looking at faxes in the Viewer. Is the fax software offended by AfterDark's flying toasters?

Toasters toasting your faxes? Is WinFax now LoseFax?

You have a conflict. AfterDark, like most screen savers, keeps tabs on system activity by monitoring the computer's communication or COM ports. Specifically, AfterDark monitors the IRQ settings. This action steps into WinFax's territory. To turn off AfterDark's monitoring COM port feature,

1. Start AfterDark.

2. From the menu bar, select Setup.

3. Disable the IRQ activity monitor option.

Using WinFax's OCR feature

Why won't the Recognize feature in WinFax's OCR fax viewer work?

Trying to play stump the host? You're not going to win(fax) this time. The OCR feature in WinFax needs the DOS SHARE.EXE command loaded in your AUTOEXEC.BAT file:

1. Make sure that you have a backup copy of your AUTOEXEC.BAT file.

2. From Program Manager, select File⇨Run.

3. In the Command Line box, type **SYSEDIT** and click OK. SYSEDIT is an editing program that shows you all the important files inside your computer in Windows.

4. Click the title bar of the AUTOEXEC.BAT file to make it the active window. You can only edit or look at the contents of a file in an active window.

5. Add the following line before the statement in the file that starts Windows:

```
C:\DOS\SHARE.EXE
```

6. Select File⇨Save.

7. Exit Windows and restart your computer for the change to take effect.

Chapter 6
Databases

Basics

Explaining database programs

I am a compulsive shopper, especially when it comes to computer stuff. A database program was on sale, so I bought it. Uh, what is a database program?

Don't tell me: You also bought the Playboy screen saver for the insightful articles.

Getting carried away is easy when you're buying computer goodies. You can always find something in the store that is bigger, better, or faster than what you have at home. (That's also what Playboy promises.)

Komando Klues

Always make a list of what you need before you go shopping, and stick to that list.

And speaking of lists, that's exactly what a database program helps manage. A database is a list of something, and that something can be your customers, friends, enemies, VCR tapes, or everything in your home or office. The phone book is a list, or database, of all the people who live near you and the places where you can spend money. The techs couldn't just leave things simple and call the software program that helps you manage lists a "list" program. Why, that would make life too easy. So they called it a database program.

The Bottom Line

The bottom line: *Database* is just a techie term for a collection of information that's on a computer. Think about it the next time you look at your address book. You could put it in your computer and call it an address database. Everyone should own one.

The big deal about database programs is that you can find information quickly. Want to know which customers bought from you in the last six months? No problem. How about finding all the customers who bought recently and live in a certain ZIP code? No problem. How about finding all the recent customers who live in a certain ZIP code and have the first name Herbert? No problem. Get the point? Good.

Rating the database programs

I don't want to read a confusing computer magazine. I don't want to read sales literature. I just want to know your opinion of the top-selling database programs in ten words or less.

Easy to use but limited in power: Alpha Four, Approach, Q&A. More powerful but more difficult to learn: Access, dBASE, FoxPro, Paradox.

Marketing uses for databases

I don't like sales and marketing. But the new VP is hot to trot on using our customer lists for databased marketing. Can you tell me what she is talking about?

She's talking about trouble. Right here in River City. Trouble and that starts with *T* and that rhymes with *D* and stands for *Database*.

You are in marketing, so I think you should learn to like it. Regardless of what your business card says or what your profession is, your company's food chain ultimately stops at customers. Pay little attention to customers or be negligent in marketing and you will find yourself in the unemployment line.

Direct marketers have known the value of databased marketing for years. For example, have you ever wondered why you receive subscription offers for only a handful of magazines? Well, a computer determined that there was a good chance that you would say yes to those offers.

Although the best direct marketing campaign produces only a 2–4 percent response rate, the odds are better than in the state lottery and most Vegas games.

Look at what McDonald's, Nabisco, and Seagram's sell and you see databased marketing in action. *Low-fat, environmentally conscious,* and *low-alcohol* are part of our everyday vocabulary. Not coincidentally, these terms are stamped on products.

The same marketing formula is available to your company, no matter what you sell. Ordinary computer technology enables you to build a *database* — that's merely the fancy computer term for an electronic list of something (in this case, a customer list).

Customer names are sorted by interests, buying patterns, age, income levels, hobbies, and more. Consider databased marketing the supreme customer Rolodex file. You know almost everything about your customers and, more important, what makes them buy.

Whether your database consists of home-grown customers or names leased from a third party, there's gold in these hills. You merely need the tools and knowledge to see the difference between real gold and fool's gold. For any substantial direct marketing effort, you need a database software program.

Several PC database personal computer software programs can help out. If your company already has a point-of-sale system, you can use, or import, these names into a database program. But any software program is only as good as the way you use it, and database programs are no exception.

The key to databased marketing is finding out why Jane Smith, John Smith, Kathy Smith, and Ray Smith buy what they buy. You have to learn what sells them on a product. Price? Advertising? The ironclad guarantee?

You start by tracking not only how many widgets are bought and by whom, but also who exactly buys them. To do so, put a survey in with every customer order. Or, if you can afford it, hire a research firm for the job. Ask customers about hobbies, interests, your competition, and anything else that helps profile them. Then put this information in the database program and go to work. The more you know about your customers, the more you can sell them.

So the next time you're ready to lay down $5 for a lottery ticket, know that the odds of making money are better if you look in your own backyard.

Differences in database and other software programs

I started a new job and my manager told me that next week I'll be working on a database program. How is a database program different from other programs on my computer? I don't want to look stupid and ask her.

I recognize this handwriting. Didn't I hire you a week ago to specialize in databases?!?

I bet you keep lists of addresses and phone numbers, lists of household goods for insurance purposes, lists of recipes, and more. Database programs help you manage these lists.

We manage words with word processors such as WordPerfect and Microsoft Word. We manage numbers with spreadsheet programs such as Lotus 1-2-3 and Excel. To manage lists of information, or databases, we use database programs such as Access, Approach, dBASE, FoxPro, and Paradox.

I'd ask your new manager a question about the database program. Try this one, "What strategic short-range goals and long-term objectives are we hoping to achieve for the data we are collecting in the database?"

Defining field and record

I just started my own crafts business. I am using a database program, and I am confused by the terms in the software. What's a *field?* What's a *record?* I'm about to have a breakdown.

A breakdown is good, but I'll get to that in a minute. For an example of records and fields, consider your customer, Wanda Bea Admiral, who bought a $1,000 painting from you and lives at 1234 Main Street, Any Town, AZ 85003. All the information about Wanda, or another customer for that matter, is called a *record. Fields* are the specific information about a customer that is contained in the record. So Wanda is your customer's first name field. Bea is your customer's middle name field. Admiral is your customer's last name field. The purchase price field is $1,000. Your customer's street address field is 1234 Main Street. Your customer's city field is Any Town, the state field is AZ, and the ZIP or postal code field is 85003. You could have more fields too, such as the customer's telephone number, fax number, notes, and so on.

It's a good thing that you asked this question now. Getting these terms straight is important when you are designing a database. The best thing to do is break down (the good part) all the information about a record, or about one particular customer, into as many parts as you can without having so many parts that it becomes overwhelming. For example, the fields in your customer database could be the following: First Name, Middle Initial, Last Name, Address, City, State, ZIP/Postal Code, Telephone Number, Piece of Art Purchased, Purchase Date, Purchase Amount, and more. When you put all the fields together and put information in the fields, you create a record. If you have 100 customers in your customer database, then you have 100 records. And if you sold 100 paintings at $1,000 each, I'm in the wrong business.

Explaining field options

When I set up fields, the program presents several options — character, numeric, and so on. How is one field type different from another field type? It has occurred to me that once again I started a project without knowing much about what I was getting myself into.

At least it has occurred to you. Most people go through life without knowing what they've gotten themselves into. The following kinds of fields are the most common ones:

➤ *Character fields* accept anything you want to put in them: letters, numbers, symbols, or a combination plate of all of them. Usually, Name, Address, City, State, ZIP/Postal Code, and Telephone Number fields are character fields.

➤ Guess what *numeric fields* take? Yes. We have a winner. Numeric fields are good for numbers only. Use a numeric field when you plan on using the number in formulas or for calculations. The purchase amount or outstanding balance should be set up as a numeric field. In some databases, you need to leave an empty slot for the result of a calculation that has been done on the numbers in the database. This field is called a *calculated field*, and it is one that you never put information into directly. A good example of a calculated field is the purchase amount plus the sales tax.

➤ Another field format is a *date field*. Date fields are good when you will be working with time-sensitive information, such as days past due on payments, or when you want to calculate the time between when an order was taken and when the order shipped. Usually, you can set the date format to look just about any way you want.

➤ Another handy field type that you shouldn't overlook is the *Yes/No* or *True/False fields*. They are sometimes called *logical fields*. My company uses a logical field in customer satisfaction surveys.

➤ *Note or memo fields* are like little Post-It notes that you can use with individual records in the database. Here you can put in specific information about particular records.

Komando Klues Before you sit at the computer to design your database, here's a tip. Get out a sample invoice, customer phone book, or whatever traditional paper-based thing you use now. Look at it carefully and pay particular attention to where you have to fill in the blanks to complete the form or entry. Then, using a pen and piece of paper, list all the fields you want to be able to save and search through with the computer. After the list is done, leave it alone for a day or so. Show it to the people who will be using the database and ask for their suggestions. Then go through the list one last time and design the database, using the software. This process will limit the changes that you need to make to the design later on.

Distinction between table and record

I read the Access manual cover to cover — truly, I did. I noticed that sometimes the manual says *table*, and other times the manual says *record*. Is there a difference?

I can see that you did read the manual — very closely I might add. A *table* holds all the fields for one or more records in a database, just as a china cabinet holds all the dishes for one or more place settings. You can add a place setting to the cabinet. You can take a place setting out of the cabinet. But the china cabinet is the structure that holds the place settings, just as a table is the structure that holds the customer records.

Tables come in handy when you want to join, or link, information from two or more relational databases. For example, an invoice database may contain an invoice table that is linked by a key to a name and address table.

You often design your fields for a database in a table, because the programmers thought people were used to seeing information listed that way. In Microsoft Access, for example, you design the table that contains all the fields and their respective characteristics in a table.

Komando Klues

You can type information for each field for each record in the table view. But here's a tip: Use the Form Wizard and let Access create a form for you to use when you are viewing each record and typing the information into each record. Using a form makes the information easier to see and so makes data entry a breeze.

If you liked reading the Access manual cover to cover, here are some other books I recommend:

➤ *Getting to Know Your Panasonic PanaPersonalPrinter*

➤ *The MS Access Database Software Program Manual, Part II: The Difference Between Tables and Records*

➤ A dictionary

Q&A Using surveys and scanners

Is there a way to scan our customer surveys into the computer and have a database program keep the results?

Probably. Quite a bit depends on the database program that you're using and how committed you are to the idea of buying extra hardware and software. Now, do you want to do this?

__Yes __No

Basically, the easiest way to scan the forms is to buy an optical card reader. Next, put the survey questionnaire in a format that the card reader can read (usually, it needs to be filled out with a #2 pencil). Yech, reminds me of all those standardized tests.

Finally, you need to design a database that can tabulate the information from your card reader. Most major database programs on the market today can handle this chore. Or better yet, you may prefer to go with a dedicated Survey/Response scoring system, such as Tabulyzer III by Business Research & Surveys (201-731-7800). One final option may be to eliminate the hard copy and go with an on-line survey administration and tabulation system.

Creating a sample travel database

I run tours in Hawaii and would like to set up a database for our reservationists to use. It should be searchable for hotels, airlines, and transportation, as well as for other goodies such as helicopter rides, island jumps, and more. Is there a way to put all this information in one file?

Aloha. Did you know that *aloha* has seven meanings? You almost need a database to keep up with it. Almost. Anyway, it sounds as if you need a relational database program. The term *relational* means that you have a number of different databases that have some things in common and can be tied together. Information from one database can be located easily from within another database. With a system such as this one, you could have a customer database that you use to store reservations. From there, you could look up available tours, accommodations, and so on from other databases.

The one worry I have is that data entry for the available tours, hotels, and so on would be a real nightmare. You'd need to enter and update a great deal of information constantly. For flights, car rentals, and hotels, tour professionals use the reservation systems SABRE and APOLLO. For more information, contact your local travel agent's association.

It could be that what you're looking for already exists, and now you know where to find it. With access to travel-specific information, you could just look up what you need. Then you'd import the booking information to your client/customer database. Any of the major relational databases on the market today can handle this job (Access, Approach, dBASE, FoxPro, Paradox, and so on).

Using a database for personnel issues

In our personnel database, I have to figure out how many weeks a person has been employed in order to determine benefits. For the life of me, I cannot figure out the formula. I always get the wrong answer.

You could just leave it to the individual employee; I've found that when it comes to benefits, all employees know perfect math.

Whenever you need to make formulas, think about the situation logically. If you forget that you're using a software program, you'll find that the formula is easier to remember.

First, make sure that you have the date fields set up in a date format. You also need a calculation field to hold the formula and result. Then subtract the most recent date from the start date and divide by 7. Voilà! The answer appears.

Switching from mainframe to networkable database software

I work for a school district and have the job of revamping the record keeping, such as student attendance and registration. It's all on the district mainframe, but the system is outdated, and any time we need a special report, the computer department takes months. Each student's attendance is kept on a card, and the cards are read by the mainframe every day. I have a feeling that a networked database program at each school would be good, with a scanner of some sort.

Database networkable software is the way to go, but you're going to have to face the district's MIS department. Tell them about your concerns and how you're trying to keep them from having to write new programs. I bet that they have more than a few suggestions, but keep in mind that your new program may eliminate some of their jobs. These people are civil servants. The school was built around some of them. I suspect that you're going to be fighting an uphill battle, especially if the district's mainframe has to hold every student's data. I'm not saying it's impossible — just be ready for a challenge or two.

About those attendance cards — check out the cards used for the SAT tests. They are pretty slick, and they work. Know that almost any scanner will make a text file that can be used by a database program. You should ask your mainframe vendor what kind of text file your mainframe needs. An older IBM mainframe, for example, uses a different text file format (EBCDIC, in case you care) than the ASCII format used in PCs. You want to avoid problems with file formats.

Mainframe tools have gotten better over the years. Ask your mainframe vendor about any report-writer software that helps upgrade old applications for today's requirements. If you want to buy a PC-based database program, start reading magazine reviews and call some computer consultants. In other words, do your homework. (You know — the thing your students avoid.) If you bid the job out, you'll get proposals and presentations on a solution. I worked for three *Fortune 500* computer companies and did bids all the time. A bid usually turned out to be a research proposal for the client, and it was full of reasons why our solution was best. I bet you can find a solution from such proposals.

Approach

Using the tutorial

I just bought Approach 3.0, ran the setup program, and then opened the tutorial. It wasn't much help: all I got was an *Overflow error* message on-screen, not any type of lessons. The system froze, so I had to reboot to get into Windows again. Did I run out of memory?

Approach's tutorial is a little bit fussy — it always wants to be on top. And this has nothing to do with running out of memory. Approach seems to need a tutorial to explain how to run the program's tutorial. I'd guess that the tutorial would start by asking you to close any other applications for Windows. It's important that you have any "always on top" programs closed since the Approach tutorial really wants to be the topmost window.

Assuming all is well, check whether you have TrueType fonts enabled in your Windows desktop: Open up the Windows Control Panel, click Fonts, and then click TrueType. When the little window pops up, make sure that there is an X in the box right before the Enable TrueType Fonts option. This should fix you right up, but if not, you need to do some more snooping.

The Approach tutorial wants to use Arial and Times New Roman fonts. See whether these fonts are installed by looking in the Control Panel Fonts window. If the fonts aren't installed, add them to your Windows desktop. To do so, highlight the font names, Arial and Times New Roman, click Add, and select the WINDOWS\SYSTEM subdirectory or the name of the directory that contains the fonts. Make sure that there is an X before the Copy Fonts to Windows Directory option. But if the Arial and Times New Roman fonts are already listed, add them again anyway. Doing so will cause Windows to reread the fonts from disk and will eliminate the possibility that corrupt font files are giving you headaches.

One last thing to check is the mouse's options. If you're using the Microsoft mouse driver Version 8.0 or later with those really cool features such as Snap to or Zoom enabled, the tutorial could fail because the tutorial wants to control the mouse. Turn these options off and see what happens. By the time you get this far, the Approach tutorial should be running.

Saving time

Our company uses Approach 3.0 for telephone order entry. The operators ask the person's address information, including the caller's city, state, and ZIP code. Is there a way for them to ask the person's ZIP code first and have Approach automatically fill in the city and state information? It sure would save some time!

Anything is possible. But in this case you have to ask yourself whether it's really worth it. You'll need to do some extensive setup work. First, you need a ZIP code database that Approach can use to associate cities and states with ZIP codes. You can find ZIP code databases on the on-line services or on BBSs. But you need to make sure that the ZIP code database file is compatible with your database. A .DBF file should work. Next, you need to have Approach open this ZIP code database and link it to your order entry database so Approach can use the ZIP code database to look up the city and state that go with the ZIP code that the operator enters.

Getting the ZIP code database to talk to a customer database can be a real challenge. Even with all the glorious years I've had programming databases, I would take the easy way out and buy a telemarketing software database program.

Or I'd call around town and find a local database guru. Better yet, I'd take an evening off and go to a local PC user's group meeting. In addition to getting tips on the project, you could start the search for a database programmer there. These groups usually have special-interest groups that are dedicated to different PC applications and even to specific software programs. Once a week or month, database enthusiasts get together to help each other. Now there's a party you don't want to miss. I'm serious. They throw the best parties because they have a huge database of people to draw from. Perhaps you'll figure out that you can do the job or find the right person to wrestle over getting the ZIP in the ZIP code field. But do yourself a bigger favor. Check out TeleMagic Software (800-835-6244). It's a full-blown telemarketing order entry and processing program specifically tailored for your business.

Writing macros

I work for a trucking firm and use Approach to handle our accounts receivables. Every day, I have the chore of opening the database and figuring out who owes my boss money. Sometimes it takes an hour, and then he gets upset because it takes me so long. Our business changes so fast; I'd like to find a quicker way.

Yeah, I understand why you don't want to get a trucking boss mad. Most of the trucking bosses I've seen have forearms like Popeye's. I suggest that you do some upfront work that will save you time in the long run — write a macro. *Macros* are little programs that contain all the commands you need to do a particular job. In your case, whenever you open the database, the macro would automatically search the database for all the folks who owe your company money. The macro also would sort these customers by date so that you could see how long the receivables are past due. Your boss would want to know that information, too.

The Approach manual has helpful information for writing macros. So crack that baby open. Here's the goal: you want to start, or launch, a macro to find the debtors. Make life easy by naming the macro Open and set the macro to run each time you open the file. That way, you can make coffee while the computer is working, and when you come back, all the deadbeat customers will be listed on-screen.

Working with different versions

I have Approach 3.0 at the office and Approach 2.0 at home. I started a database at home and finished it at the office. But now when I try to use the database at home again, Approach won't open the file.

Approach has become unapproachable. It's no wonder. After you convert Approach Version 3.0 files, the program won't "approach" older Version 2.0 files. You're out of luck. See what happens when you work at home on office things that take time away from your family?

Merging spreadsheets into Approach

I use Lotus 1-2-3 for Windows and am thinking about getting Approach. How hard is it to take information from a worksheet and put it in a database? I have sales figures that would be helpful in our database files. My overbearing boss says it will be difficult and expensive.

Sharing data between Lotus 1-2-3 for Windows and Approach 3.0 is extremely simple. The two programs were designed to work well together — unlike you and your boss. If you're used to working with 1-2-3, check out Approach's optional spreadsheet-style view of data in rows and columns. Basically, through OLE 2.0, Approach is the front end for Lotus 1-2-3. By the way, the Lotus Assistants are great. These step-by-step guides for building forms, reports, crosstabs, worksheets, mailing labels, and charts will make your job easier.

Komando Klues

If you plan to do any calculations with those sales figures, do the calculations in Lotus 1-2-3 first. Doing calculations in a spreadsheet program is much easier than dealing with calculated fields in a database program.

Creating custom menu buttons

I wrote my own database application in Approach to keep track of commercials and songs that have been aired on our radio station. The folks at the station aren't computer people. They are more concerned with keeping up with Madonna's life. Can I change the menu bars in Approach to only show the buttons that they need to press when they are using the database?

Approach makes a database just to keep up with Madonna's life. Just kidding.

Your question is an easy one to answer. You can make custom menu bars in your application so the users won't mess things up by hitting the wrong buttons. Essentially, you put only the buttons they need on the menu bar. Explain to the folks that every option they need is on the screen.

Komando
Klues

Keep the buttons to a minimum. Any more than ten options will get confusing.

Click Tools and select Customize Menus. On the screen that comes up, you can create a radio-station-employee-foul-proof menu bar that uses Approach's existing menu bars, or you can build one from scratch.

FoxPro

Making standard queries

I finally figured out how to create a daily sales report based on my customer database in FoxPro for Windows. It took me six months. I'd like to use the same query for other customer databases. Is there any way to copy the query from one database to another database? I couldn't find this topic in the manual.

Six months? You really should have written me sooner. At the rate you're going, answering your own question would take you about two years.

Sure, you can use generic queries and reports with more than one database. It's not as easy as it sounds, though. Devising an end-all query or report that works with all database types is pretty hard. A database typically contains specific information and fields for its particular contents, so different databases may have only three or four fields that are similar. Odds are, you'll have to tweak the queries or reports a bit for each database. But on the other hand, depending on the information in the database, you may be able to come up with generic queries and reports that fit all databases.

Komando
Klues

Stick with using field names instead of aliases if you venture into the generic world.

Gotta tell you — I tried this once. Note the word *once.* It's a good theory, but it doesn't work in practice. For more information on how to work with queries and reports, check the section of the FoxPro manual on creating reports. It will make your job easier.

Adjusting cursor size

My boss complains that it is hard to find the cursor when he is using FoxPro for Windows. How can I change the vertical cursor to a horizontal one? Maybe this will put him in a better mood.

I had a boss who had trouble with the cursor. Until I fixed it, he was the curser. Rim shot.

The easiest way to make the boss happy is to make the vertical cursor bigger. Microsoft's mouse drivers, Versions 8.0 and later, have options for changing the cursor's size, color, and appearance. Without knowing the specifics of your mouse, I cannot guarantee that this approach will work, though.

So I'm going to present you with an alternative that is like trekking through the Alaskan tundra in the middle of winter wearing a bikini. You can change the cursor's shape by using FOXTOOLS.FLL and calling some API functions. If the last sentence was way over your head, show this answer to your nearest FoxPro guru. Bribe your guru into the job: gurus like "Star Trek," Doritos, and "The Simpsons."

Nonetheless, you should have a sample program in the GOODIES\FOXTOOLS subdirectory called HOURGLAS.PRG, which shows how to change the cursor's shape by using the Windows API. Here's a copy of the program:

```
#DEFINE IDC_ARROW (32512)
#DEFINE IDC_IBEAM (32513)
#DEFINE IDC_WAIT (32514)
#DEFINE IDC_CROSS (32515)
#DEFINE IDC_UPARROW (32516)
#DEFINE IDC_SIZE (32640)
#DEFINE IDC_ICON (32641)
#DEFINE IDC_SIZENWSE (32642)
#DEFINE IDC_SIZENESW (32643)
#DEFINE IDC_SIZEWE (32644)
#DEFINE IDC_SIZENS (32645)
SET LIBRARY TO SYS(2004)+"FOXTOOLS.FLL" ADDITIVE
LOADCSR = REGFN("LOADCURSOR", "IL", "I")
SETCSR = REGFN("SETCURSOR", "I", "I")
OLDCSR = CALLFN(SETCSR, CALLFN(LOADCSR, 0, IDC_WAIT))
FOR I = 1 TO 300000
NEXT
=CALLFN(SETCSR, OLDCSR)
RELEASE LIBRARY SYS(2004)+"FOXTOOLS.FLL"
```

I wish there were an easier way. On second thought, there is. Tell your boss to hold a magnifying glass to the monitor.

Defining a sort order

I am using FoxPro for Windows to make our family tree. In my database, four families have the same last name (Young). When I print a report of all the records, only the first Young family prints. The rest have a blank space where the name should be. How can I make all the Youngs print out before I am too old to make the tree? I just turned 83!

You're 83? Wow, that's cool. Keep in mind that you can define a sort order within FoxPro so that when the first sort criteria yields the same results, you can have it fall back on a second criteria. This feature can be handy if you want to subsort all of the Young families on the father's first name (assuming that the father's first name is another field in the database). But back to the problem at hand.

Check to make sure that the last name is in the body of the report and not in a header. Next, open the report and double-click on the last name field. In the next dialog box, you see a check box for Print When. Click on it to see a set of radio buttons for Repeat values. It's probably set for No. Change it to Yes. Your family tree prints, and you still have many more years to spare.

Komando Klues

Here's another thought: You could just buy a family tree software program that's tailor-made for the genealogical job. The trees, lineage, and more happen in a snap; and in the newer programs, you can put photos or scrapbooks in the trees, too.

Making input forms

Every record in my FoxPro 2.6 for Windows database has 58 fields in it, so it takes me forever to fill it in. I am trying to make this job easier by using input screen forms. The only problem is that I can't find a way to easily switch back and forth between these input screens. Am I doomed to suffer with hand cramps for the rest of my life?

There are many ways to save your body. One way is to quit your job. Another is to define all of your "page 2" and subwindows as MODAL in the More dialog of the Generate command. Then, on the main screen of your page 2 button, if, for example your page 2 screen is called PAGE2.SPR, go to the Valid snippet of the page 2 button, and put the following:

```
DO PAGE2.SPR
RETURN .T.
```

In the page 2 screen, to ensure that you can cleanly exit page 2, create an Exit button and put the following in the Valid snippet of the Exit button:

```
CLEAR READ
RETURN .T.
```

Also, it wouldn't hurt to put the exact same commands in the Deactivate snippet if you've checked off Close in the Window type sub of the layout options. Happy typing!

Minimal hardware requirements

Is there any way to tweak our computer to run FoxPro on a 386SX with 2MB of RAM? I know it will run slowly, but I cannot afford a new computer.

It's a miracle! Call the *National Enquirer!* Then again, maybe not, because the performance of a computer and its software depends on whether you're talking about FoxPro for DOS or FoxPro for Windows. Using FoxPro for DOS with 2MB would be just plain annoying. Coffee breaks during sorts easily would turn into lunches at the club, extended weekends, and even vacations — unpaid, of course, because you're not making any money for the company.

If you have FoxPro for Windows running on a system with 2MB, I would be really, really surprised. The best thing you can do is to upgrade your memory so that you have at least 4 or 8MB of RAM. FoxPro will be cruising, and you'll be able to accomplish more and do it much faster too! If you do much work on this system, it's worth the investment.

Automating record numbering

I'm a used car salesman, and I want FoxPro 2.6 for Windows to automatically assign a new number to each new record I put in. I will enter the rest of the fields myself. How can I set FoxPro up so each new record will get its own number?

Even though you sell used cars, I will assume that you are not lying to me and trying to get on my good side by talking about databases. There's an easy way to have FoxPro assign the number, and there's a safe way to do it. The easy way is to tell FoxPro exactly where the field with the first number exists. Then have FoxPro increase that number by one and store it in the next record by using the Store command — `Store fieldname+1 Nextfield`. But there's a problem.

The whole thing falls apart if the first *fieldname* doesn't contain a number. So the safe method is to set up a control database where the numbers can be stored and the incrementing/counting can go on, and then just read that information into the main database. This choice is better if you re-sort the database and the order gets changed, or if records get deleted. Using this method prevents your unique numbers from being scrambled.

Exchanging FoxPro files between Macs and PCs

I created an application by using the Macintosh version of FoxPro, but now our office is changing over to PCs. Can an application created with the Macintosh version of FoxPro be read directly by the Windows version or by Access 2.0, or do I have to repeat all of last year's work?

Your best bet is probably to stick with FoxPro instead of going to Access 2.0. You shouldn't have a great deal of trouble sharing data between the Mac and Windows versions of FoxPro. And if your Mac is a more recent model, it comes with a 3^1/$_2$-inch superdrive that will read and write PC disks to facilitate the file transfer. If you have an older Mac, you may need to use a program such as Mac In DOS by Pacific Micro to enable your PC to read a disk that was formatted by a Mac.

This book has more information about using Mac disks in a PC. Can you guess the chapter? Tick. Tick. Tick. The Mac chapter. Yes, you get to go to the bonus round.

Sending a file in .DBF format

I decided to "lease" our customer names to another company for profit. The firm asked that the names be put on disk in .DBF format. How do I change a FoxPro for Windows database into the format they need? Please tell me that I don't have to type the entire thing again. The file has 300,000 names in it!

Database files saved in the .DBF format are the most common mailing list format. You're in luck. If your client wants a .DBF file, you should be able to send them your FoxPro .DBF file. And, if my name is on the list, please remove it. I hate junk mail. And stop calling me *CAR-RTE SORT*.

Eliminating old DOS message

I copied a FoxPro for DOS 2.5 application into the FoxPro for Windows directory. It works fine, but whenever I exit the program, I see a strange message: *API Library Not Found*. It doesn't seem to hurt anything. Should I just leave well enough alone, or should I fix it so the message doesn't appear?

This message won't really hurt anything, but you can get rid of it easily. So you know, the *API Library Not Found* message is saying that the computer couldn't find the C libraries referenced in the application. C routines that use the FoxPro C interface are done using FoxPro's library construction kit. Your application has a SET LIBRARY TO <name> command somewhere in it. Use the search feature to find the command, and when you find it, change <name> in the statement to where your C libraries are located. Now when you exit the program, you'll have the sense that all is right in the world. That is, until you realize that no one made the coffee again.

Troubleshooting FoxPro/SideKick problems

I have a weird problem with FoxPro 2.6 and Borland's SideKick for Windows. SideKick is in my Windows Startup Group and runs minimized. Any time I use the Alt+Tab keys when I am in FoxPro to get into SideKick, the FoxPro help screen pops up on the screen and flashes. I have to reboot my computer to make it stop. Any ideas???

Get really mad and storm out of the office. Drive recklessly through downtown screaming obscenities about FoxPro. No? OK.

FoxPro for Windows can be ill-behaved on Windows systems when you have several other applications minimized or running concurrently. This may have no bearing on your problem, but it's a thought. I have found that you can limit General Protection Fault errors and misbehaving by adding the following line to the SYSTEM.INI file of Windows (or editing an existing line):

```
DMABufferSize=017
```

If this solution doesn't work for you, contact Borland about an update for SideKick for Windows (sounds as though it may be the culprit here!).

Advice on setting colors

The computers in our company all run Windows 3.1, and we are switching from FoxPro for DOS to FoxPro for Windows. How do I set the colors in my FoxPro for Windows applications? I want everyone to use the colors I selected.

Don't push your colors on other users. Not everyone shares your love of "Hot Dog Stand Yellow."

Most Windows users set up the colors they want by using the Desktop option on the Control Panel. This feature enables users to customize the colors according to their own preferences, so all you have to worry about is developing sound code (which is your job, after all). Leave the colors on automatic when you develop the screens. Colorset commands don't always work the way you want them to, and your time is better spent on the application itself, not the frills.

Figuring out the EMPTY( ) command

The FoxPro for Windows SQL feature has an EMPTY( ) command to use when a field may be empty. I've searched high and low and can't find a damn thing about it.

Well, take another damn look. EMPTY( ) is a function call that you use in SQL code. It works anywhere in FoxPro and figures out whether a field value is logically empty. The EMPTY( ) call is a little hard to master the first or second time you use it. The biggest mistake people seem to make is that they confuse the call with a traditional null value. You really have to put on your thinking cap when you use the EMPTY( ) call. Here are different parameters for the EMPTY( ) function that you can use in your application:

➤ EMPTY for characters: either null or all blanks
➤ EMPTY for date: blank date
➤ EMPTY for logic: evaluates to False
➤ EMPTY for memo: nothing in the memo field
➤ EMPTY for numerics: equals zero

Creating applications for laptops

I'm using FoxPro for Windows. I have written an application that has many screens. I have learned that users can't see the whole screen on laptops. Is there any fix short of redesigning the screens?

Did you write the application on a machine that has the screen set to 800 × 600 video mode or better? Many folks make this mistake. I bet that the laptops use 640 × 480 video mode, and hence, the screen fits on your machine but not on theirs. If this is the case, you probably need to redo the application for the most commonly used video mode. For greater compatibility, writing applications in 640 × 480 video mode is a good idea.

Or make life better for the laptop user. Get a laptop screen-view improvement utility, such as Laptop Ultravision, and in Windows turn on mouse trails in the Control Panel. Sometimes changing the color scheme makes screens more readable. You can experiment with different colors by selecting a different color scheme through the Windows 3.1 Control Panel.

Works

Using a Works file with Office

Microsoft Works came installed on my computer. I never used the database part except to keep track of who owes me money. I upgraded to Office, and I am wondering if I will have to re-create the Works database.

You have so many people who owe you money that you need a database? Check whether I'm on it.

All you need to do is import your Works database file into Access and then save it as an Access native database (.MDB) file. I really can't give you more specifics without knowing the versions of Works and Access. You need special file import features that may not be included in the versions on your computer.

I'd try to use the file in Access anyway. It may just work, and if it does, you're in luck. Start Access and select File⇨Import/Export. Then highlight the Works database. If you get an error message on-screen, save the Works database as a comma-delimited ASCII file and then try to use that file in Access.

If neither method works, give Microsoft a call and ask for the Access supplemental converter's disk. You can reach Microsoft at 800-426-9400.

Comparing database files

I have two database files in Works. One file contains all the members of our organization, and the other file contains just the people who have made donations. The two databases have common fields, but I just want to know which names are in both databases. How can I compare the two databases?

Unfortunately, you can't use Works to compare the two databases. Nor can you use Works to add, append, or copy one database to another database. You see, these features and capabilities are found traditionally in the higher-end (read *more expensive*) database programs. I hope that the donations were made for your organization to purchase Access.

There is a workaround that you can use if you have some time and a friend who uses Access, dBASE, or another high-end database program. You can save each of the Works databases in either the dBASE III or dBASE IV format. Open each Works database, click on File, and select Save As. Then look for the Save File as Type drop-down box. Select the dBASE format and call a friend who uses a better database program. Ask your friend to compare the two databases and save the results in a .DBF file format. You can use that .DBF file with Works. It's a hassle, but it works.

Setting colors

I keep our company's inventory records and sales in Works. Is there a way to show data fields in color? Specifically, I'd like all negative numbers to appear in red on-screen.

Negative is so subjective. To me, the only negative number is *13*.

It's amazing the things you can find in a user's manual. To make negative numbers appear in red, open the database, take a look at the menu bar at the top of the screen, click Format, and then select Number. Make sure that there is an X in the box for Negative numbers in Red.

Making a mail merge

I am a mortician. I have a whole list of folks in a Works database to whom I'd like to send a letter about our new location. What's the easiest way to do this?

I'm wondering. How much repeat business do you get as a mortician?

All you need to do is set up a mail merge. A mail merge will combine all the people in your database file with the letter file. Sometimes this process is called a *print merge*, which is a term from the Works word processor. If you happen to have Works for Windows 2.0x or 3.0x, this job is a snap. Just run the Merge Wizard. When it asks for the merge file, specify your "list of folks" Works database.

Access

Learning Access

I want to use Access 2.0 for my work, but learning this program seems a little scary. The manuals seem to deal only with large database examples. Are other Access books available?

222

Different people have different ways of learning. The best thing you can do is figure out how you like to learn and then go with that. If you find the Access manuals scary, then buy a third-party Access book. So you know, software program manuals come in two basic types: those that are written as tutorials and those that are written as reference books.

Tutorials lay out lessons that teach you how to use Access with examples and problems to work through. *References* just give summaries of information; you look up these summaries in the same way you look up a word in a dictionary. Look for a book that includes a practice disk so that you can use the lessons in the book with the sample data disk.

Keep in mind that Access comes with a great deal of help built in (both tutorials and cue cards). The cue cards are great and stay on-screen, unless, of course, you become so proficient that you don't need any help. The Wizards hold your hand when you are setting up a database, too. So if you like the idea of experimental learning, try setting up a simple database yourself and search for help whenever you need it. There is nothing you can do to ruin your computer this way, and if you mess up the database beyond repair, just delete it and start from scratch. Hey, you'll learn Access so fast that you'll write a manual of your own. Then you can market it with the database you created.

Converting files from 1.0 to 2.0

I just upgraded to Access 2.0. When I try to open a database that was created in an older version, all I get is some message that Access can't open an database. Huh? Are these software companies too dumb to include such a feature?

Hey, don't knock software companies. Some of my best friends are in software companies. The folks at Microsoft (friends, mind you) want you to know that because you're opening a database that was created with Access 1.0, some of the new stuff in 2.0 won't be included or available in the old version's database. You simply need to convert the 1.0 database.

Start Access. Click File and then Convert Database. Select the name of the 1.0 database file that you want to convert, and Access does the rest of the work. After a database is converted or saved as a 2.0 database, you don't see the message anymore. Keep in mind that you can't use Access 1.0 or 1.1 to open an Access 2.0 database at all.

Making databases

What are the steps to create a database in Access 2.0? I mean, how do you type information in, look at it, and then print it out? Can you tell that I am new to databases?

Wow! You know more about databases than you realize! You've just outlined all of the steps you need to do. I'm tempted not to help you because you are almost there. But then, that's not why you bought this book.

First, you create a *form* that includes how your database will look and what kind of information it will have. Databases are made of fields and records. If you create an address book database, you may have the following fields:

➤ LastName, FirstName
➤ Street
➤ City, State, ZIP/Postal Code
➤ Telephone

You tell Access those field names and where they should appear (you don't want them all clumped up on the left side of the screen or scattered all over, so you specify where each field should go). Then you can enter data such as this:

➤ Anderson, Eric
➤ 33 Elm St.
➤ Danbury, CT 06089
➤ 203-555-1212 (Eric is a TV actor)

After you enter the data, you have one record in the database. The information in each of the fields makes up a record. You can enter more information (other records) until you're done. After your database is complete, you can view or search all of the records based on any field or combination of fields. Maybe you want to find all the people who live in Connecticut and have the last name Smith. Sometimes searches such as these are called *queries*. You can view these results on-screen, or you can design a report and send it to the printer. With this in mind, you're off to a good start, so go for it!

Modifying the Autosave feature

I work for a casino in Las Vegas, keeping track of what machines make the most payouts. How do I turn off the Autosave feature in Access 2.0? Sometimes the save happens at the worst of times, such as when I am on a roll typing in the database.

You can modify the Autosave feature in the Options menu. If Autosave bugs you, consider just changing the Autosave frequency rather than disabling it altogether. I have my Autosave feature set to 15 minutes. I don't know about you, but my rolls never last longer than that. However, since you're a high roller, you probably can make it 30 minutes or more.

Autosave automatically saves files to a location you specify (or to the directory you specify in SET TEMP=) with an .ASD extension. Should Access crash, the currently open ASD file will be copied to .BAK. Using the .BAK file may be the only way to recover work after an unexpected crash, so keeping the Autosave feature in place is highly advisable.

Evaluating locked tables and error messages

I blew it. My table is locked, and I can't access it in Access. I've copied the contents to another table, but I can't rename or delete the old one. I keep getting error message after error message. Can I fix this in Access 2.0, or will I have to wait until Access 3.0 is available?

No, with the luck you've been having, 3.0 would lock up on you too. It's a bummer, but you'll keep on getting error messages if you try to delete or rename a table that has a relationship with other tables in the database file. I've also been hurt by locked tables in Access, if that's any consolation.

You have to remove the relationships to the table that you want to delete or rename. But also know that you can't open a table in a datasheet view if you also have a form open that contains information, or rows, from that table.

Here's something to check: Look at your Database, Options, ODBC/Multiuser and then see if you set the Default Record Locking to All Records. If so, whenever the table is accessed by either a datasheet or a

225

form, every single record in the table is locked. Set Default Record Locking to No Locks, and you should be able to open the table in a datasheet view. Then get rid of the relationships to the table by clicking Edit and then Relationship. Give a right click of the old mouse on the relationship line to the table and select Delete. Now you should be able to delete or rename the table.

Using passwords

I have some very sensitive information in an Access database file: a list of my clients and potential clients. The other sales representatives are always looking for leads, and I don't want them to find mine. Is there a way to password-protect a database file in Access 2.0?

Sales is deadly. I've been there. You can password-protect a database, or you can lock some or all of its records. Start Access and open your client database. Click Security, select Password, and type your secret password. Stay away from your name, your birth date, or something else that's obvious.

Komando
Klues

A good password is between six and ten characters long and includes letters of the alphabet and numbers or punctuation marks. These password types are harder to break, but they are more difficult to remember. Never write your password down on a piece of paper and leave it in or around your desk if security is an issue. When you or someone else tries to open your client database file, the password will have to be typed or else the file won't open. If you really want to be deceptive, create a false database that anyone can access.

Setting up relationships between tables

I work for a tobacco firm. I am setting up multiple tables in our Access 2.0 database, and a customer name field, for example, is contained in many tables. It's a test database, and I have only ten

records in it. The problem is that as we make a correction to that field in that specific table, the change occurs only in that table and not in the other tables. Is there a way for the change to happen in all the tables?

Would you please put that cigarette out? You need to take another look at the way you set up the database and at the relationships between tables. Allow me. When you set up a relationship between tables and base the relationship on a common field, you can choose Cascade related records. This option means that any time you change or update the field in the primary table, all related fields in the linked tables will automatically update. It sounds as if you didn't select this option, which means that you may have to do the setup again. The common fields in both tables should be linked via those fields. Because you have only ten records, starting from scratch is easier than trying to fix the problem.

Komando Klues

But here are some things to consider in the redesign. If your customer list has a one-to-many relationship (that is, each customer record has many orders), your best bet is to use a customer ID field in all the tables. Then you won't have to duplicate all the information, just the customer ID code. The ID field in the main customer table should be a Counter type so that when you put in new customer, the Counter will automatically add the Client ID Number to the related tables.

Establishing relationships between tables

How can I see all the relationships that tables have to other tables in an Access 2.0 database?

Start Access and put the table that you want to know about on-screen. Click Edit and select Relationships: you'll see the relationship this table has to other tables. You can simply close the table or change the relationships in place.

Komando Klues

What's the golden rule of changing relationships? Break up with them before they break up with you? No. Make a backup of the database file before making any changes.

Taking precautions when upgrading

I just got Access 2.0. If I install the program, does the new version know enough to leave my database files alone?

You really have nothing to worry about because Access 2.0 handles this issue. But those are famous last words. You should take some precautions nonetheless. Stranger things have happened. If you have the hard disk space available, installing 2.0 in a new directory rather than using the 1.0 directory is not a bad idea. Also, back up all database data files before running the 2.0 SetUp command.

Other famous last words:

➤ No, it's not loaded.

➤ It's OK; I'm sterile.

➤ I don't care if it rains; I'm going golfing.

Setting up Access on a network

I see from looking in the Access 2.0 manual that the programs and database files work on a network. It would be great to have all the agents in our real-estate office using Access and the files. How do I set up the program to work on a network?

Have you noticed that real-estate agents have their own lingo? *Quaint* means *small*. A *fixer-upper* is a dump. *Easy access to all commerce* means it's under an off-ramp.

Anyway, assuming that the network is up and running, you simply need to tell Access that it's going to be installed on a network. When you install Access, put the first program setup disk in drive A, click on File from Program Manager, and select Run. In the dialog box, type the following and click OK:

```
A:SETUP /A
```

Then you need to go to each computer (called a *workstation*) that's hooked up to the network and repeat these steps.

Keep in mind, however, that when you are setting up the workstations, you can put Access on each workstation's hard disk or have the workstations use the copy of Access on the file server. If your network supports the universal naming convention (UNC), use the UNC path to avoid hassles with network drive letters.

Komando Klues

A handy-dandy file that gives detailed network setup instructions is included with Access. The file's name is ACREADME.HLP. Give it a look for the nitty-gritty stuff that's far too boring to detail in this book.

Printing mailing labels

I sell waterbeds and want to send all my customers a flier announcing a sale. What's the simplest way to print mailing labels for my customer database?

One question: Why are waterbeds always on sale? Are they ever regular price? It seems there is always a "waterbed blowout." The words together really don't do much for buyer confidence.

The Bottom Line

Use the Label Wizard to make your life easy; it creates and formats the labels from a database without much help from you.

With your database open, select Report. Select New; a dialog box opens. Click the down arrow and select a table or query that contains the names and addresses you want to print on labels.

Now, select Mailing Label from the list of options in the box. Click OK.

Next, you have to pick the fields that you want on each label. Don't forget to put spaces between certain fields; for example, the recipient's first name and the recipient's last name. When you need to put information on the next line of a label, click New Line. After you're done formatting the label, it may look a lot like this:

> First Name Last Name
>
> Company Name
>
> Street Address
>
> City, State ZIP/Postal Code

Note: These are the field names in my database; your field names may be different. Just replace my field names with the field names that are in your database.

After the labels are formatted, you can sort the labels by any field shown on the label. Often, sorting by ZIP code is handy, especially if your company sends mail via bulk mail.

Next, you're asked for the mailing label size. Avery is the name of the company that makes the most diverse selection of mailing labels. If you use Avery-brand labels, there will be a number on the box. Notice that the Avery number in Access matches the number on the Avery label box. Matching the Avery numbers makes it easy to pick the right size label in Access. If you are not using Avery labels, simply match the actual label size on the box to the label sizes shown in the Access list box.

You can change the fonts at this point, but the default fonts in Access are good for most uses. Click Finish; then select Print Preview. Print Preview shows you the labels on-screen before the labels are printed on your printer. From the Print Preview, select Print to actually print the labels.

Here's a real time-saver if you're going to be sending fliers or letters to your customers again: Save the mailing label report. This way, you won't have to use to the Label Wizard again. You can simply open the report and print the labels. To save the mailing label report, select File and then select Save. In the Report Name box, give your report a name, perhaps something like *Customer Mailing Labels*. Click OK.

Be sure to test print your report and check alignment. Use a dry run with plain paper, not those costly labels. (Sometimes it takes a lot of hit-or-miss tries to get things working just right!)

dBASE

Using extended characters

We are an international gold trader and just closed our first deal in London. I am compiling a dBASE report and find that I cannot display the British pound symbol in a field; there is no key for it on my keyboard.

You can't use "lbs"? No, I guess not; forget I said that. You have the pound symbol on your keyboard. It's hidden within the numeric keypad on your keyboard.

First, activate the numeric keypad by pressing the NumLock key on your keyboard. The NumLock light should be illuminated on your keyboard. To enter the British pound sign, press the Alt key, hold it down, and type the numbers **1 5 6** on the numeric keypad (using the typewriter number keys won't cut it).

Once you see the pound sign in the dBASE field, the next big task is to put it in your reports. The problem is: When using high ASCII codes above 127, not all printers print the same characters. Depending on your printer character set, you may get a different character or a blank in place of the British pound sign. If you have problems, check your printer manual; there should be a way to specify the ASCII characters that you need for the pound sign.

Printing lists of fields

I use dBASE III Plus to manage several construction projects. Each project includes multiple data files. Often, I get confused about which information is in which file. Is there a way to print something like a data file quick reference card?

Poof! I grant your wish. There is a way to print a reference. Open the first data file that's causing the confusion. Then, at the dBASE command or dot prompt (you know the one), type the following and press Enter:

```
LIST STRUCTURE TO PRINTER
```

The file's data structure will come out of the printer; there's your quick reference card. If the paper doesn't come out of the printer, type the following and press Enter:

```
EJECT
```

Repeat these steps to get the data structures of all the files.

Moving data to new fields

The Bottom Line

After entering in 272 friends' names in a dBASE IV file, I realized that a character field really should be a memo field. After changing the field type to memo, I lost all the information in the character fields. Do I have to redesign the database, or can I save the information somehow?

Wait a minute. You have 272 friends? I don't think I know 272 people.

You don't have to redesign the database.

First, make a backup copy of the original database — just in case. From within dBASE, you're going to make another copy of the data file to make the change you need. Open the data file and, at the dBASE dot prompt, type the following and press Enter:

```
COPY TO TEMP1.DBF
```

Change the character field in your original file to a memo field. This will, as you pointed out, wipe out the text in that field. Don't worry, you're about to get it back. Trust me.

At the dBASE dot prompt, enter the following commands and press Enter after each line. (Replace the word *FILE* with the name of your original data file, and replace the word *FIELD* with the name of the field you're changing.)

```
SELECT 1
USE Temp1
SELECT 2
USE FILE
SET RELATION TO RECNO() INTO Temp1
REPLACE ALL FIELD WITH Temp->FIELD
```

These commands tell dBASE to match the records in the two data files by record numbers (so make sure you don't add or delete records as you go through this process) and update the original file against the temporary one.

Browse the new data file and then put the cursor in the memo field. When you press the F9 key, you should see the data from your old file. Once you're sure the text is in the right places, go ahead and erase TEMP1.DBF.

32-bit capability

New PCs are 32-bit. Is dBASE a 32-bit program? Can it take advantage of my new Pentium processor?

Do you mean the one Intel ground up or the new one? Pentium should be called Pentium86 because Intel should have 86'd it when the problem was first discovered. It's fixed now, thanks.

A computer's processing capability is like the lanes on a highway; the more lanes you have, the more traffic can move during rush hour. When bottlenecks occur, your machine takes longer to do its magic. That's why that little hourglass has a bottleneck built right in.

Here's the bit shakedown on dBASE products:

> ➤ dBASE for DOS III, III+, and IV Versions 1.1 & 2.0 are not 32-bit.
> ➤ dBASE V is 32-bit.
> ➤ dBASE for Windows is 32-bit.

A 32-bit program talks to your computer's CPU in 32-bit chunks of information, rather than 8-bit or 16-bit. If you have a high-end computer, chances are that it has a 32-bit processor, an operating environment (such as OS/2 or Windows) that makes it possible, and motherboard architecture that communicates with the CPU in 32-bit chunks (this usually means Local Bus or PCI); programs will run a lot faster. You'll only realize the benefit of this if you're using Windows for Workgroups V3.11 or Windows 95 with 32-bit disk and file access enabled.

Pentium processors are capable of 64-bit processing. However, few applications are available to make use of this processing power yet. We can dream until then.

Database indexing

I am designing a database. Is there a right way and a wrong way to index my data?

Well, I can think of a lot of wrong ways to enter your data. One is throwing darts at your keyboard and hoping to strike the right key. Here's a better example: If I throw 100 items into a bag, it might take a reasonable amount of time to pull out the fifth item I threw in.

When you're first setting up a database, you need to consider how you will use your data. For instance, if you want to search for first name and last name separately, you should place this information in two fields. This will save you the trouble of *parsing* (separating) it out prior to searching. Let's face it, the less the computer has to do, the faster it can run.

If you're an advanced database developer, you may want to convert the first character of any text string that the user inputs to uppercase, so you don't have to worry about case-matching when indexing. These are only examples of how database design and indexing procedures can affect the overall usefulness of your database.

dBASE IV and higher offers extensive multilevel indexing capabilities. For more information, you might check out a great book called *Database Design: An Entity Relationship Approach* by Addison-Wesley. If you can't find the book locally, call Addison-Wesley at 800-447-2226.

Komando Klues

Use dBASE's Form Expert when you are in the design mode. After you are good at designing databases, you can turn off the expert by clicking the right mouse button while you're in the design window. To disable the Form Expert, take the X out of the box by clicking on it.

Using a mouse in a DOS-based database

I use mostly Windows programs and have no mouse problems. When I use my mouse in dBASE, I can never tell what it is going to do next. Do I need to do something to make my mouse work better in dBASE?

Your problem is not a big one. It's a small one. In fact, you have what is called a mini-mouse problem.

Mouse problems are common in DOS-based programs. If you're using an early version of dBASE for DOS, it doesn't support working with a mouse. You need to locate a shareware utility, such as NoMouse or UniMouse, and then load that utility in a batch file before loading dBASE for DOS. This will give you "light bar" mouse support in menus; it will not give you the mouse pointer you're familiar with in Windows.

If you're using the latest version of dBASE for DOS, make sure you have your DOS-based mouse driver loaded. Start by making sure that you have a backup copy of your AUTOEXEC.BAT and CONFIG.SYS files. Then, at the DOS prompt, type the following and press Enter.

```
TYPE AUTOEXEC.BAT
```

This command shows you the contents of your AUTOEXEC.BAT file. Take a peek for any mouse drivers. If you don't have any references to any mouse, you need to install a DOS-based mouse driver. Look around for the disks that contain your mouse drivers. There may have been a mouse driver's disk included with your computer (or mouse, if purchased separately). Install the mouse drivers, and your mouse should be back in action.

If you are using the Windows version of dBASE, you need to check the contents of the SYSTEM.INI file. From Program Manager, select File and then Run. In the command line box, type **SYSEDIT** and click OK.

SYSEDIT is an editing program that shows you all the important Windows system files inside your computer. Click the title bar of the SYSTEM.INI file to make it the active window. (You can only edit or look at the contents of a file in an active window.) In the [NonWindowsApp] section, add the following line:

```
MouseInDosBox=1
```

This line enhances mouse support when running a non-Windows application from Windows. Select File and then Save. Exit Windows and restart Windows to put the change into effect.

If you're using dBASE for Windows Version 1.0 with a Logitech Mouseman, make sure you have the middle button undefined and one-press double-click functions disabled. And, if you're using the Microsoft Mouse V2.0 with MS Mouse driver 8.0 or later, turn off the expanded mouse functions and slow mouse acceleration. If the problem persists, contact Borland's tech support. They've heard the problem more than once.

Displaying wide reports

When I print my reports to the screen in dBASE, I can't always see the complete width of the report. If I get a larger screen, will I be able to see the rest of my data?

I like the idea of getting a larger screen, but it probably won't do any good. You'd get the same data width with the characters — just larger — so you won't see any more data. With that logic, you would be able to see the director and crew with a bigger TV.

Newer 14-inch monitors can be changed from the standard 640×480 dpi to 800×600 dpi, or even 1024×768 dpi. This works in Windows-based applications. Remember, the higher the numbers, the smaller the icons are on-screen.

Your best bet is to redesign your report so that it doesn't exceed 80 columns when printing to your screen. Finally, try printing your report to a file instead of the screen; then open that file in your word processor. You'll get a wider view (by setting the page to landscape), and horizontal scrolling shows you the data that would otherwise be off the right side of your screen. Most Windows-based word processors support TrueType fonts, so you can select the entire report and change the font size for screen views and printouts. Plus, you can zoom in and zoom out of a document to enlarge areas of the report.

Data security

In dBASE IV, can I use a password to give users access to the fields of data that they are allowed to see? For example, users are not allowed to see a person's age, but it needs to be in the database.

Age is your most important concern? Do you work for a modeling agency?

Data protection is always a very important factor when creating a database. Your best bet is probably to create a separate table linked (Foreign Key Column) to the first table; this will allow you to selectively hide fields that you don't want users to see.

Komando Klues

While you're there, consider making it impossible for users to modify fields in another table. This protects individual data fields, by restricting access to the table containing sensitive data.

Saving databases automatically

While working in dBASE IV, I would prefer to save my work more often. Is there an automatic function that I can program (some easy keys to press) to save my changes as I go?

Unfortunately, there is no autosave function built into dBASE IV. But, if you do it manually frequently enough, saving your work becomes automatic. Here are a few shortcut keystrokes to save your file: Press Ctrl+W or Ctrl+End. If you're a menu bar type of person, select Layout and then Save Program File.

Database user groups

Is there a nationwide user group for dBASE users and developers? If so, is it available on something such as America Online?

Yes, there are support groups for this. "Hi, my name is Kim, and I'm a dBASE user." Everyone: "Hi, Kim!"

dBASE support groups are all over the country. Try checking with a local computer store or publication for one close to you.

One good source of dBASE information is *Informant* (916-686-6610). They publish a dBASE magazine that's widely accepted as the source of dBASE information (this is also a good place to find local dBASE user groups).

There is also great dBASE support available through on-line services, including America Online. On America Online, you can stop by our Komputer Klinic, using the keyword *Komando* and leave your questions in the message board. Or use the keyword *Applications*, pick Message Boards, and then select Database. You'll see discussion topics (folders) for all versions of dBASE; live chats are held weekly for dBASE developers. Check the Forum News in the Applications area for scheduling information. To access support files directly from Borland, use keyword *FTP*, select Enter and then Other Site. In the dialog box, type the following and click OK:

```
ftp.borland.com
```

Komando Klues

Once inside, select Pub and then dBASE for dBASE files.

I recommend that you download the index before searching for files.

Finally, there are dBASE support groups on the Internet (both newsgroups and mail list groups). For details, check out *The Internet White Pages* by IDG Books.

Deciding between dBASE and Excel

I'm a manager at a nuclear facility, and I need to collect monthly data on my employees who are messing up and then generate graphical reports based on the data. How should I decide whether to use Excel or dBASE for collecting data and creating bar charts?

Gee, remind me not to visit your area. Well, the novice may be better off using a spreadsheet, such as Excel. Spreadsheets are easy to learn and can make even the first-time user look good. Excel and dBASE can input and import data from a wide variety of sources, in a wide variety of formats.

First, decide how it's most convenient to store your data. If you want a lot of text-based information in your database program, go with dBASE. It's designed for your needs. If much of your data is numerical, or if you plan on using it for calculations, use your spreadsheet.

Excel does terrific charts, but if you want the best of both worlds, don't worry. Excel can read your dBASE-created .DBF files.

Special database applications

Are there any companies that have created data collection programs for the average business manager who uses dBASE?

Don't call yourself *average*. You'll never get ahead that way.

Ever since these programs were created, vendors have created specialty applications. They generally use the original off-the-shelf product and then base their entire product on it. Two companies are well known for data collection utilities that work with dBASE:

➤ Dynacomp Inc., 178 Phillips Rd., Webster, NY 14580, Phone: 716-671-6160, Toll-Free: 800-828-6772.

➤ Intex Solutions Inc., 35 Highland Ave., Needham, MA 02194, Phone: 617-449-6222, Fax: 617-444-2318.

If you're adventurous, seek a taste of the wild life. Visit your local computer software store and see what they have on the shelves and in their catalogs.

Transferring data to word processing

Can I copy portions of my dBASE report into a letter on my word processor? If so, will the report columns stay in a straight line on the word processing document? I have relatives who owe me money, and I want to send them all letters telling them how much they owe.

Gee, Aunt Helen, I hope I don't get a letter from you. I swear the deal should have worked.

Yes, just print the report to a file. This portion of your database file will be available for your word processor as a text file format. You can also choose to import your database file to your word processor as .DBF (if your word processor can import .DBF files).

Another way to transfer data to word processing is to save the database file as an ASCII, comma-delimited ASCII, or tab-delimited ASCII file. To make things line up, tab-delimited ASCII is great.

Komando
Klues

Be sure to switch to a monospaced font (for example, Courier) in your word processor. TrueType fonts use proportional spacing and the data goes all over the page. In Windows, the monospaced fonts are the ones with the small icon of the printer near them.

Other

Shareware databases

I went shopping for database software, but the programs cost too much money. I have a lot of girlfriends and I need to keep track of them. Are there any Windows-based shareware programs you would recommend for me, this poor beginner?

You have no money and lots of girlfriends? Son, you must be good.

There are many good shareware database programs. One of the better known is ButtonWare's ButtonFile for Windows (206-454-0479). ButtonFile is a Windows personal database program that is a combination address book and auto-dialer. You can store names, addresses, and multiple phone numbers on predefined cards; manage and maintain multiple address files; auto-dial any phone number and create a list of frequently used speed dial numbers; print mailing labels, reports, and 3x5 cards. If you find that you need more than ButtonFile, all is not lost. You can use the program's import and export features to move your information into Access, dBASE, or another commercial database program. ButtonFile includes 100 predefined forms, templates, toolbars, and other features common to Windows programs.

ButtonFile is not a relational database, however. A *relational database* allows you to search and sort through two tables of information in order to make a new table. Here's a real-life example: Say you had your customers listed in one table and your company's sales in a separate table. With a relational database, you can search through the customer table and sales table to find those customers who ordered in the last six months or a certain product.

Wampum from Ward Mundy Software (404-237-9420) is a relational database program; it's often called the poor man's dBASE program; it's dBASE-compatible and almost as powerful as dBASE itself. Virtually every dBASE III command and function is supported through a simple, menu-driven interface that supports nine relational databases. Although Wampum isn't a Windows-based program, Wampum's menu bar makes it easy to use. Wampum can handle databases with up to a billion records, with as many as 400 fields per record. You can also put graphics, such as scanned signatures, layouts, and drawings in .PCX format, in your Wampum records.

You can get a copy of these programs by downloading them from major BBSs or on-line services. If you don't have access to a BBS or on-line service, you can order the programs through shareware disk vendors or directly from the publisher. I always recommend registering your copy of the software and paying the fee. In addition to technical support, you'll be notified of any program updates. For more information about shareware in general, consult Chapter 17 of this book.

Chapter 7
Desktop Publishing

I can make beautiful brochures using a word processing program. Why would any sane person spend good money on a desktop publishing program?

If wasting money on software means a person is insane, wow, the world is worse off than I thought.

But, seriously, you're right: nowhere in the good book of computing does it say "Thou shalt have a desktop publishing program." Oftentimes, a word processing program does quite well — for example, when you simply want to jazz up documents. In fact, several popular word processors, such as Microsoft Word for Windows, Ami Pro, and WordPerfect, have terrific graphic- and text-handling features, making creating simple newsletters or brochures a breeze! You can use the software's predesigned templates or, better yet, tap into the Wizards, which hold your hand from concept to design.

If you try to use a word processor for a complicated desktop publishing job, however, watch your blood pressure soar. It's like trying to put together a desk by using a regular screwdriver rather than a power screwdriver. Both methods get the job done, but one takes a lot longer and tires you out.

It's time to go crazy and buy a desktop publishing program if any of the following pertains to you:

➤ You design documents that are tabloid style or perfectly bound.

➤ Your document is more than six pages and contains articles that are broken between two pages.

➤ You overlap text and graphics, invert text, or add backgrounds or screens.

➤ You work with extremely high-res graphics or color photographs.

➤ You print your document at 600 dpi or more.

➤ You don't care about any of this stuff. You just want to get a desktop publishing program.

Service bureaus

My boss told me to use a service bureau for the company's employee rah-rah newsletter. Can you give me some tips on how to work with a service bureau?

You think you have troubles. Imagine trying to put together a rah-rah newsletter for undertakers. Those are headlines that grab you by the throat: "More bad news: Plane hits White House, only the pilot perishes" or "The Law of Grave-ty: What grows up, must eventually go six feet down."

Typical service bureaus have high-resolution laser printers, called *imagesetters*, that print your document on photo-sensitive paper or film at 600 dpi or more. In addition, some service bureaus have high-res scanners and color-proofing tools.

Although most service bureaus offer a little booklet that advises you how to submit jobs, reading that pamphlet may not prepare you adequately. You need to make sure that you do the following:

Komando
Klues

➤ Because IBM PCs are less popular than Macs in the service bureau world, find a bureau that uses the same software you do to create publications. Sure, you can translate files between a PC and a Mac, but sometimes formatting or font information gets lost in the translation.

➤ Send to the service bureau every file needed to output your publication — that is, not just the publication, but also all fonts and graphics files. But to save lots of aggravation, don't send files that are not needed to print your job.

➤ Make absolutely certain your job request lists the total number of pages in the publication. And indicate whether you want the bureau to scale your publication to a specific size.

➤ Tell the service bureau the name and version number of the program used to create the publication. And list every font and their vendor (such as Adobe, Agfa, or Bitstream); sometimes fonts have the same name but look different.

➤ Do you use PostScript or TrueType fonts? Older imagesetters don't work well with TrueType fonts. Use only the fonts you need and keep illustrations simple. A long, complex document takes longer to print, and some service bureaus add huge hourly fees for difficult jobs.

➤ Most service bureaus require that you *output* (it's a verb) to PostScript. Most of the time, this process is pretty easy. Simply install a PostScript printer driver in Windows and then select that printer as the printer for the publication in your desktop publishing software.

➤ Using complex color properly often requires training and experience, so it's usually best to let your printer handle this chore.

➤ Always provide a printout of your document. The service bureau then can examine their output against your sample to see whether anything is wrong.

➤ Don't let cost be the top consideration. Your boss won't care whether you save $20 if the publication looks awful or arrives two weeks late. You should go to a firm that does quality work and has a staff that understands you're new at this stuff.

 Layout terms

What are line spacing, leading, kerning, and tracking?

Control freaks love these features, which enable you to pinpoint how text looks — down to the spacing between characters.

Line spacing, or *leading,* is the amount of space between lines on the typewritten page. You've probably seen how line spacing can be set to single, double, triple, and so forth on a typewriter (what's that?) or in your word processor.

Letters such as *w* take up more space than skinny letters, such as *I* or *l*. Letters or pairs of characters need space adjustments so that they don't sit too close to or too far from each other; either makes reading difficult. Adjusting for character spacing is *kerning*. *Tracking* is the space between characters and words in a line of text.

Kerning and tracking adjustments are more art than science. Messing around with them can be hazardous to your publication, particularly when a document is *justified*, or when the spacing between letters and words is adjusted as needed so that the beginnings and ends of all lines are aligned. (When the left and right margins are perfectly straight, a document is *fully justified*. In *left justified* text, the left margin is straight and the right is ragged. In *right justified* text, the right margin is straight and the left is ragged.) Let me put it this way: Undoubtedly, you will have to justify why you kerned when you didn't really have to kern.

Don't worry too much about leading, kerning, and tracking. The software program's automatic settings are fine for most users.

 Colors

What's the difference between spot color and four color?

The difference is, well, the number of colors.

A four-color publication (for example, any catalog, magazine, or newspaper that prints color photographs) divides the colors of the rainbow into four colors: cyan, magenta, yellow, and black, collectively referred to as CMYK (that's a dirty word in Russian). A color document is divided into four parts, each containing one of these four colors. The printing press prints these four colors on the page (either separately or at once depending on the press's size); the combination produces your full-color publication.

No, spot coloring is not CMYK that has dripped where you don't want it. Spot coloring is the addition of one color to a specific part of your publication. For example, you can use a color to make a headline jump out on the page. When working in a desktop publishing program, you pick a spot color from the computerized version of a color swatch book. The printing company uses the ink that corresponds to your color. Most high-end publishing and illustration programs accept Pantone colors, but other color models such as Focoltone, Toyo, or Trumatch may be accepted. Before choosing a swatch book, ask your printers what they prefer.

The Bottom Line

The more colors in your publication, the more the publication costs. Hence, publications with spot color are a lot less expensive than those with four colors.

Komando Klues

Here's what I do to get lower printing costs for spot-color publications: I tell the printer which color I want. Then I ask whether the printer plans to print a job in the near future using that color. Because printers can run two jobs using the same color, I ask for a 20 percent discount — but I settle for 10 percent.

Don't you just love it when I deliver a brilliant answer out of the clear blue, I mean, clear cyan?

Font etiquette

I just love fonts. What rules do professional desktop publishers follow regarding number of fonts?

Remember, too much of a good thing — even fonts — can be bad for you.

First, pick the font that your readers see the most — the body text font. I suggest picking a serif font, such as Times New Roman, because it's easy to read. A *serif* is the ornamental crossbar at the bottom of a character.

Typically, a body text font size of 9 to 12 points works best; use a larger font if your publication has wide columns and smaller for narrow columns. Reserve italics and bold for emphasis.

Next, choose a sans serif typeface (no ornamental crossbar), such as Arial, for headings. Stick to one standard heading typeface in a publication. If you want to add a decorative headline font, use it sparingly. Avoid sprinkling your document with fancy characters, which can clutter the page and give your publication an amateur look.

Don't jam-pack a page with text. Allow for white space around text blocks to help guide the reader's eye to the message. If your publication has columns, include plenty of white space between columns for easier reading, especially when you justify text across each column.

Komando Klues

Focus your eyes at a distance and then look at your desktop-published page. The blurry image you see lets you judge the overall layout.

Wow, I've given enough information here for you to write a newsletter on fonts — maybe *The Font Page News*.

Printers here and there

I telecommute to my office and do a lot of desktop publishing. The problem is when I bring the file to the office. I spend hours setting up the document to print from the office printer. Are there any shortcuts?

In this case, what the computer doesn't know won't hurt it. You need to fool your home computer into thinking that you have the same printer as at the office.

How? Simply install the printer driver for the office printer on your home computer. Then select the office printer before starting to work on the publication at home. The publication's page setup now will be the same at home and in the office. You'll find more information about installing printers in the Windows chapter.

In addition, install the publication's fonts on both the office and home computers. Without the proper fonts installed, things won't look quite right on-screen. Because you're not printing the publication on the home computer, it doesn't matter that the printer isn't there.

When you're finished, copy the publication file to a floppy disk, take it to the office, and print it.

DTP and Paper

Finding specialty paper

I'm starting my own business and need letterhead and business cards. The printer wants to charge me an arm and a leg to put color on the stationery. Worse, they won't even sell me any paper with preprinted designs. Where can I find such specialty paper?

Let me guess: Your ex-brother-in-law, who harbors a grudge against your family, runs the printer. I say it's time to find either another printer or an arm and leg that you can spare (maybe your ex-brother-in-law's?).

Specialty paper is a great image booster. The selection seems never-ending: you can buy paper with unusual colors, preprinted designs (including fancy borders), or special textures. When you find a color scheme, design, or texture you like, you usually can find the same kind of paper for business cards, envelopes, brochures, fliers, Rolodex cards, and more.

And specialty paper is easy to use — it slides into your printer. Of course, convenience costs more. Off-the-shelf specialty paper is often more expensive than hiring a printer to complete the same job, especially if you need 100 or more pages. If you need more than a few pages, ask a printer to quote a price before buying a specialty paper.

The following companies market special paper and offer free product catalogues:

Baudville (800-728-0888)

Beaver Prints (800-923-2837)

Paper Direct (800-272-7377)

Premier Papers (800-843-0414)

Queblo (800-523-9080)

Printable post cards

I want to create direct-mail postcards where the front is generic and the back is personalized. Where can I find postcards that work with my printer?

There's nothing like opening your mailbox and finding a generic postcard. My heart races whenever I receive a Publisher's Clearinghouse letter signed by Ed McMahon ("Wow, Ed took the time to address me by my first name."). I'm sure your customers will feel the same thrill.

If you're using a dot matrix printer, look for continuous form postcards. (Although you may mistake the postcards for a roll of toilet paper in the middle of the night, don't use them as such — not even in emergencies.) For inkjet, laser, and other paper tray printers, you can purchase $8^{1}/_{2} \times 11$-inch sheets, four cards to a page. (These are much better in emergencies.)

Because postcard sheets are thicker than plain paper, inkjet, laser, and other paper tray printers don't always behave. So put three or four sheets in the paper tray first and see whether the printer works. If not, you will have to stand at the printer and feed the sheets manually.

Komando Klues

Most laser printers have a back door. When this door is open, paper doesn't have to bend as much to come out of the printer. This trick is great when you're printing on thicker paper, such as postcards.

Sometimes, getting your text right where you want it on a postcard can be a challenge. It's a good idea to run a few tests with plain paper before putting the postcards in your printer.

You can find colorful postcards in specialty paper catalogs or at office-supply stores. Avery makes postcard sheets for your laser printer; the product code is 5389. If you want plain, white postcards, try Global Computer (1-800-8GLOBAL); usually, with run-of-the-(paper)mill stuff, Global Computer charges less than specialty paper suppliers.

Nonbleeding paper

For quite some time, I designed custom T-shirts by using CorelDRAW! and then printing on transfer paper with a Panasonic 2123 (a 24-pin dot matrix) printer. I switched to an HP DeskJet 560C (an inkjet), but I can't use the same paper because the ink bleeds too much. What can I do?

For high-quality output from inkjet printers, the ink has to soak in the paper quickly. Your transfer paper doesn't let the ink penetrate properly and so the ink bleeds.

Companies like Graffoto (800-888-7838) will take a file that you created in CorelDRAW! and print it to a special transfer paper from a color laser copier.

If you use a laser printer, you can make your own color T-shirt transfers. Using a special laser printer toner from a company called BlackLighting Inc. (800-252-2599), you print the picture on regular paper and then iron the image onto the T-shirt. By the way, BlackLighting publishes a bimonthy publication called *Flash Magazine* that's filled with creative ideas and desktop publishing tricks.

Do I get a free T-shirt for this answer? Size small.

Microsoft Publisher

Printing

Printing addresses on a newsletter

Is there any way to merge a database address list with a newsletter made in Microsoft Publisher so I can print a person's name and address directly on the newsletter?

Nope, you're out of luck. It's time to break out the old ballpoint pen. (Can't find one? Look between the couch cushions.)

Of course, you also can use your database program to print the names and addresses on labels; then slap those puppies one by one on the newsletters. Labels come in all sizes. For mailings printed by an inkjet or laser printer, you can purchase sheets of 30 labels (three columns, ten rows). If you have a dot matrix printer, buy a roll of labels.

I know that labels aren't very pretty, but will your customers care if the rest of the newsletter is great? If you're obsessing, you can buy transparent labels, which are almost invisible.

If you're feeling adventurous and have time to spare, check whether your database can say "Ole!" OLE (*o*bject *l*inking and *e*mbedding) is a cool way that different Windows programs share information. Perhaps you can perform a mail merge or a print merge between the database program and Microsoft Publisher.

Printing banners

Whenever I print a banner with Microsoft Publisher, the program insists on printing individual pages rather than one long strip. Is there a workaround?

249

I once saw a banner at a football game that read, "Isiah 7-14." I looked it up: it means "Block that kick."

Believe me, I've heard them all — like the time a man called my radio show because he couldn't install a Windows program. After he put the first disk in the computer and typed **setup**, the computer asked for but wouldn't accept the second disk. We went back and forth looking for a possible problem until he mentioned that the second disk would not fit in the disk drive while the first disk was in there. I wonder how he dressed himself every morning.

According to the Microsoft Publisher manual, you can't print continuously. But if you use a dot matrix printer, you can cheat and produce a banner on one long sheet. Follow these steps:

1. Get a roll of banner paper and put it in your printer.

2. Check your page setup and make sure that banner is selected and the length is appropriate.

3. Go to the Printer Setup menu and change the right and left margin settings to 0.

4. Select File⇨Print.

5. In the dialog box that appears, set the Overlap Setting option to 0.

6. Click Print. Bravo!

Test this method out by printing *Kim Komando is #1 in my book!*

Komando Klues Folks who have inkjet or laser printers can make only ugly banners, however, because they must print one page at a time and then tape all the printouts together.

Printing on envelopes

The Microsoft Publisher manual says that I can print envelopes, but it doesn't tell me how. I can't seem to get the returnee and addressee printed horizontally on an envelope placed horizontally.

I'm amazed your letter got to me.

Envelope printing is a snap after you do it once. First, you need to change your page setup to handle the envelopes. Select Page⇨Page Setup and click on Special Size. Click Print Setup, found in the upper-right corner of the dialog box. In the paper list box, select the size envelopes you plan to use.

Komando Klues

Pick Envelope #10 for standard business envelopes.

Now tell Microsoft Publisher where to find the envelopes: select Manual Feed from the Source option unless you have a special envelope feeder for your printer. Then choose the *orientation*, or how you want the text to appear on the envelopes; I pick horizontally because I slide the envelopes in the printer sideways. Click OK. Publisher is ready to print your envelopes.

Although it may sound as if a typewriter is still the best tool for addressing envelopes, there is a better way. Get a personal label printer, which is a little printer that has one purpose — it prints labels. With this time-saver hooked up to your computer, copy the address you want on the envelope to the Windows Clipboard and then click the label printer icon. The label printer spits out an address label ready for you to slap on an envelope.

Q&A *Printing faster*

I designed a simple resume in Microsoft Publisher, but it took almost an hour to print ten copies. What can I do to speed up printing in Publisher?

Boy, at that rate, you'll never get a job. Here are some tips to speed up your printing:

➤ Go to Program Manager and open up the Main group. Double-click on Control Panel. See a picture of a little printer with the word *Printers* underneath? (The engineers didn't give everything a weird name.) Double-click it. Make sure that an X is next to the Use Print Manager option. (This option works like an on/off switch. Click on the box to put an X in the box and turn on Print Manager; another click takes the X out of the box and turns off Print Manager.)

Now, when you send a publication to the printer from Publisher, Print Manager steps in and gathers all the information it needs to complete the job. You get the reins to your computer back while a job is printing. Plus, by pressing Alt+Tab, you can go back to Print Manager and cancel any print job that has yet to print.

> If the document doesn't need to be printed at a high resolution, lower the resolution — to 150 dpi, for example.

> Check your print setup: if the Collate Copies option is selected, deselect it.

> You may need more memory in your printer, especially if your Publisher documents are loaded with graphics.

> As a last resort, turn off both the printer and computer. Turn them both on again and go back into Publisher to print the resume. Restarting ensures that there is nothing lurking in the computer eating up resources.

> By the way, call your printer's manufacturer to check whether you have the most recent printer driver available. Often, the only way to find out about new printer drivers is to call and ask.

Be sure to dress neatly and smile during the interview. Good luck.

Graphics

Importing Paintbrush images into Publisher

How do I import a picture that I made in Paintbrush into a Microsoft Publisher document? P.S. I only want a piece of the Paintbrush image, not the entire thing.

Piece of cake! Rev up your Windows engine and start Paintbrush. Then go back to Program Manager and start Microsoft Publisher. After you launch Publisher, switch back to Paintbrush.

Komando
Klues

Pressing Alt+Tab toggles you from a current program to another program that's running.

Now the fun begins. Load the picture that you want to place in Publisher: Select the little scissors-and-rectangle tool, which is called the Pick tool. Draw an outline around the part of the picture you want. Copy this piece to the Clipboard (choose Edit⇨Copy).

Go back to Publisher. Pull up your publication and go to the page where you want to put the picture. Select Edit⇨Paste Object. Publisher makes a picture frame and then places the Paintbrush picture from the Clipboard into that frame. Don't worry if Publisher puts the picture in the wrong spot on the page; you can move the picture and change its size as you do any other framed picture in Publisher.

If the picture needs some tweaking in Paintbrush (don't they always?), simply double-click on the picture in Publisher; that action starts Paintbrush with the picture on-screen. When you're done editing the image, select File⇨Update and File⇨Exit to close Paintbrush and go back to Publisher.

Importing clip art into Publisher

How do I import clip art into a Microsoft Publisher publication?

What if the world's great painters used clip art? What would you pay for a Picasso Mona Lisa?

If you're using Microsoft Publisher 2.0 or higher, you can use any .BMP, .CGM, .EPS, .PCX, .TIF, .WMF, or .WPG image. Most clip art that comes on CD-ROMs is in one of these formats.

To import clip art,

1. Open a new or existing publication.

2. Use the Picture tool to make a frame.

3. Choose File⇨Import Picture. Handy list boxes show you the contents of the directories on your hard disk. To access a piece of clip art from a CD-ROM, select the CD-ROM drive (normally it's drive D).

4. Double-click on the filename of the picture you want to import. The picture appears inside the picture frame you made.

Komando Klues

Some CD-ROM discs store graphics in compressed format. Through a viewer, you can browse the images and select ones you want to use. The selected images are expanded and copied to your hard disk. As a result, you will find the filename of the picture you want to import in Step 3 — in one of the list boxes that show the contents of the directories on your hard disk. Double-click on the filename and the picture appears inside the picture frame you made.

Reversing an image

How can I reverse an image in Microsoft Publisher so the image has a black background?

To change foreground and background colors in a Microsoft Publisher picture, you need to tap into a drawing program, such as Paintbrush. You open the file and make the changes you want in Paintbrush, save the file in Paintbrush, and then import that picture into Publisher.

You also can do some snazzy things through a little Publisher feature called WordArt. For example, to reverse text in WordArt, select the object, click on the Shading icon (if you can't find the icon, choose Format⇨Shading), and change the Foreground color to White/Black.

CorelDRAW!.WMF file won't print

No matter what I do, Microsoft Publisher acts like it's possessed and spits my .WMF file made in CorelDRAW! back at me. Well, actually, I can see my CorelDRAW! file on-screen, but it won't print. What did I do wrong?

For some reason, Microsoft Publisher — that demonic software — won't use a CorelDRAW! image unless the image has a placeable header. So when you export an image as a .WMF file from CorelDRAW!, click Yes on placeable holders.

Of course, you can make life a little simpler by saving the CorelDRAW! image as a .CGM file; then you don't have to deal with the placeable header issue.

Revising WordArt creations

I love WordArt. But once my art is made, there is no easy way to change it. I want to add some effects like I do with pictures I make in Paintbrush. Any suggestions?

I can give you ten different ways or one simple suggestion. Which do you want to hear? Ah, I knew you were smart. I recommend using Paintbrush from within Publisher.

"Huh?" you ask. Well, first, go wild and create the WordArt, adding neat fill patterns and object shadows and so on. Next, click on the WordArt object to select it and then copy it to the Windows Clipboard (choose Edit⇨Copy).

Now go back to the Edit menu and select Insert Object. You may think, "Why do I want that command? I don't want to put another object in my picture." Hang in there; it works.

After selecting Insert Object, pick Paintbrush from the list and click OK. (*Note:* I usually use Microsoft Draw for this task, but I'll run with Paintbrush because I want you to be happy.) Paintbrush opens. Now put your WordArt on the Paintbrush canvas by pasting the WordArt in Paintbrush (choose Edit⇨Paste).

When you're done sprucing up your art, exit Paintbrush. A handy message pops up on-screen, asking whether you want to keep the changes or update the object. Click Yes.

Check out your WordArt in Publisher. See, it's the new and improved version. Of course, the WordArt isn't WordArt any more; rather, it's a Publisher file. So if you need to make any more changes to the image, double-click on it to start Paintbrush with the object on-screen.

Importing old .PCX files

I downloaded some .PCX files from an on-line service. I can view the images by using a graphics viewer, but Microsoft Publisher won't load them into the Clip Art Gallery. In fact, Publisher won't even import them into a document, although I tried changing the file extension (from .GIF to .PCX).

Q: How are the phrases *You look so Tony* and *My, you look nice today* like different .PCX files? A: Same language, different generations.

(By the way, just as "You look so Tony" means "Mmmm-mmm, you're looking fine" means "My, you look nice," "Don't take me to the curb" means "Don't be dissin' me" means "Please respect me." I just thought you would want to know.)

Well, Publisher doesn't speak the old graphics lingo. I suspect that the .PCX graphics you have are so old that Microsoft Publisher can't handle them directly.

If you're bent on using these graphics, try to open the files by using Paintbrush or a shareware program such as PaintShop Pro. Once the files are opened, save them in another format, such as .BMP, and then try to use the files in Publisher.

A word of caution: Changing the file extension doesn't change what's inside the file, so change that .BMP back to .PCX as soon as you can.

Of course, there is the remote chance that the file was corrupted during the download process. So try downloading the graphics again.

These must be some pictures. Care to share?

Importing/Exporting

Saving text separately

I use Microsoft Publisher to make just about every-thing, such as fliers, brochures, and even letters. How do I save just the text as a separate file?

I love easy questions. I get to look like such an expert. Highlight the text in Publisher you want to save and choose Edit↪Copy. The text is copied to the Windows Clipboard. Start your word processor and use the Paste command. Save the file.

Importing Publisher files into PageMaker

Is there any way to import Microsoft Publisher 2.0 files into PageMaker 5? I tried copying the file to the Clipboard and then using PageMaker's Paste command.

Some software programs can't import a file by themselves. They need a helping hand — a program add-on, known as a *filter*, that helps "suck" in finished files, text, or graphics from other applications.

Aldus has a filter that really sucks (in a good way). It opens Microsoft Publisher 2.0 and higher files in PageMaker 5. But don't look for this Hoover-like add-on in PageMaker; you need to call the folks at Aldus (800-628-2320) and ask them to send it to you.

Scanning text into Publisher

I tried at least 20 times to import text that was scanned using the OCR Direct software packaged with Logitech's Easytouch scanner into Microsoft Publisher. The scan completes, and I see the text fine on-screen, but Publisher won't import the text. Rather, it opens a new file or asks me which document I wish to open. I'm yelling at everyone.

Beware. Trying to solve computer problems has made people toss computers out windows, take a hammer to monitors, and kick small dogs. If you feel like doing anything like this, take a deep breath and then take another look at the problem. A fresh attitude makes a world of difference.

If Publisher doesn't cooperate or want to import the text file, you can do the same task another way: Open the text file in your OCR software, Windows Write, or Notepad. Then select all the text you want and copy it to the Windows Clipboard. Go back into Publisher and choose Edit⇨Paste.

No muss, no fuss, no wounded dogs. Besides, you're wasting your time yelling at people. You need to yell at the computer. Now aren't you glad you bought this book?

Troubleshooting

Logo Creator won't work

I can't get the Logo Creator Wizard to work with the CD-ROM version of Microsoft Publisher. Although I have 8MB of RAM and no other programs are running in the background, I receive a *not enough memory* message. Microsoft tech support told me to reinstall the program. No luck. Running MEMMAKER **didn't do the trick, either.**

Stop pulling out your hair: there is nothing you could do. I bet that you are simply one of the unlucky folks who received a sick Logo Creator.

To cure your Wizard, call Microsoft (800-541-1261) and ask for the Publisher CD-ROM patch.

Or use your modem and download the patch by dialing the Microsoft BBS (206-637-9009). Set your communications software to N,8,1. The BBS accepts speeds up to 9,600 baud.

Publisher causes general protection faults

I started getting general protection faults after upgrading to Microsoft Publisher 2.0. I get them when I print. This experience made me start drinking decaf!

OK, I'll go a little slow since you're running on unleaded now.

A *general protection fault* (GPF) generally happens when one program tries to share another program's memory space. Programs don't like other programs stepping in their memory territory.

A GPF is a clear sign that something is amiss. Perhaps a program has a bug, or maybe a file needed to make a program run is messed up in some way. Reinstalling the software program often solves the problem — but not in your case.

Many Publisher users received GPFs while printing, so a bug fix was released. To find out whether you have the update, start Publisher and pay close attention to what appears on-screen. Amid the copyrights and pictures, you should see the number *2.0* — that's the program's version number. You also should see an update letter (*a* or *b*) after the version number. (If you miss this information here, select Help⇨About.) If your Publisher version number and update letter is not 2.0a or 2.0b, give Microsoft a call and ask for the update disk. When you receive the update, reinstall the program and install the update.

Any time you get GPFs, you should do some maintenance on your hard drive. Go to the DOS prompt and run the CHKDSK program (type **CHKDSK/F** and press Enter). If you have MS-DOS 6.2 or higher, use the SCANDISK program (type **SCANDISK** and press Enter). Let either program correct any errors that it finds. With DOS 6.0 or higher, next (at the DOS prompt) run the DEFRAG program to get the hard drive back to the best organization possible (type **DEFRAG** and press Enter).

Getting zoom to work again

Most of the time, the zoom feature in Microsoft Publisher works only the first or second time I use it during a session. But it worked flawlessly the first six months. Any ideas?

Let me get this straight. Everything was working swell and then, wooomph, things started to go wrong out of the blue. Seems a little odd (if not downright suspicious). Sounds like the time you loaned your car to your teenagers: They swore they drove straight to the mall, but, for some reason, that two-mile trip took a full tank of gas.

C'mon, what did you do? Did you change anything in your computer over the last six months? Did you install any new software? Did you get a new video card or change your video resolution in Windows?

Zoom features have to do with video resolution, so check the video first. If you changed your monitor's settings or resolution, or if you put in a new video driver, try going back to standard Windows 3.1 VGA or SVGA 640 × 480. You change the video settings in the Windows Setup, found in the Main group.

It's also a good idea to perform some standard hard disk maintenance. Go to the DOS prompt and run the CHKDSK program by typing **CHKDSK/F** at the DOS prompt and pressing Enter (run SCANDISK if you have MS-DOS 6.2 or higher by typing **SCANDISK** at the DOS prompt and pressing Enter); let it correct any errors that it finds. With DOS 6.0 or higher, next run the DEFRAG program to get the hard drive back to the best organization possible. (Running CHKDSK or SCANDISK and DEFRAG is like changing the oil in your car. You get better performance when your equipment is in tip-top shape.)

Check whether you're using the most current version of Publisher available (choose Help⇨About). If your Publisher version number is not 2.0a or 2.0b, call Microsoft and request the update disk.

Finally, reinstall Publisher; doing so fixes any corrupt files.

Komando Klues

Files get messed up from time to time, especially if you turn your computer off without formally exiting the current program.

By the time you finish all the preceding steps, Publisher will be zooming.

Q&A *Publisher and Windows crash*

From time to time, Microsoft Publisher stops and Windows hangs. The only way to regain control of my computer is to press the reset button. The Ctrl+Alt+Del kill combo doesn't work. Why does a great software program choke?

You are amazing. You must be a Zenmaster. I don't know anyone who says a program is great when it hangs in the middle of a work session. Usually, people hang themselves at that point. To most, why the crash occurs isn't as important as making sure it doesn't happen again.

Be sure you have the most recent version of Publisher available. To find out what version you have, select Help⇨About. If your Publisher version is not at least 2.0a or 2.0b, call Microsoft and request the update disk.

Next, it's time for a little hard disk maintenance. (You have to take care of your hard disk so that it will take care of you.) Go to the DOS prompt and run the CHKDSK program (or SCANDISK if you have MS-DOS 6.2 or above); let it correct any errors that it finds. With DOS 6.0 or above, next run the DEFRAG program to get the hard drive back to the best organization possible.

In addition, the computer's memory may be configured wrong, or you simply may not have enough memory. Because graphics hog memory, try cutting out some of the publication's pictures.

Suppose that you do have enough memory — say, 4MB or higher — and you don't have a trillion graphics in your publication, and the problem persists. If you have DOS 5 or above, run the DOS memory management utility MEMMAKER at the DOS prompt. If you don't have DOS 5 or higher, the advantages of having your computer configure its optimum memory settings is worth the upgrade alone.

Don't run MEMMAKER through Windows. Doing so can do nasty things to your computer.

With the hard disk reorganized and the memory reconfigured, give Publisher another shot. Don't run any other program in the background. I'm sure you'll be singing the joys of desktop publishing again.

Well, at least until something else goes wrong.

 Restoring a PostScript file

After printing a publication to a PostScript file, my hard drive developed a major problem, and I lost several files, including the original Microsoft Publisher 2.0a file. I need to edit the publication, but I can't figure out how to read the PostScript file back in. P.S. I tried renaming the file with an .EPS extension and importing it into CorelDRAW! That made CorelDRAW! crash.

I bet you composed this letter on someone else's computer — after you learned that your computer couldn't survive a fall out of a second-story window.

Unfortunately, a PostScript file printed to disk isn't an editable file. (OK, the techies in the crowd will say, "Yes it is, Kim," but you don't want to try editing a PostScript file once it's outside the program that created it.) And renaming a file's extension doesn't change the file's contents. As a result, if you didn't have a backup, you are out of luck.

I know that it's no fun recreating a finished job. One thing that *might* save you some time is to print the publication and then scan it back into the computer. Some pictures and text may be saved.

PageMaker

Script too long *error message*

When I try to open templates by using the Open Templates option, I get a *script too long* error message. I reinstalled PageMaker at least 125 times. Zip. No luck. I did my disk checks and nothing was wrong. What do I do now?

You need to reinstall PageMaker 126 times. It says so right in the manual. Just kidding.

The *script too long* error message pops up when you have too many fonts installed (read: 250 or more). Use the Fonts option in the Control Panel (found in the Main program group) to select and remove fonts you don't use.

Komando Klues

If you cannot part with any fonts, invest in a font management program. These slick programs let you group your fonts by names or jobs. Then you can pick only the groups needed for the job at hand, saving the computer from loading all the fonts into memory. Of course, only the group fonts will be available.

Can't print multiple copies

Whenever I print a PageMaker .PM5 file, I get only one copy — no matter what number is in the number of copies box.

You give up too easily. What's wrong with running the printer 10 or 10,000 times in a row?

The workaround: Go to Printer Setup in PageMaker, select the Collate option, and enter the number of copies you want.

By the way, even I fall prey to these stupid little software glitches.

General protection faults while printing

When I try to print a brochure made in PageMaker 5 to my Hewlett-Packard LaserJet IIIp (equipped with 8MB of RAM), I get a general protection fault. When I click to continue, though, it prints fine. Is this normal?

No, but whose general protection fault is?

Your situation is not uncommon, but it's not how things are supposed to work. A general protection fault (GPF) usually means that something went wrong somewhere. Perhaps a file was corrupted. Or maybe two programs or processes tried to use the same hunk of memory simultaneously. I'd say your GPF lies in either PageMaker or your printer driver.

Do some routine disk maintenance by starting at the DOS prompt and running the CHKDSK program (or SCANDISK if you have MS-DOS 6.2 or above); let it correct any errors that it finds. With DOS 6.0 or above, next run the DEFRAG program to get the hard drive back to the best organization possible. Then reinstall PageMaker.

If the GPF persists, you may need to update your Hewlett-Packard LaserJet driver. Check whether your printer driver is the most recent version available (call Aldus technical support if you're unsure). Updated drivers are available from Hewlett-Packard, commercial on-line services, and BBSs.

If your printer driver is the most recent version, it may be messed up, so reinstall it. To do so, type **SETUP** at the DOS prompt in the WINDOWS directory and press Enter. This action starts the Windows Setup program; follow the directions to install new printer drivers.

You can perform the same feat in Windows, too: Go to the Main group, open up the Control Panel, and double-click on Printers. Highlight the name of your printer, click on Add, and follow the bouncing ball, I mean instructions on-screen.

Saving PageMaker 5 files as PageMaker 4

I have PageMaker 4 at the office and PageMaker 5 at home. I want to do some work at home, but my only printer is at the office. Is it possible to convert PageMaker 5 files back to PageMaker 4 files?

Someone once said, "You can never go back." Too true.

Some programs, such as CorelDRAW!, Microsoft Word, and WordPerfect, let you save work in the format of the program's last version. Unfortunately, PageMaker 5 isn't one of those programs (although you can open PageMaker 4 files in PageMaker 5). As a result, the easiest solution is to upgrade your office version.

But if cash is tight, here's a workaround: Convince PageMaker that you own a real long printer cable — from your home to your office.

First, add the laser printer driver to your home PC. From the Main group, open Control Panel and double-click on Printers. Highlight the name of the office laser printer and click Add. (Keep your Windows program disks handy. You may need them.)

Now, tell your home PC that when you "print" to the office laser printer, you want to send the publication to a file and not a real honest-to-goodness printer. After you install the printer driver, highlight the printer and click Set as default printer. (You should change the default printer back to your real printer when you are done printing to a file.) Then click Connect. From the list displayed, select File, click OK, and click Close.

When you finish creating a publication with PageMaker 5 at home, select Print. From the usual print screen, pick the pages to print (and any other print options) and click OK. A pop-up window appears, asking you to give the publication a filename. Type the filename, including the path, such as the following, and press Enter:

```
C:\TEMP\MYPRINT.JOB
```

After the file is saved to your hard drive, copy the file to a floppy disk. Bring the floppy to work and copy the file to your office computer's hard disk. (This step speeds up the printing, because the computer accesses the file quicker when it's on the hard disk.)

From the DOS prompt, go to the hard disk's subdirectory where you copied the file and type the following and press Enter:

```
COPY MYPRINT.JOB PRN /B
```

This command copies the MYPRINT.JOB file to the office printer, where /B makes sure that all the characters go to the printer.

By the way, this trick works in other Windows programs, too.

Recomposing a document

I remember reading something about an undocumented PageMaker feature that allows you to recompose a document. Do you have any idea what I'm talking about?

Many programs, including PageMaker, have secret features. Usually, the secrets are undocumented shortcuts: you won't find them inside program manuals. PageMaker's recomposition secret, known as *Pub Scout*, fixes many printing problems. In fact, this handy little trick can save you hours of frustration; invoke it when a publication doesn't quite look right after you make a series of changes.

Hold down Ctrl+Shift and select Type⇨Hyphenation. Usually, but not always, you hear a beep; if it's your lucky day, a window pops up on-screen to notify you that PageMaker is recomposing the document.

I wonder why Aldus kept Pub Scout a secret. I also wonder what else they're not telling us.

Figuring out tabs in PageMaker 5

I cannot figure out the tabs in PageMaker 5. Can you help?

Doesn't PageMaker sound like a bad horror or sci-fi movie? Now playing: *PageMaker 5, The Return of Unwanted Settings*. Or in my best Vincent Price voice: "Come see PageMaker in *Margins of Error*."

Like line spacing and indent settings, tabs are paragraph-level formatting attributes. When you want to set tabs (and indents, for that matter), click the Text menu and then click the Tabs option. In the little ruler window that pops up, you set a tab by clicking at the point on the ruler where you want the tab. You can set as many tabs as you want. When you're done, click Apply.

The little black triangles in the little ruler window, meanwhile, are margin and indent settings. The downward-pointing triangle indicates the indent for the first line in the paragraph. The upward-pointing triangle indicates the indent for the rest of the lines in the paragraph. Notice how the look of your text changes after you slide those little triangles around and click Apply. Pretty cool, eh?

Remember, the best way to learn something is to just do it.

Formatting paragraph styles globally

When I change my mind about paragraph styles in PageMaker, I wind up reformatting all the paragraphs one by one, which can take hours. Is there a quicker way?

At least you settled on one style long enough to write me. I'm proud of you.

Highlight all the paragraphs that should have the same style, select Type⇨Define Styles, and then format the paragraphs. If you later change your mind about the formatting — that is, you want Style Old paragraphs to have a Style New look — you can save considerable time by following these steps:

1. Go to Layout view. If the Control palette isn't visible already, select Window⇨Control palette. (The Control palette makes paragraph formatting easy and quick.)

2. Select the Text tool and highlight a Style Old paragraph.

3. Click on the Control palette. Highlight the style name (*Style Old*) and type a new style name: **Style New**.

4. Here's the fun part (two-fisted slingers will love it). Press Ctrl+Shift and click the name you just typed (*Style New*). A box pops up on-screen, asking whether you want to turn all Style Old paragraphs into Style New paragraphs.

5. Click OK.

CorelDRAW! 3 won't read .BMP files

I compose headlines in CorelDRAW! 3 and then save them as .BMP files. When I try to import the headlines into PageMaker 5, I get an error message — something about the image being an unsupported compressed image. Is there a quick fix?

Anything is a quick fix if you consider the alternative: using crayons.

.BMP is the Windows bitmapped graphics file format. When exporting a .BMP graphic from CorelDRAW!, you can compress it. Unfortunately, PageMaker (and many other programs) can't read compressed graphics. So when you save the headline, make sure the Compressed box is deselected.

Komando Klues

Of course, if you save your headlines as vector graphics, or in .WMF and .CGM file formats, the headlines will be cleaner and sharper.

Will PageMaker read QuarkXPress files?

I have two offices. We use QuarkXPress at one office and PageMaker at the other office. How do I import a QuarkXPress file into PageMaker 5?

Sure, sneak in that two-office thing. Most of us only work in one office, but Mr. Success here. . . .

Importing a QuarkXPress .XPD file into PageMaker 5 takes a special PageMaker *import filter*. This filter must match the version of QuarkXPress used to create the .XPD file in question.

A QuarkXPress 3.x filter shipped with PageMaker 5. If it's not available, you didn't install the filter when you installed PageMaker. No problem. Pull out the original PageMaker disks, start the installation process, and look for something about a custom installation. Then highlight the QuarkXPress filter and click on OK.

If the document was created using QuarkXPress for the Mac, you need to contact Aldus (800-628-2320) for a different import filter.

QuarkXPress

Quark won't show font characteristics

QuarkXPress only shows font names, not font styles (such as bold or italic). I tried reinstalling the program to no avail.

So you want to dress up your fonts. Do you prefer creamy Italic? Ranch? Thousand Island?

The problem isn't in QuarkXPress. It's in Windows. Go to the Main group, select Control Panel, double-click Fonts, and pick TrueType. Make sure Enable TrueType Fonts is selected. At the same time, make sure Show only TrueType Fonts in Applications is deselected.

Go back to QuarkXPress and see how your fonts look. If all is not well, go back to the Main group and again select Control Panel and then Fonts. This next step may sound a little scary, but trust me. Select all the fonts and then click Remove. (To select all fonts, click on the first font name to highlight it, hold down Ctrl, and then click all the other font names.) *Important:* After you click Remove, make sure that Delete from disk is deselected. As soon as your box of installed fonts is empty, go back and add all the fonts on your disk. Your fonts will be located in your WINDOWS directory (or in another directory if, for example, you installed a third-party font program). Select your font's directory; Windows rereads the font files and gives you a fresh start.

Seeing the whole document at once

When I select Fit in window in QuarkXPress, I can see only the left page of a two-page document. How can I get QuarkXPress to display both pages?

Seeing the entire publication in QuarkXPress is simple. Hold down Ctrl and click on Fit in windows. Yahtzee! QuarkXPress displays the Pasteboard. You see a reduced view of the publication. To see only the publication, get rid of the Pasteboard. To do so, enter 0 in the Pasteboard Width field, in the Applications Preferences dialog box.

Moving pages from doc to doc

How do I move a formatted page from one QuarkXPress 3.3 file to another?

By far, the easiest way to accomplish your mission is the *Thumbnail Drag and Drop*. Sounds gory. It's not.

To *drag* something, you select it (click on it) and then move it while holding down the mouse button. To *drop* something you're dragging, release the mouse button.

To move a formatted page from one QuarkXPress 3.3 file to another,

1. Open both publications.

2. Click View⇨Thumbnails.

3. *Drag* a thumbnail from one publication to another; then *drop* the thumbnail.

Printing faster

My HP LaserJet 4 printer takes five minutes to print a sample letterhead page made in QuarkXPress. What can I do to speed up printing?

Yes, I thought your letter was a bit late getting to me. It's a sad fact: Printing publications takes a lot longer than printing text files.

But printing QuarkXPress files to non-PostScript printers wastes even more time. So if you're always in a rush, buy a PostScript printer. Or if you want to save money, you can buy an upgrade module for your Hewlett-Packard printer so that it handles PostScript.

An even cheaper alternative: Sometimes you can almost halve printing time by printing at a lower resolution. To do so, choose File⇨Printer Setup and then change the resolution to 300 dpi (or even 150 dpi) under Options. You won't get high-quality printouts, but you'll save money as well as minutes.

With the time you'll save, you can write that next great *National Enquirer* feature about the British royal family.

Scaling down PostScript files

I just created a huge QuarkXPress PostScript file (29MB!). What can I do to reduce its size?

Unlike humans, QuarkXPress files can shed pounds without dieting or exercise. You see, PostScript files save all the doodads — and at the highest resolution. So if you play with the file's settings, you can shrink the file's size. For example, choose File⇨Printer Setup and lower the resolution and halftone frequency.

Komando Klues

Another quick weight-loss trick: Save your graphics files as .TIFF files instead of .PCX files.

Automatic hyphenation

How do I turn off the automatic hyphenation in QuarkXPress?

As you know, QuarkXPress's Preferences menu has only two hyphenation options: standard and enhanced. So where is the off button? Hiding under the Edit menu. Choose Edit⇨H&J, select Standard, click Edit, and deselect Auto Hyphenation.

God, I'm good.

Ventura

What is .EPS format?

The service bureaus in my area can't print out my Ventura files unless I output in .EPS format. Please tell me what this means and how to do it.

Carrying a computer to a service bureau is rather cumbersome, but it's easy to tote a file around. .EPS, or *E*ncapsulated *P*ost*S*cript, is a kind of file; don't worry, it's easy to produce. (The techies call PostScript a *page-*

description language, but you can think of it as the instructions that make a printer actually print something.) .EPS files are a popular file format for desktop publishing because they retain the document's formatting.

Ask the service bureau which printer it recommends for your Windows setup (the most common PostScript printer type is the Apple LaserWriter) and then install the appropriate printer driver. Here's how: First, open the Control Panel in the Main group. Double-click on Printers and select Add. From the list of printers that pops up on-screen, select the name of the printer recommended by the service bureau. Select Connect. Because you're printing to a file, select File under Port options. (Keep your Windows program disks handy. You may need them.)

Now start Ventura and open your publication. To get the publication out of the computer in PostScript format, you need to set the PostScript printer as the current printer. To do so, select Setup and click Options. Then select the Encapsulated PostScript file check box but leave the filename blank. Now print the publication; enter a filename when prompted. The resulting file is the .EPS file, so copy it to a floppy disk. Better yet, send the file by modem.

Komando Klues

I encourage you to create a publication that holds samples of the types of graphics, text, and fonts found in your regular newsletter. A small practice publication enables you and the service bureau to work out all the bugs before tackling the big newsletter.

Scanned files look bad

When I try importing a scanned image of my friend, Ventura 4.2 changes the file to an .IMG format and the resulting picture looks horrible. I've tried scanning at different resolutions, but the image always looks terrible in Ventura. Any advice?

Are you sure the scan is wrong and you're not protecting your friend?

Back in the days before Windows took over the world, Ventura used a graphical user interface called *GEM*, which worked only with bitmapped graphics called .IMG files. In fact, whenever Ventura opened a bitmapped file, such as a .TIF, the application converted the image to .IMG format. Although Ventura 4.2 is a Windows program, it hasn't forgotten its roots; it still uses .IMG files. The trick is to ignore the low-res .IMG files. Work instead with the .TIF file.

In the fall of 1993, Ventura was purchased by Corel Corp., the same company that makes CorelDRAW! Ventura 5 is, finally, a full-blown Windows program, and .IMG files are a thing of the past. In my opinion, the upgrade is well worth the price. For more information, call 800-77-COREL.

Importing WinWord files into Ventura

Every time I try to import Microsoft Word for Windows files into Ventura, the systems hangs. What's wrong?

Importing a lot could make you gain weight. I read that in a computer magazine, so it must be true.

Ventura uses *filters* to bring in files created by other programs. And only Ventura 5 can read Microsoft Word for Windows 6 files.

The quickest way to solve your problem is to save your Word for Windows 6 files as WinWord 2 files. You do so through Word's File⇨Save option; change the filename to something else (just in case) and then change the type in the list box to Word for Windows 2.0.

Know that Ventura stores a great deal of information in .INF files located in the Ventura directory. When you're not using Ventura, delete the .INF files. Also, if you see files called OVERFLOW.EMS, delete them, too. Although eliminating these files erases your preferences, all the bogus settings disappear as well. It's a hassle, but doing so speeds printing.

By the way, contact the Corel Corp. at 800-77-COREL for information about upgrading to Ventura 5; the new version fixed many problems that plagued earlier releases.

CorelDRAW!

Importing .TXT files into CorelDRAW!

How can I import a .TXT file with CorelDRAW! 4? I tried using the import command, but nothing happens.

I hate to be the bearer of bad news, but there is no Santa Claus and CorelDRAW! 4 text can be imported only via Paragraph mode. I can lessen the pain, though, because importing text is pretty simple:

1. Click on the text button (that's the icon with the letter *A*) and hold down the mouse button for a few seconds. A menu with three buttons pops out.

2. Click the second button (the one with a piece of paper on it) to select paragraph mode. (Get it? Paper and text go together.)

3. Click where you want CorelDRAW! to place the imported text and then drag the mouse to the bottom of the page.

4. Press Ctrl+T to bring up the paragraph mode dialog box.

5. Click on the Import button.

6. Select the file to import.

Attaching a drawing pad

What reasonably priced drawing pad can be used with CorelDRAW! 4? My son enjoys sketching, but he gets frustrated using the mouse.

Drawing with a mouse is like drawing with a brick. Heck, it's almost easier to draw with a real mouse.

You have a couple of options:

➤ A *digitizing tablet* looks like an overgrown pad of paper that's connected to the back of the computer. A penlike device is used to draw on the tablet. Using this combination feels more natural than working a mouse because it seems more like drawing with a real pen.

➤ An *UNmouse* also looks like a pen, but you draw on the top of your desk.

If your favorite computer store doesn't stock these devices, try contacting the following companies:

CalComp Inc. (800-CALCOMP)

Kurta Corp. (800-44KURTA)

MicroTouch Systems Inc. (800-UNMOUSE)

Here's hoping that your son becomes a high-tech Monet.

Exporting CorelDRAW! to word processors

What's the easiest way to export my CorelDRAW! 5 work for use in word processors, such as Ami Pro and WordPerfect?

Bitmapped graphics, which are made up of dots, are good for things like scanned photographs. But when you change the size of a bitmapped graphic, the picture is distorted. *Vector* graphics, on the other hand, are based on mathematical formulas. And because the picture is a formula of coordinates and objects, you can change the size of a vector graphic without losing quality.

As a result, you should save your CorelDRAW! 5 work as .WMF (*Windows Metafile*) files — the vector graphics file format of choice for Windows programs, including Ami Pro and WordPerfect.

Komando Klues

When exporting a .WMF file from CorelDRAW!, be sure to enable the Include placeable header option.

I really don't know how I keep all this information in my brain. It's crazy, I know. I tell you, I really need to upgrade to Brain 6.29a.

Shunning the AutoBackup

How can I get rid of CorelDRAW! 4's AutoBackup?

I know, I know, CorelDRAW backs up during the worst times — just like the phone always rings when you're in the shower or every stoplight turns red when you're zipping to the airport.

In the CorelDRAW! 4 directory is a subdirectory called CONFIG, which stores all the different .INI (or initialization) files. These files hold all the important settings regarding CorelDRAW!'s options. Exit CorelDRAW! and make a backup copy of the CORELDRW.INI file from your C:\WINDOWS directory. Next, use a text editor (such as Windows Notepad) to open the CORELDRW.INI file that's in your C:\WINDOWS directory. Find a line that says `AutoBackupMins=10`. To turn off AutoBackup, change this number to 0 so that the line reads as follows:

```
AutoBackupMins=0
```

Save the file. From now on, CorelDRAW!'s automatic backup feature is off.

Komando Klues

But I suggest that you think twice before disabling AutoBackup. Instead of turning the feature off altogether, try making the `AutoBackupMins` longer — say, 30 minutes. If you do turn AutoBackup off, however, please be sure to manually save from time to time. The creation you save may be your own.

Removing the scanned-in border

When I import a scanned photo into CorelDRAW!, a rectangle shows up around the graphic. How do I get rid of this box?

Are you sure you want to do this? Often, the picture frame is worth more than the painting.

First, check when scanning to see whether the rectangle appears there. If not, life's a little easier. You see, CorelDRAW! adds a thin line when importing bitmapped pictures. But this line shows up only in wireframe mode. To eliminate the rectangle, press Shift+F9 to go into full-screen mode; the rectangle should disappear.

If the picture has a rectangle in your scanning program, try adjusting the contrast settings to get rid of it. If that doesn't do the trick, you may have to remove that rectangle in the scanning program before bringing it into CorelDRAW!

Reversing text color

How can I overlap black text with a black ellipse and then reverse the text covered by the ellipse? I use CorelDRAW!.

Create the ellipse and fill it with black. Then type in the text you want; change the font style and size as desired. Select both objects (hold down Shift and click on the text and then the ellipse) and choose Arrange⇨Combine. Ta da! The part of the text that overlaps the black ellipse is now white.

Clip Art

Different file formats

I see different file extensions — such as .PCX, .GIF, and .WMF — in clip art packages. What are the different graphics file formats used in desktop publishing projects?

This ain't Baskin-Robbins. Graphics come in just two flavors: bitmapped and vector.

Bitmapped graphics are made up of dots. (Imagine taking a felt-tipped pen and drawing a face dot by dot.) *Vector* graphics use coordinates to make a picture; that is, they're based on mathematical formulas. Most important, vector images look better than bitmapped ones. And when you change the shape of a vector graphic, it isn't distorted like a bitmapped image is.

Graphics with the file extensions .PCX, .GIF, and .BMP are examples of bitmapped graphics. .WMF and .CGM are vector graphics.

A .PCX file is probably artwork — maybe a logo. A .GIF file is usually a photograph. And a .WMF (or *Windows Metafile*) can be just about anything (it's a format used by many Microsoft applications).

The
Bottom Line

The bottom line: Most desktop publishing programs handle all types of graphics, so you needn't lose any sleep.

Importing and exporting clip art

Can I use the clip art that comes with WordPerfect 6.0 for Windows with PrintShop Deluxe and vice versa?

Many word processing and desktop publishing programs get barely passing grades for graphics sharing. They have their own native graphic format, and they can import some other — but not *all* other — graphic formats.

For example, Word for Windows generally uses .WMF files, but you also can include .BMP, .GIF, .PCX, and other graphics files in WinWord documents. Similarly, WordPerfect uses .WPG as its graphic format but can handle .BMP, .GIF, .PCX, and so on.

Broderbund's PrintShop Deluxe is an exception. Whether you can import clip art from other programs depends on the version you're using. The older PrintShop Deluxe versions can import and export only images in its proprietary graphics file format.

PrintShop Deluxe has a conversion utility, called EXPORT.EXE (it's in your PRINTSHOP subdirectory), that changes PrintShop files into standard file formats. You can take your PrintShop files, save them as another format, and import them into WordPerfect.

The latest release of PrintShop Deluxe imports and exports standard graphic file formats.

Clip art packages (including pictures for business, holidays, and parties) that work specifically with PrintShop Deluxe are available directly from Broderbund.

Clip art stinks!

In search of clip art, all I find is generic people doing generic things while holding generic objects. I want some bona fide art.

You can blame your problems on capitalism. Many individuals (and companies, for that matter) who own images or original artwork won't release their stuff unless they are paid. As a result, only generic stuff is commonly available. (Of course, you probably couldn't find better art in a socialistic society.)

You can find unique clip art, however, from specialty publishers, subscription services, and BBSs. And for those truly recognizable characters, try going right to the source. For example, Mickey and Donald clip art is available from Walt Disney's software division. Call 800-688-1520 for more information.

If you buy a CD-ROM clip art disk, make sure that it has some sort of index. The last one I looked at had over 10,000 images and no real way to view or search through the images. I have better things to do than search through 10,000 images to find a picture of a heart.

Some good sources for clip art include

ArtMaker (909-625-8065)

ArtsParts (714-771-6754)

Broderbund (800-527-6263)

Chestnut (617-494-5330)

Corel Corp. (613-728-3733)

Microsoft Corp. (800-541-1261)

SoftKey Systems (800-377-6567)

T/Maker (415-962-0195)

WordPerfect (800-321-5906)

Chapter 8
DOS

Basics

DOS filename rules

I recently downloaded a zipped file. The download seemed to go OK, but a filename that started out as #1.ASSORT.JPEG somehow ended up as #1.ASS on my hard disk.

#1.ASS? You don't think that your computer was making an editorial comment, do you? What happened is that the computer came across a file with a name it didn't recognize. Mr. DOS has a few rules about filenames, and he gets a little nasty when you try to break his rules.

A file's name is like a person's name, except that it always has a dot, or period, separating the first name and last name. A filename can have only one dot. The first name can't have more than eight letters, numbers, and symbols; and the last name can't have more than three. A file must always have a first name. If the last name (the file *extension*) is omitted, then using the dot is not necessary. Because DOS reads filenames from left to right, it automatically shortened your file's last name to the three letters after the first dot.

DOS has other rules for filenames. A file's first and last name can contain only the letters *A* through *Z* (lowercase letters are translated to uppercase), the numbers *0* through *9*, and the following special characters and punctuation marks: ~, !, @, #, $, ^, &, (,), _, -, {, and }. Illegal characters are the space character, +, =, [,], ", :, ;, ,, ?, *, \, <, >, and |. DOS devices, such as LPT1, CON, AUX, and COM2, are not allowed in filenames.

In your case, DOS followed its rules and gave your file a legal DOS name. The filename #1.ASSORT.JPEG contains 12 characters and two periods. DOS stored characters as the file's name until it encountered a period, and then it stored the next three characters as the file's extension. The result is a perfectly legal DOS filename, #1.ASS.

Komando Klues

Here's a tip about file extensions: Some programs automatically assign file extensions to files saved with the program. Microsoft Word, for example, adds the file extension DOC, and Lotus adds the file extension WKS.

Searching for files

I know I saved a file, but I can't find it. How can I see all the files in my computer that end in .DOC?

You want to ask your computer, "What's up, .DOC?" right?

Well, a computer always wants to play hide and seek. (When is it ever going to grow up?) You can beat it at its own game. At the DOS prompt (the little C:\> thing that winks at you and begs you to type something next to it), type the following and press Enter:

```
CD \
```

You go to the top of the *root directory*. It's the directory that holds all your other directories. Type the following at the DOS prompt and press Enter:

```
DIR *.DOC /S /P
```

This command finds all the files on your hard drive that end in the .DOC file extension. The two items you typed next to DIR *.DOC in this command, /S and /P, are called *options* or *parameters* (or sometimes *arguments*, but why — who's arguing?). The /S tells DOS to look in all the directories below the one you are in for files ending in .DOC. Because you are in C:\, DOS looks in all the directories. The /P tells DOS to list things one screen at a time. Otherwise, if you have a large number of .DOC files, everything will just fly by before you have a chance to look at them.

Komando Klues

The DIR command has many other powerful features. To find out what they are, type **DIR /?** at the DOS prompt, press Enter, and you'll get a whole screenful of options to try out.

Setting up the mouse driver

I bought a new mouse. How do I set up my mouse's drivers?

Because the little robo-rodent doesn't have the natural instincts found in real mice (and thank God it doesn't, or you'd have little plastic pellets all over your work area), you need to give it a little training. Computer mice, like other gadgets that are plugged into your computer, need special programs called *drivers.* The driver program lets your computer and your mouse carry on a conversation with each other. Wonder what they talk about all day long? It's not cheese.

The mouse should have come with a floppy disk and a user guide. The disk contains the driver program that is designed to work with the mouse. Look in the user guide for instructions on how to set up or install the mouse. But first, check whether the computer is already set up to get the mouse working. Type the following line at the DOS prompt and press Enter:

```
MOUSE
```

If all systems are go, this command starts the mouse driver, and you'll see something on-screen saying that the driver is installed. But if you get the error message *Bad Command or Filename,* try typing this line at the DOS prompt and pressing Enter:

```
MOUSE\MOUSE
```

If you see *Invalid directory,* no mouse programs are living on your system. Use the disks that came with the mouse and reinstall the drivers. Usually, you just put the mouse drive disk in drive A and type **SETUP** or **INSTALL** from the C:\> prompt and press Enter. You'll see instructions on-screen. After the drivers are installed, the little rodent will be fine.

Adjusting background color

I am really tired of seeing white text on a black screen in DOS. How can I liven things up a little?

Well, for one thing, you need to get away from your computer for awhile. Take a class, such as dance or cooking. Broaden your horizons. When you come back to the screen, tell me if white on black is all that bad.

If it still is, you can change it, but it takes a little work. You need to add a line to the CONFIG.SYS file and then play with the colors a bit. Check the CONFIG.SYS file (in the C:\ directory) for a line that reads `DEVICE=C:\DOS\ANSI.SYS`. A simple way to see the contents of the CONFIG.SYS file is to type the following at the DOS prompt and then press Enter:

```
TYPE CONFIG.SYS
```

If you don't see the line `DEVICE=C:\DOS\ANSI.SYS`, make a backup copy of the CONFIG.SYS file to a floppy disk. Then type the following at the DOS prompt and press Enter:

```
ECHO DEVICE=C:\DOS\ANSI.SYS >> CONFIG.SYS
```

Reboot the computer. The program ANSI.SYS loads into the computer's memory so you can use it. ANSI.SYS is called a *device driver* — it enables DOS to talk to the video display. ANSI.SYS also enables you to give special commands to DOS through the keyboard, commands that tell DOS what colors to put on-screen. DOS, in turn, gives the commands to ANSI.SYS. Then ANSI.SYS translates the commands (as a foreign language translator does) into a language that the video display understands and gives them to the display.

Now, for the fun part! Type the following line at the DOS prompt and press Enter:

```
PROMPT=$e[1;33;44m$p$g
```

You should see a yellow DOS prompt on a blue background. Type **CLS** to clear the screen and press Enter. The whole screen should change to blue.

You have eight colors to work with for the *foreground color,* which is the color in which the letters and numbers appear. The same eight colors appear around the text and on the rest of the screen as the *background color.* Each foreground and background color has its own number. The following table lists the numbers for the eight foreground and background colors.

Typing **PROMPT=$e[1;34;47m$p$g** and pressing Enter yields blue text on a white background (the blue foreground number is 34, and the white background number is 47). You can try different colors by typing **PROMPT=$e[1;f;bm$p$g** at the C:\> prompt, where *f* is the foreground number and *b* is the background number. When you get the color scheme you like, add the whole `PROMPT=` line to the AUTOEXEC.BAT file. Reboot the computer to make the color changes take effect, and you'll be computing at the DOS prompt in color.

Don't make the foreground and background colors the same color.

Numbers for Background and Foreground Colors

Color	Number for Background	Number for Foreground
Black	40	30
Red	41	31
Green	42	32
Yellow	43	33
Blue	44	34
Magenta	45	35
Cyan	46	36
White	47	37

Establishing security

How can I set up my computer so that someone can't see my files when the DIR **command is used? I also want to password-protect access to my software programs.**

I can tell you're a very secretive person. I couldn't open your letter without a password.

Why limit your security to preventing coworkers, friends, or enemies from seeing your directories when they type **DIR** and press Enter at the DOS prompt? Buy a full-blown security software program that does that and more to keep nosy people from fooling around in your computer.

You can password-protect files and software programs. In other words, before people could use a file or program in your computer, they would have to type a special password. You pick the files and program to protect and how much protection is necessary. Most security programs also track the time spent using software programs and give a report on the files accessed. Security programs are a snap to install and use — well, that is, if you remember your secret password. You'll find security and password programs at almost any software store.

Understanding the license agreement

I received DOS 6.2 on 3½-inch disks with my new system. My old system uses 5¼-inch disks, but I would like to put my new DOS 6.2 software on it also. How can I copy the program to disks that are a different size?

Software is copyrighted, and this means it could be illegal for you to use the same copy of DOS on two computers. And we computer users wouldn't last ten minutes in jail.

Big Thug: What are you in for?

You: I violated international copyright protection laws.

Big Thug: I think I love you.

I hear you. I know you paid for the software. Still, check the licensing agreement that came with your computer to be sure that you can use the DOS software on more than one computer.

The best way to get DOS 6.2 on 5¼-inch disks is to contact the computer's manufacturer, Microsoft, or the store where you bought the computer. Depending on what the software policy is for your computer, often you can get disks that are a different size free or at a discounted cost. Copying the DOS files often leads to bigger headaches. DOS needs to be formally introduced to a computer through the installation process. Unless you know the little nuances of DOS that are far too detailed and boring to get into here, merely copying the files can leave you with a major mess on your hands.

Directories

Listing directories alphabetically

I want my directory listings from the DOS prompt to be in alphabetic order. Am I asking too much from life again?

You can sort directories in many different ways. The directory command has settings (DOS calls them *switches*) for your directory listings. Don't mess around. Type the following line at the DOS prompt and press Enter:

    DIR /ON

Yes! The directory list is sorted alphabetically (that's A to Z for our younger readers). You love it. I can see the expression on your face. Well, then, use the DOS EDIT program to add the following line to the AUTOEXEC.BAT file:

    DIRCMD=/ON

Save the changes, reboot the computer, and the alphabetic directory sort stays as a permanent fixture in your computer's realm.

Printing directories

Is there any way to print a listing of the files in a directory? I am working with DOS 6.22. It was easy to do with DOS 3.2.

Oh, I remember those 3.2 days of old. America was a simpler place. You could walk alone at night. People were nicer to each other. Gas was a dollar. . . . Sorry, I got lost there a second. You can print directory lists the old-fashioned way by pressing the Print Screen key when the directory listing is on-screen. Often, though, the directory list is too long and doesn't fit on-screen all at once. Hence, the entire directory listing doesn't come out of the printer. These situations call for a different approach, called *redirection*. Redirection is like a detour on a road that takes you someplace different than where you'd normally go.

DOS redirects something when it sees the > (greater than) symbol in a command line. Heck, > even looks like an arrow, pointing you in another direction. To redirect your directory listing to the printer, type the following at the DOS prompt and press Enter:

    DIR > PRN

(or type **DIR > LPT2** if you want it to go to a printer connected to LPT2).

Be sure that the printer is on and the little green on-line light on the printer is glowing before you press Enter. Otherwise, you may get an error message that says something such as the following:

```
Write fault error writing device PRN
Abort, Retry, Ignore, Fail?
```

Four very negative choices.

Don't worry. It's no big trauma. Just turn on the printer and press R for *retry*. If you have a laser printer, you need to press the on-line printer button that takes the printer off-line. Then press the form feed button to get the directory listing out of the printer.

The variations of the DIR command work for printouts, too. For example, DIR *.DOC > PRN gives a listing of all the files in a directory that have the file extension DOC. If you'd like to know more about DIR variations, type **DIR /?** and press Enter at the DOS prompt. All kinds of helpful hints pop up on-screen.

Deleting a directory

Using a multimedia setup program, I inadvertently created a directory called CD PROGS. When I tried to delete the directory, I kept getting messages that said I had too many parameters or an invalid directory. How can I get rid of this directory? P.S. I can create subdirectories to this directory, but I can't delete them.

DOS is particular about what you name directories, subdirectories, and files. Allowed characters are the letters *A* through *Z* (it translates lower-case letters to uppercase), the numbers *0* through *9*, and the following special characters and punctuation marks: ~, !, @, #, $, ^, &, (,), _, -, {, and }. Illegal characters are the space character, +,=, [,], ", :, ;, ., ?, *, \, <, >, and |. So a filename such as CD+=:;?* is really bad.

DOS also does not allow DOS devices as filenames. Some examples of device names are LPT1, CON, AUX, and COM2.

Also, if you use an illegal character, DOS usually ends the filename at that character. Although some enterprising folks manage to use one or more of the unusable characters, they typically create problems for all involved. Changing to, removing, or otherwise modifying the filename is problematic at best.

"That is all well and good," you say, "but my question is about directories, not filenames." Directory names follow the same rules. If you use DOS 6.0 or later, you are in luck because you can use the DELTREE command to delete the directory in question. Just type the following command and press Enter:

```
DOS\DELTREE C:\CD?PROGS
```

If you do not use a version of DOS that has the DELTREE command, then you will have to empty the directory so that you can remove it. After you empty it, type the following command at the DOS prompt and press Enter:

```
RD CD?PROGS
```

See, it wasn't that tough. But be more careful next time!

Don't delete a root directory

My root directory must have very long roots because I can't delete it. How do you delete a root directory?

Trust me. If you delete your root directory, you'll soon be pulling your hair out by the roots. Don't do it. Without it, all the other directories on the hard drive would be uprooted!

The root directory is really the heart of the hard drive. All the other directories are connected to it. It was probably all set up when you purchased the computer. If you decide to add another hard disk, though, you need to create a root directory for it. The only way to create one is with the FORMAT command (and pleeease don't try this on your hard drive!), which wipes out a hard disk as it does its thing.

Using dot (.) and double dot (..) to identify subdirectories

When you do a DIR **on a subdirectory, a single dot (.) and double dot (..) are the first two entries. What do these dots represent?**

Jeez, that sounds like a question for Dr. Ruth. The dot and double dot are a kind of road map that DOS uses to keep track of your travels. A dot represents the directory you are in now, and a double dot tells DOS what directory you came from.

For example, say that you have a directory called DOCS on drive C, and the DOCS directory contains a subdirectory named OLD — where you keep all those long-forgotten memos. If you type **CD C:\DOCS\OLD** at the DOS prompt and press Enter, DOS automatically sets the double dot to the value C:\DOCS and the single dot to the value OLD. When you type **DIR** to see what's in the OLD subdirectory, notice the <DIR> to the right of both the single and double dots. That's right, they are both directories! At this point, type **CD..** at the DOS prompt and press Enter to go back to the DOCS directory. This method is quicker than typing **CD C:\DOCS** and pressing Enter to go back to the DOCS directory.

You can use a single dot with commands such as COPY. If you are in the C:\DOCS directory and want to copy everything in it to C:\DOCS\OLD, for example, you just type **COPY . OLD** rather than **COPY *.* OLD.** Watch the screen during the copy process and notice the .\ that appears before each filename. The .\ tells you that files are being copied *from* the *current* directory (the directory you are now in, C:\DOCS). On the other hand, if you are already in the OLD subdirectory and want to do the same thing (copy everything from DOCS into OLD), you type **COPY ..** (which is identical to COPY C:\DOCS*.*) and save a few keystrokes.

All in all, you shouldn't even care about the dot and double dot file structures. They involve the hexadecimal side of life, which you are shielded from quite nicely if you use Windows.

Word to the wise: Never delete the single or double dot directories, or else you will erase all the files contained in those directories.

Versions and upgrading

Explaining version numbers

I looked in the manual, and it mentioned that I need DOS Version 6.x. Is this something that I have to order from Microsoft?

I'm sure Mr. Bill-ionaire Gates would love to hear from you with your credit card handy. But there is no such version as DOS 6.x, Virginia. The *x* in the version number is a shortcut. You often see the *x* used in software program version numbers when you look at software requirements or read a software manual. Instead of saying that a program or command works in all DOS versions that have the number 6 in it — 6.0, 6.2, 6.22, and so on — computer people just say 6.x. Dirty computer users often refer to it as 6-triple X.

Komando Klues

To find out what version of DOS is installed in your computer, type **VER** at the DOS prompt and press Enter.

Keep previous versions of DOS when upgrading

When I break up with a guy, I like to end it and move on. Likewise, is it all right to erase the old DOS directory when I install a new version of DOS?

All things considered, you can erase the old DOS directory after you install a new DOS version. But keeping the old DOS lying around while you break in the new version is a good idea.

When you put a new DOS version on a computer, DOS creates (unless you take special steps to prevent it) one or more floppies that you can use to uninstall (a word only a programmer could love) the new DOS version. These floppies are a kind of safety net that enables you to uninstall the new DOS version and go back to using the old version if the new version totally messes up the computer.

To get rid of the new DOS version, you need to have the directory OLDDOS.1 on the hard drive. You don't need to make this directory. DOS does it for you. If you erase this directory, the uninstall program won't work because it can no longer find the old DOS files.

Keep the old version of DOS on your computer for a week or two. Within this time, you'll probably use most of the software programs that are on the computer. After you have used most of the programs, you can safely wipe out the old version of DOS by using a file named DELOLDOS.EXE that is in the DOS directory. Type **DELOLDOS** and press Enter. Wow! DOS finds and deletes the directory named OLDDOS.1.

Komando Klues

Always keep an emergency bootable floppy of the old DOS system on hand just in case things go wrong. At least you'll be able to restart the system from the floppy drive.

Figuring out correct DOS upgrades

I have DR DOS on my computer. I have purchased an MS-DOS 6.2 upgrade kit. How should I proceed? The family has games that will not run under DR DOS, and we want to change the system. The manual does not give me clear information.

Bad news! The MS-DOS upgrade is exactly that — an upgrade from a previous version of MS-DOS. Most likely, MS-DOS will not recognize DR DOS as a valid DOS program.

I suggest that you go to your neighborhood computer store and try to find an old MS-DOS 4.2 or 5 (the full version, not an upgrade) that you can buy cheap. Then install that version. If you boot up your computer from the MS-DOS full-version disks, you should be able to set up a new DOS directory and convert your operating system to MS-DOS without reformatting. Clever, huh? That's why I get the big bucks. As a side note, a caller to my radio show who had the same problem used the MS-DOS upgrade without installing an earlier version of MS-DOS. It fouled things up so badly that he had to reformat the hard disk drive. (Wow, dude, déjà vu!)

Running DOS 6 on older PCs

I have an old Wang computer with DOS 2.01. Can I upgrade it to DOS 6?

That's like putting chrome headers on a 1976 Gremlin. You can, but why would you? Almost any computer that runs DOS can run later versions of DOS. Upgrading the DOS version in older tanks such as that Wang computer is often a worthless venture. The computer may not have enough memory to run DOS 6.x. Even if it does, the software programs may not run. DOS 6.x takes up more memory than DOS 2.01. Plus, you may not have much hard disk space left over to run programs because DOS itself has grown in size over the years.

If DOS and your software programs did work, they'd probably run very, v-e-r-y slowly. You see, today's software is designed to run on a powerful computer. Your Wang isn't very powerful, as you probably already know.

The Bottom Line

So my answer is a definite maybe, but why go to all the trouble? If it's not broke, don't fix it. That is, unless you can afford a new computer and get rid of the Wang altogether.

Running DOS 6 on older PCs, part 2

I upgraded my old XT clone from MS-DOS 3.1 to 5.0, and then to 6.0. The machine ran much better before I bogged it down with the upgrades. What would be the easiest way to take DOS down a few pegs back to 3.1?

You need to downgrade! You're going in the wrong direction. Watch out! The information superhighway is a one-way street.

You found out what many other users of older computers have learned the hard way about the newer DOS versions. They are bigger, better, more feature-laden, and are not suited for older, slower processors. The DOS directory from Version 6.0 alone eats up about 3MB. It's tough, because old XTs have an original hard disk drive of only 10 or 20MB, and you have to give up a large amount of it just to get DOS 6.0 or later on the computer.

XTs loaded with memory have 640K of RAM and will run better with the smaller kernel offered by DOS 3.1. As an additional note for users of other DOS versions, the DOS 5 kernel is smaller than any of the DOS 4 series were, so for an XT, use a 3 or 5 series for the best utilization of the system resources.

Because you have gone through several version upgrades, you probably can't use the undo disks that you created when you ran the DOS 5 and DOS 6 installation routines. Unfortunately, DOS 3.x did not have a fancy installation routine like the ones in DOS 5 and DOS 6, so you need to do a manual DOS installation. In your case, the manual DOS installation is relatively simple. All you need is a boot floppy that has the DOS version that you want to return to and the rest of the DOS version.

First, back up your computer's hard disk. Then boot from the DOS 3.1 boot floppy disk, and when you get to the A:\> prompt, type the following DOS command and press Enter:

```
SYS C:
```

When that completes, type the following command and press Enter:

```
COPY A:\COMMAND.COM C:\COMMAND.COM
```

Next, delete all the files in the DOS directory on drive C and copy all the DOS 3.1 files from drive A to C:\DOS. Reboot the computer, and you are done!

Don't forget that any commands in the CONFIG.SYS and AUTOEXEC.BAT that specify DOS 6.0 will not work in DOS 3.1, and you will get an error message when they try to run and find no DOS 6.0 files in the DOS directory. So be sure to remove any commands that belong to the later DOS versions before rebooting the computer. (You need to use the DOS `EDLIN` command instead of the DOS `EDIT` command.)

Upgrading DOS versions

I recently purchased a new computer that came loaded with IBM's PC-DOS (Version 6.1). I used the MS-DOS 6.2 upgrade, but I just get the message *DOS 6.2 already loaded* (which it is not, obviously). Do I need to create a separate partition (the thought frightens me!)? I can find nothing on this in any of the manuals.

Are your really frightened about creating a separate partition? If you are, a support group, such as Separate Partitions Anonymous, can help you through it.

Anyway, updating DOS versions is *usually* a snap. All you usually do is get a copy of the MS-DOS 6.2 Step-up Kit, and you're off and running. Unfortunately, you don't have it quite so easy because you are using PC-DOS rather than MS-DOS. The only way to upgrade is to purchase the full upgrade version of PC-DOS. Remember, you want the upgrade version, not the full version that comes with a new computer.

But don't give up too fast. The MS-DOS upgrade that you have is exactly that — an upgrade from a previous version of MS-DOS. Most likely, MS-DOS will not recognize IBM's version as a valid DOS program.

I suggest that you go to your neighborhood computer store and try to find an old MS-DOS 4.2 or 5 (the full version, not an upgrade) that you can buy cheaply. Back up your computer and then install that version. If you boot up your computer from the MS-DOS full-version disks, you should be able to set up a new DOS directory and convert your operating system to MS-DOS without reformatting. Clever, huh? As a side note, a caller to my radio show who had the same problem used the MS-DOS upgrade without installing an earlier version of MS-DOS. It fouled things up so badly that he had to reformat the hard disk drive.

Making applications work with DOS upgrades

I bit the bullet and upgraded from DOS 4.01 to DOS 6.22. What a mistake! Now some of my programs refuse to run and complain about having an incorrect version or something like that.

Program: Hey, Mr. DOS, what's your version number?

DOS: I'm 6.22, buddy. What's it to you?

Program: You don't have to be mean about it. I just can't work with any DOS that's higher than 5. Have a nice day.

DOS: No, wait. Come back. I'm sorry.

Wow, there are some real dos and don'ts to being nice. Relax and take a deep breath. Your software programs will run on your computer. DOS has a workaround for software programs that check what version of DOS is running. You see, DOS works a certain way, and some programs expect DOS to always be that way. But just as friends change over the years, so does DOS. (DOS, however, will never ask you for a loan.) And some software programs act up if they feel outdated.

You have to put the software programs back in familiar territory, and the SETVER.EXE program in DOS does exactly this trick. Because you're making some changes to the CONFIG.SYS file, make a backup of the file to a floppy disk. Then use the DOS EDIT command to add the following line to the CONFIG.SYS file (somewhere toward the bottom is good):

```
DEVICE=C:\DOS\SETVER.EXE
```

Save your changes, exit the DOS editor, and reboot the computer. Ta da. The programs should run the way they did under DOS 4.01. If this technique doesn't do the trick, SETVER doesn't know the program or programs that need the older DOS. To get them acquainted, you need to put the

293

names of the programs in a special list that SETVER looks at every time the computer is started. Find out what version of DOS each program needs by looking through the documentation or on the original program disk.

For example, if you have a program called KOOLGAME.EXE in the C:\GAMES directory and it needs DOS 4.01, you go to the DOS directory and type the following and press Enter:

```
SETVER C:\DOS KOOLGAME.EXE 4.01
```

Then you see a very unfriendly, rude actually, message similar to this one:

```
WARNING - The application you are adding to the version
table may not have been verified on this version of DOS.
Please contact your software vendor for information on
whether this application will operate properly under this
version of DOS. Version table successfully updated.
```

You have to restart your computer for the version change to take effect. Microsoft keeps DOS very compatible from version to version, so, in most cases, this check for a correct DOS version is probably unnecessary.

Upgrading tips

I received DOS 6.2 with my laptop and like some of its features. Can I install 6.2 over the 6.0 on my desktop computer without wiping out my entire hard drive, or do I have to buy a 6.2 upgrade?

First, you need to understand that DOS, like most commercially sold software, includes a license agreement that you automatically accept as soon as you open or start to use the program. This license typically allows you to install the software on one machine. Check the licensing agreement that came with DOS 6.2 to see whether it allows you to copy it to another machine. More than likely, it doesn't. And don't even think about doing it. It's bad karma, and you know how temperamental computers are anyway.

Microsoft has a Step-up Kit that you can find at most well-stocked software stores for about $10. Or, if you have a modem, you can get it free.

To save the $10 and not wait for the disk to come via U.S. mail, use your modem to call the Microsoft Download Service at 206-936-6735. The settings for the modem are Data Bits-8, Parity-none, Stop Bits-1, and speeds up to 9600. The 6.2x Step-up is a free upgrade for all DOS 6.0 users and gets you from 6.0 to 6.2x, so it's a good deal.

But here are some general words about step-ups and upgrades:

Komando Klues

➤ Unless the DOS is clearly marked as an upgrade, it's not an upgrade.

➤ If the DOS you have is part of a complete computer purchase, it may be *nonstandard* or include utilities that are specialized for the kind of machine that it came with. In addition, features that you are counting on may be missing. For example, the Texas Instruments version of MS-DOS 6.x does not support DBLSPACE.BIN, the DOS compression driver.

➤ OK, so Microsoft upgrades since 5.0 have been extremely good about installing onto existing systems without having to format or otherwise damage or destroy existing data on a drive. But always back up critical information prior to making a major change to your system. Remember, Murphy was an optimist.

AUTOEXEC.BAT and CONFIG.SYS

Examining AUTOEXEC.BAT and CONFIG.SYS

Is there a way a nontechnical person can figure out what should *not* be in the CONFIG.SYS and AUTOEXEC.BAT files? I looked in those files, and they look like they are ready for the scrap heap.

Be careful, one person's scrap heap is another person's gold. Don't delete your gold. It's a dangerous combination — a nontechnical person and the CONFIG.SYS and AUTOEXEC.BAT files. It's like that old beer commercial. These guys blow up a building and then say it's Miller Time. That's a great combo — explosives, beer, and big, fat, dumb guys.

The answer to this question depends on whom you ask. Give your shoe box full of tax receipts to 14 different accountants, and you'll probably get 14 different tax returns. Let me tell ya, sometimes even the experts have a difficult time telling what's best and guaranteed. And there's no consensus among the DOS experts. Doesn't make you feel any better, does it?

But you can take some steps to cut down on the clutter. You're treading in dangerous waters, however, and you have to be careful. Erase the wrong line, and you could mess up your sound board, mouse, memory, and more. But you asked, so I'll answer you.

First, make a backup copy of the AUTOEXEC.BAT and CONFIG.SYS files. Using the DOS EDIT command, go through the AUTOEXEC.BAT and CONFIG.SYS files and take out all the lines that start with *REM*. This change should shrink the files somewhat. (A line that starts with *REM* is a comment, and the computer ignores anything after the *REM*.)

If a line is duplicated (exactly, letter for letter and number for number), put *REM* in front of the duplicate occurrences of this line. Computers usually understand a command the first time it's spoken, unlike a big, old dog. Reboot the computer at this point to make sure that you haven't erased something you need. You can always use the DOS EDIT command again to take out the *REM* letters if something goes wrong.

There may be more than one PATH statement in the file. PATH just tells the computer what directories to look in when you type a command or program name at the DOS prompt. Sometimes, when new software is added to the system, it adds the program's directory to the PATH statement. Check the PATH statements for any duplicate directories. Usually, you can safely delete the duplicate references.

The Bottom Line

All in all, I suggest leaving the files alone. What did they do to you? Why are you setting yourself up for potential danger?

Q&A Necessary elements to CONFIG.SYS and AUTOEXEC.BAT

I have used MEMMAKER **to configure my memory. The only thing is, I need about 2K more space in the conventional memory to run a game. Are there certain things that need to be in the AUTOEXEC.BAT file and the CONFIG.SYS file?**

I'd try to use the game by starting my computer with a boot disk before I'd start tinkering. But since you asked, you probably need to have the following, at a minimum, in your computer's start-up files.

➤ Anything that says COMMAND.COM (not KOMMAND.KOM)
➤ Anything that says HIMEM.SYS

➤ Anything that says EMM386.EXE

➤ And, if you have your hard drive compressed, for gosh sakes, don't remove DRVSPACE.SYS or DOUBLSPC.SYS. Everything would really be messed up then.

Beyond that, you need to check for the CD-ROM's drivers, mouse, and video card and leave them in if your game needs these gadgets.

Komando Klues

You can usually tell where something came from by the name of the directory in which it resides. For example, a line in an AUTOEXEC.BAT file that says `C:\SSPRO\PROMODE.COM` doesn't mean much to most folks. You may not know what `PROMODE.COM` is, but `SSPRO` is the name of a video card (SpeedStar Pro).

Editing AUTOEXEC.BAT

I love crawling into bed at night with a fine wine, a fire glowing, and a software program manual. I live for these relaxing moments. The software manual tells me to edit the AUTOEXEC.BAT file. Where do I edit, and how do I get there?

From what you've written, I can tell you that editing the AUTOEXEC.BAT file is not your biggest problem. But that is none of my business.

OK, you edit the AUTOEXEC.BAT file by typing the following line at the DOS prompt and pressing Enter:

```
EDIT AUTOEXEC.BAT
```

`EDIT` is the command for the DOS `EDIT` program. It works the way that many other DOS programs work. There is a menu bar at the top. Pressing Enter gives you a blank line. The cursor keys move the insertion point around the file. You can use the Backspace and Delete keys when you make a mistake. Here's the important part: You press Alt+F and then choose the Save option to save changes to the file that you are working on. Keep in mind that you have to reboot the computer to make changes in the AUTOEXEC.BAT or CONFIG.SYS files take effect.

The AUTOEXEC.BAT file, like the CONFIG.SYS file, is important. Always make a copy of these files to a floppy disk before you edit them.

297

Troubleshooting AUTOEXEC.BAT

When I boot up, my AUTOEXEC.BAT does not execute.

When the system starts up, DOS needs to be told several things. Basically, it needs to know who handles the things you type at the C:\> command prompt. And the key word here is *command.* The command interpreter, which the computer calls COMMAND.COM, is in charge. (You've probably seen this file lurking around somewhere on the hard drive.) Without COMMAND.COM in the right place, a system can't run AUTOEXEC.BAT on its own.

First, make a backup copy of the CONFIG.SYS file that's in the C:\ directory. Then type the following at the DOS prompt and press Enter to make sure that you have COMMAND.COM on your computer:

```
DIR C:\DOS\COMMAND.COM
```

If COMMAND.COM isn't there, type the following at the DOS prompt and press Enter to put COMMAND.COM where it needs to be:

```
COPY C:\COMMAND.COM C:\DOS
```

Next, check the CONFIG.SYS file to see whether the SHELL command is in the file. (I bet it's not there or that something on the line is wrong.) Type the following at the DOS prompt and press Enter to check the SHELL command:

```
TYPE C:\CONFIG.SYS
```

You're looking for something such as SHELL=C:\DOS\COMMAND.COM C:\DOS /E:512 /P. Give up? You add the SHELL= line by using the DOS EDIT command. Type the following at the DOS prompt and press Enter:

```
EDIT C:\CONFIG.SYS
```

Add the following line as the last line of CONFIG.SYS (or change the line beginning with SHELL to this):

```
SHELL=C:\DOS\COMMAND.COM C:\DOS /E:512 /P
```

Press Alt+F and then S for save. Then press Alt+X to get back to the DOS prompt. Reboot the computer.

So what does all this SHELL= stuff mean? You told DOS to look for a command interpreter in the DOS directory (C:\DOS). You set aside 512 bytes (or characters — that is, letters, numbers, or symbols) to store things such as the PATH statement (the one found in AUTOEXEC.BAT). You made COMMAND.COM the primary command interpreter. And that's it in a nutshell! (Or is that . . . command shell?!? Ohhh . . . whatever!)

Fixing AUTOEXEC.BAT

I was playing with the AUTOEXEC.BAT file, and now my computer won't boot up. What do I do now? I know . . . I should have backed up the file first. I use DOS 6 and Windows 3.1.

Didn't anyone ever tell you that if you play with the AUTOEXEC.BAT file too much, you will go blind?

You're the type who has to learn the hard way, eh? I bet you remove parts of your car's engine without knowing what they are. And you throw out phone numbers that you find in your pocket the next day. Remember this: Before you go off and experiment with files that are necessary for your computer to start, do yourself a favor. Please. Make a backup copy of the file on a floppy disk. Now, what about this time?

Life would be good if you had a boot disk. You probably don't, so move on. With DOS 6.0 or higher, the Interactive Boot feature is the next best thing to a boot disk. After you turn on the computer, pay attention. When you see *Starting MS DOS* on-screen, press F5. You then should see a message that MS-DOS is bypassing the CONFIG.SYS and AUTOEXEC.BAT files. Bypassing these files enables you to go straight to the DOS prompt. At the DOS prompt, type the following and press Enter:

```
DIR AUTOEXEC.*
```

If you are kind to animals great and small, sometimes, even after you make changes to the AUTOEXEC.BAT file, you can find the original file. The file extension will be different, however; it may be 001 or BAK. Use the DOS editor and take a look at AUTOEXEC.BAK. It could be exactly what you need — the original AUTOEXEC.BAT file. If it is, save the AUTOEXEC.BAK file as AUTOEXEC.BAT, restart the computer, and you learned a lesson without too much pain.

Alas, if your computer doesn't start up when you use the Interactive Boot, the computer needs something special in the CONFIG.SYS file. Restart the computer, but when you see the message *Starting MS DOS* on-screen, press F8 rather than F5. The F8 option enables you to run individual statements in CONFIG.SYS and to not run AUTOEXEC.BAT at all. Say yes to statements that mention device drivers and memory managers. You should land back at the DOS prompt and at a place where you can start cleaning up after yourself in the AUTOEXEC.BAT file.

Where to put drivers

Are drivers added to the AUTOEXEC.BAT file or the CONFIG.SYS file, or are they just put in the DOS directory, or are they put in the application itself?

Imagine sitting in the back of a limo, and when your driver asks where you want to go, you say, "I want to go to the printer." And your driver takes you there. Well, it's the same with your computer, except that you don't get the free wet bar.

A driver is a special little software program that enables your computer to *talk* to a gadget that's connected to it. Monitors, printers, modems, CD-ROM drives, sound cards, and scanners all require what's known as *device drivers*. Drivers are kept in the computer's CONFIG.SYS file, which the computer reads every time you start the computer. The lines that have to do with device drivers begin with `DEVICE`.

The DOS directory contains drivers (filenames ending with .SYS) that DOS uses. The WINDOWS\SYSTEM directory contains drivers used by Windows and Windows-based programs (filenames ending in .DRV). Sometimes, driver files also are found in a separate program directory.

The Bottom Line

Don't worry about the device drivers too much. When you install new programs or add a different device to your computer, the drivers are added to the CONFIG.SYS file automatically.

Increasing buffers

I got my kid a new program, and it doesn't work. The troubleshooting guide suggests that I increase the buffers. Who? What? Where? When? How?

Let me guess, you bought a newspaper reporting program.

Who? You. What? *Buffers* are places in the computer's memory that hold information needed by your program. Sometimes, the program needs a bigger place to put and grab the stuff it needs — bigger than what you have set up on the computer. To make things bigger and, I hope, better for you, you need to poke around in a file called CONFIG.SYS. (That's the "where" part of your answer.) But first make a backup copy of the CONFIG.SYS file.

When? Now. How? By editing the CONFIG.SYS file. Type the following at the DOS prompt and press Enter:

```
EDIT C:\CONFIG.SYS
```

Scan the screen for a line that reads BUFFERS=.... If you find it, use the arrow keys to move the blinking underline, or *cursor*, to that line. If the BUFFERS= line isn't in the file, you need to buy a new computer. (Come on back, it was a joke.) There will be a number immediately to the right of = in the BUFFERS= line. Increase that number by 10 or 20. (Use the Back-space key to erase the old number, and then type the new number.) So BUFFERS=20 would become BUFFERS=30. Excuse me. I'd like to thank Miss Martinson (my first grade teacher) for my ability to add tens without a calculator.

If you don't have a BUFFERS line in your CONFIG.SYS file, don't fret. Use the arrow keys, insert a line — somewhere in the middle is good — and type **BUFFERS=40** there.

Because you made some changes to the CONFIG.SYS file, you need to save the changes. Press Alt+F and then S for save. Then press Alt+X to get back to the DOS prompt. Reboot the computer to make the changes take effect.

Configuration tips

I am in the process of rewriting my CONFIG.SYS and AUTOEXEC.BAT files to create multiple configurations, and I have come up with some questions. First, what is the best setting for the EMM386.EXE? Second, which applications need to have SHARE.EXE loaded during start-up? And does the VSHARE that came with Windows for Workgroups 3.11 replace SHARE.EXE in all cases?

While there are no *best* settings for EMM386 and SMARTDRV, there are many settings for each memory tool. In DOS 6 and higher, Microsoft provides MEMMAKER, which seems in almost all cases to do a very good job of detecting includes and excludes for the EMM386 line (which is the hardest part to do without a utility that is specially made for that task). Also, MEMMAKER does a good job of making the memory play nicely with Windows.

As for SMARTDRV, Microsoft has added write through as the default. It's a good thing. The only thing worth tuning up is the cache sizes. SMARTDRV has a default state that works well for most systems, but I always increase the DOS cache size. In an 8MB system, I use a DOS size of 3072. You most likely will be using 32-Bit File Access (BFA). When 32BFA is loaded for the first time, it disables SMARTDRV by reducing the Windows cache size to 128K; that change seems to work fine also. If you do not use 32BFA or are unable to use it, use a Windows cache size of 1024 for an 8MB system.

SHARE does not need to be loaded for a computer to boot, but programs themselves may require it, especially in a multitasking or task-swapping environment. SHARE limits access to files by more than one program at a time. VSHARE, in most cases, provides full SHARE functionality while Windows is running.

Commands

Fast help for DOS commands

I vaguely remember reading about a shortcut for getting the different parameters available to a DOS command without having to go into the help files. Do you have a better memory than I do, or did I just imagine it?

It's real, and rest assured that, just like your computer, you still have a little memory left. Just about every DOS command will give you a brief lesson when you type /? right after a DOS command at the DOS prompt and press Enter. For example, typing **COPY /?** at the DOS prompt and pressing Enter is like cracking open the DOS manual: you get a one-line description of what the COPY command does, plus information on what COPY needs to run. This shortcut is the one you read about. It works with almost all DOS commands.

Understanding BACKUP and RESTORE commands

If I want to copy all the files in a directory (there are 2.5MB worth) to 3$\frac{1}{2}$-inch disks, how do I deal with the message *diskette full*? I tried the COPY command without much luck. I have DOS 6.2.

I'll be gentle. All versions of MS-DOS include a backup program and a restore program. The backup program copies the information onto a floppy disk, and the restore program takes the information off the floppy disk and puts it back on the hard disk drive. DOS shrinks, or compresses, the files in the backup process, so more information fits on one floppy disk or a set of floppy disks. To make a copy of your directory, the DOS BACKUP command works swell.

Although users of DOS 6.0 and higher can use the `BACKUP` and `RESTORE` commands, the `MSBACKUP` program that comes with Versions 6.0 and higher is easier to use. `BACKUP` and `RESTORE` are not *friendly* utilities. By that I mean that they have no fancy user interface. They are command line utilities (yuck!), and a small error in typing can cause big-time troubles, ranging from simple failure all the way to overwriting files on the hard drive. When you use `BACKUP` and `RESTORE`, you need to check the spelling and structure of the commands carefully.

The `BACKUP` command is actually quite powerful. It enables you to select an entire hard drive, a single directory, files changed on or after a certain date, files in a directory, and all the subdirectories and the files below them. It enables you to add (computer geek talk for *add* is *append*) files created or changed to an existing backup, too.

To back up all the files in a single directory, type the following DOS command and press Enter:

```
BACKUP C:\BIGDIR A:
```

`BIGDIR` stands for the name of the directory that contains the files you want to copy onto floppy disks, and I've guessed that your 3½-inch floppies go in drive A.

The program may ask you to insert additional disks until the directory has been completely copied. To restore that directory and files to a hard drive, use the `RESTORE` command. This command has many options, but to restore the backup I just described, type the following DOS command and press Enter:

```
RESTORE A:\*.* C:\BIGDIR
```

`BIGDIR` is the name of the directory where you want the contents of the floppy disks to go.

Because you have MS-DOS 6.2, you can use `MSBACKUP` instead. It's pretty easy to use. The concepts are the same as with the DOS `BACKUP` and `RESTORE` commands, but `MSBACKUP` helps eliminate the guesswork. Just type **MSBACKUP** at the DOS prompt, press Enter, and follow the instructions on-screen. Or, if you have the Windows version of `MSBACKUP`, give it the ole double-click to start it up.

Getting the correct backup command

How can you make a backup if the computer won't let you? The other day, I started to back up some files with the DOS BACKUP command and received the message *Incorrect version*. Then I went to the DOS prompt and typed BACKUP/?, and I got the same message. This is the first time I've tried to make a backup since I upgraded from DOS 5.0.

Sometimes you can't back up on the information superhighway. You'll get hit by a speeding Pentium 100MHz. But it sure sounds as if the DOS 5 BACKUP file is trying to work in a DOS 6 world. The *Incorrect version* message means that you are trying to use a program that requires a version of DOS other than the one you booted from. It's not your fault, and I know it sounds silly, but that's the way it is.

You see, DOS 6 and higher include MSBACKUP, a special version of the well-known Norton Backup. The Windows version, MWBACKUP, is part of DOS 6 and higher too. Use the MSBACKUP or MWBACKUP program for your backups because they are better than the DOS 5 BACKUP command. Plus, they are easier to use and seem to be much more reliable.

But if you insist on using the BACKUP command (there's always one in every crowd), you need to get the DOS Supplemental Program disk, which contains a copy of the DOS BACKUP command that works with DOS 6.

Explaining FDISK

My friend used FDISK to erase my primary DOS partition. Then he made a new primary partition, and now DOS can't find any of my files. Where did FDISK hide the files?

As my dad used to say, "With friends like these, you don't need enemies." The files are not hidden; they are deleted. That is why whenever you use FDISK to change anything on the hard drive, it gives you a chance to back out when it asks, "Are you sure?" Apparently, your friend wasn't paying attention. Is there any way to get all those files back? Your friend can restore the files from a backup, if he has a backup. One last word: Do not delete your friend. It's against the law.

Using FDISK to help install DOS

When I try to install DOS on a used hard drive, I keep getting the error message *unable to setup DOS on your system—error in partition information.* When I use any diagnostic (PC Doctor, Disk Manager, and so on), they all say that the drive is fine, and they accurately report sectors, heads, MB, and type. When I boot up, I get the message *unable to find boot sector.* So I can't boot up, or format, or set up DOS (I've tried Versions 5.0, 6.0, 6.2, and 6.22). The hard drive is a Connor 116MB (762 cylinders, 8 heads, and 39 sectors); the computer is an ALR Powerflex with a 486DX option card. The BIOS is by Phoenix and is dated 1989. I've tried several new cables and a new controller card. I know that the drive is OK because I formatted it and loaded DOS onto it on another computer.

Wow, all you wanted to do was install DOS on a used hard drive, and now you're a computer expert. It's like trying to put gas in your car and ending up replacing the fuel pump.

Any time you get a message from DOS about a partition, your problem is nothing that any of those disk tool programs will handle. What you need is FDISK. Not to fear. FDISK came with DOS. You have it. Before using the FDISK command, back up any information you want. To use it, follow these steps:

1. Make a backup boot floppy.

2. Put FDISK.* on the floppy disk by going to the DOS directory, typing the following, and pressing Enter:

   ```
   XCOPY FDISK.* A:)
   ```

3. Boot from the floppy.

4. Run FDISK.

   You get several choices. Start by displaying current partition information. If you are installing DOS newer than Version 3.x, you most likely want one big "PRIMARY DOS" partition. So go to the menu thing that lets you change things. Tell it to delete what you've got (which is probably something weird, such as WIN NT, OS/2, or something that isn't DOS). Then tell it, yes, you really mean it. (That is, if you do. Did you back up all the stuff you care about on the disk?) Then tell it to create a new partition that's PRIMARY DOS, which should be a good, old, bootable partition.

The way that FDISK works should be pretty obvious; the most difficult thing is figuring out that you need FDISK in the first place. FDISK? I mean, really.

What is *FDISK* supposed to mean? (Well, it has to do with fixed disks, as opposed to portable disks, such as floppies, but you don't care about that. . . .) Anyway, if you get confused about FDISK, just open your good ol' DOS manual to the page the index sends you to when you look up *FDISK*. Read it twice, and then go to it.

Don't worry — you just got this drive, right? You don't have any data to lose. And you can't kill the disk with commands — you just can't. The worst you can do is erase data that you don't care about anyway.

Using FDISK/MBR

I recently got caught by a Trojan virus. When I booted up, DOS said *Non-System disk error*. If I used a boot disk and went to the C:\ prompt, I got the error message *invalid drive specification*. A friend suggested using an undocumented DOS command, FDISK/MBR, for recovery without loss of data. I tried FDISK/MBR, and it worked! What exactly does it do?

When your computer starts, it goes through a power-on self test, called a POST for short. After the POST is complete (or post-POST, as it were), the computer grabs hold of the boot sector. The boot sector is used to start the operating system (in the case of DOS, it points to the location where IO.SYS is stored). To ensure that the boot sector is, in fact, a valid boot sector, it has something like a signature stored inside. If the signature is corrupted, modified, overwritten, or missing, the master boot record (MBR) is not a *real* master boot record. Hence, the computer won't start.

Viruses can mess up the master boot record so well that the hard disk won't kick in and start. FDISK/MBR rewrites the master boot record without formatting the hard disk. In other words, it rewrites the master boot record without losing any information on the computer's hard disk.

307

If the code is the only portion of the MBR that was damaged, this repair works. If the data was destroyed, then what will happen next is uncertain. (Most security systems and encryption technologies will translate portions of the MBR, and then, by using FDISK/MBR, you will damage the MBR beyond repair in most cases.) Note that FDISK/MBR does not attempt to repair the partition tables, so if they are messed up, they will remain messed up. You were lucky.

You should now do the following:

1. Back up data files.

2. Back up program files.

3. Delete any infected files.

4. If you have a security package, diskwipe the hard drive.

5. Reload the previously infected applications, using the original installation disks.

6. Rerun your antivirus software.

7. Make friends who stay away from undocumented DOS commands.

The FDISK/MBR has been inside DOS but undocumented since DOS 5 at least and remains undocumented in the present version of DOS.

Note to Novell DOS users: NWDOS 7.0 has added an option to the menu choices for the FDISK supplied with NWDOS. That new option is rewriting the master boot record!

Understanding the PATH command

My PATH command is valid for only one directory at a time. If I type PATH C:\DOS and press Enter, my DOS commands will work correctly. However, if I type PATH C:\WINDOWS on the next line, all of a sudden it won't recognize the path to the DOS directory. How do I fix this?

Relax, all of us are on different paths. It appears that you have strayed from yours. Let me help you back. PATH tells DOS where to look for things, such as the programs that you use on your computer. When you start the computer, DOS asks, "Where am I, and where can I go?"

A line in the AUTOEXEC.BAT file answers these questions by using a PATH statement. After the PATH is set, you shouldn't need to set it again from the DOS command prompt. Here's the catch that's getting you into trouble: Every time you get on your high horse and use the PATH command at the DOS prompt, the new PATH statement that you type at the DOS prompt replaces the old PATH statement in the AUTOEXEC.BAT file that sets up the initial path.

Take a look inside the AUTOEXEC.BAT file for the PATH statement. You can see the contents of the AUTOEXEC.BAT file by typing the following at the DOS prompt and pressing Enter:

```
TYPE C:\AUTOEXEC.BAT
```

If the PATH command isn't there, or if you see PATH C:\DOS, you can solve the problem once and for all. After making a backup copy of AUTOEXEC.BAT, type the following at the DOS prompt and press Enter:

```
EDIT AUTOEXEC.BAT
```

Add the following line to the AUTOEXEC.BAT file:

```
PATH C:\;C\DOS;C:\WINDOWS
```

Save the file and reboot the computer. The computer will be back on the right path. If you ever want to see the PATH that DOS is using, just type the following at the DOS prompt and press Enter:

```
PATH
```

DOS shows you the PATH that it has stored for use.

Defining the SUBST command

I am a fan of your radio show. My whole family loves to listen to it. What's the SUBST command? I have it in my AUTOEXEC.BAT file.

That must be one interesting family. I can just imagine everyone gathering around the radio in the dark after dinner, all staring at the glowing dial.

Anyway, the SUBST command, short for substitute, enables you to call directories and subdirectories by much shorter names, kind of like nicknames. For example, perhaps you have a new great game that has the filename MYPROG.EXE, and it's in the C:\NEW\GREAT\GAMES directory. Type the command **SUBST H: C:\NEW\GREAT\GAMES** at the DOS prompt and press Enter. Then, instead of typing **C:\NEW\GREAT\GAMES\MYPROG** at the DOS prompt and pressing Enter to start the program, you can type **H:\MYPROG** at the DOS prompt and press Enter. To get to the GAMES subdirectory, all you have to type is **H:** and press Enter. You don't need to use the CD (change directory) command.

Although the SUBST command can save keystrokes, it has more downsides than benefits. Because many DOS commands and programs do not recognize these shortened directory names, you may find yourself in a real predicament. You can't use the DOS commands DISKCOPY, DISKCOMP, FDISK, PRINT, FORMAT, LABEL, BACKUP, RESTORE, MIRROR, RECOVER, and SYS while a SUBST is in effect. And if you use CD, MD, RD, APPEND, and PATH, all sorts of weird things may happen.

If you do venture into the unknown, get stuck, and want to set things straight again, just type the following at the DOS prompt and press Enter:

    SUBST X: /D

(where X is the letter you chose as the shortened name).

Oh, and say hi to the kids for me.

CHKDSK, SCANDISK, and DEFRAG

Understanding CHKDSK

CHKDSK **tells me that I have 51,007,488 bytes available on my hard disk. However, when I do a** DIR **of any directory on my hard drive, I'm told that I have 63,659,136 bytes free. Why the difference? How much space do I really have available on my disk?**

Gee, you're doing a lot of snooping around inside your computer. I hope you're not doing all of this at work.

The Bottom Line

CHKDSK's little nose isn't growing; it's telling the whole truth here. You have 51,007,488 bytes or about 52MB of space available on the hard drive. So is the DIR command a liar? Not really, and here's why: CHKDSK counts the space used by all the files on your system whether you can see them or not, but DIR tallies up only the space used by files that you can see. Yes, the computer has a few special kinds of files, called *system files* and *hidden files*. Don't go poking around to try to find them.

Your computer needs system files to crank itself into gear. If you delete or change the system files by mistake, your computer won't work properly. To protect the computer from your nose or the DOS editor when you try to stick either of them somewhere they shouldn't go, certain files are invisible. Hidden files are invisible for many of the same reasons. Some software programs create hidden files when they are running to save critical information about how they are set up. If you delete these files, the programs may stop working.

Difference between SCANDISK *and* CHKDSK

My computer friend and I have been arguing. Should I use CHKDSK or SCANDISK? What's the difference between the two, and is one better than the other?

Usually, when people argue over small things such as whether SCANDISK is better than CHKDSK, I find that they are covering the real source of anger in their relationship. You two need to talk. I've forwarded your letter to Ann Landers.

Now to answer the question. Use SCANDISK. CHKDSK has been around about as long as DOS, and SCANDISK is the new and improved version. Both CHKDSK and SCANDISK check the hard disk drive for potential problem areas. They report damaged directories, lost files, and areas on the disk that have become physically damaged and unusable by DOS. *Note:* They can't, however, fix the information in a file if the file has gone bad.

SCANDISK zooms ahead of CHKDSK in its ability to repair certain problems on the hard drive. It can perform a *surface test* on the hard drive to detect and report any physical defects in a bit more detail. SCANDISK also handles hard drives that have been squeezed or compressed. The truth is, they're both good. CHKDSK is quicker at what it does but not quite as thorough, so it will do in a pinch. If you have more time on your hands, use SCANDISK.

Difference between DEFRAG and SCANDISK

Is the DEFRAG command the same thing as SCANDISK?

No, or they would both be called DEFRAG.

SCANDISK is a disk repair program that keeps all the directories on your hard drive in working order. It also checks and keeps track of physical defects — places on the disk where you can't save information because they have gone bad.

DEFRAG organizes the information on the hard drive — like cleaning up shop. Over a period of time, files get jumbled up on the hard disk. Although DOS always seems to know where everything is, it's not a very good housekeeper. Pieces of a single file can get strewn all over the hard disk as the file grows and shrinks in size. This condition is known as *fragmentation* and is a normal part of how a computer works. Get it? Fragmentation happens and DEFRAG fixes it.

How often to run SCANDISK and DEFRAG

I am a clean fanatic. I like to keep my computer in tip-top shape. How often should I run SCANDISK and DEFRAG?

Well, if you are a clean fanatic, you probably need to run them less than you currently do.

The answer depends on how often you use your computer. Generally, you should run SCANDISK at least twice a month and whenever you suspect that anything strange is happening on the hard drive. You should always use SCANDISK before you run DEFRAG. Use the DEFRAG program when you think that things are starting to slow down (that is, when the programs you use take longer to start up than usual). You'll see an optimization number when you start DEFRAG. If this number is 90 percent or higher, DEFRAG won't really do much. Using DEFRAG between once a week and once a month is a good idea.

Now, when you say you like to keep your computer clean, does that include cleaning the hairs and dirt out of the keyboard, too?

Running SCANDISK *at start-up*

I'd like my computer to ask me if I'd like to run SCANDISK **every time I boot up. Is that possible?**

You need a life. You can't run SCANDISK once a week like the rest of us?

Hey, I need a life. I got your question and decided to write a little batch program just for fun. The batch file listed here will ask you whether you want to run SCANDISK when you start your computer. You get to say Yes or No. If you say Yes, then SCANDISK pops up on-screen. But if you don't, the computer starts up as usual.

Here's the plan: The AUTOEXEC.BAT file on your computer will have a command in it that *calls in* another file or program to do the job of running SCANDISK or not. (This batch file is the one I wrote for you.) First, make a backup copy of AUTOEXEC.BAT and then type the following at the DOS prompt and press Enter:

```
EDIT C:\AUTOEXEC.BAT
```

Add the line CALL SCAN.BAT as the first line in the AUTOEXEC.BAT file. Press Alt+F and then S for save. Then press Alt+X to get back to the DOS prompt. OK... now, type the following lines:

```
C:
CD\
```

Get ready, you're going to make your very own batch file. (Hold the excitement down.) Type the following at the DOS prompt and press Enter:

```
EDIT SCAN.BAT
```

Next, type everything that follows into the computer. It's the SCAN.BAT file.

```
@echo off
REM This batch file asks (Put Your Name Here) to run
     ScanDisk when the computer starts
CHOICE /T:N,10 Y FOR SCANDISK, N FOR NORMAL BOOT,
IF ERRORLEVEL 2 GOTO NORMAL
IF ERRORLEVEL 1 GOTO SCANDISK
REM NORMAL BOOT SECTION
:NORMAL
```

(continued)

```
GOTO END
REM END OF NORMAL BOOT SECTION
REM SCANDISK SECTION
:SCANDISK
C:\DOS\SCANDISK
GOTO END
REM END OF SCANDISK SECTION
:END
```

Press Alt+F and then S for save. Be sure that SCAN.BAT is saved in the C:\ directory. Press Alt+X to get back to the DOS prompt. Now when your computer starts, press Y to start SCANDISK or N to make the computer start as usual. Hey, I put a little timer switch in the batch file too. If you don't say Yes within a few seconds, the computer knows that you don't want to run SCANDISK.

P.S. You're welcome.

Understanding lost clusters

I ran SCANDISK, and it said that I had lost clusters. Where do these wandering souls come from, and how do I keep them from coming back?

Lost clusters are like torn-out pages from an old book. How? Come on, work with me on this. A file is like a book; the pages in a book are like pieces of a file, or *clusters*. A book is held together by a binding. A file's clusters are held together in what are called *chains.*

When a book is old, pages fall out and get lost in the attic somewhere. One day you find a page, but what book did it come from? Gadzooks, it's a page from your grandmother's tawdry diary. Well, DOS tries to follow every darn cluster on the hard disk. A cluster may be used by one file for awhile, but after you delete the file, the cluster is still out there. Say another file comes along: it needs a cluster, so it gets the cluster that was used by the first file. DOS keeps tabs on all this activity in a special area of the hard disk called the *FAT (File Allocation Table).*

Once in a while, DOS loses track of some clusters. Perhaps there was a power surge, or maybe the system was powered off or rebooted when a software program was running. Maybe the hard disk itself or the hard disk's controller is getting old. Whatever the reason, you end up with lost clusters. SCANDISK reports a lost cluster and gives it a home — in a new file.

To try to prevent lost clusters, you should do the following:

**Komando
Klues**

➤ Always exit a program to DOS before shutting off the computer.

➤ Always exit Windows before shutting off the computer.

➤ Make sure that you have both a TMP and a TEMP set statement that point to a directory that you do not use for anything but temporary files.

➤ Make sure that your grandmother keeps all her books locked in her drawer.

Guidelines for deleting .CHK files

I used the CHKDSK/F **command from the DOS prompt. I have more than 7MB of FILE000*.CHK files in my computer. Can I erase these files and recover the space? I looked at them, and I already have the files on my hard disk. All my friends say no, that I should keep them there for safekeeping.**

You run with a wild crowd, my friend. Most of the time, you can just do the big FILE*.CHK delete. But looking at the FILE*.CHK files with a text editor first is always a good idea. Because you already have the files and you don't need them, you can get rid of them to make room for some cool new software. The quickest way to delete all of these files is to take a walk on the wild side: use the DOS DELETE command with the wild-card option. To free up the 7MB, type the following at the DOS prompt and press Enter.

```
DEL C:\FILE*.CHK
```

All gone. Bye-bye. See ya.

HIMEM

Problems with HIMEM

I have the `HIMEM` **command in my CONFIG.SYS file. When my computer starts, I get an *Unreliable Memory Address in HIMEM* message. Am I doomed?**

It depends. How are other things going in your life? Hmmmm . . . toughie here. Are your SIMMs standard 30-pin, 72-pin, or 8 × 32s? I've seen problems with a mixture of 72-pin and 8 × 32s in the same bank/board. Computers generally don't seem to like the different parity/nonparity chips present.

Other than that, I'd check the SIMMs in different slots . . . perhaps run an eraser over their contacts to ensure a clean contact. When `HIMEM` reports unreliable memory, it usually means it.

What you need to do is determine what the problem is. Sometimes you only need to open the case and give the chips a push to make sure that they are snugly seated in their slots. Over time, SIMMs can become loose (techies call this *chip walk*). If that approach doesn't work, run an eraser or a cotton swab that's dipped in alcohol over the contacts.

If the computer still isn't working, remove one bank of memory and try it. If that helps, then the problem is with one or more of the chips in the bank that you removed. If removing one bank of memory doesn't help, single out the bad SIMM by swapping the chips out one at time until the computer works correctly (kind of like finding the bad light on the Christmas tree). You also can use this swapping procedure if the bad SIMM is in the group from the bank you removed. Just keep swapping until you get the error again, and you'll have the culprit. Then replace the bad SIMM with a good SIMM.

So you know, a computer checks its memory when it starts during the POST. But `HIMEM` checks it a little better. That's why memory can pass the start-up test but fail the `HIMEM` test.

Working with HIMEM.SYS

I'm getting an *unreliable memory address* message in HIMEM. **How do I fix it?**

HIMEM.SYS does a check of the physical memory when it loads. When the test is complete, HIMEM.SYS reports back to you that it's done. When HIMEM detects memory that fails its test, you get an error message about unreliable memory. Then HIMEM refuses to load into memory. Without HIMEM loaded, many other devices will refuse to load as well, and Windows will refuse to run, and then you can't type your report, which causes you to fail English, which causes your father to disown you. You need to take care of this problem right away.

Most computers have an option in the BIOS that tests the RAM as it counts it. If you have this option, enable it so that you can find out whether the BIOS test agrees with the HIMEM test. If both agree, you probably need a new RAM chip. Take the computer to a service center and have them test the memory chips. Such a test is the best way to find out which chip, or row of chips, may be bad.

Using HIMEM *modifiers*

I am working with my computer's memory. I have some vague recollection that there are switches for the HIMEM **command. What are the switches?**

Vague recollection? It sounds as if you should work on *your* memory before you work on the computer's. HIMEM.SYS has little in the way of switches (I like to call them *modifiers*) that can be added. In most systems, you don't need to play around with the modifiers. But for the record, here they are, along with brief explanations:

➤ /A20CONTROL:ON|OFF — The default is ON, which means that if this modifier is not part of the HIMEM.SYS statement, you get the effect of /A20CONTROL:ON. You typically use this switch (set to OFF) only if some other device has already taken control of the A20 line and you need to disable HIMEM's attempts to do so. The way that you know that you need to use this modifier is that when HIMEM tries to load, you get an error message saying that the A20 line is already enabled. This setting is rarely used.

➤ /CPUCLOCK:ON|OFF — The default is OFF, which means that without having this modifier as part of the HIMEM.SYS statement, you get the effect of /CPUCLOCK:OFF. You should use this modifier (set to OFF) only if the computer is slower with HIMEM loaded than it is without it loaded. On some systems, HIMEM affects the clock speed, but this situation is rare. (This clock is not the one that keeps the time of day!) This setting is also rarely used.

➤ /EISA — This switch does not have a default, which means that if you don't add EISA to the HIMEM statement, there is no memory effect or lack of effect relating to it. This switch is used only on EISA bus machines that have 16MB of RAM or more. Most computers do not have an EISA bus. If you have one, you probably know that you do, because everything costs more if it is for an EISA, and parts for it usually have to be ordered. Computers that are PCI, VESA local bus (VLB), MCA, or ISA are not EISA. This modifier is rarely used.

➤ /HMAMIN=*x* — The default value for *x* is 0, and valid numbers to use in place of the *x* are 0 through 63. If you have the statement DOS=HIGH in CONFIG.SYS, then this modifier is useless for you. You won't usually find this one around either.

➤ /INT15=xxxx — The default value for *x* is 0, and valid numbers to use in place of the *x* are 64 through 65535. You use this switch to reserve a specific amount of extended memory for old programs that use DOS Interrupt 15h for extended memory instead of using XMS. You won't use this modifier; don't try to understand it.

➤ /NUMHANDLES=x — The default value for *x* is 32, and valid numbers to use in place of the *x* are 1 through 128. The default works fine in almost all cases, and this switch is typically used only in response to an error message from an application about not having enough XMS handles. Each reserved handle uses 6 bytes of memory, so some memory management guru may have added /NUMHANDLES=1 to save 186 bytes of memory. Saving that amount of memory is probably not worth the errors that you will encounter, so if that is the case, remove the modifier or increase it to 32.

➤ /MACHINE:xxxx — Here is the first switch that you may run across. This modifier is used for certain hardware that HIMEM needs to change the way it loads. You know that you need this modifier if you get the following error message from HIMEM as it tries to load: *Warning! Unable to control A20 line*. Usually, you can call a hardware supplier to get the correct setting.

➤ /SHADOWRAM:ON|OFF — Informs HIMEM whether to disable shadow RAM. The default is on. Unless you get errors at boot, this switch is probably best left for DOS trivia experts. Do you think there's a market for a Trivial Pursuit game that deals in esoteric computer information? It would have to be on-screen, of course, and probably on-line too.

➤ /VERBOSE:ON|OFF — The default is OFF, and this one is fun to use but slows down the boot process a bit. Try it for a while to see a great deal of information about the memory and HIMEM as the memory is loading.

Understanding handler codes

I am having trouble setting up DOS 6.0 on my computer: I keep getting an error message that says *Error in line A20 not loading HIMEM.SYS*. I also am unable to install Windows: I get the message *bad or missing C:\DOS\HIMEM.SYS*. I checked the CONFIG.SYS file, and it does have Device=C:\DOS \HIMEM.SYS**.**

The little A20 line is on vacation. The A20 is actually a line or wire in the computer that's connected to the CPU chip and allows access to the HMA (*high memory area*). The error *Error in line A20* or *Unable to control A20* means that HIMEM could not correctly detect and control the A20. The following table lists what are called *handler codes,* with the most commonly used ones highlighted.

IBM PC/AT users need to check their user's manual or call the computer's manufacturer for the proper handler code. To use one of these handler codes, add the machine switch to the HIMEM.SYS line in the CONFIG.SYS, as shown in the example that follows. Before you add the machine switch, the HIMEM.SYS line looks like this:

```
DEVICE=C:\HIMEM.SYS
```

After you add the switch, it looks like this:

```
DEVICE=C:\HIMEM.SYS /MACHINE:12
```

Before making any changes to the CONFIG.SYS file, make a backup of the file and then type the following at the DOS prompt and press Enter:

```
EDIT CONFIG.SYS
```

Handler Codes

Code	Number	Computer Type
at	**1**	**IBM PC/AT**
ps2	2	IBM PS/2
pt1cascade	3	Phoenix Cascade BIOS
hpvectra	4	HP Vectra A & A+
att6300plus	5	AT&T 6300
acer1100	6	Acer 1100
toshiba	7	Toshiba 1600 & 1200XE
wyse	8	Wyse 12.5MHz 286
tulip	9	Tulip SX
zenith	10	Zenith BIOS
at1	**11**	**IBM PC/AT (alternative delay)**
at2	**12**	**IBM PC/AT (alternative delay)**
css	12	CSS Labs
at3	**13**	**IBM PC/AT (alternative delay)**
philips	13	Philips
fasthp	14	HP Vectra
IBM 7552	15	IBM 7552 Industrial Computer
BULL MIORAL	16	Bull Mioral 60
DELL	17	DELL XBios

Make your changes, save the file, and reboot the computer so that the changes will take effect.

Komando Klues

As a last note — and this may sound a bit bizarre — if all else fails, go back to having no handler code in the HIMEM line and try a different keyboard. The keyboard itself has a chip that is used to activate the A20 address, and I have seen this keyboard swap fix an occasional error that nothing else seemed to touch. If that method fails, go back to a typewriter and file cabinet. Computers are just not for you.

MEMMAKER

Understanding the MEM command

I have 8MB of RAM installed on my computer. When I run the MEM **command at the DOS prompt when no programs are running, I get a report that I have only 5.3MB available.**

Mary had a little RAM

Whose fleece was white as snow.

She bought 8MB, now has 5.3.

Oh, where did the little RAM go?

Komando Klues

Here's the secret. Although you bought only one kind of memory for your computer, you actually have at least two types of memory. The computer's hardware (all those little whatchamacallits inside the big box) sets up two types of memory. If you have more than 1MB, the hardware sees three types of memory. Then, depending on certain commands in the CONFIG.SYS file, three more types of RAM may be available. Each type of memory uses RAM in a slightly different way, which affects how much memory you end up with. The following table lists the types of memory and how they are used.

Types of Memory and Their Use

Memory Type	Area of RAM	Used for
Conventional	0 – 640K	DOS and programs
Adapter area	641 – 1024K	ROM from controller and adapter cards
HMA	1025 – 1088K	Area into which DOS loads high
UMB	Somewhere in the adapter area	Devices that load high
XMS	1089 – the end of installed RAM	Windows and some programs
EMS	Access is in the UMB area but EMS is actually in XMS	Programs

321

The Bottom Line

Now about that 5.3MB from the 8MB: The first megabyte is spoken for by the DOS program area and the adapter area, so that leaves 7MB. Next, another 64K is taken by the HMA, leaving 6.94MB. Hmmmm, I bet that SmartDrive loads and takes its cache area from XMS. And I bet that in an 8MB system, SmartDrive's default cache size is 2MB. Hence, this leaves you with about 5MB. Close enough. I have another 1,000 questions to answer in this book.

Tracking errors in MEMMAKER

I can't seem to get MEMMAKER **to work. Every time I try, it freezes, and I have to reboot. My friend claims that it is because my AUTOEXEC.BAT file runs another batch file. Is he crazy or what?**

Your friend may indeed be crazy. I cannot determine his mental condition based on his opinion about the AUTOEXEC.BAT file. However, if he talks only about the AUTOEXEC.BAT file, then rest assured, he's crazy.

Crazy or not, your friend is on the right track. Batch files, which are just a bunch of DOS commands run back-to-back, can call on other batch files that they run. AUTOEXEC.BAT is just a batch file that runs when you boot the computer.

A batch file can call another batch file in two ways. The first way enables you to put just the name of the batch file that you want to call on a line by itself. So in a batch file named FIRST.BAT, you have a line that reads SECOND.BAT. If SECOND.BAT finishes and doesn't have a special command that says to go back to FIRST.BAT, then FIRST.BAT is finished, too, because the rest of it won't run. The second way is much safer: you put CALL at the beginning of the line with the batch file's name on it. So CALL SECOND.BAT will run SECOND.BAT until it's finished, and then control goes back to FIRST.BAT. Then FIRST.BAT can carry on with the rest of its commands. This method is the proper way to run one batch file from another.

Because MEMMAKER needs to process anything that is started in the AUTOEXEC.BAT, including other batch files, make sure that every line that starts another batch file has CALL at the beginning of it to keep MEMMAKER from stopping dead in its tracks. Call me an old-fashioned type of gal, but I always like to use the REM statement with all batch files inside the AUTOEXEC.BAT file before running MEMMAKER, just to be on the safe side. When your computer sees the letters *REM*, short for *remark*, and then a space before a statement in your AUTOEXEC.BAT file or CONFIG.SYS file, the computer ignores the line.

MEMMAKER *versus QEMM*

Which is better, MEMMAKER or QEMM? My friends tell me I'm stupid for staying with MEMMAKER. What do you think?

Your friends have a way with words. Actually, I think that you and your friends are projecting your true anger toward each other onto MEMMAKER. All of you need to turn off your machines and talk.

Back in the DOS 5.0 heyday, the DOS memory utilities were marginal at best. Almost anyone who tried Quarterdeck's QEMM instead of the DOS utilities voted for QEMM. Microsoft upped the ante in DOS 6 and higher with a slew of memory-managing utilities.

DOS is quite the little admiral in commanding memory now. It includes a memory manager and an *automatic* configuration utility called MEMMAKER. (Bow your head in silence.) As a result, QEMM and all other add-on memory managers have worked even harder at squeezing every available bit of memory out of a computer.

For example, the QEMM 7.0x series has advanced features, which MEMMAKER doesn't include, for getting additional UMBs and increasing the lower 640K's free memory. QEMM is up to Version 7.5 (at the time of this writing), and Quarterdeck promises many new and exciting features in versions to come. Most users, however, do not need add-on memory products. MEMMAKER gives them some degree of relief from singing the out-of-memory blues.

The Bottom Line

Should you use a third-party memory management program? If MEMMAKER works, stick with it. Save your money. But if you still need that little bit extra, QEMM is worth a try. After all, it is one of the top add-on memory managers.

Troubleshooting MEMMAKER compatibility

I have a Conner 1.08GB hard disk formatted with Disk Manager (Ontrack). Ever since I installed the new drive, I have been unable to run MEMMAKER**. I get as far as the reboot, and then my machine stops at the *Starting MS DOS* statement. I have to copy the AUTOEXEC.BAT and CONFIG.SYS files from the backup in order to go back to the original start-up.**

MEMMAKER is not 100 percent reliable or 100 percent compatible with all software drivers. But I guess you don't need me to tell you that. You need me to tell you this: Many of the things MEMMAKER does, you can do yourself without turning over control to the computer and having it determine what the best configuration is. It's best to follow simple trial-and-error techniques, remembering to load devices high that can be loaded high and loading the larger drivers first so that smaller fragments of contiguous memory are still available for the smaller drivers.

MEMMAKER and mouse driver

I tried to load the mouse driver high, but my computer is not cooperating. The MEM **command shows that I have enough upper memory left, so what is the problem?**

You've been caught in a trap set by a mouse.

Mouse drivers, like all other device programs that run in memory, carry excess baggage when they start up. Because the program doesn't know which features it needs to keep in memory so that you can use the device, it assumes at the beginning that it needs to keep everything.

After the mouse driver program knows how the mouse is configured or set up, it can discard the features that aren't going to be used. To determine what features it can get rid of, it looks at, or *reads,* a configuration file that you help make when you install the mouse drivers. Thus, it frees up some memory for your computer to use.

Try running MEMMAKER with different options than you have used in the past. Sometimes, choosing different options opens up larger sections of upper memory. A quick way to increase the number and size of these memory blocks is to answer no to the question *Do you use any programs that require the use of EMS?* EMS is a type of memory that is above and beyond the basic 640K found in most PCs. Usually, only high-end graphics programs or games use EMS memory. Unless you're absolutely sure that your software needs EMS memory, don't use it because EMS likes to borrow UMBs. By saying no to this question, you save yourself 64K of memory, and that should be enough to run the mouse. I have yet to see a mouse that didn't fit into a 64K UMB.

Caching

Working with caches

I recently added a caching controller that has 4MB of RAM on board. Can I save some conventional memory and do away with SmartDrive?

Cash by any other name is *cache.* If you have 4MB of RAM on the controller, then you have what is called a *hardware cache* and, yes, you can do away with SMARTDRV. Doing so will free up memory both in conventional memory — the first 640K of memory — and in extended memory (XMS), where the cache actually loads.

The new caching controllers are getting more and more popular. These little gadgets speed up certain functions that your computer performs, such as reading and writing files to and from the hard disk. So more space is free. That's my gift to you. Merry XMS!

Komando Klues

To those of you who are running Windows on computers that have less than 8MB of memory, adding RAM to the motherboard will benefit you more than any amount of memory on a caching controller. If you do not use SMARTDRV, remember that you will not be able to cache things such as floppy drives and CD-ROM drives with the caching controller.

Getting around caching

The program wants me to disable disk caching such as SmartDrive, but I don't know how. Be gentle. I'm new to this junk.

Junk?! Please, I ask you not to speak that way. This junk is my career.

It's a little weird for a program to make such a demand because many programs actually work better with a cache. Oh well, there's always one bad apple, or PC for that matter.

I wouldn't get rid of caching altogether, however. I'd opt for something called the *Interactive Boot,* which is part of DOS 6.0 and later (or IBM PC-DOS 6.1 and 6.3 as well as Novell DOS 7.0). The Interactive Boot enables you to pick the lines in the AUTOEXEC.BAT file that you want to use when you start the computer. Like, wow! SMARTDRV is started from the AUTOEXEC.BAT file, so we have a match.

Using the Interactive Boot is easy. When you see *Starting MS DOS* on-screen when you start the computer, press F8. DOS asks you to say yes or no to each line of the CONFIG.SYS file and then gives you the option to not run AUTOEXEC.BAT at all. Say no at this point to have the SMARTDRV cache turned off.

Using disk caching to improve performance

My computer is running a little slower since I compressed the drive by using the DOS compression utility. How can I speed up DoubleSpace?

You can speed up DoubleSpace somewhat by using disk caching. SmartDrive is a fast and reliable cache that works well with compressed drives. SmartDrive isn't always so smart, though. It needs to be told to cache only the physical drive. If you use SmartDrive on a DoubleSpace or DriveSpace drive, you get an error message when the computer tries to load the cache.

To cache a DoubleSpace or DriveSpace drive, you first need to identify the host drive letter. If you're not sure what it is, type the following at the DOS prompt and press Enter. This command gives you a mapping of the drive letters and host drives.

```
DBLSPACE /LIST
```

Armed with this information, you need to tell SMARTDRV to cache only the host and not the compressed drive. Make a backup of the AUTOEXEC.BAT file and use the DOS EDIT command to add to or modify the following line in the AUTOEXEC.BAT file:

```
SMARTDRV /X C- H+
```

Save the changes and reboot your computer to make them take effect.

There is no such thing as a free lunch, and compression is no exception. When you get from 50 percent to 150 percent additional disk space for *free,* there is a cost. If your computer is processor-challenged, meaning a 386DX or lower, the additional work imposed by the compression/ decompression cycles will slow down the system noticeably. Take a peek at the earlier questions in this chapter for a little more information on CPUs and hard drives with compression.

 Caching your CD-ROM

I have DOS 6, so why won't SmartDrive cache my CD-ROM drive?

Gee, it's not such a SMARTDRV after all. Well, you can show it a thing or two. First, check which version of SMARTDRV is running. It should be the one that came with DOS 6.2. If you run Windows, the version of SMARTDRV may be out of date. Check the AUTOEXEC.BAT file for a line that uses SMARTDRV from the WINDOWS directory. *Note:* Older versions of SMARTDRV do not come equipped with CD-ROM caching.

You may need to back up AUTOEXEC.BAT and change it to use the right SMARTDRV program. Check the options that SMARTDRV is using to start up. If you see /U on its command line in AUTOEXEC.BAT, then CD-ROM caching has been shut off or disabled. Remove the /U. If the SMARTDRV line appears before the MSCDEX line in AUTOEXEC.BAT, there will be no caching of CD-ROMs. When you load SMARTDRV, it sets up caching for all drives that DOS knows about at the time, so until the MSCDEX line runs and gives the CD-ROM a drive letter (D or E, for example), the CD-ROM doesn't exist in the DOS world. You need to put the MSCDEX line before the one that starts up SMARTDRV.

Compression

 Backing up a compressed hard drive

How do I back up a compressed hard drive? Are there any catches? Do I just say, "Back up Drive H," the name of my compressed drive, or what?

Simply put, yes. When I talk about *compression,* I am referring to any program such as DoubleSpace, DriveSpace, or Stacker because they all do pretty much the same thing: squeeze information to a fraction of its original size. To back up a system with or without compressed drives, you should do a complete backup of the drives that contain the program, configuration, and data files that you want to save.

Compression adds one or more drive letters to the system, so on a system with only a drive C, the letter for the new drive will be another letter — *H,* in your case, for example. All programs and data will be on the compressed drive H, as well as on drive C. Drive C is known as the *host drive* because it holds the compressed drive (really just another special kind of file on the hard drive). On drive C, you will find a small DOS directory, a few files in the root (C:\), and, if you use Stacker, a small Stacker directory with a few files.

All the files on the host drive are also duplicated on the compressed drive, except for a few files used by the compressed drive (DBLSPACE.000, DRVSPACE.000, or STACVOL.DSK, depending on which disk compression program you use). If you back up the host drive as well as the larger compressed drive, you back up files that are duplicated on the compressed drive and also the container file (often referred to as the *Compressed Volume File,* or *CVF*). A CVF is typically quite large; in fact, it may exceed 90 percent of the drive's size, so both the backup time and the amount of backup media would increase. I know few users who enjoy making the backup procedure longer than necessary.

Using DoubleSpace

I use DOS 6 at my office. Will DoubleSpace prevent me from bringing files home to work on if my home DOS version does not utilize DoubleSpace?

It depends. Probably. I guess that you could. (Look at that. One question, three answers. Does this mean that I can skip the next two questions?) Odds are, you shouldn't have a problem as long as — here's the catch, so pay attention — you copy your office files to a normal *uncompressed* floppy disk. But if you compressed the floppy disk at your office using DoubleSpace, then, no, you can't use the files at home. You need DoubleSpace on your home computer to use a floppy disk that is compressed with DoubleSpace. As a side note, Stacker has the ability (starting in Version 3.0) to make compressed floppies that can be accessed for reads and writes on computers that do not have Stacker installed. Go figure.

Komando
Klues

In almost every instance, the terms DoubleSpace and DriveSpace can be interchanged. Microsoft's compression utilities are nearly identical; the only difference is the version of MS-DOS with which they are packaged.

Finding the compression ratio

How can I tell what my computer's DriveSpace or DoubleSpace compression ratio is? I looked all over and couldn't find it anywhere.

Did you try under the bed?

Both DriveSpace and DoubleSpace have handy-dandy menus. Just type **DBLSPACE** (for DOS 6.0 through DOS 6.21) or **DRVSPACE** (for DOS 6.22) at the DOS prompt and press Enter. To get information about a compressed drive, choose Drive from the choices in the menu bar. When the next menu drops down, choose Info. The piece of information that you want (the compression ratio) is shown on-screen.

If you're a C:\> prompt type of person, type the following at the DOS prompt and press Enter to get the compression ratio:

```
DBLSPACE/INFO C:
```

To get nitty-gritty details on a file or directory, use the /C switch with the DIR command. That switch tells the DIR command to display compression information as well as the other file statistics that you are used to seeing.

Troubleshooting DoubleSpace command

Drive C is too fragmented to resize. What does this DoubleSpace error message mean in English, and how do I work around it?

Your computer's hard drive is like a big drawer that holds many pieces of paper. After a while, the drawer gets a little messy. You take things out of manila folders, put some things back in the wrong folders, and lo and behold, the day comes when you need to reorganize everything again. Well, fragmentation is like a very disorganized drawer — perhaps too disorganized for DoubleSpace's liking. But cleaning out the computer's drawer is much easier than cleaning the one in your desk. Why? Because you won't have to decide whether you should finally throw out those 1980 Pink Floyd ticket stubs.

When things get fragmented on the hard drive, you can use DEFRAG, a utility that DOS provides for cleaning up shop. DEFRAG defragments files and directories on the hard drive and reorganizes them into a neater package. To organize your hard disk's files, type the following at the DOS prompt and press Enter:

```
DEFRAG C: /F/H
```

Komando Klues

A word to the wise: Be sure not to run any tools such as MIRROR or IMAGE before or after you reboot because the files that these two animals create will cause the same error message.

Compression effect on computer speed

I'm in desperate need of more hard disk space, but I don't want to compromise my computer's performance to get more space. It's important to me that my computer runs fast. If I use DriveSpace or Stacker, will my programs run slow?

Where are you going in such a hurry? Sit down. Relax. Play a game of computer golf and come back to me. I'll wait. . . .

Didn't help? OK. The computer's processor plays a much bigger role in performance than the hard drive does. But you have a point. The time it takes to load a program and keep it running smoothly can be affected by the hard disk's compression. Still, if you have a fast processor and a reasonably fast hard drive, you shouldn't see too much of a change just because you compress the hard disk.

If I were pressed to define processor types and speeds of hard drives that are *fast*, I would say that a fast processor (for this purpose) is a 386DX 33 or higher and a hard drive that has an access time of 16 milliseconds or lower.

Here is the scoop on speed and compression in general:

Komando
Klues

➤ Most computers in use today have a fairly fast processor.

➤ Most hard drives in use today have fast access times.

➤ Processor time is faster than hard drive access time.

➤ Compressed information occupies less physical space for the same amount of information (usually half as much space). Remember this fact and follow me on this next thought. Reading less physical area of the disk (one of the slowest parts of computer) plus decompressing it in the CPU (one of the fastest parts of the computer) usually takes less time than reading more physical area (one of the slowest parts of the computer) and not spending any time in the CPU.

Defining actual compression ratios

How come DoubleSpace didn't double my space? Is Microsoft lying again?

Gee, are you just a little angry? Why was your letter written in blood?

Disk compression utilities are often incorrectly called *disk doublers.* They are really just information or data compression utilities. Your hard disk drive doesn't get bigger — your data gets smaller.

The truth is that actual mileage may vary, depending on whether your hard disk truly doubles in size by using a compression utility. The type of information contained on your hard disk has a great deal to do with the compression ratio. For example, graphics, program files, and other files compressed with PKZIP (referred to as *ZIP files*) are already compressed, and as a result, no additional compression is gained. But you can get a 4 to 1 compression ratio for documents, spreadsheet files, and database files.

Guidelines for uncompressing drives

I think I blew it this time. How do I use the DBLSPACE/UNCOMPRESS **command in DOS 6.22 if I have more files than will fit on my drive uncompressed?**

You said it. You took a five-gallon pail and found a way to get ten gallons of water into it. Basically, DOS 6.2 will figure out that you have too many files and give you an error message telling you that you cannot uncompress the drive while it is filled to the brim. You can remove enough files from the compressed drive so that the remaining files fit on the uncompressed drive. However, I'd be more inclined to leave the disk compressed, assuming that there aren't many traumas lurking in the midst.

Don't push the panic button just yet. I have to guess that you have some reason to uncompress the drive. Did you buy a better computer with a bigger hard disk? Are you adding another hard disk to your computer or replacing the hard disk that is in the computer? If so, your best bet is to make a backup of the compressed drive and then restore the information on the new hard disk. Be sure that the new hard disk is a little bigger than the current compressed hard disk. Check the compression ratio, and you'll see a number, 2:1, for example (or something a little higher or a little lower). A ratio of 2:1 tells you that if the hard disk you have now is 100MB, you need 200MB to restore the information. See, I can multiply without using a computer. What a gal!

Unexplained Files

Finding hidden files

When I run CHKDSK, **it says that I have 12MB in five hidden files. I ran** SCANDISK, **but the hidden files are still there. How can I see the hidden files and then get rid of them? I want more hard disk space so that my wife will leave me alone. She keeps asking me to take my architectural drawing software off the computer to make room for her software.**

Be cool. Marriages have ended over hard drive space. And if you divorce, she gets half your software. The solution: Buy your wife a computer that's all her own.

As for you, leave those hidden files alone. You shouldn't mess with them — that's why they're hidden. All versions of MS-DOS have two hidden files in the main C:\ root directory, and DOS 6.x and later have at least three hidden files. If you use compression software, more hidden files lurk on the hard disk. And a permanent swap file in Windows is yet another hidden file.

Fooling around with hidden files is dangerous. The following table lists hidden files that may be in your computer.

Hidden Files

Filename	Purpose	DOS Version
IO.SYS	Boot file needed to start DOS	All, 1.0 through 6.22
IBMIO.COM	Boot file needed to start DOS	All, 1.0 through 7.0; IBM, DR, and Novell DOS
MSDOS.SYS	Boot file needed to start DOS	All, 1.0 through 6.22
IBMDOS.COM	Boot file needed to start DOS	All, 1.0 through 7.0; IBM, DR, and Novell DOS
DBLSPACE.BIN	Preloading compression driver	MS-DOS 6.x, IBM PC-DOS 6.1 through 6.3
STACKER.BIN	Preloading compression driver	Novell DOS 7.0
DBLSPACE.xxx	Compressed Volume File	MS-DOS 6.x, IBM PC-DOS 6.1 through 6.3
SSTACVOL.xxx	Compressed Volume File	Novell DOS 7.0
386SPART.PAR	Permanent Windows swap file	All, when running Windows with a permanent swap file

To see the hidden files in the C:\ root directory, type the following at the DOS prompt and press Enter:

```
DIR C:/AH
```

Now that you can see the hidden files, forget you ever saw them.

Unknown batch files

I have mysterious batch files appearing in my root directory, and I don't know where they are coming from. They all have names similar to B546.BAT. Do I have a computer virus?

Files that appear out of nowhere are kind of like poltergeists. Makes you wonder who came up with the idea of naming batch files with a .BAT extension. Well, short of chasing ghosts and goblins out of your computer, better down-to-earth cures and scientific methods are available to eradicate the problem.

Your mysterious batch files don't sound like the work of a virus. Computer viruses usually destroy files instead of creating batch files. But running a virus-scanning program on your system certainly isn't a bad idea.

Next, use DOS editor to take a look inside the batch files. Type **EDIT B546.BAT** at the DOS prompt and press Enter and look for any DOS commands, files with an .EXE or .COM extension (these files normally start a software program), or directory names. Program filenames and directory names are a good clue to get to the source of which program may have created a batch file.

If you are still in the dark about these files, copy the batch files to a floppy disk. Then delete the questionable batch files from your hard disk drive.

Leave the AUTOEXEC.BAT file alone, because this batch file helps your computer work. Reboot your system and run a few programs. If everything seems OK, then you can safely delete those batch files.

Just so you know, the following types of software programs sometimes create batch files on a computer without first asking your permission:

> ➤ Games
> ➤ Programs that install or set up new software on the computer
> ➤ Older (that is, really old) programs that don't know what subdirectories are
> ➤ Programs that use what's known as *copy protection schemes* to keep people from making copies of the programs illegally

If you're up for an adventure, be brave. Run one of those batch files and see where you land.

What are .TMP files?

I was snooping around in my computer's directories and found bunches (14MB) of files with the .TMP extension. Where do these files come from, and can I get rid of them?

Files that came out of nowhere? Makes you feel as if your computer is seeing other operators on the side, doesn't it? Do you feel cheated on? Is that why you're snooping through directories?

Software programs create certain files that are needed for the programs to work. Most of the time, these annoying TEMP files are not permanent files; instead, they exist only when the program is in use. Usually, when you're done using a software program, the TEMP files go to the great cosmic garbage dump. You don't have to worry about getting rid of them because the programs that make and use them do the job for you before they finish running.

Sometimes, though, the computer may lock up while a software program is still running, and you have to reboot the computer to regain control of it. Or you may turn off the computer without exiting a software program. These scenarios don't give a software program the chance to clean up after itself. The result is TEMP files that have no home but take up space on the hard disk.

Generally, you can safely delete TEMP files. Some programs are terrible housekeepers, and you may see more and more TEMP files appearing over time. But don't delete any TEMP files while a DOS program or Windows is running: you may get rid of something that's important. Also, if you're not sure what's inside a TEMP directory, check the file's date and time; they should give you a clue about which program you were using when the file was created.

It's a good idea to set up a special TEMP file holding area called — come on, guess — a TEMP directory. If you don't have a TEMP directory, you can create one by typing the following at the DOS prompt and pressing Enter:

```
MKDIR C:\TEMP
```

Make a backup copy of AUTOEXEC.BAT because you need to change its contents. You need to add a line that tells the computer to put all the TEMP files in one place, the TEMP directory. To change the AUTOEXEC.BAT file's contents, type the following at the DOS prompt and press Enter:

```
EDIT C:\AUTOEXEC.BAT
```

Take a look in the file for a line that has SET in it. It should be in the middle of the AUTOEXEC.BAT file. Add or change the SET statement in AUTOEXEC.BAT so that it reads like this:

```
SET TEMP=C:\TEMP
```

And add the following line to catch any programs that may use TMP to look for TEMP directories:

```
SET TMP=C:\TEMP
```

After you put all the TEMP files in one place, you can track them down and delete them more easily.

Deleting TEMP files

Is there a way to program my computer so that it automatically deletes TEMP files whenever I start it? I do it myself, but I want the computer to do the job for me.

You could hire a temp to do it. Ha, ha. I just kill myself. Although the computer can delete TEMP files for you, I don't recommend the big automatic delete because you just never know. . . . Then again, I've never wanted a TEMP file that I've erased back.

To automatically delete TEMP files when you start the computer, you need to add a line to the AUTOEXEC.BAT file. (You know the rule: make a copy of the AUTOEXEC.BAT file before you make any changes.) Type the following at the DOS prompt and press Enter:

```
EDIT AUTOEXEC.BAT
```

Add the following line somewhere near the middle of the AUTOEXEC.BAT file.

```
ECHO Y | DEL C:\TEMP\*.*
```

The ECHO Y part of the statement automatically answers yes for you when DEL asks whether you are sure that you want to delete all files in this directory. Save the file, and the next time you turn on the computer, away go TEMP files into the intergalactic bit bucket. In the old west, it was called a *bittoon*.

336

CHKLIST.MS files

Where do CHKLIST.MS files come from? I have hundreds of them all over my hard disk, like a bad rash. My friend deleted his, and things are working just fine. He wants me to do the same.

Don't! Get a new friend instead.

Microsoft's Anti-Virus software makes the CHKLIST.MS files so it can figure out unauthorized changes made by viruses. Every time you run Detect or Detect and Clean, Anti-Virus checks out the CHKLIST.MS files that contain information. If it finds changes in the file size, date, DOS attributes, and so on of the executable files, it asks you to give the okeydokey to the changes.

If you wipe out the CHKLIST.MS files, Anti-Virus is outta luck because it doesn't have any reference points to run with for the next scan. So leave those little puppies alone. They don't take up much space on the hard drive; they provide a good degree of protection; and the next time Anti-Virus scans for viruses, it will overwrite them with new CHKLIST.MS files.

Troubleshooting

Diagnostic tools

What's inside my computer? (Actually, what I'm trying to ask is, how can I tell how much RAM or disk space I have or what kind of video card I have, short of taking off the cover and looking inside?)

Don't worry. You don't have to take a wrench to your computer to find out how much power you have inside it; special programs can reveal what's inside. Norton Utilities, PC Tools, and WinSleuth Gold Plus are among the more popular powerful snooping tools, and if you subscribe to any of the popular on-line computer services, you'll find numerous programs under shareware library categories such as PC Tools and System Utilities.

337

In addition, Microsoft has included a fine utility called MSD (Microsoft Diagnostics) with Windows 3.1 and with DOS since Version 6.0. I often refer to MSD reports as "More than you ever wanted to know about your computer and then some." The amount of information is overwhelming, especially to newcomers in the PC crowd. Give MSD a shot by going to the DOS prompt and typing **MSD** and pressing Enter. Don't use MSD through Windows, though, because you may get the wrong information.

All you asked was how to find out how much memory (RAM) you have, how much disk space you have, and so on. It doesn't sound as if you want to earn an engineering degree or find out who did what to an interrupt vector. Fortunately, your computer tells you quite a bit about itself automatically, and DOS shows you the rest if you know where to look beyond the MSD report.

➤ *How much RAM does your computer have?* The amount of RAM is one of the things the computer stores and checks each time it starts up. The boot (start-up routine) counts each itsy-bitsy byte of RAM installed and compares this number to the amount of RAM that's inside the computer. Watch next time you start your computer. You'll see the RAM count up on-screen. If you don't see it, try again, and look all over the screen. Listen closely, too — you'll probably hear a ticking sound. Divide the memory counted by 1,024 and round up to the next whole number to get the total RAM in the computer. Users of DOS 6.0 and higher can type **MEM** at a DOS prompt and press Enter to get a nice display that includes the total amount of memory.

➤ *How much disk space do you have?* When the computer is booted and running, type **DIR** at the DOS prompt and press Enter. After the scrolling list of the computer's directories stops, you see a line that reads something such as 261,861,376 bytes total space. Divide this number by 1,024. If my calculator didn't fail me, in this example the computer has 255.7MB of hard disk space to fill up with cool software.

➤ *What kind of video card do you have?* All video cards store important details about themselves and show their vital statistics when you turn on the computer. Just watch the screen. You should see the name of the video card's manufacturer, the amount of video memory, and then some.

Fixing a faulty environment

Help! I have a bad environment. When I run MSD, I get a message that says *Environment StringIs Invalid TEMP=C:\DOS;C:\WINDOWS TEMP*. Now what do I do?

You need to recycle the computer's environment, but first take a look at the environment from a program's point of view. Almost all programs make changes to the AUTOEXEC.BAT file when you first install them or set them up on the system. One command line in particular that the programs add is SET. This line tells a program where to find certain information, including something known as a *working* or *temporary* file directory, which stores information while the program runs. Most programs expect to find a working directory by checking either a TEMP or TMP environment variable. The SET command is responsible for *setting up* TEMP and TMP with a directory name.

Having TEMP and TMP working correctly reduces the risk that a program will damage files in any other directories. Because the program is using only this TEMP or TMP working directory, having this directory also protects against losing information should the system lock up. Also, some programs are not good about cleaning up after themselves, and having a TEMP or TMP directory makes it easy to remove annoying little files that just take up space in a directory listing.

If TEMP or TMP is not set, then programs often use the DOS directory. Why DOS? Well, just about every computer has DOS on the hard drive, so it's the only place that programs can count on being there.

If you don't have a TEMP directory, you can create one by typing the following at the DOS prompt and pressing Enter:

```
MKDIR C:\TEMP
```

Make a backup copy of AUTOEXEC.BAT because you're going to change its contents. You need to add a line that tells the computer to put all the TEMP files in one place, the TEMP directory. To change the AUTOEXEC.BAT file's contents, type the following at the DOS prompt and press Enter:

```
EDIT C:\AUTOEXEC.BAT
```

Take a look in AUTOEXEC.BAT for a line that has SET in it. Add or change the SET statement so that it reads like this:

```
SET TEMP=C:\TEMP
```

And add this line to catch any programs that may use TMP to look for TEMP directories:

```
SET TMP=C:\TEMP
```

Save the file and reboot. You are probably getting the message about an invalid environment because your SET statement for the TEMP variable looks like this:

```
SET TEMP=C:\DOS;C:\WINDOWS TEMP
```

That path is not valid, and the TEMP statement is out of whack. Oh, you need to have 2MB or more of free disk space available to use the TEMP statement, too. Just make the changes I've described, and all should be fine.

Defining the system environment

I am encountering the message *Out of Environment Space* each time I boot and each time I go to the C:\> prompt. It has not seemed to cause any problems thus far, but it sure is annoying!

Five things that tell you that you have too much furniture in your real-life environment:

- ➤ You can play musical chairs with every kid in the neighborhood.
- ➤ You have a bed for every night of the week.
- ➤ Your grandmother sat down somewhere and hasn't been seen since.
- ➤ You have a TV for every channel.
- ➤ You don't remember whether you have hardwood floors or carpet.

The system's environment is a great deal like the environment inside your home. *Out of Environment Space* is the computer's way of telling you that you can't put more furniture in a house than the house can hold. And you know when that happens. Your home starts to look like your parents' house even though you swore that you would never let things get that way.

When you start your computer, the AUTOEXEC.BAT file sets up the environment. The SET and PATH commands set up the environment space and move in the furniture or environment variables. The *Out of Environment Space* error message tells you that some statements in the AUTOEXEC.BAT that are used to set the DOS environment are working right. And the SET, PATH, and PROMPT commands will no longer work because the house is full.

If you don't tell DOS to set the *size* of the environment, it sets it to 256 bytes. (Think of a byte as a letter or number, so the command SET DIRCMD=/ON would take up or occupy 14 bytes of environment.) To find out how much environment you are using, type the following commands at the DOS prompt (press Enter after each command):

```
SET > SIZE.ENV
DIR SIZE.ENV
```

The size of the SIZE.ENV file in bytes is equal to the amount of environment you are using. If you do not have a SHELL statement in the CONFIG.SYS file and SIZE.ENV is close to 256 bytes in size, you need to increase the size of the environment.

To change the size of the environment, you need to have a SHELL statement in the CONFIG.SYS file. If you already have a SHELL statement, it should look something like this:

```
SHELL=C:\DOS\COMMAND.COM C:\DOS /E:512 /P
```

In this case, the environment size is set to 512 bytes (/E:512). To increase it to 1024 bytes, change 512 to 1024 so that the statement reads /E:1024. If you set the size of the environment, remember to make a backup of CONFIG.SYS first and observe the following rules:

➤ You cannot set a size lower than 160.

➤ You cannot set a size larger than 32,768.

➤ If the size that you set is not a multiple of 16, DOS automatically rounds up to the next largest multiple of 16. So an /E:513 parameter will set up an environment of 528 bytes.

➤ Each byte of environment that you set up is taken directly from computer memory, but normally this use of memory should not affect any programs. Even a 1024-byte environment is a small amount of memory in comparison to what programs use, but it is considered large as far as environment sizes go.

Where's DOSSHELL?

Why won't DOSSHELL **work since I upgraded to DOS 6.2?** DOSSHELL **is listed in the manual, but I can't seem to find it on the installation disks.**

You stopped reading the manual too soon, my friend. DOSSHELL is no longer included with DOS versions after 6.0. Now that Windows is so popular, not too many folks need a DOS-based file management and menu program, so Microsoft stopped putting DOSSHELL on the DOS disks. But you can still get DOSSHELL by ordering the DOS Supplemental disk from Microsoft. This disk also contains many of the *old* DOS utilities and programs, such as ASSIGN, COMP, EDLIN, GRAFTABLE, JOIN, MIRROR, and PRINTFIX.

If you can't wait for the disk to arrive by mail, then use your computer. Some on-line services, such as America Online and CompuServe, as well as Microsoft's own download BBS, have the disk available for download. Because the download takes quite some time unless you connect at a high speed, ordering the disk by telephone is often cheaper.

To get the Supplemental disk from Microsoft's BBS, you need to use your communications program. The phone number is 206-936-6735, and the modem settings are Data Bits-8, Parity-none, Stop Bits-1, and speeds to 9600.

Reading different file formats

Is there any way to view or read a file that has all these odd symbols and stuff instead of words? I have tried to use Norton Diskedit and view the file as text, but I still just get gibberish. Is this because the file is encrypted or what?

Computers speak different languages for a reason. It all goes back many years to the time when all the computers got together to build a tower of Babel to get to their god, UNIVAC. But UNIVAC struck them down, and they all speak differently now.

Your question is difficult to answer without knowing what kind of file you're trying to look at on-screen. The last three letters in the filename, the ones after the dot, often provide a clue about what kind of file it is. This part of the filename is called the file's *extension*. Any file that has an extension of .COM, .EXE, or .DLL is a program file that is written in a language that only the computer can understand. Files that have a .ZIP extension, on the other hand, are compressed or squeezed down in size so they take up less space on the computer. ZIP files may have started out as words or sentences — stuff that people understand — but now they make no sense until they are *uncompressed* or inflated to the way they used to be. Some files, on the other hand, are truly encrypted, regardless of the file extension.

Norton Diskedit is a very powerful tool that can change any file on your computer up to and including the physical disk drive. One slip on your part, and you could destroy a program. Don't use Diskedit for viewing files, period. But if you need to look at a file with this tool, make a backup copy of the file first. Then, if something gets changed, you won't have to worry too much. But be careful anyway. I'd hate to get a question from you that starts out with, "I used Norton Diskedit to look at a file, and now my computer won't start."

Using Remark to get back Ctrl+Alt+Delete

Since I used MEMMAKER, **I can no longer do the three-finger salute (Ctrl+Alt+Delete). Strangely enough, if I REM out the line** DOS=UMB **in my CONFIG.SYS, everything works fine. Any ideas?**

Of course, I have all answers. Go ahead. Use the Remark statement on the EMM386.EXE line instead of the DOS= line, and the same thing will happen. EMM386.EXE is involved in switching the computer between protected mode and real mode. When you tell the computer to restart by using the Ctrl+Alt+Delete key combination, the computer must check the mode that it is in and possibly switch modes.

Some computers react strangely, or don't react at all, to Ctrl+Alt+Delete when EMM386.EXE is loaded. EMM386.EXE must use what is termed a *handler* to reboot the computer. Do you care? Me neither. I assume that you have a line in the CONFIG.SYS file that looks like this:

```
DEVICE=C:\DOS\EMM386.EXE NOEMS X=E000-EFFF
```

To get the three-finger salute back, you need to change the `DEVICE=...` statement. First, make a backup copy of the CONFIG.SYS file. Then add `ALTBOOT` to the device for EMM386.EXE, as in the following example:

```
DEVICE=C:\DOS\EMM386.EXE NOEMS X=E000-EFFF ALTBOOT
```

After you make this change to the `EMM386.EXE` line, be sure to save the changes and exit the editor. Restart the computer (you need to use the reset button one last time), and when you are at a DOS prompt, try the Ctrl+Alt+Delete keystroke. It works.

Deleting a file for good

How can I delete a file and make sure no one can ever undelete it or recover it in any other way?

What's the big secret? Are you in the CIA or something?

When DOS erases a file, the information is still there. The file is simply marked as a space that the computer can use the next time you save a file. Each time you save a new file, the computer uses the space from the file you last erased. Because the computer works this way, you can use `UNDELETE/UNERASE` utilities to recover files that you may have deleted days or even weeks ago.

Because DOS preserves the erased space for as long as possible, anyone with an `UNERASE/UNDELETE` utility or a disk editor can find files that you have deleted. For some folks, this capability presents a big-time security problem. To solve it, you can buy special software programs that truly erase a file from a computer's hard disk or floppy disk. XTGold (newer versions only) and Symantec's Norton Utilities are two of the software programs that can perform this trick. If you do not have Norton Utilities or something like it, try using `DEFRAG` or another DOS disk optimizer.

To use `DEFRAG`, type **DEFRAG** at the DOS prompt and press Enter. After you are inside `DEFRAG`, choose the full optimize option. It arranges the hard disk in file size from largest to smallest. Run `DEFRAG` again and put the files in order from smallest to largest. By shuffling the files this way, you should be able to overwrite areas on the drive that contain erased files. Then `UNERASE` won't work on them anymore.

By the way, if you are at the CIA, check whether there is a file on Komando.

Partitioning a hard drive

I own a chain of restaurants, and I'm using a great deal of hard disk space for new programs and data. If I partition my hard disk, will I get more hard disk space?

Have you heard about the restaurant on the moon? The food is great, but it has no atmosphere.

First, think of your hard drive as a big room full of books. You decide to organize those books, so you buy one of those temporary wall dividers. You set the divider so that it splits the room in half. You put all the fiction books on one side of the room and all the nonfiction books on the other side of the room. You've *partitioned* the room into two parts, but the room is still the same size.

This arrangement is similar to what goes on when you partition a hard drive. That is, you split the hard disk in half or into two unequal parts, but the hard disk is still the same size. After you partition the disk, you have a drive C and a drive D. I have my computer set up this way. All my software program files are on drive C. All the information that I create by using the software programs is on drive D.

Komando Klues

Partitioning helps you organize the information on your hard disk. Also, making backups of the hard disk is easier because you have to back up only drive D. Why? Well, because you still have the original distribution disks for the software programs that are contained on drive C, you can reinstall the software if something goes wrong.

Saving power on a laptop

Can you save my marriage? My wife swears she'll divorce me unless I can figure out how to make the laptop last longer off a charge. I hear that a new DOS command can do just this.

Isn't it just like a woman to want a longer charge from her man? Many laptops (even older ones) are power conscious. That is, if the computer is turned on but is not being used for a given length of time, certain parts of the computer will go to sleep. This feature saves valuable laptop battery life. The formal term for power-saving features is *power management*.

Check the laptop's manual and look for something called *Advanced Power Management (APM)*. It may be listed as *APM*. Or features that conserve battery power, such as display sleep (which turns off the display screen after a few minutes of nonuse), may be listed separately.

POWER.EXE ships with DOS 6.0 or higher and improves a laptop's power management. The catch to using POWER.EXE is that your machine must abide by the Advanced Power Management Specification — a fancy way of saying that your laptop must know APM. If a laptop supports APM, POWER.EXE can boost battery life by about 25 percent, and if not, by about 5 percent.

To get POWER.EXE rolling, first make a backup copy of the CONFIG.SYS file that's in the C:\ directory. Then use the DOS EDIT program to add the following line to the CONFIG.SYS file:

```
DEVICE=C:\DOS\POWER.EXE STD
```

The next time you start the computer, you'll be saving the charge in the laptop's battery, and maybe your marriage, too!

Duplicate files in DOS and Windows

I have noticed that some of the files in DOS are the same as those in Windows. What duplicate DOS and Windows files can I delete? Or should I just let bygones be bygones?

Microsoft has provided several files that seem to be everywhere! The following files are the most commonly found duplicates that occur in both Windows and DOS directories:

➤ HIMEM.SYS

➤ EMM386.EXE

➤ RAMDRIVE.SYS

➤ SMARTDRV.EXE

➤ MSD.EXE

➤ EXPAND.EXE

Why does Microsoft duplicate these files? Doesn't it know that you are almost out of hard drive space and you need to make room for just one more game? Well, the answer is actually simple and sensible. Each time Microsoft introduces a new version of DOS or Windows, it typically updates several very commonly used utilities that are either needed or desired for Windows to run or for DOS to be utilized to its maximum. You can safely delete the older of those duplicated files, whether they are in the DOS directory or in the Windows directory. Just be sure that if you are using HIMEM, EMM386, RAMDRIVE, or SMARTDRV in the CONFIG.SYS file or SMARTDRV in the AUTOEXEC.BAT file, you correct the path used in the device line.

Of course, if you just leave well enough alone, all will be fine. Besides, deleting those six files only saves between $^1/_5$ and $^1/_4$MB. If your drive is so full that a few hundred thousand bytes will make a difference, then you need to do some more radical house cleaning. For example, think about adding another hard disk to the computer. Remember, though, if you screw up, it's a hard drive to the computer repair store to explain what happened.

Switching from PC-DOS to MS-DOS

I recently purchased a computer with IBM PC-DOS 6.1 installed on it. I have no complaints but want to switch to MS-DOS 6.2 or later. All attempts at eliminating PC-DOS have failed miserably. I have followed suggested methods and have asked others but can't get it to run.

It bothers me that you have not even given 6.1 a chance. What did it do to you? Is this the way you are with everything? Will you trade me in for a younger, more attractive, advice giver?

Anyway, the IBM and Microsoft versions of DOS are very nearly the same. The only exceptions are some of the additional utilities that are supplied with each company's version of DOS. IBM has added utilities from Central Point Software with PC-DOS. At last count, it was up to release 6.3, which is about equal to MS-DOS 6.20 through 6.22.

From what you are saying, the MS-DOS software you have may be an upgrade kit rather than a full-fledged installation version. If so, you need to get a full MS-DOS 6.x version running on the system to use a DOS 6.22 upgrade kit. The box that your version came in or the installation requirements in the documentation should tell you whether you have an upgrade kit. If you do, try installing a full DOS 6.x version.

One thing to be aware of when you are switching from PC-DOS to MS-DOS is SUPERSTOR/DS compression. If you change to MS-DOS, SUPERSTOR/DS compression will probably work, but all the IBM DOS tools may disappear along with your IBM DOS files. So before switching from PC-DOS to MS-DOS, be sure to back up all the files and data that you cannot afford to lose. It's the cheapest and best insurance you can get during a system upgrade. Although your tendencies are toward the latest and greatest MS-DOS version, PC-DOS 6.3 is more or less equal to MS-DOS Versions 6.2 through 6.22, and IBM offers a PC-DOS 6.3 upgrade.

Creating batch programs

I set up all of my kids' games in a menu program. The idea was to make the games easy to use. But they have to change directories and so on to get to their games, and this kind of defeats the purpose. How can I set things up so that they just need to type MENU from anywhere?

Well, the time has come for you to become a programmer (wearing a pocket protector is optional). Actually, this programming job is not difficult, and it's kind of fun, depending, of course, on what your idea of fun is. (It's less fun than playing your kids' games but more fun than doing laundry.)

You need to write a little program that will run from any directory on your system. This program, called a *batch* program, contains a bunch of DOS commands — actually, the same commands that the kids use now to run the menu program.

Don't be intimidated by this job — batch programs are easy to write. A batch file is just a collection of commands, saved in an ASCII text file. The commands are the same ones that you would type at the DOS prompt. Batch programs use the file extension .BAT. For example, a MENU.BAT program would contain commands at the DOS prompt to run the menu:

```
CD\MENU
MENU
```

If you created a text file with these lines in it, named it MENU.BAT, and placed it in the DOS directory, then every time you typed **MENU** at the DOS prompt, the commands in the file would execute, one line at a time.

The DOS editor is a great tool for creating .BAT files because it uses almost all ASCII text. .BAT files written by a word processor usually aren't usable as .BAT files because word processors use special codes, not just plain, old ASCII text. An interesting way to create simple .BAT files is to type directly to the hard drive. To try this method, change to the DOS directory and type the following at the DOS prompt, *exactly* as it appears here:

```
CON MENU.BAT
C: CD\MENU
MENU
```

After you type these lines, press F6 and then press Enter. You should see a message on-screen that is similar to this one:

```
1 File copied
```

That's it! You created a batch file, typed it, and saved it as a file on the hard drive. The batch program that you have written into the file MENU.BAT is ready to use. Change to any directory on your system, type **MENU**, and the menu program should appear. Just make sure that the PATH statement includes the DOS directory.

Come on. Ruffle your feathers. You did it. Don't get too cocky, though. It's time to do the laundry.

Komando Klues To avoid confusion, always type the whole name of program files, first name and last name, when they appear as part of a command in batch programs.

Solving run-time errors

I have a DOS flight simulator program that generates run-time errors when I try to use it. Oddly enough, it worked fine on my old computer, but it just can't get along with my new Pentium. Is there something I should do with my memory configuration?

I don't think that memory configuration is the answer here. I hate to be the bearer of bad news, but your system is just too fast for that program. Some older programs just weren't written to accommodate your speedy machine.

Of the three basic kinds of run-time errors, only one kind appears outside of programming and program compilation. The run-time errors that you get when you try to run a program are execution errors and usually have nothing to do with memory configuration. Intel worked very hard to ensure that the Pentium is fully compatible with earlier CPUs. The Pentium itself is a member of the X86 family, or *architecture*, so the new chip is not likely the cause of the problem.

Without knowing the specific error message that you are getting, the best I can offer is a set of suggestions that may lead you to a solution:

➤ Check the program's documentation to see what DOS versions it is compatible with. If the latest DOS version mentioned as a supported version is an older version, then the error could be due to timing. Games (flight simulators are classified as games), especially older ones, may rely on timing.

➤ Be sure that you don't have any memory-resident programs that conflict with the program that you are having difficulty using.

➤ If the computer has a turbo switch, sometimes you can get a program to run by pushing the switch to turn off turbo mode. This change slows the system down. If that approach doesn't work, you can disable the external cache from the CMOS and really slow things down.

➤ Try reinstalling the program in case a file or files that the software program needs to run have become corrupted. When files are corrupted, you get an error message.

➤ Upgrade the software. Call the software's publisher and find out if you have the latest and greatest release of the problem program.

➤ Do a virus scan. (You probably aren't dealing with a virus infection, but I never miss a chance to plug safe computing!)

➤ Boot as cleanly as possible and try the program again.

Understanding DISKCOPY *error messages*

I think you people are into sabotage. If it weren't for incompetent computer designers, I would never have system failures. When using DISKCOPY **in DOS 6.2, I get the error message** *Error creating image file. DISKCOPY will revert to a multiple-pass copy.* **How do I get around this message?**

You have an attitude problem, buddy. You have bigger issues to deal with than computer error messages.

You use DISKCOPY to make an identical copy of one floppy disk to another floppy disk when both floppy disks are the same type. DISKCOPY uses the hard disk as an interim storage area where the image file is created. You don't have to swap floppy disks, and you can make multiple copies of the same disk.

You get the *Error creating image file* message when the hard disk is just about maxed out or the drive is write protected. You can try erasing some files that are on the hard disk, but if you don't want to part with any of your files, tell DISKCOPY to use conventional memory instead of hard disk space to make the copy. To do so, type the following at the DOS prompt and press Enter:

```
DISKCOPY /M
```

Komando Klues

Here is a bonus tip: If you have enough RAM to spare and you want to make faster copies, have the SET TEMP= statement use a RAM drive of at least the size of the largest disk you might copy. RAM drives are much faster than hard drives.

Solving disk reading problems

A coworker sent me a Verbatim DataLife MF2-DD disk that holds some spreadsheets. When I try to use the disk, I get the *General failure reading drive A* message. Why? Is it because the disk was formatted on a lower-density drive? (I have a 1.44 high-density disk drive.) If so, is there any way for me to get the data off this disk?

Verbatim makes some pretty good media, so unless the disk was stored improperly or physically damaged, I doubt that the disk is bad. Is it possible that your coworker gave you the wrong disk? If not, then I think that the disk once had data written to it by a low-density drive and this data was erased in a high-density drive. Then the data that you are having difficulty reading was written by a high-density drive.

How do I come to such a conclusion, you ask? Problems such as this one pop up because the tracks written by a low-density drive are physically wider than the tracks written by a high-density drive. So imagine that the wide data tracks were erased by a narrow read-write head, which left some traces of the old tracks to either side of the new tracks. Then the new data was written to the new narrow track between the remnants of the old tracks. When a read head tries to access the drive and get data, unless it is the same read-write head that did the erase and write of data, there is a chance that it will be reading parts of the new and old tracks. Hence the error.

The Bottom Line

Try SCANDISK or Norton Disk Doctor to repair the disk. Either normally can do the trick.

Chapter 9
Fonts

Basics

Font types defined

What's the difference between bitmapped and vector fonts? And what are TrueType fonts? If all I do is some light desktop publishing and word processing, which font type should I use?

Relax. It's rather easy to understand.

A *bitmapped* or *raster* font generates a character by displaying a picture (made up of dots) of the character. To use a bitmapped font, you need a picture of every character in every size that you want.

A *vector* or *TrueType* font generates a character by a mathematical outline to a fixed pattern of pixels tailored to the resolution of a screen or output device (say, a printer).

Vector fonts are *scalable*: as long as you have the mathematical description, you can produce a character in any size. Thus, you need not store a copy of every typeface in every size, saving valuable hard disk space.

Both TrueType (TT) and Adobe Type Manager (ATM) are brand names of vector fonts; TrueType is produced by Microsoft and Apple, ATM by Adobe.

The Bottom Line

If you're a casual user, TrueType is great because it's part of Windows. If you do a lot of desktop publishing work and you often send work to service bureaus, you're better off going with ATM fonts.

There's your answer. Happy, now? Good. I love these one-way conversations.

More types of fonts

What are the different types of fonts (screen, printer, PostScript, ATM, TT, and so on)? And why are there so many?

Lots of companies make lots of fonts in order to make lots of money. But relax, there really are only two kinds of fonts: bitmapped and vector. *Screen*, meanwhile, refers to fonts that appear on-screen, and *printer* refers to fonts used by a printer. *PostScript, Adobe Type Manager (ATM)*, and *TrueType (TT)* are brand names of vector fonts.

Bitmapped fonts work fine as screen fonts because most users don't often change the size of on-screen characters; as a result, you need only a few sets of characters — one for each size of each font you use. In other words, because you don't have to store a copy of every typeface in every size, you don't have to worry about wasting hard drive space.

But people aren't happy with just one or two font sizes when they create and print their work. And yet, they still can't afford to fill up their hard drives with dozens of files to cover all the sizes of all the fonts they need. Enter vector fonts, which are generated mathematically. A vector font's description can be recalculated to produce characters of any size. (Don't worry. The fonts figure everything out without your help.)

Adobe has developed many vector fonts — once referred to as Type 1 PostScript fonts, now called Adobe Type Manager (or ATM) fonts — and font managers to make these fonts useful for the Mac and Windows. With the advent of Windows 3.1, Microsoft jumped into the font game, too; TrueType (TT) fonts (developed in cooperation with Apple) are vector fonts built into the Windows interface.

Font characteristics

I'm so confused. What in the world are typeface, style, and size?

Typeface, style, and size define and describe fonts:

> ➤ *Typeface* refers to the name (for example, Arial) given to a set of characters that have a similar look. Typefaces are frequently

categorized by their purpose: either decorative (also known as display) or body text. Decorative faces are appropriate for headlines or special circumstances. Frequently, decorative faces are elaborately styled.

➤ *Style* refers to a font's slant and/or weight. If a font is slanted, it is usually called italics. The weight, which refers to how dark a font is, can range from regular to bold. (*Note:* A script face is not considered italicized; it is merely decorative.)

➤ Font *size* is measured in one of two ways: pitch (characters per inch) or points (character height). Pitch as a measurement standard is a relic from the typewriter days, when most fonts were *monospaced,* meaning that each character takes the same amount of space on the page, no matter how narrow or wide the character is. Meanwhile, there are 72 points in an inch, so a 24-point font stands one-third of an inch tall.

(Look! You bought a computer dictionary and a question-and-answer book all in one.)

All three factors combine to make a font. To define a font, you must use all three — for example, Arial, bold, 72 point.

Speaking of which, have you heard the legend of Arial, the bold volleyball player, who once scored 72 points in a single game? Me neither.

Font file extensions

Are .FON files the same as .FOT and .TTF files? Can I delete the .FON files?

Leave those .FON files alone, just as you would leave an eating dog alone. Trust me, replacing the files is no FON.

.FON files are Windows's desktop screen fonts. If you delete them, Windows will be really unhappy. Of course, you will be sad, too, because you may not see any text under your icons. .FOT files, meanwhile, tell Windows which TrueType fonts you have and where to find them on your computer. And .TTF files are the actual TrueType fonts themselves.

To summarize,

Extension	What File Is
.TTF	TrueType font
.FOT	TrueType font for printing
.FON	TrueType font for display on-screen

If you delete the .FOT or .FON files, the files will be re-created. So, what's the sense?

What fonts come with Windows?

What are the names of the fonts that come with Windows 3.1?

A fontastic question. Windows 3.1 includes the following fonts in regular, bold, and italic:

➤ Arial

➤ Courier New

➤ Times New Roman

➤ Symbol

➤ WingDings

The Windows font files are in the C:\WINDOWS\SYSTEM directory with the following filenames: ARIAL.TTF, ARIALBD.TTF, ARIALBI.TTF, ARIALI.TTF, COUR.TTF, COURBD.TTF, COURBI.TTF, COURI.TTF, TIMES.TTF, TIMESBD.TTF, TIMESBI.TTF, TIMESI.TTF, SYMBOL.TTF, and WINGDING.TTF.

Hanging with Mr. Control Panel

Duplicate fonts?

Many of my fonts seem to be listed twice in my WINDOWS\SYSTEM directory, under slightly different names. Here's the kicker: Several fonts appear both as expected (name and .TTF extension)

and under what looks suspiciously like an alias (name, underscore, zero, and then the .TTF extension) — for example, SMOKE.TTF and SMOKE_0.TTF. Do I need both files, or is one just taking up space on my hard drive?

It's difficult to know for sure whether any two files are the same font. You see, there are so many shareware and commercially sold fonts floating around these days, they could simply be variations of the same font.

Komando Klues

To find out whether a font is a shareware font, open your word processor and try typing all the characters. Many shareware fonts are missing characters. (Sounds more like sheisterware, eh?)

If you have more than one of the same font installed, it's OK to delete one of the files. Here's how:

1. Go to the Main program group in Windows.

2. Select Control Panel and then Fonts.

3. Remove a font by highlighting its name and selecting Remove. Be careful not to select Delete from disk.

To help you sort your fonts, you can get a font cataloging utility, such as FontMinder by Ares. Such a program prints the filename, its Windows font name, and a sample.

WARNING

Avoid deleting .FON files, which are Windows system fonts (that is, screen fonts). Your fonts need these files like a duck (or a human, for that matter) needs water.

Installing fonts

I want to use the fonts that I've downloaded from an on-line service. My computer guru friend said to set up the fonts in File Manager, I think (actually, maybe he said DOS). How do I do whatever I need to do? P.S. I have Works.

Your guru is gu-wrong. You don't set up fonts in File Manager or in DOS. You set up fonts by using the tools that come with Windows:

1. After you download a font, unzip it and copy it to your C:\WINDOWS\SYSTEM directory.

2. Go to the Main program group in Windows.

3. Go to the Control Panel and double-click Fonts.

4. Select Add.

5. Highlight the name of the font you downloaded.

6. Click on TrueType. Make sure that Show Only TrueType Fonts in Applications isn't selected.

7. Click OK when you're all done.

The new font should appear in Works's Fonts menu. If not, try removing and reinstalling your printer from within Works.

Komando Klues

By the way, if you try opening a font from File Manager, you'll probably get a weird message asking which file you want the font *associated* with. (If Windows can't run something, it asks you to link it to something that it can run.)

Sheesh, now you're a computer guru.

Locating lost fonts

I was playing around in the Control Panel for kicks one night and my fonts disappeared. Now, when I open PageMaker or Word, I see a list of just six fonts — I had hundreds. Where did my fonts go?

Call out the bloodhounds. Let 'em sniff the six you have and then turn them loose inside your hard drive.

With luck, your missing fonts really didn't go anywhere. I believe that you have accidentally turned off the TrueType fonts display switch in your Windows desktop. It happens. To check this possibility out,

1. Go to the Main program group in Windows.

2. Select Control Panel and then Fonts.

3. Select TrueType. Make sure that Enable TrueType Fonts is selected and Show Only TrueType Fonts in Applications isn't selected.

4. Click OK.

When you next open PageMaker or Word, welcome back those wayward fonts.

Applications won't show TrueType fonts

I want my fonts! I want my fonts! Although my TrueType fonts show up as installed in the Control Panel (and they are enabled), no applications show them.

Is that why you wrote your letter using a crayon? Interesting, very interesting. A number of things may be happening. Let's check things out:

1. Go to the Main program group in Windows.

2. Select Control Panel and then Fonts.

3. Select all fonts and then Delete. However, be sure Delete from disk is deselected. You want the fonts to stay on your hard disk because you'll need them in a second.

4. Highlight all available fonts and select Add. (See why you didn't want that nasty Delete from disk option checked?) This action forces Windows to reread your font files from disk. Any corrupted fonts are replaced.

Try your fonts again. If the above steps didn't work, it's time to call in the troops.

1. Open the WIN.INI file with Windows Notepad.

2. Look in the [TrueType] section and make sure the following line is there:

```
TTEnable=1
```

This line enables TrueType fonts for use with Windows applications.

If your fonts don't reappear, make sure that you have the right printer driver installed. If the right driver is installed, be sure that it isn't corrupted; from the Control Panel, remove and reinstall your printer driver. You'll find more information about printers and drivers in the Printers chapter.

TrueType fonts aren't displayed

In the Control Panel, I see all my fonts installed. But when I fire up Write, I only see the Modern, Roman, and Script fonts. Where is Arial? For that matter, where are my other fonts? Even stranger, if I choose Character⇨Font and enter a font name, I can use it even though it's not listed in the Font menu. What's going on?

Your fonts are ghosts in the machine. You must exorcise them. To do so,

1. Go to the Control Panel and double-click Fonts.

2. Select TrueType. Make sure that Enable TrueType Fonts is selected. In addition, select Show Only TrueType Fonts in Applications; enabling this option gives you a wider selection of font sizes.

Nonetheless, Write may not show all your installed fonts or in all available point sizes; you may simply own too many fonts.

Komando Klues

As you discovered, you still can use fonts not in the menu by selecting Character⇨Font and typing the desired font name in the Font Name box. OK, it's a hassle, but at least you can access any of your fonts.

Saving deleted fonts

Help! I accidentally deleted a font I need. Can I get it back? I use Windows 3.1.

If you're lucky, and so far you haven't been, the font is not too far gone. But you can retrieve the font easily — as long as you deleted it from Windows but not the hard disk.

1. Go to the Main program group in Windows.

2. Select Control Panel and then Fonts.

3. Look for your missing font in the list of available fonts. If it's there, select Add.

If this series of steps doesn't work (that is, the font is still missing in action), go back to the source — your Windows disks, an add-on font program, or wherever you initially got the font — and put the font on the computer again.

Q&A *I lost my Windows fonts!*

I got lost in the Control Panel and Fonts windows and now all my fonts are lost. No TrueType font files appear in the C:\WINDOWS\SYSTEM directory. How do I get back the basic Windows fonts?

Getting the Windows fonts back on your computer is not fun, but it is possible. You have some preparatory work to do:

1. Go to the Control Panel and select Fonts.

2. Select TrueType.

3. Click OK.

Get out your original Windows disks. The TrueType files you need are on your original Windows disks and have the .TT_ file extension.

Komando Klues

If you are using Windows 3.1, start with disk number 5; then use disk numbers 6 and 9. Windows for Workgroups users should start with disk numbers 6 and 7. (Who else knows this stuff? This book should be twice the price! I'm calling the publisher.)

Here goes the real work:

1. From the Fonts window, select the Add button.

2. Put one of the original Windows disks that contain TrueType files in the floppy disk drive.

3. Select the drive letter where the disk is located. In no time, the Windows TrueType font names appear in the installed fonts window.

4. Click the Select All button and then OK. The fonts from the Windows disk are back on your computer, in the C\WINDOWS\SYSTEM directory.

Repeat the preceding four steps for all the Windows disks that contain TrueType files. I suppose I really don't have to tell you, but please be more careful next time.

TrueType fonts make my computer crash

I've seen more crashes on my computer than in 30 years while hanging out at the track. The latest: With TrueType fonts enabled, Windows crashes and I get the message *Invalid TrueType Font Detected*. How do I get out of the pits?

Let me take a look under the hood. You get this message if one or more of your installed TrueType fonts is corrupt — that is, if the font file bit the big one. Or perhaps you have a TrueType font that's not set up exactly right. Some shareware fonts, for example, do not adhere completely to the Windows TrueType font specifications and thus cause errors when you try to use them.

To find out which font crashed,

1. Go to the Main program group.

2. Select Control Panel and then Fonts.

3. From the list of fonts, click each font name. Corrupt font files give you an error message or show a file size of 0K or 2K.

4. Remove the bad font(s) by selecting Delete. However, be sure not to choose Delete from disk.

5. Exit and restart Windows.

6. Return to the Main program group. Select Control Panel and then Fonts. Reinstall the bad font.

Have a beer and take a victory lap.

Moving fonts to a new directory

How do I give my fonts a new home? I want to move my fonts from C:\WINDOWS\SYSTEM to another directory, and I want the system to recognize the change.

OK, let me get this straight, you're looking for a new homefont?

It's not a bad idea to clear the fonts out of your C:\WINDOWS\SYSTEM directory. TrueType fonts can reside in any directory, even on another hard disk; heck, they don't have to reside in a pathed directory. The catch: You must install the fonts back in Windows after you move them to their new home. You see, when you install fonts, Windows creates appropriate .FOT files (which go in the WINDOWS directory) to point to the font files' actual location. If the .FOT files are current, Windows applications can find the actual TrueType files.

To move fonts, you move the files with the .TTF extension:

1. Go to the Control Panel and double-click Fonts.

2. Select all the TrueType fonts that you want to move and choose the Remove button. Another window pops up, asking you whether you want to delete the font file from disk. Say yes.

3. Exit Windows.

4. At the DOS prompt, change to the C:\WINDOWS\SYSTEM subdirectory.

5. Use the DOS MOVE command to move the font files with the extension .TTF to the new font directory. For example, if you want to move fonts to the directory C:\MYFONTS, you should type

   ```
   MOVE *.TTF C:\MYFONTS
   ```

6. Restart Windows and again double-click the Fonts icon in Control Panel.

7. Select the Add button.

8. At the bottom of the Add Fonts dialog box, enter the directory name where the fonts are now located. (In my example, you would type **C:\MYFONTS**.)

9. Deselect the Copy Fonts to Windows Directory option.

10. Choose the Select All button and click OK. All should be well in font land.

Preferences

Easy-to-read fonts

I have so many fonts on my computer. Is one font easiest to read on-screen?

You need me to answer that? For me, how easy a font is to see when you view it on-screen depends on

- ➤ Font type
- ➤ Font size
- ➤ The program you're working with
- ➤ Video resolution

In general, simple fonts such as Times Roman, Helvetica, Courier, and Arial (TrueType) are easiest to see on-screen. If you need to view information in your word processor, you may want to use a monospaced font; Courier is a good choice. Each character is a monospaced font, meaning that each character occupies the same amount of horizontal space. For example, the letter l is the same width as the letter m.

If you are using a WYSIWYG (*what you see is what you get*) program and you eventually plan to print out your work in a difficult-to-read-on-screen script font (such as an old English font), you may be more comfortable using a font such as Arial or Times Roman as you work and then switching to your fancy font just prior to printing.

Q: What's the easiest font you can read on-screen?

A: Hooked on Fontics.

Changing system font

I'm old and so are my eyes. How do I change the system font in Windows? I find that the default is too hard to read at high resolutions, but I do like my screen set at 1024 × 1024 mode.

How many fingers am I holding up? Wrong. Three.

Before you do anything else, try reinstalling your video driver. When you do, see whether there's an option for Large Fonts. Many recent video drivers offer a choice between small and large fonts. If the large font option is available, go with it; it's the easiest solution. If not, don't worry, there's still something you can do, but it involves editing some of your Windows system files.

Note: Please remember to make backup copies before changing the system fonts. Hey, it's a good idea to back up all your Windows .INI and .GRP files regularly anyway.

With a backup of the WIN.INI file in a safe place — for example, on a floppy disk — take the plunge:

1. Use Windows Notepad to open the WIN.INI file found in your WINDOWS directory.

2. In the [Desktop] area, add the following line:

   ```
   SystemFont=FontName
   ```

   where `FontName` is the name of the font you wish to use.

3. Save the file, exit Windows, and restart Windows.

The preceding procedure may change the fonts in places you didn't expect, such as dialog boxes. In addition, some programs may not look right because they were written to expect a certain size font — and you just changed that default!

If the changes bother you, you can install a software program that enlarges the screen's contents. Of course, you also can go back to 640 × 480 mode.

Changing Program Manager's fonts

Is there a way that I can change the fonts that appear in Program Manager under the icons and on the group windows? I have trouble seeing the little letters below the icons.

Can't read the words? Icon.

To change the font of the text shown below icons on your Windows desktop, you simply have to add the necessary lines in the WIN.INI file. Here's how:

1. Back up the WIN.INI file.

2. Open the WIN.INI file with Windows Notepad.

3. Go to the [Desktop] section of the WIN.INI file and add the following three lines:

```
IconTitleFaceName=FontName
```

where `FontName` is the name of the font you want to use, not the font filename. You can denote a TrueType font (for example, Arial), a vector font (Modern), or a raster font (Courier), as long as the font has a corresponding .FON file. To avoid any errors, pick a font name that's in the [Fonts] section of the SYSTEM.INI file. The Windows default is MS SansSerif.

```
IconTitleSize=PointSize
```

where `PointSize` is how large (in points) you want the font to appear. The Windows default is 8.

```
IconTitleStyle=x
```

where `x` is a value that corresponds to the font style (bold or not bold). When x = 0, icon titles appear as regular text; when x = 1, icon text is bold. The Windows default is 0.

The larger the font, the more space necessary for each icon. If you make the font too big, the titles overlap and your desktop looks messy.

The following is how the WIN.INI lines look if you want the icon text to be 10-point Arial and bold:

```
[Desktop]
IconTitleFaceName=Arial
IconTitleSize=10
IconTitleStyle=1
```

 Komando Klues You can change the font name and size shown in File Manager, too. To do so, in File Manager select Options⇨Font.

 ## Changing Write's default font

I added some fonts recently. For some reason, a really ugly font is now the default font in Write. How can I get my old default back?

Write's default font is the first one it finds under [Fonts] in your Windows initialization file (WIN.INI). You need to use a text editor, such as Windows Notepad, to change the order in which the fonts are listed so that your favorite is at the top of the [Fonts] section.

Remember, make a backup of the WIN.INI file before you start messing around.

If the idea of editing your WIN.INI file gives you the shakes, fear not. There's a special workaround. You can force Write to use a specific font type and in a specific size:

1. Open Write and change the font, size, and margins or whatever else you want Write to use every time you use the program.

2. To put your font changes into effect, press the spacebar.

3. Press the left-arrow key to return the cursor to the beginning of the document.

4. Save the document; use a descriptive filename (DEFAULT.WRI, for example).

5. Exit Write.

You now need to make this file a read-only file so that your new settings won't be overwritten:

6. Open File Manager and find DEFAULT.WRI. *Hint:* If you're not sure where DEFAULT.WRI is located, invoke File⇨Search and type **DEFAULT.WRI**.

7. Select DEFAULT.WRI.

8. From the File Manager menu bar, choose File⇨Properties.

9. Click in the Read Only box and then OK.

You can either use the Open command to open DEFAULT.WRI each time you use Write, or you can configure Write to always use the settings in DEFAULT.WRI. The latter method is easier:

10. Click once on the Write icon.

11. Choose File⇨Properties.

12. To the end of the command line, add a space and then type **DEFAULT.WRI** so that the line reads

```
WRITE.EXE DEFAULT.WRI
```

From now on, each time you use Write, the font is the one that you set and saved in the DEFAULT.WRI file.

Komando Klues

You can create different Write documents that contain settings for the different documents you use — for example, FAX.WRI, MEMO.WRI, LETTER.WRI, and so on. But remember, if you ever want to change the contents of the DEFAULT.WRI file, you need to retrace the steps that made the file read-only. In other words, to change the settings, you need to disenable the file's read-only property.

Adobe Type Manager (ATM)

 Figuring out ATM

No one here at chef school can figure out Adobe Type Manager, which was installed automatically with another software program.

It's OK, I can't make a soufflé stay up.

Adobe Type Manager (ATM) makes it possible for you to use Adobe Type 1 PostScript fonts. If you don't have any such fonts installed on your system, ATM won't do much for you.

As you discovered, ATM is sometimes coupled with other software. For example, ATM is included with recent versions of WordPerfect for Windows.

To track down the necessary documentation, I suggest calling the vendor who sold you the software program that accompanied ATM.

 Which fonts are better — ATM or TT?

Should I use Adobe Type Manager or TrueType fonts? I have both.

Some argue that Adobe Type Manager (ATM) fonts are better than TrueType (TT) fonts, particularly at very small sizes. However, just as many TrueType fans dispute this claim.

The Bottom Line

The convenience of TT fonts outweighs any other consideration unless you do serious desktop publishing work, when you should use ATM fonts and a PostScript printer.

The biggest reason most professional desktop publishing folks work with ATM fonts is service bureaus; if you create a document and send it to the service bureau only to find that printer doesn't have the TT fonts you used, life can get complicated!

If you are simply doing word processing, number crunching, or presentation work, and all you want is a few extra choices of how your documents look, TT fonts are fine.

Komando Klues

Even if you use ATM fonts, be sure to include a complete list of the exact fonts used in any work you send to a printer or service bureau. Doing so helps prevent nasty surprises later.

Of course, all this talk is as pointless as arguing about which flavor is better: strawberry or vanilla. (Obviously, strawberry.)

Service bureaus and True Type fonts

The service bureau that I use told me that TrueType fonts come out bitmapped on their equipment. Is this a fact of life?

When my parents sat me down to explain the facts of life, the first thing they covered was how TrueType fonts come out bitmapped on service bureau equipment.

They said, "Daughter, sometimes a TrueType font is printed as a bitmapped font if fonts are not loaded properly or if a document is printed on older equipment that can't handle TrueType fonts." This tidbit has made a difference in my life. Just don't look under my bed.

Find a service bureau that knows what it's doing or isn't using old equipment. Look in the Yellow Pages or call your local PC user's group.

Deleting PostScript fonts through ATM

I use Adobe Type Manager and want to get rid of all traces of the PostScript fonts I don't want anymore. How do I do this?

Adobe Type Manager (ATM) takes the prize for aggressive programs. The program is downright rude, actually.

ATM changes the single most important line in your SYS.INI file, `system drv=system.drv`, and converts it into two lines, as follows:

```
system.drv=atmsys.drv
atm.system.drv=system.drv
```

369

Reminds me of the time I invited my aunt to stay at my house: while I was at work, she rearranged all my furniture.

After reworking your SYS.INI file, ATM ends up handling all system driver calls. If a call is not font related, ATM passes it to the `atm.system.drv`, which is now the system driver.

To remove ATM, therefore, you must delete these two lines and replace them with the original `system.drv=system.drv`. After you do so, you can safely remove the actual ATM files and fonts from your hard drive.

Troubleshooting

 Speeding up Windows for the Master of Fonts

I'm a fontaholic. I have 382 (that's right, 382!) fonts in WIN.INI. Windows takes *forever* to start; I guess that the computer is reading all the font files. Short of deleting (gulp) some of my beloved fonts, is there anything that I can do to speed things up?

Font, by definition, means a source of abundance — but 382? Most folks say that 255 is the speed/sanity limit. I suggest that you seek counseling to slowly reduce your font intake. Weekly meetings, 12 steps, group readings: you know the drill. If you don't actually attend the meetings, you write to your group sponsor; try to use one less font each week.

As you surmise, Windows tries to load every font it can find when starting. You need a font grouping utility, such as FontMonger (by Ares Software) or Font Monster (shareware by Steven Fox of Leaping Lizards Software). If you have such a utility, you can have Windows load only certain groups of fonts. For speed's sake, try to keep to 50 fonts at a time.

Storing fonts on floppy disks

I don't need many fonts. I noticed some files with the extensions .FOT and .TTF in my WINDOWS\SYSTEM directory. If I save the .FOT files to a floppy disk and then try to recover them in the Control Panel font window, I get *No fonts found* message.

Oops! Sounds like you fonted up.

You moved the wrong files. .FOT files must remain in the C:\WINDOWS\SYSTEM directory; they tell Windows where to find your TrueType font files (the .TTF files). If Windows can't find an .FOT file, it won't know where to look to find the TTF file.

So put those .FOT files back in the C:\WINDOWS\SYSTEM directory. Then you can move the .TTF files around if you want!

Same font, different name

It seems that the same font can go by several different names. Can you list the most common fonts and their names or aliases?

A font by any other name would spell just as sweet.

Arial is not Helvetica is not Gill Sans is not HELV, although they look the same. And Times New Roman is not Times Roman is not TMS RMN is not CG Times.

Yeah, it's confusing. And unfortunately, there's no easy answer. There are just too many sources for fonts and no widely accepted naming conventions. Not only can different fonts go by very similar sounding names, but the same font also can go by very different names. To make matters worse, shareware font vendors have gone hog-wild converting fonts from one flavor to some variety of the same flavor.

For starters, you can contact major font producers, such as Adobe or ZSoft, and ask the folks there for lists of their fonts. Then try categorizing fonts on your system against these basic types. If you find fonts with different names that look identical, eliminate all but one.

By the way, a font cataloging and sampling program, such as FontMinder by Ares, comes in handy for this chore!

371

Shareware fonts are incomplete

A few shareware fonts I downloaded are missing random characters. I see outlined boxes rather than letters. Am I doing something wrong?

It's not you. Those boxes are a clue. Some shareware fonts are missing characters, especially accented and typographic ones. If you detect something wrong with a shareware font, get it off your system immediately, for it can cause all kinds of problems.

Foreign language fonts

I need to send letters in languages other than English. Windows fonts and typefaces don't work well. Suggestions?

You can find fonts for just about any language and within any price range. The good news is that the price of the fonts is not tied to exchange rates or the Eurodollar.

Monotype, the company that designed the Arial and Times New Roman fonts that ship with Windows, offers three flavors of their Times New Roman font. These variations are good for letters going to Eastern Europe and Greece:

➤ Times New Roman Efo, a Roman face with the accented characters used in Eastern Europe
➤ Times New Roman Greek
➤ Times New Roman Cyrillic

For more information, call Monotype at 800-666-6897.

If you need other language fonts, call Linguist's Software. The company markets a TransRoman font for virtually all European, African, and Native American languages. In addition, Linguist's Software offers fonts in the following languages:

➤ Armenian
➤ Cambodian
➤ Cherokee
➤ Cyrillic

➤ Georgian

➤ Gujarati

➤ Hebrew

➤ Hindi

➤ Inuit

➤ Laotian

➤ Punjabi

➤ Thai

➤ Tibetan

➤ Vietnamese

You can reach Linguist's Software at 206-775-1130.

If your letters are heading to India, remember that the Devanagari alphabet used in Hindi, Sanskrit, Marathi, and other languages of India is very specialized. Contact Cantext Publications at 204-275-1598.

Komando Klues Foreign language fonts are easier when you're using a foreign language version of your word processing software. Check with your software program vendor for available foreign language versions.

Chapter 10

Graphics

File Formats

File formats and CorelDRAW!

Which file formats can I import into CorelDRAW!?

CorelDRAW! imports just about any file format imaginable, including those with the following extensions:

➤ .AI	➤ .JPG	➤ .SEP
➤ .BMP	➤ .JTF	➤ .TGA
➤ .DIB	➤ .PCD	➤ .TIF
➤ .DOC	➤ .PCT	➤ .TXT
➤ .DRW	➤ .PCX	➤ .VDA
➤ .DXF	➤ .PIC	➤ .VST
➤ .EPS	➤ .PIF	➤ .WK*
➤ .GEM	➤ .PLT	➤ .WMF
➤ .GIF	➤ .PS	➤ .WPG
➤ .ICB	➤ .RLE	➤ .XLS
➤ .JFF	➤ .SAM	

Pronunciations

How do you pronounce the graphics file formats .GIF, .PCX, and .BMP?

OK, class, take your seats, please. Your first word for today is *.GIF*. The correct pronunciation is "Jif," as in the brand of peanut butter. Your second word is *.PCX*; all together now, "Pea See Ex." Your last word, *.BMP*, is pronounced "Bee Em Pea." (Computer folks in the know, however, call .BMPs *bitmaps* in everyday conversation.)

Choosing a file format

Wow. When I choose File⇨Save As in CorelDRAW!, all these options pop up on-screen, including .BMP, .GIF, .PCX, and .WMF. Which format is best if I want to use my CorelDRAW! picture in another program?

You need to check which graphics formats are supported by the other program. *Hint:* Look in the other program's user manual under *Graphics*.

Komando Klues Before you crack open any manual, however, let me share a great insider's tip. Paint programs seem to lean more toward .PCX or .TIF files, and Windows-based programs prefer .BMP or .WMF files.

.GIF and .TIF — universal file formats

I need to scan a piece of clip art so that my client can use it in Mac, DOS, Windows, or even UNIX layout programs. Which file format should I save the art in?

Only one format is standardized and common to Mac, DOS, Windows, and UNIX platforms: .GIF. Unfortunately, .GIF resolution is quite low and unsatisfactory for use in layout programs.

As a result, the best format is standard .TIF, either 8 bit (256 colors) or 24 bit (16 million colors). Most commercial layout programs import the .TIF format. In fact, any .TIF file created and readable on a PC platform should be readable by commercial programs on all other platforms.

Scan a small image and import it on your client's systems. This test can save you some time and frustration later.

Printing .GIF files

I work in the Department of the Interior. How do I print .GIF files? I have an HP 550C inkjet.

The government, huh? This answer will cost you $6,000.

All you need is software that displays or imports and then prints .GIF files. Check your user manuals, but most top commercial software (including word processing, spreadsheet, database, and page layout programs) let you insert a .GIF picture. Printing the file prints the .GIF, as long as your printer is set up properly in Windows.

Oftentimes, a graphics program works best. In addition, you can touch up the picture or enhance its colors. One of the best Windows shareware utilities for this job is Paint Shop Pro from JASC. With Paint Shop Pro, you simply open the .GIF file and print it. If you are more adventurous, you can use Paint Shop Pro to enhance the image's colors and contrast before printing. Paint Shop Pro works well if you need to change .GIF-format pictures into .BMP-format pictures, too.

If you are strictly a DOS user, get Graphics Workshop from Image Mindworks for its easy-to-understand interface. Besides, the folks at Image Mindworks claim that their program supports color printing with all inkjet printers.

Best format for selling clip art

I created some graphics that I want to sell as clip art. Which file format(s) should I use to give the art the most appeal?

Save your clip art in the most popular graphics formats: .BMP, .EPS, .PCX, .TIF, and .WMF. Why all five? It's not too much work, and you can package each format separately.

I suspect that your product will appeal tremendously to folks who are tired of the generic clip art contained in today's popular software programs. The old stuff is as interesting as carpet.

By the way, try distributing your art as shareware first and then go retail.

Make certain that the clip art is 100 percent your original work and not a variation of existing clip art. That is, don't take a Mickey Mouse scene and change it by adding a tree. If you do, you probably will lose the ensuing copyright lawsuit.

Bitmap vs. vector

Thumbnails

How can I get a clear thumbnail image from a large .PCX file? Do I need a vector program? My ex-wife mentioned a Thumb something-or-other program.

Your ex-wife? You trust her?

Forget about the vector program; you would need to change an apple into an avocado. See, .PCX is a *bitmap* format — that is, the image is made up of tiny dots, or *pixels*. A *vector* image, meanwhile, is made up of connecting lines. A vector image is stored as a mathematical formula that describes all the lines.

Note: Bitmap graphics lose quality when made larger or smaller. Vector images scale with precision; in other words, you can make them larger and smaller without losing quality.

Do you simply want to catalog .PCX images? Many thumbnail applications can do the job quite well. Thumbs+Plus for Windows (shareware from Cerious Software) is an excellent choice, for example. Thanks to an easy-to-understand interface, it's no trouble to thumbnail and catalog directories, disks (hard and floppy), or discs of images. You then can display the thumbnails on-screen or print them out. If you just want to reduce an image and thumbnails are too small, Thumbs+Plus also allows you to rescale and save an image to any size. You can find Thumbs+Plus on most BBSs and on-line services, or from shareware disk vendors.

If you need a utility more sophisticated than Thumbs+Plus, check out ImagePals 2 (from U-Lead Systems; call 800-858-5323). This program offers something called *album folders*, or holding areas for thumbnails. You can search for a graphics file by keyword, description, file size, and resolution. ImagePals 2 also converts more than 30 raster- and vector-based image formats. And, as an added bonus, it supports JPEG, LZW, and RLE compression schemes.

Komando Klues

Those who work only occasionally with images typically don't bother with image-management functions, but such features help users who manage large numbers of graphics. For example, DOS's eight-character file-naming system isn't very helpful when you're searching for a specific image in a huge catalog of files; a browser utility that lets you preview thumbnails of stored images certainly helps alleviate this headache.

Animations

.FLI, .FLC, .FLH, and .FLX

Someone was fired, and they gave me her old computer. A directory contains files with .FLI and .FLC extensions. What do these files have to do with the restaurant industry?

Odds are, the woman who previously used your computer was more into creating animations than doing her job.

Files with .FLI and .FLC extensions are made with an animation software program. The difference between .FLI and .FLC files relates to the animation's screen size: .FLI files are limited to a 320 × 200 screen size, but .FLC files can have any screen size.

By the way, .FLH and .FLX files also are animation files. They differ from .FLI and .FLC files only in that they can include more colors. An .FLH file is the same as an .FLC file, but the animation can have up to 32,000 colors, not just 256. .FLX files are the same as .FLC files, except they can have up to 16,000,000 colors, not just 256.

Before you delete the files, however, tell your manager what you found. It's unlikely that the animations have anything to do with the restaurant business, but stranger things have happened.

.GL

What is a .GL file? Do I need to use a special program to see it?

.GL is an animation file format created by Grasp, a commercial animation and presentation package from Paul Mace Associates. Displaying Grasp animations usually requires

➤ A VGA system

➤ A copy of Grasp or the .GL player GRASPRT

GRASPRT is an easy-to-use DOS program. Suppose that you want to see a Grasp animation called BUGEYES.GL that's located in your GRASPRT directory. To use GRASPRT, go to the GRASPRT directory, type **GRASPRT BUGEYES.GL**, and press Enter.

Creating Art

Making art

I want to start drawing pictures and making animations on my computer. What software do I need? Which shareware program(s) do you recommend as learning tools?

You need a drawing program and an animation program. Or an animation program that has drawing capabilities.

One of the better shareware draw-and-paint programs for DOS is NeoPaint from USCS. The menu system makes it easy for beginners, yet NeoPaint has features powerful enough for advanced users.

A very good shareware draw-and-paint program for Windows is PictureMan (a.k.a. PMAN) from Popatov Works. A fully integrated Windows program, PMAN uses both the video and printer driver that the user has installed in Windows.

Another good shareware draw-and-paint program for Windows is TopDraw.

In my humble opinion, the best shareware animation program is Animagian from Kavik Software. Animagian, which rivals commercial 2-D animation applications, has a complete built-in draw-and-paint program for creating traditional cel animations.

You can find any of these shareware programs on a major BBS or on-line service, or through shareware disk vendors.

Are you the next Walt Disney? I have this idea: You know how cartoon characters always have the same first and last initial (Donald Duck, Fred Flintstone, Roger Rabbit)? Why not Kim Komando? If you go with this idea, remember that I steered you in the right direction, and I want royalties.

 ## Making slides

I want to make 35mm slides of some sales charts and figures for an important presentation. How do I turn a graphics file into a 35mm slide?

You need professional help. Sure, you can spend thousands on the computer equipment necessary to turn a graphics file into a 35mm slide, but a better approach is to find a local copy shop or service bureau that already has the equipment and makes a living turning graphics into slides. To find a local copier or service bureau,

> ➤ Let your fingers do the walking: consult the Yellow Pages.

> ➤ Ask your local PC user's group for recommendations.

> ➤ Check the advertising or classified sections of computer magazines for national mail-order service bureaus.

Usually, national mail-order service bureaus are the least expensive outlets due to the sheer quantity of orders they fill. Make certain, however, that you find a bureau that can meet your deadline, give or take three business days. In addition, make sure that the bureau sends the slides back to you via an overnight delivery service so that the package is traceable. If the slides are lost in the mail, the inevitable fallback plan — shadow puppets — can be pretty darn embarrassing.

Making screen shots

I work in payroll. After getting bugged day in and day out by folks who don't know how to use Microsoft Word, I decided to write a short guide. I want to include screen shots, as in, "You are here." How do I capture them?

You know, you don't have to do everything yourself. There are these special stores, for example, that sell only books. Really. Maybe you've heard of them. In these, ahem, bookstores (novel term, eh?), you can find at least ten different how-to books on Microsoft Word. If you buy just one, you have your guide.

Now go back to what your cohorts really want from you: their checks!

To capture the entire screen shown in a Windows application, press the Print Screen key, which is normally located in the top row of your keyboard. Sometimes, this key is abbreviated on keyboards as PrtScn. Pressing PrtScn takes a snapshot of the screen and copies that image to the Windows Clipboard. You then can paste the contents of the Clipboard in a Windows application. For example, it's a snap to incorporate the screen shot in a word processing document. Just remember the Clipboard rule: The Clipboard's contents are automatically replaced whenever you cut or copy.

(Where does the old Clipboard contents go? No one knows, but I bet someone is writing a program right now to recover old Clipboard contents.)

To capture just the active window, press Alt+PrtScn. The active window is copied to the Windows Clipboard.

If you want to capture just an icon (or part of an active window), you should get a screen capture utility. (Sure, you can edit any picture that you paste to the Clipboard in Paintbrush, but you'll want a better way. Trust me.) For my company's software user manuals, I use ImagePals 2 from U-Lead Systems. The screen shots are accessible in *album folders*, or holding areas for thumbnails. You can search for a screen shot (or any other graphics file for that matter) by keyword, description, file size, and resolution. ImagePals 2 also converts more than 30 raster- and vector-based image formats. And, as an added bonus, it supports JPEG, LZW, and RLE compression schemes.

Signature as art

I want to add a personal touch — my signature — to the faxes I send from my computer. If I don't own a scanner, how can I turn my signature a graphics file? I use WinFax and WordPerfect for Windows.

The easiest way to turn your signature into a graphics file is to sign a piece of paper and mail it along with a check (the going rate is around $100) to Orbit Enterprises. Orbit returns your signature as a graphics file in .BMP, .PCX, or .TIF format. For more information, call Orbit at 800-767-6724.

Orbit's work is kind of pricey, so you may want to include your middle name so that you get your money's worth.

If you're the adventurous type and have access to a fax machine, you can turn your signature into a graphics file without Orbit:

1. Sign your name with a fine felt-tipped pen on a blank sheet of paper. *Tip:* Make your signature twice as large as normal. You then can resize the signature later without distorting it.

2. Set the fax machine to fine resolution.

3. Set your WinFax software to receiving mode.

4. Fax the page with your signature from the fax machine to your computer.

5. After your computer receives your faxed signature, choose File⇨Save As in the WinFax viewer and save the page as a .PCX file.

6. Open the saved page in Windows Paintbrush.

7. Clean up any rough spots and stray dots around the signature.

8. Use the cropping tool in Paintbrush to cut out just the signature.

9. Save the trimmed signature as either a .PCX or .BMP file.

You can use the resulting graphics file in any application that lets you bring in graphics.

Copyright

Understanding copyrights

Is it true that artwork I create on my computer is automatically copyrighted? A minister told me so.

Why doubt your minister? He gets his information from a higher source.

In the United States, a work is copyrighted as soon as it is created. Here are some excerpts from the 1976 Copyright Act (Title 17, US Code), which specifically states that protection

> . . . does not afford to the owner of a copyright in a work any greater or lesser rights with respect to the use of the work in conjunction with automatic systems capable of storing, processing, retrieving, or transferring information.

Other excerpts of this act that relate to your question:

> Copyright protection subsists . . . in original works of authorship fixed in any tangible medium of expression, now known or later developed, from which they can be perceived, reproduced, or otherwise communicated, either directly or with the aid of a machine or device. *17 U.S.C. 102(a).*

and

> A work is "fixed" in a tangible medium of expression when it's of the author, is sufficiently permanent or stable to permit it to be perceived, reproduced, or otherwise communicated for a period of more than transitory duration. *17 U.S.C. 101.*

The Bottom Line

In real life and in simple terms, as soon as you create original work, it's copyrighted. But the "either directly or with the aid of a machine or device" provision is important. The copyright stands whether you've printed your work or it's still sitting on a hard drive or floppy disk. No formalities are required.

In case you're wondering, copyright notices stopped being a requirement when the U.S. signed the Berne Convention and enacted the Berne Convention Implementation Act in 1988.

Komando Klues

Still, it's a good idea to register a copyright that will stand up in a court of law. You can save some money by registering the copyright yourself, but if your work is important, I'd hire a lawyer.

Establishing copyrights

I just started a computer graphics design company. I want to copyright the artwork I create on my computer. Whom do I contact at the government? When I tried to find out, I got the usual runaround.

To file copyrights yourself, you need to obtain the necessary forms from the U.S. Copyright Office, return the completed forms, include copies of the works to be registered on disk or hard copy (the office prefers printouts) and the fee (currently $20). You can register as many works as you wish at one time and still only pay a single registration fee. For more information, write to The Copyright Office, Information and Publication Section LM-455, Library of Congress, Washington, DC 20559. Or call 202-707-3000.

I suggest getting a handle on dos and don'ts now while your business is young. The Graphic Artists Guild publishes an excellent book about copyrighting, *Graphic Artists Guild Handbook: Pricing and Ethical Guidelines* ($24.95). Call the guild at 212-463-7730 for details.

Another excellent resource is *The Legal Guide for the Visual Artist* from Allworth Press; to order, phone 800-247-6553.

Getting permissions

How do I get permission to scan someone else's drawing and then use the drawing in a newsletter?

Contact the person who owns the drawing. It's tough to track down the artist unless the artist is a friend or you know a good private investigator. But fear not, we live in America, where capitalism rules.

For $20 an hour, The Copyright Office will perform a copyright-registration search. Write to The Copyright Office, Library of Congress, Washington, DC 20559, Attn: Reference and Bibliography Section. Or call 202-707-6850.

If you need permission quickly, go outside the government and hire an agency to hunt down the copyright holder. Hourly rates range from $50 to over $200. Two such agencies are

➤ BZ/Rights & Permissions (212-580-0615)

➤ Thomson & Thomson (800-356-8630)

By this point, I bet you're thinking that some original art done by your 3-year-old will suffice.

Copyright law

If I use clip art from CorelDRAW! while creating a line of greeting cards or stationery, am I violating any copyright laws? What if I alter the clip art?

I think that you can expect a greeting card that says, "Hope you get out of jail soon."

Generally, clip art included with commercial software programs (including CorelDRAW!) can be used as the purchaser sees fit — as long as the purchaser doesn't resell the images.

Adhering to copyright law is definitely a case of *Better safe than sorry*. In other words, don't guess when dealing with other folk's property. Read the user's manual, the fine print on the disk's packaging, and any other documentation. If you can't find the information you need, contact the source of the images. And if you cannot reach the source, don't use the images! Modifying an existing image doesn't change the copyright unless the end image bears *no* similarity to the original. And even if you think that the resulting image "bears no similarity to the original," remember that similarity is a judgment call, so you still risk potential litigation.

The truth is, the copyright laws haven't kept up with technology. The laws are ambiguous and out of date. If you have any doubts, consult a lawyer.

Copyright law, part 2

I want to use the clip art from the CorelDRAW! CD-ROM in some business fliers and advertisements. Can I get into trouble?

Hey, it's a moral thing. And you're the one who has to look at your reflection in that CD-ROM disk every day.

It's legal to use the clip art that comes on the CorelDRAW! CD-ROM in business fliers and advertisements as long as the person (or company) who purchased the disk is the person (or company) who's using the clip art. The license agreement allows only the purchaser to use the images.

So if you borrowed the disk from someone, you're not licensed to use the artwork. And if your employer owns the CD-ROM and you're using the clip art to launch a new business on the side, you may get burned in legal hot water. (You'll probably lose your job to boot.)

Clip art copyrights

I understand that clip art is protected by copyrights. Is it OK to use store-bought clip art on T-shirts and then sell the T-shirts?

Most software packages give you full reign to use clip art as you see fit. Well, almost full reign. Clip art publishers still retain the rights to distribute clip art electronically.

After you purchase CorelDRAW!, for instance, the product license allows you to use the clip art for personal use, business ads, logos, or any other creative endeavor. You are free to distribute your work in any printed manner.

You see, publishers have what is known as a *royalty free agreement*, thus enabling you to use their images for free. Basically, this phrase means that the clip art publisher doesn't get any compensation — other than a sense of pride, of course — if you decide to go into T-shirt business and use their clip art on your T-shirt.

Corel, however, draws the line at distributing or selling the company's images in electronic form. If you do so, expect a letter from Corel's lawyers. (Quick, send them some T-shirts.)

Not all companies are so generous. T/Maker's ClickArt Gold, for example, has much the same license agreement as Corel's licensing agreement. But T/Maker has a different view of people who use ClickArt Gold images in a commercial venture. In fact, ClickArt Gold users have to walk a fine line between selling a product with T/Maker ClickArt Gold images on it and selling T/Maker ClickArt Gold images on a product. In other words, T/Maker ClickArt Gold images can't be a substantial part of a product. For example, you can distribute a newsletter for profit that incorporates T/Maker ClickArt Gold artwork because the value of the newsletter is not based on the artwork. But you can't sell T-shirts with ClickArt images on them.

Other publishers have even stricter licensing agreements. You can use any of the clip art included in Softkey's PFS:Publisher in your company advertisements, brochures, stationery, and so on. But forget about using this clip art on any kind of product that you sell. Softkey's license lets you distribute a product that uses PFS:Publisher clip art as long as you don't charge for the product. Ask for money, and you need specific, written permission.

Your best source of information is the license agreement included in the software package. Yeah, you know the message; it's the one that no one ever reads but agrees to by opening the package of disks. Amid all the legalese and warranty disclaimers on the wrapper is a pretty straightforward note detailing how you can use the product. If you have any questions, call the software publisher's sales line or public relations department.

Be sure to write down the date you called, the time of day, the representative's name, and that person's exact reply to your questions. If a claim ever arises, you probably can use your notes as evidence.

Komando Klues

Even if the software publisher says that it's OK, you still may want to get a second opinion. So call a lawyer. It's better to be safe than sorry, especially if you want to keep your money in your pocket and not give it to some lawyer.

Using someone else's computer

I use my company's computer to make artwork. Who owns my art, my company or me?

Artists (or authors, for that matter) own the copyrights to their work automatically unless their art (or prose) was done as work-for-hire, in which case the employers own the copyrights. Makes me wonder what

Rembrandt would be doing today — probably creating screen savers for some company.

Check your company's employee handbook and human resources department for any applicable policies. Sometimes, generous employers let employees use company equipment during nonworking hours for personal use; of course, in most cases, the company must give explicit written permission.

Also look into your company's policy for keeping nonwork-related information on a company-owned computer. I've seen some pretty strict policies; the consequences can range from probation to termination. Don't be afraid to ask your employer or your lawyer. The job you save may be your own.

Scanning

Basic definitions

 What's a scanner?

I hear all this talk about image processing. Is this some high-tech public relations campaign? What's a scanner?

Image processing is taking some picture, such as a photograph, and transforming it into a computer file. After the picture is processed into a computer file, it's no longer merely a picture or photograph: it's an *image*. You can use this image as you do any other graphics file in your applications.

A *scanner*, which is a gadget that hooks up to your computer and works a lot like an ordinary copy machine, makes an image possible. A scanner takes a snapshot of something — photo, page of text, logo, artwork, and so on — and puts it inside your computer.

In days of yore, your parents' photographs rotted away in some old album, slowly developing a yellow tint. When you looked at those faded pics, you said, "You're old."

But you can preserve all your photos on disk. And years from now, when your kids look at you on-screen, they'll say, "You're old."

Ain't technology great?

What's resolution?

I just bought a hand scanner. The manual says to set the switches on the scanner for the picture's resolution. What is resolution? And how do I figure out which resolution to use?

I want you to learn all this stuff by the end of the year. A New Year's *resolution*, so to speak.

Look closely at a newspaper photograph, or place your nose up against a computer screen. See the tiny dots that make up the image? That's resolution in action. *Resolution* is the total number of dots per square inch, or dpi (*dots per inch*). The higher the resolution, the greater the number of dots. The greater the number of dots, the sharper and cleaner the image. But the greater the number of dots, the more hard disk space the image takes.

For example, raising the resolution from 150 dpi to 300 dpi for a 256-grayscale picture earns you a sharper image. But the extra 150 dpi takes four times as much disk space. A 24-bit color image — that is, a 24 million colors image — scanned at 300 dpi can take up 20MB.

Which resolution is best? There is no hard and fast rule. In fact, a lot depends on the printer eventually used. Scanning a picture in at 1,200 dpi is worthless when your printer prints out at only 300 dpi. If you scan an image at 1,200 dpi, you should use a service bureau that has a printer that can generate images at 1,200 or 2,750 dpi (or even higher). Moreover, it's not worth the hassle to scan images in 24-bit color when your computer can display images in 256 colors only.

Komando Klues

Most folks find that scanning at 600 – 1,200 dpi is more than adequate for desktop publishing or multimedia work. Black-and-white line art actually looks better scanned at a lower resolution, such as 300 dpi.

Note: Scanning an image at too high a resolution just wastes hard drive space and increases printing time.

Usually, you set the resolution in the scanning software. I suggest experimenting with different resolution settings for different types of images. When you find a resolution that works, make a note of the settings and save the information for future reference.

What's a bit?

What's a bit? What's the difference between 8-bit and 24-bit images?

An image's quality is based on both the bits of data per pixel (called *bits*) and the resolution.

Images are made up of dots, or *pixels*. You can squeeze anywhere from 1 to 24 bits per pixel. The higher the number of bits per pixel, the more colors you can squeeze into a pixel.

One bit equals one color and uses one bit per pixel; four bits equals 16 colors and uses four bits per pixel; eight bits equals 256 colors and uses eight bits per pixel; and 24 bits equals 16 million colors and uses 24 bits per pixel.

Komando Klues

The bits count, but resolution (that is, dpi) really determines an image's quality. That is, the more dots per inch, the clearer the image.

Image file size

Is there a rule of thumb for figuring out the relationship between resolution and file size? How much disk space, for example, will a standard 5 × 7 black-and-white scanned photograph consume?

Sounds like a joke. "I don't know. How much disk space will a standard 5 × 7 black-and-white scanned photograph consume?" "As much as it wants." Hey, I didn't say that it sounded like a *good* joke.

Each dot (or pixel) in an image takes about a byte of information (to represent the image and color). So if you scan a photo at 300 dpi, each square inch is made up of 300 dots × 300 dots — 90,000 bytes. You do the math: a 5 × 7 photo has 35 square inches, and 90,000 bytes multiplied by 35 equals around 3MB of hard disk space.

Note: Depending on the software you use for the scan (the software may use some kind of compression technique), the file size may be smaller.

For the record, a graphics file consisting of a 256-grayscale image quadruples in size each time you double the resolution.

Komando Klues

If hard disk is at a premium, scan your grayscale photographs at 150 dpi rather than 300 dpi. Most times, the extra 150 dpi is hardly noticeable.

Hardware/software

 What determines scan quality?

Assuming that the photo to be scanned is in great shape, is the quality of a scan more dependent on the hardware or software used?

Scanning isn't as easy as it sounds. It isn't even as easy as running a copying machine (which, come to think of it, isn't really that easy if your copier likes to eat every sheet of paper you feed it). Making a good scan of a photo is a delicate combination of science (hardware, software) and artist (the person who is scanning).

The three hardware areas that affect image control are

> ➤ *Scanner:* If you are scanning photographs or pages of text, you need a desktop unit, not a hand scanner. The quality of output and ease of operation are well worth the price difference.

> ➤ *Hard Drive:* Scans takes up hard drive space. An uncompressed, scanned 24-bit image at 640×480 resolution takes up almost a full megabyte of hard drive space.

> ➤ *Video Card:* For proper WYSIWYG (*what you see is what you get*) operation, you should buy a 24-bit video card — especially if you're scanning color photos. Good scanning software is hamstrung by a 256-color system. In fact, the combination of powerful software and 8-bit video card may make you feel as if you're doing needlepoint; the image appears on-screen in a cross-stitch pattern as the software and card attempt to convert the 16,000,000-color scan down to 256 colors for display.

A good scanning program should offer different image-manipulation options, including

> ➤ Sharpening controls
> ➤ Color, contrast, and hue adjustments
> ➤ Dithering methods
> ➤ And more

Most scanners include good starter software. Some of the more popular and powerful scanning tools are ZSoft's PhotoFinish, Aldus PhotoShop, and Aldus PhotoStyler. *Note:* Shareware applications lack the sophistication of their commercial counterparts.

Producing high-quality scanned photographs takes time. Experiment with different settings and save samples, noting the settings used.

Scanning software

Do scanners come with software, or do I need to buy special software separately?

Most times, the software you need (both to scan a photo and then to edit the resulting image) comes with scanners. Depending on the scanner software bundle, you normally get one or more of the following:

➤ Scanner driver(s) needed to run the scanner with your computer

➤ Scanning software

➤ An image editor, which you use to modify or clean up an image after the scan is completed

➤ An image-file organizer, which helps you find images quickly on your computer's hard disk

➤ An optical character recognition (OCR) program, which translates a page of text into an editable file (OCR programs take a snapshot of text and then try to identify the letters)

You should buy a scanner because of its performance; think of the accompanying software as bonus features. Oftentimes, a scanner may ship with a scaled-down version of a full commercial program. This software will work, but it won't have all the features you want. Generally, the less expensive the scanner, the more likely you need to buy a commercial image editor or OCR program. And the more money you'll have to shell out. If your scanner doesn't include good OCR software, for example, you can buy Caere Corp.'s OmniPage Professional, which boasts a 99-percent hit rate. But the manufacturer's suggested price is $695! That's over $7 per percent!

What's TWAIN?

Prices for 24-bit color scanners range in the thousands. It seems that all have drivers for the TWAIN standard and a minimum optical resolution of 300 dpi. What is TWAIN? And what does it mean when a scanner has an automatic document feeder and an attachment for scanning transparencies?

Time to crack open the Komando dictionary. It's in my brain, so be gentle.

Twaddle: Foolish, trivial, or idle talk. For example, *Kim twaddles on and on about scanners.*

TWAIN: An acronym for *Technology without an Interesting Name.* Think of TWAIN as the one-size-fits-all-scanners driver type.

Twang: A sharp nasal tone. Associated with blind dates.

An automatic document feeder, meanwhile, is a hardware add-on that automatically feeds a new document into a scanner, allows the scan to take place, removes the document, and feeds in the next document to be scanned. This attachment is useful if you plan to scan many pages at once or are too lazy to feed the sheets manually. (It's also something that's handy when you go on vacation; you don't have to worry about your scanner starving to death.)

An attachment for scanning transparencies is a device that lets the scanner take a good picture of transparent images (such as 35mm slides). This is a handy add-on if you have to give a lot of presentations.

Understanding OCR

I'm currently using a flatbed black-and-white scanner. I'm looking for a utility that will let me scan a full page into PageMaker 5.0 and then edit as needed. Any program that enables me to input a full page and has editing and printing capabilities will do.

When is a picture not a picture? When it's a picture of a page of text.

The type of scanning that you're talking about is called OCR (*o*ptical *c*haracter *r*ecognition). An OCR program takes a picture of text and then tries to identify or recognize the letters.

One of the better OCR programs is OmniPage Professional 5.0 (from Caere). OmniPage Pro is a Windows application that supports the TWAIN scanner interface; that is, it works with any scanner that has a TWAIN driver, which is just about any recently made scanner. Don't worry, Mark Twain has nothing to do with scanners. TWAIN is YAA (*yet another acronym*); it stands for *Technology without an Interesting Name* (honest!).

After OmniPage Pro takes a picture of your text, it tries to recognize the characters that make up the words. If it doesn't recognize a letter, the program lets you type in the missing letter. The program even learns how to recognize letters as you use it. After OmniPage Pro works its magic, you can place the text in a PageMaker document.

OmniPage Pro comes with Image Assistant, which lets you save any pictures on the page as well.

You can find OmniPage Pro at your local computer store. Or call Caere for more information at 800-535-7226.

Komando Klues Be sure to check the list of supported scanners before you buy any OCR program.

Troubleshooting

Scanning options

Should I set the scanner software for line art, half-tones, or grayscale?

It's pretty safe to pick the *line art* option when scanning simple art. Of course, you don't get any color with line art — line art is black and white. On the other hand, because line art consists of 1-bit scans, the image's file size is small.

By the way, you shouldn't have to change the scanner's software settings for line art.

Komando Klues Most times, the default is the best setting.

Selecting *halftones* works well with drawings that have a lot of shading. Select *grayscale* for photographs (black-and-white or color) that you want to convert to grayscale images.

Diet software

I just bought a scanner and am running Adobe PhotoShop LE. I can save my files as .BMP and .TIF but not .GIF. What do I need?

Money, money, and more money.

PhotoShop LE, which has just half the calories of real PhotoShop, does not save to .GIF format. In fact, PhotoShop Limited Edition gives you only enough tools to get started. (Hey, not everyone needs to save files in the .GIF format.)

In the PhotoShop LE manual, you can read about how to upgrade to the full version. Normally, the upgrade price is a fraction of the product's original purchase price. Order it. You need it.

Komando Klues

Until your upgrade arrives, you can save your images to .BMP or .TIF and then convert them to .GIF with other programs, such as the shareware programs Paint Shop Pro, Thumbs+Plus, and VPIC.

Scanning a signature

I want to use my hand scanner to scan my signature and make a graphics file for use in my faxes. How do I do so? Which file format should I use? Which resolution is best? I use Microsoft Word and WinFax.

Ask and ye shall receive:

1. Sign your name on a blank sheet of paper with a fine felt-tipped pen. Your scanned signature should be about twice as large as the one you plan to use in your documents. A graphic looks much better when you reduce it rather than enlarge or stretch it.

2. Scan your signature as you scan any other image.

3. Save the scanned image as a .PCX or a .BMP file. Faxes print at 200 dpi in high-res mode, so there's no need to scan your signature at a higher resolution.

4. Create a document that you want to fax in Microsoft Word.

5. When you're ready to insert your signature, make a picture frame by selecting Insert⇨Frame. Make the frame as big as you want your signature. You may have to fiddle with it a little before the size is right.

6. Choose Insert⇨Picture.

7. Select your signature's filename. Bingo. Your signature is, so to speak, signed, sealed, and delivered.

Now be careful that your kids don't get hold of that file, or they'll be using it to sign their report cards.

Filters

I have a scanned .TIF photo. I want to give it a watercolor appearance. Do I need a filter?

Actually, just get some watercolor paints and a few brushes. . . . Oh, you want to use your computer? Then yes, you need a filter.

A filter keeps certain things out and lets certain things through. Kind of like a teenage cheerleader's mother around the school football team.

Filters, which have become popular in both shareware and commercial paint programs, alter the appearance of pictures, making them look as if they've been painted on canvas, made out of ceramic tile, and more.

In the shareware realm, Paint Shop Pro (JASC) for Windows and Improces (John Wagner) come with predefined filters but also enable you to create your own. Creating original filters is quite confusing and takes a lot of experimentation, but the result is well worth the effort.

Commercial programs, such as Adobe PhotoShop and Aldus PhotoStyler, also come with predefined filters and better picture-handling tools. If you need more filters, don't worry. You can buy add-on filters — most notably, Gallery Effects from Aldus. Gallery Effects currently comprises three volumes of filters. Volume 1 has an excellent watercolor filter.

Most folks start out with the filters and then want more artist tools. At that point, they should get a progressive paint-and-draw program, which allows the artist to define mouse or stylus strokes to appear as if they were made with traditional artist tools. The commercial applications Fractal Design

Painter and Fauve Matisse, for example, offer tools such as watercolor brush and paper, felt markers of various styles, charcoal, and much more. (By the way, a shareware version of Fauve Matisse is available, but it does grayscale only.) As usual, you can find the commercial software programs at software stores and through computer mail-order houses. If you want the shareware, check a local BBS, on-line service, or shareware disk vendor.

Faulty scanner driver

The images I scanned at 300 or 400 dpi are herky-jerky from side to side on every scan line.

The herky images probably are caused by a jerky scanner driver (that's the software, not the person driving the scanner). Contact the technical support department of your scanner's manufacturer to see whether updated drivers are available. Most companies will ship updated drivers free of charge. If you cannot wait, use your modem to connect to the manufacturer's BBS and download the drivers.

Until you get the new drivers (or if no new drivers are available), try reinstalling your scanning software and the drivers. Sometimes, a scanning problem is the result of a corrupted software file or driver. A reinstallation is often a quick fix.

Komando
Klues

Finally, here's a tip for using a hand scanner: Use a thick ruler or other straight edge as a guide; that is, place the ruler alongside the image and run the scanner along the edge.

And limit coffee intake.

Dithering

I scan near-photographic images at 300 dpi. When I reduce my scans to 640 × 480, I get nothing like the photo quality on most 640 × 480 .GIFs. Is there a secret to this process? I've tried about ten graphics utility programs without much results.

Actually, you do get results, you just don't like them.

Listen carefully. Don't tell anyone. The secret: Software makes the scan.

As a result, you definitely should experiment; but follow the same steps with different programs. Then save each image under a different name and compare results.

Are you sure that you gave your scanning software a real honest-to-goodness try? It's the first place I look when trying to improve the quality of my scans.

When scanning, follow these steps:

1. Leave the scan in 24-bit format and load the image into your program.

2. Rescale the image to the desired size.

3. If the image is somewhat blurry, apply a slight bit of a sharpening filter.

4. Reduce the number of colors. Many programs offer different *dithering* methods for converting a 24-bit scan (up to 16 million colors) to an 8-bit image (256 colors). Three of the most common dithering methods are

   ➤ *Nearest* causes color blobs, not smooth changes between shades of color.

   ➤ *Ordered* causes a cross-stitch pattern.

   ➤ *Diffusion*, the least of the three evils, often causes random color pixels to appear where there should be a smooth transition between shades of color.

Komando Klues

The best utility for color reduction is DyeWorks (by Stefan Reich), a tiny DOS-based freely distributable utility. You can find DyeWorks on major BBSs and on-line services, and through shareware disk vendors. Although it's a DOS utility, it's easy to use; there are no confusing parameters or settings. To use DyeWorks, save the image to TGA (Targa) format after Step 3 of the preceding procedure.

My job is done here. Next question.

Wrong video driver

My scans look horrible. I recently discovered that my Diamond (Stealth 24) video adapter was a VGA (640×480 resolution). Is this why my scans are bad? Please help. These scans are making me look bad where I work.

OK, relax. This may take a couple of days, so you may want to bring in doughnuts for a few mornings until you can straighten things out.

Many users prefer a 640×480 resolution. But resolution is a personal call and doesn't have much to do with scan quality.

Stealth 24 is a 24-bit card, so you should be seeing some great images. I bet, however, that you're running Windows with a 16- or 256-color video driver. These video modes make your scans take on a needlepoint or cross-stitch effect when displayed in 24-bit mode. Most Windows scanning software applications automatically display 24-bit scanned images with an ordered dither unless Windows is running under a 24-bit video driver.

To check this out, go to the Main program group and select Windows Setup. If a 256- or 16-color display driver is listed, you need to install the 24-bit driver made for your video card. This driver should have come on a diskette with your video card. You also can obtain it free of charge from the manufacturer; in fact, this route may be your best bet because video drivers are updated regularly.

Excluding memory ranges

I have a Microtek ScanMaker IISP with SCSI that uses certain memory addresses with a TWAIN driver. I am using the memory address E400-E7FF. But something is conflicting, even though I used an EMMExclude statement in SYSTEM.INI to exclude that memory area. I called technical support; they were clueless.

I'm impressed. You took a step that few people think of: You told Windows to exclude the range of memory that the scanner is using. But because you didn't mention it, I bet that you didn't think of telling DOS not to use that same memory range. Ah, don't fret, that's why they pay me the big bucks.

As always, first make a copy of your AUTOEXEC.BAT and CONFIG.SYS files and put them in a safe place. Next, using a text editor like DOS's EDIT, open your CONFIG.SYS file. Near the top of your CONFIG.SYS file is a line that says something like

```
DEVICE=C:\DOS\EMM386.EXE...
```

where in place of the ellipsis are things such as I=, WIN=, and X=, as well as a bunch of numbers and words. These things tell DOS's memory manager which address ranges to include and which other memory ranges to use for Windows.

Add the letters *REM* and a space to the front of this line. *REM* informs the computer that the line is a *remark* and that the computer should ignore it.

The line should now look like

```
REM DEVICE=C:\DOS\EMM386.EXE...
```

Next, add the following line directly below the REM line:

```
DEVICE=C:\DOS\EMM386.EXE NOEMS X=E400-E7FF
```

This line tells DOS to exclude the memory range that's used by the scanner.

Save the new CONFIG.SYS file and restart the computer. Go into Windows and see whether the scanner is working properly now. If so, exit Windows and run MEMMAKER at the DOS prompt. When asked whether you want to run an express or custom setup, choose Custom. Then tell Windows to keep the current settings for EMM386 inclusions and exclusions. After MEMMAKER runs through all its calculations, run Windows again to make sure that the scanner is still working properly.

Other Troubleshooting

Compressed file

Right before my sister left the country, she sent me a disk with a JPEG picture. When I tried to open the picture in Paintbrush, all I saw was error messages.

Why did your sister leave in such a hurry? Is someone after her? Is she Carmen Sandiego? Perhaps the secret is in the picture.

A JPEG file isn't really a graphics file. JPEG is a way of shrinking (what techie types call *compressing*) a graphics file. I bet your sister JPEGed the graphic so that it would fit on the disk.

No offense, but your sister must not be too familiar with the graphics compression field. Although JPEG reduces the size of a picture file, it simultaneously reduces the quality of the image. It's a trade-off: you get a smaller file size, but the picture quality suffers.

You need a JPEG viewer to look at your sister's file; as you discovered, Paintbrush isn't enough to open the file. If you have access to a BBS, on-line service, or shareware disk vendor, get a copy of the Windows-based shareware program Paint Shop Pro.

Otherwise, drop by your nearest computer store and pick up a copy of Inset Systems's $169 HiJaak Pro for Windows. This program, which is an *imagebase* (that is, a database management system for images), supports over 70 graphics file formats. In fact, I bet HiJaak can handle your sister's file even if it isn't JPEG.

Komando Klues

By the way, if you're going to compress a graphics file, use PKWare's PKZIP. This compression utility won't compress the file nearly as much as a JPEG, but the picture quality won't suffer, either. Don't expect a huge difference in file size after using PKZIP; graphics files don't compress much because the files already are sorta compressed.

Encoded file

A friend sent me a .GIF file with a .UU file extension. When I open it, all I see is garbage characters and numbers on-screen.

You know what they say: "Garbage characters and numbers in, garbage characters and numbers out."

I bet that your friend sent you the .GIF via the Internet. Messages sent over the Internet can contain only regular letters and numbers. Picture files, such as .GIFs, contain special characters.

The .UU extension indicates that the file was encoded or changed to contain just regular letters and numbers. To put the file back into its original form (so that you can see the picture), you need to decode it.

Several DOS, Windows, and Mac shareware programs are worthwhile. Check with your Internet provider for a .UU file decoder. Indeed, because many Internet providers include basic file and mail utilities in their membership kits, you already may have the decoder needed. You just need your Internet provider to tell you where it's hiding in the membership software.

Or you can get Extract by David Penner. One of the most popular shareware programs, it runs either in DOS as a command line application or in Windows as a full-blown program.

CorelDRAW! and .TIF file

My logo is blue and gold, with no background. I want to place this art — saved as a .TIF file — on a shaded background. When I try to do so in CorelDRAW! 3.0, the background doesn't show; instead, I see a white rectangle around the logo. My deadline is near! What can I do?

Uh, change the logo to include a white, rectangular box?

CorelDRAW! is a great drawing program, but it's not the right tool for this particular job because a .TIF file is a bitmap graphic and CorelDRAW! puts graphics in a vector format. Sure, CorelDRAW! lets you import .TIF files, but you can't edit these images much. In your case, CorelDRAW! assumes that your logo already has a background — the white rectangle. And you cannot make that white background disappear.

Your best bet is to use a drawing program, such as Corel Photo Paint. In drawing programs, you can cut out your logo and then paste it on a background. In other words, the process is similar to clipping a picture out of a magazine, carefully removing any unwanted background, and pasting the trimmed image on another piece of paper.

Import formats

I have made a healthy collection of graphics in CorelDRAW!. At my new job, I need to convert these files to another format to use in programs that won't import .CDR files. Which format do you recommend?

CorelDRAW! graphics are vector graphics, so save them in any other vector graphics file format, such as .WMF or .CGM.

Note: You can edit vector-based graphics in any vector-based graphics editing program.

If you need a graphics file conversion tool, drop by your nearest computer store and pick up a copy of Inset Systems's $169 HiJaak Pro for Windows, which supports over 70 graphics file formats.

Komando Klues

Each graphic must be loaded individually into CorelDRAW! and then saved in the format of choice. Because converting graphics can be a time-consuming process (especially if the images are big or your system has just 8MB of memory), consider using a service bureau or a commercial printer.

Printer driver

My Instant Artist for DOS (by Autodesk) does not list my HP 550C printer, so I have to choose the 500C, which does not work in color. The printer works fine in Windows. What's going on?

Here's the problem in a nutshell (or DOS shell, for that matter): The version of Instant Artist that you're using was made before your printer was made.

You see, printers and other devices speak their own languages; *drivers* are interpreters that translate information sent from programs to the device. Your version of Instant Artist doesn't list the 550C printer because it doesn't have the appropriate driver; because the program doesn't have the appropriate driver, it doesn't know exactly how to talk to the printer.

To solve your problem, you need to upgrade to the latest version of Instant Artist for DOS. Or, if you're running Windows, get Instant Artist for Windows. (Windows programs don't need to know how to talk to a printer; if the proper driver is installed in Windows, the picture prints out.) Either way, call Autodesk at 415-332-2344.

Ooooh, here's an idea: You can always downgrade your printer.

Speed

I have Windows (8MB of RAM) and use DOS 6.2, PhotoShop, and CorelDRAW!. What can I do to speed up screen redraws? Now, I press Enter and go out for coffee and a cigarette. If I put in a large picture, I have time to grow my own coffee and tobacco.

Your computer simply may need a tune-up.

Start with some disk maintenance. SCANDISK is a disk repair program that keeps all the directories on your hard drive in working order. The program also checks and tracks physical defects — places on the disk that have gone bad, places where you can no longer save information. To run SCANDISK, exit Windows entirely, go to the DOS prompt, type **SCANDISK**, and press Enter.

Then run DEFRAG, which reorganizes the information on your hard drive. Over time, files get jumbled up on your hard disk. Although DOS always seems to know where everything is, it's not a very good housekeeper. For example, pieces of a single file can be strewn across the hard disk as the file grows or shrinks. DEFRAG fixes this *fragmentation*. To run DEFRAG, type **DEFRAG** at the DOS prompt and press Enter. Reboot the computer and restart Windows.

After you finish tuning up your computer, double-check two factors that affect speed: swap file used and colors displayed.

➤ A *permanent* swap file helps speed up Windows's performance. From the Main program group, select Control Panel and then double-click the Enhanced icon (which looks like a computer chip). When you click on the Virtual Memory button, Windows tells you the type of swap file it's using. If necessary, click on the Change button and change the swap file type to permanent; be sure to take the suggested value for the new swap file size. In addition, make sure that the Use 32-Bit Disk Access button is checked. Then click OK. When Windows asks whether it should restart again, restart Windows.

➤ You also can speed up Windows's display by decreasing the number of colors used. Although it's nice to see pictures in 256 colors (or more), Windows and the video card then must move a lot more information. If you're not going to work with images in 256 colors, change the video driver back to 16 colors. You can do so within Windows by selecting the Windows Setup icon (found in the Main program group). Speaking of video drivers, make sure that you have a current video driver. Contact the manufacturer if you need an upgrade.

If things still are running too slow, you're going to have to buy an accelerated video card designed to work in Windows. In addition, although Windows, PhotoShop, and CorelDRAW! all work with 8MB of RAM, you need 16MB to do heavy-duty work with reasonable speed. Finally, know that CorelDRAW! 5.0 requires a math coprocessor: if you own a 386 or 486SX computer, you will enjoy a significant boost in CorelDRAW! speed by upgrading to a 486DX or Pentium computer. (In fact, all your Windows programs benefit when you have a faster CPU.)

File management

I come from a religious family. According to our tradition (so to speak), .GIF's have to be hidden from the mother. What's the best way to do so? I used ATTRIB **to hide some files, but my mother found them.**

You know that mothers have a sixth sense and eyes in back of their heads. I never could put anything past my mom.

I don't know how computer-literate your mother is, but you can try the following:

➤ Set up your File Manager so as not to show hidden files. Choose View⇨By File Type. Then deselect Show Hidden/System Files.

➤ Don't leave the files on the hard drive. Copy them to a diskette and keep them in your private stash.

➤ Try renaming the files with a different extension, such as .DOC. When you want to use the files, rename them back.

Chapter 11
Hardware

 Spotting a floppy disk

My computer is hard to reach. Is there a quick way to look at it and tell whether a floppy disk is in the disk drive?

You may want to get Footstool 6.2. It's two inches higher than Footstool 6.0. Ah, technology.

You can tell whether a disk is in the floppy disk drive by looking at the drive latches. On a 5¼-inch drive, you close the disk drive latch door by moving the knob to a vertical position. So, when the little latch is vertical (up and down for those younger readers), a floppy disk is in the drive. The smaller-size disk drives use 3½-inch floppy disks, and they have a button instead of an open-and-close knob. If the button is pushed in and you can hardly see it, no floppy disk is in the disk drive. When you slide the 3½-inch floppy disk in all the way, you hear a click, and the open/close button pops out.

Komando Klues
Here are some tips about floppy disks and drives: If you take a closer look at the disk drives, you will see a tiny light bulb. When the computer is putting information on or taking information off a floppy disk, the light goes on. Never, ever take a floppy disk out of a drive when the light is on. You can do some damage. Also, after you're done using a floppy disk, take it out of the disk drive. If you are using 5¼-inch floppies, be sure to keep them in their protective sleeves.

Why is the hard disk faster?

Whenever I load my fantasy baseball game from a floppy disk onto my computer, it seems to take forever. Loading the game from my hard disk is much faster. How come I can load information from the hard disk faster than I can load information from a floppy disk?

Fantasy baseball striking out? Hitting foul? Remember, baseball is a slow game. Not the answer you wanted? Let me take another swing at it.

The simple answer is that hard disk drives are faster than floppy disk drives — for several reasons.

First, hard disk drives and floppy disk drives spin at different rates. Floppy disk drives normally spin at 300 RPM (*r*evolutions *per m*inute). The exception to this rule (there always is at least one exception to every rule) is the 5¼-inch high-density floppy drive. This puppy spins at 360 RPM. On the other hand, the slowest hard disk drives spin at 3600 RPM, which is ten times faster than floppy disk drives. Faster hard disk drives can spin up to 6500 RPM and beyond. Go, speed racer!

Another reason hard disk drives spin so much faster than floppy disk drives is that they are made out of different materials. They use a different method for getting, or reading, information from the disk. The part of the floppy disk that actually stores information, as you might guess from the word *floppy,* is the flexible piece of plastic that's coated with a magnetic compound. When information is written to or read from the disk, two heads in the floppy disk drive physically grip the disk. Although the pressure is extremely light, their touch does create a small degree of friction — kind of like the friction you feel when someone calls you now by your grade-school nickname. This friction is responsible for the limited speed at which floppy disks can rotate.

Hard disks, on the other hand, have one or more platters that are made of either an aluminum metal alloy or glass. These platters are — you guessed it — hard and also very lightweight. In contrast to the heads in a floppy disk drive, the heads in a hard disk drive do not touch the platters while they are spinning. Instead, the heads float on a cushion of air a minute distance away from the platter. The technology is incredible. Because the heads don't touch the platters, there is little friction. Hence, hard drives spin at far greater speeds than the speeds at which floppy disk drives spin. This rotational speed translates into faster data transfer.

But, to really understand why things are the way they are, you need to know a little bit about the way hard and floppy disks store information. Information is put in concentric rings around the disk. Each ring is called a *track*. Each track is broken down into smaller sections, called *sectors*. Moving from one sector to another within a track is a relatively quick activity because only the disk needs to spin under the heads. What takes up the most time is moving from one track to another because the heads of the drive have to move back and forth, parallel to the disk. The average time required by the head to move from one track to another is called the *seek time*. Again, the lack of friction enables hard drives to seek faster than floppy drives. As a result, hard disk drives are faster than floppy disk drives.

What's my bus?

I just bought a sound card, and I need to know whether my computer has a VESA local bus. How can I find out?

They call VESA a bus, but it's really a jet.

The VESA local bus is designed to significantly speed up the 486 computer's ability to process video output and communicate with hard disks. It accomplishes this feat by offering a slot that has direct access to system memory at the exact same speed as the processor. This design eliminates much of the bottleneck that occurs on computers that have MCA 8-bit and 16-bit slots. These slots can send only 8 or 16 bits of data to a processor that can handle 32 bits of information. As a result, the processor cannot get data as fast as it can handle it, so much of the processor's speed is wasted. Not a good use of resources. But with the new VESA local bus, the processor is kept busy with data that is sent as fast as the processor can receive it.

The maximum rated speed of the VESA bus is 128 – 132MB per second, compared to a maximum speed of 8MB on a computer that has a 16-bit ISA bus. Just a teensy bit of difference between the two! Windows and OS/2 love the VESA bus because it greatly speeds up screen redraw.

The
Bottom Line

So, do you have a VESA local bus? Well, if you have a 386SX or older computer, definitely not, because those computers have only a 16-bit or slower bus and can't handle the VESA bus. If you have a newer, faster 386, such as the 386DX 40, or an older, slower 486SX 40, you may have a VESA bus. It's hard to tell. However, if your computer is a 486DX2, DX4, or Pentium, it is extremely likely that you have a 32-bit VESA or a 64-bit PCI bus. The best way to know for sure is to check the documentation that came with the system to find out the motherboard type. Wow, this answer turned out to be a long one.

Killing time while the memory adds up

How can I avoid counting memory when my computer boots up? It just takes soooooo long for it to count up to 32MB!

Ah, what a problem to have. Sort of like Uncle Scrooge complaining that it takes too long to count his money. Why do you want to bypass the memory check? You run the risk of having the computer fail to warn you that a memory chip is bad. You really should learn to have more patience in life.

You could just leave the computer on all the time so that it's ready when you are. But that's a bad idea for a novice user. I would recommend that a new user understand the pros and cons before making that type of system decision. A better solution: Simply get into the habit of switching the computer on a few minutes before you need to use it. How about playing along: turn it on and try to review everything in your memory while the computer counts its memory.

You can speed up memory count by not having the computer check its memory. If you have an AMI or Award BIOS in your computer, pressing the Esc key during the memory count will cause the computer to zip through the memory count. On a Phoenix BIOS, pressing the spacebar does the same thing. On most computers, you could go into the computer's CMOS and make sure that error checking beyond 1MB is disabled or turned off totally. (*Note:* I do not recommend this method, and if you did it while I was nearby, I'd slap your hands with a ruler.) The CMOS stores information about your machine that the computer uses each time the computer starts. On most computers, you can access the CMOS by pressing the Delete or F1 key as soon as you turn on the computer. Be careful not to change anything in the CMOS that you aren't sure about. Otherwise, you could find that your computer doesn't recognize your hard drive, or you could have other such nasty problems.

If you have DOS 6.2 or later or Windows for Workgroups 3.1 or later, these programs automatically perform error checking on all extended memory more thoroughly than most BIOS checks. You can disable the memory checks by editing the HIMEM.SYS line in the CONFIG.SYS file. Just add the following switch to the end of the HIMEM.SYS line:

```
/TESTMEM:OFF
```

The Bottom Line

If you're not sure how to edit the CONFIG.SYS file, the answer is in the DOS chapter of this book.

Hey, leave the memory check alone. The few seconds you save could be the best seconds spent.

What are BIOS and CMOS?

I don't want to look stupid in front of my friends who speak computerese. What are BIOS and CMOS?

You shouldn't let your friends intimidate you. Remember, these people are the same computer geeks you used to laugh at in school. Don't let them push you around. Inside, they're just as scared as everyone else.

Gee, if those terms are the only ones that stump you, you're doing pretty good. Computer techies just love to impress their friends by throwing around acronyms. BIOS and CMOS are often used in the same breath because they are closely related.

BIOS stands for *b*asic *i*nput/*o*utput *s*ystem. That's helpful, isn't it? The BIOS is stored in *ROM* (*r*ead-*o*nly *m*emory) on the motherboard. It's becoming clearer now — I can see it in your eyes. Just think of the BIOS as all the rules and regulations, called the *instruction set,* that the computer needs to know so that it can use all the equipment inside it — the hard drive, the floppy drives, CD-ROM — and attached to it — the keyboard, the monitor, and more.

CMOS stands for *complementary metal oxide semiconductor.* (What a mouthful! Go ahead. Try to say that three times real fast without stuttering.) The CMOS is where the computer saves information about itself. It keeps track of what kind of drives you have, the date, the time, the keyboard type, and much more. The CMOS settings are maintained by a rechargeable battery. The battery keeps it from forgetting the computer's vital statistics when the computer is turned off.

411

Some computers have a special long-life battery, but many computers use standard AA batteries. Eventually, the batteries need replacing, and this is often a computer user's first experience with computer-induced panic. The CMOS battery dies, and you receive an ugly message, such as *No boot device present*. But of course, when this happens to you, you'll know not to panic. Why? Well, because you heeded my advice and went into your computer's CMOS zone and wrote down all the settings and stored this information in a safe place. You need this to reenter the information into the CMOS settings after you buy and install a new battery.

CMOUSE failure *message*

My sister is getting a *CMOUSE failure* message when she turns on her computer. There's no DOS prompt or anything. She turns it on and the message sits on-screen. She's ready to sell the computer and buy a new one.

Your sister gives up pretty easily. Has she been married several times?

I bet the message your sister is getting refers to a CMOS failure. The CMOS is where the computer stores its vital statistics. It keeps track of what kind of hard and floppy drives it has, wait states, RAM, bootup sequence, and other technical details. It's a sure bet that the battery that powers the CMOS when her system is off is running down or is no longer working. She needs to replace the battery and restore the CMOS settings.

When she gets the error message, it probably also tells her to push a key or some combination of keys to resume or enter the setup screen. That action will take her to the CMOS setup screen. It's a scary-looking place. But, if she is lucky, there will be an option to use the power-on default system settings. If not, she should probably take the computer to a service center and have the settings restored by a professional. If the settings are wrong, the computer won't boot correctly, if at all.

Adjusting the CMOS settings

I thought I would improve my system by installing a VGA card, and I messed it up big time. I also noticed that the hard drive was marked "not installed," so in a moment of madness, I set the hard drive to Type 1 in the CMOS. Now, nothing works. Please offer some suggestions even if they involve dropping heavy objects on the motherboard.

Suggestions, hmmm. Have you considered auto repair? Computers don't seem to be your thing.

First, let's assume that you did indeed remove the old video card and not some other card, such as the sound card. And let's assume that you correctly seated the new video card. If you are scratching your head now and thinking, "Er, I was supposed to remove the old video card?" or if you're wondering what is *seating* in computer talk, you need to go back to square one: reread that otherwise useless manual that came with the video card.

If all of the settings are gone in the CMOS, check the CMOS battery inside the computer. Your attempt at making the computer better may have coincided with the death of the battery. Or perhaps you disconnected the battery when you were futzing inside the computer. Check that the CMOS battery works and that it is snug.

Now that you've got everything connected correctly (yeah, right), you need to fix the CMOS settings. Make sure that all the information is correct for everything except for the hard drive; check the information about the floppy disk drives, the date, the time, the amount of memory, the screen type, and all of the computer's other gory details.

Here comes the tricky part: choosing the hard drive's settings. Somewhere in the hard drive's documentation or the computer's paperwork, there should be a list of specifications. If you don't have the documentation, oftentimes the information is listed right on the hard drive itself. You're looking for any mention of the hard disk type; the number of cylinders, heads, and sectors that it has; and other words you wouldn't normally use in one sentence.

If you can't track down the hard disk's facts and figures, call the hard drive's manufacturer for the information. You need to obtain the hard drive's size and the number of cylinders, heads, and sectors. With that information in hand, go back into the computer's CMOS settings. Chances are, despite the many types to choose from, your computer's hard disk type is the user-defined type — 47. Enter the information about the hard disk, save your changes, and the computer will restart. If you are wondering how you will know whether you got it right, don't worry. The hard drive won't work if the CMOS settings are wrong. Isn't that special?

Now that I have solved your problem, I have an '88 Honda that needs a new timing chain. Can you help?

Do I need more RAM?

I may be the stupidest person ever to operate a computer, but I am at my wits' end! I have an IBM/PS1 with 6MB RAM, and it is a 386SX. I have Windows 3.1 and have upgraded my DOS from 5.0 to 6.2. I have installed a CD-ROM drive and a 72-pin, 4MB SIMM card. My problem is this: I purchased PrintShop Deluxe for DOS and followed the directions precisely on its installation. But when I tried to run the program in DOS, a message stated that there was not enough memory in RAM to operate the program. Do I need to shell out more money to buy another SIMM card?

Wow, you are not the stupidest person ever to operate a computer. You almost lost *me* there. Now relax. Your computer has enough memory to run PrintShop Deluxe. You see, although you put more memory in the computer, but DOS doesn't know it's there. DOS looks at only the first 640K of memory; memory beyond 1MB gets used, but differently. Another SIMM probably won't do anything except make your charge-card bill a little higher.

Time for a little history lesson. The reason that DOS looks at only the first 640K of memory goes back to the original 8086 chip that was used in the very first personal computers. That chip could only see, or *address*, 1MB of memory. The first megabyte of memory in a computer is called *conventional memory*. Unfortunately, early computers used only 640K of that memory. The other 360K or so was reserved for the hardware. Chips developed later can use more memory, but a problem remains. Because of the way older operating systems access memory, older programs don't run on the newer machines. And even worse for owners of the older computers, the new programs don't run on older machines. So to keep everything backwards and forwards compatible, DOS to this day can address only 1MB of memory.

The message that you received tells you that you don't have enough conventional memory — the first 640K of RAM in your computer. PrintShop Deluxe for DOS, like all DOS programs, needs a certain amount of conventional memory. Most programs sold today need somewhere in the neighborhood of 580K to 620K. Look at the PrintShop Deluxe box and see how much conventional memory the program needs. If it's not listed on the box, look in the user's manual or call the software's technical support department. But wait a minute, I hear you, you should have 640K available. You'd think so, wouldn't you, but the truth is never simple. Type the following at the DOS prompt and press the Enter key:

```
MEM
```

You'll discover that the largest executable program size is significantly smaller than 640K.

Where is all of that missing memory going? DOS takes some, as do device drivers, terminate-and-stay-resident programs (TSRs), and other programs in your computer's start-up files. If you're curious to see exactly what's hogging all that memory on your system, type the following at the DOS prompt and press Enter:

```
MEM /C /P
```

As you saw before, the MEM command tells you how the memory is being used. Adding /C as a switch to the MEM command causes device drivers, TSRs, and programs to be listed, along with the specific amounts of memory they are using. The /P switch simply causes the computer to pause when the screen is full so that you can read the information on-screen and then press any key to continue on to the rest of the information.

Now that you know that lots of stuff is taking up precious memory, you are probably wondering what to do about it. The answer is simple. No, no, no, don't delete all the drivers! You need them. You have to move as much stuff as possible out of the user portion of conventional memory — also known as *lower memory* — and into the reserved portion of conventional memory — also known as *upper memory*. Because you use DOS 6.2, this change is a piece of cake. All you need to do is run a program that came with DOS, MEMMAKER, which will automatically optimize memory by finding the most efficient way to load drivers into the upper memory area. Type the following at the DOS prompt and press Enter:

```
MEMMAKER
```

Choose the Express Setup — it's easier to use than the Custom Setup. If, after running MEMMAKER, you still don't have enough memory, you may be able to use other third-party programs, such as QEMM386 and NetRoom, to obtain a little more conventional memory.

 ## Can I add a coprocessor?

My friend bought a 486SX 25 and would like to add a coprocessor. Is it cheaper to add a coprocessor without the clock doubler?

Sure, your friend can get a math coprocessor for the 486SX 25 chip without doubling the clock. Whether it is cheaper depends on what he hopes to gain now and in the future. To make a good decision, your friend should understand exactly what he is thinking about buying. He may be surprised by the answers.

The 486SX 25 chip is the exact same chip as the 486DX 25 except for two tiny differences: the math coprocessor on the 486SX 25 chip is disabled, and it's cheaper than a 486DX 25. So your friend decides six months later that the machine is too slow. It happens to almost everyone. Well, now he can add the 80487SX chip.

What's an 80487SX chip? You think it's a math coprocessor chip? Surprise! It's a 486DX 25 chip. And when it's inserted into its little socket, it completely shuts down the 486SX 25 chip and takes over. So now you have a 486DX 25 system that has the math coprocessor with an extra 486SX 25 chip on the motherboard as decoration. Aren't those guys and gals down at Intel clever?

OK, the machine is still too slow. If your friend wants the clock doubler chip, he has to add an overdrive processor to the system. The so-called overdrive processors are the 486DX2 series of chips. The 486DX2 chips are 486DX chips with the clock doubled. Like the 80487SX chip, the 486DX2 chip can be popped into the empty math coprocessor slot. It too takes over the system and shuts down the 486SX 25 processor.

As you may have gathered by now, the so-called math coprocessor slot on the 487SX motherboard is simply an upgrade slot. It enables you to easily transform your computer into a faster machine. Although the 80487SX chip is cheaper than the 486DX2 chips, there's a catch. When your friend eventually wants to double the clock, he will need to remove the 80487SX chip and replace it with a 486DX2 chip. So in the long run, buying an 80487SX chip now will cost more money because he will have to purchase two different chips. Unless, of course, he waits for the next generation of chips to come out and push down the prices.

Komando Klues

Before you upgrade to a chip that has a math coprocessor, make sure that your software programs will use a math coprocessor. Number-crunching programs, such as spreadsheets, and graphics programs, such as CAD programs, use a math coprocessor. Word processors don't use a math coprocessor. If you don't have an application that uses a coprocessor, there is no sense in buying one.

Wow, that answer took up a lot of space. If I had an 80487SX math coprocessor or a 486DX2, I could have answered this question in half the space.

Is C: drive failure *bad?*

When I started up my computer, I got a very scary error message: *C: drive failure insert boot disk.* Is this as bad as it sounds?

Are you sitting? Are there any sharp objects nearby? Do you love yourself enough to hear the truth? The message *C: drive failure insert boot disk* means exactly what it says. The computer tried to read the drive for the information it needs to work and discovered that the information wasn't there. Because it was expecting to find the operating system on drive C, it is wisely asking you to insert a boot disk into drive A.

Many different things could be wrong with the hard drive, but they all have one thing in common — hardware failure. In other words, something is physically wrong with the hard disk or its controller. If it were merely a problem with the information on the disk or the material holding the data, you'd get a different error message — something about failure to read the hard drive, a missing operating system, a nonboot disk, or an invalid partition table.

The most common reason for hard drive failure is that the drive is not responding to the CMOS configuration sent to the hard drive controller. The controller card for the hard disk is inside the computer. Usually, this problem is caused by an incorrect drive-select jumper setting; a loose, broken, or incorrectly inserted control cable; a loose or damaged power cable; a bad power supply; or a damaged controller.

Another common reason for hard drive failure is that something on the hard drive's logic board has failed. The logic board (some drives have more than one) is mounted directly onto the hard drive and controls the spindle and head as well as the transfer of information off the hard disk to the hard disk controller. What commonly happens is that one of the tiny circuits or diodes blows on the board. If this happens, you can usually smell that something has burned and see some smoke traces on the bad circuit or diode. Perhaps you can see a corresponding smudge on the inside of the case. The good news is that these parts cost pennies. The bad news is that unless electronics is your hobby, the very minor labor involved could cost a fortune. Replacing the board or even the complete hard drive is much cheaper. However, the only companies that will replace the hard drive circuit board for you are ones that specialize in data recovery. They bank on the fact that most people don't back up the information on their hard disk. Of course, you're not one of those people.

Another possibility is that the hard drive controller card failed. If you have the most common type of hard drive, IDE, the problem is the same as having the logic board fail because the main controller is directly mounted onto the IDE hard drive. If, however, you have a SCSI controller, the quite rare ST-506/412, or the ESDI, you can replace the controller card very easily because it is not mounted on the hard drive. If you are not sure of what you have, you probably have an IDE because it costs less. People who have other kinds of controllers spent more money, and they usually are quite proud of them and brag about them a great deal. That's why you are quietly happy when they get a *C: drive failure insert boot disk* message.

The next most common reason for hard disk failure is *stiction* — the techie term for static friction. In other words, the heads are stuck to the platters of the hard drive so firmly that the motor is not strong enough to lift the heads from the platters and start them spinning. This problem can occur if the hard drive overheats — particularly if the computer has been overheated and then turned off for more than a week. Then the heads have time to firmly glue themselves to the platters.

Take the computer in for service. But at least you know about some possible problems when the technician explains what needs to be done to fix the computer. Aren't you glad you have been backing up your data files on a regular basis?

Understanding AMI BIOS

I've pulled all my hair out trying to understand the Advanced CMOS Setup in an AMI BIOS system. I desperately need information describing what each individual setting does and what to set them for on a 486DX 33 system. Do you have any idea where I can obtain answers to these questions?

You've pulled all your hair out? Are you sure you are not using your problems with the Advanced CMOS Setup in an AMI BIOS system to disguise your hair loss?

You've asked one of those questions that mere mortals were never meant to ask. Unless you *know* what you're doing, don't mess with the advanced CMOS settings. You can end up leaving your system in a very bad state (such as making it very, very slow). In some cases, you may not even be able to boot up the computer. If that happens, you have to unplug the little battery from the motherboard (this can be as easy as unplugging a couple of wires or as complex as unsoldering the battery from the motherboard). Then you have to reconnect the darn thing. Most CMOS setup programs have an option to reset BIOS to factory defaults. These defaults are generally best for the computer. You can also reset the CMOS to the factory defaults inside the advanced CMOS option usually by pressing the F7 key. An easier way is to simply unplug the battery that helps the computer remember its settings.

If you have a burning need to know what all those little options in the Advanced CMOS are, the best place to get information on the AMI BIOS Advanced CMOS Setup is in the user's manual that came with your motherboard. What's that? The dog ate it? You never got one? Too cryptic? OK, maybe that wasn't the best suggestion. Here's a basic rundown of the settings.

Two important settings are Cache write Wait State and DRAM write CAS Wait State. The default settings for these two are 0, and they should be left that way. The other setting, 1, is for factory testing only. These settings set the speeds of the memory chips; it's best to leave them alone until you know what you're doing.

On to the next settings, for Shadow Cacheable. Remember the Advanced CMOS Setup? In it are four settings for shadowing various portions of ROM BIOS. When ROM BIOS is shadowed, the BIOS instructions load much faster RAM, which makes the BIOS much faster. Unfortunately, shadowing also takes up some valuable upper memory blocks that are oh-so-useful for loading the zillions of devices that no computer is complete without.

Depending on the way your computer is configured, you may or may not have room to shadow all or parts of the RAM without risking the loss of too much conventional memory. If you try to load more things in upper memory than your system has room for, they will simply be loaded low, and you may wind up without enough conventional memory to run your favorite programs.

If you do choose to shadow the RAM, you can enable these settings to cache any or all of the shadowed RAM. Caching will further speed up the system, although you sacrifice even more memory. The default settings are to enable only C000h 32K SHADOW CACHEABLE and F000h 64K SHADOW CACHEABLE. If these settings are enabled, then the video and system BIOS also must be shadowed.

If your inquiring mind wants to know more, contact the company that made the computer or the company that made the motherboard. They sometimes make the "tech specs" available. As a last resort, contact the company that made those BIOS chips. American Megatrends Inc. (AMI) can be reached in Norcross, Georgia, at 404-263-8181.

And remember, I'm not only president of the Advanced CMOS Setup club, I'm also a member.

What's the difference between serial and parallel?

How can I tell the difference between a serial port and a parallel port?

Well, if it gets all soggy when you add milk to it, it's a serial port. (Bad, bad, bad.) The easiest way to tell them apart is to look at the connectors on the ports. A serial port is *pronged*, meaning that the pins are sticking out, and it has 9 or 25 pins. A parallel port is prongless and has 25 holes.

Modem kills mouse

I have two serial ports, called COM 1 and COM 2, in my 386DX computer. I've just put in an internal modem, but now my mouse doesn't work. What should I do?

Go back to your dealer and trash his place of business. No, don't do that. Only do that if this answer doesn't work.

It sounds suspiciously like you've got an IRQ conflict. "Of course," you say, "why didn't I think of that? Uh, what in the blazes is an IRQ?" Communication ports, called *COM,* or *serial,* ports, are particular little devils. Many people run into trouble because they simply don't know the COM ports' purpose and hence, cannot figure out how to make them work.

Think of COM ports as merely a means to enable your computer to use things outside the actual system unit box. For example, almost everyone has a mouse. The pointing device is necessary to talk to, or work with, Windows. Almost always, the mouse connects to a COM port.

A modem enables your computer to talk to another computer over an ordinary telephone line. The modem takes a COM port, too. Most people use modems to connect to on-line services, such as America Online. A big piece of the COM port puzzle is the computer's center of activity, or the central processing unit, or the *CPU* for short. The CPU has a lot to do when you're using the computer or a device connected to the computer. Basically, the CPU controls the flow of information and traffic that goes in and out of the computer.

When you use your mouse or modem, the serial port interrupts the CPU as if to say, "Hey, buddy, we need you down here." The ports interrupt whatever the CPU is doing to get its attention. Not surprisingly, techies call this occurrence an *interrupt.*

Interrupts are given numbers so that the CPU distinguishes between interrupts. It's like each device has a little flag with a number on it that the serial port waves in front of the CPU.

Here is a listing of COM ports and the interrupt flags:

➤ COM 1 uses interrupt 4.

➤ COM 2 uses interrupt 3.

➤ COM 3 uses interrupt 4.

➤ COM 4 uses interrupt 3.

Note that both COM 1 and COM 3 use interrupt 4, and COM 2 and COM 4 use interrupt 3. If two devices use a COM port and also share the same interrupt, they wave the same numbered flag to get the CPU's attention. This causes the CPU to get confused; it doesn't know what it to do, so it does nothing. In other words, your mouse or modem may not work.

To see whether the mouse and the modem are trying to use the same COM port, leave the mouse COM port alone and check the COM port that the modem uses. If the modem is set to either COM 1 or COM 2, change the COM port number of the modem to COM 3 or COM 4. Depending on the modem type, you may have to move the jumpers on the modem's board. A quick peek at the manual will tell you how to change the modem's COM port settings.

If you have your mouse on COM 1 and nothing on COM 2, set the modem to COM 4. Because COM 2 and COM 4 use the same interrupt and you don't use COM 2 for anything, there will be no way for the CPU to become confused. Now your modem will work fine.

After you get the modem COM port settings under control, you need to take one more step: make sure that your communications software knows the modem's COM port. Usually, you do this in the communications software setup menu. What you need to do is let the communications software know in what part of memory the location of the port will be stored. You also need to give the port an interrupt. The interrupt is referred to as an *IRQ*, or *interrupt request.* It is called an *interrupt* because whatever is using the line must interrupt the processor to send or receive information from it. The IRQ number is the line it will be assigned to use when it is trying to communicate with the processor.

If you don't feel comfortable tinkering around with the COM ports, seek help at a computer repair center.

Old computer, new floppy drive

What is the recipe for success when mixing antique computers and new floppy disks? My old dinosaur of an XT has only a 5¹/₄-inch floppy drive. I added a high-density 3¹/₂-inch floppy drive to try to spruce it up, but I can't seem to get the new drive to work.

The problem is that your dinosaur XT was built long before they had high-density 3¹/₂-inch floppy drives. The XT's BIOS simply has no way of recognizing the high-density drive. But never fear, help is here.

The solution is to purchase a special high-density floppy controller for the XT. The controller will provide the BIOS level support needed to run the high-density drive. Before buying the drive, however, be sure to check with the manufacturer to find out whether their controller card can handle your machine's version of BIOS. You can find this number in your computer's documentation. If hunting through the manual isn't your idea of fun, turn on your computer and watch the screen. One of the first things you'll see is the computer's BIOS and a version number.

Floppy drive bombs out

I can't get my 3¹/₂-inch floppy drive to work. I used Check-It to test the floppy, and it failed with many errors in the read/write test. How can I fix it? Or do I need to buy a new floppy drive? My drive still reads disks, but it gets about halfway through copying a disk and bombs out.

I know the feeling: When I'm in bed, I get about halfway through a book, and then I bomb out.

Whenever you have a problem, don't just run out and replace the hardware. There's nothing worse than upgrading to the very same thing you already have. It's more like even-grading.

The first step in troubleshooting a floppy drive that is having read errors is to clean the drive heads. Special floppy disk drive cleaning kits come in two flavors: wet and dry. The wet kind uses a liquid that you apply to wash the heads, and the dry kind uses an abrasive to scrape the heads clean. The wet kind is safer because the dry kind's abrasives can harm the heads with repeated use.

If the drive is still having problems, the next step is to make sure that all the jumpers and cables are still set correctly. Also be sure to check the CMOS to make sure that the drive is properly configured. Another possibility is that the drive is out of alignment. Either the drive is no longer reading and writing in the right places on the floppy disk, or the floppy drive controller is malfunctioning. The only solution to these problems is to replace the drive. Because the price of drives is so low, fixing the old one is more expensive than buying a new one.

Write protection error

My 3¹/₂-inch disk drive is driving me insane! Every time I try to use it, I get an error message that says that the disk is write protected. The little tab is down so the hole is closed. I even tried it with the hole open — no dice!

Hardware — do they call it that 'cause it's so hard to figure out? Remember, there are two rules in life: Don't sweat the small stuff, and it's all small stuff.

When the little tab is down and the hole is closed, the disk is write enabled, so it is really no surprise that opening the hole didn't help. The good news is that there is probably just some dust in the floppy disk drive. The write protect sensing device on some floppy drives uses an optical mechanism, and it could be blocked by dust. Get a can of compressed air at your favorite computer store. Put the little straw in the nozzle and blow some air in the slot where the floppy goes.

If that procedure doesn't do the trick, try to clean the floppy disk drive. Kits are available to help you clean it properly. Choose the kind that uses liquid rather than an abrasive because the liquid method is safer for your floppy drive. The sensor that detects that the hole is closed may simply be dirty. Of course, if cleaning doesn't help, it may be broken. If it is broken, then you need to buy a new one. (Sadly, in our mass production/throwaway culture, replacing the floppy drive is cheaper than repairing it. So much for ecology.)

A remote possibility is that the cable connecting the floppy disk drive to the controller card is bad (bad cable, bad cable). The cable could have come a little loose, or it could be broken. If this is the case, the solution is simple and cheap. Replace the cable.

Floppy drive won't update

My computer must either be stubborn or have a hard time letting go of the past. Whenever I put a new disk in the disk drive, the computer thinks that the old disk is still in the drive. When I load another floppy, the computer thinks that the first one is still there. Do you have a clue?

Hmm . . . how about Col. Mustard in the ballroom with the candlestick? Or how about Col. Mustard in the kitchen with Miss Scarlet?

Computers use a combination of device access speed and available memory to give you the quick results you have grown to love and respect. Sometimes, when commands are repeated, the computer looks first to its memory for the answer before doing a physical check. If this is the case, and if you are using Windows File Manager, you need to press the F5 key to refresh the disk drive information. Unfortunately, if you are at the DOS prompt, you need to do a directory of another drive: that is, do a directory of the floppy drive, followed by a directory of the hard drive, and finally another directory of the floppy drive. Checking the hard drive's directory clears out the memory buffers from the preceding directory command. If this sequence of events works, you may want to change your buffers in your CONFIG.SYS to Buffers=20,0, depending on your version of DOS. *Note:* Use the DOS EDIT command to make changes to your CONFIG.SYS file, but remember the golden rule: Always make a backup copy of the CONFIG.SYS file before you start messing around inside the file.

Reassigning drive letters

It is becoming more and more evident to me that 5¹/₄-inch floppies are going the way of the dinosaurs. Everything you see in the store is now on 3¹/₂-inch disks. For this reason, I would like to make my 3¹/₂-inch drive be drive A. Presently, my 5¹/₄-inch drive is drive A. How can I switch them?

First, you need to open up the case. Inside you will find a ribbon cable connected to each of the floppy drives. Switch the ribbon cable connectors. If the 5¹/₄-inch drive is currently located above the 3¹/₂-inch drive, you may want to swap them because most people expect drive A to be on top, but this change is not necessary. On some systems, you need to change jumpers or switches; check the documentation for your system or contact the manufacturer. The only other thing you need to do is get into the CMOS setup screen to inform the BIOS that the change has been made.

Computer ignores boot disk

I have this great new game I want to play, but I need a boot disk to use it. Making the disk was fairly easy, but when I put it in the drive, the system still boots off drive C. What am I doing wrong?

The fact that it won't run is God's little way of telling you that you play too many games and you need to get back to work. Now finish your work, and I'll answer the question for you. I'll wait.

. . . Finished? Good. The first thing you need to do is make sure that the floppy is inserted in drive A and not in some other floppy drive. The computer is stubborn about this one, and there is just no reasoning with it. However, if you are absolutely positive that you have placed the boot disk in drive A, then there is only one other reason for the computer's failure to boot off the floppy: your system is not set up to start off drive A. Not a good situation. If your hard drive were to go adios, amigos, you would be up the proverbial creek without a paddle.

Luckily, the situation has an easy fix. Boot up your system and access the CMOS when it first starts up. You usually do this by pressing the Delete key, the Esc key, or the F1 key. Watch your screen when the computer starts, and it will tell you which key to press. Or look in your computer's manual. After you're in the CMOS zone, go to the Advanced CMOS Setup screen (not the Standard CMOS Setup screen).

Look for a line similar to `System Bootup Sequence`. This line tells your computer which drives to look to for the configuration files. I would bet that yours says `C:, A:`. All you need to do is change it to `A:, C:`. Then exit the CMOS and, yes, you do want to save those changes. This change will force your system to check for a boot disk in drive A before it looks at drive C. If no disk is in drive A, the computer simply goes straight to drive C.

Homemade computer won't recognize floppies

I built my own computer last year, and it worked great until recently. Now whenever I turn it on, the computer beeps, and an error message pops up. It says I have an *FDD controller failure*. My computer recognizes drives A and B, but my drives don't recognize any disks! Could both of my floppy disk drives be going bad at the same time?

Well, anything is possible, but in your situation the answer is much simpler. I doubt that both of your floppy drives would go out at the same time. The problem is more likely to be with the controller card or ribbon cable.

The warning *FDD Controller Failure* is a message from the BIOS that the floppy disk drive controller has failed. The floppy disk drive controller acts as an interface between the computer and the floppy disk drive. The controller is on a separate adapter card that is plugged into the motherboard or, more commonly, it is on the same card as the hard drive controller. If the controller is not responding, the cables that connect the controller to the floppy drive may be loose or frayed. But because neither of the drives responds, more than likely you need to replace the card. Fortunately, this card is one of the cheapest things to replace on the system.

General Failure reading *message*

I have a 486DX with both 5¹/₄-inch and 3¹/₂-inch floppy disk drives. The other day my son tried to play a game from drive A (5¹/₄-inch), and he got a *General Failure reading* message. Now when I try to access that drive, it just tells me that the current drive is no longer valid. Please tell me how I can cure this frustrating problem.

Simple, keep your son away from the computer.

General Failure reading is a DOS error message telling you that the computer can't read the information off the floppy drive. The problem could be with the floppy disk or the floppy drive.

Most 5¹/₄-inch floppy disks that hold computer games are high-density 1.2MB diskettes. Some older computers have 5¹/₄-inch drives, but they are low-density 360K drives and cannot read the higher format. You should try the floppy in another machine to see whether it is readable.

You get the message *current drive no longer valid* when the computer tries to use a drive that is not there. Typically, with a floppy drive this message means that no floppy disk is in the drive, or in the case of a 5¹/₄-inch drive, that the door latch is not closed. If a floppy disk is in the drive and the door latch is closed, the error message must indicate that the floppy drive is no longer responding to the system.

To check, try inserting other floppies into the drive. If you still get a *General Failure* message, then the drive is definitely to blame. First, resist the temptation to hurt your son. Next, check whether all the wires of the floppy drive ribbon cable are all right inside the computer. If one or more wires are loose, broken, or frayed, replace the cable. If the cable is OK, then something must be wrong with the drive itself. The solution is a new floppy drive because drives cost more to repair than they do to replace. I suggest a paper route for junior. He'll earn that disk drive back in no time.

Devoted to my 286

I've been using my trusty old 286 for about four years, and I'm really comfortable with it. Is there any kind of gizmo I can get to upgrade my 286 to 386 capability? I'd love to be able to run things like WordPerfect 6.0 and QuattroPro 5.0, but they all require a 386.

If I were you, I would bury the 286. I can understand your reluctance to part with that faithful puppy, but there is no magic gizmo that can make a 286 processor act exactly like a 386 machine. In fact, a 286 will never run fast enough to handle the complex operations of newer software programs because the 286 processor is a 16-bit processor, while the 386 is a 32-bit processor.

With double the number of bits in the processor, the 386 can execute many more instructions per second than the 286 can. The speed of a processor is measured in megahertz (MHz), meaning how many million cycles can be performed in a second. Although this amount may seem large, when you consider that it takes at least two cycles to complete the simplest instructions and that it can take hundreds of instructions to accomplish the most trivial of tasks, the eight million cycles per second of a 286DX 8 really don't get you very far today. The 386, on the other hand, can run at speeds of anywhere from 16 to 40MHz, and even that speed can seem slow when running many of today's hottest programs.

Another 386 capability that is lacking in the 286 is the addition of a new mode of operation called *virtual real mode* or *virtual 86 mode.* This mode is the one that gives Windows and OS/2 their power. In virtual real mode, the processor can simultaneously run multiple programs as if each program were running on its own machine, thus enabling the computer to act as if it is two or more computers at the same time.

Now that you know a little bit about why a 286 can't really become a 386, you may want to consider upgrading your machine. You can't merely pop in a new CPU because the pin sets for connecting the 286 and 386 CPUs are different, but you can swap the motherboard. You can still keep the same monitor, keyboard, floppy and hard drives, and probably most of the cards in the computer. You'll almost certainly need to swap your memory chips for some faster ones, and you may end up wanting a video card with a bigger cache, depending on the type of monitor you have and what kind of applications you will be using.

Rather than upgrade all the 286 bits, bytes, and pieces, why not pick up a used 486? Upgrading your computer doesn't necessarily mean that the comfort zone (that is, familiarity and trust) of your 286 will disappear. In most cases, the only things you will notice are an increase in speed and the capability to run programs you couldn't before.

My floppy drive is too loud!

I just bought a new computer, and when I start it up, the drive check on one of my floppy drives seems to be really loud. Should I be concerned? It works fine, but it is kinda noisy.

It depends on how noisy it is. Do the neighbors bang on the walls when you are running File Manager in drive A? Do all your pets stop what they are doing and stare at the computer? Does it drown out your spouse so much that you find yourself going into drive A unnecessarily?

When it comes to noise, floppy drives are a great deal like dishwashers. Having a quiet one is pleasant, but it doesn't have anything to do with how well it works. They are two separate issues. If the sound really bothers you, try taking the drive back to the dealer and asking for a different manufacturer's floppy drive. But, from a usage standpoint, nothing is wrong with it.

Is there a standard motherboard size?

I wanted to replace my Packard Bell motherboard with an Intel motherboard. Do motherboards come in a standard size?

All men may have been created equal, but all computer cases were definitely not created equal. Computers come in standard desktop, slim-line desktop, mini tower, or medium- and full-tower case sizes. When shopping for a new motherboard, it is very important to measure the inside of the case to see how large a board it can accommodate. Checking the size is even more important for a desktop case than for a tower (upright) case because many desktop cases have a very limited amount of room inside them. Sometimes the screws in the board are in a different location than the ones in the case, but you can usually work around this problem. Most new cases are designed to accommodate nearly all motherboards.

When you buy the board, if you have any doubts about whether it will fit, ask the dealer whether you can exchange it if it is too big. Most dealers will be happy to accommodate you if the exchange is made in a timely fashion. Anything longer than 14 to 30 days isn't considered in a timely fashion.

Should I RISC buying a new computer?

I keep hearing a lot of talk about a new RISC computer. What is a RISC computer, and why would I want to buy one?

Careful. A question like that will keep you in the store for hours. Apple is playing a risky (get it? RISC) game by betting the farm (or the *orchard*, perhaps) on this new type of chip. RISC is an acronym for *Reduced Instruction Set Computer* (or Computing). Most computers use a CISC (*Complex ISC*) CPU, such as the Intel 80x86 or Motorola 680x0 chips.

A RISC processor uses fewer computer cycles for its instructions. And since a computer's speed is measured in millions of cycles per second, or MHz, a RISC processor can substantially out-perform a CISC processor that is running at the same speed.

Only a handful of computers on the market use a RISC processor. The Power PC is one of the more popular RISC computers. However, because a RISC processor requires special software and not much has been written for it, sales have been sluggish. IBM's OS/2 is currently the only operating system that will run on an IBM-compatible RISC processor, and few programs thus far have been written specifically for OS/2. Apple also manufactures a RISC-based system. In fact, IBM and Apple joined forces to create a single RISC platform that can run both OS/2 and Apple software. IBM and Apple hope to put a dent in the Windows user base. Intel is putting off the transition by producing faster and more efficient versions of its CISC CPUs. Whether you move to RISC depends on what you want to do with computers in general. If you want to use a Mac, a Power Mac is the way to go. If you'd rather use a PC-compatible, CISC is it for the time being.

486SLC

I have a 386SX 16 and want to upgrade the CPU. The problem is, I'm broke. The 486SLC chip seems too good to be true. Is something wrong with it, or will it speed up my computer's graphics enough so I can finally play my golf game?

Only computer users could find a way to make golf less strenuous.

You sound like a nice person, so I'll be gentle. The 486SLC chip, made by Cyrix, is designed to be plugged into your 386SX socket. Essentially, it's a 486SX chip that is specially designed for low power consumption. Like the 486SX, it does not have a math coprocessor. The chip is intended for use with laptop and notebook systems to increase the amount of time the computer can run off its batteries before being recharged.

The 486SLC chip will give you a great deal of extra speed and may be a good choice for you, but I want you to understand something: this operation isn't without risks.

First, if you want to upgrade from a 386SX processor, you need to purchase a new motherboard, not just a new processor. You need the new processor because the 386SX, although a 32-bit processor, uses a 16-bit bus rather than a 32-bit bus like the 386DX and 486 processors. The bus sends information to and from the computer. This, in turn, affects the way the memory is organized. On a 16-bit bus, the memory is organized into banks of four slots apiece, but on the 386SX system the banks have only two slots. That aside, there is nothing wrong with the 486SLC chip, and it certainly offers more than ample speed to properly enjoy your golf game — but don't confuse it with a 486DX chip.

Second, the SL processor is much smaller than an SX or DX processor and is designed for a much smaller motherboard. And guess what? Everything that plugs into this smaller motherboard also has to be smaller. Suddenly, the SL processor is not such a great deal after all, is it? If you cannot afford a 486 motherboard, you may want to consider a 386DX processor. It is quite a bit cheaper than the 486 motherboard, and any speed 386DX would run considerably faster than your SX because it has twice the number of buses as your current system. Plus, a 386DX would enable you to run just about any of today's newest software, as long as you have sufficient memory.

I think that the cheapest thing for you to do is go out and play a real game of golf.

486SLC2 vs. 486DX2

IBM 486SLC2 66 motherboards seem to be a lot cheaper than the current 486DX2 66 systems. What's the catch? Are the 486DX2 66 systems that much better?

So you're interested in taking route 66 on the old info superhighway. Well, before you can get your kicks, consider this. The 486SLC2 line of chips is IBM's version of the Intel 486DX2 chips. Like the 486DX2, the 486SLC2 has a clock doubler and a 16K cache on board. In addition, the 486SLC2 line includes low-voltage circuitry that enables it to conserve electricity. It is intended primarily for laptops and notebooks that run off batteries. Assuming that the systems that you are comparing are both laptops or notebooks, the difference in price is mainly attributable to one thing — the brand name Intel. If, however, the 486SLC2 66 is in a desktop system, it also may be cheaper because it is not normally found there and some people may be leery of it.

Can I upgrade a DX2 66 to a DX4 100?

I have a 486DX2 66 computer. Can I replace my CPU with a DX4 100, or am I doomed to forever lag behind my tech friends?

If your tech friends jumped off the Empire State Building, would you? Sorry, I don't mean to sound like your motherboard.

The DX2 66 and DX4 100 chips are very similar in that they are both based on the 486DX 33. The DX2 is clock doubled, and the DX4 is clock tripled. What sets them apart is the voltage requirement. The 66 is a 5.0-volt chip, and the 100 is a 3.3-volt chip. Replacing a DX4 100 chip with a 486DX2 66 chip should not cause any problems. The only possible snags: making sure that the memory in your machine is fast enough for the new processor and that your new system can handle the increased heat of the faster processor.

Komando
Klues

You may want to invest in a heat sink chip to help draw the heat away from the processor if you don't already have one.

DX4 100? Show me the math!

If a DX2 66 chip is a clock doubled DX 33, then is a DX4 100 a quadrupled SX 25 or a doubled DX 50?

If you failed Algebra II, skip reading this answer.

Fortunately, Intel, in a rare sympathetic moment toward customers, chose to be very consistent with its conventions for naming the chips. The members of the 486 family stay together in a product line. The *4* after the *DX* refers to the 486 processor family and has nothing to do with the chip's performance. The DX4 has a 16K on-board cache that's twice as large as the 8K cache in all other 486 chips. The DX4 includes a math coprocessor like the 486DX and 486DX2 chips, too. But a DX4 100MHz chip is a tripled, not quadrupled, 486DX 33MHz chip.

You should, however, be aware that there are some limitations to what you can accomplish by increasing the speed of a clock. A 486DX2 50 is a little slower than a 486DX 50. The more *times* the clock is sped up, the more speed is lost in the cracks during the process. For example, the 486DX2 100 is faster than the 486DX4 100 but slower than a theoretical 486DX 100 would be.

I told you that most of you wouldn't get it. All of this doubling and tripling and quadrupling of clock speeds can be confusing.

What is a P24T slot?

What are P24T slots? I know they have something to do with Pentium upgrades.

Welcome to the highly confusing and ever changing world of computer technology. If you thought Detroit had cornered the market on planned obsolescence, think again. Silicon Valley is giving it a run for its money.

The P24T socket on your motherboard is for the highly touted Pentium OverDrive chip that Intel is supposed to make . . . someday. At this point, it is purely vaporware (that's techie talk for "it doesn't exist yet").

Just like the 486DX OverDrive chips that gain speed by doubling, tripling, and even quadrupling the clock, the Pentium will eventually have the same options. The P24T slot is there to provide users an easy way to pop in a new processor. The new processor will shut down the old processor and take over the running of your computer.

As for putting an actual Pentium chip on your 486 board, it just doesn't work like that. A Pentium chip needs a motherboard designed to handle it. It is quite a bit different from the 486.

Pentium or 486 100: Which uses more power?

How much electricity does a 486 100 scarf down as compared to a Pentium-60? I'm considering both, and I want to know which is going to cost me the most to operate. Also, do you know of any Pentiums that will power down after a certain period of inactivity?

Do you really care about the electricity? You're that penny-pinching? I bet you're a fun date. Do you spend your spare time looking for change in the couch? Anyway, Mr. Ben Franklin, by the 486 100 I assume that you mean the 486DX4 100. The new DX4 chips are 3.3-volt. The Pentium 60 and 66 chips are 5-volt, but the newer 90 and 100MHz Pentiums are 3.3-volt.

How much electricity a particular system will draw depends on other things besides the processor. You have to consider the amount of memory on board, the video adapter, the floppy drive(s), the hard drive, the number of fans, the power supply, and how frequently the parts are in use; so there is no end-all answer.

As for the processor itself, the difference in the electricity drawn by a 486DX4 100 and a Pentium 60 costs pennies an hour. Electrical consumption is not normally a thing that most people take into consideration, although maybe they should. In terms of powering down the system during inactivity, the system already uses very little power when it is inactive. The SL family of chips, which is designed for laptops and notepads, has special circuitry built in to minimize power consumption when the computer is inactive. But these were created to extend the amount of time the system can run before the batteries need to be recharged because they contain so very little power. It was not done in the interest of saving money on an electric bill.

Right now, green PC motherboards are politically correct, and almost everyone is jumping on the bandwagon. These 486 and Pentium motherboards have built-in BIOS features that can turn the display and hard drive off after a certain amount of time to help extend equipment life and save a little electricity at the same time.

Time (and chips) to kill

I have an AMD 40MHz chip in a clock-selectable AMI motherboard with AMI BIOS. If I set the jumpers for a 50MHz chip instead of the 40MHz, everything seems to work OK. But I say it will cause the chip to overheat and quit working. My friend says it won't. Who's right?

Who cares? You guys have too much time on your hands. Most chips are capable of having their clocks doubled, tripled, and even quadrupled, so increasing the clock speed by 10MHz shouldn't harm it. Of course, if you really want to be on the safe side, set the jumpers back to 40MHz. Keep in mind that CPUs are rated at a certain speed for a reason and that manufacturers guarantee and warranty chips to work only at a certain speed.

Increasing speed without a new computer

I have a 486SX with a 25MHz CPU clock. I was wondering if there is a way to get a faster time (33MHz or more) without buying a whole new computer. Some of these new programs require speeds that are faster than I can run.

Maybe. It depends on your particular motherboard. The majority of motherboards are upgradeable, but not all of them are. Upgrading a motherboard usually consists of removing the old chip, putting in the new one, resetting jumpers on the motherboard, and resetting the CMOS. Not exactly an operation for beginners.

If you have a 486SX 25 computer, you can increase the speed of the computer by purchasing a faster chip and placing it in the math coprocessor slot. The poorly named math coprocessor slot is really an upgrade slot. Any processor chip placed in it will cause the new processor to take over the running of the computer and shut down the original processor. The reason for this is that the 486SX chip is really a 486DX chip with the math chip disconnected.

The 80487SX chip that is advertised as an add-in math coprocessor is really a full-fledged 486DX that shuts down the old CPU and takes over the running of the computer. So you don't need a whole new computer if you want to step up to something a little or a whole lot faster. For relatively little money and effort, you can turn your system into a 486DX 33 or even a 486DX2 100. You just have to make sure that the memory in your system is fast enough for your new processor. If it's not, the memory can usually be upgraded for faster chips at a fraction of the cost of actually buying the new memory.

Gee, is there nothing I don't know? Come on. Try to stump the great Kim Komando!

Cache is screwing up the floppy drives

I just upgraded to an Intel 486DX2 66. When I try to read from a floppy disk, all I get is garbage on-screen. It won't read anything from either floppy. I have tried two different VL (VESA) bus controller cards. The weird thing is that when I disable the 256K cache, the drives work fine.

Ah, don't disable the 256 cache. Check to make sure that all of the jumpers are set correctly and that you plugged everything in correctly (careful, that's *in correctly,* not *incorrectly*). Your best bet is to check with the manufacturer of the motherboard to find out whether there are any compatibility problems between your new motherboard and the kind of floppy drives that you have. It sounds as if there may be a problem with the motherboard itself. Since you just upgraded the board, it should be under warranty. Check with your supplier about exchanging it.

My Pentium thinks it's a 486

I paid for a Pentium, but when I run Microsoft Diagnostics, it says I have a 486. Did I get ripped off or what?

Microsoft Diagnostics (MSD) is just playing a bad joke on you. Older versions of MSD were written before the advent of the Pentium chip. As a result, they won't identify a Pentium. They see the CPU, become confused, and call it a 486. So, no, you didn't get taken, unless you bought it from the inside of a guy's sports jacket off a downtown side street.

If you want to be sure, open up the case and look at the processor. Its name is on the chip. You also may want to try getting your hands on a diagnostics package that does recognize the Pentium, because, if by some small chance the chip is defective, it may not run at the speed you paid for.

Will a new disk controller speed up disk access?

I have a 486DX2 50 computer with a 340MB Western Digital hard drive. Would a different or newer style disk controller speed up how fast I get information from the hard drive?

Well, it depends on what kind of hard drive you have. If you have an IDE drive, you can't change the hard disk controller because it is directly mounted to the hard drive. If you have a SCSI hard drive, you may find a faster disk controller to work with your system. SCSI hard drive controllers come in the following flavors: Standard SCSI, Fast SCSI, and Fast/Wide SCSI. Not all drives and adapters will work in all systems.

If you really want to improve the access speed, the quick fix is to *cache* it. Caching moves information from the hard disk to faster RAM memory. The DOS SmartDrive command does this trick, and some controller cards have caching built in. These cards are called — come on, guess — *caching controllers.*

Will SCSI and IDE controllers get along?

Can I have both a SCSI controller and an IDE controller in my computer? I'm looking for new ways to stay ahead of my friends.

Jeez, two controller cards. I bet it's safe to say that you like to be in charge of things, that you are a type A personality. But you most certainly can win the envy of your friends by having a SCSI controller and an IDE controller. In fact, adding a SCSI hard drive to a system is easier than adding a second IDE. The reason is that on an IDE system the controller is mounted directly to the hard drive. If you want to add a second hard drive, you have to first disable the controller on the new drive and let the first hard drive's controller handle the second drive as well.

All you have to do to add a SCSI drive is pop in the new SCSI hard drive and its controller card. The only restriction is that the IDE drive must be the primary or boot drive for both drives to be accessible at the same time.

I think my hard drive is dying

My computer is acting kind of flaky. I'm getting messages like *error reading drive C* from time to time. Also, files take a long time to appear on-screen. My friend says this isn't a good problem to have.

I don't know of any problem that is a good problem to have. The message *error reading drive C* means that the computer is having trouble reading information from the drive. This Windows message is the equivalent of the DOS *read fault error, reading drive C* message. Most of the time, this message means that the magnetic media on the hard drive has weakened. You see, information on the hard drive is stored on a coating of a magnetized substance. This material is usually a form of iron oxide — that is, rust. Isn't it comforting to know that all of your precious data is stored on rust?

Before the hard disk can be formatted by DOS, it first has to be physically formatted. This physical formatting is referred to as a *low-level format.* Most of the drives on the market are IDE drives. These drives, unlike SCSI drives, are always low-level formatted at the factory. When they come to you, they only need a logical — also called *high-level* — format by DOS. Over time, the signal on portions of the hard drive's magnetic media weakens, and the low-level formatting disintegrates. If you have an IDE drive, redoing the low-level formatting is rarely possible because each manufacturer uses its own unique method. However, sometimes you can get the low-level format from the manufacturer or use a utility such as Spinrite to replace it.

Be aware, however, that doing a low-level format removes everything from the hard disk.

The typical solution to read errors caused by weakling media is to run a disk utility, such as DOS's SCANDISK, Symantec's Norton's Disk Doctor, or PC Tools, on the hard drive. These utilities can scan the drive and determine whether the hard drive has any bad sectors. If they discover any bad sectors, they can block them out so that DOS does not use that particular area of the hard drive. Although this solution decreases the amount of space available on the hard drive, it usually eliminates the read fault errors if the problems are not extensive.

Sometimes read fault errors signify that the hard disk controller is failing. If that happens, you will notice more and more read fault errors over time. If you have an IDE drive, you generally have no choice but to replace it. If you have a SCSI drive, you can replace the controller. In any case, making sure that all data is backed up as soon as you notice a read fault error is always a good idea.

One additional note: A read fault error on a drive that has been compressed with a program such as Stacker or DoubleSpace usually indicates a logical error in the drive's look-up table and not a physical problem at all. That is, these programs fool the operating system into thinking that there is a new physical drive when in actuality they are storing all of the compressed data in one big file (only they understand where all of your data is located). If the look-up table gets messed up and the program can't find the data, DOS thinks that the problem is physical. The solution is to run CHKDSK at the DOS prompt. Or you can run a program that comes with the compression utility, such as CHECK from Stac Electronics.

MS-DOS 6.0 or higher has another useful utility called DEFRAG. This program puts files and parts of a file saved on a hard disk in order so that the parts of the files are contiguous. Having parts of a file located in many different places on a hard drive is normal. However, it takes time for the computer to search for all the pieces of the file. DEFRAG enables programs to find and load files much quicker. To use it, type **DEFRAG** at the DOS prompt and press Enter. (You cannot run DEFRAG from Windows.)

DEFRAG then displays the recommended optimization method, which, even if it says otherwise, selects full optimization the first time. If DEFRAG says, however, that no optimization is necessary, press Esc and then Alt+X to go back to DOS.

Gee, if this answer were any longer, I'd have to write another book. Another book? Hmmm . . . now that's a good problem to have.

Hard Disk Controller Diagnostics Error *message*

I attempted to install a second 3$^1/_2$-inch floppy disk drive, but when I tried to use it, I got the following error message: *Hard Disk Controller Diagnostics Error*. I double-checked all the cable connections because the setup was not passing the floppy drive test or the hard drive test. I finally got the floppy drives to pass one at a time, but the setup still stops on the test for the fixed drive. Maybe this second drive isn't worth all the trouble.

Yeah, maybe Mr. Important can get by on one drive like the rest of us. The best thing to do is start at the beginning. Open your case and recheck your handiwork. Make sure that the card is well-seated in the slot and that all of the ribbon cables are well-seated. Recheck all of the switches and jumpers on the floppy drive that need to be set. How they need to be set depends on the type of system that you have and which drive letter you want the floppy to take. Unfortunately, all manufacturers have unique requirements for setting these things up, so you're on your own, kid. You'll have to rely on the documentation that came with the drive and whatever help you can get from the manufacturer. Sorry.

When you set up the floppy, you need to notice what type of cable you have in the computer. Most cables have the *IBM twist*, which means that everything beyond the part that is twisted is reversed so that if you have a drive set up to be at the first DS position (drive A), it will really be set up to be at the second DS position (drive B). Why did they do this? I don't know.

You can tell whether your cable is twisted by looking to see whether the ribbon wire appears to be in three sections and one of the sections has a twist just before the connector. A terminating resistor needs to be placed on any drive that is at the end of the untwisted cable. Most 3$^1/_2$-inch drives have the jumper permanently enabled to spread the resistance across the drives.

441

After you have given the hardware the OK, you can proceed to check the CMOS. Then check to see whether you have settings for drive A and drive B. Do they match the types of your two floppy drives? If only one floppy drive setting is available, your CMOS may not be able to support two floppy drives. This is sometimes the case with older systems.

If everything in the CMOS and inside the case checks out, you may need a new I/O Controller card. I'd say you sound a bit frustrated, and it may be worth any amount of money to have someone else fix your computer for you. Hey, sorry about that Mr. Important crack earlier.

My PC forgets it has hard drives

After my computer has been on awhile, it seems to forget it has hard drives in it. If I turn the computer off and wait 20 minutes, everything works fine. I changed the ribbon cables; I even swapped out the controller board. No change.

Intermittent problems are the worst kind to track down. Things just don't seem to act up when you want to prove that something is wrong. It's like when your car makes a strange sound, so you take it to the mechanic . . . and it purrs like a kitten . . . and the mechanic looks at you like you are insane. And if you're not insane, it can be very frustrating.

You know, the same situation you describe happened to one of my computers. I bet your computer's fan is on its last leg. It doesn't take long for your computer's innards to warm up without a fan or with a fan that's not working up to par.

If the vent gets clogged, the computer can't keep itself cooled properly. So try cleaning out the vent between the computer's fan and the back of the computer. Using a can of compressed air works like a charm. Open the computer's case, with no power to the unit of course, and look for the fan's vent. It's behind the fan on the back side of the computer. Spray the vent from the inside of the computer toward the outside of the computer. That way, the fuzzballs go out the back of the computer and not toward the inside, where they can damage the circuits and stuff.

Komando Klues Make sure that you give your computer plenty of breathing room. Some folks put their computers right up against a desk or wall to save space. This doesn't allow enough air to circulate in and out of the system unit properly.

But if a little cleaning doesn't solve your problems, you probably need to replace the computer's fan. A computer service center can do the job for you, or you can replace the fan yourself. Either way, be sure that the fan you get is the same size as the original fan and that it meets the manufacturer's specifications. Check whether your present fan is under warranty too. A quick call to the dealer or manufacturer could save you some money.

Can I add a new hard drive to the existing one?

My brother is a know-it-all, but sometimes he's right. He told me that it is possible to put a new hard drive in my system and still keep the old one. Is this true?

Survey says, "Probably." Whether you can add another hard disk also depends on the hard drive type currently in your computer and the hard drive type you want to add.

If you have a SCSI-type hard drive, adding another SCSI hard drive is fairly easy. That's because SCSI drives can be daisy-chained together and need only one controller.

If you have an IDE drive, which is probably the case, adding another IDE drive is rather tricky. The controller for the IDE hard drive is mounted directly to the hard drive itself and is unique to each manufacturer. To add a second hard disk drive, you have to disable the controller of the new hard drive so that the first hard drive's controller can run both hard drives. In some cases, you may have to use the same manufacturer's hard drive when you add a second one. Buying the same manufacturer's drive is a good idea, even if you don't have to, because installation is easier.

Basically, using two IDE drives in the same system is known as *slaving them together*. That's computer talk for hooking the two hard drives up together. The original drive C is the master, and the additional drive D is the slave.

When you get a new hard disk drive from the factory, the jumpers usually are set for the drive to be used alone in a system. You can move the jumpers to designate the drive as either a master or a slave. If the jumper settings are not included with the drive, you need to call the manufacturer to get them.

Most hard drive kits come with pretty installation guides that walk you through the process. It's not terribly difficult. Before you start the installation, practice good computing. That is, make a complete backup of your system and write down every little detail in the computer's CMOS settings. Know, too, that you never want to mix SCSI-type hard drives with IDE-type hard drives. Don't ask why . . . just trust me on this one.

My PC won't recognize hard drive D

I am trying to install two drives by two different manufacturers. They have been properly configured according to instructions, but I just can't get the system to recognize drive D. By the way, I did set up drive D in the CMOS. I just can't master this slaving drives together thing.

Master? Slaving? Technology's great, but I'm not so sure about the direction of this conversation!

If you are trying to install IDE drives from two different manufacturers, you may be fighting a losing battle. Sometimes there is no way to get them to work together.

Theoretically, you should be able to slave IDE drives together. It works great in theory, but in practice . . . well, you already know how it goes. Older drives are kind of picky about the master/slave thing and don't always cooperate. Luckily, the newer drives usually cooperate just fine. You need to make sure that the second drive's controller is disabled so that the first drive's controller can take charge of both drives. This step is the one that seems to get most people into trouble.

Should I partition my hard drive?

I just bought a large (340MB) internal hard drive for my home computer. My office computer has one disk drive, but it also has two drive letters, C and D. Is this the way to go?

The computer wizardry that divides one real hard disk into two or more hard disks is called *partitioning*. You don't get more disk space than the size of the original hard disk; the hard disk is merely split into parts. It's sort of like having a closet and dividing it into different sections for organizational purposes.

Here's a little trivia: Prior to DOS 4.0, partitioning wasn't popular because there was a 32MB limitation. Back in those days, computers had a 40MB hard drive divided into drive C with 32MB and drive D with 8MB. Of course, in those days, 8MB was a lot. (Yes, I remember those days well.

You were too young to remember this, but in those days we had only three TV channels.) Now, with DOS 4.0, partitioning (and cable TV) has become the preferred choice.

Partitioning a drive is a good thing because it helps you find things quickly. For example, you may want to store all your games on one drive and all your business stuff on another drive.

Another good reason to partition your drive is if you want to be able to use different operating systems to start your computer. For example, if you want to be able to use both DOS and OS/2, you need to have two primary partitions. A primary partition is a drive from which the computer boots, and it is designated drive C. You may have up to four primary partitions. When you boot under one drive C, the other drive Cs are not accessible.

The chief disadvantage of partitioning a hard drive is that free space is used less efficiently. For example, perhaps you want to install a program that needs 32MB of disk space. Furthermore, you have only 25MB of disk space on drive C and 17MB on drive D. You have plenty of free disk space, 42MB in all, but that free space doesn't do you any good because the space is on two different drives. So the only solution is to move some programs and other stuff from one partitioned drive to another. With today's large applications, this scenario is very common. And, of course, the more drives that you have, the more you will run into this situation.

If you want to know more about how to partition a hard disk, that topic is covered in the DOS chapter.

Cheap hard drive space

I'm a software junkie. I love to add new programs to my computer. What inexpensive options are there for expanding hard drive space? I have a 60MB hard drive on a PS/2. I've heard about stackers and disk compressors, but I really don't know what they do.

They stack and compress. Next question.

What? More? OK. A disk compression utility can dramatically increase the amount of free hard disk space. Programs such as DOS 6's DoubleSpace, DOS 6.22's DriveSpace, and Stacker by Stac Electronics play tricks. The programs fool the computer's operating system into thinking that there is a new physical drive. Actually, compression programs squeeze information into one big file. When information is written to or read from the disk, it is automatically compressed and decompressed as needed.

Not all information compresses equally well. Pictures, program executable files, and graphical games don't usually compress very well. But database and spreadsheets files, as well as word processing documents, usually do compress very well. You can expect a 2:1 compression, meaning that a 60MB hard drive effectively doubles to become a 120MB hard drive. And Stac's latest version, Stacker 4.0, claims a 2.5:1 average compression ratio, meaning that a 60MB hard drive effectively becomes a 150MB drive.

Komando Klues

Disk compression utilities are, as you say, a good alternative to buying a new drive. When you are using any compression program, however, you need to remember to keep the drive defragmented (most compressors come with a utility to do this) and to keep at least 5MB of uncompressed space on the drive. Remember, too, that compression programs eat up some valuable conventional memory. But all in all, disk compression is a quick fix for more hard drive space.

Will a bigger cache help me?

I currently have a 486DX 33 with 4MB RAM and 128K cache memory on board. I am toying with the idea of upgrading my cache to 256K. What will this do for me?

It will slice, dice, mix, and grind. It will change the way you see yourself. You will lose weight, discover a soul mate, and unlock your spiritual powers. And if you think that's good, wait till you see what it does for your computer.

OK, back to earth. *Cache memory* is really fast RAM that is used to store the most often-used information. How much faster is cache memory than regular RAM? About $3\frac{1}{2}$ times faster. OK, now your day is complete.

Think of a cache as a special holding area. A computer is pretty smart. It holds onto the information that it thinks you may want to see next. The computer first looks at the cache for the information. If that piece of information is there, a *cache hit* occurs, and the data is transferred at the cache's speed. If the information isn't in the cache, a miss happens, but the computer updates the information held in the cache for next time.

The Bottom Line

The larger the cache, the larger the holding area, and the more hits will happen. If you increase the on-board cache size from 128K to 256K, the computer will waste less time waiting and more time computing, thus helping it realize more closely its true capabilities.

Do I need shadow RAM or a new roommate?

My roommate keeps talking about shadow RAM and how great it is. I would love to know what shadow RAM is and how I can take advantage of it.

When you shine a bright light on a RAM chip, that dark area behind the chip is shadow RAM. (I just crack myself up sometimes.)

Seriously, computer memory (RAM) is relatively fast but volatile. When the computer's power is shut off, the computer loses everything held in RAM. It's kind of like high-tech amnesia.

Nonvolatile read-only memory (ROM) is slower but permanent. Your system's BIOS (*Basic Input/Output System*) is a set of instructions, burned into a ROM chip, that tells the computer how to perform its most basic, low-level, primal functions (such as sex, hunting for food, and finding shelter). Video cards, controller cards, and other adapter cards also can contain instructions on ROM.

The Bottom Line

Some systems have the ability to remap, or *shadow,* the BIOS instructions from the ROM chips into the faster RAM memory on start-up. This speeds things up a bit. A disadvantage to enabling shadowing is that it takes away from the RAM memory that's available for programs to use.

Shadow RAM is turned on and off in the CMOS. Your computer either has the ability to use it or not. Be careful, and write down anything you change in the CMOS settings — you can really screw things up if you change the wrong parameters.

Defining SRAM and DRAM

My computer has 256K SRAM and 2MB Video DRAM. What do SRAM and DRAM stand for, and what do they mean to me?

Your techno-mumbo terms have to do with memory and improving the computer's performance. Caches, to be exact, perform this feat of memory trickery. Disk caches improve performance because the computer's main RAM is faster than the hard disk is. Oh, no, I feel a limerick coming on. . . .

There once was a guy with some RAM,
but not enough, so he got DRAM.
It was slow, I'll admit.
Slow as . . . well, really slow.
To him, it was just a big sham.

OK. I'm back. *SRAM* stands for *static RAM*. Now, doesn't knowing that fact make you feel fulfilled? SRAM, which is also called an *on-board cache*, improves processor performance by shortening the amount of time that the processor spends waiting for incoming data. SRAM is much quicker than system memory, and the processor wastes less time getting information from it. So if the processor speed is the same, the computer with the larger SRAM will be the faster one.

DRAM stands for *dynamic RAM*. DRAM is used to store video images, but it's a slowpoke. Most computers can handle information as high as eight times faster than DRAM can throw their way. Video DRAM is the space available for storing images on the card. The more space available, the less time is wasted waiting for images to be read from the hard disk or CD, and the faster the screen refreshes.

Upgrading RAM and troubleshooting

Like almost every other new computer user, I soon found out that the 4MB of memory my computer came with was not enough. I added four more 1MB SIMM chips and began getting memory errors every so often. Since the memory was under warranty, I returned it for four new SIMMs, but I'm still getting occasional memory errors.

Maybe you're not getting more errors at all. The upgrade to 8MB has increased the computer's speed, so you get the same number of errors, but now you get them faster. (How convenient!) You need to play Sherlock Holmes to solve the memory error mystery. Because I can't solve it in this book, I'm going to give you some clues. There isn't one end-all clue to solve this memory mystery; there are several to follow. Sorry.

If it makes you feel better, the numero uno cause of memory problems is a bad SIMM. You have to pretty much replace one SIMM at a time to rule it out as a possibility.

Then again, SIMMs that are not seated properly or SIMMs that have dirty connections don't work right. When the heat is on, or the chips are in use, the chips lose contact. But having new chips that are not the same speed as the chips that are already in the computer is a problem, too. Check your motherboard book to see whether you are using SIMMs that are the correct speed for your board. Most SIMMs work with anything faster than 80 nanoseconds (ns), but some are more particular.

Also, some motherboards are so finicky that all of their chips have to be from the same manufacturer. Some systems *choke* (that's tech talk for *won't work*) with certain makes of chips.

Yet another possibility is that the bank that you added the new chips to is not correctly soldered to the motherboard. This problem is called a *cold solder,* and it can cause intermittent errors.

Wait — I have one last clue for you. Yet another thing to consider is the location of cards in relationship to the memory bank that you added the chips to. Noise from cards can cause memory errors, so try moving the cards around.

A less common possibility is what the techies call the *chip walk.* Sometimes chips on the motherboard come loose and no longer make adequate contact with the board. Push down on the SIMMs lightly with your fingers — not the soldered SIMMs, just the ones in sockets.

How to upgrade RAM

I have a 386DX 40 with 4MB of RAM. I would like to upgrade it to 8MB. The type of SIMM that the computer uses is three tiny chips on a single, plug-in type circuit board. My computer currently has four of these boards, filling all four slots. What specifically do I have to do to boost the memory to 8MB?

Hundreds of motherboards are out there, each with its own way of doing memory upgrades. Your 386DX motherboard should have two sets of banks, each with four slots. The first bank is filled with four 1MB SIMMs, and the second bank should be empty. You need to buy four 1 ×9 SIMMs. (Here's a tip: *1 ×9* means that you need nine chips to get 1MB of RAM.) Check your computer's manuals for, among other chip details, the correct speed. If you buy the wrong speed, you're asking for memory errors.

Komando Klues

If you can't find the information in the manuals, call the computer's manufacturer. Or, if you're feeling brave, pop the case on the computer and read the speed on one of the chips. Go memory shopping and double-check with the vendor that you are buying the right SIMMs for your computer.

When you're home and ready for the adventure, don't drink any coffee — you need stable fingers so that you can carefully insert the memory. Here's a list of ten things that can help you remain calm while you are inserting the SIMMs:

- ➤ Do it between naps.
- ➤ Intone a mantra an hour before the adventure.
- ➤ Pray.
- ➤ Listen to any radio station with "Easy" in the title.
- ➤ Read *Zen and the Art of Memory Installation*.
- ➤ Play the *Chant* CD.
- ➤ Watch my infomercial (it's very calming).
- ➤ If you smoke, light up.
- ➤ If you don't smoke, don't.
- ➤ Do it during your yoga class, using your third eye. It helps.

The computer should be turned off but still plugged into a power source while you insert the SIMMs. To be on the safe side, minimize static electricity, which can harm the chips, by wearing sneakers or rubber-soled shoes and standing on a floor that doesn't have carpeting. Put one hand on the power supply to ground yourself and help discharge static electricity. Don't worry — the reason for taking all of these precautions is to minimize the chances of damaging the SIMMs, not to prevent you from being electrocuted. The SIMMs are fragile, but you are not in danger.

With your hand still on the power supply, carefully insert the SIMM into the slot at a slight angle to the connector slot and then press it forward into the clips. You should here a *snap* as the chip is seated. It should be at a 90-degree angle to the motherboard. Repeat this process with the rest of the chips. After installing the SIMMs, you need to enter the CMOS and change the setting for the amount of RAM in the system.

Before you attempt this job, remember that if the computer is under warranty, you could void the warranty by playing around with the SIMMs. But if the machine isn't under warranty or if you want to test your skill with basic computer upgrades, go for it. However, if you are at all uncomfortable about installing the SIMMs yourself, haul the computer into a service center and watch a technician do the memory upgrade. And while you're there, find out what the technician does to relax.

Using the same SIMMS

I saw some SIMMs on sale that may work with my computer, but the SIMMs are different from the ones in my computer. Can I mix and match memory speeds?

Hmmm . . . let me put it this way. It's easier to leave Las Vegas with money. It's easier to turn on a hard rock station and hear Perry Como. It's easier to get Elvis's autograph. In short, no.

Some people will tell you that it is flat-out impossible, while others will claim that it's fine as long as you don't mix and match speeds in the same bank. Yet you may hear claims that alternating two different speeds of memory within a bank is the way to do it.

The Bottom Line The truth is that memory is very finicky. Whether it works depends on the interactions between the processor and the chips, and no two combinations of various manufacturers will produce quite the same results.

Although all PC-compatible motherboards are supposed to be interchangeable, memory is not always interchangeable. Memory is extremely volatile, and the slightest hair of a difference can spell *parity error*. Some people even find that all of the memory chips in their board must be from the same manufacturer or that only certain makes of chips will work. And the SIMMs must be no slower than the slowest speed the board allows. In other words, if your computer's motherboard needs 80-nanosecond SIMMs, 70-nanosecond and 80-nanosecond SIMMs should work, but 100-nanosecond SIMMs won't.

Komando Klues Playing it safe and sticking with the same speed and chip manufacturer is best. But if you have to mix and match chips (and really, who is putting a gun to your head to make you do that?), put the slowest chip in bank zero.

Many computer stores trade old chips for higher-speed chips for a relatively small price. Remember, though, that if you succeed in getting the chips to play nice together, the memory works at the speed of the slowest memory and not at an average of the two.

Understanding banks

Can I put one 4MB SIMM in a bank? Currently, I have a 386SX with two $1 \times 9 \times 70$ ns SIMMs. I have the chance to trade them for one $4 \times 9 \times 70$ ns SIMM. I have always heard that you need to keep them in pairs (that is, I would need two $4 \times 9 \times 70$ ns chips). Is this a myth?

No. In ancient Greece, Simmcrotes told the Greeks to always pair their chips. And the rule holds true even today. Care to know why?

First, look at the way SIMMs are organized and accessed by the computer's processor. A 386SX has a 16-bit data bus that sends information to the processor and receives information from it. Memory on the board is grouped into banks, and each bank must contain 18 bits of memory (16 bits for the data and 2 bits for error checking, or 1 bit of error handling for every 8 bits). So a bank must contain two 9-bit chips. Chips are placed in slots in the banks.

The type of motherboard and the kind of SIMMs that you are using are directly related to how many slots are in a bank. Rule number one about memory banks: A bank must be either completely full or completely empty. But having all banks full is not absolutely necessary. The bottom line: You are limited in the ways that you can configure memory on the motherboard.

Most 386SX motherboards contain four banks and bank the SIMMs in groups of two. You see, many 386 motherboards weren't around yet when the 4MB SIMMs hit the streets. Unless you use 256K chips, the next step up from 2MB of memory is to use four 1 x 9 x 70 chips to fill two banks. If you want to use 4 x 9 x 70 SIMMs, you need to put two in the first bank for a total of 8MB of memory.

If all of this is getting you down, cheer up; you could be trying to upgrade memory on a 386DX motherboard. Each of the banks on a 386DX motherboard needs four chips!

Using a RAM board to expand memory

I don't know if I am being greedy, but I have this strange desire to have more and more RAM in my computer. According to the manual, though, I now have the maximum RAM installed. I read somewhere that there is a RAM board that I can use that will boost the memory and speed. Can I cram some more RAM on board with a RAM board?

After you buy a computer and turn it on, it's the strange glow that makes you want more and more and faster and faster. Yes, it's a disease, but we all have it.

So some motherboards have a dedicated expansion slot for an add-on memory card. Typically, the card provides two more banks to install additional SIMMs. It's perfect for people like you who just can't get enough of a good thing. Check the documentation for your motherboard to see whether your board has this capability.

Some cards come with memory on board, and other cards make you buy the SIMMs separately. Know that memory on a card, like soap on a string, isn't as good as the real McCoy. It's kind of like the Muzak version of a Beatles song. Close, but no cigar.

Comparing 30-pin and 72-pin SIMMS

What's the difference between 30-pin and 72-pin SIMMs?

Forty-two pins? OK. OK. The major difference, without getting into technical terms, between 30-pin and 72-pin SIMMs is what's inside. The 30-pin SIMM has 9 bits on a SIMM, and the 72-pin SIMM has 36 bits. The 30-pin chip is smaller than the 72-pin chip. Chips can be on only one side of the SIMM or on both sides. The pins transmit information between the chips and the processor.

With 30-pin chips, you need to use four chips together to fill one entire bank to get the required 32 bits. Such a system is less flexible because you have less choice about how much memory you can add to it. For example, if you have four 1MB 9-bit SIMMs for a total of 4MB in one bank, you cannot simply add two more megabytes for a total of 6MB. Instead, you have to buy four more 1MB SIMMs to fill up the entire second bank, or else the computer will not work. This setup makes adding memory more expensive than it needs to be. In contrast, if you want another 2MB and you have 36-bit SIMMs, you just add them as desired without having to worry about filling up a bank.

The 72-pin SIMMs are ideal for 386DX systems and higher because they provide all 36 bits that are needed to fill a bank on one chip. These systems are set up this way because a 386DX or higher has a 32-bit bus for communicating with the memory. The bus needs to be connected to a full 32 bits. The 72-pin SIMM provides 32 bits for data, plus 4 bits for parity checking, or 1 parity bit for every 8 data bits.

Back here on earth, you can put 72-pin chips in one at a time. Plus, you can put chips that are different speeds next to each other. This capability can result in cheaper upgrades because you can keep the lower capacity memory. However, before you get too excited about 72-pin SIMMs, first check the motherboard's documentation for what kind of memory it uses. Often, you have no choice. Your computer has to be designed to use 72-pin chips, and if your computer uses 30-pin memory, you're probably stuck with it.

But look at it this way. This limitation gives you an excuse to get a new computer sooner. You can explain to your spouse that the old one cannot be upgraded any more: "Dear, I've tried. Kim Komando has said it can't be done. There is no other choice. Just ask Kim for yourself. Go ahead. I dare you. Honey, can we go shopping this weekend? I love you."

Troubleshooting add-ons

I am trying to add both a SCSI hard disk and a SCSI removable disk to my system. When both disks are connected to the SCSI bus, the power supply does not even turn on the fan. The system appears dead. When one of them is unplugged, the system boots normally. Help!

I see two possibilities in my crystal ball. Either the drive is not connected correctly, or the extra drive is the straw that broke the camel's back and less power is available than is needed to run your system.

As for setting up the SCSI drive correctly, the most common problem is incorrect termination. Both ends of the bus must be terminated. If a host adapter is located at one end of the bus, it has to be terminated. If the host adapter is in the middle of the bus and both the internal and external buses are present, then the adapter must be terminated. Some devices have resistors for termination built in, and the resistors are controlled by jumpers that you have to set, or sometimes you have to actually remove the resistors from the device. Double-check the drive's connections, too.

Most of the time, if the fan doesn't even kick in, odds are that you need a bigger power supply, say 300 watts or more. You see, no fan means no power, no power means not enough juice, and not enough juice means no fan. And no fan means no power. . . . You get the picture. Sometimes you can solve this problem by configuring the system so that all the SCSI drives do not start to spin as soon as the system is turned on. If multiple drives are drawing on the system at start-up, the system may overheat and not turn on. Check your documentation to find out whether you can delay the spinning of the drives.

What's a heat sink?

What's a heat sink? I have one in my computer.

Show-off. Braggart. Snob. A *heat sink* is a tiny chip that is mounted onto the processor and helps to draw heat away from it. It, along with a computer's fan, helps to keep the computer's innards cool. You need it, and just be glad you have it.

Is a CPU fan/heat sink necessary?

When I upgraded to an AMD DX2 66, the dealer insisted that I use a CPU fan/heat sink. They are quite inexpensive, but are they really necessary? Shouldn't a serious heat sink use that special silicone paste to conduct the heat? I feel like I'm doing more harm than good.

Wow, you've done your homework. Makes me feel special that you still need me after all that research. The AMD processor has 1.2 million transistors on it. It dissipates approximately ten watts and can get as hot as 170° – 190° without a heat sink. The heat sink spreads that heat over a larger surface, enabling the heat to dissipate faster. However, a combination of a fan and a heat sink provides better cooling. Don't be a cheapo — spend the few extra dollars. Any chip bigger than a 486 33 needs a fan to keep it cool.

Overheating concerns

I keep hearing all these horror stories about the 486 chips overheating and melting down the system. What can I do to avoid this problem in my new 486DX2 66?

You worry too much. Today's 486 and Pentium computers have fans or heat sinks that draw the heat away from the CPU. The only thing that can melt 486 and Pentium chips is some of the talk in the Flirt's Nook on America Online.

The Bottom Line

It's a safe bet to say that your computer is OK with the heat. Although 486DX2 processors operate at incredible speeds and generate heat in the process, chip meltdown is very rare. I had an old VW Bug that overheated all the time in the summer. What did it do? It shut down on its own. Same with your computer: It will shut off automatically if it begins to overheat.

Heat can be a problem, though, in systems that have clocks that have been doubled. If you are concerned about it, take some precautions.

First, make sure that the computer's case is an adequate size for the number of expansion boards and drives installed. If you try to cram too much into a smaller case, such as a slim desktop, you may not have sufficient space for air to circulate properly. Also, keep the vents on the back of the computer free of dust, and don't block the airflow. Next, always make sure that the fan attached to the power supply is running while the computer is operating. You should be able to hear it hum. Sometimes the fan shorts out, but the system continues to work.

If you are really concerned about things warming up, go to a computer supply store and purchase a fan card. I doubt that you need it, but this inexpensive card slips into an expansion slot and provides two more fans to cool the system. You may want to invest in the kind of power supply that has two fans to help keep the machine cool. If the room you work in is hotter than 80° and you're too cheap to turn up the air conditioning, aim a fan at the computer to be on the safe side. The hotter the room is, the harder it is for the computer to dissipate the heat it generates.

Understanding monitor sizes

My monitor says it's the 15-inch type, but it doesn't measure 15 inches. I sure hope I didn't get ripped off again like I did the time I bought a used car from a little old lady who only drove it once a week to the market. She forgot to tell me that the market was in Mexico City.

Did you buy your computer south of the border, too? The size of a monitor is the size of the actual display area and does not include the monitor's plastic casing on the sides. You measure a monitor on the diagonal and not on the horizontal or vertical. The reason is not to confuse you or make you think that you are getting a bigger monitor than you are, but to simplify things. Monitors are not square; programmers are square. Monitors are rectangular. If a horizontal measurement were used, a vertical measurement would have to be provided too. On a 15-inch monitor, the viewing area is approximately 13¹/₂ inches. Hasta la vista, amigo.

Understanding monitor pitches

My buddy told me I should trade in my .28-dot-pitch monitor for one with a .32-dot pitch. Should I listen to him?

If your buddy told you to jump off the Microsoft State Building, would you? Don't listen to your buddy's advice. He's wrong.

If you look closely at a monitor, you'll see that the picture is made up of thousands of tiny dots. The *dot pitch* is the amount of space between the dots, measured in millimeters. A .28-dot-pitch monitor has .28 millimeters of space between each itty-bitty dot. The closer the dots are together, the better the picture, or *screen resolution*. The smaller the pitch, the closer the dots, and the crisper the image. The way the dot pitch works is the reverse of what your friend is telling you. As the size of the monitor increases, say to 17 inches or 20 inches, you want a smaller dot pitch, say .26 or lower.

Care for a bit of trivia? The first IBM PC color monitor had a dot pitch of .43 mm, while today's top-of-the-line monitors have pitches of .28 mm or less.

Two computers, one monitor

I have two desktop PCs and one monitor. Do I have to buy another monitor?

You can buy a special device called an *A-B switch* at a computer or electronics store. It enables you to select which computer is using the monitor while they are both running. Most switches enable you to use one keyboard for two computers, too.

Monitor flashes

My monitor seems to jump out at me when I change applications. I have a 17-inch *state-of-the-art* (last week) monitor with a 486DX2 66 with Windows for Workgroups and DOS 6.2.

Cool your jets. Many multisynching monitors give you a slight flash and may even go dark for a split second when you change from applications in DOS to applications in Windows. If you get the flash only when you change programs, you have nothing to worry about.

You may not have the correct drivers installed for the monitor. If that's not the problem, take the monitor back to the people you got it from and get this week's monitor. That's what your warranty is for.

Electronic interference

My monitor recently started getting wavy lines through it. At first, these lines just reminded me of the ocean, but now they are ticking me off. Is it time for a new monitor? I live in Nebraska.

Well, if you live in Nebraska, the ocean may be a refreshing change. I really wouldn't do anything unless you're hit by a tidal wave and the real estate prices suddenly go up because you have beachfront property.

Wavy lines are often telltale signs of electronic interference. Anything from a neighbor's food processor to computer stereo speakers that are not magnetically shielded to a passing police car can disturb the computer.

If interference isn't the problem, the video card may be at fault. If so, you may need to replace it. But first, if you feel comfortable opening the computer, push down gently on the video card: possibly the connections are loose. While you're at it, check the connection from the computer system unit to the monitor. Or you may need to replace the monitor itself. Some monitors come with a test or diagnostics program. You'll find it in the monitor's directory on the hard disk or on the monitor's setup software. Run the test and see what happens. Check for sea salt and crustaceans.

Whatever you do, don't open the monitor, even to take a peek, because curiosity can kill the cat. The circuits can retain charges of up to 35,000 volts for weeks after you last turn off the computer, and that amount is more than enough to electrocute you.

Troubleshooting monitor problems

For some strange reason, my monitor sometimes turns to a yellow background. This problem affects all the colors my computer displays, even in Windows. Is my monitor going bad?

Yellow? Your computer is suffering from jaundice interruptus.

When your computer screen's background turns yellow, try turning off the computer and leaving the monitor on. If the screen is still yellow even with the computer off, then the problem lies with the monitor. If not, it's the video card. If the video card is the problem, replace it. If the monitor is the problem, make sure that all of the cables are firmly connected.

If the monitor has a cable that can be disconnected on both ends (from both the monitor and the computer), then try a different cable and see whether the problem persists. If that doesn't work, then the monitor is bad, and the only choice is to replace it unless it was very expensive. For an expensive monitor, find a factory-authorized service center because few other repair facilities have the necessary documentation to repair a monitor.

Don't even think of fixing the monitor yourself. You could be electrocuted. The monitor's circuits can retain as much as 35,000 volts for weeks after you last turn off the monitor.

Power supply problems

My monitor intermittently goes blank for five minutes or so. Although it gives me a great excuse to make another pot of coffee, I would like to know what the problem is and what it takes to fix it. My boss thinks I'm just goofing off.

Your computer goes down, and you run and make coffee? That's not goofing off; that's hard work. No one likes to make the coffee in the office. Tell your boss that. While you're at it, ask for a raise.

If possible, try to use the monitor at another computer workstation in the office. If you continue to have the problem, the monitor needs to go to the computer doctor or to a repair center. Odds are, the power supply inside the monitor is on the blink.

If the problem magically disappears, check the power supply to the monitor at your desk. You may have a short in one of the cables that connects the monitor to the computer or to the outlet. Make sure that everything is connected securely and see whether replacing the cables and the power cord gets rid of the problem. Regardless of the outcome, go talk to the boss. Either enjoy your coffee breaks or get a new monitor, unless it is a very expensive monitor. In that case, you should find a factory-authorized service center to repair it. Few other places can repair a monitor because documentation on monitors is scarce.

Warning, warning, danger, danger! Do not even think about opening the monitor. It is extremely dangerous. Internal circuits can retain high voltages, as much as 35,000 volts worth, for weeks after a monitor has been disconnected!

Troubleshooting video card problems

I think my video card is croaking. Whenever I use a game, the screen goes wacko. But in other programs, it works fine. What's going on?

It sounds to me as if you've invented a new computer game called Wacko. Either that, or you're having problems with resolution. Resolution means how good the stuff looks on the screen, and it boils down to pixels. You see, a monitor isn't just one big picture.

A monitor is really a bunch of dots, or *pixels,* that create the picture. In VGA mode, the resolution is 640 × 480 pixels, and in Super VGA mode (SVGA), the resolution is 800 × 600 pixels. Sounds to me as if you are trying to use a game that needs SVGA but you have only a VGA setup.

You need a middleman from the computer to the monitor or a video card that also sets the resolution. Having an SVGA monitor and a VGA video card won't give your SVGA resolution. You need an SVGA card to work with the SVGA monitor.

Comparing digital and analog

I have a digital monitor. My brother has an analog monitor. He keeps telling me that his is better. What's the difference?

This sounds like a sibling rivalry that has gone on far too long. The question is not who has the better video monitor, but whom did Mom love more? Come on, face the truth.

You can sum up the difference between digital and analog monitors in one word: color. Well, maybe in four words: the number of colors. A digital monitor works by firing red, green, and blue electron beams on and off. You get eight possible color combinations. But digital monitors can display the eight color combinations in either high-contrast or low-contrast mode. So you have a whopping 16 possible colors.

Your brother's analog display also uses red, green, and blue beams to create various colors. It can display these colors at 64 different levels of intensity, so analog monitors can produce more than 262,144 different colors. So, his is better . . . maybe. It depends on whether the video card in his computer can show him all the colors. The VGA card can display 262,144 different colors but only any 256 at one time. The SVGA cards offer various improvements on the VGA cards, depending on the card's manufacturer. SVGA generally gives users a greater number of color choices, the ability to display more colors at the same time, and greater speed.

Understanding monitor resolutions

My video card offers several resolutions. Before I start fiddling around, please help me. What is the advantage of going from a VGA 600 x 480 to, say, 1280 x 1024 resolution?

The advantage of going from a VGA 600 x 480 to 1280 x 1024 is a much sharper image. The measurements refer to the maximum number of pixels that can be displayed on-screen. The more pixels on-screen, the denser the graphics, the more detailed the images it can handle, and the more stuff shown on-screen. The downside: At 1024 x 1024 mode, displays are a little harder to read because the characters and graphics are smaller. It's the same screen, but it seems as if it's a foot farther away.

Magnetic interference

I have a monitor that pulls in from the sides and has even lost the entire screen momentarily. Where do I start looking for the cause?

In your heart. Did you skimp and buy a monitor on a street corner?

The first thing I'd check for is magnetic interference. Are you getting interference from any other appliances or devices, such as a TV, the neighbor's vacuum cleaner, a portable telephone, or planes that are flying overhead? None, you say. Well, then, something is wrong with either the video card or the monitor.

Try hooking a friend's monitor up to your machine and see whether the same problem happens. But if doing that doesn't change the situation, the video card is out, or the monitor is at fault. Troubleshooting will not take much time. Why? Simply stated, there are very few things that can be repaired on a monitor.

If the video card is at fault, try reinstalling the video card's drivers just to make sure that they haven't been corrupted. Make sure that the cables on the monitor are in good shape and tightly connected. You can play with the little knobs that control the vertical shift, horizontal shift, brightness, and contrast. If the screen shakes, the vertical control or the horizontal control could be loose.

Never, never, never, under any circumstance, open a monitor to see whether you can play "Home Improvement." Doing so is extremely dangerous. Internal circuits can retain high voltages, as much as 35,000 volts worth for *weeks* after a monitor has been disconnected! The power has to be discharged by a person who knows how to do the job properly.

Unless you have a very expensive monitor, having it serviced rarely pays. In addition, the required documentation isn't readily available. If you decide to have the monitor repaired, make sure that you take it to a factory-authorized service center.

Monitor and video card compatibility

I recently purchased a Trident SVGA card with 1MB on board. It is supposed to give you the capability for 16 million colors or true colors. On my system, I can get only 800 × 600 resolution with 256 colors. I have copied all the supplied drivers, and I am still having no luck.

Two parties are always involved in displaying images: the video card and the monitor. It sounds as if you have a pretty spiffy SVGA video card, but you may not have a monitor that is capable of taking advantage of the card's full range of features.

A Trident card can show 16 million colors, but probably only in 600 × 480 resolution. You need to have more than 1MB of video memory to get a higher resolution. But you should be able to change from 800 × 600 resolution showing 256 colors.

If you have a VGA monitor, it can't display more than 256 colors at one time. Another possibility is that at the greatest resolution that the monitor offers, the card is designed to display only 256 colors. Or perhaps you need to set a jumper on the card for different modes of operation. Check your documentation carefully. If you are certain that your monitor is capable of a higher resolution, call Trident and get the new video drivers for your computer.

Installing monitor drivers

You are my last hope. Please answer my question so that all those who come after me won't suffer as I have. I put in a video card and used the DOS COPY command to put the drivers on my computer's hard disk. I tried to use the video drivers, but all I get is Windows error messages. What am I doing wrong?

Hey, relax. It's gonna be OK. The DOS COPY command is the problem. You have to install the video drivers by using either the Windows Setup or the driver installation program that's included with the video drivers disk.

Get out the manual that came with the video card and read the first or second chapter. It should be called something like "Installation" or "Installing the Video Drivers."

Here's the *Reader's Digest* version of what you need to do: Put the driver's disk that came with the video card in drive A. From Windows Program Manager, select File and then Run. In the command line box, type **A:SETUP** (sometimes it's **WSETUP**), and click OK. This routine usually creates a new program group in Windows that contains your video drivers. Have your original Windows installation disks handy because you may need them.

Speeding up graphics

I don't like waiting in lines, and I don't like waiting for my computer to refresh the graphics. If I shell out more cash for video card memory, will the graphics in my programs speed up?

Yes, but watch out. Many people are buying software these days. You may run into a line at the store. Get your new video card during off hours — like during a nationally televised football game.

The more memory on the video card, the faster the screen can refresh and the faster the graphics will appear. It makes sense. The more images that can be stored in memory, the less time the system has to waste waiting for the information to be sent from the hard drive. The only hitch is the refresh rate of the monitor. The *refresh rate,* also known as the *scanning frequency,* is the speed at which the system can send new images to the screen.

Images on-screen are created by three guns (one for each of the three primary colors: red, blue, and green) that shoot electrons at the screen. The faster these guns move, the faster your screen can draw an image. Obviously, no matter how fast a card you get, you are going to be limited by your monitor's refresh rate. Fortunately, most monitors on the market today are *multisynch,* which means that the monitor can detect the scanning frequency of the video card and adjust accordingly. However, if the monitor is a fixed frequency, you need to make sure that the video card that you buy matches the scanning rate of the monitor, or the monitor won't work with the card and may even be damaged. Check the documentation that came with the monitor to be on the safe side.

465

Komando Klues When you add most memory (video memory especially), getting the same chips as you have — including the same speed — is always best. If you're looking for more speed from your video card, simply adding more video RAM will not usually help you much. You would be better off investing in a *graphics accelerator* type of video card. There are many such cards to choose from these days. They've been designed to give you top performance when you're running Windows. And if you do get stuck in line, bring this book along. It will make the wait that much easier.

Understanding turbocharged speed

My new computer has a TURBO switch on the front that is supposed to slow it down. Why in the world would someone want to spend good money for a fast system and then slow it down on purpose?

Once upon a time, computers used to have to work at two speeds. The new turbocharged computers had faster brains, but some programs couldn't work that fast. The computer designers had to give computer users a way to slow down the computer so it could work with the old programs. Nowadays, the turbo button is rarely used. It is left over from the good old days of computing.

Arcade-style games written for the 8086 and 286 computers are particularly notorious for using the system clocks to regulate speed. As a result, these golden oldies are unplayable on the newer computers, even when the turbo switch is off. There are, however, special programs available that will slow the processor down even further for people who want to continue to play their old favorites. Imagine that! Spending money on a program to make your new system slower! It's like buying a first-class ticket and sitting in coach near the toilets.

Dirt in keyboards

I am having a p oblem with my keyboa d. I can no longe type the lette of the alphabet that is afte Q and befo e S. Fo give my poo typing, but as you see, I'm in need of that one key!

We forget how important R letters R until they R all gone.

466

Almost all keyboard problems can be summed up in one word — *dirt*. Yes, day after day, poor keyboards have crumbs dropped into them, coffee dripped on them, and paper clips lost in them; yet, amazingly, they continue to work flawlessly. It is not until one of the keys finally goes on strike (or maybe *doesn't strike* is more accurate) to protest the harsh working conditions that someone finally thinks to clean the keys.

To clean a keyboard, you need either a keyboard vacuum cleaner or a can of compressed air. If you use compressed air, hold the keyboard upside down while you shoot the air at it. This technique will blow out the dirt and other less attractive stuff that has accumulated within the keyboard.

To fix a sticking key, you first need to pry the cap off the key. You can buy a special tool to do that, or you can improvise and use a paper clip. After the cap is off, spray the exposed switch with contact cleaner, or if that's not available, with distilled water. Check the spring too; perhaps it is bad. Let the switch dry completely before trying it. Repeat if necessary.

If you have to replace the key, a new one shouldn't cost more than a few dollars. Or, if you have to replace the keyboard, it's about $50 for a new one. In the interim to get the R key, press and hold down the Alt key and type the number **114**, using the numbers on the keyboard's numeric keypad.

Keyboard error messages

I keep getting the error message *Press F1 key* and error number *301* when I turn on my computer. After I dutifully press F1, everything proceeds as normal and seems to work fine. I also notice that I can no longer use the Ctrl+Esc keys in Windows to access the task list. Although this is no huge problem, I'd like to know how to solve it.

When you turn on your computer, it goes through a pretty extensive self-test. The techs call it the *POST*, or *power-on self test*. Pretty advanced, huh? Wouldn't it be great if all our appliances did that? Like the toaster would come on and say it was going to burn the toast. Or the VCR would say that it was going to have trouble taping "I Love Lucy" and was going to tape the food dehydrator infomercial again. The POST is performed every time the system is turned on. It does a very thorough check of almost everything in the system and then informs you if there are any problems. Of course, it would be more helpful if the test actually told you what the message meant instead of giving you a number. For your information, error code 301 means *Keyboard reset or stuck key failure.*

As you have noticed, the Ctrl+Esc key combination does not work. The POST is telling you that one of the keys is stuck. You should experiment with these keys individually to see which key is the problem. You can clean the keys by using either a keyboard vacuum cleaner or a can of compressed air. If you use compressed air, hold the keyboard upside down while you shoot the air at it. This method will blow out the dirt and other less attractive stuff that has accumulated within the keyboard. To fix a sticking key, you first need to pry the cap off the key. You can buy a special tool to do that, or you can improvise and use a paper clip. After the cap is off, spray the exposed switch with contact cleaner, or if that's not available, with distilled water. Check the spring too; perhaps it is bad. Let the switch dry completely before trying it. Repeat if necessary. If you have to replace the key, a new one shouldn't cost more than a few dollars.

Installing an MS Ballpoint mouse

I purchased an MS Ballpoint mouse for my laptop and want to use it with my desktop. Will it work at all?

Hey, is there always a line at the bank? Does the TV cable company make you wait all day at home until they come to hook the cable up? Do you always catch every stoplight on the way to the airport? Does the phone always ring while you are in the shower? Sure, it's easy stuff. Just use the installation software that came with the Ballpoint mouse on your desktop computer. The connection on the end of the Ballpoint mouse should fit the computer's connection. If not, you get to use that weird-looking thing, a pinout converter, that is inside the Ballpoint's box.

Cleaning the mouse

My mouse is very temperamental. It sticks constantly, and I have to yank anything that I want to move. Is it time for a new mouse, or can I fix it?

468

You are talking about the mouse that goes to your computer, right? You're not talking about a pet that you are mad at. Your little rodent spends all of its time crawling around your dusty old desktop, so it doesn't take long for its little feet to get dirty. Sounds like you need to clean out the old mouse. If you have never cleaned it before, you will be amazed at the amount of gunk that gets stuck to the little bars that the ball rolls against. The mouse is very sensitive, and even the smallest piece of hair or the tiniest bit of lint can make it impossible to use.

Special kits are available for cleaning the mouse, but most people are content to use their fingers, which, while not usually dangerous to the mouse, is not recommended. All you have to do is turn the mouse upside down, turn the panel in the direction the arrows point, turn the mouse right side up, and the ball falls out. Use a cotton swab to clean any dirt out from around the edges, and do it gently. If the ball is dirty, clean it with some water, dry it completely, and then put it back in. Slide the panel back in place, and you have a clean mouse, ready for action.

The standard Microsoft style mouse seems to be the worst offender at sucking up dirt from the mouse pad — no matter how clean the pad appears to be. If you have this kind of mouse, you'll want to clean it once a month or so. On the other end of the spectrum, the Honeywell mouse never needs cleaning because it has wheels that roll along a surface, and the interior of the mouse is totally sealed from contamination. If cleaning doesn't do the trick, you may have a short in one of the wires inside the cord that connects to the computer. In that case, you have to replace the mouse. I prefer the pads with a smooth laminated top. The pads with a fabric top tend to trap the dust and the grime.

Installing game cards

I just installed a game card so that I can use two joysticks and cream my brother in my basketball game. For some reason, my computer will not recognize that the game card is even installed.

Does the computer belong to your brother? It could be loyal. Better check this angle out before reading any further. The next thing you need to do is look at the documentation that came with the game board to see how it selects which IRQ to use. The game card needs to be assigned an IRQ number in order to communicate with the processor. You need to make sure that the IRQ that the game board uses is not already being used by something else, such as a sound board, modem, or mouse.

If the machine is not recognizing the game card, maybe something else is taking the IRQ that the game card is set up to use. When the computer starts up, it checks the slots in the computer in order — either right to left or left to right. It assigns IRQs on a first-come, first-served basis. So you have to change either the game board's IRQ or the IRQ of one of the other devices.

If the board still doesn't work, another possible problem is noise from one of the other boards. Sometimes a board, such as a sound card or modem, can interfere with the workings of another card. The solution is to keep rearranging the order of the cards in the slots until you find an order that works.

Then again, this problem is fairly common in installing multiport game cards when other game ports are already on the computer. When this is the case, you need to disable all other game ports on the system. You often can find a game port on the I/O controller card that needs to be disabled by moving a jumper. Dig through all the little books that came with your system (you did save them, I hope), and find the manual for the controller card. If you don't have it, contact the manufacturer and have someone walk you through the job over the telephone. And good luck with your brother.

Motherboards and the Pentium

I have a Choice (I think that's the name) motherboard with a 486DX2 66MHz CPU. Can this motherboard take a Pentium CPU chip? If so, what kind?

Currently, no 486VLB motherboards can run the Pentium CPUs. At least, none that I've been able to find. The "Pentium Ready" and later "Pentium Technology Upgradeable" motherboards are supposed to take the P24T CPU, which Intel has promised will be a "Pentium Technology Processor." Haven't seen this beast yet; don't know if we ever will. But if Intel puts it out, it should work on your motherboard. So the answer is a definite yes. And no.

Choosing graphics cards

I have a Packard Bell 486 33. The bus is an ISA/ classic bus. It has four AT-compatible expansion slots (16 bit). Just what does this mean when I go to choose a graphics card?

What this means is that if you go shopping for a video card, don't let someone talk you into a local bus, or VLB, video card. You don't have a VLB slot on the motherboard. It won't work. You need to stick with an ISA accelerator — a Diamond Stealth 24, Diamond Speedstar, Trident 8900C, Oak S3, ATI MACH32 ISA, or something from these groups. Any of them will do fine and work with your computer.

Troubleshooting clock problems

I've noticed that my clock does not keep accurate time. It seems to lose between one and three minutes a week. Is this symptomatic of impending motherboard hardships? Also, my computer has twice lost its CMOS settings. My PC clone is less than a year old, but I hate this motherboard already!

Don't hate your motherboard. You don't know what she's been through.

Does it help knowing that your problem has nothing to do with the motherboard? Inside your computer is a little battery that keeps the computer's date and time. All the important stuff, such as the date, the time, and other computer vitals, are kept in the CMOS that is powered by a battery. So it's time to change the battery. No time like the present. Don't wait another minute. Time's a wastin'.

Komando Klues
Before you do anything, however, write down your computer's CMOS settings. On most computers, you can access the CMOS by pressing the Delete or F1 key as soon as you turn on the computer. Be careful not to change anything in the CMOS that you aren't sure about. Just write everything down on a piece of paper. Or send a copy of the screen to the printer by making sure your printer is on-line and pressing the Print Screen key on your keyboard.

Store those settings in a safe place. Check the computer's manual and find out what type of battery you need. Usually, you can pick up a battery for about five or ten dollars at just about any computer store. If the system is still under warranty, you will probably want to take it in and let a technician do the job. Do-it-yourself repairs can void the warranty.

Using plastic computer covers

I have a friend who is considering a computer purchase, but she has some reservations. She lives on the beach, and she leaves her windows open most days. The salt spray has affected some of the iron stuff inside her house (accelerated rusting), and she would like to know how it would affect a computer.

Computers are durable, and the humidity and salt air combination shouldn't pose too much of a problem. Your friend should invest in some plastic computer covers, though, to protect the CPU, the monitor, and the keyboard when she's not using the computer. But please tell her not to put the covers on right after she turns off the computer. The computer is hot then, and she needs to give it a few minutes to cool off.

Sometimes humidity causes one strange problem. I found this out while working during a vacation in Hawaii. Humidity causes envelopes to get sealed while they are going through a laser printer — which makes it pretty tough to put a letter inside them. You can prevent this problem by drying out the envelopes before they go into the printer. To do so, spread about ten envelopes on a plate so the gummed edges aren't touching each other. Then put the plate in a microwave oven and nuke the envelopes for a minute. After they cool, load them into the printer. Sounds strange, but it works! It also serves five to ten. I recommend a glue stick as an appetizer and an eraser for dessert.

Chapter 12
The Internet

The Basics

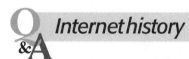 *Internet history*

Perhaps I'm dopey, but what exactly is the Internet?

You're not dopey, but I can tell you're getting grumpy. I hope this answer won't make you sleepy.

The *Internet* is a worldwide network of computer networks. Like the U.S. government, it's so large (how large is it, Kim?) there's really no accurate way to measure it or even count the number of people who are using it.

Started in the late '60s, the Internet, or the *Net*, has recently become amazingly popular with regular people. Over the years, it has grown well beyond its original scope — it now includes over 19,000 networks. And it's still growing every day, like the fungus in my refrigerator.

You may hear the buzzphrase *information superhighway* applied to the Internet. They really aren't one and the same. The information superhighway, or *National Information Infrastructure* (NII), is a yet-unrealized computer network in the United States. The Internet is the NII's foundation, just as dirt roads were the starting point for today's interstate highway system. By the way, most developed nations are working on plans for NIIs; all NIIs likely will be connected to each other in much the same way that the Internet is connected today.

On the Internet, you can hop from Florida to Bombay to Brazil in the blink of an eye. The Internet brings the global community and its accumulated knowledge to your doorstep. And it takes you as far as your imagination allows.

Internet requirements

I'm ready to become a productive member of society. What do I need to use the Internet?

Yeah, as I always say, there's no better way to feel like a productive member of society than holing up in a room and exchanging e-mail with (other) computer nerds.

To use the Internet, you need

> ➤ A computer
> ➤ A modem
> ➤ Live phone line
> ➤ Computer communications software
> ➤ An Internet account

Because the Internet connects computers, you need a computer. The type of computer doesn't matter; you can use an IBM-compatible, a Macintosh, a Sun workstation, a Commodore Amiga, and so on. Although the Internet itself is usually run on minicomputers or mainframe computers that run an operating system called *UNIX*, you don't need a computer running UNIX to access the Internet.

A *modem* lets computers talk to each other over telephone lines. When communicating over the phone, computers can talk in a few languages; the language of choice is controlled by the communications software. Modems work at different speeds; the higher the number, the faster the information flows between computers. Modem speed is measured in *bits per second*, or bps.

Komando Klues

The word *baud* is used interchangeably with bps.

Although you can access the Internet with a modem of any speed, you want to go as fast as possible. (Even if you're not paying long-distance charges, you may pay an hourly rate.) By the way, on the Internet, information flow ranges from 56,000 bps to over 10 million bps.

Although you can use any type of computer, the communications software you use has to be written for your specific computer type. Just like you can't play an 8-track tape (remember those?) on a record player, you can't run a Macintosh program on an IBM-compatible. The program also has to know the language of the Internet: *TCP/IP* (Transmission Connect Protocol/Internet Protocol). I discuss some of the different types of software in more detail later in this chapter.

A *service provider* is an organization that lets you establish an Internet account. Of course, you usually must pay the service provider for the account, much as you pay for a newspaper or magazine subscription. Before you get any bright ideas about circumventing the system, know that you need an account to access the Internet, just as you need a library card to check out books from the library.

Paying for an account buys you a name and a password. The password is like a key: it keeps other users from tapping your account. (If we didn't have car keys, for example, anyone could borrow our cars. On the other hand, locks don't stop determined thieves. I recommend The Club.) I talk about the different types of accounts later in this chapter.

As you know, there are exceptions to every rule, and the preceding rules are no exception:

➤ You don't need a computer or modem if the company or school where you work is directly connected to the Internet. If your company/school has a direct connection, you can use a *dumb terminal*. (They call a dumb terminal "dumb" because it doesn't have a brain or CPU chip; it's wired to some big computer.)

➤ You don't need a special communications software program. A plain ol' program such as Procomm, Qmodem, or Microphone can do. With these programs, your computer pretends that it's a dumb terminal after it connects to the service provider's computer.

➤ You don't need a service provider. It's possible to get some Internet features from an on-line service, such as America Online, CompuServe, and Prodigy. In fact, even some local BBSs (*b*ulletin *b*oard *s*ystems) provide limited access to the Internet.

Internet search programs

Are there things on the Internet named after comic book characters? My friend told me so, but I think he's pulling my leg.

Archie, Veronica, and Jughead are all real Internet programs. (I'm waiting for Reggie and Betty to show up soon.) Who said computer geeks have no sense of humor? It's just a bit warped.

> ➤ *Archie* is a program that helps you search for files on the Internet. *Archie servers* are computers dedicated to passing out Archie information.

> ➤ *Veronica* searches for keywords in Gopher menus around the world. (Gopher makes so many menus available that it's often difficult to know where to start.) For more information about Gopher, refer to the "Surfing the Net" section, later in this chapter.

> ➤ *Jughead* is a little lazier than Veronica; it only searches for keywords in the names of Gopher menus.

Which 'toon will appear on the Internet next? I know! How about Spiderman as a search program for the World Wide Web!

Internet shell accounts

When I went to sign up for an Internet account, they tried to sell me a SLIP or PPP account. Is this just a way to get some extra money out of me?

So you think the Internet provider is trying to slip it to you, eh?

If your company or school has a direct connection to the Internet, you can access the Internet via a *shell account* (that is, a UNIX shell account). A shell account is less expensive than a SLIP or PPP account, but it's harder to use and isn't as pretty.

In fact, working with a shell account is like working at the DOS prompt: to do things, you have to enter commands. (To list a directory, for example, you have to type **ls**.) I bet you don't want to learn the commands for a new operating system. And if you think DOS is hard, wait until you see UNIX!

A quick proof:

1. UNIX is pronounced "YOU Nix."

2. *You* means *you, the user*.

3. *Nix* means *to forbid or stop*.

4. Therefore, you must stop using UNIX.

With a shell account, you don't need to use special communications software to access the Internet. You can use regular communications programs, such as Procomm, Qmodem, and Microphone.

The Bottom Line

SLIP and PPP are types of Internet accounts. *SLIP* (*Serial Line Interface Protocol*) and *PPP* (*Point to Point Protocol*) accounts let you use graphical software to access the Internet. Wading through the oceans of information on the Internet is much easier when you can point and click rather than type command after command.

You can find SLIP and PPP communications software for Windows, Windows NT, OS/2, Macintosh, Amiga, and even UNIX. (UNIX computers must be running X Windows.) SLIP and PPP accounts are a little more expensive than shell accounts, but they're well worth the extra money. With a SLIP or PPP account, you get a certain number of hours each month to use. If you go beyond the allotted time, you pay an hourly rate.

Komando Klues

If you can choose between SLIP and PPP, get a PPP account: they cost the same, but PPP is newer and it has a few extra features.

A final word: SLIP and PPP software can be difficult to set up. But once you have the programs set up, life is good.

Navigating the Internet via World Wide Web

I bought the hype and got an Internet account. And I'm not impressed. Maybe I'm just looking for love (of technology, of course) in all the wrong places. How do most people use the Internet?

There's no way to define *most people*. Heck, no one even knows exactly how many people are using the Internet.

You see, no one central organization controls the Internet. This is both a blessing and a curse (IDG won't let me print the curse). Either way, it's tough to define who is using the Internet, let alone how.

But according to the Internet Society, an international organization that *attempts* to coordinate Internet activities, the most common type of transaction on the Internet is electronic mail (or e-mail). The most information, meanwhile, is transferred via the *World Wide Web* (*WWW* or *the Web*), an attractive and easy-to-understand hypermedia system that enables you to browse the Internet without breaking a sweat.

You see, if you have a plain-Jane Internet account (that is, if you have a shell account), you don't get a lot of cool-looking stuff. You're left at a prompt that looks like

    $

or

    %

Not very exciting, eh? Still, with a lot of practice, a good book (try *The Internet For Dummies* from IDG Books), and a little luck, you can find most of the goodies on the Internet.

Using a graphical account (SLIP or PPP account), however, opens up the Internet in an exciting fashion. Just as Windows is a lot nicer to look at and easier to navigate than DOS, a graphical account (combined with the right graphical communications software) makes wandering through the Internet a much more enjoyable experience. Those who use the Web, for example, can cruise the information superhighway in the fast lane — no more getting stuck in the slow lane behind the student driver.

Imagine that you're looking at a screenful of information about hang gliding. As you read through the screen, you see a reference to the origins of hang gliding. And you notice that the word *history* is displayed on-screen in a different color. Because you've always wondered who first jumped off a cliff clinging to an overgrown kite (oh, that brave pioneer), you place your mouse on the word *history* and click. In a sec, you're connected to a computer that's sitting in Australia. (The different color is your clue that the word *history* is a launching pad.) In other words, despite not knowing how to get to the second computer, you navigated halfway around the world and logged into another computer system with a single point-and-click.

Without the Web, you would have had to type at the $ prompt

> ➤ The name of the computer system
> ➤ How to get there
> ➤ How to access the computer
> ➤ The name of the document you wanted to read

I get sore fingers just thinking about it. Where would you get all this information? Programs such as Gopher search through databases for keywords. Of course, you have to know where a Gopher server is, how to get to it, and how to look for something.

Getting the picture? Getting a headache? Getting off the Internet?

Komando Klues

On-line services such as America Online also allow Internet access, but that road is still under construction.

Q&A Using school accounts at home

I have an Internet account at school and I want to use it at home. How do I do so?

Just because there's a gym at school doesn't mean that you can use it any time you want.

In the same vein, you need permission from the school to access the computer system during nonschool hours. Remember the movie "War Games"? Matthew Broderick almost ended the world because he failed to ask for permission.

If your school allows after-hours access, you need the standard tools for on-line communications: computer, modem, live phone line, and communications software. Check with your school's computer science department to identify any restrictions, as well as which type of software you need.

After you dial into the school's computer system, you can work as though you were sitting in a chair in the computer lab. Everything that you can do at the lab, you can do at home. Of course, anything you can't do at the lab, you can't do at home either.

Komando Klues

Keep in mind that stuff will appear on-screen at home slower than you're accustomed. That's because the school has a high-speed link to the Internet, while a modem is a slow-speed link.

Of course, because you're accessing the Internet purely for educational and intellectual purposes (yeah, right), you won't mind a little inconvenience, will you?

"Surfing the Internet"

Who coined the phrase *surfing the Internet*, and how does this describe Internet users? I mean, how does some green-skinned programmer geek ever resemble a bronzed surfer dude?

One possible explanation: The Internet is a tidal wave of information.

Another: More and more people are spending time browsing the Internet. And it sounds much cooler to say *surfing the Net* than *looking up information with the aid of my computer*.

Besides, if sitting in your underwear on a couch while pressing the TV remote control is called *channel surfing*, then looking up stuff on the Internet can be called *Internet surfing*.

And come to think of it, some underwear can pass as bathing suits. See, nerds and dudes aren't that different.

Internet user courtesy

What does *spamming the Net* mean? Is it a good or a bad thing?

Spamming the Net sounds, and is, dirty. If you're spamming, you're breaking the Net's unwritten rules:

> ➤ *Never do anything to endanger the Internet.* For example, using the Net for commercial purposes was taboo because nobody wanted to upset Uncle Sam (remember, the Internet began as a government-funded network). Devoted users didn't want to risk losing the government's funding of the Internet.

> ➤ *Don't waste bandwidth.* Bandwidth is another term for capacity. Although the Internet is huge, only a fixed amount of information can be moved through at a time. So if a computer (or worse, the network itself) is busy working with useless information, then useful information can't be transferred or accessed during that time.

One of the most famous incidents of spamming the Net occurred in 1994. A company advertised its services by posting messages to over 5,000 newsgroups. The reaction was fast and furious. Enraged Internet users around the world started *flaming* the guilty company (that is, sending the electronic equivalent of hate mail). Users also flamed the service provider that the company had an account with. The result: In just a few days, the service provider received several thousand megabytes of e-mail objecting to the heinous advertising; the provider's computer system crashed.

To send that much e-mail wasted a lot of Internet bandwidth. But worse, many people reading the postings in the newsgroups posted other messages to say how outraged they were at the company. So more bandwidth was wasted.

Just think: All the messages posted in the newsgroups are stored on tens of thousands of computers. Even if a message is only 1,000 characters long, it can take up millions of characters of space worldwide. Some of those characters could have been used to store more worthwhile messages, like your valuable question. And my answer.

Firewalls

What's a firewall? How do I get around it?

A *firewall* limits access to a network or group of networks. A firewall, which works like an electronic fence, is located between the network it serves and the Internet. It may be a device specifically designed for the purpose, such as an *NES* (*n*etwork *e*ncryption *s*ystem), or just a dedicated computer workstation.

A firewall typically keeps unauthorized people off a network. This type of security measure was developed after some people (called *hackers* or *crackers*) broke into a number of commercial and government networks and caused serious damage. The movie "War Games" was imaginary, but the basic idea underlying it was real.

Fences can keep things in, too. Firewalls are sometimes used to keep employees from accessing Internet features. For example, many companies use the Internet for sending e-mail; some employers fear that without firewalls, employees would spend hours and hours surfing the Internet on company time.

Here are some other terms you should know:

➤ *Slacker hackers* are 20-something people who break into computer systems.

➤ *Meatpacker hackers* are Green Bay computer pirates.

➤ *Tracker hackers* are private investigator fence hoppers.

E-Mail

E-mail basics

I don't understand how e-mail works. I heard that I can send a letter to the president by using the Internet. What do I do?

E-mail is a lot like regular mail, which is affectionately referred to as *snail mail* or *Phony Express* by Internet folks. With regular mail, you write a note on a piece of paper, put the paper in an envelope, write the recipient's address and stick a stamp on the envelope, drop the envelope in a mailbox, and wait, and wait, and wait for the person to get the letter. (When you think about it, *postal* and *service* just don't belong together.)

With e-mail, you write a letter, using an e-mail program. When you address the letter, you don't have to know ZIP codes, state names, country names, or street addresses because e-mail addresses follow an easy pattern:

    person@place.typ

For example, President Clinton's e-mail address is

    president@whitehouse.gov

But not for long. Soon it will be

    shlub@ark.hom

The `person` part of the address is an electronic name chosen by the recipient. It's sort of like a CB handle.

The `place` is where the person has an account (what techies call the *service provider*). For example, the `whitehouse` part of the president's e-mail address gets the message to the computer at the White House that's connected to the Internet. Some place names may have several parts.

The `typ` is a three-letter name for the type of place the e-mail address is at. For example, `gov` means governmental. Some other common type names are

> ➤ `com` for commercial
> ➤ `org` for organization
> ➤ `edu` for educational institution

The @ is an at sign (you make it by pressing Shift+2).

The . (pronounced "dot") tells the computer where the place name ends and the type name begins.

Here are a couple of rules governing e-mail addresses:

> ➤ No spaces are allowed anywhere in the address. Use dashes or underscores instead.
> ➤ No capital letters are used. (UNIX computers treat capital letters and lowercase letters differently.)
> ➤ Spelling counts! The name has to be spelled correctly. Likewise, the address has to be correct, too.

A place name may be broken down into several parts. To handle Internet traffic, for example, a given place may have more than one computer on the Internet. For example, the computer serving the House of Representatives is at

`@hr.whitehouse.gov`

This address is only the computer, not any person. You know that because no name precedes the @. (There's no such thing as *occupant* with e-mail.)

Once upon a time, e-mail systems were islands. That is, CompuServe users couldn't send mail to or receive mail from MCI users. Now that all commercial service providers, and even some local bulletin board systems (BBSs), are hooking up to the Internet, you can send e-mail to anyone anywhere if you know their e-mail address.

By the way, you *say* Clinton's current address as *president at white house dot gov*.

Junk mail

I'm a mail carrier and I hate junk mail. I'm getting garbage notices, advertisements, and even chain letters in my Internet mailbox. Please, no more.

I get leery when an employee of the U.S. Postal Service uses the word *hate*.

Junk e-mail is annoying. Fortunately, most on-line systems don't charge you to receive e-mail, just to send it.

Some e-mail software programs, such as Eudora from Qualcomm, let you download or transfer e-mail to your computer. If you do so, you won't spend valuable time on-line reading messages. The catch: All your e-mail — worthwhile and junk — is transferred.

Some e-mail packages for the UNIX environment (including Procmail and Deliver) can filter, forward, delete, and send automatic replies for you. For these packages to work, however, you must build a list of return addresses that you want to filter out. This filtering feature soon will find its way into regular PC e-mail packages.

Don't forget, you can always treat junk e-mail the same as you do junk real mail: Don't read it. Throw it away. In other words, *junk* it.

Wait — I was just joking. Put down the rifle, OK?

Reading e-mail off-line

Can I download my Internet mail and read it off-line?

Fortunately, someone had the good sense to develop a *mail reader*, or a program that allows you to login remotely, download and send mail, and then logoff automatically.

I find a mail reader particularly useful when I'm away from the office; I can download my mail messages to my "notebook computer" disk and then view them at my leisure (which, by the way, I seem to have less and less of).

Several commercial programs designed for PCs have a mail reader built in or as an optional add-on package. For example, Chameleon (a TCP/IP product for Windows) allows you to set your mail facility to determine when you download and send mail. Frontier Technologies SuperTCP, another outstanding Windows-based package, provides TCP/IP protocol and mail.

If you're connecting to the Internet via a service provider, check whether its software has mail reader capability. Many Internet membership kits include one.

Finding e-mail addresses

I want to send e-mail through the Internet to my brother, who is in the Air Force and stationed in Nagoya, Japan. I'm afraid that he'll be out of the service before I figure out what I need to do.

Are you your brother's keeper? Or does he simply owe you money? What if your brother joined the Air Force just to get away from you? Why do I suddenly feel like a psychiatrist?

To send people e-mail, you need to know their e-mail addresses. And the easiest way to discover someone's e-mail address is to ask. You can check some of the different Internet directories that exist — they work like phone books — but there is no comprehensive list of all computer users. Why? Because

> ➤ There's no Internet central governing body.
> ➤ People change e-mail addresses often.
> ➤ Privacy and/or security is at stake.

Nonetheless, you may be able to track down your brother without talking to him . . .

The U.S. military, for obvious reasons, doesn't advertise its users' e-mail addresses. But most military bases include their name (or an abbreviation) in the name of the computer system that's hooked to the Internet. For example, the computer that's hooked to the Internet at Eglin Air Force Base is at `eglin.af.mil`, while Wright Patterson Air Force Base calls its Internet computer link `wpafb.af.mil`. The base in Nagoya, Japan, probably calls its Internet computer link `nagoya.af.mil`.

Each computer system on the Internet has a *postmaster*, or a person in charge of the e-mail. So send an e-mail to `postmaster@nagoya.af.mil`, saying that you want to get in touch with your brother.

If `nagoya.af.mil` isn't a known address, you will receive a message saying that your mail was undeliverable. But don't give up yet. Send a brief e-mail to `postmaster@af.mil` (the address of the postmaster who oversees the e-mail operations of all U.S. Air Force bases), asking for the Nagoya base postmaster's address.

In next to no time, you will be able to tease your brother unmercifully about his silly haircut.

 Komando Klues If your brother sends you a piece of e-mail, the return address is automatically part of the message.

 Finding e-mail addresses, part 2

I want to send my son (he's enrolled at Rutgers University) an e-mail note. How can I find out whether he has access to the Internet and, if so, what his address is?

The low-tech approach garners the quickest response: call your son and ask him. (I know, you swore that you wouldn't talk to him until he got married. This is the last time, I promise.)

 Komando Klues If your son sends you a piece of e-mail, the return address is automatically part of the message.

In the preceding answer, I described how you can send e-mail to an Internet postmaster to find out an e-mail address. Although that approach works in this case, too, take pity on the poor college postmaster (imagine fielding e-mail requests from the parents of every student). Luckily, there's another way to find out an address — *netfind*.

To use netfind, you have to *telnet*, or connect, to a computer on the Internet that's running the netfind program. A couple of computer systems that run netfind are

> ➤ `ds.internic.net` (in New Jersey)
> ➤ `bruno.cs.colorado.edu` (in Colorado)
> ➤ `eis.calstate.edu` (in California)

Don't worry. If any of these computers busy, it lists other computers that run the netfind program. Pick a computer close to you and give it a whirl.

Some computers tell you to use the login name `netfind` to run the netfind program. Others don't.

While running netfind, you see a menu with five options. To search for your son, select option 2 — search. When you're asked for some keywords to search for, type

> ➤ Your son's name
> ➤ Rutgers and university

Press Enter. Choose a computer from the list of possible computers with information and let netfind search for you. (Choose help to get more information.)

Yahtzee! There's junior. Write down that address and surprise him with an e-mail from home. Remind him to study and be a good boy.

Komando Klues

Keep in mind that there's no guarantee that netfind will find someone. Some computers on the Net don't bother to make their lists of users available.

Surfing the Net

Gopher basics

What does a furry little rodent (Gopher) have to do with the Internet?

What does a mouse have to do with your computer? Don't judge what you don't know.

Gophers keep the Internet running, à la hamsters and their little wheels. Wait, don't call the Humane Society. I'm just joking. Actually, they put that "Love Boat" actor-turned-politician in the little wheel.

The Internet has so much information that it's hard to even know where to start looking for something. That's why you need *Gopher*, a program that "goes for" information on the Internet. It was developed at the University of Minnesota, whose mascot is the Golden Gopher. (What can I say? Computer geek humor.)

487

Gopher is the Internet waiter, sort of. Gopher offers you a menu to help you search for things. After you pick an item, Gopher shows you another menu. And so on.

It may take a bit of work to find the exact piece of information you want. But while you're searching, Gopher will show you things that you never dreamed existed.

Komando Klues

Depending on the communications software you're using, Gopher may even help you retrieve the information.

Telnet

My economics professor wants me to telnet to someplace, but I haven't a clue what he means.

Hey, while you're at it, why don't you ask me an economics question?

To *telnet* is to connect to another computer on the Internet. That computer can be anywhere. After you telnet, you can use your computer to work with the other computer as if the two computers were connected by cable. Telnetting is the next best thing to being there.

Telnet is a UNIX command. If you have a shell account with your service provider, you can type **telnet,** followed by the name of the computer you want to connect to. For example, to try to find someone on the Net, you can connect to the InterNIC's computer and run the netfind program by issuing the following command:

```
telnet ds.internic.net
```

Komando Klues

To use the netfind program, type **netfind** when asked for a login name. The netfind program shows a menu with five choices (including help).

If you have a graphical account such as SLIP or PPP, you should have a terminal program. WinQVT, for example, is a shareware program that lets your computer *emulate,* or pretend, that it's a plain old terminal. When you run this program, you can telnet to a computer just as if you were at that ugly old UNIX prompt.

Some computers on the Internet are more open and friendly than others. You can telnet to these computers and read the information that they make available. Some computer systems are like exclusive clubs, however; they don't let just anybody in. In fact, if the computer isn't set up to be accessed by the public, you need a user name and a password that's recognized by that computer.

When on the road, I telnet to the computer that receives my e-mail. After I log into the computer system with my name and password, I can check my messages.

By the way, thanks to the World Wide Web, telnetting has become less and less popular.

Even though you didn't ask, here's my answer to any economics question: As the supply goes down and the demand gets higher, the price goes up.

File Transfer Protocol

I've heard that you can get Internet files by using STP. I thought that was something you put in your oil to make your car run better. Can you set me straight?

It's *FTP*, not STP, and it stands for *File Transfer Protocol*.

FTP is a way of *downloading* (or transferring) files from a computer on the Internet to your computer. (A *protocol*, by the way, is an agreed-upon set of standards for doing something.) FTP makes sure that the file you copy to your computer arrives in perfect condition. Of course, you can use FTP to *upload* (or send) a file to another computer.

The purpose of the Internet is to share information. In fact, the Net is full of computers storing vast numbers of files. And these files are just waiting to be copied to your computer. No matter what type of computer you have, you probably can find a bunch of programs, including

➤ *Shareware.* Try before you buy. If you like the program, you send the author some money.

➤ *Freeware.* You pay nothing, but the author holds the copyright.

➤ *Public domain ware.* The author lets anyone use in almost any way.

➤ *FAQs* (*f*requently *a*sked *q*uestions, pronounced "FAKs"). Compilations of questions and answers about the Internet.

Naturally, to access some of these storehouses of information and programs, you need an account on the corresponding computer. But you don't need an account on the more public storehouses; this process is called *anonymous FTP*.

Checking for available users and servers

What does it mean to ping or finger someone? Sounds illegal.

Ping is the sound of a pin dropping after you announce that you've just fingered someone.

Actually, *ping* means to check whether a computer is connected to the Internet at that moment. You see, computers sometimes have bad days. They may be shut down for repairs. Or they may stubbornly decide to stop working for a time. (OK, sometimes the cables connecting the computers are accidentally disconnected or broken.)

By the way, a submarine sends out *pings* to find out whether anything is near it. The sound bounces off any nearby object and returns to the sub.

With the Internet, you ping a computer by sending a bunch of information, called a *packet*, to the computer in question. If the packet doesn't come back, there's a pretty good chance that "It's worse than that, Jim. It's dead."

Finger lets you reach out and (electronically) touch someone. It's a way to see whether a person has an account on a particular computer. Of course, you need to know your friends' e-mail addresses to see whether they're there. Think of fingering as going back to your hometown and looking up that long lost high school friend in the phone book. (She never did repay that money she borrowed, did she?)

Depending on how much the person you're fingering knows about the Internet, you may see a bunch of information displayed after the basics. UNIX allows people to set up `.plan` and `.project` files. (Yes, the period is part of the names; remember, this is UNIX, not MS-DOS.) The information in these files proudly appears for all the world, or at least the person fingering, to see.

Working with Usenet

How do I subscribe to a newsgroup on the Usenet? Is Usenet the same as the Internet?

Usenet is a digital discussion forum on any of 10,000 topics. The Internet is the primary way that this massive amount of missives is moved between computers.

Because there is no Usenet central governing body, it's easy to start a discussion group, called a *newsgroup*, on just about any topic. You just have to show that there's enough interest in the topic. (It's a big world, so you probably can get a newsgroup going about something as esoteric as Esoterica cold cream.) Think of newsgroups as big bulletin boards that people can tack pieces of paper to.

Newsgroups are broken down into broad topics, or *domains*. The domain name is found at the left-hand side of a newsgroup name. Common domains are

comp	Computer-related topics
misc	Miscellaneous topics
news	News about the Usenet and related programs
rec	Recreational activities
sci	Scientific topics
soc	Social issues
talk	Controversial cultural and social issues

Some domains, meanwhile, relate to specific companies (hp for Hewlett-Packard, apple for Apple Computer Corporation), universities (mit for Massachusetts Institute of Technology, asu for Arizona State University), geographic areas (ca for California, phx for Phoenix), and countries (de for Germany (or Deutschland), se for Sweden).

Each newsgroup can have subgroups. To find discussion about Windows, for example, you can read any of the following newsgroups:

```
comp.os.ms-windows.advocacy
comp.os.ms-windows.announce
comp.os.ms-windows.apps
comp.os.ms-windows.misc
```

Many more Windows-related newsgroups exist, but you get the idea.

Komando Klues

Just like in e-mail addresses, the periods in newsgroup names are pronounced "dot."

Like the Internet, Usenet is freewheeling and without many constraints. The `alt` domain, in fact, has practically no restrictions at all. If you can dream up an idea for a newsgroup, you can start it in the alt. domain. All sorts of wild and wonderful topics are found here, from `alt.fan.piers` (discussion about Piers Anthony's books) to `alt.barney.die.die.die` (people who are sick and tired of Barney). Some newsgroups in this domain contain adult material; for this reason, some service providers don't carry the `alt.binaries.pictures` newsgroups.

On the opposite side of the spectrum are *moderated* newsgroups. Any message posted to a moderated newsgroup is first sent to a person overseeing the discussion (the *moderator*) for approval. The moderator not only decides whether the message is appropriate, but edits the message (if necessary).

Most pieces of information on the Internet are stored on a particular computer. If you want to read the latest information about robotics from Stanford University, for example, you must access the appropriate computer by telnetting there or using the World Wide Web. Copies of Usenet messages, however, are kept on each service provider's computer. So, when you're reading Usenet news, you're going no farther than the computer at the Internet provider's offices. Because there are tens of thousands of Internet providers, each message is thus stored tens of thousands of times — which is why spamming the Net is a bad thing. Spamming the Net wastes megabytes of disk space on tens of thousands of computers around the world.

After you connect to your local service provider and read the messages in a particular group, you can join the conversation by posting a message. Posting is like sending an e-mail, but it's easier, because you don't have to worry about an address: every computer system that carries the newsgroup will get your message within a few hours of your posting. In fact, some Internet providers have a satellite dish hookup to the Usenet and constantly send out messages.

The Usenet is a great place to find information. A word of *caution*, though: Just because someone writes a message in a newsgroup doesn't mean that it's a fact. People have a tendency to trust anything they read on-line. A phrase comes to mind: *Believe none of what you read and half of what you see.* Or a more modern adage: *Garbage in, garbage out.*

World Wide Web

Is Mosaic the program that lets me read World Wide Web? Can I get on the Web from DOS, too?

The World Wide Web (WWW or the Web) is the darling of the Internet community. It's fast becoming *the* way to access information on the Internet.

Mosaic is a program that lets you browse through the pages of information found on the Web. Developed at the University of Illinois at Champaign-Urbana, Mosaic can be found for Windows, Windows NT, Macintosh, and X Windows (a graphical front end for some UNIX computers).

The pages of information on the Web are like pages in a book. With Mosaic, you can read any page as if you were reading text in a word processing program. By the way, the pictures on a Web page often look like photographs.

Words on a Web page can have different styles, just as in a book. Some words are underlined or in a different color (or both); these words are hot links to other pages of information. Clicking on one of these special words, or *URLs* (*U*niform *R*esource *L*ocators), moves you to another page.

URLs (pronounced "earls") are written in a special way. Here's a favorite URL:

```
http://akebono.stanford.edu/yahoo/
```

This URL is the Yahoo server at Stanford University, a place that lists tens of thousands of other URLs (by category!). Check out Yahoo sometime; it's a great place to start exploring the Web.

The first part of an URL (before the colon) is the *access method* — that is, how you're going to get at the information stored on this computer. (Don't worry what it stands for; it means that you're going to be getting a Web page.)

The second part (after the two slashes) is the name of the computer where the information is located. After the computer name is the name of the directory that contains the information. Because the Web is running on the Internet, and most computers on the Internet use the UNIX operating system, the slash (/) is used in directory names, not the backslash (\) used in MS-DOS.

Sometimes, the URL points to a specific file on a computer, but in this case, it points to the main page (or the *home page*) for Yahoo.

Mosaic lets you retrieve different types of information from the Internet. For example, you can use Mosaic to read newsgroups. To read the newsgroup with information for Mosaic users, for example, use the following URL:

```
news://comp.infosystems.www.users
```

You also can use Mosaic to telnet to another computer. The URL to try to find someone on the Internet is

```
telnet://ds.internic.net
```

You even can use Mosaic to go for information with Gopher.

If all this stuff seems like magic, let me bring you down to earth. Mosaic has to be set up (or *configured*) to work with other programs to do some of these things. For example, Mosaic doesn't have telnet capabilities built in, so you have to configure it to use a program such as WinQVT. You also must configure Mosaic to play sound files and display graphics files.

Although Mosaic is already a great program, some companies have been improving it. Netscape Communications, who hired most of the Illinois folks who programmed Mosaic, created a Web browser called Netscape, which has all the capabilities of Mosaic plus better built-in graphics viewers. Two other browsers are Cello from Cornell University and WinWeb from EINet. And for those Internet users who don't have a graphical account (yet), a program called Lynx, developed by the University of Kansas, lets you see the text of Web pages. You just don't get to see the pictures. (In fact, Lynx works faster than any graphical browser, because you don't have to wait for the pictures.)

Using the Net

Internet Relay Chat

Where are all the live discussions for which the Internet is so famous?

It's there, but you have to dial a 1-900 number to get at it. Just kidding.

The Internet's version of a party line is known as *Internet Relay Chat* (IRC). With IRC, people type messages to each other; these messages appear on-screen instantaneously. (Well, almost. And if the message has to go to the other side of the world, it takes a few more seconds, of course.)

Believe it or not, at any hour of the day (even as you read this sentence), hundreds, if not thousands, of people all over the world are banging out messages.

Many people can chat at the same time about the same subject. And discussion topics are as varied as the people who participate. Some discussions are conducted on a regular basis, while some are held almost nonstop. Each subject or discussion group is referred to as a *channel*.

IRC is addictive. Many college students have watched their grades suffer after getting hooked on IRC.

On the other hand, IRC played a prominent role during the Second Russian Revolution, as people sent spot reports to other IRC users.

To learn more about using IRC, I highly recommend reading *More Internet For Dummies* from IDG. Chapter 15 is "Internet Relay Chat: The Ultimate Solution to Free Time."

Before long, people will be able to send live video of themselves as they talk on the Internet. Although this concept, called *teleconferencing*, is still new, it will undoubtedly become more popular when faster connections to the Internet become more common.

I don't know, though. A picture takes a lot of the romance out of the Internet. Sometimes, you just don't want to see what these people look like.

 Foreign language newsgroups

I want to communicate on Internet message boards in other countries. Can I use English or will I need to type in another language?

What? You can't find anyone interesting among this country's 240 million people?

Fear not, English has become the international language of computers. But you can find message boards, or *newsgroups*, intended for use by non-English speakers. For example, you can find German, Spanish, Italian, and Swedish boards somewhere among the world's collection of 10,000 newsgroups.

Because many people who use the international ranks of the Internet learned English as a second language, you may see grammar and spelling mistakes in the newsgroups. (Of course, given America's educational system, you may find the same problems in messages written by native speakers.) Keep in mind that the person from Moscow has a far better grasp of the English language than you have of Russian, so skip past the errors and concentrate on the message's meaning.

Komando Klues

Here are a couple of tips for native English speakers when corresponding with people in other countries electronically:

➤ Use proper spelling and grammar. Slang and misspelled words may be hard to decipher.

➤ Humor is hard to convey electronically, even to someone who is fluent in your language. So unless you *know* that the message's recipient will get the humor, avoid using jokes. (That is, stay away from Nazi references when chatting with Germans.)

Scientific newsgroups

Where can I get the latest news and research about AIDS and cancer?

Come on. Don't you want to use the Internet for serious questions, such as *How many "Gilligan's Island" episodes featured plots about Ginger?* PooPooPeeDoo.

The Internet is a great way to keep tabs on the latest research in medicine, science, computers, and more. Check out some of Usenet's 10,000 discussion topics, including `sci.med.aids`, `clari.tw.health.aids` and `misc.health.aids`.

Cancer information can be found in `sci.med.diseases.cancer`. You also can find discussion groups about specific types of cancer, such as `alt.support.cancer.prostate`.

You can use tools such as Veronica or Gopher to find sources of information — perhaps an electronic *mailing list* (that is, an e-mail subscription that's automatically sent to you). For example, if you send an e-mail to `cancernet@icicb.nci.nih.gov`, you'll receive the latest cancer research information from the National Institutes of Health.

Finding a pearl in an oyster is a great reward. Finding the information you need on the Internet is just as rewarding.

Marketing on the Internet

I am a consultant who helps companies solve problems. I want to use the Internet to find troubled companies and develop marketing lists. Do you have some pointers?

Remember, the Internet was originally a government-funded network for the military. (After a short time, colleges and universities joined the Net.) Lately, though, commercial companies have come on board, and these companies are paying for more and more of the connections as Newt's New Government is getting out of funding the Internet. (Companies are in business to make money. Government is in business to spend it.)

Marketing on the Internet is a touchy subject, however, because many users want the Net to remain the same as when the government was footing the bill, when the Net was forbidden to carry out commercial pursuits. So you can conduct business on the Internet, but you have to be careful about how you do it.

For example, it's OK to post an informative message about your service in the appropriate area; the Internet community will not react negatively. However, posting a typical marketing hype press release to inappropriate newsgroups doesn't sit well with other computer users (this practice is affectionately known as *spamming the Net*). In other words, Internet users frown upon those who send unsolicited material, but creating a place for people to come to for information about your goods or services is widely accepted.

In fact, this practice is becoming more popular, thanks to the World Wide Web and graphical browsers (such as Mosaic). When using the Web, people read through pages of information — sort of like this book, only a lot less interesting. Some of the words on a Web page are hot words — they are in a different color or are underlined. When you click on these words, other pages appear.

Some other Web facts:

➤ Pages can contain pictures as well as words.

➤ Your own page of information is called a *home page*.

➤ Pages can contain forms. Any information filled in by the reader is saved on the computer where the pages are kept.

> ➤ Pages can contain a catalog, a brochure, an order form, pictures of your products, and more.

> ➤ Some pages that list by category other peoples' home pages. (It's not uncommon to find over 100 new additions since the preceding day.)

Komando Klues

Remember that most of the people on the Internet are computer-literate. A marketing approach that works for the average consumer may not work with Net users.

Searching for Net users

I need help locating relatives (I'm developing a family tree). Is the Internet a good place to search? If so, where do I start?

Win the lottery and you'll find all the relatives that you need.

You can search for individuals on the Internet with a variety of tools. However, the process can be time-consuming, frustrating, and costly — especially if you don't have much information to start. As a result, I recommend that you obtain as much information as possible about the people you're trying to find before you attempt to locate them on the Internet.

The most cost-effective Internet search method is a Usenet inquiry or search; it can be performed by users who only have e-mail capability. This method will suffice, even if a name is all you have. Keep in mind that Usenet inquiries look for people who have recently accessed the Usenet, so an occasional user may not show up in your search.

Start by sending an e-mail message to `mail-server` at either of the following Usenet servers:

```
mail-server@pit-manager.mit.edu
mail-server@rtfm.mit.edu
```

Don't bother placing anything in the subject line of your message, because the server will ignore it. In the body of the message, type **send usenet-addresses / john doe**. A space must separate the `john` and `doe` *keys*; in fact, a space must separate any additional information keys (used to narrow a search), such as city and state (for example, `send usenet-addresses / john doe pensacola`). You can perform multiple Usenet inquiries with the same e-mail message by adding additional `send usenet-addresses` lines.

Note: Less-specific inquiries may give you more information than you want.

Komando Klues

If your inquiries fail to produce the desired results, consider sending an e-mail message for help to whois@whois.internic.net.

Multiple player games

What's a MUD?

What kid doesn't like to play in the mud? What kid doesn't enjoy the eerie sensation mud evokes as it squishes between your toes? What kid doesn't laugh at the splatting sound mud makes when you throw it against a tree, a wall, a face?

But our infatuation with mud doesn't dissipate altogether when people stop calling us kids. Some big boys and girls like to wrestle in mud (the rest of us like to watch), and even the president and fellow politicians sling some mud now and then. Internet users, who are just big kids, are no different; they like playing in their MUDs, or *Multi-User Dungeons*.

A MUD is a mythical world. It's a world where monsters and magic abound. It's an escape from the real world.

But a MUD isn't your typical multimedia computer game. A MUD doesn't have realistic-looking settings with bone-chilling sound effects or stirring soundtrack. In fact, when you're playing in a MUD, all you see are descriptions of your surroundings and the other players' actions.

MUDs are inspired by such books as J. R. R. Tolkien's *The Lord of the Rings* trilogy. Accordingly, MUD players can be elves, wizards, or even warlords (if they've been playing long enough and have the phone bills to prove it). Interacting with the other players, you go on quests, learn new magic spells, and battle monsters and enemies.

For some people, it's the *multiuser* aspect of a MUD that's so appealing. No computer game can be as sophisticated and unpredictable as another person.

Like any fun thing, MUDs are addictive. MUDs have caused many a sleepless night and many a failed class.

True, the realistic simulations encountered on the USS Enterprise's holodeck (please, a moment of silence for the passing of "Star Trek: The Next Generation") are a long, long way away. But MUDs are the best thing for the moment.

Troubleshooting

 Viewing ASCII graphics

The Internet holds a significant number of graphic files posted as ASCII code. I tried to use a graphic viewer to no avail. What is ASCII? And how can I see these files?

Your problem stems from how the Internet transfers information. Don't worry, I'm not going to get into an esoteric discussion of packet switching or other propeller-headed things.

ASCII (pronounced "ass-key"; insert your own dirty joke here) is regular letters and numbers. In other words, ASCII comprises the alphabet (upper- and lowercase), numbers zero through nine, and a few extra characters, such as the space and the end of line character.

Computer graphics files use many more characters to save the picture to a file. When you try to examine a file that contains an electronic version of a photograph, for example, you see all kinds of other weird characters, such as smiley faces. These other characters enable us to have files that contain photographs, program files that help run the computer, and so on. These files are *binary files*.

The Internet's computer network can only handle ASCII information; you can't directly post a picture as a binary file in newsgroups. So before a picture or program file can be posted in a newsgroup, it has to be converted from a binary file to an ASCII file.

The standard way to do this conversion is called *uuencoding*. The *uu* part means UNIX to UNIX. (Remember, the Internet started out as an all-UNIX network. To this day, it remains predominantly UNIX-based.) The uuencoding program translates the binary information into plain ASCII. The plain ASCII version of a picture or a program can be posted to a newsgroup or included with e-mail.

To view the picture or use the program, you must decode the file. The uudecode program does the trick, changing the ASCII file back to its original form. Then you can view the picture or run the program just as if someone had given it to you on a floppy disk.

Some Internet computers split long messages with encoded information into several smaller messages, because it's more efficient for Internet computers to deal with small packets of information.

International e-mail delays

It took me 25 minutes today to send mail to Guatemala City. Does it normally take a long time to send e-mail internationally?

Imagine standing by the mailbox waiting for someone to receive your letter. Better pack a lunch — and a sleeping bag.

You don't have to wait on-line while the message is being sent. After you give the command or hit the send button, the program takes care of getting your message to the Internet. Then the Internet determines the best way to get your piece of information to its destination. In some cases, the process takes minutes; in some cases, it takes hours.

To test sending times, I sent pieces of e-mail from my Internet account in Scottsdale, Arizona, to my America Online account in Vienna, Virginia. The messages took an average of five seconds to make the several thousand mile journey. Sending something to another country will certainly take longer.

Of course, your mileage may vary, especially in the city.

User unknown *error message*

I have tried several times to send e-mail to an Internet address. I keep getting the same *User unknown* message. What exactly does this error mean, and what am I doing wrong?

Return to sender! Last address unknown! Boy, wouldn't Elvis be proud that I'm singing his song. (You know what I hate about e-mail? No reason to lick the King's stamp.)

User unknown is the Internet's way of telling you that it can't deliver your e-mail because no person is registered with the computer system that you specified.

You can do a few things at this point:

1. *Hit your computer.* The action won't do any good, but it may make you feel better. Not too hard, though. You don't want to break the darn thing, do you? Wait, don't answer that. I don't want to know.

2. *Double-check the address.* Remember, the name has to be in lowercase letters — and no spaces. In addition, spelling counts.

3. *Double-check the name of the computer system you're sending the mail to.* You may have accidentally sent the e-mail to a computer system with a similar name.

If none of these steps helps you get the mail through, try sending a message to the computer system's *postmaster* — the person who manages the computer system's e-mail accounts. To send a message to the postmaster, address a message to

`postmaster@place.typ`

`place.typ` is the same as in the e-mail(s) that didn't get through. Send the postmaster a copy of the returned mail that you received and ask whether there's a user by the name you're trying to reach.

E-mail configuration problems

I tried to send a message to the University of Zimbabwe, but it was returned with the following errors: *Insufficient Permission* and *Unknown Mailer Error*. What do these error messages mean, and what do I do next?

I could give you a lengthy technical explanation, but I don't want you to nod off on me just when you're about to get the answer. The short answer: You more than likely have an e-mail configuration problem.

Mail can be *bounced* (that is, returned) for several reasons. The question is: Is the problem at your end or the other end? You can determine the answer for yourself by looking at the e-mail *header* (the section of your e-mail that tells you who sent the message and whence it came).

You see, something called a *mailer-daemon* is in charge of sending a bounced message back and offering an explanation. In fact, the mailer-daemon tells you which system had the problem: you simply look at the header and see which e-mail address is listed in the error message. If the problem is on your end, contact the person who runs your mail server by sending an e-mail to

```
postmaster@your mail server
```

If the problem is at the destination address, you can try sending an e-mail to

```
postmaster@distant end server
```

Of course, if that other mail configuration is incorrect, this second e-mail also will be returned to you. If this is the case, ask your system administrator or postmaster for help. If no one has the answer, dig into your pocket for 32 cents, slap on an Elvis stamp, and mail your note.

Unbalanced *error message*

When I tried to send a letter, it came back *unbalanced*. What does that mean?

The Internet can determine your emotional stability. It's that smart.

Actually, despite what people tell you, computers are dumb. They don't even try to understand what you mean to say; rather, they look at exactly what you say.

Sometimes, e-mail addresses use angled brackets (< and >) as comments. For example, say that your friend Joe Doe has an account with a service provider called `thenet.com`. His e-mail address is `joe-doe@thenet.com`. Suppose that he added a comment to the end of the address so that you knew who sent the message. The sender's address thus looks like

```
joe-doe@thenet.com <Joe Doe>
```

When you replied to the message, however, you probably accidentally chopped off the last character, making the line look like

```
joe-doe@thenet.com <Joe Doe
```

Without that last angled bracket, the programs that take care of receiving the mail at `thenet.com` didn't know what to do with the message. So the e-mail was sent back to you with the unbalanced message.

503

Finding pen pals

I want to get a list of Internet users from other countries. How can I do so?

Finding pen pals (I call them *keyboard kompanions*) on the Net can be easy. If I were you, I'd start by picking out a few good newsgroups.

Of course, if I were you, who would answer this question?

Every message in a newsgroup contains the e-mail address of the sender. Most e-mail addresses outside the U.S. end with a country code. In other words, the last two or three characters in an e-mail address after the type of service provider give the country code. Here are a few examples of country codes:

> ➤ . au (Australia)

> ➤ . ca (Canada)

> ➤ . dk (Denmark)

> ➤ . us (United States of America)

Note that some service providers in the U.S. put . us at the end of their computer names.

Now, send an e-mail to a person in another country, introducing yourself. Should be easy. After all, you have a common interest — the newsgroup topic.

In very little time, you can compile a list of people around the world to send electronic mail to. Later, you may even want to use Internet Relay Chat (IRC) to converse. Use e-mail to schedule a time. Don't forget that high noon where you're at is midnight somewhere else.

Chapter 13

Macs and PCs — Working Together to Build a Better World

Sharing

Disks and other stuff

 Old Mac disks

I have a bunch of old Mac disks lying around. Can I reformat them for my PC?

Five uses for old Mac disks:

> ➤ Give them as inexpensive toys. Call them *Computer Starter Kits*.
> ➤ Sell them as jumbo guitar picks.

➤ Use them to pick cheap locks.

➤ Package them as *Geek Party Coasters.*

➤ Make them PC disks.

Mac floppy disks look the same as PC floppy disks; only the formatting is different. When a computer *formats* a disk, it gets the disk ready so that you can use it in the computer. Among other things, formatting establishes how much information the disk can hold and on what computer platform the disk can be used.

Although you can reformat old Mac disks in PCs and old PC disks in Macs, you occasionally may run into a few stubborn disks that won't want to be reformatted. Bulk erasing the old floppy disks should take care of those problems. You can pick up a bulk eraser at an electronics store such as Radio Shack. The bulk eraser is an electromagnet that erases everything off floppy disks, audio tapes, and even video tapes.

IBM disks in a Mac?

I recently bought a lot of disks labeled IBM. Can I use them in my Mac?

I don't want to be flip (or floppy for that matter), but it depends on the disk. Both Mac and IBM computers use 3¹/₂-inch floppy disks, but they format disks differently. Nonetheless, you can use IBM diskettes in a Mac as long as you reinitialize the disk first. Just as the same book can be written in two different languages, the Mac and the IBM use different formats to store information on floppy disks.

Mac floppy disks come in three sizes:

➤ 400K (or single-sided)

➤ 800K (or double-sided)

➤ 1.4MB (or high-density)

IBM-compatible 3¹/₂-inch floppy disks come in two sizes:

➤ 720K (or double-density)

➤ 1.44MB (or high-density)

There are also 3¹/₂-inch 2.88MB, or *extended-density*, IBM-compatible floppy disks, but they're very uncommon.

When you buy new floppy diskettes, make sure you get the right type for your computer. (For example, newer Macs take high-density disks; Mac Plus and older SE models use double-sided disks.) A double-sided disk will work in a high-density floppy disk drive, but a high-density disk won't work in a double-sided floppy disk drive.

Mac virus on a PC?

Can my IBM PC get viruses if it reads infected Mac disks?

Remember that computer viruses are programs. And just as Mac programs can't run on an IBM-compatible computer without some special board or software, neither can Mac viruses.

An IBM-compatible virus can infect a DOS volume on a Mac, however. The Mac volume, however, ignores the virus because the virus is trying to get the Mac to do things the same way it would try to make an IBM-compatible computer do them. *Note:* You can get an IBM-compatible virus from a disk given to you by a Mac user who runs DOS or Windows, though.

The Bottom Line

All in all, don't worry about Mac viruses on your IBM-compatible, but maintain the usual vigilance against all computer viruses.

Reading Mac files in DOS

I am currently running MS-DOS 6.2 on a 486DX IBM-compatible. Can I convert a double-density Mac disk so that it can be read and printed from an MS-DOS system? This disk contains a great deal of information and the person who maintained this information on the Mac system skipped town. We have no Mac systems available to us.

Fortunately, just as you can find utilities for reading DOS floppies on Macs, you can get DOS and Windows utilities for accessing Mac floppies and translating files. Some examples are

➤ Hypro's MacAccess

➤ DataViz's PC Link

➤ MacSEE (shareware)

Unfortunately, these utilities only work with high-density floppy disks. IBM-compatible floppy drives cannot access double-density Mac disks because they are formatted with an encoding method not supported by IBM-compatible floppy drives. If you need to access information on 800K Mac floppies, you must use a Macintosh.

If you have a Mac (or if you can rent, beg, or borrow a Mac), check out a package called PC Connect. It lets you hook an IBM-compatible and a Mac together with a special cable and a special communications software program. I prefer Traveling Software's LapLink, which works like PC Connect, and is a little easier to use.

You can also contact your local Mac user group and ask to borrow a Mac for the disk transfer. A user group is a volunteer organization run by people who love computers and like helping other people. Apple has a user group information line you can call to find your nearest group. The number is 800-538-9696.

Finally, check the Yellow Pages for a business that can translate information from one type of disk to another. If you don't have a company like this locally, check in the classified section of computer magazines.

Reading 800K disks on a PC

I recently purchased an IBM. I need to access three years of Mac files, and these old files are stored on 800K disks — too small for the 1.44MB disk minimum required for Mac 'n' DOS software. Please don't tell me to buy that computer that operates in Mac and DOS. It's too late for that.

Problem: PCs can't access double-density Mac floppies.

Solution: You need to find someone with a Mac who can move all those files to PC disks. Or you can ask this someone to send the files via modem or other serial communication.

For more detail, see the preceding question. (Wow. I just saved a tree — maybe an Apple tree — by not repeating myself.)

CD-ROMs for Mac and Windows?

Will the CD-ROMs that I use with my IBM-compatible work on my Mac? After all, music CDs work on both computers.

A good way to save money: Shopping on double-coupon days. A bad way to save money: Trying to use CD-ROMs made for IBM-compatibles on Macs.

Music CDs aren't Mac- or IBM-oriented, so using them on either platform isn't a problem. Some newer CD-ROM disks, called hybrids, can work on either Mac or IBM-compatible multimedia computers, too, but not all CD-ROM programs are created equal. (Earthshaking news, eh?)

The Bottom Line

Macs and IBM-compatibles run different software; whether the programs come on floppies or CD-ROMs makes no difference. Unless you buy a CD-ROM that specifically states that it works on both Macs and IBM-compatibles, it probably won't work on both.

To use IBM-compatible CD-ROM programs on a Mac, you need special hardware or software for running DOS or Windows on your Mac. Even then, be sure that all the CD-ROM's program requirements are available on the Mac. IBM-compatible games that need Sound Blaster support, for instance, run silently on Macs. Apple and other companies are working to change this limitation, but, in the meantime, the best platform for running most IBM-compatible CD-ROMs is an IBM-compatible computer.

Mac hard drives in a PC?

My local computer store is having a sale on Mac hard drives. Can I buy one for my PC?

As long as your IBM-compatible computer has a SCSI card and you have DOS SCSI formatting and driver software, you shouldn't have any problems with a Mac SCSI drive. SCSI is SCSI. Just make sure you get the right cable for your card; most PC SCSI cards have 50-pin connectors, while the built-in SCSI port on Macs has 25 pins. Since the Mac is a more limited market, you might find that SCSI hard drives for Macs are a little more expensive than the same size SCSI drive for IBM-compatible computers.

Used monitors

I can cheaply acquire a refurbished SVGA monitor from a local Mac dealer. The catch: I don't own a Mac. Will this monitor work with my PC?

Are you buying this monitor out of the trunk of a '75 Cadillac?

You're in luck, as long as the dealer did a good job of refurbishing and you have a decent SVGA video card. SVGA is an IBM-compatible standard, not a Mac standard, so you're in business. *Note:* You might need a special adapter to make that monitor cable fit the Mac, depending on the model of Mac and the model of the monitor.

ImageWriter for the PC?

My Mac friends are shaking their heads in disbelief because I bought an IBM-compatible. Can I recycle my old Apple ImageWriter and use it with my PC?

Gee, aren't Mac people soooooooo snobby? (I'd like to say something meaner, but I prefer to be PC — politically correct.)

Can you recycle your ImageWriter? Yes, with some work. Should you? No. Sell it and spend the money on a better printer.

The only reason to use an impact printer such as an ImageWriter is to print forms with carbon copies. Inkjet printers cost about the same, print a little faster and much more quietly, and produce dramatically superior output.

If you need an impact printer, buy a 24-pin printer (such as one from the popular Panasonic KXP series), which produces much better output than the 9-pin ImageWriter. Otherwise, buy an inkjet; used Hewlett-Packard DeskJets and Canon BubbleJets are easy to find.

Komando Klues

A used ImageWriter I typically sells for around $75 or $100, while an ImageWriter II fetches $150 to $200. You can get a good used 24-pin dot-matrix printer for about $100 and a decent used inkjet printer for under $200. If you get a decent price for your old printer and shop wisely, your net cost will be virtually zip; if you have an ImageWriter II, you may even come out ahead.

Using an Epson printer on a Quadra

I broke the bank to buy a laser printer. Now, my old Epson Stylus is collecting dust. Can I hook the Stylus up to my Quadra? There's no plug in the back that fits the printer cable.

Epson offers Mac upgrade kits for many Stylus printers, so check with the folks at Epson. If they can't help, GDT Softworks's PowerPrint package will allow you to use any of hundreds of PC printers with the Mac, including your Epson.

For help, call GDT Softworks PowerPrint at 604-291-9121 or Epson Direct at 800-374-7300.

Will SIMMs work in both platforms?

My girlfriend's father has a Performa 450 and wants to upgrade to 8MB of RAM. The documentation says to use 72-pin SIMMs. Are these the same SIMMs that work in an IBM-compatible computer? If I know this answer, he may let me marry his daughter. P.S. I'll invite you to the wedding.

Get down on one knee and tell him that as long as his 72-pin SIMM is rated for at least 80ns, he's all set. If that answer doesn't clinch his daughter's hand, remind him that the Performa 450 has only one SIMM slot (4MB of RAM are soldered to the motherboard), so any RAM he buys now will have to be discarded when he needs to upgrade again. As a result, I suggest buying as large a SIMM as he can afford (I'd opt for at least 8MB).

I hope this info helps you get the girl of your dreams. If not, you can always elope through Windows.

Information

The bottom line – Mac or PC?

I am torn between choosing a Mac or a PC. I hear that Apple makes a computer that runs Mac and DOS programs. Is this true?

A special version of the Quadra 610 has a DOS card (based on 486SX 25 technology) and runs both Mac and DOS programs. But the DOS programs don't always run like they should or as fast as you want.

The Quadra 610, whose special card inside the Mac is often referred to by its code name, *Houdini*, is a good, low-cost machine with the following advantages:

> ➤ Its processor is expandable to 16-bit.
> ➤ You can buy a logic board upgrade (to Power Mac 6100/60).
> ➤ Ethernet is built in.
> ➤ The colors look cool on 16-inch monitors.
> ➤ And more.

But Houdini has disappeared as computer companies race to build bigger and better computers. Currently, Apple is developing the PDS (*processor direct slot*) card, based on a 486DX2 50 chipset. Unlike Houdini, the PDS card has networking and Sound Blaster support. (Today, this card works in Power Macs, but many 7100 and 8100 users may have to sacrifice video features for DOS because of the way video is implemented.)

Orange Micro (Apples and Oranges, get it?) is a company that sells DOS cards that are more powerful than Houdini. It's too bad they cost as much as, or more than, a whole computer.

The Bottom Line

The bottom line: If you want a Mac, buy a Mac. If you want an IBM-compatible, buy one. The gap between platforms is slowly narrowing, but I'm not convinced that these cards are as great as some people say, especially if you are running application software that's not native to the Mac.

DOS programs on a Mac?

I recently heard that DOS programs can be run on Macs with special software. Is there such an animal that not only reads files but actually runs programs?

Yes, but that animal is a snail. Insignia Solutions has long produced a family of products, known as *SoftPC*, that runs DOS on any 680x0 Mac. But on anything below an '040, it's pretty slow going. SoftPC 3.x allows you to run Windows on top of DOS on an '040 Mac, but the speed is simply unacceptable. Basically, SoftPC is OK for running DOS on an '040 (or a very fast '030) Mac.

Power Macs with at least 16MB of RAM can run SoftWindows 1.0 — Insignia's Windows emulator that directly incorporates Windows 3.1 code. The current version supports only Windows's standard mode, which is strictly 286 compatible — albeit at roughly 486SX 25 speeds (video-based functions suffer the most). Programs requiring 386 enhanced mode (for example, WordPerfect 6 or FrameMaker 4) won't run at all under SoftWindows. Sorry.

By the time you read this book, however, Insignia may have shipped a version of SoftWindows that supports 386 enhanced mode. The new SoftWindows may promise better performance and compatibility, and many traditional problems may disappear, but I still wouldn't recommend SoftWindows for anything other than light Windows usage. For heavy usage, I suggest getting a fast 486 or Pentium PC.

By the way, Utilities Unlimited claims to be readying a DOS emulator that's more powerful than Insignia's, but at press time it's strictly vaporware.

Taking fonts across platforms

I have a great font collection at work on my PC. Is there any way I can use these fonts on my Mac at home?

I hate people who brag about their great font collections. They're the biggest bores at parties. ("Look at this one; it's called Mistrel.")

You must convert the fonts between platforms. In my humble opinion, the most powerful utility is Altsys's Fontographer, which comes in both Mac and Windows flavors and can translate fonts in either direction. Fontographer, though, does much more than font translation; it's a full-fledged font design program. Of course, its price tag matches its heavy-weight capabilities.

Also noteworthy is Ares Software's *FontMonger*. Although a bit less expensive, it has some design features and is a great entry-level font converter and editor. It's available for both Mac and IBM-compatible computers.

What about shareware (try before you buy) and freeware (no cost) programs? Unfortunately, I don't know of any utilities that translate PC PostScript fonts to the Mac. The Mac utility TTConverter, though, is useful for translating TrueType fonts in either direction.

TTConverter has trouble with some fonts; that is, some converted from Windows won't print on PostScript printers, and some won't convert from Mac to Windows at all. Also, the developer says that the current version (1.5) is the final version. But, hey, for $10, you can't go too wrong.

On the PC side are Refont and Mac2PFB. Refont is a $20 shareware utility that converts Mac TrueType and Type 1 PostScript fonts to PC TrueType and Type 1 fonts, respectively. Refont doesn't convert TrueType to Type 1 or vice versa, and it doesn't convert from PC to Mac. Mac2PFB, meanwhile, is an older, public domain, Type 1-only Mac-to-PC font converter. Although not as full-featured as Refont, it works with some fonts that Refont has trouble with. Besides, Mac2PFB is free.

Finally, a word about copyright violations: If your employer purchased the font collection at work, you don't have the right to convert the fonts and take them home for your own use. You have to buy your own fonts. If you own the license to the office fonts, read that license to see what your rights are. More than likely, you're OK, but check that fine print. A conversion program is not a license to steal.

Transferring information from PowerBook to PC

I have a 165 PowerBook and an IBM PC. What's the best way to transfer information contained on a PC disk to my PowerBook? Right now, I'm typing everything twice. I don't think that's what they mean by office automation.

Congratulations! You've identified one of my favorite hundred ways to waste time. Your parting gift? A Polaroid camera for all your office photo-copying.

What you need is a program that enables you to use DOS floppies on a Mac. (*Note:* It doesn't matter whether you're using a desktop or a portable Mac; these programs will work for you.) Several commercial options exist, including Dayna's DOS Mounter Plus, Insignia's AccessPC, and Apple's PC Exchange.

You can use PC Exchange, which comes with System 7.5, to assign certain DOS file extensions to specific Mac applications. For example, you can tell your Mac that all your DOS files with a .DOC extension should be used with Microsoft Word.

If your Mac programs can't translate your PC documents, you need a file translation utility, such as DataViz's MacLinkPlus or PC Connect. If you buy System 7.5 on CD-ROM, the DataViz translators are included. With PC Connect, though, you get more goodies and timesaving tricks. For example, it lets you hook an IBM-compatible and a Mac together with a special cable and a special communications software program.

Komando
Klues

By the way, I prefer Traveling Software's LapLink, which works like PC Connect but is a little easier to use.

Taking Lotus across the great divide

I have a PowerBook Duo, but the company I work for supplied me with an IBM clone and data-intensive Lotus worksheets. I want to use my Mac to do the work and my color printer to print the graphs and charts. Can I do so?

515

Hey, has man walked on the moon? Are delicious foods fattening? Is Congress useless? You can import Lotus worksheets into any popular Mac spreadsheet program, including Microsoft Excel or even the spreadsheet module in ClarisWorks. When you're done working with the files, you can resave them as Lotus files.

.GIF files on a Mac

A friend sent me .GIF files from his Mac. Why won't they work with my GIF viewer?

Mac programs put a special header on IBM-compatible .GIF files. Don't worry, you don't need to know what a header is; just know that its existence is why you can't see the files. Before an IBM-compatible user can view the .GIF files, the header must be removed.

A legitimate .GIF file starts with GIF87a (or GIF89a) at the top of the file. With a text editing program such as Windows Notepad or DOS editor, you can see that your .GIF file begins with some other extraneous text, such as Giffer or Bozo — not GIF87a or GIF89a. This extra text is the Mac header and corrupts the PC .GIF. You can strip these headers out easily by using AOMAC2PC, a shareware utility available on most commercial on-line services. AOMAC2PC installs like any other extension: drop it into your System folder and the Mac will put it into the Extensions folder. Every time you start the Mac, the new extension runs automatically.

Komando Klues

Mac filenames can hold a lot more letters than IBM-compatible filenames, which are limited to eight letters and a three-letter extension. The only way to be sure that a Mac file is in .GIF format is if your friend tells you that it is.

Which machine should be the translator?

Is it more efficient to load a DOS translation program on a Mac (in my case, an LC II with 8MB of RAM and 80MB hard drive) or put Mac translation software on my new Compaq 486 laptop (160MB drive)?

Good question. You have your thinking cap on today. If you can, do the translations at the Mac end. Because the Mac is "the other platform," Apple and Mac developers have had to work hard to accommodate DOS users. Hence (we feel so regal when we use that word), the best hardware and software cross-platform support is on the Mac side.

Komando Klues Either way, make sure you check out the translated files while you're at home; you don't want to discover that the important document didn't translate properly after you're on the road!

From Appleworks to ASCII

I need help converting a single file created under IIGS Appleworks into an ASCII file. Any pearls of wisdom? The file is a small but very important mailing list.

What kind of mailing list? Was it perhaps once a little black book of phone numbers?

Sign on to a commercial on-line service and download Peter Watson's MS-DOS Utilities for Apple IIGS, which lets you access MS-DOS disks under ProDOS on a IIGS. If you need a file translation utility as well, try the commercial utility Cross-Works.

If you don't have access to a IIGS, but you do have access to a Mac, you can use a DOS mounting utility on the Mac to mount the ProDOS disk; then copy/translate the file to a DOS disk for use on a PC. If a Mac is available, check out a package called PC Connect, which lets you hook an IBM-compatible and a Mac together with a special cable and a special communications software program. By the way, I prefer Traveling Software's LapLink, which works like PC Connect but is a little easier to use.

P.S. Is my name in your address list?

File translation problems

I have an IBM-compatible and Quick Link II, and my friend has a Mac with Microphone. We can use the chat box OK, but we have been unable to transfer files between us. What's the secret?

I'll tell you the secret, but you have to promise not to tell your friend. He didn't buy the book.

Make sure that both programs are using the same communications protocol and that Microphone has MacBinary mode turned off. (MacBinary corrupts incoming PC files and makes outgoing Mac files appear corrupted on the PC.)

Loading a Mac backup on a PC

I backed up my Quadra 605 by using an Iomega tape backup system and QIC-80 tapes. Can I restore this backup to my PC?

No way, José. Forget that, Pat. It won't do, Lou. Restore the files on a Mac first; then worry about translating them for use on a PC.

Two platforms, one printer

I own an IBM-compatible (486DX2) and a Mac (Performa 550 with CD-ROM). I want to hook them up because a) I want to print on the same printer and b) I often work on my PC's word processor and then transfer the file to my Mac to add graphics.

If you can forgo exchanging files, all you need is a LocalTalk card for the PC and some PhoneNet connectors.

If not, the easiest way is to connect the computers and the printer via Ethernet. Of course, all three must be Ethernet-equipped (the computers need Ethernet cards, for example). To exchange data, first install Telnet on the Mac and set up the PC with any TCP/IP (*Transmission Control Protocol/Internet Protocol*) software package; then you can use FTP (*File Transfer Protocol*)/Telnet to transfer files back and forth.

You also can buy Novell Personal NetWare, but that gets complicated.

A more low-tech approach is to get a printer switch box that lets you hook up both a Mac and an IBM-compatible. With this box, you just switch back and forth between the Mac and the IBM-compatible. Depending on the printer you have, you *may* need to reset the printer between the Mac and IBM-compatible computers (refer to your printer manual). Some newer printers include automatic switching, with built-in connectors for both Macs and IBM-compatible computers.

To share the files back and forth, you could use some techniques mentioned in this chapter. Macs and IBM-compatible computers are still in two different worlds, but they're getting closer every day. Until the magic day when they work alike, we will have these issues to deal with.

Software

 Word processing

When I tried opening in Microsoft Word for the Mac documents that were created in Microsoft Word for Windows, a bunch of funky characters showed up on-screen. Are my files corrupted?

No. Those funky characters are not gibberish. They are computerese for "Please, get me the latest and greatest versions of Microsoft Word on both the IBM-compatible and Mac."

I know firsthand that the translators in Word got much better with each new version. You see, the person who transcribes my video scripts from a dictation machine uses a Mac, while I do much of my work on a Pentium. And Word for Windows 6.0 imports the Mac Word file with less fuss than ever before. Until Word for Windows 6.0 hit the streets, I had to spend a fair amount of time cleaning up the file before I could use it.

PageMaker 5

How similar are the PageMaker 5 versions for Mac and Windows?

You'll need practice like a duck needs practice to quack, a lawyer to overbill, or a politician to lie.

In other words, the two versions are extremely similar. In fact, the versions are so similar that Aldus (oops, Adobe just bought Aldus — old habits die hard) sends out the same manual, regardless of the platform you're using.

The only potential problems: graphics and fonts. Just be sure that your graphics files are supported by both the Mac and the IBM-compatible (for example, use TIFF or EPS files) and that your font names are the same.

QuarkXPress

I recently designed a newsletter for a client on QuarkXPress 3.3 for Windows. My client has QuarkXPress 3.2 for the Mac. Do I have to re-create the file in QuarkXPress 3.2 for Mac or can I use the one I made? My profit depends on your answer.

You'd better get another client real soon.

You need to re-create your masterpiece in 3.2 for Windows, or your client needs to upgrade to 3.3 for the Mac. Upgrading to 3.3 is a good idea for numerous reasons; most important, 3.3 is a free upgrade for 3.2 owners.

Komando Klues Even when working with the same version numbers of programs on a Mac and an IBM-compatible computer, you must be sure both sides have identical fonts. In addition, pay careful attention to graphics translation so that file format won't be a stumbling block.

PowerPoint

I just received via Microsoft Mail a PowerPoint for Mac 3.0 file, and I can't get my PowerPoint for Windows 4.0 to read the file. Is there anything I can do?

I have forwarded a copy of your question to Bill(ionaire) Gates. For reasons known only to Microsoft, PowerPoint 4.0 for Windows doesn't open PowerPoint 3.0 for Mac files.

Short of getting your colleague to upgrade, what can you do? One possibility is to keep PowerPoint 3.0 for Windows installed alongside 4.0. You then can open the Mac file with PowerPoint 3.0 for Windows, save it as a PowerPoint Windows 3.0 file, and finally open that file in PowerPoint 4.0. Also, check with the folks at Microsoft to see whether they have an Apple File Exchange translator for PowerPoint 3.0 for Mac files (they did for PowerPoint 2.0).

If you already have *parallel versions* (the same version number of programs for both the Mac and the IBM-compatible computer) of PowerPoint, your trouble may lie with Microsoft Mail, which reportedly has bugs related to file transfers. Try transferring the file by another method.

PowerPoint for Windows v.4c supposedly corrects this import problem. However, Microsoft Office v.4.2 doesn't recognize PowerPoint v.4c as an Office product. Microsoft says that it has just released Office v.4.2c, which can find PowerPoint v.4c. Both upgrades (Office and PowerPoint) are free to registered users. Give Microsoft's tech service line a jingle at 206-635-7056.

The Bottom Line

All in all, convince your colleague to beg for PowerPoint 4.0; upgrading will make your life easier.

HyperCard for Windows?

I'm looking for a Windows program that does what HyperCard does and can read HyperCard stacks.

Well, you're going to have a hyper-tough time finding it. Apple has made noises about HyperCard for Windows, but the ship date is anyone's guess. Similarly, Allegiant is talking about SuperCard for Windows, but it's too early to say when we'll see it.

Your best bet for now probably is Asymetrix's ToolBook or MultiMedia ToolBook in combination with Hypermedia Group/Heizer Software's ConvertIt. ConvertIt converts many HyperTalk scripts to ToolBook's OpenScript; you still need to write (or find) the equivalent of XCMDs and XCFNs to re-create your HyperCard stacks as ToolBook books. Although you may have to fix some things in ToolBook — the more complex the stack, the more fixing — the language isn't all that different from HyperTalk.

521

You also can buy Spinnaker's Plus, but there hasn't been much development in terms of features or bug fixes.

Finally, WindowCraft purports to translate HyperCard stacks, but it just isn't ready for prime time.

Developing multimedia for both platforms

I want to develop multimedia titles for both the Macintosh and IBM-compatible. Should I do the development work on a Mac or IBM-compatible computer?

You can do it all on one platform, although you may need to tweak your files a bit on the other side. I suggest doing the bulk of your work on the Mac because it has better Windows development tools than Windows has for the Mac.

On-line

Compressed Mac files

I downloaded a Mac file called CAROUSEL.SIT from America Online, but I can't seem to unzip it or execute it. What am I doing wrong?

In the Mac world, almost everyone uses Aladdin's StuffIt — much as ZIP is the standard for DOS and Windows. Mac files or programs that are *stuffed*, or compressed, have the three-letter .SIT extension.

A little trivia: Compressed archives are one of the only areas in the Mac universe where filename extensions are used. (Doesn't this nugget make you SIT up and take notice?)

To unstuff a StuffIt archive, you can use several utilities, including Aladdin's commercial StuffIt Deluxe, shareware StuffIt Lite, and freeware StuffIt Expander.

In addition, with America Online (and some other commercial on-line services), StuffIt is built right in. Under the Members menu, select Set Preferences and then choose Downloading Preferences. You can set AOL to automatically decompress StuffIt archives after you quit or logoff from AOL. Heck, you can even have your AOL software delete the compressed copy after the file has been extracted. You also can use AOL's File⇨Open command to open any StuffIt archive; you are given the option to delete the archive after decompression on the fly.

On occasion, you may want to use a Mac .SIT file on an IBM-compatible. Aladdin makes a DOS program that will decompress a Mac file. It's a freeware program that can be found in Aladdin's forum on AOL.

AOL interfaces in different platforms

America Online sure looks different on a Mac than on my Gateway IBM-compatible. It seems that there are different options available. What gives?

All the versions of America Online have different interfaces and slightly different features, including access to platform-specific areas. Windows users have to search for Mac areas and vice versa. Don't worry: The principal features are the same.

PCs on a Mac BBS

Can your IBM-compatible computer sign on to Mac-only BBSs? When I tried with the local Mac user's group BBS, the screen freaked.

I'm freaking out. How do you know which kind of computer I have?

You'll have to check with the individual BBSs to see whether they allow, I mean support, IBM-compatible users.

By the way, even Mac users need special software to use graphical Mac-oriented BBSs, so don't feel slighted. The popular Mac BBS sign-on software programs are

> ➤ Spider Island's TeleFinder
> ➤ SoftArc's FirstClass
> ➤ ResNova's NovaLink

Normally, you can get the sign-on software programs directly from the BBS operators.

Komando Klues

Of course, I wouldn't waste my time looking for files on Mac BBSs if I used an IBM-compatible. It's a hassle. Plus, odds are you'll find the coolest piece of shareware known to mankind on the Mac BBS but be unable to use it because you don't have HyperCard. You will, however, be able to read and write messages on that Mac BBS.

Downloading Mac files on a PC

Can I use my 486 PC to download Mac files from a BBS and then load the files into a Mac later?

Yes, but it's not worth the hassle.

Mac files are very different from IBM-compatible files. In particular, a Mac file usually has one or two *forks*, including an information fork and a resource fork. Neither IBM-compatibles nor standard communications protocols used on on-line services understand forks. Therefore, Mac files downloaded to an IBM-compatible can get hopelessly munged.

The workaround: Make sure the files you want to use are saved in a MacBinary format. This encoding method keeps the two Mac forks intact. (This step is necessary for Mac-to-Mac modem transfers as well.) Because you plan to store the Mac files on your IBM-compatible temporarily, you want to be sure not to un-MacBinary the file as you download it, because data the Mac needs will be lost. Then you must remove the file from its MacBinary envelope when you get it to the Mac. Many utilities can do this, including Aladdin's freeware StuffIt Expander.

Chapter 14
Music and Sound

Basics

Sound cards

 Are sound cards necessary?

I noticed that some computers have a sound card and speakers attached. My computer already has a speaker built in. Is this a gimmick to get more money from us computer buyers?

It's no gimmick. Take a trip to your local computer retailer and listen to an F15 fighter's sounds reverberating from a pair of stereo speakers. Now go home and listen to your computer. Go ahead and admit it — your computer sounds like an AM station on a cheap clock radio.

Most PC built-in speakers were designed to generate beeps and chirps and not much else. And those are good only if you like programs that feature lots of cars and birds. If you use your computer only to type the occasional letter or do taxes, then perhaps the PC speaker is adequate. But a sound card can add a whole new dimension to using your computer when you're playing games, using CD-ROMs, listening to music, and a whole lot more. In fact, many commercially available computer games today offer built-in sound capabilities (such as music and sound effects) that can be harnessed *only* with a sound card.

Certain sound cards allow you to hook up musical instruments to your computer and use the computer as a recording studio. Also, a sound card coupled with a CD-ROM player allows you to play regular audio CDs as well as run CD-ROM-based multimedia applications. All in all, a sound card can make your computer a much more fun thing to use — never a bad thing.

Want to liven up your Windows desktop? Windows comes with the capability to assign sounds such as cool beeps, toilet flushes, parts of songs, and snippets from movies to accompany certain events. You need a sound card and a set of stereo speakers, however, to make the experience worthwhile.

What's the best kind of sound card?

There seem to be a million sound cards out on the market. I'm so confused. What's the best sound card for me?

Pick a card, any card. Pick the right card and you're a winner. If you don't do a little research before buying a sound card, you may as well be taking your chances with a sidewalk hustler. And just like hustlers, sound cards come in all different sizes, interfaces, and yes, price ranges. Here are some factors to consider when buying a sound card:

➤ *What's the sound card's job?* If you're simply playing games and listening to audio CDs, you don't necessarily need a top-of-the-line card. By the same token, if you plan on making MIDI recordings, you shouldn't buy a cheapo 8-bit card.

➤ *Does the sound card comply with the MPC 2 standard?* The Multimedia PC Level 1 and Level 2 standards were developed by the Multimedia PC Marketing Council (MPC) to ensure that manufacturers were making equipment that would be compatible with equipment from other manufacturers. But forget about the outdated MPC 1 and look for the MPC 2 logo. Plug-in expansion cards that are compatible with the MPC 2 standard must record and play back wave-form audio with 16-bit resolution at 44KHz. This is CD-quality audio, which is far more than you'll need for voice annotation.

Boards that comply with the MPC 2 specification must be capable of playing MIDI music, have a joystick port (which can be used as a MIDI interface instead), accept Red Book audio from a CD-ROM player, and interface with and control a CD-ROM player. In fact, the lack of a CD-ROM interface is the major reason some products are classified as sound boards rather than as MPC 2 boards. If you buy a multimedia PC-compatible sound card now, adding a CD-ROM drive will be much easier in the future.

➤ *Will you be adding a CD-ROM later?* CD-ROM drives are most often plugged into the interface built into the sound card, saving an expansion slot for other neat gadgets that you may want to add later down the line.

➤ *Does the card have a SCSI or a proprietary interface?* SCSI interfaces are generally faster. Take heed: Not all sound cards have a CD-ROM interface.

➤ *Is the manufacturer well known?* It's not wise to buy a cheapo, no-name sound card because, despite the MPC standard, you could be asking for trouble. How? Well, some applications will not work with your card. Go for the brand name (such as Sound Blaster or Pro Audio Spectrum); you'll do better in the long run.

➤ *How much money do you have to spend?*

To research the performance of specific cards, check computer magazines for editor evaluations. These evaluations rate sound cards on everything from ease of setup to quality of sound. Also, most major computer magazines have their back issues available on various on-line services for easy searching. Whether you're into serious digital recording or multimedia presentation creation, or you simply want cool sounds for computer games, there's a sound board out there to meet your needs.

Will my PC support a sound card?

My friend has a computer with a sound card, and I'm amazed at how many different sounds his computer can make. How can I tell if my computer can support a sound card?

If your computer has an empty expansion slot, it will support a sound card. Check to see whether you have an 8- or 16-bit slot available before you buy a card because sound cards come in both sizes. A couple of new models are 32 bit.

Don't forget a set of external speakers. PC speakers were never designed for anything more than beeps.

What kind of sound card do I have?

I'm tempted to buy a cool game that needs a 16-bit sound card, and I'm not sure whether I have one. I mean, I have a sound card, but how can I tell whether it's 8 or 16 bits?

Sauté it with a little onion, serve it with a nice red wine, and if you can eat the whole thing in 8 bites, it's an 8-bit card.

The easiest way to tell is to look in the manual. Isn't it funny, though, how those manuals have a way of disappearing into thin air when you need them? They end up in a part of the universe with your sunglasses, the missing sock from the dryer, and the TV remote. If you don't have or can't locate the book, then look at the actual card. The 8-bit sound cards have one tab that fits into an expansion slot, whereas 16-bit cards have two tabs.

Sound ports vs. sound cards

I made the mistake of buying one of those computer magazines that said *899 Sound Cards Evaluated* on the cover. I can't say I understood much of the article. Before I try reading it again, what's the difference between a sound port and a sound card?

You'd better hurry. By the time you go back to that magazine, there will be 1,899 cards to evaluate.

"Any port in a storm" may be good advice, but not just any sound device works in a port. If you need a sound device for your PC, your choices are a sound port or a sound board. A sound port clips on to the parallel port of the computer, whereas a sound board plugs into an empty expansion slot.

The advantage to sound ports is that they are easy to install and configure, and they are the only current alternative for portable computers, which don't have expansion slots. The downsides to sound ports are that they can monopolize the parallel port (as a result, you can't print without removing the sound port or using an AB switch), and have limited fidelity. In addition, very few can play MIDI music. Because few programs written today include drivers to support sound port devices, the sound port usually has to emulate a low-end 8-bit Sound Blaster card or it won't work at all with that particular program.

Sound boards offer good-to-excellent fidelity, are easy to use once they are installed, and can double as CD-ROM, MIDI, and joystick interfaces if you choose the multimedia variety. The downside is that sound cards are the second most cantankerous cards to install and configure. (Network cards are often considered the most difficult.)

The good news is that sound boards and ports come with a variety of capabilities and prices to fit most needs.

Speak to me, computer

 Bored with the beep

What types of sounds can I get out of my computer? I am starting to get bored with that same old beep. I want more from my computer.

Starting to get bored? You mean you still find it even a little interesting? The most basic Windows sound is the plaintive beeping of the computer's built-in speaker. It's about as exciting as homework. You can liven things up by adding a sound card and assigning sound files — known as .WAV, or *digital audio,* files —to common system events. This is done through the Control Panel in Windows.

With a sound card, a computer can play or record lots of different types of noises. Here is a list of the more common ones:

> ▶ *Digital audio* is analog sound that has been recorded by a computer using Digital to Analog Converter. Most consumer-level sound boards (such as Sound Blaster and Pro Audio Spectrum) use the DAC technology to record sounds. Common digital audio file formats are .WAV (Windows native format) and .VOC (Sound Blaster sound files).

> ▶ *Synthesized audio* is generally MIDI music that is created with a musical instrument. However, some speech and sound effects are also synthesized. A common synthesized audio format is .MID.

> ▶ *Red Book audio* is music from a regular audio CD. If you have a CD-ROM drive attached to your sound card, you can play regular audio CDs.

Make my computer talk!

I want my computer to talk to me, as in the movies. Do I need a special program to make my sound card talk?

You can make your sound card talk to you, but don't expect it to be much of a conversationalist. Does it require a special program? Yes. Many cards come bundled with speech synthesis software when you purchase them. For instance, Sound Blasters often come with a Windows program called Monologue for Windows and a DOS program called SBTALKER. Monologue can read text from the Windows Clipboard or from Microsoft Excel spreadsheets. SBTALKER is a very simple command-line program that can read short phrases or entire text files.

Definitions

What's the frequency, Kenneth?

Why can't anyone in computers talk normally? I asked a salesperson what frequency was, and he entered a different planetary frequency.

The most important thing to know about frequency is the higher, the better (unless you're talking about trips to the bathroom). Of course, the higher the frequency, the higher the price.

If you want to impress your friends with techno-nerd facts, here are a few to throw around. Frequency is usually mentioned when discussing sampling rate. When you record an analog sound source (a human voice, a guitar) with your computer, the computer turns the sound into digital data (those infamous ones and zeros). *Sampling rate* is the number of times per second that the computer converts the analog signal into numeric data.

The sampling frequency determines how often the board measures the level of the sound being recorded or played back. I'll skip the math for now, but the bottom line is that you have to sample at about twice the highest frequency that you want to produce, plus an extra 10 percent to keep out unwanted extra signals. The generally accepted limit for human hearing is about 20,000 cycles per second, or 20KHz. Double it, add 10 percent, and you get 44KHz — almost exactly the 44.1KHz sampling rate used by high-fidelity stereo audio-CD recordings.

The other part of the sound specification is the number of bits per sample. An 8-bit sample is only capable of describing 256 steps between the quietest and loudest sounds in a file, which in audio terms is known as the *dynamic range*. These 256 steps work out to just 48 decibels. Newer audio cards are capable of 16-bit sampling, however, doubling the dynamic range to 96 decibels. This increased range is sufficient to handle everything from near silence to a salvo from a full symphony at point-blank range.

As a guideline for evaluating the quality of sound files, 8-bit/11.025KHz sampling (recording) is roughly equivalent to AM radio quality. The 8-bit/stereo/22.05KHz sampling is comparable to FM radio quality, and the 16-bit/stereo/44.1KHz sampling provides quality equivalent to that found on audio CDs. The quality of the digital sound depends on your sound card, the quality of the microphone or other sound source, the size of the sample (8 or 16 bits), and the sampling rate at which the sound is digitized.

MIDI

What are MIDI files?

Remember the miniskirt fad of the early '70s? (Boy, am I dating myself.) Wait, do you remember the miniskirt fad of the late '80s? (There, that's better.) MIDI files could be considered the miniskirt of computers. Have you heard of miniskirt works? These shortened versions of traditional sound files are the latest fashion craze in computer sound technology.

Rather than store the entire sound (like a wave file does), a MIDI (or *M*usical *I*nstrument *D*igital *I*nterface) file stores information about the type of instrument that created the musical note and information about the note itself (how loud, how long, and so on). MIDI files are quite a bit smaller than .WAV files for this reason.

When MIDI first came out, standardization throughout the industry was a big problem. As with any new computer technology, every company wanted its format to be the standard. International MIDI Association stepped in and created the General MIDI System, Level 1 standard. This standard, much like the Multimedia PC standards, was created in an effort to make sure that MIDI files had some degree of uniformity. Most MIDI files on BBSs and on-line services are General MIDI-compatible. If you intend to use a card with MIDI capabilities, making sure that it complies with the association's standards is important.

.WAV

Almost every bulletin board and on-line service offers a ton of .WAV files. The files have high download counts, too, so they must be popular. What are they?

Like any computer file, a .WAV (pronounced "wave") file is just a collection of ones and zeros. It's what you can do with those ones and zeros that makes .WAV files interesting.

To play sounds on your computer, the sounds have to be converted to something a computer can understand. Files ending in the extension .WAV are in a format native to Windows. These files can be played on any Windows machine that, at least, has the Windows Sound Driver for PC Speaker installed. Because playing them requires no additional hardware, .WAV files are the preferred method of exchanging sound files. Trust me, they actually sound much, much better with a sound card and a pair of speakers.

To see whether you have the PC Speaker driver, go into the Drivers icon in the Windows Control Panel and see whether it appears in the list. If it doesn't, you need to obtain the SPEAKER.EXE file. This file is a self-extracting archive containing the Windows PC Speaker driver and instructions on installing it. You can get it from the computer's manufacturer and as a downloadable file on many BBSs and on-line services (including America Online).

To hear a .WAV file, you can play it by using the Windows Sound Recorder or Media Player. Both applications are included in the Accessories group.

Troubleshooting

Too little noise

 This sound bites!

I finally saved up enough money to buy a sound card and, boy, was I disappointed. I get music now, if you can call it that. It sounds terrible and works only in DOS. In Windows, I don't get any sound at all. Is my sound card defective, or what?

What, you don't like tinny, hollow music? In my day, that's all we had and we liked it.

It is very unlikely (but not impossible) that you have a defective card. Ninety-nine percent of the time the problem is operator error. That's you! You probably goofed up something during the installation. Don't feel bad. Sound cards are great once they start working, but they can make you pull your hair out in the meantime.

By the way, did you crack that wallet open far enough to purchase a pair of speakers when you bought the sound card? Although you can use the built-in PC speaker, it was never designed for anything more than chirps and beeps. A sound card without speakers is like Mickey without Minnie, bread without butter, government without scandal.

The solution to your problem could be one of a million things. Here are some things to try:

Make sure that the card is firmly seated in the expansion slot. You also can try removing the card and putting it in another slot. On more than one occasion, a novice installer has put a 16-bit card in an 8-bit slot.

Make sure that the IRQ and DMA settings don't conflict with any other cards or ports. DOS 6.*x* and Windows 3.1 come with a diagnostic utility, called Microsoft Diagnostics. To use it, go to the DOS prompt, type **MSD**, and press the Enter key. In MSD is a screen that shows what is using all your computer's IRQs. *Note:* Even if there is no conflict, you may want to try using another available IRQ.

Reinstall the software that came with the card. Check the sound volume settings on the card. Make sure that the sound isn't distorting because the sound is turned up too loud.

If the sound at the DOS level is still crappola, it's time to call tech support and discuss returning the card. If your DOS problems are solved, skip ahead to the next question to get things working in Windows.

Windows won't squeak

I went through and checked everything in my computer's setup, but Windows is as silent as a lamb, and I'm ready to kill it. Why can't I get any sound?

For a moment there, I could swear Anthony Hopkins was in the room warming up the fava beans. That movie just sends shivers up my spine. Oops, I'm supposed to be talking about computers. Hey, cut me a break. You answer 1,001 computer questions and see how you feel.

If you don't hear sounds from Windows, there are at least four things to check:

First, go through the troubleshooting steps outlined in the last question and make sure that your card works in DOS. Drivers that make your sound card work in DOS are not the same drivers necessary to make the card work in Windows. Check the disks that came with your card to see whether there is a Windows support disk that you may not have installed. Also, check the user manual that came with the card for information on using the sound card with Windows.

Second, check the Control Panel in Windows to see whether system sounds are available. If you double-click the Sounds icon and all your choices are grayed out, reinstall the Windows sound drivers. While you're there, make sure that the necessary .WAV files are in your WINDOWS directory.

Did your sound card come with a mixer? Even if you see a volume-control knob, there may also be a software utility that lets you adjust volume, bass, treble, and other output settings. (Sound Blaster owners use SBMIXER.EXE; for the Pro Audio Spectrum, look for PMIX.EXE.) If the volume is set too low in the utility, you'll hear nothing.

Finally, a DMA conflict can cause digital audio to be distorted or not play at all. A DMA conflict also can cause your system to lock up, spontaneously reboot, or generate parity errors. To change the DMA setting, use the Setup dialog of the Control Panel's Drivers utility.

No sound

I think my daughter shut off the computer while a program was running, and now that program doesn't recognize my sound card. Can you find the culprit?

Are you ready? It's your daughter. Question: Is the problem only with this one particular program, or are all your programs silent? If you hear no sound in all programs, run the sound card's configuration program and/or reinstall the sound cards drivers. When the computer was shut off, the driver files probably were damaged. But if the other programs use the sound card, you should check the program's sound configuration. The worst-case scenario is to reinstall the program that has difficulties using the sound card.

Komando Klues

Give the children a little etiquette lesson. You never leave a room without saying good-bye to your friends, and you never turn off the computer without exiting the program that's on-screen.

Silent MIDI

Why won't my MIDI files play? I've gone into my Control Panel and opened the MIDI Mapper. A number of drivers are listed, but I don't know what to do with them. I've got the no-music blues.

OK, are you ready to rock and roll? Ready to jazz things up? This is one of those questions that could take all day to answer. Rather than drown you in techno-nerd terms and explain every detail of the MIDI Mapper, however, I'll just go through the steps required to get it to work.

When you go into the MIDI Mapper icon (say that three times fast), you should choose the General MIDI option. Depending on the card, you may have Extended MIDI or All. Selecting the General MIDI option ensures that you will be able to play most MIDI files that you come across.

Most of the setups will say *This references a nonexistent driver.* Don't bother with those. Create a new setup. Call it *Mine* or name it after your cat or something. Also, give it a description that means something.

OK, now you see a screenful of channel maps. The center column of each channel should say *none*. Check the names of the drivers; one should say OPL, SAPI, or TAPI somewhere in it. Unless you have a WaveBlaster or other wavetable board, choose that driver. If you have a wavetable, then check for an appropriate-sounding driver.

Now, you have a slight problem. Most sound cards use either 10 or 16 as a percussion track. So you need to either map 16 onto 10, or 10 onto 16. Chances are you should map 10 onto 16. If percussion sounds weird (like different piano notes or whatever), then map 16 onto 10 instead.

This should work until you buy a different sound card, in which case you need to do this all over again. Also, you may want different setups if you own an external MIDI keyboard.

PC speaker won't play all .WAV files

I don't get it. Why can I play some .WAV files but not others through my PC speaker?

Internal PC speakers were never designed for anything more than beeps and buzzes. You'll find better speakers at a convention for stutterers. To make matters worse, the PC Speaker driver for Windows just gives you minimal sound capability.

The Bottom Line

The Windows PC speaker driver is capable of playing only very basic 8-bit sound files. The PC Speaker driver will not play stereo .WAVs, 16-bit .WAVs, or .WAVs sampled at a rate higher then 22MHz.

Komando Klues

If you're receiving these unplayable .WAV files from a BBS or on-line service, check the description of the file before downloading it to make sure that the sound file is only 8 bit. If the file size is relatively small (less than 100K), chances are that you can play it.

You know, you could always let those moths out of your wallet and shell out $20 for a set of real computer speakers. Trust me, they are well worth the investment. If you do decide to buy the new speakers, be sure to uninstall the PC Speaker driver so that your sound card knows which speakers to use!

.WAV files won't finish

Sometimes my .WAV files stop in the middle of playing. Is it because I am using a PC speaker?

Yes, but there is a workaround. Go into the Drivers icon in the Control Panel. Click Sound Driver for PC Speaker and then click the Setup button. The horizontal scroll bar in the middle of this dialog box controls the maximum time limit that a .WAV file can play. Sliding the elevator all the way to the right sets no limit on how long a sound file can play through the PC speaker.

Be warned, though. When a sound is playing, you can't use your computer. If you set up your computer to play 60 seconds of *The 1812 Overture* every time you open Windows, you have to wait for it to finish before Windows completes loading, which isn't fun when the boss has just pulled up outside and you need that computer now!

Cannot play the selected sound *message*

I have been trying to assign sounds to system events, but it isn't going well. I'm a comedy writer, and I want my computer to laugh at the end of every paragraph. Why do I receive the message *Cannot play the selected sound* with some .WAV files and not others?

You sound like a very insecure comedy writer.

Sometimes you receive this message — or no message and no sound — when you play certain .WAV files using the Sound section of the Control Panel. That's because the Sound option plays only 22.05KHz .WAV files; it won't play 11.025KHz .WAV files. However, Sound Recorder plays both 11.025KHz and 22.05KHz .WAV files but saves files only in 22.05KHz format.

To play the 11.025KHz .WAV files, first make sure that the sound functions are working by playing a sound from the WINDOWS directory. If this doesn't work, you have driver or hardware problems; check your sound card setup. Otherwise, you then can load the .WAV files into the Sound Recorder. Save them in 22.05KHz format so that you can play the file using the Control Panel's Sound utility. Hee hee. Ha ha. Hope this works. Hee hee. What a card! Ha ha.

537

DOS game won't scream in Windows

I have a DOS game full of great sound effects, but the sound effects don't work if I run the game through Windows. If I run the game through DOS, they work fine. Is there something I can do to make the sounds work in Windows?

People often ask how to make their DOS-based games access their sound cards under Windows 3.1. If you're getting error messages (such as *Sound Card in Use by Windows*) when you try to run DOS games from Windows, here's why: All Windows applications share the same sound card drivers, so as long as Windows is running, the drivers are loaded. DOS applications use sound cards in different ways, depending on how they're programmed. Although some games work with Windows still loaded, many try to load their own drivers, which conflict with the Windows drivers that are still resident.

Often, running Windows in standard mode (to do so, type **WIN /S**) resolves some of these conflicts, but there's no guarantee. Even if you could resolve the conflict, launching DOS games from Windows is usually not a good idea. If the publisher supports this approach, it usually includes a .PIF file for this purpose. The system overhead of having Windows resident cripples the performance of many DOS games, especially those that require the use of extended or expanded memory — for example, high-performance programs such as X-Wing and other real-time simulators. The only game programs that can operate under this pressure are Snail and Turtle Races. But even they will limp along with noticeably reduced frame rates and other problems if run from Windows.

TADA

Upon starting Windows, I used to hear the familiar "TADA," which told me that everything was fine. But of late, nothing, no sound when I "start her up." I checked my Windows files, and I see the TADA.WAV and other .WAV files (all of which should work but never have). I'm not that bad at

taking instructions, but reading them. . . . Ugh, I'd rather watch every rerun of "Hee Haw" in a row. I have a basic 486SX, 220MB, DR DOS 6, 8MB RAM — nothing fancy.

The Windows Control Panel is the central command post for the settings on your desktop. Open up the Control Panel and you see a bunch of little icons. Double-click the one that says Drivers to bring up a nice little list of all the drivers you currently have installed in your system. Highlight Sound Driver for PC Speaker and go to setup. (If you don't see this driver, you need to reinstall it.) Turn the volume all the way up . . . or to a 10. Or, if you like "Spinal Tap," set it to 11. Close out the driver section when you have finished.

While you're in the Control Panel, go ahead and check out your setup. Find the icon that shows a musical note to the left of an ear. Double-click on it. Select Windows Start from the left box and then select TADA.WAV (or whatever sound file you wish to associate with the Windows start event) in the right box.

Also, make sure that the Enable System Sounds option is selected.

Sound Blaster won't use the speakers

My new Sound Blaster keeps playing over the PC speaker. What do I have to do to make it use my new speakers?

You're hearing the .WAV files out of your PC speaker because the PC Speaker driver is still installed. Because your PC Speaker driver is installed, Windows wasn't sure what "sound" driver it should use. If you reinstall your Sound Blaster drivers, Windows should get the hint that you want to use it for all your audio stuff.

Here's what you need to do. First, make a backup of your SYSTEM.INI file (found in your WINDOWS subdirectory). You will be editing this file, so you want to be sure that you have a good copy of it somewhere else.

Now, go into your Sound Blaster program and check the current setup. Make a note of the DMA, IRQ, and address settings.

Next, you need to reinstall your Sound Blaster drivers. Depending on what version of Sound Blaster you have, you may need to exit Windows completely (check your manual to be sure). Reinstall the Sound Blaster software and let it run through the test procedure. Take a look at what settings are recommended and compare that to the numbers that you wrote down when you were in Windows. They should be the same. If they're not, make a note of what settings the test program recommended and use them.

Connecting computer to stereo

I have Pro Audio Spectrum 16 and would like to hook my computer to my stereo system amplifier. I ran a cable from the back of my sound card to the stereo's amplifier. But I have to crank the volume full blast to hear anything. What can I do?

I know, you crank it up, and the sound still sounds like it's coming from an AM radio inside a jar. Alas, poor Pro Audio Spectrum 16 user, I can help. The Pro Audio Spectrum (PAS) 16 card's output jack is a Line Out jack; that's where the connection is made to the Line In jack on your stereo. For some stereos, though, there's not enough power on the line. Try plugging into an Auxiliary In jack, if you have one. Doing so should amplify the signal coming into your stereo.

Also, make sure that you buy shielded stereo cable. Look for one that has a male miniphone on one end and two male RCAs on the other. The miniphone plugs into the PAS16, and the two RCAs plug into a Line In on your recording equipment. The plug costs about $5 at any Radio Shack. It works, it's shielded, and it's stereo.

By the way, I bought a second cable and ran it out the back of my Pioneer cassette deck. I often play tapes or the radio through the Line In on my PAS16, which serves as a good amplifier when you have powered speakers set up. Because MVSOUND.SYS is in my CONFIG.SYS file, using it as an amplifier doesn't get in the way of any software programs.

Too much noise

Windows exits noisily

My sound card makes loud noises when I exit Windows. Is this Windows's way of punishing me for leaving?

So, it kind of sounds like DOS and Windows are having a cat fight, does it? Hell hath no fury like a Windows scorned.

On occasion, Windows can be selfish and greedy. It may fight to retain control of the sound card rather than release it to DOS. In time, and with a little persuasion, Windows allows the sound card to see other drivers on the side. With a small change or two to your system setup, you can probably teach it to be a little more generous.

First, try to update your Windows sound drivers. The easiest way is to contact the manufacturer of your sound card and ask it to send you the latest and greatest version. If the new card doesn't clear things up (hey, I have been wrong on a few rare occasions), then try configuring your sound card to use a different IRQ or DMA channel. A device you are using under Windows (modem, scanner, and so on) may be trying to share a channel with your sound card and thus causing a conflict.

Static and noise

Static and noise are coming from either the CD-ROM or the Windows programs. I have tried changing the speakers and the sound card, but nothing helps. What should I try next? Buying another computer isn't an option.

You could learn to enjoy static.

As much as I hate to say it, I suspect that you are having a DMA or IRQ conflict. Those types of conflicts can often cause fuzzy, static sounds or no sound at all. See whether changing the settings helps.

If changing the settings doesn't clear up the sound, then you need to buy another computer. Wait, that's not an option. So start looking at hardware problems. Are you certain that the plug you have your system plugged into is *fully* grounded? If it's not, then that could be causing your static. Also make sure everything hooked to your system is well-connected.

Computer components (such as hard drives, modems, video adapters, and so on) often produce quite a bit of noise. The noise you hear is picked up by the amplifier on your sound card and amplified just as an audio signal would be. If the CD-ROM's audio output cable is near a cable from the hard drive or video near the video circuits, noise produced by these components will leak into the cable. Try rerouting this cable or moving the sound card to a different slot.

You also might try buying a cable with heavier shielding (the wire braid that surrounds the two audio wires) that will work with your CD-ROM. *Note:* Make sure that the connectors look like the original cable's connectors. One other thing: Double-check that this braid is connected to the pins that say *ground* on your audio card or CD-ROM's audio connector (check your manuals for pin assignments). Most have two connections, but only one needs to be connected unless there are two separate cables in the cable assembly. Make sure that it is grounded at both ends.

Lunar static syndrome

I recently moved, and now I hear static in my speakers. Maybe the moon is too close to the Earth on this side of town. What do you think?

I think the moon has affected your judgment. During the move, something could have jarred your computer, causing the sound card to become unseated. Open your case and make sure that the card is securely positioned in the expansion slot. Next, carefully push on the wires to make sure that they are snugly in place.

An improperly grounded outlet also can cause static. Try plugging your system into a different outlet. If the problem doesn't clear up, it may be time to call an electrician.

Is this cereal or a sound card?

I have an 8-bit Sound Blaster card that is making snapping, crackling, and popping noises in Windows. Is the card defective?

Are you sneaking a cereal ad in here?

If you have Sound Blaster 1.0 or 1.5, you need to upgrade the Digital Sound Processor chip on your card to Version 2. The version of DSP chip you probably have right now is 1.05, and that version can not process sound fast enough to accommodate Windows. The upgrade can be purchased from Creative Technologies directly for about $30. However, think about buying a whole new card because the one you have is rapidly approaching obsolescence.

Cranking up the speakers

I'm using a Pro Audio 16 Sound Card and Labtec CS1000 Computer Speaker System. I can raise the sound in Windows by using the keyboard controls, but I can't make the volume control on the front of the Labtec CS1000 function. How do I get the volume control to work?

After you hear this answer, you will want to hit yourself on the head and shout, "Why didn't I think of that!" Don't feel bad; it's the little things that we forget the most. OK, are you ready to feel stupid?

For the volume control on the speakers to work, you have to put batteries in or use an AC adapter and plug it in the wall. You see, your sound card puts out just enough juice to power the speakers but not their built-in amplifier. If you use the keyboard to change the volume, you are actually increasing the signal before it gets to your speakers so that you don't have to use their amplifier.

543

Adjusting volume

The sound on my computer is way too loud when the system first starts up. I immediately have to turn the volume down. Is there any way to set my Pro Audio card to a lower volume? My neighbors are pounding on the walls and screaming as I write this.

Are you sure they're complaining and not doing something else?

Most sound cards allow you to set the volume for the speakers when the system first boots up. Pro Audio cards are no exception. The driver MVSOUND.SYS has a command line switch that lets you select the start-up volume of the PAS. If you need 20 percent volume, for example, simply add the following line to your CONFIG.SYS file:

```
DEVICEHIGH = C:\PROAUDIO\MVSOUND.SYS [...] V:20
```

The Bottom Line

If you don't include the switch in the command, the volume defaults to 80 percent, which can be rather deafening. Reboot the computer for the changes to take effect.

Sound device driver

Do I need a driver?

I just got an "as is" computer with a Sound Blaster card installed. The hard drive has an SB directory, but the configuration files do not mention a driver for the card. Am I missing something?

Sometimes, people who buy "as is" often find that they've made "as is" of themselves.

As you have learned, purchasing an "as is" computer often means that you have to become a detective to make the darn thing work. Your mission, should you choose to accept it, is to track down which model Sound Blaster card you have installed. You could probably crack the case by cracking the case of your computer and taking a look at the card itself. Creative Labs usually prints the model name and number on the card.

544

Before you pull out your trusty screwdriver, however, make sure that you haven't overlooked a clue. The default directory name for the original 8-bit Sound Blaster card is \SB — the name of the directory on your hard drive. Could that mean that you have an original Sound Blaster card? You're darn tootin' it could. Although it is possible to change the default directory name during installation, most people are too lazy to do that. Chances are good that you have an 8-bit Sound Blaster there. It may be an older model card, but there's something to be said for maturity. It is a good basic sound card that is supported by almost all software that utilizes a sound device. After all, it is the industry standard.

Another cool thing is that it doesn't require special drivers for sound at the DOS level. DOS programs that support sound cards have the drivers built into them. To utilize the card, you need to set up two statements in the AUTOEXEC.BAT file:

```
SET BLASTER=A220 I5 D1 T1
SET SOUND=C:\SB
```

A220 is the default address; I5 is Interrupt 5; D1 is DMA channel 1, and T1 means that it's the original Sound Blaster. Keep in mind that these are the default settings and you may have to modify them to avoid hardware conflicts.

If you also want sound in Windows, you need to obtain the drivers from Creative Labs. Heck, while you're on the phone with tech support, go ahead and ask to have a manual sent out, too.

Missing sound device driver

When I start a DOS-based program from Windows, I receive yet another helpful message: *Unable to Play Sound: Sound Blaster Is in Use by Another Application.* Why?

What does Windows have in common with a child and her toys, a monkey and his banana, a dog and his bone? Answer: None of them like to share. Although many DOS applications support audio, running them under Windows in 386 enhanced mode sometimes causes problems. Windows doesn't like to share sound hardware with DOS applications.

The easiest fix is to try the DOS program running Windows in standard mode rather than enhanced mode. To start Windows in standard mode, type **WIN /S** at the DOS prompt and press Enter.

An alternative is to add a line to the Windows SYSTEM.INI file. Usually, the error message you received means that the virtual sound device driver is missing or invalid in the SYSTEM.INI file's [386enh] section.

You see, Windows needs a certain file called VSBPD.386 in the SYSTEM.INI file. Apparently, it's not there. Using Windows File Manager, select File⇨Search to make sure that you have VSBPD.386 in your C:\WINDOWS directory.

Next, make a backup copy of the SYSTEM.INI file because you're going to make some changes to it. Then, using Windows Notepad, open the SYSTEM.INI file that's located in your C:\WINDOWS directory. Look for the [386enh] section and add the following line:

```
device=vsbpd.386
```

If you can't find the file, reinstall the Sound Blaster software, or call Creative Labs and ask for a new copy.

Sound Environment Not Found *message*

I am trying to install a Sound Blaster 16 card but every time I try to add the driver, I get the message *Sound Environment Not Found*. What am I doing wrong?

You are probably either missing your SET BLASTER statement from your AUTOEXEC.BAT file, or the statement contains incorrect settings for your card. DOS uses the SET command to set up environmental variables for other programs or batch files to use. The SET BLASTER statement lets DOS know which IRQ, I/O port, and DMA channel your sound card will use.

The exact syntax should be in your Sound Blaster documentation. In fact, I'm surprised that this wouldn't have been automatically added during the software installation. Did you run the installation program with the Sound Blaster disks?

If the statement is there, but things still don't work right, try using the Sound Blaster SBCONFIG.EXE utility found in your \SB16 directory. It will allow you to change the settings to something compatible with the card.

DMA/IRQ

No DMA/IRQ combinations available *message*

When I set up my Pro Audio sound card, I got a *No DMA/IRQ combinations available* message. What does that mean? The last combination plate I ordered was at a Mexican restaurant.

As much as I hate to use the techie terms, I don't see a way around it this time. Don't worry. Just take a deep breath, clear your mind, and put down that burrito. I'm sure you can handle it.

It sounds like you're having a DMA or IRQ conflict. What does that mean? It means that there is a civil war going on inside your computer. You have some other card (SCSI adapter, scanner interface card) or port (serial, parallel, or game) active in your computer that is conflicting with your Pro Audio sound card. Something is using a DMA or IRQ that your Pro Audio wants.

Let me start with the basics. An IRQ (*i*nterrupt *req*uest) is a direct line from a device (port, SCSI card, sound card, and so on) to the CPU. When a device needs the CPU's attention, it sends a request to the CPU via these lines. Fourteen IRQs (2–15) are available for your devices to use. However, only one device at a time can use a given IRQ. As a result, your mouse and your sound card can't be assigned to the same IRQ. But you can usually give your printer and your sound card the same IRQ because you are unlikely to use both at the same time. In a typical system, IRQs 3, 4, 6, and 14 are assigned to the modem, mouse, floppy controller, and hard drive controller. Don't assign these IRQs to other devices.

A DMA (*d*irect *m*emory *a*ccess) channel is used by the computer to efficiently transfer information in and out of memory. Once again, two devices can't use a given DMA channel at the same time. Sound cards, network cards, scanner cards, SCSI controllers, and so on all use DMA channels. In a typical system, DMA 2 and 4 are assigned to your floppies and to memory refresh, so don't assign these to other devices.

Unfortunately, there is no easy fix for DMA and IRQ conflicts. First, make sure that all the hardware is properly installed and connected. Something as small as a cable put on backwards can cause this error. In the end, most IRQ/DMA problems are solved by trial and error.

Next, use the Microsoft Diagnostics program to check how many serial and parallel ports you have. If MSD reports that you have three LPT ports, chances are you can afford to disable one of them to make its IRQ available. Beyond that, you will have to start reconfiguring other cards and/or ports to make the necessary IRQ and DMA combinations available.

Now comes the fun part: Make a backup copy of your CONFIG.SYS file. Use a text editor, such as Notepad in Windows or the EDIT command in DOS, to edit the file. You will need to try different IRQ and DMA settings until you find a combination that works. Look in your user's manual; it normally includes sample CONFIG.SYS files for you to copy and try with your computer. Remember, you need to reboot each time you make a change to the file.

DMA conflict

I recently installed a Pro Audio sound card in my system and have been having a weird problem ever since. When I try to run a program off my floppy, the computer locks up. I don't know whether the sound card has anything to do with it, but the timing is a little too coincidental, don't you think?

Very good. You've made me proud. One of the first rules of diagnosing computer problems is to figure out what has changed in your system recently.

You are definitely experiencing a DMA channel conflict here. I bet you have set the Pro Audio to use DMA channel 2. DMA 2 is usually reserved for the floppy drives. If a program tries to use the floppy and the sound card at the same time, a small-scale war breaks out in your system. The problem is that computer components can be rather greedy and absolutely hate to share system resources.

When the computer locks, you have to give the old three-finger salute to make your system operational again. That is, take out the floppy disk from the drive and press Ctrl+Alt+Del. If you're mad, you may want to give the one-finger salute first. Try setting the DMA channels for the Pro Audio card to 3, and I bet there is a cease-fire.

IRQ conflict

My computer locks up and gets stuck in parts of .WAV files. Does this mean I have some kind of hardware problem or a bad sound card?

If your sound card gets stuck playing one syllable, you haven't slipped into the Minimalist Composer Zone — you probably just have an IRQ conflict. It could be worse: it could be an IRS conflict. When that happens, you need to create a lot more hidden files. (You didn't hear that from me.)

When the sound card's interrupt is set incorrectly, the sound driver may play only the first 2K of data in the sound file, over and over again. In some instances, your system can lock up. Here's what to look for to prevent that from happening:

Make sure that the sound card's interrupt is correctly specified in the Control Panel's Drivers dialog box. (Highlight the sound card's driver and click the Setup button to get there.) Look for IRQ conflicts. Creative Labs's Sound Blaster Pro cards, for example, typically default to IRQ 5, whereas Media Vision's Pro Audio Spectrum cards use IRQ 7.

The repeating sound problem also may occur when the jumper setting on the sound card and the interrupt specified in the driver are not the same.

If you're certain that the driver settings for the sound card are correct, but .WAV sounds still repeat, the problem may be caused by a defective parallel port card. One of these can lock the interrupt lines so that the controller can't receive interrupt signals from the sound card.

Unknown IRQ setting

I'm trying to play Day of the Tentacle on my new 486DX2 with a Sound Blaster set at IRQ 10. The game doesn't have a setting for IRQ 10. Where do I put the IRQ setting?

Some people just have to do things their own way no matter what. When LucasArts released Day of the Tentacle, the company simply never expected people to have their Sound Blaster cards configured to an IRQ setting of 10. Instead, the company expected the IRQ to be 5 or 7, and it is in 99 percent of the systems.

549

You're not out of luck, though. Give LucasArts a call and ask for George. See if he has a patch that will help you. Even if he doesn't, it's still good to let him know. If enough people call in with the same problem, a software publisher will announce a fix or an update for a program. It's the squeaky blaster that gets all the oil.

Your second option is to use the Sound Blaster configuration program, SBCONFIG, to temporarily change the settings of your card. You'll find the SBCONFIG program in your Sound Blaster directory. You should be able to change the IRQ setting there.

Word to the wise: Before you change the IRQ settings, write the existing ones down in case the computer locks when you try the new settings. This action may save you hours of trying to figure out the settings that once worked and allow you to restore the card to its previous (and working) settings without pulling your hair out.

Other

Attaching sounds to events

I want to add sound to different events (such as when I open MS Works), but I can't seem to make it work. What am I doing wrong?

Are you sure you want to? That Beavis and Butthead sound clip might be fun the first time, but after a week or two, the novelty wears thin.

Still, some Windows system events benefit from the judicious application of a sound clip. For example, you can replace the default beep with a louder, more distinctive sound — that way you'll receive unmistakable feedback when it's time to swap disks during a lengthy installation.

To attach sounds to system events, open the Control Panel and double-click the Sound icon. System events are listed on the left side of the dialog box, available .WAV files on the right. By default, the dialog box lists only .WAV files in the WINDOWS directory, but you can browse through other directories in search of other sound clips. Highlight a system event and a matching sound clip; then click the Test button to preview the sound. Make sure that the Enable System Sounds box is checked; then press OK.

Although some of Windows's events are predefined (opening and closing Windows, for example) for you to attach sounds to, Windows doesn't have the capability to attach sounds to any other events. Adding a clip to the opening of MS Works, then, becomes a little trickier. To do this, you will need a third-party program such as Whoop It Up! from Advanced Support Group or Wired For Sound Pro by Aristosoft. Either of these programs will allow you to associate sounds with a myriad of events, ranging from launching applications to clicking OK in a dialog box.

Converting .VOC to .WAV

I'm fairly new to the world of computing, newer still to SBPro, and a babe in the woods when it comes to Windows. I've made a neat .VOC file (screaming babies) that I want to assign to a system event. At one point, a message stated that I needed to convert from .VOC to .WAV. How can I convert my Sound Blaster .VOC files to .WAV format?

As you have noticed, Windows doesn't support .VOC files, which are sound files that have been made using Sound Blaster's DOS-based sound recorder. You can make things a whole lot easier on yourself next time by using Sound Blaster's Windows-based sound recorder. For that matter, the Windows Sound Recorder in the Accessories group works just dandy with Sound Blaster cards for basic recording needs. You then can save the files as wave files (with the .WAV extension) and save yourself lots of time.

Because you have already gone to all the trouble of creating .VOC files (at least it was a good learning experience), the least I can do is help you convert them. If you bought your SBPro recently, you probably have a DOS utility called VOC2WAV in the SBPRO\VOCUTIL directory. At the DOS prompt, type the following and press the Enter key:

```
VOC2WAV BABIES.VOC BABIES.WAV
```

where the filename is BABIES.

Lack of memory

I just installed the Pro Audio 16 sound card in place of my old 8-bit Sound Blaster. Now Flight Simulator 5 tells me that it lacks conventional memory. X-Wing won't play the digitized sounds because it doesn't have enough memory. Why are these programs suddenly short of memory?

Basically, to support your new card's sound capabilities (hooray!), the manufacturer sent along with it new drivers that take up more conventional memory (boo!). You should try to squeeze every K of conventional memory out of your computer. This is covered in Chapter 8. If you don't feel like reading every question in Chapter 8 (I can't blame you — it's about as interesting as a C prompt), look in the index under *MEMMAKER*. But, even after you maximize your computer's memory, sometimes the darn game still won't work.

A boot disk is the 99 percent cure. A *boot disk* is a floppy disk that you put in drive A when you start your computer. The disk contains the bare minimum configuration necessary to play the game. *Note:* Make sure that you copy the device drivers for the sound card to the disk, too.

Start your computer with the boot disk and try the game again. Many folks have this problem, and I've noticed that game manuals are starting to include sample AUTOEXEC.BAT and CONFIG.SYS files. Remember: Make backup copies of your AUTOEXEC.BAT and CONFIG.SYS files before you start changing these files.

Adding memory to a card

I have a Gravis Ultrasound sound card and would like to add memory to it, bringing it up to 1MB (256K comes with the card). What kind of chips do I need?

Erik Estrada was always my favorite. If you want to upgrade the memory on your GUS, you should probably skip the Latino actors and purchase some Dynamic RAM chips, or *DRAM*. You need to get 256K × 4 DRAM chips with a speed rating of between 70 and 100 nanoseconds. The guys at the local computer repair shop can probably order them for you. Or you can order them through a mail-order dealer. You'll find lots of companies that sell memory chips in the back of almost any computer magazine. But the computer store around the corner will put the chips in the computer for you, too.

Computer is too fast

I have a 486, and many games can't find my Sound Blaster card. Sierra tells me the machine's bus is too fast. Does this mean I'll never get to play Leisure Suit Larry?

Many older software computer games use CPU-dependent methods for calculating the delay between commands. So, when the CPU becomes faster, the delay is shortened, and the game doesn't work properly.

There is a temporary and a permanent fix for your predicament. The temporary fix is to disengage the turbo button on your CPU while the game loads. When you hear the game's music, reengage the turbo button. Makes a lot of sense, doesn't it? Spend all that money on a fast machine and then slow it down on purpose. Go figure. (There is a super-duper turbo to slow it down even more: the power switch. Ha ha, sometimes I'm just too much.)

I prefer the permanent fix. Call Creative Labs's technical support at 405-742-2345 and ask them to mail you the 486BDRV.EXE driver update. If you have a modem, you can download the file from the Creative Labs's BBS. The telephone number to call is 405-742-6660 (14,400 bps, 8 bits, 1 stop bit, no parity). If you have an account with an on-line service, check there, too. Most times, software program updates are also available on company forums, such as the Creative Labs forum on CompuServe.

Sound card won't support Adlib

Why won't my sound card work with programs that call for Adlib support in Windows? It seems to work fine when I run the program through DOS.

For some strange reason, people like to go poking around in the Control Panel. They just get these unexplained urges to see what's in there. You wouldn't believe the things they do. Everything from password-protecting screen savers (and then, of course, they forget the password) to changing the color scheme. One guy changed all the colors to black and then couldn't see anything on-screen. The point is this: By any chance, did you play around in the Drivers section?

On more than one occasion, people have "cleaned up" the drivers they felt they didn't need and removed the Adlib driver. After all, they have a Sound Blaster or a Pro Audio card. Why in the world would they need an Adlib driver? But a lot of programs still use Adlib sound. Almost all sound cards sold today have the capability to emulate an Adlib card, so this isn't usually a problem — as long as the driver is installed.

Take a look in the Driver section of the Control Panel and see whether Adlib is listed. You can install it very easily from your Windows 3.1 disks.

Windows/Sound Blaster conflict

Why does my 8-bit Sound Blaster card keep locking up Windows? I'm 18, and I want to play some video games.

How does it feel to be 18 years old and behind the times? Imagine how I feel, and I'm not even old enough to be your mother.

You're not giving me enough information to answer your question. But here are some typical problems that cause a sound card and Windows to enter into a lip lock.

Often, some older Sound Blaster cards are not fully compatible with the new audio schemes used by today's programs. At the DOS prompt, change to the Sound Blaster directory in your computer. Once there, run the Sound Blaster test program by typing the following and pressing Enter:

```
TEST-SB
```

Check the DSP version number. If it's version 1.05, upgrading the DSP to 2.00 should fix your problems. The older DSP couldn't keep up with the new multimedia standards such as Windows 3.1 and newer games that use digitized audio extensively. The DSP upgrade costs around $30 and is available from Creative Labs. Call Creative Labs technical support to order the DSP upgrade.

You might be better off to take this opportunity to buy a better sound board (such as an SBPro or SB16). Or, if the Sound Blaster is still OK, you can buy the Sound Blaster 2.0 for around $75. It will give you a line-level input for recording and has a 2.01 DSP.

Another very common problem with sound cards is bad configuration settings. If the IRQ or DMA selected for your card is also being used by something else in your computer, all kinds of strange things happen. Try experimenting a little with different settings and see whether that clears things up. Do yourself a huge favor first. Make a backup copy of your original AUTOEXEC.BAT file. Then use the SBCONFIG program found in your Sound Blaster directory. It will let you try different configurations to see what works best.

Compressing sound files

Is there a way to compress sound files? They take up so much room!

Imagine if you could listen to a sound file while it was still compressed. You could have a whole evening's entertainment in six minutes and still have time for "Northern Exposure."

You're right, a stereo-quality file of my voice recorded for one minute at 44.1KHz in 16 bits takes 10MB of disk space. Clearly, a handful of high-quality sound files adds up quickly. But normal compression techniques don't work. In fact, sound files aren't compressed well, if at all, by DriveSpace, Stacker, or PKZip. A special form of compression works best. A number of sound board manufacturers use ADPCM (*A*daptive *D*ifferential *P*ulse *C*ode *M*odulation), a form of audio compression that compresses files by as much as 4:1. Motion Picture Experts Group (MPEG) has put out another standard for both audio and video that can compress files up to 12:1.

Unfortunately, compressing sound files removes some fidelity from the original recording. And software-based compression can place a considerable strain on the processor. However, the worst problem is portability: virtually no sound device plays the files compressed by another device unless the devices share a standard.

The Bottom Line

Sound-file compression isn't easy or practical for most users. Newer sound boards, however, have built-in, real-time compression as well as the capability to compress speech data to one-eighth or one-tenth of its original size. Unless you have a sound board that offers enhanced compression, do your recordings at a lower frequency, which results in smaller files.

Recording

Recording on the dark side of the moon

I want to record some Pink Floyd as either a .WAV or a .VOC file. How can I record more than 60 seconds using the Windows Sound Recorder?

I don't know, 60 seconds is more than enough Pink Floyd for me. Otherwise, all my computing becomes depressing and suicidal. I hope you have lots of tissues, Prozac, and hard disk space available. Sound files tend to take up lots and lots of disk space. For an entire Pink Floyd song, I'm talking megabytes. Even Megadeth requires megabytes.

To record a .WAV file longer than 60 seconds with the Windows Sound Recorder (found in the Accessories group), open the application and choose File⇨New. Disconnect the microphone (or other sound input source) from the back of the card. This action will keep you from accidentally recording room noises. Click the record button and let the Sound Recorder run for 60 seconds. When it finishes, save the file as BLANK.WAV. Then choose File⇨New again. Select Edit⇨Insert File and insert BLANK.WAV. Each time you insert BLANK.WAV, you make the file 60 seconds longer.

You can keep doing this until the file is long enough to accommodate your Pink Floyd taste. Then just rewind and record your tunes right over this blank file. Remember to reconnect the sound cables to your sound card before you start recording.

Making .WAVs

I am a '70s disco music fan. I want to put certain parts of certain songs on my Windows desktop. For example, when I start Windows, it would be great to hear "Do the Hustle." What do I need to make my own .WAV files?

"Do the Hustle"? Yeah, that won't get old fast. I bet you won't be a '70s music fan for long.

Basically, you need to play the song "Do the Hustle" on your stereo and record that clip as a computer file. To do so, you need a sound card, a microphone or some other sound input source, and a recording program. Most sound cards come with their own .WAV file recorder/players. For example, Pro Audio cards come with Pocket Recorder. If, by some strange twist of fate, you don't have the software that came with your sound card, you can use the Windows Sound Recorder in your Accessory group.

Raising the recording volume

I have been trying to record something for my wife as a .WAV file, but the sound comes out so low I can hardly hear it. I want to figure this out so that I can surprise my wife by having it play when Windows starts. Any suggestions?

Yeah, marry the bionic woman. She had great hearing.

Sound cards usually come with a mixer program for Windows that enables the user to turn on and off channels, control equalization (bass and treble), and control volume. Check the manual that came with your sound card for information on how to use this mixer program. After you have located this program and are familiar with its general use, make sure of the following:

- ➤ The microphone channel is turned on.
- ➤ The input level for the microphone is turned up.
- ➤ If the input channel has a switch for choosing line input or microphone input, then set it for microphone input.

Changing sound defaults

Why does Windows default the microphone to off? Whenever I start Windows, I must turn the microphone on in the Sound Blaster settings box. Is there any way that I can change the default?

Here's a novel idea: The next time you turn the microphone on, save the settings.

No matter what model of Sound Blaster you have, the Windows Sound Blaster mixer has the capability to save settings. The location of this command varies from model to model, but it is usually in a drop-down menu in the mixer or in the command menu in the upper-left corner of the mixer. After you change the microphone setting to on, save the settings. That way, no matter how many times you close and reopen Windows, the microphone will default to being on.

Hooking up the musical keyboard

How do I hook up a MIDI keyboard to my computer?

I've always envied people with musical talent. Unfortunately, I'm about as melodic as a piano tumbling down the stairs.

To hook up that MIDI keyboard to your computer, you need an expansion card with MIDI support built into it. You may want to buy a sound card with MIDI capabilities. Most of the sound cards today have a MIDI port, and some even include basic MIDI editing software. You will also need some kind of MIDI composition software, such as Midisoft Studio for Windows or SuperJAM! by Blue Ribbon Soundworks. These programs allow you to record, arrange, and play back music.

What effects will higher frequency have?

Is there a downside to recording a sound file at a higher frequency?

Yes, a mega downside. For instance, a 60-second, 16-bit .WAV file recorded at 44.1KHz can take 10MB of hard drive space! Yikes! Not exactly the best way to use drive space. The question is, is there an upside? It sounds better. But if you record at a higher frequency and share the file with other people who don't have sound cards as sophisticated as yours, they won't be able to play the file.

Chapter 15
OS/2

 OS/2 features

I've seen the OS/2 Warp commercials, but I have no idea what it is? Do I need it?

Basically, OS/2 is a 32-bit multitasking operating system that offers some significant advantages over DOS and Windows.

It runs nearly all of your DOS and Windows programs; most DOS programs run somewhat faster under OS/2, while Windows programs seem to run about the same (some a little slower, some a little faster). As a result, if you use one program at a time, things will be about the same. But OS/2 goes further and lets you run them all at once. For example, you can work in Word for Windows while you run your DOS Links386Pro golf game while you download a file from your favorite on-line service while you format a floppy disk and so on. I have no idea why you'd want to, but you could. No particular application may work that much faster, but you will be a lot faster because you don't have to wait for one thing to finish before you go on to the next. It feels as if the computer is working for you, rather than the other way around.

The graphical interface that comes with OS/2, the Workplace Shell, is object-oriented and very powerful. Do you want to delete a file? Just drag it to the shredder. Copying and moving files is just as easy. And you can print a document by dragging it to the printer. You can organize the Workplace Shell (that is, your desktop) any way you want, making folders that are task-specific and contain a variety of different types of objects, so you can open one folder that holds everything you need for a project.

If you choose to use the High Performance File System (HPFS), you can use long filenames, such as *Letter to Mom for Money, December 1, 1995* instead of *Letter2.Mom*. (While DOS and Windows applications will run on the HPFS system, they'll probably only be able to save files with the traditional 8.3 naming convention though. Bummer.)

Plus, if you're tired of fighting DOS for memory, you can take advantage of the fact that OS/2 sees all installed memory the same — no more 640K limits.

If you have a modem, the superb Internet Access Kit that is included with the latest version of OS/2 hooks up to the Internet very easily, connecting to IBM's service provider or the local provider of your choice. Be careful: This can be addicting!

The Bottom Line

To sum it up: If you are happy with everything about your computer now, don't make the change. If you want to increase your productivity and fun, though, OS/2 is worth a serious look. And I don't even make a percentage from OS/2 sales.

OS/2 for Windows

I've heard that OS/2 for Windows is lightweight compared to regular OS/2. What's the deal? How does the vanilla OS/2 compare to Windows?

Contrary to popular belief, OS/2 for Windows isn't OS/2 lite. It is full-blown OS/2 that takes advantage of the Windows 3.1 already installed on your computer. In fact, when you have OS/2 for Windows and Windows 3.1 on your computer, you have a full copy of OS/2. (The "for Windows" lets you know that the program is designed to run with Windows.)

The Bottom Line

There are two major differences between regular OS/2 and OS/2 for Windows. First, OS/2 for Windows costs less. IBM doesn't have to pay Mr. Gates for the Windows code because he got his cut when the manufacturer or you put Windows on your system. Second, OS/2 for Windows takes up less hard disk space. When you install full OS/2, you are essentially installing a second copy of Windows if you already have Windows on your system.

The latest and greatest version of OS/2 — OS/2 Warp — is also "for Windows" and is far from lightweight. It has tons of enhancements and new features, from cosmetic changes (such as more desktop color schemes and glitzy animated icons) to significant functional additions (for example, built-in Internet access). In addition, it is designed to run on a computer with only 4MB of RAM; of course, fast computers with lots of RAM will always outperform their weaker cousins.

Q & A *Learning OS/2*

At my new job, the company uses OS/2 for Windows. I have used Windows 3.1, but I'm a little concerned about the OS/2 part. Does it work pretty much the same? Are there any tips that you can give me that would help me survive my first days of using OS/2 for Windows? I feel like I'm losing something that is close to me.

Hey, come back to earth. It's just a computer program. It's not your cat they're replacing.

Komando
Klues

Use your knowledge of Windows in the Windows applications you know; all your favorite Windows functions are still there. If you get homesick for the Windows gestalt, launch a full-screen Win-OS/2 session.

Nonetheless, here are a few reasons to enjoy the switch:

➤ To make the desktop more comfortable, open the OS/2 System folder on the desktop and double-click on the Command Prompts folder. Double-click on the Full-screen Win-OS/2 icon. Look: There in the Main group is the Control Panel, where you can customize the desktop settings as if you never left home. When the day's work is done, exit the Windows session just like you normally would (mouse clicks or Alt+F4) back to the OS/2 Program Manager. A right-click brings up the OS/2 System menu. Now, choose Shut Down.

➤ Try out the multitasking by formatting a floppy while you open and use an application. Try dialing up an on-line service and downloading a file while you play a game and play some music from a CD. (Wait until your boss is away, or if you're the boss, wait until your secretary is away.) After you do these sorts of things, you'll begin to multitask everything, never fearing that things will crash.

➤ Now that you feel more at home, go crazy. Try making icons so that you can launch Windows applications directly from Program Manager. To do so, open the OS/2 System folder and then the Templates folder. Drag a program template (by holding down the right mouse button) to a blank space on the Program Manager and drop it (release the mouse button). A notebook will open, waiting for you to make a few decisions. You can find an application by clicking on the Locate button to search for the application you want. When you've found the application, click on the Session tab of the notebook to define whether this will be a windowed or a full-screen session (you can always change your mind later). The default settings for WIN-OS/2 Settings are fine for most applications. Click on the General tab and fix the program name. You'll probably want something more appropriate than the default, which is Program. This is where you can change or edit icons associated with the application, too. When you're done, double-click on the upper-left-hand corner of the notebook to close it (or press Alt+F4).

OS/2 manuals and help

My new computer had OS/2 on it, but there were no OS/2 manuals in the box. Three days after I bought my computer, the store went out of business. How do I find help?

How do *you* find help? How about that computer retailer? He should have bought my audio learning system, "50 Ways to Make Money with Your Home Computer." (Hey, it's my product and this is my book. I'll plug what I want.)

The truth of the matter is no one got a manual for OS/2 2.0. IBM never made one. (Not that anyone actually reads the software manuals, but they do make good doorstops.) Manuals are included with Versions 2.1 and 3.0, but they are only designed to help you get started; that is, they tell you how to install OS/2 and configure it, give some help for installation problems, and explain how to do basic procedures.

In place of a three-inch thick manual, IBM gives you the most extensive on-line help system around. If you ever feel befuddled, just press the F1 key. OS/2 sends in the cavalry: the help files appropriate to your current activity are instantly brought to the screen.

IBM also provides a tutorial that has been completely reworked for Warp. It'll lead you through the essentials of working with the Workplace Shell, the object-oriented desktop. Sure, most people will ignore the tutorial and just start working, but it'll prevent a few headaches.

If you're really bored and feel like perusing the help files, just use the Master Help Index. Just double-click on the program object that looks like an address book with a question mark and while away the hours.

If you need more help, go to a bookstore and scan the computer section for OS/2 how-to books. But do yourself a favor before laying down the charge card. Take a peek at the book's index and first few chapters to get an idea for the level of reader the book is geared toward. And, check out the books with a disk or CD-ROM in the back.

Hey, I hope you're not reading this book in some store. If you are, don't be such a cheapo. Buy the book. My mother needs new shoes.

OS/2 compatibility with Windows 3.11

I have used the Windows 3.11 patch on my system. Can I still install OS/2 for Windows? The system requirements call for Windows 3.1.

The first version of OS/2 for Windows came out before the Windows 3.11 patch. When the patch came out, OS/2 for Windows initially could no longer work with Windows. A fix was soon prepared, though, and all later copies work with Windows 3.11. All copies of the newest version of OS/2 for Windows will work just fine with Windows 3.11.

OS/2 system requirements

I have a 386SX 16 with an 80MB hard drive and 4MB of RAM. Will OS/2 or OS/2 for Windows work on my system?

If you are a good person, kind to little animals, and the powers that be smile down on you, then maybe OS/2 will work. Your system barely meets the minimum system requirements for OS/2, and we all know that *minimum system requirements* is doublespeak for *maybe*. You'd certainly be happier with a better, faster, and more expensive computer. But wouldn't we all?

OS/2 needs, at the very least, a 386SX CPU. If you have one of those handy little chips that upgrades a 286 to a 386, get outta here. OS/2 wants the real McCoy. A 386DX 33 machine works pretty well, and, of course, a 486 or Pentium is great. The bare-bones amount of RAM is 4MB, but anyone who has ever used OS/2 will tell you to get more. Having more applications open at the same time requires more memory, and, ultimately, everyone wants to run a lot of things at the same time with OS/2. The latest version of OS/2, Warp, runs fairly well with 4MB of RAM, but for real multitasking power, 8MB is the bottom line.

A
563

No one will ever accuse OS/2 of being a lightweight program: it commandeers about 30MB of hard disk space. As a result, OS/2 won't leave you much room for your programs or data files if you stay with that 80MB hard drive.

The Bottom Line

The system you really need for OS/2 is a 486 machine with at least 8MB of RAM and a large hard drive (300MB or higher).

Q&A *Converting to OS/2 from DOS and Windows*

I use DOS 6.22 and Windows 3.1. I'd like to change my system to be all OS/2. Must I erase DOS and Windows altogether, or will the OS/2 installation take care of this for me?

OS/2 is different from the DOS of yesterday and today: OS/2 gives users a great deal of flexibility in configuring their systems. You don't have to make any decisions — there is a default installation — but you will probably be happier with your system if you take the time and effort to plan ahead. You have a few options.

OS/2 will live in harmony with your current DOS and Windows installations and applications, if that's what you want. Because you already have Windows 3.1 on your machine, there's no need to buy Windows again, which is what you do if you buy the "full" version of OS/2. Get OS/2 for Windows; it will find and use your existing Windows code. All versions of OS/2 contain their own DOS in the OS/2 directory MDOS. It is this DOS that is used for running DOS applications in OS/2. Although you don't really need to keep MS-DOS 6.22 on your machine at all, you might someday want to boot DOS instead of OS/2. If you have decided to run only OS/2's High Performance File System (HPFS), which allows for long filenames (among other things), then you can make your old DOS go away. *Note:* Installing the HPFS means reformatting, which means reinstalling all of your applications, including Windows.

Remember, while OS/2 for Windows will save you a couple of dollars, the installation will expect to find Windows. If you've just reformatted for HPFS, OS/2 won't find Windows because Windows must have an operating system to install to, and DOS is gone. You don't have to chase your tail in this apparent Catch-22 situation, however: You can install OS/2 for Windows without Windows. When the system is up and running, use the OS/2 Selective Install function to add Windows support.

If you don't want to think, the default installation for OS/2 Warp will detect your system hardware and install OS/2 to the computer's C drive. Keep feeding it disks until it's done. By the way, have your Windows installation disks handy. The OS/2 installation program will want to update the Windows files, too.

DOS utilities in OS/2

I use the DOS utilities SCANDISK and DEFRAG to maintain my hard disk. Should I be using OS/2 utilities instead of DOS utilities?

You might be able to continue using your DOS-based utilities without a problem; on the other hand, you could end up thoroughly trashing OS/2 if you run SCANDISK on an OS/2 bootable drive. Your best bet is to buy OS/2 utilities, such as SoftTouch Systems's GammaTech Utilities for OS/2 (405-947-8080). This program offers optimization, reporting, and maintenance utilities comparable to those found in Norton and PC Tools.

The DOS utilities that you use find and repair some routine problems that crop up from time to time on a disk drive. In case you're wondering, the most common errors are lost clusters, file size mismatches, and crosslinked files. These problems sound pretty horrible, but SCANDISK is the DOS utility that makes the errors all better — most of the time, anyway.

Want to know more about those errors? Good. I like people who are on a quest for knowledge. Plus, if you understand the error messages, you'll better understand my answer.

Lost clusters are partial file entries taking up room on the disk without corresponding entries in the FAT table. The FAT table is like a table of contents; it is where DOS keeps track of which file is written to which cluster. The clusters are "found" when SCANDISK clears out the FAT for those clusters.

Similarly, if the size of a file does not match the FAT entry, an adjustment is made. (In the days before SCANDISK, utilities performed these services with the surgical precision of a chainsaw: they simply cut off part of the file to make it fit.)

Crosslinked files happen when two different files have been assigned to the same cluster on the disk, according to the FAT. The DOS CHKDSK command doesn't have a clue about fixing crosslinked files, but SCANDISK is better. In essence, one of the files is copied, the original is deleted, and then the copy is rewritten to a new location and the FAT is updated accordingly.

OS/2's EAs, or extended attributes, are file attributes that go beyond the usual Read-only, System, Hidden, and Archive attributes that track a file's or program's characteristics. OS/2 keeps these characteristics in a special file, called *EA DATA*. Although DOS utilities should overlook a file completely if it has "illegal" characters in its name — say, spaces — EAs are not safe from the actions of a utility program. In fact, the EAs may get mangled by a disk utility.

The Bottom Line

The bottom line: OS/2's CHKDSK will take care of lost clusters and size mismatches, and the RECOVER utility will move files from bad sectors on the hard drive and mark those sectors out; both utilities are, necessarily, "EA-aware." Still, all in all, get GammaTech Utilities for OS/2. You can thank me later.

Advanced hardware compatibility with OS/2

I currently run DOS 6.2 and Windows for Workgroups 3.11. I have a 486DX 33, 270MB hard disk, 8MB of RAM, CD-ROM, Sound Blaster 16-bit card, Diamond Stealth Pro VLB, and an HP 550C printer. I have read a little about OS/2, but other than 32-bit processing, I can't see much reason to switch. Am I missing something by not using OS/2 or OS/2 for Windows? Would you see any problems with my computer setup and using either variety of OS/2?

Are you missing something? IBM thinks so, but OS/2 is its product.

Forget the *bit processing* in the phrase *32-bit processing*. Instead, picture a 32-lane freeway. See the cars. See the trucks. See the carpool lanes with no cars in them. The point is that you can move more traffic on a 32-lane freeway than on a 16-lane freeway. But this is not just a freeway. It's a highway. But it's not just a highway. It's the (c'mon, everyone) information superhighway.

Since creating the 80386 chip, Intel has manufactured a line of computer chips that can handle 32-bit processing. DOS is a 16-bit operating system, whether the name on the box is IBM, Microsoft, or another DOS vendor. The 32-bit system handles more traffic — or in computer talk, has more *processing power* — than its predecessor chips.

Now, in order not to abandon users who had invested in software for their XT (8-bit Intel 8088 CPU) and AT (16-bit Intel 80286 CPU) machines, DOS has been maintained specifically to be *backward compatible*. The reasoning is that people who spend lots of money purchasing software will not be inclined to change to a new operating system that doesn't run that software. As hardware gets better diversified, and software developers create ever-more-complex programs, the limitations of DOS have become more troublesome. Memory management is a prime example.

With 16-bit DOS as the operating system, it doesn't matter whether you have 4MB of RAM or 40MB of RAM — you still need to provide enough *program memory* (between 0 and 640K; also called *conventional memory*). Programs need conventional memory to run; then they squeeze device drivers and TSRs into the next 384K of memory. The need for memory management has not decreased at all; if anything, the situation is worse, thanks to the development of new devices and their necessary device drivers (MSCDEX for CD-ROM drives comes to mind).

With OS/2, you are no longer responsible for managing memory: if you add RAM, the operating system configures the memory. In fact, with 32-bit OS/2 applications, you *cannot* adjust program memory settings. Heck, there's no need to.

OS/2 has maintained backward compatibility for DOS and Windows applications, so you won't have to abandon your investment in software. OS/2 generally does such a good job of running programs designed for the DOS or Windows environments that developers are not inclined to write 32-bit versions. On the other hand, sticking to 16-bit applications (and backward compatibility) means that your DOS and Windows programs cannot take full advantage of the processing power of the 32-bit CPU. It's rather like intentionally de-tuning a high-performance engine because you can only get low octane fuel. When you use an application written for DOS, you have to live with DOS rules. Fortunately, in OS/2, each DOS application can have its own settings and, for the most part, the generic configuration is just fine.

OS/2 does Windows, but buy the newest OS/2 for Windows release, called *Warp*, because older versions didn't support Windows for Workgroups. Of course, OS/2 doesn't support the networking stuff in Windows for Workgroups yet, so if you use Windows for Workgroups for the peer-to-peer networking capability, you may want to wait until it is supported (or until IBM develops its own peer-to-peer capability).

567

You're concerned about your hardware, though. The early versions of OS/2 didn't include the drivers — software that allows hardware to interact with the operating system — to support a lot of video cards, and IBM received a lot of criticism. IBM had hoped that the video card manufacturers would write the drivers for their products, but this turned out to be a long and slow process; in the end, IBM wrote many of them. Now, however, OS/2 Warp comes with the drivers to support most printers, video cards, sound cards, CD-ROMs, and so on; most manufacturers are keeping up on their own, so new video cards, for example, are likely to come with OS/2 drivers.

Note: Ultimately, this answer is about money and who tries to separate you from it. The computer industry is a multibillion dollar industry — and we helped create it. We, users, wave our dollars around, yelling, "Hey, we want more, and we want it better, and we want it faster." Hardware and software developers scurry, trying to make us happy enough to give them our dollars. Today, computers are the new status symbols, cutting across socioeconomic boundaries: you don't have to be wealthy to own a top-of-the-line personal computer.

Using OS/2 for Windows without using Windows

Call me nuts, but I just can't get the hang of Windows. I saw OS/2 for Windows, though, and I'd like to put it on my computer. Can I use OS/2 for Windows if I don't have Windows? I am a DOS man.

You're nuts. I mean, you bet!

OS/2 for Windows actually means *OS/2 without Windows* because it doesn't include any Windows code. You may use your own copy of Windows with it, but OS/2 does just fine without it. You'll save a few megabytes of hard disk space, too, if that's a concern.

By the way, DOSman sounds like a new comic book character. I can see it now: "Join DOSman as he flies into adventure, leaping from Windows with only a blinking cursor by his side."

OS/2 compatibility with DOS programs

I have tons of DOS programs. Will OS/2 run *all* my DOS programs?

At once? No. Actually, the answer depends on which of the gazillions of DOS (and Windows) programs you have. The following categories of programs do not work correctly with OS/2:

➤ DOS extenders that require exclusive access to the 80386 control registers, such as the Virtual Control Program Interface (VCPI). These are mostly older programs (including some games).

➤ Programs that directly address the physical disk sectors to perform disk-write operations. This category includes most DOS undelete programs, AutoCAD XII, Bound Checker, Comanche, Fax Concentrator, Magic-CV, MusicPrinter Plus 4.0, Oracle (there is an OS/2 version of this program), PharLap DOS extenders prior to Version 4.0, Smartfax, Soft-ICE, Splash 1.01, Turbo Debugger, and Ultima VII.

WIN-OS/2 does not support real-mode programs. Also, Windows enhanced mode programs that load specific Windows 3.1 virtual device drivers (.386 or .VXD) will not run in WIN-OS/2 enhanced compatibility mode; this mode uses an unsupported method. Some of these programs will run in WIN-OS/2 standard mode. To run these programs, set the WIN_RUN_MODE setting to Standard.

Installing OS/2 on compressed hard drives

My hard drive is compressed with DriveSpace. Can I install OS/2, or will I have problems?

The disk-compression software that is included with MS-DOS is not compatible with OS/2 and should be removed prior to installing OS/2. If you're tight on hard disk space (and you probably are, or you wouldn't be using disk compression), this means you'll probably need to back up your data and then restore it after OS/2 has been installed.

But wait! You still may not have enough room after the installation, especially because OS/2 takes up quite a bit of space. You can buy disk compression products for OS/2, however, notably Stacker for OS/2 by Stac Electronics and DCF/2 by Proportional Software. But you're going to have to spend a bit of money. You can find these programs at a local computer store or in computer mail-order catalogs.

  Komando Klues With the costs of hard drives falling fast, you might consider buying a second, larger hard drive instead of a compression program.

Using unmatched SIMMs with OS/2

I am about to totally give up on installing OS/2! I have tried disabling the cache, the shadowing, the turbo, everything, and I still can't get it to install. A friend of mine said it might be because of my SIMMs. I have four 1 × 9 chips and four 1 × 3 chips. What do you think?

I think your friend should write a computer advice book, because that's probably the answer. OS/2 demands quite a bit from your hardware; if there are any problems, OS/2 finds them. In this case, it doesn't like the fact that your SIMMs are different. Because of the way OS/2 uses memory, it requires that all of your SIMMs work the same way, at the same speed. Unfortunately, your only solution is to get matching SIMMs; fortunately, you can probably trade in the old ones.

Exiting OS/2

What do I have to do to safely turn off the system in OS/2?

To turn off the system, either click the Shut Down button on the Launch Pad in the Warp version or choose Shut Down from the desktop menu. (Shortcut: Point to a blank part of the screen and click the right mouse button; from the system menu that appears, choose Shut Down.) The main advantage to these methods is that they force OS/2 to clear its cache and write everything to the disk that shouldn't be lost. You'll probably hear some disk activity, and then a box will appear that says that it is safe to shut off your system.

If you fail to use Shut Down, you may lose data that is held in the cache. You see, to speed up interactions with the user, OS/2 doesn't write everything to the hard disk right away; instead, it waits until things have slowed down a bit. This feature is known as Lazy Write. (It can be turned off if you prefer, but most people like it.)

Shut Down bugs

When I click on Shut Down, all I get is some message that says the system is shutting down. The message stays on-screen until I flip the big on/off switch. Although the system never shuts down, it starts fine and OS/2 loads the next time I turn it on. Kind of weird, huh? I mean, didn't those programmers ever once shut down their system?

This bug appeared in Version 2.1 of OS/2; the system actually shuts down fine but never tells you that everything is OK. This bug was fixed in the service pack, and it is also no longer a problem with Warp. If you are using a version with this problem, just wait until all disk activity has stopped after you choose Shut Down; it'll then be safe to switch off the computer or reboot.

OS/2 compression software

I really need more hard disk space, but I can't afford it. Which compression software programs are compatible with OS/2?

Times are tough right now. It's all a matter of perspective, though. I once felt bad because I had no shoes, until I met a man who had no feet. I asked, "Can I borrow your shoes?"

The two main compression programs that are compatible with OS/2 are Stacker for OS/2, by Stac Electronics, and DCF/2, by Proportional Software. Both have good reputations for reliability, safety, and speed. Plus, they promise the same 2:1 compression ratios that are available with the DOS compression utilities. As with those DOS programs, the OS/2 compression programs work invisibly in the background, compressing and decompressing on the fly. After installation, you have little to worry about.

The one confusing aspect of this is that OS/2 can see and use both the FAT and HPFS file formats. As yet, Stacker works with FAT systems but not with HPFS. DCF/2 does its compression onto HPFS partitions, but it can place FAT volumes there; DCF/2 cannot, however, compress FAT files onto a FAT-formatted partition.

The Bottom Line

Confused? Well, it's actually pretty easy: If you only use the FAT file format, your only choice is Stacker. If you only use the HPFS file format, your only choice is DCF/2. If you use a mix, you must decide which partitions to compress.

Komando Klues

By the way, other options are becoming available as more vendors become involved in OS/2. And you should pay attention to the falling prices of hard disks; they are becoming more affordable every day.

Choosing a boot system for OS/2

What is the difference between Boot Manager and Dual Boot? When would you choose one over the other, and why?

Both can start different operating systems. With Dual Boot, you go to a command line and type a command that reboots the computer in the other operating system; it's a convenient and easy way to switch between OS/2 and real DOS. If the OS/2 installation program detects DOS on your system, it will set up the Dual Boot option as the default unless you tell it differently.

The Boot Manager offers a bit more flexibility. When you boot the computer, you are given a choice of operating systems. You can install DOS, OS/2, UNIX, Windows NT, and so on or just other versions of OS/2 or DOS. Many people find that, even if they plan on installing only OS/2, it's useful to make a small (perhaps 0MB) partition for bare-bones OS/2 that can be used for tending the main OS/2 partition, if necessary; it's a lot faster than booting from a floppy.

If you intend to use the Dual Boot option, the installation procedure for OS/2 will handle all the details for you. If you use the Boot Manager, you must plan how you intend to organize before you start; be sure to read the sections in the User's Guide before you begin. Many OS/2 aficionados consider the Boot Manager the better choice because of the greater flexibility, but make sure you know ahead of time what you are going to do. Plan, plan, plan.

Komando Klues Whichever method you use, if you intend to keep real DOS you must remember that it can only see FAT-formatted drives. Don't make everything HPFS and plan on booting into real DOS. Of course, OS/2's version of DOS (included automatically) has no problem with the HPFS format.

Using Boot Manager with partitioned hard drives

I use OS/2 with a C startable partition and D drive. Both are compressed with Stacker for OS/2 and DOS. When the system is up, I thus have C, D, E, and F drives. Most of my DOS and Windows programs are on the C drive. I want to install OS/2 on the D drive. Is there any way I can put a Boot Manager partition on the D drive?

Wow, you have more drives than a rabbit in spring. Boot Manager resides in its own 1MB partition, so you must make space for it, and that space must be on the C drive. When your computer starts, it checks the A drive for a bootable floppy, if it doesn't find one, it checks your C drive. Your computer has no way of knowing that it should then go on and check the D drive. A software solution would be nice, but all this checking occurs before the operating system is even loaded, so there isn't a good way around it.

The Bottom Line So, you have to put the Boot Manager on the C drive somewhere, and it needs its own partition: you need to use FDISK to create the partition. FDISK can enlarge and shrink partitions that it has already created, but Stacker-created partitions are another story. As a result, the process of creating the Boot Manager partition will, unfortunately, clean off your C drive. Back it up, and then restore it again after you reinstall OS/2. (Ouch!)

Extended filenames

I have used DOS for years, but a few OS/2 terms have me scratching my head. What is the HPFS and what does it do for me?

Basically, DOS keeps a map of filenames and file locations. This is the File Allocation Table, called the FAT for short. The FAT is also where DOS charts your disk's bad sectors so that files aren't written to a damaged part of the disk.

OS/2 has a supercharged file system, called the High Performance File System (HPFS). This file system allows filenames as long as 254 characters, including the path. Longer filenames make it possible to give your files much more meaningful names. Instead of calling a file 93ENDYR.DAT, you can call it 1993 END OF YEAR MONEY TO GO SHOPPING. HPFS also is more resistant to file fragmentation, uses smaller cluster sizes, and can handle disks as large as 512 GB (that's 512 gigabytes, not megabytes!). On the downside, HPFS takes approximately 500K of system memory. If your system doesn't have more than 6MB of RAM, HPFS is not for you. It would slow your system down to a crawl.

Multitasking with OS/2 and Windows applications

When I was installing OS/2, I received a warning that said something about my video card not being able to support seamless Windows at a particular resolution. What is meant by *seamless* Windows, and is this something I should be concerned about?

There's not a thread of truth in it. The very fabric of truth falls apart at the seams.

Actually, *seamless* refers to the ability to run a Windows application on the OS/2 desktop in a window, right next to DOS and OS/2 applications. If you intend to do much multitasking, and you probably will after a while, it is a very nice feature; you don't have to shut down a full-screen Windows session to switch to another application. Most makers of video cards now provide drivers so OS/2 can run Windows in seamless mode (and full-screen, too). Call your video card's manufacturer and ask for the updated drivers for OS/2.

OS/2 video installation

I want to try a higher resolution for graphics. Do I have to reinstall OS/2 from scratch, or can I adjust the video card settings?

You don't need to reinstall OS/2, but the procedure for switching resolutions depends on the video card that you have. With some cards, you just need to choose a new resolution from the System object in the System

Setup folder. The resolutions that your card supports are listed in the window on the first page. Pick a new resolution from the list and reboot; that's all there is to it.

A few cards, though, require a different installation program that sets the resolution. This program is not complex or difficult, but does require you to answer a few questions and (possibly) insert a floppy with the appropriate driver. At the command prompt, type the following and press Enter to start the program:

```
DSPINSTL
```

If you really mess things up and are too embarrassed to ask for help, you can restore VGA mode by rebooting and then waiting for a small white box to appear in the upper-left-hand corner of your screen. When you see it, press Alt+F1. You'll be given some Recovery Choices (sounds ominous), from which you should choose V. You can now try your new driver again.

What if you buy a new video card? Put in your card, reboot, and then restore your system to VGA mode. After boot-up is completed, open the System Setup folder (usually within the OS/2 System folder) and choose Selective Install. Choose Primary Display from the window that appears, select the driver from the choices presented to you, press OK, and follow the instructions. If this process sounds complex, don't let it scare you; it is actually very simple and straightforward.

Compatibility with Phoenix BIOS

I just installed OS/2 for Windows on a Dell Latitude 433c with a Phoenix BIOS 486 S v.1.01. Everything seems to work, except when I start DOS and Windows programs from OS/2. They are still accessible from DOS through a dual boot. I get a SYS3176 message that says, *An illegal instruction exception was generated when an attempt was made to execute an instruction whose operation was not defined for the host machine architecture.* **What does this mean in real life, and how do I fix it?**

In real life, it means there is some lonely engineer at Phoenix BIOS who wants you to call and ask him to explain its meaning. No ordinary human can figure that out. Fortunately, I am no ordinary human.

Some older Phoenix BIOSs have problems with OS/2; a BIOS chip upgrade is probably the solution. Call the manufacturer of your computer and tell them that you are having problems running OS/2 with their computer; they should be able to tell you what you need to fix it.

Speeding up OS/2

What can I do to speed things up in OS/2? I have a 486DX2 66 computer with 8MB of RAM, but the thing is so slow. Are there any memory tricks you can tell me about? The biggest program I run is Lotus SmartSuite, and it crawls.

The amount of RAM you have is adequate to run one program. If you are going to multitask, 8MB probably isn't really enough to move at good speed with large programs. Getting more RAM is probably the best solution.

There are other things you can do to tweak the system. Open the settings for your SmartSuite applications and make sure that DOS is loaded high and that UMBs (upper memory blocks) are enabled. (Although OS/2 doesn't have a 640K limit, DOS programs need to think that they're running on a traditional DOS system, so OS/2 pretends to be DOS.) In the same settings, you can increase the amount of EMS (expanded memory), XMS (extended memory), or DPMI (DOS *p*rotected *m*ode *i*nterface *m*emory), whichever your application happens to need. For SmartSuite, try increasing the DPMI limit to 8 or 12MB. Don't worry about not having that much RAM; OS/2 will make use of the Swapfile if the application actually needs that much space.

Software caching

I'm trying *real* hard to get OS/2 running, but I am always encountering crosslink errors. There is nothing wrong with my hard drive. It works fine under MS-DOS and passes the system diagnostics. Under OS/2, the problem is so persistent that I often can't even run the DIR **command!**

How are you shutting down? OS/2 (and Windows) uses software caching to store data temporarily until it is convenient to write the data to the hard drive. This speeds up the performance of the system like a magic carpet, but adds an element of vulnerability: if the computer is turned off before the cache has been flushed (the data written to the drive), the cache has had the magic carpet pulled out from under it. The operating system can no longer direct the writing of the data, and the results can be just what you're seeing — massive check disk errors.

First, always shut down OS/2 with software; don't just turn off the machine. Use the Shut Down button from the Launch Pad, or click the right mouse button to bring up the system menu and then choose the Shut Down option. Wait until the system message appears, telling you that shutdown is complete and that it is now safe to reboot (or power down) your computer. If you have a caching controller (a hardware cache on the controller card), it still may not be safe to turn off (or reboot) the computer; wait until all drive activity has stopped.

You can disable the write-delay cache for FAT drives by editing the OS/2 CONFIG.SYS line DISKCACHE=256,LW to remove the LW. Your data will be written directly to the hard drive, even if you have to wait for it; the downside of disabling the Lazy Write cache is that the system performance suffers.

On HPFS drives, the cache is enabled (by default) in the OS/2 CONFIG.SYS by the line IFS=F:\OS2\HPFS.IFS /CACHE:256 /CRECL:4 /AUTOCHECK: [dd]. If you want to disable the cache during an OS/2 session, you can enter **CACHE /LAZY:OFF** at an OS/2 command prompt. There is no equivalent command line for a FAT drive. To make such a change permanent, add RUN=[d]:\OS2\CACHE /LAZY:OFF to the OS/2 CONFIG.SYS. The cache can be disabled for both FAT and HPFS drives, making certain that data will not be lost in a buffer, but properly shutting down the system is a better route.

Moving and duplicating program objects

How do I put program objects on the desktop instead of in folders?

How do you move a refrigerator upstairs? Drag it. How do you prove that your hot rod is better than the guy's next to you? Drag it. What do you do when you want to dress up in women's clothes and parade around the house. . . My point is: To put any object on the desktop, just drag it from its folder with the right mouse button depressed.

577

However, you might find it best to keep program objects (.EXE files) in their folders (directories); instead, place a program reference object on the desktop. A *program reference object* is not the .EXE file itself, but an object that launches the program.

Sure, if you double-click on the program reference object, the program will start just as if you double-click on the program object, but there are some other advantages: First, the program reference object contains fields for entering command line parameters, so you can start a program with switches and change the way the program runs. Second, since the program reference object is not the program itself, if it gets deleted (for example, if you accidentally drag it to the shredder), the program still resides safely in its own folder, unaffected. And, third, many programs require access to other files within their directories (folders); if you drag the program object out of that folder, it may not know where its auxiliary files are located.

Object shadows

Should I shadow an object? I'm afraid I might screw something up.

Shadows and Objects. Sounds like a Fellini movie.

Don't be afraid of your shadows. A *shadow* is a kind of copy of an object, but it is still connected to the original object; changes made to a shadow are also seen in the original object. The exception: If the shadow is deleted, the original object is not; this is one of the advantages of using shadows.

The other main reason is convenience. For example, suppose that you want to create a folder on the desktop with everything that you need for a particular work project: a word processor, a spreadsheet, and the files that those applications use. Well, you could drag the program reference objects for the word processor and the spreadsheet into that folder, but then what happens when you want to access them from other folders? You would have to open that work project folder each time. Instead, you can make shadows of those program reference objects and have them available from within that work folder. The same goes for the data files; you can keep them safely in their home folder but still have access to them through the work folder.

Disabling animations

Those explosions when I open a folder or a window have grown old. How do I get rid of them?

What a party pooper! IBM tries to jazz things up a little, but you're still not happy! Hey, I have an idea. How about keeping the explosion and putting a disgusted sigh after it?

You can get rid of the explosion animations if you really want. Open up your OS/2 System folder and rummage around till you find the System Setup folder. Open it up and look around for the System object. From your handy-dandy System Notebook, click on the Windows tab and then click on the Disabled button under Animations. The party's over.

Changing the window font

Is it possible to change the standard OS/2 system font (the font used for window titles and window text)?

Yes. Open the System Setup folder and then the Scheme Palette. Open the scheme that you are currently using (it's the one that's highlighted) by double-clicking on it; then browse the list on the right to find Icon Text. Click on this option to choose it. There you can change the font. (You can even change the font color, if you want! Anything to procrastinate.) You can see your changes in the sample window, on the left. When you are done, close the scheme window and then drag (hold down the right mouse button) the scheme icon to the desktop. If you want the changes to apply to every folder window, hold down the Alt key as you drag.

Adding printers

How do I install a second printer in the Workplace Shell?

Open the Templates folder and drag a Printer template to the desktop to create a new printer object; an automatic window asks for information about this new printer. Give it a name and select the port where it is connected; then select the right printer driver from a list and hit the Create button. You'll be asked if you want to *install an equivalent WIN-OS/2 printer configuration* for Windows support. Choose the appropriate answer, and you'll end up with a new printer object on the desktop.

Komando Klues
You can further customize the printer's properties by right-clicking on the object and choosing Settings, selecting the Printer Driver page, and then right-clicking on the printer driver icon.

Fonts for OS/2

I have a whole bunch of TrueType fonts that I use with Windows. OS/2 doesn't seem to have the fonts that I like. Can I install Windows TrueType fonts in OS/2?

Windows programs running on OS/2 can use their TrueType fonts, but OS/2 does not yet support TrueType fonts for other applications. OS/2 supports the Adobe Type 1 font file format, for which there are thousands of fonts.

The Bottom Line
Either learn to like the fonts you've got or shell out the cash for Adobe Type 1.

Recovering deleted files

Help! I just finished a big report that's due in hours, and I sent it to the shredder. I'm panicking. My wife is pregnant for the third time in five years, and this mistake could cost me my job. How can I get the report back?

Panic isn't the answer. The solution depends on a few configuration parameters within your system and one caveat: Do not write — that is save — anything to the drive containing the file that you want to recover. You see, when a file is deleted, the first character of the filename is changed to a unique little squiggle character that tells the operating system that the cluster is available to be (over)written. Undeleting a file changes that special character back; it just takes a special utility to find the files with that character.

If the file was deleted from a FAT (DOS-formatted) partition, you can recover it with the DOS utility UNDELETE. You can even run the DOS undelete program from a DOS window in OS/2, if you change to the drive and directory where DOS is located (usually C:\DOS). Your favorite third-party utility (PC Tools, Norton Utilities, XTree, and so on) and its file-recovery function also may work, but it will probably politely decline to work in a multitasking environment, so you will have to boot DOS to use it.

If the file was deleted from an HPFS partition, it is still recoverable. In the OS/2 CONFIG.SYS is a line that says

```
rem SET DELDIR=C:\DELETE,512;D:\DELETE,512
```

By default, this function is not enabled — it is "remarked out" when the CONFIG.SYS file is first created. If you remove the *rem* from the start of the line, each partition listed will have a directory named DELETE, and the OS/2 undelete function will work. If you haven't un-remmed the DELDIR line, there is still hope, but now you need a utility that you have previously installed, can install to a different partition than the deleted file, or will run from a floppy disk.

The GammaTech utilities (commercial software) recover deleted files without the DELDIR option enabled in the CONFIG.SYS. But remember not to write anything to the partition containing the deleted file! Don't install anything to that partition or download from a bulletin board if it will happen on that partition; both actions can overwrite your errant file.

Another option is restoring from your tape backup. (There are only two types of computer users: those who have lost data and those who will.)

Finally, as a preventative measure to reduce the chances of repeating such an accidental deletion of a critical file, move the shredder. The icon looks just a bit too much like the printer icon, especially if you are bleary-eyed after long hours at the computer. The shredder doesn't need to be on your desktop — you can move it to a folder of your choice — and getting it out of the way will make it almost impossible to shred something without some conscious thought. If you have OS/2 3, and the shredder is one of the buttons on your OS/2 toolbar, you can delete the icon by dragging the button from the Launch Pad to the shredder icon. The shredder will then shred itself (an interesting Zen-like experience). This works because the Launch Pad button was a shadow of the original shredder icon, which is stored out of the way in the OS/2 System folder.

581

Chapter 16
Printers

Basics

 dpi

Which is better: 300 or 600 dpi?

The dpi setting relates to print quality, or *resolution*. Specifically, *dpi* is the total number of dots squeezed into one square inch (that is, *dots per inch*). Any printout — graphics or text — is composed of dots, in the same way a Matisse painting is made up of small brush strokes. The higher the dpi setting, the clearer and sharper your printouts are.

I bet you're thinking, "Well, Kim, I'll just leave the printer set to 600 dpi all the time."

The problem: All good things in life have a downside, and print quality is no exception. You see, the higher the dpi setting, the longer it takes for the file to print.

Komando Klues
Text-only documents look fine at 300 dpi, but documents with graphics look much better at 600 dpi. Rough drafts, meanwhile, don't require higher settings, so you can save time and printer toner by printing files at a lower density (75 or 150 dpi, for example); when it's time to print a final version, switch to a higher dpi setting.

By the way, Matisse set his canvas on 30 dpi. (Betcha didn't think I knows about art, too.)

Laser printers unveiled

My friend and I made a bet. He insists that laser printers burn images onto paper. I say that he's wrong. What do you say? A steak dinner is riding on your answer.

Go back and up the ante because you win.

Laser printers don't burn either text or graphics onto paper. Instead,

1. Laser printers draw the image with a laser on an internal drum.

2. Toner is attracted to those places on the drum touched by the laser.

3. The toner passes from drum to paper.

4. The printer heats the paper to make the toner stick.

Most laser printers can perform this sequence of steps with 6 pages per minute. Some can print as many as 11 (or more) pages per minute. Of course, the faster laser printers cost more money.

PostScript levels

What's the difference between Adobe's PostScript levels 1 and 2?

A universal computer rule of thumb whether you're talking microprocessors or PostScript levels: The higher the number is, the newer (and, usually, the more expensive) the technology. (The numbers game isn't proportional, though. Windows 95 is an improvement over Windows 3.11, but it's not 91.89 better.)

PostScript level 2 gives you more options and increases printer performance. If you need three of the following characteristics, check out PostScript level 2:

> *Increased print speed.* Level 2 makes all printer memory available to all printing tasks. In addition, level 2 stores patterns and forms in a special memory holding area, called a *cache*. As a result, the printer doesn't need to generate patterns and forms each time they're needed. Level 1 stores fonts only in its cache.

> *Additional support for color imaging, data compression, and pattern manipulation.* Level 2 also has color extensions for color printing and generates higher-resolution images.

> *Support of PPDs* (printer description files). A PPD lets you make a PostScript file for a printer that isn't actually attached to your machine. Typically used in high-end desktop publishing programs, such as PageMaker.

> *Multitray compatibility.* Level 2 enables you to choose the paper tray in a multitray printer.

Note: You may be able to jump up to level 2 by adding a special cartridge to your printer. Ask your printer manufacturer and have your credit card handy.

Printing from DOS

Do I need a special printer to print from DOS? I wanted to buy a laser printer at a wholesale club, but the box indicates that it "prints from Windows." I have Windows, but I like DOS, so I asked the salesman whether the printer would print from DOS. He said no.

Wholesale clubs are great, but that same "computer" salesman was probably selling bulk diapers a few minutes later, saying, "Oh, yes, one size fits all."

The slogan *works through Windows* is a marketing angle. A printer that works in Windows works in DOS. Period. No more news to report. No film at 11.

Maybe you can profit from the salesman's ignorance. Go back to the store, grab him by the, ahem, hand, and either negotiate a better price because the printer "doesn't work in DOS" or make a bet — if you can prove that the printer works in DOS, then you get a discount.

Say that he bites (one born every minute). Here's how to show that no-good salesman that the printer works from DOS:

1. At the computer where the demonstration printer is connected, exit Windows and go to the DOS prompt.

2. Create a screenful of text (using the DOS command DIR a few times should work).

585

3. Make sure that the printer is on-line and press Shift+Print Screen. This action takes a snapshot of what's on-screen in DOS and sends it to the printer.

4. With some printers, the screen shot automatically comes out of the printer. With others, take the printer off-line and then press the form feed button to eject your printout.

Printouts per toner cartridge

How many sheets of paper can I print from one toner cartridge?

You can expect 3,000–6,000 printouts per toner cartridge. If you print a great deal of graphics or at higher resolutions, you use more toner per printout and so the number of printouts per cartridge decreases.

> *Q: How many licks does it take to get to the center of a Tootsie Roll Pop?*
>
> *A: It depends on the size of your tongue.*

Print Manager

What is Print Manager?

What does Windows Print Manager do?

Print Manager is a traffic cop inside your computer, directing the flow of printing jobs from Windows to your printer.

The best part of Print Manager is that it works in the background. In other words, when you send a file to the printer, Print Manager baby-sits the printing. You can do something else.

When you send more than one job to the printer, Print Manager hands the jobs to the printer in the order you sent them; that is, the *print queue* works on a first-come-first-served basis. But you still can override this order, stop files from printing altogether, or pause files before they're printed.

If some problem arises with a print job — for example, the printer runs out of memory — Print Manager pops up a small window to tell you so.

Sometimes, disabling Print Manager can improve performance:

➤ Print Manager only takes 50K to run, but occasionally another program won't run properly without that lost memory.

➤ Print Manager needs enough hard disk space to save the temporary files required to print a job.

All in all, unless your memory is limited, using Print Manager is a good thing. It gives you tremendous flexibility and control.

Turning off Print Manager

How do I tell Print Manager to take a hike? My new printer drivers recommend turning Print Manager off.

I love telling managers to take a hike. Maybe that's why I run my own company.

1. Open Windows Control Panel.

2. Select the Printers icon.

3. Disable the Use Print Manager option.

Print Manager's limit

How many print jobs can I send to the printer before Print Manager chokes?

One hundred. The 101st file sent won't enter the print queue until one of the 100 files already in the queue has finished printing or is deleted from the queue.

Note: Print Manager works on a first-in-first-out basis.

Caring for your printer

Clogged ink cartridges

How do I clean my Epson's clogged inkjet cartridges?

Most printers do the job themselves when prompted. The Epson Color Stylus, for example, cleans its own heads:

1. Press the Pause button.

2. Press the Alt+Economy/Condensed buttons to clean the color heads.

3. Press the Alt+Load/Eject button to clean the clogged black heads.

Refilling inkjet cartridges

My Epson Stylus ink cartridge is empty. Can I buy ink and refill the cartridge, or do I need to purchase an entire cartridge?

It's less expensive and more ecologically correct to refill an ink cartridge than purchase a new cartridge; you save about $15 per cartridge and make Mother Nature happy, too.

An inkjet cartridge can take anywhere from 0 to 10 refills. The number depends on whom you ask, the printer manufacturer or refill vendor. (Guess who says what?)

Most inkjet refill kits come with a needle (plastic or metal). You just fill the needle up with new ink and then inject the ink into the cartridge.

But be careful:

➤ Inkjet cartridges have built-in circuitry and print heads that don't respond well to mishandling.

➤ Don't go buy any ink. You need the type of ink used by your printer. Sources for inkjet refill kits include office-supply stores, computer retailers, and mail-order supply houses.

➤ Check your printer warranty before refilling: doing so may void the warranty.

Q&A Replacing toner

I'm a poor writer who temps in offices to make ends meet. I can save over $100 by buying a used toner cartridge, but I don't want to be penny-wise and pound-foolish. P.S. The toner cartridges at work look more and more tempting.

Don't do it. Taking Post-Its is one thing, stealing toner cartridges is, well, stealing.

Whether buying a used toner cartridge is a bad deal depends on where you're buying it. But you must be cautious because there are different flavors of used toner cartridges. Specifically, ask your supplier whether the toner cartridge is recharged, reconditioned, or remanufactured.

> ➤ *Recharged* cartridges are refilled with fresh toner.

> ➤ *Reconditioned* cartridges are overhauled. The drum is recoated, not replaced.

> ➤ *Remanufactured* cartridges are cleaned, disassembled, and then put back together (with new parts).

You can find a used toner cartridge in several places, including office-supply stores, computer retailers, mail-order supply houses, and even printer manufacturers. Wherever you buy the cartridge, be sure to ask what gets replaced inside the cartridge. The toner is the least costly element; the drum is the most expensive. And get a written guarantee from the vendor: you don't want to have to vacuum two cups of toner out of a laser printer because the cartridge fell apart. In addition, check your printer's warranty because using recharged, reconditioned, or remanufactured toner cartridges may void the warranty.

I never buy new toner for my company's printers. (See what happens when you let a computer person approve the budget?) I always get remanufactured cartridges. Other budget-conscious rules regarding printing at The Komando Corp. are

Komando Klues

> ➤ Think twice about printing.

> ➤ Turn the printer's controls to light density. Some printers are sold with the density cranked up; this setting is unnecessary for normal home and office use.

> ➤ Before you replace a toner cartridge because it's empty, take the cartridge out of the printer and give it a little shake, rattle, and rol' Often, shaking a cartridge redistributes the remaining toner and extends the life of the toner cartridge a bit.

Ener-G Saver

I'm really into helping save our planet. I can't afford the new printers that power down automatically. Is there a way to turn my printer into an ecologically correct printer?

For starters, you could have e-mailed me this letter. And for $99.95, you can buy PC Ener-G Saver from PC Green Technologies (800-984-7336). It's a software-controlled power outlet that has separate three-amp outlets for the monitor and printer. The software is a memory-resident utility and comes in DOS and Windows versions.

With PC Ener-G Saver, you plug the keyboard and power cords into an external box, install the software on your PC, and then set a period of time after which your components automatically power down. PC Ener-G Saver turns on the power to the printer as soon you send a job to the printer. Pressing any key wakes up the monitor.

In case you forget to turn off your computer sometimes, you also can set your computer, monitor, and printer to shut off at a given time every evening. EPA calculations show that you can save up to $135 per year by shutting off a monitor and laser printer when you're not using them.

Sharing

One computer, two printers

My wife lets me hook my HP Color DeskJet to her computer. Problem is she already has an Epson. As a result, whenever I want to print, we must unplug the laser. It's a royal pain, and I'm afraid she's going to revoke my printing privileges. Can I install both printers on the computer?

....ddy, does she give you an allowance, too?

You can install two printers on one computer in two ways:

> ➤ Install another printer port (that is, put a parallel printer card in an empty expansion slot inside your computer).
>
> ➤ Buy a printer switch box.

Adding another printer port isn't hard or expensive. Right now, you're using printer port LPT1 for both printers. After adding another printer port, you can use LPT1 for the HP printer and LPT2 for the Epson printer (or vice versa).

After you install the parallel printer card inside the computer, you set up the printers from the Printers window in the Windows Control Panel:

1. Highlight a printer.

2. Click Connect.

3. Highlight LPT1.

4. Highlight the other printer.

5. Click Connect.

6. Highlight LPT2.

A printer switch box, meanwhile, sits outside your computer and turns one printer port into two printer ports. That is, you connect both printers to the switch box rather than the computer's LPT1 port. Then you connect the switch box to the printer port.

Komando Klues

Look for an electronic and not a manual switch box. Electronic switch boxes offer extra protection for a laser printer's memory and components. In addition, if you use an electronic switch box, the document is automatically sent to the printer that's selected in the application. If you use a manual switch box, you must remember to select the right printer in your application *and* then make sure the switch box is connected to the correct printer.

You can find electronic and manual switch boxes at your local computer dealer, Radio Shack, or in computer mail-order catalogs. Switch boxes range in price from $140 to $400 (manual switch boxes are less expensive).

Check both printers' warranties. Sometimes, using a manual switch box voids the manufacturer's warranty.

Two computers, one printer

I have two computers but only one printer. Do I have to network the computers so that the printer can be shared? The computers are in my house and I'd hate to string cable all over.

I understand: You trip over one wire and your whole business crashes to the floor.

You don't need to install a network. Instead, you can use an electronic switch box (for more information, see the preceding answer) — unless you share the printer with another person and both of you work in different rooms or print frequently. If so, consider purchasing a print-sharing device with built-in memory; such a device works as a print buffer. These things are best when you want to connect two to six PCs to a printer via standard parallel, serial, or telephone cables. Prices range from $400 for a four-port model to $800 for an eight-port model with extra memory.

Printer Drivers

Printer driver

How can I tell whether my HP 550C printer is set up to use the Windows-supplied printer driver or the Hewlett-Packard printer driver?

Ask it. Open the Windows Control Panel, double-click on Printers, and then look at the listing in the Installed Printers window:

➤ If you're using the HP DeskJet printer driver supplied with Windows 3.1, your printer will be listed as HP DeskJet, HP DeskJet Plus, or HP DeskJet 500. *Note:* The Windows 3.1-supplied printer driver filename is HPDSKJET.DRV.

➤ If you're using the Hewlett-Packard printer driver, your printer will be listed as HP DeskJet 500 Printer, HP DeskJet 500C Printer, HP DeskJet 550C Printer, HP DeskJet 510 Printer, HP DeskJet Plus Printer, or HP DeskJet Printer. *Note:* The Hewlett-Packard printer driver filename is DESKJETC.DRV.

Although both drivers work, use the Hewlett-Packard printer driver; it's a little slower but provides better color and grayscale printouts.

By the way, if you try to install an HP Color DeskJet, you need to get a printer driver directly from Hewlett-Packard by mail or download the driver from Hewlett-Packard's BBS or a commercial on-line service such as America Online or CompuServe.

 Installing printer driver

Why does my Citizen printer work great with some Windows programs but not at all in others?

Are you registered to vote? You may not have the correct print driver installed. Although some applications can send the correct information to the printer by using one of several printer drivers, other apps may have some characters that only a specific print driver can handle.

I ran into the same situation once: I was using an Epson LaserJet 1500. The recommended printer driver is an HP LaserJet III, but I set up the HP LaserJet II driver. When I printed from Excel 5, everything looked fine. But when I printed from Word 6, I got pages and pages of garbage. At least that's what my publisher said. (Publishing lesson #1: Blame your printer.)

Contact Citizen for the latest, greatest printer driver. When you get it,

1. Open Windows Control Panel.

2. Select the Printers icon

3. Click the Add button.

4. A new window appears. Highlight the first option, Install Unlisted or Updated Driver.

5. Click Install.

6. You may be asked to put one or more of the original Windows disks in your floppy disk drive. (Windows automatically assumes that you will put the disk in drive A. If you want to put the disk in drive B, delete the A: and type **B:** to continue.)

7. Click OK. Windows finishes the job.

Reinstalling printer driver

Whenever I print from Windows, all I get is a bunch of hearts, number symbols, and other strange characters. The printer works great under DOS. Is this a Windows bug?

Nah. It's the secret computer programmer's code for *Wrong printer driver installed* or *Printer driver file is corrupted*. I guess it's not a secret.

Did your printer come with a setup disk? If so, take a look on the disk and find out which command installs the printer driver in Windows. Then put the disk in drive A. Go to Program Manager and select File⇨Run. In the command line box, type the setup command that you found. (Normally, it's Setup or WSetup.) Click OK. When you next try printing, everything should be fine.

No setup disk, you say? Then you have to install the printer driver the old-fashioned way:

1. Open the Windows Control Panel.

2. Select the Printers icon.

3. Make sure that the name of your printer is listed in the Installed Printers window. (If it is, the printer driver file simply may have gone to the intergalactic bit bucket. It happens. And it's not your fault.)

   If you can't find your printer listed at all among the available printers, look in your printer's user manual under *emulation*. Emulation is a trick whereby a certain printer brand and model number pretends to be one of the more popular printer brands and model numbers.

   If you have two or more printers installed on your computer, highlight the name of the printer you use the most and click the Set as Default Printer button.

4. Highlight the name of your printer.

5. Click Remove. Say yes when asked to confirm. Don't worry, you're going to put it right back.

6. Click the Add button and highlight the name and model number of your printer.

7. Click Install. You may be asked to put one or more of your original Windows disks in the floppy disk drive. Or you may be asked to put the disk that came with your printer in the floppy disk drive.

After the printer drivers are under your control, those hearts and symbols should disappear.

Deinstalling printer

I sold my old LaserJet and bought a new color model, but the old printer is still listed as a printer option in my software. How do I let my computer know that the printer is no longer attached?

Have you ever noticed that it's easier to remove something from your life than it is to try to make it work? You'll have to write Ann Landers for more details. Now on to the more important things — your printer fix.

1. Open the Windows Control Panel.

2. Double-click on Printers.

3. From the Installed Printers list box, highlight the name of the old printer.

4. Click Remove.

5. When Windows asks, "Are you sure?" click "Don't question my judgment."

6. Close the Printers box.

Your computer will never, ever, ever again look for that old LaserJet.

Printer driver version

How can I tell what version printer driver is installed? I've asked everyone, and no one knows.

Sure, leave me for last. I feel slighted.

Open the Windows Control Panel and select Printers. Highlight the name of the printer in the Listed Printers list box and click Setup. Now click About, and there you should see the printer driver and its version number.

Now you know to come to me first.

Emulation

I've searched high and low for a Tandy 8-pin printer driver. How else can I get this printer to work in Windows?

First, clean that thing up. Take the cover off and look inside. Yeeech. Tangerine peels. Rubber bands. M&Ms. And hair, lots of hair.

If you still have the printer manual, pick it up and look in the index under *emulation*. Many printers can pretend that they're another printer brand and model number.

Even if you can't find the printer manual, don't lose hope. An 8-pin printer is a dot-matrix printer, so it's a good shot that the printer will work if you tell the computer that the printer is an Epson.

How, you ask?

1. Open the Windows Control Panel.

2. Select Printers.

3. Click Add.

4. Highlight Epson FX.

5. Click Install. You may be asked for one or more of your original Windows disks.

See whether the printer works now. If it doesn't, you have another alternative:

1. Go back to the Windows Control Panel and double-click Printers.

2. Click Add.

3. Highlight Generic Dot Matrix printer (it will be at the top of the listing of possible printers).

4. Click Install and feed Windows the original disks it requires.

The downside to choosing this option: Graphics don't print, only text.

Star printer driver

I recently purchased a used Star printer at a garage sale. How do I get the printer driver?

More garage sales? Flea markets?

The easiest way is to contact the printer manufacturer, Star Micronics (908-572-3300). Or you can hop on a BBS or on-line service. Just make sure the printer driver matches the model number on the printer.

Until you get the Star driver, you can set up the printer to use the Windows generic printer option.

You won't be able to print any graphics, though.

To set up a printer to use the generic printer option,

1. Open the Windows Control Panel.

2. Select Printers.

3. Click Add.

4. Highlight Generic Dot Matrix printer.

5. Click Install.

6. Feed Windows the original disks it requires.

This solution should tide you over until the right printer driver arrives or is hunted down.

Troubleshooting

On-line

How do I get my printer to come on-line and show me its little green light?

You can't expect a printer to show you its green light right off the bat. Printers like to be wooed a bit.

1. Slowly plug the printer in. (Be gentle.)

2. Connect the printer to your computer. (Most IBM-compatible computers use parallel printers, so you should use a parallel printer cable to make the printer-to-PC connection.)

3. Turn the printer on.

4. Turn the computer on.

5. Press the printer's reset (or on-line) button.

Bingo, there's your green light.

Memory

Sometimes, my Hewlett-Packard color printer says *out of memory* and nothing prints. What does this mean, and how can I avoid it?

Do you know anyone who talks so fast that you can't keep up with the conversation? Back in the '70s, for example, most of us talked fast. (Come to think of it, I bet our memory was affected, too.) A printer *out of memory* message means that the computer is sending information faster than the printer can handle.

Like computers, printers have RAM. When you print a document, the printer stores it page by page in its RAM. An *out of memory* message means that the printer doesn't have enough memory to print a page.

This problem often crops up when the printer has only 512K or 1MB of RAM and you want to print a lot of fonts or graphics at 300 dpi or higher. To avoid the error message, try to reduce the number of images on the page and the print resolution (perhaps as low as 75 or 150 dpi). If reducing the print quality isn't a viable alternative, try fiddling with the printer's setup:

1. Open the Windows Control Panel.

2. Double-click on Printers.

3. Highlight the name of your printer.

4. Click Connect.

5. Disable Fast Printing to Port.

6. Click OK.

7. In the lower-left corner of the Print Setup window is the Use Print Manager option. Disable Print Manager.

8. If you're using a laser printer, click Options and disable the Print Type as Graphics option.

9. Click OK to return to the Control Panel.

If that annoying *out of memory* message appears, you must add more memory to your printer. Most printers are sold with a minimum amount of RAM — usually 512K or 1MB. Check your printer's manual or call the printer's manufacturer for more information about the type of memory your printer uses. For most home uses, 1MB or 2MB of printer RAM is good. Professional desktop publishers and graphic artists may need 8MB or higher.

Often, purchasing memory from third-party vendors is less expensive than buying from the printer's manufacturer. Your local computer retailer, for example, should carry printer memory upgrade kits; it may even install the memory for free.

You also may want to check mail-order memory vendors that advertise in computer magazines. The downside: You have to put the memory in the printer yourself. On the other hand, adding memory to an HP color printer is very easy: First, you buy a card containing the additional memory. (An HP color printer supports only one add-on memory card.) Then unplug your printer, locate the memory expansion slot, unscrew the slot cover, and gently insert the board. Connecting it to the printer system board port shouldn't take more than five minutes.

Printer error 20

Why do I get a printer error number 20 with my Hewlett-Packard LaserJet? What do I do?

It's that twenty-something, slacker, Generation X angst that we've read so much about. Twenty-something error messages often accompany print-outs that are missing characters. In fact, a *20* error message means that your printer doesn't have enough memory. You can get rid of the error message by adding more memory to your printer, removing objects from the page, or printing at a lower resolution.

When you get a *20* error message, take the printer off-line by pressing the on-line button on your printer and then press the Continue button on your printer. Your printout will emerge on two pages.

Speed

I use an HP 560C to print graphics. Will a Windows graphics accelerator card speed up the process?

Teenagers are complex. The food chain is complex. Just imagine a teenager printing graphics of the food chain. It boggles my mind.

The short answer: A graphics accelerator card helps speed up screen redraw; it won't help your printing time. You should check with your HP dealer for more printer memory. Or try a software store for a print caching program.

The detailed answer: A graphics accelerator card allows three major things in Windows — enhanced resolution, enhanced color depth, and video acceleration. Depending on your monitor type and the amount of memory on the card, a graphics accelerator can allow resolutions of up to 1024 × 768 and colors in lower resolutions of up to 16 million. By processing much of the image, a graphics accelerator frees some of the processor's resources. So, as you scroll through or change views in a document, the image refreshes quicker than normal.

Printer fonts

The fonts on my printout don't match those great fonts on-screen. What's wrong?

Whether the fonts you see on-screen come out of the printer depends on a few things.

There are three basic types of fonts: printer, TrueType, and screen:

> ➤ *Printer* fonts are available when you have your printer selected. They appear on-screen just as they do on the printout.

> ➤ *TrueType* fonts also appear on-screen as they do on the printout. Most TrueType fonts are available to all printers; printer fonts are available only to a specific printer.

> ➤ *Screen* fonts often come with your video driver for Windows. They usually don't print well, so Windows sets up a substitute font. For example, Windows may substitute Arial for a flower font.

Komando Klues If your software offers a print preview feature, use it to get an accurate representation of how the hard copy will look.

To make sure that your printout matches what's on-screen, use TrueType fonts only:

1. Open Windows Control Panel.

2. Select Fonts

3. Select TrueType.

4. Make sure that the Enable TrueType Fonts in Applications option is selected. And deselect the Show Only TrueType Fonts option.

When you return to your software program, use only the TrueType fonts. Your printouts then should look the same on paper as they do on-screen.

Lost printer fonts

I received a driver disk for Windows 3.1 with my new Stylus printer. The driver installed OK, but I can't find any of the printer's built-in fonts in any of my applications. Why did I spend all this money if I only get one boring font? Sniff Sniff. Help.

Wow, are those real tears?

It sounds as though the Show Only TrueType Fonts in Applications is enabled. You just have to disable the option:

1. Open the Windows Control Panel.

2. Select Fonts.

3. Select TrueType fonts.

4. Disable the Show Only TrueType Fonts option.

5. Click OK.

Printer sounds

My printer sometimes sounds as if it's gearing up to print a page. Is my printer haunted?

Ah, a printergeist.

Don't worry. Inside your printer is a fuser roller that lasts longer if it's rotated. This strange phenomenon happens usually every 30 minutes or so.

Printer is busy *message*

Whenever I try to print a document in Microsoft Word 6.0, I get this message: *Printer is busy . . . cannot print. Try again when printer is free.* **After I click OK, it starts to print. In all my other applications, the printer prints right away. I have a DeskJet 500C printer, but it shows as DeskJet Series V2.1.**

You want to know something worse? The first three printers I called gave me the same response. It's a conspiracy, I think, or perhaps a governmentally funded program.

First, try loading the correct printer driver. If you do not have the correct printer driver, you can find the latest driver for that printer on Microsoft's bulletin board.

The Word 6.0a upgrade, by the way, corrected some printing problems. If you have the upgrade installed, consider reinstalling it.

Testing printers

My LaserJet printer says *Call Service.* **What tests can I run?**

Why? Just to make sure that the printer absolutely doesn't work? Have you called service? Apparently not.

You can perform your own tests, but you probably will need to call Hewlett-Packard anyway. A *Call Service* message means that your printer's power supply or fuser is going or gone. That's why printers are sold with warranties. And the clock is tick-tick-ticking away.

Nonetheless, here are three tests:

> ➤ The *Printer Self-Test* tests the printer's RAM, ROM, internal fonts, and LED lights. Take the printer off-line and hold down the Print Fonts/Test key. This is the same test that the printer performs every time you turn it on.

➤ On the right side of the printer is a tiny hole, about the size of a pen. Insert a pen in the hole and the LED status panel should display *Engine Test*.

➤ Shhh. The *Service Test* trick is only known by real printer repair personnel. Holding down the Continue, Enter, and On-line buttons, turn on the printer. Press the Continue button and then the Enter button; the LED will display *Service Mode*. When the printer is done with the test, press the Test button. You'll get a printout of the printer's grayscales and resolutions.

Editing WIN.INI

When I tried to install a new printer, Windows gave me a *Cannot connect printers because the [ports] section of the WIN.INI is bad* message.

It's bad, but it's not that bad. Normally, this message means that something is wrong with the WIN.INI file.

First, open the WIN.INI file (located in the C:\WINDOWS directory) by using Windows Notepad. Check whether the [ports] section looks as follows:

```
[ports]
LPT1:=
LPT2:=
LPT3:=
COM1:=9600,n,8,1
COM2:=9600,n,8,1
COM3:=9600,n,8,1
COM4:=9600,n,8,1
EPT:=
FILE:=
LPT1.OS2=
LPT2.OS2=*
REM Kim Komando is Kool
```

If any of the preceding lines are missing, add the applicable line(s), save the file, and retry the printer driver installation. (By the way, your fax modem also may be listed.)

Note: The line REM Kim Komando is Kool is optional.

If you can't open the WIN.INI file because it's damaged or the printer driver reinstallation still didn't work, copy your backup copy of the WIN.INI file (you do have a backup, right?) to your C:\WINDOWS directory and then try to reinstall.

If you can't find your backup copy of the WIN.INI file,

1. Haul out your original Windows disks.

2. Exit Windows.

3. Put the first Windows disk in drive A.

4. At the DOS prompt, type **C:\WINDOWS\EXPAND A:WIN.SRC C:\WINDOWS\WIN.INI** and press Enter.

5. Start Windows and head into the Printers section of the Control Panel for one last chance at romance, I mean, reinstalling the printer.

If this last try doesn't work, you have no choice but to reinstall Windows entirely. Before you do, though, make backups of all files that have the .INI, .GRP, and .SYS extensions. You just never know what can happen.

Color

I have a Panasonic KX-P2123 with color option printer. When I print images in Windows, I only get black-and-white copies. I followed all the directions in the manual, but I only get color when I print in DOS.

Manuals, who needs them? They're only as good as names you can't pronounce.

The default setup for your particular printer driver is set to no color. Remember, color is an extra option with the 2123. To cure your woes,

1. Open the Windows Control Panel.

2. Select Printers.

3. Highlight the name of the Panasonic printer.

4. Select Setup.

5. Click Options.

6. Enable the Color option.

Ta da! You now can print in color through Windows.

True black

My HP DeskJet prints a black that looks like dark green. How do I fix it?

Did you skimp and buy cheap ink cartridges? Hey, maybe you can do some counterfeiting. If so, you then can afford the good cartridge and go legit.

Wait, there's an easier way. Many HP DeskJet drivers have an option for True Black printing:

1. Open the Windows Control Panel.

2. Select Printers.

3. Highlight the HP DeskJet printer.

4. Click Setup.

5. Click Options.

6. Make sure that you have True Black selected.

With True Black enabled, printing time is longer, and you have to wait a little longer for the ink to dry on your printouts.

You also may need an updated printer driver. Call Hewlett-Packard (303-339-7009) and ask for one. Any HP DeskJet user should have Version 3.1 or higher installed.

Paper

I have an HP 560C. Do I have to use the glossy paper that came with the printer, or can I use normal paper?

Normal paper won't hurt your printer, but it may damage your image.

If you're printing drafts or informal letters, plain paper is fine. If you're printing something important, however, such as a resume, you should use laser paper or a piece of nice flat-grain linen stationery.

On second thought, don't use the glossy paper. Doing so can cost between 75 cents and $1 per sheet, including ink used by the printer. And the output is so great that you'll want to use it all the time; then you won't have any money left over to feed the kids.

Komando Klues
Next time you need to do a presentation, print on a transparency slide rather than paper. Watch out, though: The thickness of transparency slides can cause printer jams, so use the manual feed option.

Printing out of house

My resume looks terrible when I print it on my dot-matrix printer. What can I do?

Many copy shops rent computers and laser printers by the hour. In addition, some libraries and colleges have equipment you can borrow by the hour. If wrestling with a foreign computer and printer doesn't thrill you, consider taking the disk to a service bureau. (Who knows, maybe you can even get hired there.)

Regardless, before you leave your house, make sure that the computer at the other end can read your resume without hesitation — in other words, make sure that the computer has the same fonts and version of software installed as you have on your computer. If you can't find such a beast, you can, as a last resort, save your document as a text-only or ASCII file. The upside: You won't have to retype the entire resume because any word processor or desktop publishing program can import a text file. The catch: This end-all file format eliminates all your formatting. Making the resume pretty again will take some time.

Good luck.

Chapter 17

Shareware and Other On-line Stuff

Basics

 What is shareware?

What is shareware? And how is it different from commercial software?

The software packages that line store shelves and fill catalog pages is called *commercial* software. To use a commercial program, you need to buy it.

The alternative to buying commercial software is tapping into the world of *shareware*. You can find shareware on just about any bulletin board system (BBS) or on-line service.

Most times, if a commercial program isn't what you want, you're stuck with it. So unless you have money to burn, you should think ahead before you commit to any commercial software. But shareware's motto is *Try before you buy*. If you try and like a piece of shareware, you send the author a registration fee. If you don't like the program, you trash it.

Shareware works by the honor system; no shareware police will ever crash down your door.

Literally, every kind of software program imaginable is available as shareware, including business programs (from accounting systems to checkbook managers), databases, spreadsheets, word processors, graphics programs, games, utilities, and even operating systems.

Casual computer users should not consider trying a different operating system.

Usually, shareware is created by individuals and not big software companies. Because there is little overhead, the registration price usually ranges from modest to reasonable (quite often under $50).

Paying for and registering shareware entitles you to technical support and updates. You can call the author or company and get answers to your questions. In addition, you typically receive a printed manual, the latest version of the program, and information about future releases. Oftentimes, the registered version has more features, too.

Although not all shareware authors make their living by writing programs, an increasing number do. As such, the authors rely on your honor; after all, they expect and deserve compensation for working — just as you do. Most shareware documentation suggests how many days you can try the program before you should register or remove it.

Frankly, not all shareware is good. Some are barely passable: you may feel that the authors owe you money. Then again, some shareware is better than commercial software.

Where do I find it?

Where can I find shareware? I went to three software stores and none carried shareware nor could recommend where to find it.

People who sell software haven't heard about shareware? Sounds fishy. Software stores sell commercial programs that compete with shareware. The salespeople probably just didn't want to tell you that shareware is on just about any BBS and on-line service, as well as on disks available from shareware vendors.

➤ Try looking for BBSs in your local area. (To find them, ask friends, check with computer stores, ask at a user's group meeting, and scour computing publications.) If the first BBS you try doesn't have a lot of files you'd like to download, don't be discouraged. Keep trying!

➤ You also can join a major on-line service, such as America Online, CompuServe, Delphi, GEnie, or Prodigy. The shareware selection there is usually larger than on a BBS. After you access an on-line service, look for a means of searching for shareware quickly and easily. For example, America Online has a shareware search utility, keyword *QUICKFIND*. This utility enables you to enter search criteria — program name, author, or description. You then can download directly from the list of files matching your criteria that pops up.

➤ If you don't like the idea of downloading, you still can get your hands on plenty of great shareware; just hook up with a shareware vendor. The back of your favorite computer magazine likely includes different shareware vendor advertisements. Two of the biggest IBM-type shareware vendors are Public Brand Software (800-242-4775) and Public Software Library (800-444-5457). Macintosh users can call The Amish Outlaw (800-947-4346) or Educorp (800-843-9497). Some shareware vendors put together CD-ROMs with hundreds or even thousands of shareware titles. Computer user groups often sell a shareware library to members, too.

 Is it the same no matter where I find it?

Are the shareware programs found on BBSs and on-line services the same as the shareware sold in catalogs?

Yes, for the most part. Most shareware authors not only upload their programs to BBSs and on-line services, but they also distribute their programs through vendors. Sometimes, though, a shareware program found on a BBS is just a demonstration version of the same shareware program found in a catalog.

If you're wary about downloading something sight unseen, you may prefer to browse a shareware catalog. Some shareware catalogs include pictures and sample screens from the programs they advertise.

 Komando Klues

And you don't risk getting a virus from reading about the program in a catalog.

Did it; can't find it

I can't find downloaded files. Windows. On-line service. Help.

You are a person of few words but many problems. (I got this fortune at a Chinese restaurant. Never went back there again.)

Most on-line services have something called a *Download Manager* that keeps track of files you download — and, equally important, you select the download destination. If you can't find files that you downloaded, you may want to check the default DOWNLOAD subdirectory in your on-line service's program directory.

To find these downloaded files, you also can use the Search command in the File Manager; look for common download file extensions, such as .ZIP or .TXT.

You also may want to keep a notebook (yes, an old-fashioned pencil-and-paper notebook) by your computer to keep track of where you have been. I know that this log helps many people, especially those who routinely access BBSs and on-line services, where there is so much information for you and your computer to ingest.

Tracking current releases

I want to update a shareware checkbook program I found on a BBS. How can I find out whether the author has updated the application?

The very best way to find out whether shareware authors have updated their programs is to pay the appropriate registration fees and become a registered owner. Most shareware authors send free updates or at least notify registered owners of available updates. So balance that checkbook (by hand if you must), find the funds, and register the program with the author!

Komando Klues

Another way of staying current is to keep your eye on a good local BBS or on-line service; use the available file search utility to search for new versions of a desired program. Remember, however, that searching for the exact filename is a bad way to find files. For example, if you own PKZ110.EXE and want to know whether there's a newer version of PKWare's ZIP utilities, looking for the filename PKZ110 won't tell you what you want to know. Instead, search by the author (Katz) or company name (PKWare) to keep updated on all available software, including program updates (such as PKZ204G).

Releasing your own shareware

I am interested in releasing my own shareware programs. Where can I get more information?

Undoubtedly, the best resource is the Association of Shareware Professionals (ASP). The folks there should be able to fill in all the details and answer any questions. ASP also can give you the lowdown on getting your shareware included on BBSs, on shareware disk vendor CD-ROMs, and in shareware catalogs. ASP's newsletter is a good resource, too. For more information, contact ASP at

> 545 Grover Rd.
>
> Muskegon, MI 49442-9427
>
> Phone: 616-788-5131
>
> Fax: 616-788-2765

You also may want to check with disk vendors or BBSs for Shareware Author's Kits, which describe the steps you need to take to have that particular distributor carry your program.

In addition, your local PC user's group often has a special-interest group dedicated to authoring and marketing commercial and shareware programs. Many top commercial games and utilities originated as shareware. Maybe your program will too!

Cost

 Scared of the free lunch

In my spare time, I've been browsing the incredible selection on BBSs and on-line services. But is freeware really free? I can't believe that no one is making money off this really great stuff.

Sounds too good to be true, doesn't it? But *freeware* (also known as *public domain* files/programs) is free. Amazing, we live in a culture where we pay for water but can get free software.

When a program or file is in the public domain, the author has given up all claims to copyright. In other words, the author no longer can charge you money. And you can use or modify the program or file any way you want.

So you know, an author of a *freely distributed* file or program still owns it, holds the copyright, and may rule how the work is distributed or used. But rarely does a freely distributed program cost anything. Authors of freely distributed programs may request a donation, however; if so, toss some change into their thinking caps.

Most freeware and shareware vendors, BBSs, and on-line services clearly identify whether a program is public domain, freely distributed, or shareware. In fact, when you're looking at files on-line, you may see an appropriate abbreviation: PD, FD/FW, SW.

 How do I register?

How do I register my shareware? I feel guilty because I use a shareware football program that I haven't paid for. P.S. I'm Catholic.

Say three Hail Marys and go deep.

Ah, there's no need to surprise your priest with "Father, forgive me, for I have downloaded." Registering shareware is easy! Most times, just look in the program's documentation for registration information. You should always find an author's mailing address and the registration amount. Then send a check to the author for the requested amount and mail it to the address indicated in the documentation.

It's always a good idea to include a note with your name, your mailing address, program name and version, and the preferred disk size. That way, you're sure to get the most recent version and in the right format.

Registration forms usually lurk somewhere in the shareware program or the program's documentation. And like a bad rash, some forms show up every time you use the program (they stop appearing, however, when you receive the registered version).

The program's registration also may come in the shape of a README.TXT file or in a REGISTER.DOC or REGISTER.TXT file. To get a copy, simply open and print the file with your favorite word processing program. If you're still hanging at the DOS prompt, make sure your printer is on-line, type **TYPE REGISTER.DOC >PRN**, and press Enter.

Now, go in peace.

Where's Ralph Nader when you need him?

When I go to download files on a BBS or on-line service, I see only a paragraph about the program. How can I tell whether a program is any good? I've wasted a lot of time and money downloading junk.

You could call the psychic hot line. But it may be cheaper just to download the program and give it a test-drive.

Actually, it's pretty hard to tell the good from the bad from the ugly without test-driving the programs. But there are some steps you can take before downloading the file:

> ➤ Scan the on-line service's description of the file for any mention of Association of Shareware Professionals (or ASP). An ASP membership usually means a program is good, because it meets the association's standards. Plus, the unregistered version of an ASP program is fully functional. (Sometimes an uploaded piece of shareware is merely a demo or sample of the entire program. Then you have to send the shareware author the registration fee to get the entire program.)

> ➤ Check the user ID or screen name of the person who put the file on the on-line service. If the person who uploaded the file is a software company or the author's name, you can safely bet that the author will be available for comment and support. If the screen name is *RipOff* or *Gotcha$*, though, stay away.

➤ Check whether your on-line service has a system where you can ask questions about a file. At the bottom of America Online's description screen, for example, is a button marked *Ask the Staff*. If you click this button, the America Online forum leaders will help you determine whether a file is worth the download time and try.

Komando Klues

Don't ask, "Hey, is this program any good or is it a piece of trash?" Ask questions about features. Or tell the staff how you plan to use the program and ask, "Will this program do x, y, and z?"

➤ Many BBSs and on-line services track *download counts* — that is, how many times a program has been downloaded. Download counts is a good way to judge a program's popularity. Of course, this kind of popularity is no guarantee because none of the users who downloaded the program had seen it in action yet either.

➤ Next time you're sitting around talking to your computer friends, ask for recommendations of good shareware programs. In addition, most computer magazines list top shareware hit lists.

Once it's mine, can I sell it?

Can I copy shareware and give it to my friends? Do they have to pay if I've already paid? Can I sell shareware to my friends?

Yeah, go ahead and make a profit off your friends. I bet you invite friends over for dinner and after dessert hand them a bill.

Shareware programs come in two flavors: unregistered and registered. You find unregistered versions on BBSs, on-line services, and disks you get from shareware vendors. It's OK to pass out unregistered versions to as many friends as you want. Heck, you can even upload it to your local BBS. (By the way, shareware vendors encourage this practice; it helps get the word out about their programs.)

If you sent the shareware author a registration fee, however, you are entitled to one copy of the program — a registered version. And that copy is just for your own use, so you can't pass that program to your friends or upload it to a BBS. If your friends like the unregistered version, tell them to send the shareware author the fee and receive their own registered copy.

I used it once; do I still owe?

I downloaded a shareware program that I only needed once. Do I need to send the shareware author money?

If you take a piece of candy at the market, do you put money in the box? If you find a wallet, do you keep it? It's all a matter of conscience.

Keep in mind that the entire concept of shareware is based on the honor system. If we want authors to keep writing programs, then those of us who benefit from using the programs need to pay for the programs.

Ask yourself whether you benefited from the shareware. Could you have done what you did without the program?

Problems

Files look like foreign language

When I try to read downloaded files, they look like they were written in Egyptian. Why?

I have to ask the obvious: Did you download anything from Egypt?

Be sure that the files you are trying to read are, in fact, text files. If you think a file is a text file, open it by using a program (such as Microsoft Word or WordPerfect) that can figure out what the file is.

Note: Text files (also called *ASCII* files) usually have a .TXT or .DOC extension.

If an open file looks like Egyptian still (or any other language besides English for that matter!), it may require a specific word processor. Or perhaps the files really were written in another language. In any case, go back to where you downloaded the file; you may be able to find some clues in the file's description.

615

ZEN.TXT and the art of file opening

I downloaded a text file (called ZEN.TXT) but can't view it. It's unzipped and on a floppy disk. I use Windows.

ZEN.TXT. Hmmmm. Try meditation, self-contemplation, and intuition.

If that doesn't work, put the disk containing ZEN.TXT into the floppy disk drive. The extension .TXT means that the file is a text file, so you shouldn't have any problem viewing the file: in fact, it should open in any word processor.

If you have a word processor, open the file just like you do any text file. That is, choose File⇨Open, choose the correct drive, and then select ZEN.TXT. If the file won't open, try using the import or insert command in your word processing software.

If you don't own a word processing program, use Windows Write or Notepad to open the file.

Avoiding viruses

A friend told me never to download lest I get a computer virus. If I download a file that has a virus, do I contract it automatically? Or will I get the virus only when I run the program?

Your friend has a point. Computer viruses can cause serious, irreparable damage; they can even wipe out *all* the information on your hard disk. And, yes, you can download viruses when you download any software. (On the other hand, downloading files is only one way to get a virus. You also risk contracting a virus, for example, whenever you swap disks between computers.)

Viruses that attach to a program's executable files are the most common encountered via download. They are tricky little devils because they remain inactive until you actually access the file that you downloaded. In other words, you won't see the virus until you run the program (or the program's installation file).

You needn't avoid downloading altogether, however; you just need to be careful. Check with the BBSs or on-line services that you access about their virus-scanning policy. All major on-line services and most good BBSs check all files for known viruses before they make them available to the public.

But this protection isn't enough. You need to protect your system by doing your own virus scanning. In fact, it's a good idea to scan your system each time you add a new program, regardless of the program's source.

Here's how I work with downloaded files:

1. I download to my computer's hard disk.

2. I copy the downloaded file to a floppy disk.

3. I extract the file's contents on the floppy disk.

4. I use my antivirus software on the floppy disk before I install the program on my computer's hard disk.

You can buy a virus scanner, such as Central Point AntiVirus or Norton AntiVirus. Of course, if you're using MS-DOS 6.0 or later, you already have Microsoft AntiVirus (MSAV). You also can download a very good shareware virus-scanning program called Scan, by McAfee and Associates. You can find DOS, Windows, and OS/2 versions of Scan on most BBSs and on-line services. Or you can download the program from the McAfee BBS:

1. Call 408-988-4004.

2. Set your modem for parity none, 8 start bits, and 1 stop bit.

3. Speeds up to 9600 baud are accepted.

The problem with antivirus software is that the programs only find viruses known at the time that the program disk was made. Although antivirus software is updated regularly, it takes time after a virus appears before the updated virus-scanning software hits the streets. To make sure you have the most recent version of your antivirus software, call the software's publisher. Having the most recent virus checkers is paramount to protecting your computer.

Komando Klues

To be absolutely safe, your virus protection strategy should combine virus scanning and hard drive backups. Remember, you are more likely to lose data to an equipment problem than a computer virus. Backups keep you ready for anything that may strike!

Limited shareware or demos

I downloaded a shareware program that has some menu options in gray. No matter what I do, some program features are never activated. Is this what they call crippleware? How is crippleware different than nagware?

Crippleware? Please, in these politically correct times, the term is *limited shareware* or *shareware demos*.

As you discovered, not every shareware program has all its features turned on. Often, to encourage registration, authors leave out features or limit the scope of certain features. For example, a videotape catalog may only let you index 50 tapes unless you register the program. Or perhaps an inventory control program only lets you print one kind of report. So look for shareware written by authors who belong to the Association of Shareware Professionals (ASP); these programs are fully functional.

Nagware refers to shareware whose authors encourage registration by reminding you to register on the opening screen, on the closing screen, and/or at random intervals while you're using the program. The request is often accompanied with a delay so that you can't continue using the program for a few seconds. These authors are the kind of people you don't want to borrow money from; they like to remind you of your debt every time you see them.

Be sure to check with your shareware disk vendor or BBS about their policy on describing shareware programs. Most good vendors or BBSs warn you about programs that are severely limited.

Printing downloaded articles

How do I get articles I download to print out?

I'm at a loss here because you didn't tell me what computer platform and on-line service you're using.

Nonetheless, here's a fairly generic answer: The easiest way is to print the document or article while it's on-screen. (Then you don't have to play hide-and-seek on your hard disk to locate the file and appropriate word processing program.) On your on-line menu screen is a picture of a little printer; click it. Or select the Print menu option. (It's normally under the File menu; if it's under Edit, it may be hidden again underneath Copy.)

What is OMBUDSMN.ASP?

What is the file OMBUDSMN.ASP? A lot of shareware programs have it.

OM*BUDS*MAN n. 1. A government official who investigates citizens' complaints against the government. 2. One who investigates complaints from consumers. 3. A quick and easy way to report a deadbeat programmer. 4. A transcendental meditator who drinks beer.

The presence of OMBUDSMN.ASP indicates that the shareware author is a member of the Association of Shareware Professionals (ASP) and is distributing the program in accordance with the association's guidelines. Members must adhere to the association's standards regarding quality of programs (for example, the programs should be bug-free and fully functional). ASP authors also must support the program by providing technical help to registered users and updates or bug fixes as appropriate.

The file called OMBUSMN.ASP lists the name and address of an ASP ombudsman, whom you can contact if you feel that the shareware author isn't living up to his or her end of the deal. It's kind of like Ralph Nader going high-tech.

Zzzzzzip

What is a .ZIP file . . .

Every shareware program I download ends in .ZIP. Why?

If you're like most people, when you pack for a trip, you figure out a way to fit all you need inside a carry-on bag. Move things around here, rearrange things there, make sure nothing's hanging out, and then sit on the suitcase until it closes! After you arrive at your destination, you open the case and take out your clothes so that you can wear them.

Well, computers work the same way (although your cologne won't explode en route). The information you download is squeezed (or *compressed* or *zipped*) to just a fraction of its original size. When the information is where you want it, you unpack (or *decompress* or *unzip*) it so that you can use it. Whoever first came up with file compression was a pretty smart cookie.

Almost all downloaded files that are compressed have the .ZIP file extension. Other extensions of compressed files are .ARC, .ARJ, or .LZH.

Note: You must restore a compressed file to its original size before you can use it.

Why do people compress files? The following are a couple of the advantages:

➤ Compressed files travel faster from one computer to another. (And when dealing with BBSs and on-line services, faster means cheaper.)

➤ A whole slew of files can be shrunk into a single .ZIP file (for example, the file BOOK.ZIP can contain the files CHAPTER1.TXT, CHAPTER2.TXT, and so on).

. . . and how do I unzip it?

I just downloaded my first file from an on-line service. When I try to use it, I get error messages. Did I do something wrong when I downloaded? P.S. The file ends in .ZIP.

Wow, your first download. (And don't worry, the download went fine.) I'm so proud. I remember my first download — seems like just yesterday.

Programs that end in .ZIP are compressed. Compression saves you download time and, as a result, money (man, those hourly on-line service charges are a killer). Before you can use a compressed program, though, you need to decompress (or *unzip*) it.

Lots of programs can unzip files; the most popular utilities are PKUNZIP and WinZip (a Windows-based unzipping program). But before you run out and grab one of these programs, find out whether you really need it. Many BBSs and on-line services can unzip files for you. For example, America Online unzips files when you logoff from the system. To turn this feature on, select Members⇨Preferences⇨Download and then put an X in the Automatically decompress ZIP and ARC files when I sign off box. You will find the program downloaded on your hard disk in a separate directory within your America Online software directory.

If your BBS or on-line service doesn't offer automatic decompression, you need an unzipping utility, such as PKZ204G.EXE. You can download PKZ204G.EXE from just about any BBS or on-line service. Or you can download it directly from the authors, PKWare, by calling 414-354-8670; set your modem program for N, 8, and 1. After you download PKZ204G.EXE, make a PKZIP directory and move the file you just down-loaded into that directory. You can decompress the file by double-clicking on the file from the File Manager in Windows. From DOS, change to the file's directory and type **PKZ204G.EXE**; the file will *explode*, or decom-press. *Note:* Don't forget to pay your registration fee to PKWare.

PKZ204G.EXE is a DOS program, so you need to be in DOS to unzip any other files. Change to the directory where PKUNZIP is located (to do so, type **CD \ name of directory**). The syntax for unzipping is PKUNZIP {pathname of file to unzip} {pathname of destination to place files}.

For example, if you want to unzip the file TEST.ZIP that is located in the directory BLUE on drive C and then place the decompressed files back in the directory BLUE, change to the directory where PKUNZIP file is located and type **PKUNZIP C:\ BLUE\ TEST.ZIP C:\ BLUE** and press Enter.

What is an .ARJ file?

Is an .ARJ file Mac or PC? Where can I find an appropriate decompression program?

Many different compression schemes coexist out there. For example, PKZIP.EXE creates .ZIP files, LHARC.EXE creates .LZH files, and ARJ creates .ARJ files. Generally, .ARJ files are intended for PCs.

To decompress .ARJ files, you need ARJ V2.41 by Robert K. Yung. You can download this file from most BBSs or on-line services (it's usually called ARJ241.EXE). Unlike ZIP utilities, which require two different programs, ARJ.EXE both compresses and decompresses files. For a list of available ARJ commands, type **ARJ -?** at the DOS prompt and press Enter.

.ZIP files on multiple platforms

I use an IBM PS/1 running DOS and Windows. My brother has an AST Advantage running OS/2. Does the operating system matter when sending/receiving .ZIP files?

Sending the file is not a big deal. You can send a .ZIP file to any IBM-based system easily; it won't matter whether the file ends up on a different class of system. You also can send a .ZIP file to completely different computer platforms, including OS/2, UNIX, VAX, and Macintosh. Even Brother.

PKWare works on DOS and OS/2 platforms, meanwhile, so you shouldn't have any problems decompressing the file. You also can easily find utilities that can unzip a PC .ZIP file for Mac, UNIX, and other systems. To avoid any problems, tell your brother which version of PKZIP you used to create the file. And give him some idea about the file's contents so that he knows what to look for.

My .ZIP file is soliciting me!

Sometimes, a text file that looks suspiciously like an advertisement pops up on-screen when I unzip a file. How do these ads get in my .ZIP files?

To add advertising or other comments to a .ZIP file, people use the -z switch. You can do so either when you originally create the file or later. (By the way, you can update these *ZIP comments* without rezipping the file.)

Pretend you're creating a .ZIP file called MYSTUFF.ZIP, and suppose you want to add a comment to it. To do so, type **PKZIP -z MYSTUFF.ZIP** and press Enter. When you are prompted for your comment, type

```
Give Kim Komando's IDG book to your friends & family.
Call 800-KOMANDO today to find out about Kim's products!
```

(Incidentally, I recommend putting this ad in all .ZIP files.)

622

ZIP comments, which are stored with the .ZIP file and displayed whenever the file is unzipped or viewed, can be up to 127 characters — hardly enough characters for an advertisement. If you need more space or want to show an ANSI graphics screen as a ZIP comment, create the advertising file and save it as a text-only file.

Say that you name the file AD-EXTRA.TXT, for example. The ZIP command to include the AD-EXTRA.TXT file is

```
PKZIP MYSTUFF.ZIP -z < AD-EXTRA.TXT
```

If you go hog-wild and include ANSI graphics with the AD-EXTRA.TXT, the command is

```
PKZIP MYSTUFF.ZIP -zq < AD-EXTRA.TXT
```

The preceding command gives you a comment with graphics up to 4096 bytes (about three-quarters of a page).

Komando Klues

A comment (or advertising) text file doesn't compress and is limited to 64K in size. If you usually are long-winded, you're better off leaving the bigger message inside the program file — for example, in the help file or registration document file.

What's the best format for my on-line text?

I ran an ad on an on-line service describing my company's services. I need to send respondents more information (about 3,500 words). Should I zip it up or put in an e-mail note?

On most BBSs and on-line services, e-mail messages have a size limit. As a result, you're probably better off sending a zipped file.

When you zip up text, make sure that it's in a text file format or ASCII (the standard text format that just about any word processing software can use or open).

You also have to make sure that the people who receive the zipped file can decompress it. You may want to include a little primer in an e-mail note about how to do so. Or suggest that they buy this book.

Sorry, since you're selling, I thought I would, too.

What version do I have?

How can I tell which version of PKZIP I have?

You registered the program, didn't you? Just look in the program's documentation. If you can't find the user manual or program disk, change to the directory where your PKZIP utilities are located. At the DOS prompt, type **PKZIP /?** and press Enter. The screen that pops up will report the version number.

Wait a minute. Why can't you find the documentation? Don't tell me your dog ate it. Did you download the program without paying for it? In that case, are you reading this answer in the bookstore instead of buying the book? Shame on you.

How many versions do I need?

I have PKZIP 2.04G. Some BBSs compress files with Version 1-point-something-or-other. Do I need that version, too?

Like most software, PKZIP is *backward compatible* — meaning newer versions of a program can read (or in this case, unzip) files created (in this case, zipped) by older versions of the same program. You don't need PKZIP Version 1.10 (which is distributed as PKZ110.EXE) because Version 2.04G is a higher version number than 1.10. That is, files compressed with PKZIP Version 1.10 can be decompressed with either Version 1.10 or Version 2.04G.

Pleasing those with lesser versions

Before I upload files, I compress them by using PKZIP 2.04G. But I get complaints from people who use PKZIP 1.10. What can I do?

Files compressed with PKZIP 2.04G can be decompressed with PKUNZIP Version 2.04G but not PKUNZIP Version 1.10. To upload compressed files that folks who still use Version 1.10 can read, you can do one of two things:

➤ Grab a copy of PKZ110.EXE and use it to create your .ZIP file. If you do so, however, don't extract PKZ110.EXE to the same directory where your 2.04G files are located, because the 2.04G files will be overwritten. Your best bet is to extract PKZ110 to another location and then rename all the files to indicate that they were zipped by the older version — for example, rename PKZIP.EXE as PKZIP11.EXE. The renamed file functions normally and you won't confuse it with the file compressed by Version 2.04G.

➤ After you use PKZIP Version 2.04G to create your .ZIP file, use ZIP2EXE.EXE to convert the file to a self-extracting format. The resulting file doesn't require any version of PKUNZIP; users can extract it simply by typing the name of the file. Converting to a self-extracting format is easy; just type **ZIP2EXE FILENAME.ZIP** (where FILENAME is the name of your .ZIP file) and press Enter. You can decompress the resulting file, which is called FILENAME.EXE, by typing **FILENAME.EXE** at the DOS prompt or double-clicking the file from Windows File Manager. Creating a self-extracting file only adds about 20K to the file and makes things more convenient for folks who want to download your file.

Komando Klues

If you decide you want the older PKZIP version, look for PKZ110.EXE. If your BBS or on-line service no longer carries this file, you can download it directly from the PKWare BBS by calling 414-354-8670; set your modem program for N, 8, and 1. Don't forget to pay your registration fee to PKWare.

And send me the file, too. My screen name on America Online is KOMANDO.

Zipping in front of the Windows

Is there a version of PKZIP for Windows? I don't like DOS.

You can find several Windows-based file compression utilities on most BBSs and on-line services. Normally, the files are found in the Windows areas of forums, under the Utilities category.

One of my personal favorites is WinZip, by Nico Mak. With WinZip, you don't even have to venture into the DOS prompt zone. PKZIP and PKUNZIP are built in, but you need the original .EXE files for *disk spanning* (that is, storing a large file on multiple disks) or password protection. WinZip has a powerful point-and-click and drag-and-drop interface (and step-by-step help files to boot) that enables you to easily view, run, extract, add, delete, and test files in .ZIP, .LZH, and .ARC files, including self-extracting archives. *Note:* Be sure to check out WinZip's CheckOut feature.

Troubleshooting

Where do I find PKZIPFIX?

When I tried to decompress a shareware file that I downloaded, I saw the message *Error in Zip — use PKZIPFIX*. What's going on? Where can I get PKZIPFIX?

This message means that the downloaded file is damaged. This damage can be brought about simply by some noise on the telephone line during the download. Crazy, I know, but these computer things are more sensitive than a teenager with pimples.

With PKZIPFIX, which is included in PKWare's ZIP utilities PKZ110.EXE and PKZ204G.EXE, you can try to fix the file — but it doesn't always work. To give it a shot, change to the directory where the PKZIP utilities are located, type **PKZIPFIX FILENAME.ZIP** (where FILENAME is the downloaded .ZIP file's name), and press Enter. You receive a message back, notifying you whether the file has been fixed. There's no in-between here.

Komando
Klues

If your attempt to fix the file fails, or you simply don't want to try, you needn't worry. Most on-line services offer credit to members when downloaded files are damaged and need to be fixed. So request a credit for the download and try again.

Komando Klues
Many BBSs and on-line services let you interrupt a download and resume later. If you interrupt and then try to unzip the partially downloaded file, the odds of getting this error message are great.

My compressed file didn't shrink!

I tried zipping a file before sending it to my mother through an on-line service, but the file didn't get smaller. Did I do something wrong?

First, kudos to your mom for having a computer, subscribing to a service, and using it. My mother refuses to give up her Betamax. Worse, she uses the 486DX2 66 I bought her solely as a $2,000 solitaire machine. I should have bought her a deck of cards.

You probably didn't do anything wrong. Not all files that are zipped will shrink. For example, encrypted files, files that have already been compressed, and certain file types won't get much smaller than their original size:

> ➤ You may be able to shrink the file's size if you protected the file by using an encryption method. (*Encryption* garbles the file's contents; to ungarble the information, you need the encryption code.) Try first saving the file without encryption and then use PKZIP's encryption feature.

> ➤ Files distributed with commercial applications often are already compressed, so compression is a waste of time.

> ➤ Graphics files, program executable files, and sound files don't compress much either. Text files compress the most.

Note: Those using Stacker, DoubleSpace, DriveSpace, SuperStor, or other hard drive compression utilities should take special note that you can't compress an already zipped file. Because these utilities can't compress .ZIP files further, the files will seem to take up a great deal of space. It's best to remove .ZIP files from compressed drives if possible.

Zipping subdirectories

I want to zip up my data directory and all its subdirectories to send to my boss, who lives in another city. Whenever I try to zip this directory, though, he never gets the subdirectories. What am I doing wrong? If my boss doesn't see these files, he won't know that I really am working.

Boy, lots of trust in this company.

You must tell PKZIP that you want the subdirectories to be included in your .ZIP file. To talk to PKZIP about subdirectories, you need to use appropriate switches.

Change to the directory that has the subdirectories you want included in the .ZIP file. Then type **PKZIP -rp FILENAME.ZIP** (where FILENAME is the .ZIP file's name) and press Enter. *Note:* This command assumes that the directories that hold your PKZIP software are listed in the PATH statement of your computer's AUTOEXEC.BAT file.

This action creates FILENAME.ZIP in the current directory and includes all the files in all the subdirectories. The subdirectory names and path information are all stored in the .ZIP file, too, making it possible to unzip an exact duplicate of your current directory and subdirectories on another system.

Be sure to use the lowercase -rp because -rP does something altogether different.

You can get very fancy with storing directory information in a .ZIP file. Refer to the PKZIP manual for more information.

When it's time to unzip the directory, along with all the subdirectories, you must tell PKUNZIP that it should look for all this nifty path or directory information so that the original directory can be re-created. To have the directory structure re-created, your boss needs to use the -d switch (*d* stands for directories): that is, type **PKUNZIP -d FILENAME.ZIP** (where FILENAME is the .ZIP file's name) and press Enter.

Note: Again, this command assumes that the directories that hold your PKZIP software are listed in the PATH statement of your computer's AUTOEXEC.BAT file.

If you download a .ZIP file and aren't sure whether it has path information stored inside, you can check by typing **PKUNZIP -t FILENAME.ZIP** (where FILENAME is the .ZIP file's name) and pressing Enter. This action makes sure that the archive file is OK and shows you its contents. If you see files listed with directories such as \DATA\MYWORK.DBF, you know to use the -d switch when unzipping. You also can use the -v switch to view the files in the archive without testing archive integrity. If you're a techie type, try using the -vt switch, as in

```
PKUNZIP -vt FILENAME.ZIP
```

where FILENAME is the .ZIP file's name. This action reveals more about the files in the .ZIP file than you have ever wanted to know!

More and more people are working at home. In fact, I've compiled a short list of advantages:

➤ It's a short commute from the bed to the desk.

➤ You can work in your underwear.

➤ You're not forced to listen to soft hits on the radio all day.

Saving large .ZIP files to floppies

I frequently need to zip many files to a floppy disk. Unfortunately, the size of the .ZIP file still exceeds the size of the disk. What can I do?

If you own the latest version of PKZIP (2.04G), you can make a .ZIP file that's too big to cram on a single disk. So PKZIP 2.04G actually spreads this file over several disks — called *spanning*. (Yes, just like the French, computer techies have a word for everything.)

The command you need to span your .ZIP file over several disks is

```
PKZIP -& A:\FILENAME.ZIP
```

where A: is the drive letter of the floppy drive and FILENAME.ZIP is the name of the .ZIP file. You can use the -& option only when creating a .ZIP file on *removable media* (that's nerdspeak for floppy disk).

If you think that this command can be used as a sort of hard drive backup program, you're right! To find out more about using PKZIP as a backup program, check out the user manual.

629

Be sure to use the `-ex` switch for maximum compression. You may able to get more of the compressed files on one disk this way. The command should look like

```
PKZIP -&ex A:\FILENAME.ZIP
```

where `A:` is the drive letter of the floppy drive and `FILENAME.ZIP` is the name of the .ZIP file.

Note: The `-ex` switch works on programs that you don't span. And, come to think of it, the `-ex` switch works for spouses from hell, too.

PKZIP 2.04G won't work on my machine

I cannot get PKZIP 2.04G to function through Windows or DOS. I have an IBM clone 486DX2 66 with 8MB of RAM. Every time I try to execute the command, the screen blanks and the system locks. What's the problem?

Hey, don't get download on yourself. If I were you, I'd try downloading PKZ204G.EXE again.

First, delete the old PKZ204G.EXE from your hard drive. If you're not sure where it is, type **DIR PKZ240G.EXE /S** at the DOS prompt and press Enter.

Make sure you delete PKZIP.EXE, PKUNZIP.EXE, PKZIPFIX.EXE, ZIP2EXE.EXE, and PKUNZJR.COM before you download PKZ204G.EXE again. Then run `CHKDSK /F/V` or `SCANDISK` from the DOS prompt on your hard drive to eliminate the possibility of corrupted files.

Type **PKZ204G** at the DOS prompt and watch carefully for any errors. Then change to the directory where you decompressed PKZ204G.EXE, type **PKUNZIP /?**, and press Enter. See whether you get the help screen. Now try to unzip a file.

If you still get a system lockup, you may have problems with extended/expanded memory on your system. Attempt to unzip with the following PKUNZIP command line option:

```
PKUNZIP -3-+) FILENAME.ZIP
```

where `FILENAME.ZIP` is the name of the .ZIP file. The troubleshooting `3-+` switches are explained in the PKUNZIP help screen, page 2 — it has to do with memory. It's a little complicated, but this trick often is a quick fix.

Unzipping produces incomplete filenames

Some of the files I unzip have incomplete extensions (for example, SETUP._XE). Have these files become as corrupted as Congress?

Depends on what district you live in.

The download went fine. An underscore (_) in the extension normally means that the file is still compressed. Typing **SETUP** usually (but not always) decompresses the file automatically.

If the installation program isn't SETUP, use INSTALL instead. Either way, this should decompress the file for you.

Speeding up the zipping process

Every day, I do more zipping and unzipping of files than Madonna does dresses. I'm falling behind in my other responsibilities. Is there anything I can do to speed up the process?

You can do a few things to make PKZIP zippier:

➤ If you like to do things at the DOS prompt, consider writing batch files for repetitive commands. For example, you can create a batch file to copy all the files you want to zip into a single directory, run PKZIP, and copy the resulting .ZIP file elsewhere. Similarly, you can simplify unzipping by creating another batch file.

➤ If you're using PKZIP 2.04G, you can create a configuration file with all your frequently used ZIP/UNZIP options listed. Then you won't need to specify so much on the command line.

➤ If you don't get your kicks by typing a novel at the DOS prompt, you may want to go with one of the ZIP menus or shells. PKWare, for example, has a menu called PKZMENU that lets you automate unzipping and lets you tag multiple files for unzipping at a single whack.

➤ If the speed is contingent upon the computer, not the user, play the memory game. You can speed up PKZIP by making it use a RAM drive to store the temporary files it needs while creating the .ZIP file. Basically, you edit the computer's AUTOEXEC.BAT file by adding the following line:

```
SET PKTMP=D
```

where D is the RAM drive's letter. The catch: Your RAM disk requires free disk space equal to the size of the largest compressed file. (This method involves DOS commands. For more information, type **HELP RAMDRIVE.SYS** at the DOS prompt and press Enter.)

And don't knock Madonna. She's a friend.

Q&A Launching downloaded files from Program Manager

I downloaded a couple of applications to my WINDOWS directory. Can I launch them from Program Manager? Using File Manager to start .EXE files is such a hassle.

In this answer, I describe how to run a file from Program Manager without adding it to a bona fide program group.

Start with some basic hard disk organization: make a directory and call it DOWNLOAD and then create a few subdirectories.

For example, I have the following subdirectories in my DOWNLOAD directory:

➤ NOTTESTD, where I download all my files before I copy them onto a floppy disk and virus-check them

➤ TESTAREA, where I copy the virus-checked files back and test-drive downloaded files

After a file has made it back into TESTAREA from Windows Program Manager, select File⇨Run. If you know exactly where the file is that you want to test and what it's called, type the following in the command line box:

```
C:\DOWNLOAD\TESTAREA\TCHAOS.EXE
```

Bee kareful bekaws speling kounts! Also, be sure to use the backslash (/) and not the forward slash (\).

If you get a message stating that Windows can't find your file, you may just be spelling it wrong or looking in the wrong place. Don't worry, all is not lost! Click the Browse button and then select the directory where you think the file may be. Next, use the up and down arrows to scroll through the list of files in that directory. When you find the one that looks like it runs your program, click on it.

Komando Klues

This method works great when you're trying out a downloaded program because it's much easier to get rid of any program you hate. Just delete the TESTAREA subdirectory.

If you love this program, however, and want to add it to your Accessories program group, select the Accessories group. (Either click on a part of the window to bring it to the top or pick it from the Window menu.) From Program Manager, select File⇨New⇨Program Item and then choose the file's name to start the program. If you're not sure of the program's start-up filename, use the Browse feature.

You may be asked to pick an icon for the program. If so, click on Change icon to choose one of Windows's icons. Windows automatically writes all the techno jargon needed to link the icon to the application. From here on out, the program starts when you double-click the icon.

VBRUN

Q&A *Where should I put the VBRUN files?*

I download a number of files that require VBRUN100.DLL, VBRUN200.DLL, or VBRUN300.DLL, but I don't know where to put the VBRUN files after I download them. Do I have to create a directory?

Nine times out of ten (heck, maybe 99.9 percent of the time), the VBRUN files, which are run-time modules required to run programs written in Visual Basic, go in the WINDOWS\SYSTEM directory — assuming that Windows is in your AUTOEXEC.BAT path statement. You can check your path statement's contents by typing **PATH** at the DOS prompt and pressing Enter.

In case you care, DLL stands for *Dynamic Link Libraries*.

VBRUN300.DLL too big for Notepad

I recently downloaded VBRUN300.DLL. I received a message saying that the file is too large for Notepad. What do I do?

You do not edit VBRUN100.DLL, VBRUN200.DLL, or VBRUN300.DLL files, which are run-time modules required to run programs written in Visual Basic. These files should be placed in your WINDOWS\SYSTEM directory.

But I bet, for some reason, files with the .DLL extension are associated to pull up Notepad in your WIN.INI file. You associate file extensions with programs in File Manager.

Make a backup copy of your WIN.INI file. Then use Notepad to open your WIN.INI file. Go to the [extensions] section, which is where the associations are saved. If you find the line

```
DLL=C:\WINDOWS\NOTEPAD.EXE ^DLL
```

or something that looks a lot like it, delete it. Then save the changed WIN.INI file.

Is my VB shareware royalty-free?

I wrote a great program that I want to distribute as shareware. I used Visual Basic and want to know whether I have to pay Microsoft any run-time royalties.

Microsoft, like most providers of development tools, allows you to distribute the VBRUN300.DLL run-time library for free with your programs. In fact, Microsoft's Visual Basic run-time DLLs are freely distributed.

As a result, you can include them with your files. And users can download them from a variety of sources, including most BBSs, on-line services, and the Microsoft Download Service. Because these run-time DLLs are so readily available, most folks already have them.

They're also pretty large, so you may not want to include them with your program. If you don't, be sure to specify which version of Visual Basic your program is written in and which run-time is needed to run it:

> If your program is written in Visual Basic 1.0, users need VBRUN100.DLL.

> If your program is written in Visual Basic 2.0, users need VBRUN200.DLL.

> If your program is written in Visual Basic 3.0, users need VBRUN300.DLL.

It's a good idea to tell users where they can get these DLLs if they're not included in your program and what to do with them once they have them (usually, placing them in the WINDOWS\SYSTEM directory is a safe bet).

Remember, these three DLLs are not interchangeable! No fair trying to mix and match!

Case Examples

 WINDUPE runs correctly only once

I downloaded WINDUPE, installed it, and ran a test run. It worked great. Later, I went back in, clicked on WINDUPE, told it "I agree" and "OK." WINDUPE then gave me an error message, saying that SHARE.EXE wasn't loaded. I erased the whole thing and started over. Again, the test run immediately after installation worked OK. But after I left and returned to Windows, I saw the same error message. Am I going to have to reinstall the program every time I want to use it?

Sounds like you've been WINDUPEd.

You don't need to keep reinstalling the program. Instead, try loading SHARE in your AUTOEXEC.BAT file.

If the AUTOEXEC.BAT file, which is one of two files that your computer reads each time it starts up, gets messed up, your computer may not start up exactly as you're accustomed. So it's important that you practice safety first when changing the AUTOEXEC.BAT file. In other words, make a backup copy of this file.

Here's how, if you don't remember:

1. Put a blank disk in drive A.

2. Type **FORMAT A:\S** and press Enter. The disk is formatted. When the procedure ends, you get a *System transferred* message.

3. Label the disk *Emergency Boot Disk — My Loving Computer*.

If ever your computer won't start from the hard drive, you can stick this disk in the drive and reboot. This backup is a good thing to have around when editing your start-up files — just in case something weird happens.

Next, using Windows Notepad, open AUTOEXEC.BAT file and add the following line somewhere in the middle of the file:

```
C:\DOS\SHARE.EXE /F:1500 /L:500
```

Some folks preface this line with Loadhigh, but problems can develop when SHARE is loaded high, so don't try it. Save your changes.

Note: It is very important when editing an AUTOEXEC.BAT file that you save the file as ASCII text only.

Reboot your computer for the changes to take effect. Try running WINDUPE again; it should work like a charm.

DEMOBILD causes confusion

I downloaded a program and unzipped it. The instructions said to do something with a file named DEMOBILD, but I didn't understand. I think the directions were written by a nuclear scientist instead of someone at Lotus.

You make it sound like the people at Lotus are dumb.

A program can be downloaded to and stored on a hard drive without being installed. Some demo programs use DEMOBILD to turn downloaded files into their installation disks. Make sure you type the appropriate command in the directory where the DEMOBILD.EXE utility and your demo data files are located.

I bet I can guess your problem. Lotus shipped some demos of Organizer with a goof in the documentation: it said to type **DEMOBILD DISK1 A:**. The problem is there isn't any DISK1.DAT in the archive. Try putting a blank formatted disk in drive A and typing

```
DEMOBILD LOTORG A:
```

If you still have trouble, just contact the folks whence you downloaded the program for a new copy. Or call Lotus Development at 800-872-3387 and ask them to send you a demo disk in the mail.

What and where is QBasic?

The file description for a shareware game says that I need QBasic or QuickBASIC. What is it, and how do I get it?

QuickBASIC, sometimes called QBasic (to be quick to the punch), is the BASIC language that comes with more recent versions of MS-DOS. It replaces the slower GW Basic, or Gee Whiz BASIC.

You probably have QuickBASIC already. And the file you need, QBASIC.EXE, is probably in your DOS directory. Generally, you can run a QuickBASIC program by typing the following at the DOS prompt and pressing Enter:

```
QBASIC FILENAME.BAS
```

where FILENAME.BAS is the name of the program you want to run.

Downloaded file causes crashes

When I try to use the F15 game that I downloaded, I get a choice of sounds. After choosing one, the system locks in Windows or reboots in DOS. What am I doing wrong?

Your system may be rebooting/locking due to a memory conflict or a problem with the way the program accesses your sound card. (Or maybe you've been shot down by a Soviet missile!)

If the file has an installation or setup program, make sure that you ran it. Sometimes, you need to set your computer's configuration to work with games. You can find more information in the program's help file or documentation.

Next, try *clean booting* your system. Do what? Good question!

➤ If you're using DOS 6 or higher, reboot your computer. As soon as you see *Loading MS-DOS* on-screen, press F5. This action bypasses your CONFIG.SYS file. See whether the program will run now.

➤ If you're using a version of DOS prior to 6.0, boot your system with a bootable floppy and then see whether the program will run.

If you still run into problems, try contacting the sysop (system operator) or staff where you downloaded the program or get in touch with the program's author. Be sure to include as much information about your system hardware and setup as you can.

The root directory: Decompress equals mess

I downloaded family tree software and PKZIP. Unfortunately, I downloaded them into my main root directory. And when I decompressed all the files, I wound up with a mess on my hands. How do I clean up after myself and not get rid of anything real important?

What do you mean by *real important*? Are you willing to delete stuff that's *somewhat important*? I don't think so.

Let's do this the safest way possible. I don't want to tell you to just delete whatever you don't think you need from your root directory. That advice could prove disastrous. So here's what you should do:

1. Copy both programs to an empty subdirectory on your hard drive and unzip them there.

2. While in that directory, turn on your printer and type **DIR >PRN**. This command prints a list of all the files in the subdirectory. These are the files to delete from your main root directory. If you are using a laser printer, you may need to press the form feed button on the printer.

Komando Klues

To be extra, extra safe, make a backup copy of your root directory and have a bootable floppy disk available before you delete anything.

"I can't see"

I downloaded some pictures of models. How do I look at them?

Models of what? Airplanes? Drag cars? Naked women? Perhaps you should download some psychological models and see which one you fit into.

Graphics information can be stored in several formats, including .GIF, .TIF, .PCX, and .BMP. Different formats need different viewers. For example, WINGIF for Windows or CSHOW for DOS are good viewers for .GIF files. For other formats, consider an all-purpose viewer, such as Paint Shop Pro by JASC or Graphics Workshop by Alchemy Mindworks.

The Bottom Line

So you need to determine which format the pictures you downloaded use.

By the way, you also should identify the computing platform used when the pictures were made. For example, if the picture is a .GIF created on a Macintosh, you need a utility (such as GIFSTRIP) to remove the file's 30-byte header or else you won't be able to view the picture with a PC-based .GIF viewer.

Installing downloaded screen savers

I recently found on a local BBS some airplane and jet screen saver add-ons that work with Windows's built-in screen saver. How do I make them work?

Sounds like you have really learned to harness the power of technology. All you have to do is unzip or copy those screen savers (probably .SCR files) to your WINDOWS directory.

To do so, open the Windows Control Panel and select Desktop and then Screen Saver. From the list, select a screen saver. Set other options as desired (usually you can set blank time, colors, patterns, speed, number of wiggle things, and so on). Click Test to see whether you like the new screen saver. If so, stick with it: close the Desktop and Control Panel.

To see your handiwork, wait patiently for the screen to blank.

I want Program Manager back!

I downloaded a program entitled Control Panel for Windows. When I installed it, I used the option that makes it become the Windows shell. Now, I don't like the program but can't get rid of it. I tried writing the author, but the e-mail address is no longer valid.

First, start Windows and look in Control Panel for an uninstall option. If available, this option will offer the cleanest deletion available.

If no uninstall option is available, make a backup of your WIN.INI and SYSTEM.INI files in your WINDOWS directory.

Then use Windows Notepad to open WIN.INI and look in the [windows] section. Make sure `Control Panel` doesn't appear in your `load=` or `run=` lines. If it does, remove the mentions and save your WIN.INI file as a text file. Close the WIN.INI file.

Now open the SYSTEM.INI in Notepad. In the [boot] section, you'll see something like

```
[boot]
mouse.drv=mouse-driver-name
shell=control-panel-program name.
```

Change the `shell=` line to read

```
shell=progman.exe
```

and save the SYSTEM.INI file as a text file. Restart Windows.

If Control Panel is still there, you may want to buy a really cool program called UnInstaller. (I promise that it's not written by the guy who wrote Control Panel.) UnInstaller finds all the installed applications on your Windows computer and then helps you get rid of them. All you have to do is click on the program name; UnInstaller goes out and safely does the dirty work for you.

Smile, You're on Komando Camera

Smileys

I'm new to the world of on-line communications. What's the cryptic symbol language that everyone uses? It makes me nervous and uneasy. I don't know what anyone's saying.

You should be nervous and uneasy, because we've been talking about you!

Because it's hard to get a point across in on-line or e-mail messages, computer users far and wide use combinations of characters called *emoticons* to give life to their electronic words. These combinations of normal keys make faces, frowns, and more.

The following is a listing of e-mail symbols. Noses are optional!

Emoticon	Translation
:-)	Basic smile.
;-)	Winky smile. A "Don't hit me for what I just said" smile. In other words, denotes a flirtatious and/or sarcastic remark.
:-(	Frowning smile. User did not like last statement or is upset/depressed.
:-I	Indifferent smile.
:->	Denotes a cutting sarcastic remark that's worse than ;-).
>:->	You'd probably get your hand slapped if the reader of your note was near.
>;->	Denotes a lewd or crude remark.
(@ @)	Raised eyes. As in, "You're kidding!"
Less common smiles.	
(-:	Left-handed.
:-"	Pursed lips.
:*)	Drunk.

(continued) **641**

Emoticon	Translation
{:]	Robot.
8-)	Wearing sunglasses.
B:-)	Wearing sunglasses on head.
::-)	Wearing normal glasses.
B-)	Wearing horn-rimmed glasses.
g-)	Wearing pince-nez glasses.
8:-)	Little girl (bow in hair).
:-)-8	Big girl.
:-()	Mustachioed.
:-{}	Wearing lipstick.
{:-)	Wearing a toupee.
}:-(	Wearing a toupee in an updraft.
@:-)	Wearing a turban.
:-{	Count Dracula.
:-[	Vampire.
:-E	Buck-toothed vampire.
:-F	Buck-toothed vampire with one tooth missing.
%-)	Glazed eyes (brought upon by staring at a screen for 15 hours straight).
:-7	Wry comment.
:-*	Oooops (mouth covered by hand). Or ate something sour.
:-B	Drooling (or has overbite).
:'-(	Crying.
:'-)	Happy crying.
'-)	Winking.
:-@	Screaming.
:-#	Wearing braces. Also, censored (muzzle over mouth).
:^)	Broken nose.
:v)	Broken nose (the other way).
:<)	Ivy League education. (Or hairy lips.)

:<)=	Bearded.
:-&	Tongue-tied.
=:-)	Hosehead.
-:-)	Punk rocker.
-:-(	Real punk rockers don't smile.
:=)	Two-nosed.
+-:-)	Pope (or holds another religious office).
`:-)	One eyebrow missing.
,:-)	The other eyebrow missing.
|-I	Asleep.
|-O	Yawning.
:-Q	Smoker.
:-?	Pipe smoker.
O :-)	Angel (at heart, at least).
:-w	Speaking with forked tongue.
:-W	Shouting with forked tongue.
:-S	Incoherent.
:-D	Laughing (at you!).
:-X	Sealed lips.
:-C	Disbelieving (jaw dropped). Or bummed.
:-T	Keeping a straight face (tight lips).
<|-)	Chinese.
<|-(	Chinese and unhappy.
:-/	Skeptical.
C=:-)	Chef.
=|:-)=	Uncle Sam.
*<:-)	Santa Claus (or wearing Santa's cap, at least).
E-:-)	Ham-radio operator.
P-)	Pirate.
:-9	Licking lips.
%-6	Braindead.

(continued)

Emoticon	Translation
[:-)	Wearing a Walkman (or headphones).
(:I	Egghead.
<:-I	Dunce.
K:P	Kid wearing propeller beanie.
@=	Pro nuclear war.
More.	
o=	A burning candle (for flames).
-=	A doused candle (to end a flame).
OO	Headlights.
:-J	Tongue in cheek.
:*)	Clowning.
:-x	Kiss kiss.
:/i	No smoking.
:/)	Unfunny.
:_)	Nose out of joint.
:-O	Shhhhhh (no yelling, please).
:-:	Mutant smile.
	Invisible smile.
.-)	One-eyed.
,-)	One-eyed and winking.
X-)	Dead.
8 :-)	Wizard.
O-)	Megaton man on patrol (or scuba diver).
:-P	Nyahhhhh!
<:-O	Eeek!
:-8	Talking out both sides of mouth.
(:-)	Wearing helmet.
C=}>;*{))	Megasmile! That is, a drunk, devilish chef with a toupee in an updraft, a mustache, and a double chin (whew!).
|-(	Late-night message.

:^)	Teasing people about their noses.
:-{#}	Teasing people about their braces.
(:-$	Ill.
(:-&	Angry.
(:-(	Very sad.
(:^(	Concerning people with broken noses.
(:<)	Concerning blabber mouths.
:-(=)	Big teeth.
&:-)	Curly hair.
@:-)	Wavy hair.
?-(	Black eye.
.	Fuzzy things.
*.**	Fuzzy things with fuzzy mustaches.
%-)	Broken glasses.
+<:-|	Monk/nun.
{0-)	Cyclops.
(:-|K-	Formal message (bow tie).
...—...	S.O.S.
@%&$%&	Not said in polite company.
||*(	Handshake offered.
||*)	Handshake accepted.
<&&>	Rubber chickens.
><><	Wearing argyle socks.
2B|^2B	Shakespeare.
(-_-)	Secret smile.
<{:-)}	Message in a bottle.
<:-)<<|	Message from space.
(:-...	Heartbroken.
<<<<(:-)	Hat salesperson.
(O—<	Fishy.

(continued)

Emoticon	Translation
(:><	Thief (hands up!).
(l==l)	Four wheels.
:^{	For those with mustaches.
@>--->--	A rose.
:-o	Uh oh!
#:-) :-)	Matted hair.
#:-o	Oh, nooooooo! (à la Mr. Bill).
(8-o	It's Mr. Bill.
*:o	Bozo the Clown.
3:]	Pet smile.
3:[	Mean pet smile.
d8=	Pet beaver is wearing goggles and a hard hat.

Then, there are the midget smiles.

:)	Midget smile.
:]	Gleep. A friendly midget smile.
=)	Variation on a theme.
:)	Happy.
:D	Laughter.
:I	Hmmmm.
:(	Sad.
:[	Real down.
:O	Yelling.
:,C	Crying.
[]	Hugs and . . .
:*	Kisses.
|I	Asleep.
|^o	Snoring.

More and more.

:-` Spitting chewing tobacco.

:-#|	Bushy mustache.
:-$	Jaw wired shut.
:-%	Banker.
+:-)	Priest.
<:>==	Turkey.
(:-)	Big face.
:-q	Trying to touch tongue to nose.
:-a	Lefty trying to touch tongue to nose.
:-e	Disappointed.
:-t	Cross.
:-i	Semismile.
:-1	Smirk.
:-o	Singing national anthem.
:-p	Tongue sticking out.
:-r	Bleahhh.
:-[	Blockhead.
:-s	Bizarre.
:-d	Lefty razzing.
:-j	Lefty smiling politely.
:-l	Smile.
:-\	Undecided smile.
:-|	Disgusted.
:<	Forlorn.
:-z	Cross.
:-v	Talking head. (Also, profiled.)
:-V	Shouting.
:-o	More shouting.
|-P	Yuk.
|-D	Ho ho.
|-)	Hee hee.

(continued)

Emoticon	Translation
:-8(	Condescending.
>:-<	Mad.
(:-(	Frowning.
:-) :-) :-)	Guffaw.
:-))-:	Acting.

By the way, at least you passed the first test of on-line message writing, because YOU DIDN'T USE CAPS. You see, all capital letters means you're screaming at someone. However, you failed the second test of on-line protocol; you always should address important people (ME!) as *Your royal highness*. Your e-mail notes get answered quicker when respect is demonstrated.

OK, OK. I'm joking. Sorry.

[] and :*,
Kim Komando
8 :-)

Chapter 18

Spreadsheets

Basics

Spreadsheets defined

My computer came with a spreadsheet program. What is it?

Ever make a home budget using a calculator, a pencil, and piece of paper? It's tedious to set up the categories, put all the numbers in the right columns, add the numbers, and then to find that a number changes and it's a do-over. Accountants have been using columnar pads with wide pages to line up numbers into nice neat columns for years. The idea behind spreadsheets is to provide an electronic version of the accountant's pad. You type numbers in the proper columns and have the computer do the math.

So, a spreadsheet is a program that stores information and does calculations on that information. Sometimes, the calculations are simple. At other times, you can be very fancy. With a spreadsheet, you can make charts or graphs or even manipulate data based on certain criteria.

A spreadsheet program is a lot better than a calculator. A spreadsheet not only lets you store lots of numbers and see them on a screen, it lets you change one number and see the result immediately. Because the computer makes it so easy to change numbers, you can use spreadsheets to answer a lot of "what if" questions, such as, what if I didn't buy Excel? How much would I have saved?

Most spreadsheet programs do a lot more than crunch numbers. You can make graphs, create presentations, and handle a database with a spreadsheet program, too. Macros are popular in spreadsheet programs. Think of a macro as a way to take all the steps you take to make a pot of coffee and save them into one big step. To make a pot of coffee, all you would have to do is play the coffee macro.

Try out the spreadsheet program with something simple: a home budget. Put the months January, February, March, and so on across the columns. List the categories of how you spend your money down the left side with one category in each row. Where the column and row meet, say January Rent, enter the amount. Play around. You can't hurt anything. Pretend that you just won the lottery and are trying to manage your new-found riches. Don't forget to put in a category for books. Buy one of mine for all your friends.

What goes in a cell?

In my spreadsheet program, there are different types of cells. What type of information can I put in a cell?

You can put three types of information in cells:

➤ Numeric information that holds numbers only; for instance, the $20 that you hand over to your teenager to go to the movies or the $.27 that you get back.

➤ Formulas, which perform calculations on the numbers in the spreadsheet and cause a result to be displayed, such as $20 times 2 when your teenager takes a date to the movies. You would type the formula into the cell, 20*2, and a cell with a formula in it would show only the result, or $40. You don't always have to type numbers in formulas; you can use cell addresses. For example, if cell B4 contains the number 20 and cell C7 contains 2, the formula B4*C7 will display the number 40 in the cell holding that formula. In spreadsheet programs, the following operators are used in mathematical formulas:

*	multiplication
/	division
+	addition
-	subtraction

➤ Cells that hold descriptions, titles, and other free-form notes. Rows or columns of descriptive information are sometimes referred to as labels. Titles usually are column headings. Money Spent, Total Dollars, and Now I'm Flat Broke are examples of labels. January, February, March, and Yearly Total are examples of titles.

Letters and numbers

I'm having trouble understanding what all the letters and numbers on-screen mean when I am using a spreadsheet program. I feel like I'm playing battleship — A1, B4, D19.

When I play Battleship, the first thing I always say is "I One." Then my opponent asks, "What do you mean, you won?" Oh, I get the biggest kick out of that.

An accountant's pad has lines going up and down and left to right on a page. The lines make it easier for the accountant to put the numbers in the right place. A spreadsheet program works the same way. The lines divide the spreadsheet into rows and columns. It's easy to remember columns because they are up and down, just like columns on buildings such as the White House. Rows go side to side, just like rows of corn in a field. To keep track of which column you're in, a spreadsheet program uses alphabetic letters. You start at the very left-hand side of the spreadsheet and call this column A, the next column is B, and so on. To keep track of rows, you use numbers. The top row is number 1, the row under the top row is 2, and so on.

Because you can have so many cells or boxes in your spreadsheet, you need some way to keep track of them. Remember, each column has its own letter, and each row has its own number. Well, guess what? You use these numbers and letters as an address for each box, or cell; a cell is the place where a row and a column meet.

A cell is like a post office box; each cell has a unique address. An address of D15 means that the cell is in the D column and the 15th row.

Some spreadsheets let you work with more than one worksheet at a time. You may see A:A1 as a cell address. The first A tells you that this is the first spreadsheet you have open, the colon is just a separator, and the A1 is the cell you're working in, the active cell. Usually, the active cell is the one on the spreadsheet outlined with a dark box. The cell pointer is similar to a cursor, and by being highlighted with a contrasting color or border, the cell pointer indicates your current location on the worksheet. (When you're editing the contents of a cell, you will see a regular cursor indicating your position within that cell.)

Most spreadsheet programs will also show the cell currently selected somewhere underneath the menu bar. You can put descriptions, called *labels, numbers,* or *formulas,* in the cells.

Excel

 Help me understand this!

I took a computer class on Excel and failed it. For the life of me, I just can't get a handle on using a spreadsheet. It's so hard. Any ideas for me? You can call me Numberless in New Jersey.

What really scares me is that your mother will need to sign your report card.

Komando
Klues

Microsoft Excel has great help available from within the program up to and including step-by-step instructions. Select Help from the Excel menu bar and click the Examples and Demos button. Try using some sample worksheets that Excel includes. Select File, then Open, and change to the Examples directory (it's usually an Excel subdirectory) to see sample worksheets and macros.

Don't forget about the TipWizard, Excel's answer to holding your hand through worksheet tasks. When the TipWizard is on call, hints appear on how to do whatever you're doing more efficiently, and you receive a tip-of-the-day when you start Excel. To turn the Wizard on and off, click the TipWizard button. It's all the way to the right side of the Standard toolbar and has a lightbulb on it.

Sounds as though you could use *Excel For Dummies* from IDG Books. And Cruncher by Davidson & Associates (800-545-7677) is a software program designed to teach spreadsheets to kids aged 10 and up. But it's great for adults just getting started, too.

Adding features to toolbars

I frequently use certain tools that are not on the toolbar in my spreadsheet program. Can I add the Find tool, or another tool for that matter, to a toolbar?

A toolbar sounds like a place where you'd meet some very tough drinkers. But a toolbar in a software program is the row underneath the menu bar that contains lots of icons representing shortcuts to frequently used options.

Most programs allow you to customize your work area, from customizing the buttons shown on a toolbar to getting rid of the toolbar altogether. For instance, Lotus 1-2-3 Version 4.0 for Windows or later, Quattro Pro Versions 1.0 and 5.0 for Windows, and Excel Versions 4.0 and 5.0 all allow you to assign items to a toolbar. You can modify the toolbar by removing the buttons for items you don't use and adding new ones.

Most Windows programs have a Customize Toolbar shortcut available. Try this: Place the mouse arrow on the toolbar, not on an icon, and click the right mouse button once. A toolbar-specific pop-up options window may appear on the screen that lists the Customize option. Click Customize and the new window appears. Usually, you select the category (File, Edit, View, and so on), select the button that you want on the toolbar using your mouse, and then drag the button to the position where you want it on the toolbar. It's quite simple.

If the right-click didn't do anything, you may have to do the job through the program's menu bar options. Take a peek in your software program manual under *Customizing* or *Toolbar*, or use those as search words in Help.

Some programs also allow you to change the toolbar buttons from small to large. With luck, your program offers the Customize Toolbar feature. You'll be able to see the new buttons all the way across the room. Having the right tools makes any job easier.

Changing options

Surely, there is a way that the cursor box will move automatically after I type a number and press Enter in Excel 5. It's probably as easy as turning off a light switch.

Normally, pressing the Enter key after typing a number or formula causes the active cell to move down one row automatically. Someone's been sitting in your chair, someone's been lying in your bed, and someone's been messing with your program settings, and they still are! Let's fix it.

Select Tools⇨Options. Click the Edit tab and then put an X in the box before Move Selection after Enter option. Clicking an option box does in fact work like a light switch; it takes the X out to deselect an option or puts the X in to select an option.

While you're in the Options menu, customize how you work in other Excel features. Click the General tab to set the font for all new workbooks, the number of sheets in every new workbook, and also, where you keep your data files. Click all the tabs in the Options area; there are all kinds of neat ways to make the Excel desktop your own. Click OK when you are done and the changes take effect immediately.

Defining a print range

My entire worksheet is really big. I need to print only a certain area, but to get it, I print the whole thing. It seems to be a waste to pick 12 pages out of the printer and look at only one page. Is there a workaround? I'm tired of making paper airplanes.

Well, have you tried playing NBA with your trash can? I always miss the basket.

The quickest way to print just a section of a worksheet is to first highlight the area that you want to print. You highlight an area using the mouse; click the left-most and upper area of the worksheet, drag the mouse across the worksheet, and release the mouse button when the entire area that you want is selected. Select File⇨Print. Under Print What, click Selection. Then click OK.

If, however, there is only one area — or range — of a worksheet that you continually print out of an entire worksheet, there's a better way. Choose File⇨Page Setup. Select the Sheet tab and then click the Print Area box to move the cursor. You can type the cell addresses, or you can move the cursor onto the worksheet and highlight the area that you want to print.

Next, under Print Titles, click the Rows to Repeat box to leave the cursor there. Select the row title to appear on every page by highlighting it from the worksheet or typing a new row title in the box. To get column titles on the left of every page, click the box after Columns To Repeat At Left box to drop the cursor and highlight the column title from the worksheet, or type a new column title. Click OK to close the Page Setup box. Select Print and from now on, until you change it, the only area of your worksheet that will print is the area that you highlighted in the Page Setup.

Komando Klues Take a moment and select File⇨Print Preview. You'll see on your screen what will come out of your printer, and you can play around with the margins and setup, too. If everything looks swell, click the Print button. Otherwise, click Close and you'll return to your worksheet.

Excel won't print entire worksheet

I am so frustrated. No matter what I do, Excel just won't print my entire worksheet. The Print Preview is quite selective in that it chooses to display only portions of the spreadsheet — the start and the end. I'm sure the reason is obvious.

Well, not that obvious or you wouldn't have asked. It sounds as if you accidentally told Excel to print just the beginning and end of your worksheet. OK, it was Excel's fault, really. Let's set the program back.

Press the Ctrl+Shift keys and then the space bar to select the entire worksheet. Select File⇨Page Setup⇨Sheet. Remove the information in the Print Area box and click OK. Click Print Preview and you should be able to see your entire worksheet as it will be printed. Make sure that your printer is plugged in and on-line. Click Print and you have your entire worksheet.

Counting calories with Excel

I run a diet center and keep clients' progress in Excel. I need to track not only pounds lost, but ounces, too; for example, 167 and 2/16th of a pound. I figure out the ounces part with decimals now but have to convert the decimal back to ounces or else the result doesn't make sense to the client.

You count the ounces? Your clients could effectively lose weight if they get a haircut, remove their glasses, or take a bath.

The easiest way to perform calculations on pounds and ounces is to keep the pounds and convert the ounces to a fraction. There are 16 ounces to a pound, so enter the 167 and 1/8th pounds in your worksheet as follows:

```
167lbs 2/16oz
```

You don't have to put the "lbs" and "oz"; doing so may just make the numbers more identifiable on the screen. *Note:* The fractions automatically reduce to the lowest common denominator, but all the numbers will calculate.

Recovering corrupted data

I know — I should have listened to the warnings and used backup files. But I foolishly didn't. I have recently been informed by my program that my file has *corrupted data*. Is there any way I can get even part of the data back?

Wait, are you in the Mafia? Your computer may be making a social commentary. I know, I know — it's no time for jokes. You cannot get to the file you need.

If you selected the Always Create Backup option when you saved the file, you may be in luck. The worksheet backup file has the same name as the original but has the .BAK file extension. Simply rename the file with the .BAK file extension so that it has an .XLS file extension.

If you didn't have Excel automatically create backups, there is an alternative you can try, but I'm not making any promises. Here are the steps:

1. Open the corrupted file and keep it as the active worksheet if you have more than one worksheet on the screen.

2. Choose File⇨Save As⇨Options. Type a filename, perhaps GETBACK, and then look near the bottom of the Save As window. Click the down-arrow button near file format and highlight SYLK (Symbolic Link) as the file format. Click OK to save the file in a SYLK file format, GETBACK.SLK.

3. Close the file but don't exit Excel yet.

4. Open the GETBACK.SLK file; you need to change the file format to .SLK to see the file and you highlight the file to select it. You can open a new worksheet and copy the GETBACK worksheet contents to a new worksheet, or save the GETBACK.SLK worksheet as an Excel worksheet.

5. Select File⇨Save As⇨Options again as you did in step 2. This time, select Microsoft Excel Workbook for the file format. The file will be saved as GETBACK.XLS. Click OK.

Komando Klues Corrupted data is often a sign that you need to do some hard disk maintenance. Now is a good time to run the SCANDISK and DEFRAG commands. There is more information about these commands in Chapters 8 and 11, "DOS" and "Hardware."

Setting new page breaks

I went through my worksheet and spent a great deal of time figuring out where the page breaks should be, but Excel 5 doesn't care. It prints the pages where it wants to print them.

No, you're wrong. Excel does care. Give it another chance. I know you two can work it out. I know, I hear you. "Kim, answer the darn question."

Common problem; easy fix. Select File⇨Page Setup. Look under Scaling; I bet you have selected the Fit to Page option. No matter where you set manual page breaks in a worksheet, Excel takes control when you use the Fit to Page option. It puts the page breaks in the worksheet where it thinks they should be.

Want to know a workaround? Deselect Fit to Print and use the Adjust with a percentage. Play around making the percentage smaller or larger by clicking the down- or up-arrow button. Click Print Preview to see what the page will look like before you actually send the worksheet to your printer. It's the old trial-and-error method, I'm afraid. But once you get the Adjust and percentages down, you're all set, and Excel will pay attention to those page breaks again.

Hiding rows in Excel

I work on a governmental electorate committee, and I need to hide rows from the staff in an Excel 5 worksheet. Is there a quick and easy way?

Hmmmm, governmental electorate. Those hidden rows wouldn't happen to be payola or a trip to the Bahamas, now would they?

Just highlight the row you want to hide and then click the right mouse button. A pop-up menu specific to actions you can take with rows appears. Hide and Unhide are near the bottom of the pop-up window. Simply select the one you want: Hide or Unhide. The trick works with columns, too. Just select the column you want to hide or unhide and click the right mouse button.

This isn't a great way to protect the information in your worksheet from prying eyes. People can unhide rows and columns too easily.

You can give the file a password, but this won't hide rows from people who know the password to open the file. Next time you save the worksheet, select File⇨Save As. You can keep the same filename. Select Options and then you can protect your files with two types of passwords: protection and write reservation.

A protection password asks the user for a password before the worksheet appears on the screen. A write reservation password lets anyone open the file, but no one can save any changes made to the file unless it was opened by typing the protection password.

A password can have up to 15 characters and case matters: The password TOPSECRET will not open the file if the password set is TopSecret or topsecret.

Inserting time and date stamps

I'm an old-fashioned gal and would like to know whether there is a way to input the time and day on an Excel 5 sheet just like we used to do with rubber stamps on paper before the computer age.

Hey, old-fashioned gal. Did you know that accounting is the second oldest profession? You know the oldest one, right? Well, they had to find some way to keep track of the money.

Sure, here are two ways to do it, a hard way and an easy way. The easy way is to enter the date in the active cell and press Ctrl+;. To enter the time in the active cell, press Ctrl+Shift+:.

Or use the Now function to return the serial number for the current date and time, and then convert the format to the date/time format that you want to have displayed. I use the shortcut keys.

And speaking of shortcuts, I'm an old-fashioned gal, too: I like to use the keyboard more than the mouse. Because this answer is awfully short, here are some more shortcuts I use:

Action	Shortcut
Display Function Wizard	Shift+F3
Move to next workbook sheet	Ctrl+Page Down
Move to preceding workbook sheet	Ctrl+Page Up
Apply percentage format	Ctrl+Shift+%
Apply two-decimal place format	Ctrl+Shift+!
Format as currency	Ctrl+Shift+$
Copy a formula from the cell above	Ctrl+'
Copy the value of the cell above	Ctrl+"
Move to the beginning of the sheet	Ctrl+Home
Move to the last cell in the sheet	Ctrl+End

Excel will date and time stamp your file when saving it, too. These dates and times can be used to easily locate the file when searching via FindFile in Excel or in Windows File Manager.

Saving an Excel sheet as text

I need to save a spreadsheet as a text file back to our home office. How can I do this? I asked the computer manager and he told me to look in the Excel 5 manual, which is — you guessed it — at the home office.

Those manuals end up all over the place, balancing refrigerators, keeping doors open ... but in most cases they make great bedside soporifics.

You can save your document in a text file a few ways. The easiest way is to select File⇨Save As⇨File Format⇨Text. The file extension automatically will change to .TXT, for text.

Using Excel with the A drive

They just don't make ambidextrous computers yet. I would love to use my A drive (3½-inch) and Excel 5 at the same time. But when I try, Excel gives me an hourglass, yet the drive doesn't do anything. Even after I close Excel, the drive does nothing and I have to reboot my computer to begin again. I also use Norton Desktop. Could this be affecting it?

Hey, that thing in front of you can do so much, and now you want it to be "ambidextrous"? Look at the other appliances in your house. How about that vacuum cleaner? Can it clean the carpet and wash the dishes?

The Common Dialog Box Dynamic Link Library (COMMDLG.DLL) file and SHELL.DLL are used by many applications to provide a consistent interface for common tasks. These dialog boxes include the File⇨Open, File⇨Save, File⇨Print, and Format⇨Font dialog boxes. The Microsoft Excel installation program checks for an existing COMMDLG.DLL in the C:\WINDOWS\SYSTEM directory and replaces it if the file date is outdated. It doesn't look in other directories for this file, therefore, multiple or older versions of the file may remain on the hard disk or network directory.

A problem occurs if you install Norton Desktop after installing Excel because it will install an older version of these files. Replacing these files from your Excel install disks will fix the problem. You may also want to turn off your Norton FileSave and FileSaveAs macros to avoid other problems with Microsoft Excel 5.0 and Word 6.0.

Placing Excel charts in a WinWord file

I want to put some (there are 18) Excel 5 charts in a dissertation written using Word 6.0. Is there a better way to get the charts in the dissertation other than using the Copy and Paste commands?

Yes and no. You could set up a link with some programming DDE in a macro if a chart will appear on every page at a certain spot on every page. My point here is that a pattern must be established before the charts know automatically where to go in the dissertation document.

I do have an idea that may save some time. Windows comes with a Recorder icon found in the Accessories program group. Start Recorder and let it record the steps of copying the active chart from Excel, switching to Word, and pasting the active chart in your dissertation.

Then you just have to find the proper place in your dissertation for the next chart, activate the next chart, and use a hot key to run your Recorder macro. Depending on how your report and chart files are set up, you may be able to automate things even further. Recorder is a great resource for repetitive jobs. Too bad they don't make a macro for computer questions. I'm going crazy here.

Entering ZIP codes in Excel

I have ZIP codes in an Excel 5 spreadsheet. When I type the ZIP code, I lose the leading zeros. For example, 07060 appears as 7060.

Knowing the Post Office, it'll probably get there faster.

Excel drops leading zeros unless told otherwise. You have to create a custom format so that the leading zeros will appear in numbers that have five places.

First, select the range of cells that have the ZIP codes. Then click the right mouse button to make the format-specific pop-up menu appear. Select

Format Number and then click Custom. In the Code box, type the following and click OK:

```
00000
```

You'll have your leading zeros in the range selected.

Lotus 1-2-3

Quick menus or quicksand?

I get cranking using Lotus 1-2-3 for DOS, but then I'm lost in the quick menus. Is there a fast way to get back to the worksheet mode?

The long, winding road that leads back to the ready mode is to keep pressing the Esc key. There is an easier way, alone worth the price of this book: Press Ctrl+Break and you're out of the menus totally, ready to enter numbers, formulas, or labels in a Lotus 1-2-3 for DOS worksheet.

Can I have two print ranges?

I have one Lotus 1-2-3 for DOS worksheet with different areas for my income and my expenses. Often, I want to print only certain columns or rows. Can I print two ranges instead of just one?

You can do anything you want. This is America.

Sure you can, but the method depends on where the ranges are in your worksheet.

Say you set the ranges up all over the worksheet, with the first range located at A1 through D12 and the second range at F22 through K45. Select the first range, put in a comma, and then select the second range. The print range looks as follows:

```
A1..D12, F22..K45
```

If you have different ranges going across columns, it's a little easier; you just hide the ranges that you don't want to print. For example, with the first range located at A1 through D12 and the second range located at F1 through K45, just hide the column between the two ranges — the E column — and then select everything from A1 to K45 as the print range. The print range looks as follows:

```
A1..K45
```

Running 1-2-3 for DOS from Windows

I'm trying to use Lotus 1-2-3 for DOS, release 3.4, from Windows. I double-click the program icon, and the program tries to start, but then I end up back in Windows. The program works fine in DOS 6.2. How do I get the program to work from Windows?

Perhaps Windows is jealous of Lotus 1-2-3. Or you may have a *very* personal computer.

The symptoms you describe are clear-cut signs that there isn't enough memory for the Lotus program to run from Windows. Lotus is particular about memory; it likes a special type of memory called *expanded memory,* or *EMS memory.* EMS memory is your computer's RAM above 1MB. Your computer has to be told to use it.

Try managing your computer's memory better by using the DOS memory management tool, MEMMAKER. MEMMAKER sets up your computer to use its memory efficiently and give Lotus the EMS memory it wants. First exit Windows and then, at the DOS prompt, type the following line and then press Enter:

```
MEMMAKER
```

Choose the Express setup option and when MEMMAKER asks you if any programs need EMS memory, choose Yes. After MEMMAKER gets done, start Windows and give the Lotus program another shot.

Not working still? Poor baby. Let's try something else. Take a deep breath. It's going to be better.

Make sure you have a backup copy of the CONFIG.SYS file, exit Windows, and go to the DOS prompt. You're going to open the CONFIG.SYS file and take a peek. Most times, there is one little line that causes headaches typical of your situation. The downside to this memory configuration change is that other software you use in Windows may not work properly or will work slowly. If you're willing to sacrifice performance in your other programs, continue reading this answer. Otherwise, run Lotus 1-2-3 for DOS from DOS and not from Windows.

So, you continued reading? OK. At the DOS prompt, type the following line and then press Enter:

```
EDIT CONFIG.SYS
```

Look for a line like this:

```
DEVICE=C:\DOS\EMM386.EXE RAM
```

Change the word *RAM* to a number (2,048 will create just over 2MB of expanded memory, and it's a good estimate for what you need). The editor you are in works like most word processing programs. Use the cursor keys to move around in the file and the press the delete keys to erase items. Modify the preceding line of code so it reads this way:

```
DEVICE=C:\DOS\EMM386.EXE 2048
```

Select File⇨Save to save your changes. Reboot your computer and try to use Lotus 1-2-3 for DOS from inside Windows again. It should work now.

Hiding a row from sight

Is it possible to hide a row like a column in Lotus 1-2-3 for DOS? I've looked in Help. I've checked the manual. I called Lotus and got put on terminal hold, so I hung up.

Gee, maybe I shouldn't help you, either. Do they know something I don't know?

Actually, it's easier hiding a big body in loose jeans than hiding a row like a column in Lotus 1-2-3, but I do know a workaround.

Set the row height to 1; this makes any information in the row virtually impossible to read. Move the active cursor to the row that you want to vanish. Select Worksheet⇨Row⇨Set Height. In the height box, type 1 and press Enter. When you want to see the information in this row, you'll have to go back and reset the row height to its original size.

Undo won't undo

I make a lot of mistakes. I tried to enable the Undo feature in Lotus 1-2-3 for DOS. I can't. I get more mistakes, specifically *Out of Memory* messages.

Wouldn't it be great if life had an Undo feature? Imagine it: You go home to your parents for the holidays, have a lousy time, and then undo it. This way, everybody's happy.

Undo takes a lot of memory, some conventional and perhaps some EMS memory, too. Short of reconfiguring your computer's memory or adding memory, here's a way to possibly get the Undo feature to work.

Pay attention. To pave the memory path for goodies like Undo, clear out some other features. Usually, temporarily disabling the program's add-on features allows you to enable the Undo option.

Select Add-in from the menu — or press Alt+F10 to do the same thing — and select Clear. You just cleared all the add-ins from memory. Now, to enable the Undo feature, it's a long process. Select Worksheet⇨Global⇨ Default⇨Other⇨Undo⇨Enables⇨Update⇨Quit. When you press the Undo keys, or Alt+F4, you can reverse the last action performed.

Use @DAVG to average

I am no mathematical genius, but I do know that one plus one make two. (Of course, in sex ed, I was taught that one plus one make three.) I rely heavily on Lotus for DOS. I have a long column of numbers that increases by one cell daily. Is there a way to automatically @AVG the column when I add a new entry to the column?

Hey, about that whole sex ed thing. You are no comic genius, either.

Use the @DAVG function instead of @AVG. This offers an advantage over working with @AVG, because it resets your data range each time you add new data. In later versions of Lotus for Windows, you can use @AVG along with @INDEX to average items relative to a position. That makes this process even easier! Look in your Lotus manual under @INDEX for more information on this function.

It's better to rewrite than convert

I've been trying to convert 1-2-3 for DOS 2.x macros to 1-2-3 for DOS, release 3.4. Is it better to rewrite a macro than to convert it? Frankly, I think it would be easier to convert to Judaism from Greek Orthodox Catholicism.

I think you're right. I know someone who was Jewish but recently converted to metric.

Lotus has been great at keeping version compatibility for most of its DOS and Windows versions. Current versions of Lotus 1-2-3 for Windows will open worksheets created with any prior version of Lotus 1-2-3. That's the good news. The bad news is that (as you've noticed) macro conversions aren't perfect.

The Bottom Line

Nine times out of ten, it's easier and quicker to rewrite 2.x macros than it is to troubleshoot where the conversion process has failed. Plus, you'll be able to compose the macro so that it takes advantage of new features available in Lotus 1-2-3 release 3.4.

Commenting on formulas

My boss is constantly changing her mind about what to include in our budget. I make the formulas, and she tells me what items to include. First, we're allowed money for morning doughnuts, then she puts on a few pounds and morning doughnuts are off. Is there a way to make a formula and attach a note to it?

You mean a note like, "Don't take out your self-hate on us."

Make the formula and put a colon at the end of the formula. A colon tells Lotus that the rest of the formula is a comment. The formula with a comment inside may look like this:

```
@sum(B3..B25)-B22 : Her mood swings are noticeably
larger. We probably have a day or two left on the dough-
nuts.
```

In the cell-viewing area, you'll see the formula and the note. Only the result of the formula will continue to appear in the cell.

Salvation from universal grid lines

It amazes me how much damage you can do by hitting only one little button accidentally. I have tried numerous ways to delete the universal grid lines, but this works only for the current file in release 4 of Lotus 1-2-3 for Windows. Is there a way to eliminate the grid lines in all the files at once?

Hitting one little button accidentally could ruin people's lives. Just ask the people at NORAD. Fortunately, your solution is a bit less complicated.

In Lotus 1-2-3 for Windows 4.*x*, just as in many other Windows programs, information on how the program is set up and formatted is stored in an .INI file. The .INI file you want to change can be found in the WINDOWS directory, labeled as the 1-2-3R4.INI file. Exit Lotus 1-2-3 for Windows — if you have it running — and make a backup copy of the file 1-2-3R4.INI, which located in your C:\WINDOWS directory. Afterward, open the Windows Accessories program group and then double-click on Notepad. Open the 1-2-3R4.INI file.

Once the file opens, you will see a lot of high-tech computer guru information that maps out specific information about how your program works. Now if you thought hitting a wrong button *before* could get you into trouble, understand that changing a bit of information in this file without knowing what it does can cause your program to run worse than ever before — or not at all. Be careful.

Select Search from the Notepad menu bar and, in the search box, type the following and click OK:

```
grid_on=1
```

To fix your problem, you will need to change just one number at the end of the line. Change the number 1 to a 0 in the preceding line so the line now reads as follows:

```
grid_on=0
```

Just like a light switch: 1 for on and 0 for off.

From the Notepad menu bar, select File⇨Save. Exit Notepad; the next time you start Lotus 1-2-3 for Windows, the grid lines are gone.

That'll take care of things for any new worksheet you'll work in from this point forward, but not for any old worksheets. Older files that had grid lines will still have them because the grid lines were saved with the files. When you open files that were saved during the grid line fiasco, you can undo the grid formatting for each file by selecting View⇨Preferences and choosing options to match the way your program runs now. Unfortunately, if you worked on and saved a lot of files with the grid lines, you will have to repeat this process for each file. I know, yuck!

1-2-3 counts the days

I keep staff's time cards in a Lotus 1-2-3 file. Can you tell me the easiest way to have Lotus input into a file the number of days in a month? (There's no big hurry — I'm the only one who works for the company.)

You're weird. Anyway, you could look at a calendar, or you could use Lotus's @DAY and @TODAY functions in your worksheets. The formula that automatically figures out the number of days in a current month is as follows:

```
@DAY(@TODAY-@DAY(@TODAY))
```

There's another useful date-sensitive formula that's helpful in calculating employee time records. When you need to figure out the total number of weekdays between two dates, where the start date, for example, is in cell A1 and the end date is in cell A2, use the following formula:

```
(@INT(A2/7)-@INT(A1/7))*5+@MAX(0,@MOD(A2,7)-1)-
@MAX(0,@MOD(A1,7)-2)
```

Hiding columns and ranges in Lotus

My worksheet file contains inventory control figures. There is so much information in the file that it would be easier to work in if I could simply hide columns or ranges. How can I do this?

Hide is great. Again, wouldn't it be great if we could hide some people in the office? Like that guy in the copy room who flirts with everyone. Or the gossip at the reception desk who listens to everyone's calls. Or how about your boss? No . . . that might mean *me* at my company.

It's easy to hide columns, ranges, and even cells in a Lotus 1-2-3 file. And although they are hidden from view, cells, columns, and ranges can still be used in formulas. When you want to hide a cell or a range, select Style⇨Number Format. A list of formats appears in a dialog box. Find the option Hidden; click the box in front of Hidden so that there is an X in the box. When you want to see the hidden area, simply retrace your steps. Select Style⇨Number Format⇨Reset.

Hiding columns is a little different, but not much. Select the columns in the worksheet you want to hide. Next, select Style⇨Hide. When you want the columns back in clear view, select Style⇨Show.

Komando Klues

Don't hide cells, columns, or ranges thinking that no one will be able to see their contents. They can — on the edit line. To hide a cell's, column's, or range's contents from screen view and edit line view, select the cell or range, and then select Style⇨Protection.

Mapping the globe

On the side of the box for Lotus 1-2-3 for Windows, release 5, it says that the program has maps. Where are they?

In the glove compartment.

Don't worry. Making a map with Lotus 1-2-3 is easier than . . . well, easier than 1-2-3.

Select the information that you want in the map. Select Tools⇨Map⇨Insert Map Object. Your mouse pointer turns into a spinning globe, and you can click on the worksheet where you want the map to appear. Here's a hint: The upper-left corner of the map will be placed where you click.

Lotus figures out what to put in the map and voilà— you have your map. When information changes in your worksheet, the map updates automatically, too!

Successful logos

I am making a big presentation to our company's board of directors and would like to impress them. I want to put our company's logo, which is a .BMP file, on the worksheets of Lotus 1-2-3 for Windows, release 5. What are the steps to success?

You've come to the right place. There are two steps to success. Step one: Kiss the behinds of the board of directors. Step two: See step one.

Start Lotus 1-2-3 for Windows and open the worksheet file that will contain the logo. Press the Alt+Tab to return to Program Manager. Don't exit Lotus; you'll be back in just a moment.

You have an option here regarding the logo. You can open the logo file in the draw or paint program you used to create the logo, or you can use Windows Paintbrush for the same job. To keep things simple, use Paintbrush. So, open the Windows Accessories group and start Paintbrush. From Paintbrush, select File⇨Open, highlight the name of the logo file, and then click OK. This shows you the logo in Paintbrush. Now, you need to copy the logo to the Windows Clipboard; to do so, select Edit⇨Copy. Exit Paintbrush.

Press Alt+Tab again to go back to your Lotus 1-2-3 worksheet. Select Edit⇨Paste to copy the logo from the Windows Clipboard to your worksheet file.

Komando Klues As long as you don't cut or copy any other information to the Windows Clipboard, you can keep opening worksheets and pasting in the logo until you're done.

SmartIcon wisdom

I love how smart the SmartIcons are in Lotus 1-2-3 for Windows, release 5. But I find myself constantly going from palette to palette to find the icon I want. Can I create one SmartIcon palette that contains only the icons I use daily?

It's scary when the SmartIcons are smarter than you, isn't it?

Select Tools⇨SmartIcons. A dialog box appears. The column on the left shows icons available for you to put on your SmartIcon palette; the column on the right shows the icons you have already put on your SmartIcon palette.

Before you start messing around, take a look above the column on the right. Make sure it says Default Sheet. If not, click the down arrow and select Default Sheet from the list box.

Select the Next Set of SmartIcons. A list of icons appears, and this is the area you want to work in — the listing of icons on the right side of the window. Remove any SmartIcon that you don't want on your palette by clicking on the icon to select it and then dragging it away from the SmartIcon window.

Don't worry. You're only removing them from your palette, not from your program. You'll see some Spacer icons; these are used to put some breathing room, or *space,* between groups of similar icons on a palette. You remove Spacer icons just like you do SmartIcons. Click the icon to select it, and then drag it out of the SmartIcon window.

Now, you get to be yourself.

Pick the SmartIcons you want by choosing them from the Available icons window on the left and placing them in your SmartIcon window on the right. Keep selecting and dragging, scrolling down the list until you've reached the last option: Display Cells in Default Size Icon. You can move the SmartIcons around on your palette and, once you have the SmartIcons arranged in groups, use the Spacer SmartIcon.

When you get done making your SmartIcon palette, click Save Set in the SmartIcons window. In the box after Name of set, type your palette name, maybe — ahem — Im-Smart, for example. Click OK for Lotus to save your palette and click OK to close the SmartIcon window.

Any time you want to use your Im-Smart palette, just click through the palettes you did before until the palette you want appears inside Lotus.

Macro rumor dispelled

I've used Lotus for years and have never written a macro. I hear it's hard to do. How do I record a macro in Lotus 1-2-3 for Windows, release 5?

I've written a lot of macros in my life and to this day not one of them has written back. Get it, like a letter?

671

The place to start is with a new worksheet on-screen. You don't want to ruin your last year's work. After that, there are just four things to do: turn on the macro recorder, do the steps in the macro, stop the macro recorder, and give your macro a name. It's not that hard, really. Then, any time you want to repeat the steps in a macro, you just type the macro's name to run it.

I'm going to show you how to make a simple macro that puts my mailing address automatically into your worksheet any time you run this macro. It's the process I want you to understand; there's much more you can do with macros other than mailing addresses. So as you use my address to create your first macro, think of the formulas and other information you can use a macro with in order to save time.

Put the cell pointer in A1 and then select Tools from the main menu. Select Macro Recorder to turn on the recorder. Type the following in A1 and press Enter:

```
Kim Komando
```

Go to cell A2 and type the first line of my mailing address and press Enter:

```
4400 N. Scottsdale Rd., 9-139
```

Go to cell A3 and type the last part of my mailing address and press Enter:

```
Scottsdale, AZ 85251
```

Use the cursor arrow keys and go back to cell A1. It's the end of your macro, so it's time to turn off the macro recorder. Select Tools⇨Macro⇨ Stop Recording.

If you want to look at the script, or transcript, of the macro, Select Tools⇨Macro⇨Show Transcript and you'll see the transcript of the macro. The macro transcript contains all the steps of the macro. The Transcript feature also comes in handy when you're troubleshooting macros that don't work.

Click the Transcript Window and highlight all the text in it that selects all the steps of the macro. Next, you need to copy this text to the Windows Clipboard. Select Edit⇨Copy, and your macro is on the Clipboard. Go to cell K1 now. Go ahead. Cursor on down there.

Select Edit⇨Paste to put the macro's transcripts in this part of the worksheet. Don't fret about it. Lotus will fill up cells K2 and K3 and so on if it needs more room for the macro. The last step is to name the range, which will ultimately become the macro's name. Put the cursor box in cell K1 and select Range⇨Name. Here's the deal about macro names: you press the Ctrl key and a letter, usually, to run a macro. Type the following for the name of the cell and click OK:

```
/k
```

The slash represents the Ctrl key, and the letter is the one you press with the Ctrl key to run that macro.

Now go to cell D1 or F12 or wherever you want to run the macro in your worksheet. Press Ctrl+K. Voila! You have my address any time, anywhere, by just pressing Ctrl+K.

Komando Klues

Lotus uses the Ctrl key for shortcuts. Stay away from naming macros with the same Lotus shortcut keys. For example, name a macro Ctrl+B and no longer will pressing the Ctrl+B key combination turn on and turn off bold. It will run your macro. Other macro-naming no-nos include

Ctrl+E	Centers text
Ctrl+I	Adds or removes italics
Ctrl+L	Left-aligns cell contents
Ctrl+N	Removes all the bold, italics, and underlining from the cell selected
Ctrl+R	Right-aligns cell contents
Ctrl+U	Adds or removes underlining

Quattro Pro

Q&A

Frustration case

I'm very particular about my uppercase and lower-case letters. When I type an @function in upper-case, lowercase, or mixed case, Quattro Pro for Windows gives me all uppercase letters. I want my @functions in lowercase!

The Bottom Line

Well then, you'd better get a job on the board of directors at Quattro and state your case, cause otherwise it ain't gonna happen. No matter what case you type letters in @functions, Quattro Pro for Windows always converts the letters to uppercase.

673

Named ranges

OK, I made it this far. I would like to use named ranges instead of keeping numbers in formulas in a Quattro Pro for Windows, Version 6, worksheet. The only information I still need is the steps to name the ranges.

It's always a good idea to try something different with a new worksheet on the screen. This way, you won't lose anything, like your job.

First, go to the cell you want to name. I like cell K1, so go there. Select Block⇨Names, and a dialog box pops up. You get the same menu option by right-clicking on the cell or by pressing Ctrl+F3.

Give the range a name, the cell K1, in the Name box. Type, for example, Kim. Click Add and select Close to go back to your worksheet. Let's talk for a moment about names: they have to start with a letter and can be up to 64 characters long. Avoid using spaces and the plus sign, the minus sign, the division sign, or the subtraction sign. This leads to later confusion; trust me.

If you want to name more than one cell, or a range of cells, the steps are the same. Highlight or select the cells you want to name and then name them using the Block⇨Names command.

Komando Klues

To go from one named cell or block to another in your worksheet, press the F5 key.

Row/column switcheroo

I screwed up in a Quattro Pro for Windows, Version 6, worksheet. My rows should be columns and my columns should be rows. Is there anything I can do to avoid retyping all the worksheet data?

That's not screwing up. Screwing up is when you throw your wife a surprise 40th birthday party and you find out she's only 38. That's screwing up.

Sure, we can switch them around without reentering the information. It's called *transposing*.

First, select the row that should be a column. You can select an entire row by clicking on the row number. Select Block⇨Transpose, and a dialog box appears. In the From box, you see the row you selected. In the To box, type the column or column's cell address where the information should really be located. Repeat the preceding steps for every row and every column, but not before you read the following very important Komando Klue.

Komando Klues

Quattro Pro is rude. The program automatically overwrites any information contained in the cells that you transpose the data to. It's a good idea to make the switcheroo in an empty area of your worksheet. Then you can use the Edit⇨Cut command to copy the contents to the Windows Clipboard, and you can use the Edit⇨Paste command to copy the cells to where they should be in your worksheet. But if you do make a mistake, select Edit⇨Undo. Or exit the program without saving the changes to the worksheet.

Easy graphing

I was enthusiastic about being able to put graphs in my Quattro Pro for Windows, Version 6, worksheets. Then I looked in the manual and found it too hard to read. Please tell me how to make a graph the easy way.

I'll make it easy as pie. In fact, I'll make it as easy as a pie *graph*.

All you have to do is select the information you want to put in the graph and let Quattro Pro finish the dirty deed. Let me explain.

Say, for example, that your home budget worksheet is contained in the cells A1 to K56. Click on A1 to select it and keep the left mouse button pressed. Drag the mouse all across and down your worksheet until you reach K56. Release the left mouse button.

Look at the Main toolbar and find the icon with a little graph on it. This is Quattro Pro's graphing tool. Click on the Graph button, and the mouse pointer turns into a graph. Isn't that cute?

Put the mouse pointer, which is a graph, in your worksheet and drag it so it makes a box about the size that you want for your graph. Release the mouse button. Quattro Pro for Windows figures out the graph type, where the information should appear in the graph, and rolls with it.

Keeping column headings in sight

My Quattro Pro for Windows, Version 6, worksheet is pretty huge. When I start scrolling down into the unknown depths of rows, I lose my column headings. I have to scroll back to the top of the worksheet to figure out which column is which in order to put information in the proper rows. Is there a way to keep the column labels on top of the worksheet all the time?

Every guy brags about how big his Quattro Pro for Windows 6 worksheet is. Every gal knows that guys have a weird perception of distance. To answer your question: Yes, there is.

You can lock one or more columns and/or rows to always appear in your worksheet — regardless of where the active cell is located in the worksheet. Suppose your column headings run horizontally across row 1 and your row headings run vertically down column A. Put the cell pointer in cell A1. Select View⇨Locked Titles.

The Locked Titles dialog box appears. Your options are to Clear titles that you have already locked, lock the Horizontal titles, lock the Vertical titles, or lock both the Horizontal and Vertical titles. Select Horizontal titles to keep the column headings in row 1 by clicking the radio button before Horizontal. Click OK, and your column headings will always be displayed in your worksheet.

If you want to remove the locked titles later, select View⇨Locked Titles. Select Clear, and those locked titles are gone.

Formula for adults

I'm becoming an adult and accumulating debts. I can't figure out the formula to put in my budget that calculates the monthly loan payment for a house I want to purchase.

The formula to calculate loan payment is as follows:

```
@PMT(amount of the loan, interest rate/number of annual
payments, term of the loan)
```

So, if you were requesting a $100,000 home loan, the interest rate was 8 percent, and the term of the loan was 30 years, the formula would look like this:

```
@PMT(100,000,8%/12,30)
```

Komando Klues

When you need help with formulas, Quattro Pro has a cool feature called the Formula Composer. Select the cell to contain the formula. Select Tools⇨Formula Composer. A dialog box appears with an outline window on the left, where you can select parts of a formula, and an @function window on the right, where you can read about and select @functions. If you need help from within the Formula Composer, click the question mark button. If you need help with a formula, click the button that has a question mark and the @.

Other signs of adulthood include:

➤ You know all eight verses of the "On Top of Spaghetti" song.

➤ You realize that the fatty, cholesterol-laden pieces are the only tasty part of a chicken.

➤ You start getting gray hairs on places other than your head.

Cure for password memory loss

I can't seem to move past the passwords in my life. I always forget them. How do I remove a password from a Quattro Pro for Windows file? Also, does the case matter when I enter a Quattro Pro password?

You forget all your passwords? I bet you don't know where your car keys are right now. Or your sunglasses. Or that other gray sock. I'll help you with the password. With the rest, you're on your own.

In many programs, passwords are case sensitive. A password entered as EyeSpy isn't the same as EYESPY. If you ever run into trouble with Quattro Pro (or another software program, for that matter) accepting a password, check the obvious — the Caps Lock key. Make sure the Caps Lock key is off when you are typing your password, and if you have to use capital letters, use the Shift key. Sounds silly, but nine times out of ten, that's the problem when a password is not accepted.

To remove passwords from a Quattro Pro for Windows, Version 6, file, select File⇨Save As, using the name of a file appearing in the filename box. Then click the password field and press Enter. The message *File Already Exists* will appear. Click OK, and the file is saved with the same name but without a password.

Unlimited printing possibilities

I'm not sure if my formulas are correct in my Quattro Pro for Windows, Version 6, worksheet. Is there a way to print only the formulas and not the formula's result in a Quattro Pro worksheet?

Is it possible? Hey, do we have a Republican Congress? Are stamps 32 cents? Is Elvis alive and well and bagging groceries?

It's easy. Select File⇨Print⇨Options. Select the option Set to Cell Formulas and the formulas will be printed regardless of what is displayed on-screen at printing time. Enjoy!

Dimension conversion simplified

We own an interior design and home remodeling company. It's very annoying that all our formula results are in inches and not feet. Is this a Quattro Pro limitation?

No, just *your* limitation. Let me set you free.

You simply need to tell Quattro Pro that you want feet and not inches. Here's where the @CONVERT function is numero uno. It allows you to convert inches to feet. The formula is as follows:

```
@CONVERT(number of inches,"the measurement to convert
from","the measurement to convert to")
```

So, if you measured a picture, for example, that had a 39-inch dimension, and you wanted this converted automatically to feet, the formula in your worksheet would look like this:

```
@CONVERT(39,"in","ft")
```

You can also use the @CONVERT function to change days to minutes, miles to feet, feet to yards, and much more. To use the other conversion features, replace the measurements in quotes with Quattro Pro's abbreviations. Here are some commonly used abbreviations that are used with the @CONVERT function:

Statute Mile	mi
Nautical Mile	nmi
Yard	yd
Year	yr
Day	day
Minute	mn
Second	sec

Clearing peer-to-peer confusion

What causes the message *Unable to open overlay file* to appear when a second user tries to access Quattro Pro for Windows on a peer-to-peer network?

Let's think about it for a minute. You open a file and start to make some changes. Another user opens the same file and makes some changes of his or her own. Whose information should the computer keep? I know you are thinking *yours,* but hold on. Software programmers have established rules to handle this type of problem.

The *Unable to open overlay file* message will appear on a peer-to-peer network if the files in the Quattro Pro directory have not been designated as read-only. Read-only files are like fine art in a museum. You can look, but you can't touch. Definitely no mustache painting here.

But, files that aren't specifically designated as read-only automatically become read/write files whereby you can look and touch the file's contents. In a peer-to-peer network, two users cannot have read/write access to an .OVR (overlay) file at the same time.

A simple solution would be to use the Properties feature in the Windows File Manager to make all of the files in the Quattro Pro directory read-only, so that they may be shared over the network. Open File Manager and select the Quattro Pro program directory by clicking once on the directory file name. Select File⇨Properties. In the dialog box, you'll see, among other things, four boxes of attributes that a directory can have. Click the box marked Read Only so that there is an X in the box. Click on OK, and now the Quattro Pro program directory is set up for network use.

The error message you received could also appear if the Q.OVR file in the Quattro Pro subdirectory is missing or damaged. If this is the case, use the Search command in File Manager to ensure that the Q.OVR file is in the Quattro Pro directory. If it's not, well, you could troubleshoot for hours or you could take 15 minutes and reinstall the program. Which would *you* do? You got it. Reinstall the program.

If the Q.OVR file is in the Quattro Pro directory, I want you to do some hard disk maintenance just in case the file is damaged.

1. Exit Windows completely and go to the DOS prompt.

2. At the DOS prompt, type **CHKDSK/F** and press Enter. If you're using MS-DOS 6.2 or above, use SCANDISK instead because it is much more thorough than CHKDSK. To use SCANDISK, type the following at the DOS prompt and press Enter:

   SCANDISK

3. If you're told that there are errors on the disk and asked if you should save them to files, say no. You usually can't make heads or tails of the information, anyway.

When you've finished checking out the hard drive, I want you to reorganize it by running the drive defragmentation program that comes with MS-DOS 6.0 or above. This program will put the files on the hard drive back in order. To run this program, type the following at the DOS prompt and press Enter:

DEFRAG

You should be crunching numbers with users on the network now.

Chapter 19

Word Processing

What is word processing?

I finally emerged from the dark ages: I put my typewriter in the closet and bought my first computer. I plan mainly on writing letters. Is this word processing?

I've seen closets like yours before. Next to that typewriter is a Betamax, an 8-track player, and a hulking 13-inch black-and-white tube TV. Come to think of it, maybe it was my closet.

Computers are more than big, overgrown calculators. True, they work with numbers very, very well, but they also work with words much better than your rusty (I mean trusty) old typewriter. The type of program a computer uses to work with words is called *word processing*. Just as a food processor lets you slice and dice vegetables to create the ultimate cuisine, a word processor lets you slice and dice phrases to create the ultimate correspondence.

Microsoft Windows ships with Write, a basic word processing program; with it, you can write letters to your heart's content. To start up Write, open the Accessories program group and double-click the Write icon.

If you find that Write isn't, ahem, right, you have options. The three word processing biggies in the world today are

> ➤ Word by Microsoft
> ➤ WordPerfect by WordPerfect/Novell
> ➤ Ami Pro by Lotus

Although these fancy programs do everything except the dishes, don't think that they're too powerful for you. Many people start out tapping into only about 10 percent of a word processor's power. But it's not like buying a Ferrari just to go to the corner store; you'll grow into the other 90 percent. Popular advanced features deal with mail merge (form letters!), graphics, and desktop publishing.

Note: Using a top-selling word processor increases your stock in the job market; more and more businesses want computer-literate employees.

You can find less powerful word processors that are designed for small-office and home users. For example, the word processing component of programs such as Microsoft Works and ClarisWorks (which combine word processor, database, and spreadsheet) is usually powerful enough to handle most people's correspondence needs.

Finally, if you really like being thrifty, go with a shareware word processor, such as Word Express by Microvision. Shareware programs are found on BBSs and on-line services (such as America Online or CompuServe).

Special symbols

I know that you can put special characters, such as the copyright symbol, in a word processing document. But I don't know which characters exist nor how to get them on paper. I use the Times New Roman font.

In the Accessories program group is Character Map, which shows all the special characters that can be included in any document. To use Character Map,

1. Double-click on the Character Map icon to start the program.

2. A page of characters appears. You can change the font displayed by clicking on the button at the end of the font name (in the upper left-hand corner of the Character Map window) and then selecting a new font from the drop-down list.

3. Click and hold down the right mouse button to turn the mouse pointer into a magnifying glass.

4. Move the mouse pointer over the page of characters. When you find the special character you're looking for, release the mouse button. *Note:* Not every font has every special symbol.

5. Click the Select button. The special character shows up in the Characters to copy blank.

6. Click the Copy button. This action copies the special character to the Windows Clipboard.

7. Start your word processing program.

8. Move the cursor to the spot in your document where you want the special character.

9. Select Edit⇨Paste. Or use the Paste command's keyboard shortcut (usually Ctrl+V or Shift+Ins).

Whew, I know that seems like a lot of work, but the results are worth it. Using special characters gives your document that professional touch.

Komando Klues Some fonts such as Symbol and Wingdings are all special characters. Some word processing programs such as Word 6 for Windows allow you to insert symbols in your documents too.

Word 6 for Windows

AutoCorrect

I'm a TV meteorologist, and I write my weather reports with Word 6 for Windows. Every day I write the word *degrees* in my script. I want to use the symbol for degree instead. How?

I've never understood how TV meteorologists can be wrong day in and day out and still keep their jobs. It must be the slick-looking scripts you write.

Word for Windows (or *WinWord* to its friends) has a feature, called AutoCorrect, that can automatically correct mistakes for you as you type. For instance, a lot of people type *teh* rather than *the*; Word for Windows can automatically correct this error. But you can use AutoCorrect to change ordinary text into the degree symbol. Here's how to invoke this shortcut:

1. Select Tools⇨AutoCorrect.

2. A little window pops up on-screen. One blank in this window says Replace, the other says With.

683

3. Type in an easily remembered character sequence in the Replace blank. In this case, you may want to enter **(o)**.

4. Type in the keyboard command for the degree symbol: Alt+0176. *Note:* You must use your keyboard's numeric keypad (looks like a calculator) to type in these numbers.

5. Click Add.

6. Click OK to close the AutoCorrect window. Make sure the Replace text as you type box is checked.

As you write your scripts from now on, type in the shortcut — (o) — everywhere you want the degree symbol to appear. Word for Windows automatically changes (o) to the degree symbol for you.

Komando Klues

I suggest using WinWord's AutoCorrect feature for any common symbol, word, or phrase. For example, when writing this book, I set AutoCorrect so that when I typed *CDR*, WinWord changed it to *CD-ROM*. After all, computers are supposed to make things easier for us, not harder.

Search and replace

When I import a DOS text file into Word 6 for Windows, a hard return shows up at the end of each line. Changing the import parameters doesn't help. I don't want to delete the hard returns manually. Any tricks?

Tricks? How about making your problem disappear?

I clean up imported text files by using the Search and Replace command. That is, I search for hard returns and replace them with other things.

As you note, an imported text file has a hard return at the end of each line. In addition, paragraphs are separated by a line space, so they are separated by two hard returns. Although you want to eliminate the gratuitous hard return at the end of each line, you need to keep the two hard returns between paragraphs or the entire document becomes one big paragraph. Here's how:

You first need to replace two consecutive hard returns with another character. I use the tilde (~).

1. Press Ctrl+H to start the Search and Replace function.

2. In the Find What blank, type **^p^p**. To Word for Windows, ^p represents a hard return. To enter the first character, called a *caret*, press Shift+6. *Note:* Case matters. Be sure that you don't type capital *P*s.

3. In the Replace With blank, type ~.

4. Click the Replace All button.

Next, you need to replace every remaining hard return with a space to make sure that the last word in a line doesn't run into the first word in the next line.

1. Press Ctrl+H.

2. Type **^p** in the Find What blank.

3. Press the spacebar once in the Replace With blank.

4. Click the Replace All button.

The last step is to put back all the breaks between paragraphs.

1. Press Ctrl+H.

2. Type ~ in the Find What blank.

3. Type **^p^p** in the Replace With blank.

4. Click the Replace All button.

This trick can save you a lot of reformatting time. Keep in mind that you still may have to do *some* manual editing.

For my next trick, I will successfully answer the next question.

Default font

How can I change the default font in Word 6 for Windows?

Everyone needs to update their look now and then. Just ask Michael Jackson or Madonna.

To change the default font in Word 6 for Windows,

1. Choose File⇨Open and click OK to open a new document.

2. Type a word in this document.

3. Select this word by double-clicking the mouse pointer on it.

4. Change the font to the new size and style you want to use.

5. Select Format⇨Font.

6. Click the Default button.

7. Click the Yes button.

Word for Windows changes the default font to the one you selected.

Disappearing fonts

Oh where, oh where have my little Word fonts gone? Oh where, oh where can they be?

Fonts are such finicky things. Here today, gone to Maui.

Most users chase their fonts away by tinkering; they try to make things better, but they sometimes end up making them worse. I bet your fonts aren't showing up in your other programs either.

Here's how to get your fonts back:

1. Select the Main program group.

2. Double-click on the Control Panel icon.

3. Double-click on the Fonts icon.

4. Click on the TrueType button.

5. Click the mouse pointer in the Enable TrueType Fonts check box.

When this option is enabled (that is, the X is in the check box), the TrueType fonts are available to Word for Windows — and your other programs, too.

Footers

I have never seen the footers in Word 6 for Windows. I feel as if I'm missing out on something. The Header and Footer command only shows headers.

Wow, now I feel like I've really lived. Why? Let's just say I've seen some footers in my life.

WinWord's footers are within your grasp, too. All you need to do is to click on the right button. Here's how to see footers in Word for Windows:

1. Select View⇨Header and Footer.

2. The screen changes to show a box with a dotted line around it and the word *Header*. A small rectangular toolbar shows up on-screen with *Header and Footer* appearing in the title bar.

3. Click the first button on the left in the rectangular window to switch from the header to the footer.

That's it. Clicking this button switches you back and forth between header and footer. When you're finished working with the header and footer, click on the Close button.

Komando Klues

To learn what any of the other buttons do, rest the mouse pointer over it; a short description pops up on-screen.

If finding Prince Charming was only that easy. I'm trying, Mom. I'm trying.

Combining files

They call me Mr. Messy. Pieces of my Word 6 for Windows documents are spread over a bunch of files. How can I tidy up my filing system and get all my documents grouped together?

Mr. Messy, please meet Miss Calculate. The two of you are headed for disaster.

Word for Windows lets you take those pieces (I call them *little files*) and combine them to make a big file:

1. Select Insert⇨File.

2. Select the first little file to put into the big file.

3. Click OK.

4. The file appears on-screen, and the cursor moves to the bottom of that file.

5. Select the next little file to put into the big file by using Insert⇨File again.

6. Click OK.

7. Repeat Steps 5 and 6 until all the little files are in the big file. Save the big file the same way you save any file.

If only it was as easy to get your tax files together.

Networking

Why is my Word 6 for Windows complaining? It keeps saying things such as *Word cannot create this file*. I have 8MB of memory and am connected to a Lantastic network.

That's gratitude for you. You give the program a home, and it still complains.

Computer networks are wonderful things; they let us share printers and files between computers. The trouble is that you have to tell the network to play nicely. Remember when your kindergarten teacher told you that sharing was a nice thing to do? Networks flat out don't work if they don't share things.

The first time you save a Word for Windows document to a network drive, it gives you the *Word cannot create this file* message if someone hasn't set up the program or network settings properly. You see, for a networked hard drive to let some computer write something on it, it has to keep track of what's going on. When the network is set up, a certain amount of space is allocated to keep track of what files are being shared. If this space is too small, the network refuses to let files be written to a network drive by other computers.

The workaround: Save the document you're working on to your own hard drive first, and let the *network administrator* (that is, the person in charge of running the network) know that your computer needs some more elbow room.

You also can try asking for a milk-and-cookie break and time for an afternoon nap, but that could be pushing your luck.

Hard drive space

I don't want any converters on my Word 6 for Windows any more. They are taking up too much room on my hard drive. Can I get rid of them, or am I stuck with them forever?

Amazing. No matter how big a hard drive you buy, there's never enough room. Why?

Come to think of it, how is there always just enough news to fill the newspaper? And why do people always die in alphabetic order? And ... OK, I'll stop.

Removing unwanted converters from Word for Windows is easy:

1. Exit Word for Windows.

2. Select the Microsoft Word program group from File Manager.

3. Double-click on the Word Setup icon.

4. Click the Add/Remove button.

5. Click on the Converters check box.

6. Click the Change Options button.

7. Click on the check boxes of the text converter(s) you want to remove. You can uninstall as many converters as you need at once.

8. Click OK.

9. The setup program removes the selected converter(s) and adjusts the settings for Word for Windows.

Mailing labels

Now that I've drawn up my will, I want to write my inheritors and tell them what to expect. Is there a way to print multiple copies of my return address label?

Hey, where there's a will, there's a way.

I like this kind of question. There's an easy way to do what you need, as long as you know where to go:

1. Select Tools⇨Envelopes and Labels.

2. Click on the Labels tab.

3. Type in the information you want to appear on the label.

4. Click the Full Page of Same Label radio button.

5. Click the Options button and then pick the type of label you're using.

6. Select the type of printer you have — laser or dot matrix.

7. Select the type of label you have from the list at the bottom of the window.

8. Click OK.

9. Click the Print button.

689

Mail merge

I do a mail merge to send out press releases from Word for Windows. I keep the addresses in a Word table. Can I select who receives a particular press release, or does everyone necessarily get every press release?

I hope your client isn't Greenpeace. Form letters kill trees.

Computers are supposed to let us work with information in intelligent ways. When doing a mail merge, Word for Windows lets you query or specify the items you want to work with in the list. Because you already know how to mail merge, I describe how to query in this answer.

The Mail Merge Helper has three main steps. In the third step, you see a Query Options button. Click on it. The window that appears shows two tabs: Filter Records and Sort Records.

1. Click Sort Records tab. Computers work with lists of information much better when the lists are sorted. When sending letters, it's often useful to sort the list by ZIP code.

2. Click on the button after the first blank.

3. From the list of fields in your address list, click on the ZIP code field.

4. Click on the Ascending radio button.

The records are now sorted by ZIP code. Next, it's time to decide who's going to receive the letters.

Say that you want to send this press release to all your California-based clients. Here's how:

1. Click the Filter Records tab.

2. Click on the button after the first blank.

3. From the list of fields in your address list, click on the State field.

4. Click on the button after the second blank.

5. Select the Equal To option.

6. Click the mouse pointer in the third field.

7. Type in **CA** (for California).

8. Click the OK button.

Word for Windows now knows that you want to do a mail merge for only those clients who live in California.

The Bottom Line

The query option offers you a lot of power and versatility. You can make the mail merge even more specific by adding another option.

Now that you have the knack, play around with queries a little bit.

Printing envelopes

When I try to use the print envelope feature in Word 6 for Windows with #10 envelopes, the address prints at the top, bottom, left, or right — never in the center. What am I doing wrong? I have an HP LaserJet III.

Looking for addresses in all the wrong places, eh? Sounds like you've been messing around with the envelope settings.

Word 6 for Windows lets you change where the address prints on a label. It's not a good idea to change the settings just for the sake of changing them. When you want to print an envelope, Word 6 for Windows makes a recommendation based on the type of printer you're using. I suggest accepting this recommendation.

To return to the original envelope setting,

1. Select Tools➪Envelopes and Labels.

2. While you're here, you can change the standard return address.

3. Click the Options button. A new window appears. Select the Printing Options tab.

4. The Feed Method shows six different options. For your HP LaserJet III, the proper option is the second one from the left. Click on this option.

5. Make sure the Clockwise rotation check box is selected.

6. Click the Face Up radio button.

7. Click the OK button. After the screen changes, click the OK button again.

When you print your envelope, everything should line up as it's supposed to. If not, you can use that newfangled invention called the typewriter.

Komando Klues

When testing envelope printing, print on regular sheets of paper. They are easier to work with and a lot less expensive than envelopes.

Exporting to WP

When I try to use a Word 6 for Windows document in WordPerfect 5.2 for Windows, all I get on-screen is a bunch of garbage. How can I prevent this?

A long, long time ago, the software publishers of the world gathered together to build a tower to Heaven. But as those great architects approached the pearly gates, the tower collapsed. Amid the ensuing babel, no one could understand each other. Worse, the software created by those fine people also spoke in different languages.

Programs save files in their own language. As a result, WordPerfect 5.2 for Windows doesn't know how to read Word 6 for Windows files. When WordPerfect tries to open up the WinWord document, it doesn't know what to do with all the extra things that WinWord puts in its files.

You have two options to make your files readable:

➤ Get the latest version of WordPerfect for Windows (Version 6.1).

➤ Save the Word for Windows document in something that WordPerfect for Windows 5.2 understands — for example, a WordPerfect 5.1 document or a text file.

Getting the upgraded version of WordPerfect is probably your best bet. Not only can WordPerfect 6.1 read WinWord 6 documents, but also it's faster, easier to use, and has more features than your version. Call WordPerfect at 800-228-1029 for information about upgrading.

If you can't afford to upgrade yet, here's how to save a Word 6 for Windows file in WordPerfect 5.1 format:

1. Select File⇨Save As.

2. Type in a name for the file.

3. Specify the directory where you want to save the file.

4. In the Save File as Type section, click on the button after the words *Word Document*.

5. Scroll through the list and click on the WordPerfect 5.1 for MS-DOS option.

6. Click OK.

Importing from Publisher

I import my champagne from France, my clothing from Italy, and my cars from Germany, but I can't work out how to export a graphic from Microsoft Publisher to Word for Windows.

So you're the one causing the deficit problem.

A quick way to import a graphic into Word for Windows is to use the Windows Clipboard. With both Microsoft Publisher and Word for Windows running,

1. In Publisher, select the picture you want to export.

2. Select Edit⇨Copy.

3. Switch to Word for Windows.

4. Move the mouse pointer to where the picture should go and click the left mouse button.

5. Select Edit⇨Paste. The picture shows up in the Word for Windows document.

Printing clip art

I don't think that my computer likes my choice of art. I often insert clip art into my Word 6 for Windows documents. When I save these documents to a floppy and then try to print them on another computer, the clip art doesn't print.

Computers know nothing at all about art. So if your computer isn't printing your clip art, the art must be horrible. Or really, really bad.

Word for Windows only cares about how the pictures are placed. You can include a picture in a document in two ways:

➤ Link the picture by using Object Linking and Embedding (OLE). By the way, OLE works not just with pictures, but also charts, diagrams, sounds, and more.

➤ Paste the picture.

Komando
Klues

When a picture is linked, double-clicking on it starts the program that created it. And the picture is opened up, ready to be edited.

When Word for Windows saves a file with a linked picture, it puts a little flag in the document. This flag says, "Open this picture." When the Word for Windows file is saved to the hard drive, you have no problems printing because the picture is on the hard drive, too. But when the Word for Windows file is saved to a floppy disk, only the flag is saved — not the picture. When you try to print that file from another computer, the printer sees only the flag.

Don't worry though, you can work around this problem. You can place the piece of clip art in the document:

1. Select Insert⇨Picture.

2. In the window that pops up, choose the piece of clip art you want to insert.

3. Click the OK button. The graphic becomes a part of your document.

Note: Documents are considerably bigger when they contain actual clip art and not just flags.

Printing speed

I'm losing a lot of time and money because large Word 6 documents take an eternity to print. How can I speed up the process?

No matter how fast computers are and how much time they save, they never seem fast enough. Here are several hints for speeding up printing from Word for Windows:

Komando
Klues

➤ Turn off screen savers. They're cute and they're nifty, but they require the computer's attention.

➤ Make sure you have at least 6MB of free hard drive space. Word for Windows needs to write temporary information to the hard drive as it's printing.

➤ If you don't need to keep working while Word for Windows is printing, turn off the background printing option. To do so,

1. Select Tools⇨Options.

2. Select the Print tab.

3. Deselect the Background Printing check box.

4. Click OK.

> ➤ Add more memory to the computer. You need more than 4MB of RAM to do serious work in Word for Windows (and other advanced Windows programs).

> ➤ Do some hard drive housekeeping. Run `SCANDISK` and `DEFRAG` to clean things up.

> ➤ Buy a faster printer. Some printers can churn out paper at 12 pages per minute (or more).

> ➤ If you just need a draft of the document, select draft printing. To do so,

>> 1. Select Tools⇨Options.
>> 2. Select the Print tab.
>> 3. Click in the Draft Print check box.
>> 4. Click OK.

It also may be time to buy a new computer. If you're still working with a 386SX 16, you're losing time because the computer can't handle the workload given it by the newer, more powerful programs such as Word for Windows.

If none of the preceding suits you, try this list of five things to best economize your time while that huge document is printing:

> ➤ Eat. Your mother is worried about you.

> ➤ Get on the phone and find more work. Or call your mother: she'll give you more to do.

> ➤ Read the rest of this book. You may learn some life lessons — stuff your mother didn't tell you.

> ➤ Feel guilty. Your mother wants you to.

> ➤ Relax. You're killing yourself by feeling that you have to fill every moment.

Forgotten passwords

My brain has taken a vacation without my permission. And I can't remember where it went or when it said it would be back. In the meantime, I need to know the passwords on some private files in Word 6 for Windows so that I can actually access them.

Don't worry, most people get by without using their heads.

So you want me to tell you about some secret backdoor. Well, there isn't one. What good would passwords be if anyone could get around them?

But just as locksmiths can open your house if you lose your keys, some people specialize in unlocking password-protected files. When people access your locked files without your permission, they're called hackers; if they do so with your permission, you call them gods. Try checking the Yellow Pages under *computer security specialist*.

In addition, a program called WDPASS from Access Data Recovery (801-224-6970) unlocks Word for Windows documents (and PKZip files too). You have to decide, though, whether the document is worth the program's $185 list price.

Komando Klues

Many people forget that passwords in Word for Windows are case sensitive. In other words, the password *KEYS* is different than the password *Keys* or *keys*.

WinWord add-ons

I write TV scripts for a living. I know that the next great movie is in me if only I would stop struggling with Word 6 for Windows. Are there any special add-ons that would help me?

So you're sitting there Home Alone, and you want to upgrade Word 6 for Windows. Here's my advice — it may seem Rocky at first, but soon you'll be Shining. For some people, that may be Rocky II, but stick with it, and you'll be the next Godfather of screenwriters.

There are some terrific screenwriting add-ons for Word 6 for Windows. Better yet, many are shareware. These add-ons provide you with an appropriate style sheet/template and macro set. My favorites include

> ➤ Scrnsty by Emmett Loverde
> ➤ Screen by Brian Jay Johnson
> ➤ Sw_Help by Guy Gallo

Just to whet your appetite, here's a description of Loverde's style sheet:

ScreenStyle is a Word 6 for Windows template created specifically for the needs of screenwriters. Version 3.0 includes several new shortcuts.

ScreenStyle conforms to the specifications outlined in *The Complete Guide to Standard Script Formats — Part I: The*

696

Screenplay, written by Hillis Cole Jr. and Judith H. Haag. These specifications include margins, tab settings, and capitalization requirements. Several automated features make this a welcome alternative to dedicated screenwriting programs such as Scriptor.

The Writer's Computer Store (800-272-TWCS) is an excellent resource for computer-literate Hollywood mogul wannabes. Don't forget to mention me during your acceptance speech.

SHARE.EXE

If I try to save anything in Word 6 for Windows, I get error messages like *Can't read Drive C* or *Current Drive is Write Protected.* Is there a way to save me?

Word for Windows usually gives this type of message when the document you're working with is opened by another program. The computer has a way of keeping track of which programs are using which files. The program that does so is SHARE.EXE.

SHARE.EXE should have been loaded automatically in the AUTOEXEC.BAT file when Word 6 for Windows was installed. Here's how to check whether SHARE.EXE is working:

1. Exit Windows.

2. Make a backup copy of the AUTOEXEC.BAT file to a floppy disk for safekeeping. Put a formatted floppy disk in drive A, type **COPY C:\AUTOEXEC.BAT A:**, and press Enter.

3. Type **CD ** and press Enter.

4. Type **EDIT AUTOEXEC.BAT** and press Enter.

5. Scroll through the **AUTOEXEC.BAT** file and look for a line that says SHARE (the word LOADHIGH or LH may precede it; some numbers may follow it).

If SHARE isn't in the AUTOEXEC.BAT file, you can add it:

1. Within the AUTOEXEC.BAT file, move the cursor to the line before the word WIN.

2. Press Enter.

3. Type **SHARE**.

4. Press Alt+F,S for File⇨Save.

5. Press Alt+F,X for File⇨Exit.

6. Restart the computer.

When the computer restarts, the SHARE program will be loaded into memory. Because SHARE keeps track of which program has which file open, the error message you described shouldn't appear.

Komando Klues

If you're using Windows for Workgroups 3.1 or 3.11, you don't need to add SHARE to the AUTOEXEC.BAT file. A part of Windows for Workgroups already has SHARE built in.

Buying paper

I make certificates and awards for the people where I work. The borders that come with Word 6 are so boring. I don't want these certificates to look like cheap computer awards; I want people to be proud enough to hang them. Any suggestions?

Well, first I have some suggestions about the types of awards. Perhaps

➤ Biggest Instigator

➤ Best Gossip

➤ Best Instinct to Turn Off Tetris Before the Boss Arrives

➤ Best Butt-Kisser

OK, now the real answer. Sometimes, the best answer to a computer question is to not use a computer. True, you can use Word for Windows to add borders around cells in a table, but it always looks like something you designed on a computer. I suggest buying preprinted certificate paper to put in your laser printer; this is absolutely the best way to get professional-looking certificates and awards. You can order this paper from

Baudville (800-728-0888)

Beaver Prints (800-923-2837)

Paper Direct (800-272-7377)

Queblo (800-523-9080)

Also check with your favorite computer software and accessory store.

On-screen colors

Black and white are too dull for me. How can I change the colors on my Word for Windows 6 screen to something more interesting?

Word for Windows sits on top of Windows. Whatever colors are used for Windows are used for Word for Windows (and other programs). Luckily, Windows lets you change the palette you're working with.

I can tell you how to change the colors in Windows, but you can't hold me responsible for the color combinations you come up with, OK?

1. From Program Manager, double-click on the Control Panel icon. It's usually in the Main program group.

2. Double-click on the Colors icon.

Windows comes with some color schemes already. To select one of those schemes,

1. Click on the button after the Color Schemes blank.

2. Select the name of a color scheme by clicking on the name. The sample window on-screen changes to show you the color settings.

If you can't find a color combination that you like, you can make your own (finally, your first-grade art schooling comes in handy):

1. Click the Color Palette button.

2. Click on the part of the sample screen where you want to change the color (for example, click on the words Window Text).

3. Click on one of the colors on the right-hand side of the window. The item selected in Step 2 changes to that color.

4. Save your color scheme by clicking on the Save Scheme button.

5. Type in a name for your color scheme (spaces are allowed).

6. Click OK to apply the color scheme.

You can come up with some really obnoxious color schemes if you spend enough time playing around. For most people, one of the basic Windows color schemes does the trick.

WordPerfect 6

Single-spacing

My boss really wants me to use single line spacing in my reports, letters, and so on. WordPerfect 6 seems to automatically double-space everything.

Because all your documents have double-spacing, you need to change the line spacing in the template:

1. Select File⇨Template.
2. Select the Standard template from the list.
3. Click OK.
4. Select Layout⇨Line.
5. Click on the Spacing option.
6. Change the 2 to a 1.
7. Save the template. Now every new document will be single-spaced.

To change the line spacing from double to single in an already created document,

1. Open the document.
2. With no text highlighted, select Layout⇨Line.
3. Click on the Spacing option.
4. Change the 2 to a 1.
5. Save the document.

Bullets

What are bullets? And how do I make them in WordPerfect 6.0a for Windows?

The first bullets were dangerous projectiles — only Superman was faster. Along came bullet bras and bumper bullets. Now this.

A typographic *bullet* is a mark (a symbol, letter, or numeral) beside a paragraph. Designers use bullets to make paragraphs stand out.

I usually use bullets when I want a list of things or a series of steps to stand out from the rest of the information on a page.

WordPerfect for Windows makes it easy to add bullets to your documents:

1. Select the paragraphs where you want bullets to appear.

2. Select Insert⇨Bullets & Numbers.

3. From the list of bullet types and numbering styles, select the desired mark.

4. Click OK. WordPerfect puts the desired bullet character in front of each of the selected paragraphs.

Note: WordPerfect even lets you designate a starting number for a bulleted list.

Komando Klues

Here's a WordPerfect 6 shortcut: After you highlight the paragraphs where you want bullets to appear, simply click the right mouse button. From the list of options that shows up, select Bullets.

Styles

Can I apply a style in WordPerfect 6 to the whole document at once, or do I have to do so paragraph by paragraph?

Here's how to look like a computer genius in six easy steps:

1. Select Edit⇨Select.

2. Click All (the entire document is highlighted).

3. Click Layout.

4. Click Styles.

5. Click the name of the style you want applied.

6. Click the Apply button.

All the paragraphs now have the style you selected.

When at Step 5, you can create new styles by clicking the Create button.

Deleting buttons

How do I get rid of unneeded buttons on my WordPerfect 6.0a button bar?

I may be putting my button the line, but here goes:

1. Move the mouse pointer to the button bar.

2. Click the right mouse button.

3. Select Edit from the list of options. The Button Bar editor window pops up.

4. Click the left mouse button on the button you want to get rid of and then drag the mouse pointer to the Button Bar editor window.

5. Release the left mouse button.

6. Repeat Steps 4 and 5 until all the unwanted buttons are gone.

7. Click OK.

Say good-bye.

Adding buttons

I often check how many words are in the document I'm typing. A custom button would make this action easier. How do I add a button to the WordPerfect 6.0a button bar? (Incidentally, that question was 32 words.)

You're different. I bet you stack quarters, dimes, and nickels into separate piles before you go to sleep.

Nonetheless, here's your answer:

1. Move the mouse pointer to the button bar.

2. Click the right mouse button.

3. Select Edit from the list of options. The Button Bar editor window pops up.

4. Select the Feature Category you want to work with (in your case, select File).

5. Click on the Document Info command.

6. Click OK.

The new button appears on the button bar.

If the bar holds more buttons than can be displayed at once, the right-hand side of the button bar will have an up-and-down arrow button. Click the down-arrow button to see more buttons.

(Incidentally, that answer was 112 words. I'm weird, too.)

Moving button bar

How do I move the button bar in WordPerfect 6.0a to the left-hand side of my screen?

Some people dream of owning a home beside a golf course. Others don't want people in funny pants walking around in their backyard pretending to look for a lost ball while they're peering into your bathroom. Screen real estate is funny, too. Some people like seeing button bars at the top of the screen; others like to see them on one side or another. Well, that's just bar for the course.

WordPerfect 6.0a lets you easily move the button bar on-screen:

1. Move the mouse pointer to the right-hand edge of the button bar (where there's a gray space and no button). The mouse pointer changes into a hand.

2. Click the left button and drag the mouse pointer to the left-hand side of the screen.

3. Release the mouse button.

When you start WordPerfect again, the button bar will appear on the left-hand side of the screen.

You can move the button bar around any time you want.

Video drivers

I don't know where to begin to get the right video drivers to work with WordPerfect for Windows. Can you give me a hint?

What do you mean you "don't know where to begin"? You came to me. And let me add, you came to the right place.

Video drivers present one of the biggest problem areas for computer users. In fact, a problem with the video driver may cause your computer to crash every time you use WordPerfect for Windows — even though you have no problems using File Manager.

A *driver*, in computer terms, is an interpreter. It translates what a program asks a computer device to do so that the device can understand. For example, a Windows video driver interprets what WordPerfect for Windows wants to display on-screen so that the video card understands; otherwise, the video card won't know what information to put on-screen.

Most video cards come with their own video drivers. In fact, different video cards from the same manufacturer require different video drivers. If the video card driver you selected is not working, try choosing the generic VGA driver; you can use it with just about every VGA card. If you're not already using this standard video driver, here's how:

1. Exit Windows completely.

2. Change to the WINDOWS directory by typing **CD \ WINDOWS** at the DOS prompt.

3. Type **SETUP** and press Enter.

4. A screen showing your Windows setup appears. Move the cursor to the line that says Display and press Enter.

5. Scroll through the list until you see an option that reads VGA (and nothing else) and press Enter twice.

6. When Windows asks, place the appropriate Windows installation disk in the floppy drive and press Enter.

When the setup program finishes, you are at the DOS prompt. Type **WIN** and press Enter to restart Windows. Try running WordPerfect for Windows again and see whether your problems are solved.

The standard VGA driver is like plain vanilla ice cream. For a more flavorful on-screen display, contact the company that made your video card and ask for an updated Windows driver for your make and model of video card. (You also may be able to download this driver from an on-line service.) After you receive the driver, follow the preceding Steps 1–4. In Step 5, scroll through the list until you see the line that reads Other (it's at the bottom of the list). You'll then be asked to type in the drive and/or subdirectory name where the new drivers are.

Komando Klues

If your video driver is more than six months old, contact the video card maker for an updated version.

Printer drivers

My printer must have lost its license. I can't find a WordPerfect 6 for DOS driver for my printer. I know how to install printer drivers, but how am I supposed to know which one to use?

Printer lost its driver's license? Hey, do what every teenager does: print a fake one. Oh, yeah, you can't get anything to print.

You're in luck, my friend. WordPerfect must have the largest collection of printer drivers on earth. Contact WordPerfect at 800-861-2450 if you have a dot matrix printer or 800-861-2440 if you have a laser printer.

Most printers *emulate*, or pretend, that they're another type of printer. Check the printer manual to see which type of printer your printer wants to be. Sometimes, you need to change some switches to make the printer change its personality. I cover this information in the Printers chapter of this book.

Printing envelopes

Talk about a communications breakdown: my HP Deskjet 560C and WordPerfect 6 just can't get together to print an envelope. How can I get them back on speaking terms? Now my roommate and I aren't talking either.

Well, I'd better hurry before this plague spreads uncontrollably, or no one will talk to anyone.

To print envelopes on any HP Deskjet printer,

1. Select Layout⮡Page⮡Paper Size.

2. Select Create. Give this new envelope a name, such as *My Envelope*.

3. Select Type⮡Envelope. The envelope macro recognizes only one description.

4. Select Size⮡User Defined Size and type **9.5 x 4.50**. This action makes WordPerfect override the standard size settings.

5. Select Wide Form. Make sure that the icon of the page is in landscape mode (long side runs up and down). Don't select rotated font.

6. Select OK.

WordPerfect may tell you that it doesn't like your paper size. It may even talk to the Deskjet behind your back. But don't worry. Remember, you're the boss, and what you say goes. And at least your word processor and printer will be on speaking terms again.

Faxing from within WP

I can't afford a stand-alone fax machine, but I've heard that I can fax from within WordPerfect 6 for DOS. Is this true?

Yes. If you have a fax modem, you can fax directly from WordPerfect 6 for DOS. In fact, WordPerfect 5.1+ for DOS, which came out after Version 6 (go figure), also lets you fax directly from within. These programs support a wide variety of fax modem boards, but call WordPerfect Corp. at 800-861-2066 to make sure your fax modem is supported.

To fax from within WordPerfect, press Shift+F7 (to print) and select the fax as the printer type. In the screen that pops up, enter the fax number that you want to send to.

Note: WordPerfect doesn't let you receive faxes from someone else. To do that, you need a program such as DOSFax from Delrina. Or you can use the fax program that usually ships with the fax modem.

General protection faults

My computer crashes as consistently as waves hit a beach. Why am I getting so many general protection faults when using WordPerfect for Windows 6.0a?

Computer programs are complicated things, and bugs crop up no matter how much a program is tested before it hits the market.

WordPerfect 6.0a, for example, corrected several bugs that were found in Version 6.0, but it introduced a couple of new ones, too. WordPerfect has released Version 6.0c, which corrects some bugs found in Versions 6.0a and 6.0b. Version 6.1, meanwhile, not only corrects all known bugs but includes a few new features.

You can obtain the 6.0 series of bug-fix disks for a small shipping and handling charge. Version 6.1, however, is considered an upgrade and costs a bit more. Contact WordPerfect at 800-228-9907 for more information.

.BIF

WordPerfect keeps telling me that it's *Unable to create or find .BIF file*. What on earth is a .BIF? This is so infuriating.

.BIF is Muffy's preppy boyfriend. Everybody knows that.

Actually, a *B*inary *I*nformation *F*ile stores the settings for how WordPerfect is started.

Unfortunately, WordPerfect 6.0 had some bugs. In your case, at least one .BIF file was damaged. WordPerfect 6.0a corrected several bugs that were found in Version 6.0, but it introduced a couple of new ones, too. WordPerfect has released Version 6.0c, which corrects some bugs found in Versions 6.0a and 6.0b. Version 6.1, meanwhile, not only corrects all known bugs but includes a few new features.

You can obtain the 6.0 series of bug-fix disks for a small shipping and handling charge. Version 6.1, however, is considered an upgrade and costs a bit more. Contact WordPerfect at 800-228-9907 for more information.

Importing graphics

WordPerfect 6 for Windows doesn't let me put pictures in my documents. It says *no conversion DLL is available for the requested file type* and *detected file format is invalid*. What's going on?

Your computer is just being stuck up. You just need to let it know who's boss. (Pssst, you are.)

Different types of graphics file formats save information in different ways. WordPerfect needs the right conversion file (usually called a *filter*) to translate a graphic into something that it can understand. Without the proper filter, WordPerfect can't read the graphic properly.

One of two things is happening in your case:

➤ The proper filter has been damaged.

➤ The proper filter was not installed when WordPerfect was set up.

I want you to do some hard disk maintenance first in case the filter was damaged:

1. Exit Windows completely and go to the DOS prompt.

2. At the DOS prompt, type **CHKDSK /F** and press Enter. If you're using MS-DOS 6.2 or above, use SCANDISK because it's much more thorough than CHECKDISK. To use SCANDISK, type **SCANDISK** and press Enter.

3. If either program finds errors on the disk, it asks whether you should save them to files; say no. You usually can't make heads or tails of the information anyway.

4. After you finish checking out the hard drive, reorganize it by running the drive defragmentation program that comes with MS-DOS 6.0 or above. To run this program, which puts the files on the hard drive back in order, type **DEFRAG** at the DOS prompt and press Enter.

After you clean up your hard drive, it's time to install (or reinstall) that filter. Get out your original WordPerfect for Windows installation disks.

1. Start Windows.

2. From the WordPerfect group in Program Manager, double-click on the WPWin 6.0 Setup icon.

3. Click the Install button.

4. Click the Custom button.

5. Click the Files button.

6. Click the Unmark All button.

7. Click the Additional Conversion/Printer Docs button.

8. Click the OK button.

9. Click the Start Install button.

10. WordPerfect tells you which floppy disk to put into the drive. Insert the required disk and click OK.

11. Repeat Step 10 until the installation is complete.

When you start up WordPerfect again, it will have all the information it needs to place the picture in your document.

Speed

To speed up WordPerfect 6 for Windows, should I use a math coprocessor or up my RAM to 8MB?

A math coprocessor has the cushiest job I know: it only works when a program knows how to talk to it, and most programs, including WordPerfect, don't use a math coprocessor. (Man, you know that has to be a union job.) Advanced graphics programs, such as CorelDRAW! 5, and computer-aided design (CAD) programs, such as AutoCAD, do use the math coprocessor. Spreadsheet programs, such as Lotus 1-2-3, use a math coprocessor if it's available, but you have to get into some real advanced spreadsheets before it's useful.

Windows speeds up significantly when you add more memory. In fact, Windows 3.1 has the most noticeable performance improvement when you go from 4MB to 8MB of RAM.

Not enough memory

I'm puzzled. When I start WordPerfect 6 for Windows, I get the message *WP DRAW error* and then *probable reason insufficient memory*. What's the problem here? I'm using virtual memory already.

Although you should pay attention to error messages, they do not always communicate the absolute truth. You may not have enough memory, but the problem may simply be that some of the drawing program files are damaged.

Computer memory is like a wading pool. Just as you can fit only so many kids in a pool, there's only so much memory for programs to use. When big kids are in the pool, fewer kids are splashing. In the same way, some programs use more memory than others; and when the space is filled, late-arriving programs just have to stand by and watch the others having fun.

You have two choices:

➤ Get a bigger pool (get more memory).

➤ Tell some of the kids to get out of the water (close down some programs).

Windows works pretty well with 4MB of memory, but it's not really enough room for some of the big kids (including WordPerfect) to feel comfortable. *Virtual memory*, where Windows lets you take a chunk of hard disk space and use it as RAM memory, is a good start. But if you only have 4MB of RAM, you should consider upgrading to 8MB. (The biggest noticeable performance increase in Windows performance occurs when you up from 4MB to 8MB of memory.)

Of course, adding memory costs money. If your budget can't handle the upgrade, it's time to kick some kids out of the pool. Which other programs are running when the error message comes up? To find out which programs are running currently, press Ctrl+Esc to bring up the Windows Task List. Maybe you should think about closing down that game of Solitaire. Do you really need Paintbrush open now? To close down any program you don't need,

1. Click on the name of the program.

2. Click on the End Task button.

RAM memory is one of the most precious resources you have. With some thought, you can make it go a long way.

But save your spare change so that you can eventually purchase more memory. It's a fact of computing: The more you do, the more you want to do. And those really neat, powerful programs need a lot of memory.

Komando
Klues

Not all programs clean up after themselves. When you close down some programs, they leave behind little souvenirs that take up memory and/or something called system resources. It may be necessary to close down Windows and start it up again so that every byte of memory and every system resource is available.

 Uninstalling

How do I remove WordPerfect 6.0 from my computer?

The folks who make WordPerfect realize that having an easy way to uninstall a program is just as important as having an easy way to install it. That's why the program is called WordPerfect and not WordPrettyGood.

1. If WordPerfect is running, exit it.

2. From either Program Manager or File Manger, select File⇨Run.

3. Type **A: SETUP** or **B: SETUP**, depending on which drive the floppy is in.

4. Click OK.

5. Click on Standard.

6. Click OK.

7. You have one last chance to change your mind: click OK again if you're sure you want to uninstall WordPerfect 6.0.

8. At the end of the process, you need to click OK one more time.

Poof. No more WordPerfect for Windows. Well, almost. One or two subdirectories may remain because WordPerfect can't delete a file or subdirectory that's in use by the setup program. Here's how to remove what was left behind:

1. Run File Manager.

2. Change to the drive that WordPerfect was installed on (if necessary).

3. Click on the subdirectory (file folder) named WPC20 (on the left-hand side of the File Manager screen).

4. Press the Del key.

5. Click the Yes to All button.

6. If there's a subdirectory (file folder) named WPWIN60, repeat Steps 4 and 5.

Icons in a DOS program?

My WordPerfect 6 for DOS has icons and stuff just like the Windows version. Did I buy the wrong package? How can I get rid of all the icons and stuff?

You didn't pick up the wrong box. WordPerfect for DOS has a split personality: it has two different faces, or what techies call *modes*. One mode, the one with all the pretty pictures and icons, is called WYSIWYG (*what you see is what you get*) mode. The other mode, text mode, is for people who are used to working with WordPerfect 5.1 for DOS.

In WYSIWYG mode, you work much as you would if you were using WordPerfect for Windows. To go into text mode, which works faster and seems a lot more like WordPerfect 5.1, select View⇨Text Mode.

Ami Pro

You say Amy, I say Ah-mee

I'm so humiliated. Every time I say "Ami Pro" at work, everyone laughs. What's the correct way to pronounce Ami Pro?

No matter how you say the Ami in Ami Pro, somebody gives you a funny look. People who think that they know what they're talking about tend to say "ah-MEE." The rest of us usually just mumble "aw-me" — as in "Aw, me. Are they laughing again?"

If you really get embarrassed, you have two options: Say "Ami" the way most of your coworkers do. Or carry the Ami Pro manual around all the time and point to the cover whenever you want to talk about the program.

Cursed screen

An evil witch has cursed my 486DX screen. Whenever I type, the right-hand side of the screen turns into bizarre symbols. Do you have a magic potion that can fix this problem? I have Windows 3.1 (enhanced) with DOS 6.22 and Ami Pro 3.

Some of my staff members think that I'm a witch. I know, of course, that they mean Glenda, the good witch of the North.

If the problem crops up only in Ami Pro, you probably have to reinstall Ami Pro. If these mysterious symbols show up in every program, something is wrong with Windows.

Of course, if the computer can't read the information from the hard drive properly, all kinds of strange things can happen. So before reinstalling anything, do some disk maintenance.

Click your heels three times and follow these steps:

1. Exit Windows completely.

2. Because you're using MS-DOS 6.2 or above, type **SCANDISK** at the DOS prompt and press Enter. (If your version of DOS predates 6.2, you have to use the less thorough CHECKDISK. At the DOS prompt, type **CHKDSK /F** and press Enter.)

3. If SCANDISK (or CHECKDISK) finds errors on the disk, it asks whether you should save them to files; say no because you usually won't be able to make heads or tails of the information.

4. After you finish checking out the hard drive, reorganize it by running the drive defragmentation program that comes with MS-DOS 6.0 or above. To run this program, which puts the files on the hard drive back in order, type **DEFRAG** at the DOS prompt and press Enter.

Now that you've cleaned house, it's time to see whether things are acting properly. If the Ami Pro screen still looks bewitched, it's time to reinstall the program. If the other screens in Windows also are messed up, it's time to reinstall Windows.

Reinstalling Ami Pro (and Windows, if necessary) should eliminate the curse. Just remember not to break any mirrors or walk under any ladders.

Komando Klues

When reinstalling Ami Pro, back up at least the Ami Pro directory, its subdirectories, and all the Ami Pro .INI files found in the C:\WINDOWS directory. When reinstalling Windows, back up at least the WINDOWS directory and all its subdirectories. By the way, after you reinstall a program such as Ami Pro, you usually have to reset all your preferences (including where the files are stored and custom toolbars). Reinstalling Windows, on the other hand, just copies back all the Windows files, replacing any that are bad; as a result, you keep all your groups, color preferences, and settings.

Spell checker and hyphens

The Ami Pro 3 spell checker thinks that most hyphenated words are misspelled. Is there a way to tell the spell check function to automatically ignore hyphens?

If Ami Pro runs into a word that it doesn't recognize, you can

➤ Click Ignore.

➤ Click Replace to accept Ami Pro's suggestion (for example, *spell checker* rather than *spell-checker*).

➤ Click Add to add the word in question to your dictionary. Ami Pro won't ever again think that it's misspelled.

Table lines don't print

When I create a table in Ami Pro, I see the table's lines on-screen, but the lines don't print.

Table lines show on-screen to help you maneuver through cells and rows. Unfortunately, they don't print automatically. If you want the lines to print, you have to tell Ami Pro:

1. Tell Ami Pro where you want the lines to appear. To select an entire table, you can either highlight the whole table by using the mouse or put the insertion point inside the table and then choose Table⇨Select Entire Table.

2. Select Table⇨Lines.

3. Select Color and go to town.

Komando Klues

While you're playing around with the colors, pick the line position and style, too. (You can use the line style to make certain areas of your table — such as column titles — stand out.)

Q: What do an actor, a draftsman, and a drug addict have in common?

A: They all need lines.

Using oddly sized labels

How do I add label sizes to the LABEL.STY style sheet? I tried to use the macro MAKELABL.SMM but ended up where I started: nowhere. This burns me up.

Sounds like a macrowave accident.

Exit Ami Pro. Make a backup copy of the AMILABEL.INI file (located in your C:\WINDOWS directory). Open the Windows Accessories program group and double-click on Notepad.

Open the AMILABEL.INI file, which contains all the label style sheet settings. Press the End key to get to the bottom of the file. Then write down the last label entry, which is the total number of labels in the style sheet (you will use this number in a minute).

Press the Home key to return to the top of the file. From the Notepad menu bar, select Search. In the command line box, type **NextCustomLabelKey=** and click OK. Change the number that appears after the equal sign to the total number of labels in the style sheet (remember, that's the number you found at the end of the file) *plus* one.

Press the End key to go to the end of the file again. Now add a description of the custom label to the bottom of the file. Type the label information exactly as follows:

```
Headings=Part Number, Label Type, Label Height, Label
Width, Number Across, Number Down, Top Margin, Side
Margins, Horizontal Pitch, Vertical Pitch, Page Type
```

For example, if my 25th label used Avery Part Number 5972, the entry would look like

```
Label25=5972,Address,1.000,2.625,3,10,0.500,0.188,2.750,1.000,
8.5" x 11"
```

Select File⇨Save. Exit Notepad and go back to Ami Pro. You should see the new label on the style sheet.

Say good-bye to SwitchKit

I thought that only humans had difficulty ending relationships. I used Ami Pro's WordPerfect SwitchKit, but the SwitchKit won't stop loading when I start Ami Pro.

Exit Ami Pro. Make a backup copy of the AMIPRO2.INI file (located in your C:\WINDOWS directory). Open the Windows Accessories program group and double-click on Notepad.

Open the AMIPRO2.INI file. Scroll to the section marked [SwitchKit] and find the line that reads as follows:

```
AutoStart=2
```

Change the 2 to a 1 so that the line now reads

```
AutoStart=1
```

From the Notepad menu bar, select File⇨Save. Then exit Notepad. The next time you start Ami Pro, the WordPerfect SwitchKit relationship will be history.

Komando Klues

If you have second thoughts, you can rekindle the fire: Select Help⇨For WordPerfect Users. Then select On. The WordPerfect SwitchKit will not be automatically loaded during that particular Ami Pro session.

If only ending human relationships was that easy.

Searching for key phrases

I lost an Ami Pro document. I know I saved it, but I can't remember the filename. How do I ask Ami Pro to search for certain phrases so that I can track down the file? I know one key phrase is *knife wound*.

I don't even want to know what this file is about.

Ami Pro 3 searches files for certain phrases with the FINDFILE.SMM macro. From the Ami Pro menu bar, select Tools⇨Macros⇨Playback. Type in the appropriate search phrase, select the directories (or subdirectories), and then click OK.

Lost font

My company uses only the Courier font. But half of us use WordPerfect, the rest Ami Pro. When I import a WordPerfect document into Ami Pro, I lose the Courier font. Is there a way to keep it?

You can have a messenger bring you the Courier. (OK, that was dumb, even by my standards.)

Exit Ami Pro. Make a backup copy of the AMIWP.INI file (located in your C:\WINDOWS directory). Open the Windows Accessories program group and double-click on Notepad.

Open the AMIWP.INI file. Scroll to the [FontIgnore] section and find the line that reads as follows:

```
Courier New=12
```

Tell Ami Pro to ignore this line. To do so, put the letters *REM* before the line so that it reads as follows:

```
REM Courier New=12
```

From the Notepad menu bar, select File⇨Save. Exit Notepad. You shouldn't have any problems the next time you import a WordPerfect document into Ami Pro.

Chapter 20
Windows

Basics

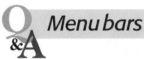
Menu bars

I just got some programs for Windows. But I'm not so sure about the menu bars. Why do some of the menus on the menu bars have lines underneath certain letters?

The menu bar in a Windows-based application is similar to a restaurant menu. When you go to a restaurant, a waiter hands you a menu so that you can make a selection. The *menu bar* is a horizontal bar at the top of the screen, and it lists all the different things you can do while you're using the software program. Even better, the menu bar groups different selections, or *commands*. These groups are called *menus*.

If a program's commands were all typed out, you would have almost 50 pages of commands, so Windows-based programs use *pull-down* menus to keep the screen free of clutter: the menus are hidden along the menu bar. To open a pull-down menu, you click once on the menu.

The underlined letters are for convenience. Instead of using the mouse to open the pull-down menu, you can use the keyboard. How? As an example, *File* on a menu bar has the letter *F* underlined. To use the keyboard to open the File pull-down menu, press the Alt key and the letter that's underlined. In other words, press Alt+F.

Keyboard vs. mouse

I'm more accustomed to a keyboard than a mouse. This is a problem in Windows. You seem to need a darn mouse for everything.

For some tasks, using a keyboard is actually easier and quicker than using a mouse (for example, for cutting and pasting information from one Windows-based application to another or for multiple pastes from the Windows Clipboard). The following table lists some timesaving keyboard shortcuts to use in files and documents and on the Windows desktop. The plus sign in the Keystrokes column means that you press the first key and hold it down, press the second key, and then release both of them. It's a snap!

Komando
Klues

Task	Keystrokes
Cut selected text	Ctrl+X or Shift+Del
Copy selected text	Ctrl+C or Ctrl+Ins
Paste contents of the Clipboard	Ctrl+V or Shift+Ins (works for word processing, not with faux pas)
Undo most recent action	Ctrl+Z or Alt+Backspace
Move cursor right one word	Ctrl+right-arrow key
Move cursor left one word	Ctrl+left-arrow key
Move cursor to beginning of line	Home
Move cursor to end of line	End
Move cursor to start of document	Ctrl+Home
Move cursor to end of document	Ctrl+End
Change program item or group properties	Alt+Enter
Select another program item	Press first letter of label
Save current Program Manager settings	Alt+Shift+F4
Move program item to another group	F7
Copy program item to another group	F8
Tile windows	Shift+F4
Cascade windows	Shift+F5
Close Program Manager and exit Windows	Alt+F4

Now, cut and paste this list from my book, er, I mean your book, to a place where you can see it.

Mouse speed

I'm faster than my mouse. I want to make it move quicker. Maybe I should take a whip to its back end.

Keep it up, buster, and the Animal Defense League will be knocking on your door. Speeding up a mouse is pretty simple, and no violence is required. Just open the Windows Main program group and then open the Control Panel. You'll see an icon of a mouse — the computer kind.

Click the Mouse icon and move the Sensitivity slider all the way to the right. This trick works on almost every system, except for notebook computers such as IBM's ThinkPad or other computers that have a built-in pointing device. Of course, maneuvering a built-in mouse at warp speed is tough. On those systems, the Sensitivity slider should go almost all the way to the left.

While you're at it, switch on Mouse Trails. It's fun for about ten seconds, but then you begin to experience flashbacks.

Double-click speed

The kids have trouble holding the mouse still and double-clicking at the same time. Is there a way to make it easier for them?

Most kids have a tendency to move the mouse each time they click the button. You can solve this problem by making a little edit in the WIN.INI file.

First, however, make sure that you have a backup copy of the WIN.INI file. Then use Windows Notepad to open the WIN.INI file that's in the C:\WINDOWS directory. Look for the [Windows] section and then add the following lines:

```
DoubleClickHeight=8
DoubleClickWidth=8
```

The Windows default setting for DoubleClickHeight and DoubleClickWidth is 4. Making the setting 8 enables the kids to move the mouse around a little more during a double-click.

Come to think of it, kids have a hard time holding still period.

Note: You also can change the speed of the double-click setting so that it recognizes slower double-clicks. Open the Windows Main program group and then open the Control Panel. Click the Mouse icon and move the Sensitivity slider all the way to the left.

Time format

While serving in the military, I grew to like their way of keeping time. Why doesn't Windows offer this option?

A small covert operation would have informed you of the International icon.

To customize the clock, open the Main program group and the Control Panel. Then click on the International icon. You can set the time format to the 24-hour clock. You can change the colon used to separate the numbers to some other symbol. You can even add a leading zero to the time so that you see 0400 hours rather than 400 hours.

Moving and resizing windows

When I try to resize a window by using the mouse pointer, the border of the window that I am attempting to resize skips around on-screen. Sometimes the window moves off-screen, leaving only a small portion of itself visible.

Windows is a pane, eh?

First, a word about those borders. They are there to define the limits of the windows. You click and drag any window border or corner to resize it. When you are doing it correctly, you see a double-edged arrow.

You may not be holding down the left mouse button all the way when you are resizing the window. When you lose a window, just click Window on the Program Manager's menu bar and choose Tile or Cascade. Windows tiles or cascades the windows that are open, and vwaaa-laaa, you get back your lost window.

If resizing hasn't ever worked right, you may have the wrong mouse selected. Of course, if Windows is corrupted, you need to reinstall it. (Yuck!)

It takes practice to get window sizing, tiling, or cascading down. Give it time and be patient.

Resizing windows

One side of an application window is out past the edge of the screen. I have no way to resize the window to make it smaller. Please help. I want my window back.

Windows giving you a pane? Not a problem. Just choose Window from the Program Manager title bar and select Tile or Cascade. All your open windows are tidy now.

Or grab the uncooperative window's title bar with your mouse and move the application until it's all the way on-screen. You can resize that window to your heart's content by placing the cursor on the very edge until it has two arrow heads. Then just hold the mouse button down and drag the edge of the window to the size and location you want.

Floppy disk size

File Manager is ripping me off when it formats disks! If I format a 1.2MB floppy from Windows for Workgroups, it formats to only 1.15MB. A floppy that is supposed to hold 1.44MB formats to 1.38MB.

It is really just a math thing. A formatted $3^1/_2$-inch high-density disk holds approximately 1.44 million bytes of information. Such a disk is quite commonly, although not entirely correctly, referred to as a 1.44MB disk. You see, the true definition of a megabyte is 1,048,576 bytes. The File Manager in Windows for Workgroups now uses the true definition of a megabyte in its calculations. If you multiply the 1.38MB that your File Manager is reporting by the number of bytes in a true megabyte, you get exactly 1,447,034 bytes, or approximately 1.44 million bytes.

How much RAM do I have?

I checked the About Program Manager and, wow, something is wrong. Windows tells me I have over 7MB of RAM. I'm supposed to have only 4MB of RAM. I'm not complaining, but do you think maybe the computer dealer made a mistake?

Rule of thumb: A salesperson never makes a mistake in the consumer's favor.

When Windows looks at memory, it sees more than just RAM. Windows takes into account the size of the permanent or temporary swap file, too. It adds the total amount of RAM available inside the computer to the total amount of RAM available through Windows virtual memory tricks. *Note:* You need to run Windows in 386 enhanced mode to use a swap file.

To check the type of swap file you have and the amount of RAM available through your swap file, open the Windows Main program group. Select the Control Panel and then the 386 Enhanced Icon. Select the Virtual Memory button and you'll see the current settings of your swap file, including type and size.

Add the total amount of memory inside your computer to the size of the swap file and you should be pretty darn close to the amount of memory that Windows says is available.

System resources

How can I tell how many system resources I have available?

I have five nickels and take away two nickels. How much do I have left? Not much. Better spend it now, inflation is rising.

To determine the available system resources, just click Help from the Program Manager menu bar and select About Program Manager. Toward the bottom of the window that opens, you will see the Windows mode that you're using, available memory, and system resources. The system resources should never drop below 20 percent; if it does, exit and restart

Windows. Try to keep your system resources above 65 percent to prevent any *insufficient memory* messages. I like to open and close different applications just to see how they affect the system resources. Try it sometime; it's kind of interesting. It's certainly more interesting than doing that English paper that's due in two hours.

What's multitasking?

What exactly is multitasking? Is it possible to, say, copy files to a disk and work on a spreadsheet at the same time?

Open a program such as Solitaire. Then hold down the Alt key and press the Esc key once. Pressing this key combo displays the open programs, or the *Windows Task List*, and lets you switch to another application or close an application that's running. You can, for example, open your word processor or any other program and work away. Or say that you want to download a nifty file from America Online, but you're going for that Tetris championship. Just start your download, press Alt+Esc, and work or play away. When the download is done or a program needs your attention, Windows switches back automatically to America Online and lets you log off.

Once you have Alt+Esc down pat, try pressing the Alt+Tab combination. Each time you press Alt+Tab, a title box appears in the middle of the screen. When you see the title box of the program that you want to use, let go of the Alt+Tab keys. This shortcut gives you a quick way to work in several applications at once. (It is especially useful when you're playing Solitaire and your manager walks into the room. Press Alt+Tab and in a split second your screen shows that report you should have been completing. No, wait — it's Chessmaster 2100. Quick, pull the plug!)

Making a screen saver

I'm really into self-motivation. I'd like to make a personal message for a screen saver. What's the easiest way to do this in Windows?

"Go for the gold." "Run with it." "I'm in your corner." "You can go all the way with it." You can use any of those messages for your screen saver. No charge, other than the charge for the book, of course.

Open the Main program group and then the Control Panel. Inside the Control Panel, double-click the Desktop icon to open the Desktop. Here, among other things, you can create your motivational message and set the time that the keyboard is idle before it appears.

Look for the Screen Saver box and click the down arrow in the Name box. Select Marquee and then click Setup. OK, the generic Windows 3.1 message that comes with Windows is probably not what one considers a kick in the butt, so you want to change it. Click in the Text box and type a new message. (Mine says, "What are you doing right now to follow your dreams?") You also can change the background color from black by selecting Background Color. The Position option enables you to put the marquee in the center of the screen or in random places.

Next comes the fun part, changing the marquee's font. Click the Format Text button to see the Format Text dialog box and then select the font, font style, color, and size for your message. Click OK when you're done. Back in the Marquee Setup dialog box, look at the sample. If you're satisfied, click OK and then click the upward- or downward-pointing arrow in the Delay box to increase or decrease the time the keyboard is idle before the marquee shows. I set mine for two minutes as a little reminder to get to work.

Attaching sounds to system events

I downloaded a whole bunch of sound files, like breaking glass, from a BBS. How can I put these sounds with certain things I do in Windows?

I hear what you're doing: every time you open a window, you want to hear the sound of breaking glass, like on David Letterman's show.

Bulletin board systems (BBSs) and on-line services are great places to find all kinds of neat sound files. You name it, it's probably available for downloading from somewhere. You can find everything from MIDI to .VOC to .WAV files and more.

Although you can play all of these kinds of files on your system (provided you have a sound card that supports those formats), you can't use just any sound file for system events. The Sound option that's available in the Control Panel will work only with .WAV files — it won't play files made in other formats, such as MIDI. If the files you downloaded have the .WAV extension, all you have to do is copy them into your WINDOWS directory and then use the Sound icon to assign them to different events in Windows.

To attach sounds to system events, open the Control Panel and double-click the Sound icon. System events are listed on the left side of the dialog box, and available .WAV files are on the right. By default, the dialog box lists only .WAV files in the WINDOWS directory, but you can browse through other directories in search of sound clips, too. Highlight the system event and a matching sound clip; then click the Test button to preview the sound. Make sure that the Enable System Sounds box is checked and then press OK.

Although Windows has some of its own events predefined for you to attach sounds to, it does not allow you to attach sounds to any other events.

 Tracking saved files

I want to set my system so that my files are saved automatically in a certain subdirectory. Right now, I have files all over my computer's hard disk, and this makes it hard to find things.

Windows 3.1 has a little feature that not many people use (that is, until this book hits the shelves and I blow this whole secret wide open). It's called the *working directory,* and normally this directory is where the program is located (not the *subdirectory,* where the information created with the software program is located). You can change a software program's working directory by changing the *properties* of a program. Here's how to do it.

With the Program Manager on-screen, choose the program that you want to change the working directory for by clicking it once. Click File⇨ Properties. The Program Item Properties window pops up on-screen. If you want, you can change the title that appears under the icon in Program Manager. You can change the command line, too, but don't. (It tells Windows where the program file is located and how to start up the program.) The next line in this window, the Working Directory, is the one to change. Select this line and type the drive letter, a colon, a backslash, and then the name of the subdirectory that the files are in. Click the OK button to save the changes.

When you start the program by double-clicking its icon and then clicking File⇨Open, you will be in the subdirectory that you told the program to use in the preceding steps. Also, when you save a file, the program will point to this subdirectory. This handy little trick can save you extra mouse clicks every time you open or save a file. And you'll have a better handle on hard disk management, too.

 ## Backing up vital Windows files

It must be me. I've never heard of anyone having as much trouble keeping Windows working as I do. Whenever I add a program, Windows acts up. Is there any way to set up my computer so that I back up the most important Windows files every time I exit Windows? It must be me.

Don't be so hard on yourself. I know people who can't turn computers on.

By "the most important Windows files," I suppose you mean the ones needed for Windows to run. These files have the .INI and .GRP extensions, and they are in the C:\WINDOWS\SYSTEM directory.

The best method of backing them up is to have your computer do a few extra steps for you so you won't have to work too hard. First, make a special holding area, or *subdirectory*, for your important Windows files. If you are in Windows, exit Windows. At the DOS prompt from the main root directory, type the following and press Enter:

```
MD 911
```

where 911 is the name of your emergency Windows files directory. You can call me 411. I'm your information directory.

Your computer's hard disk now has a 911 directory on it. Because you've admitted that you're not so good at this computer stuff, copy the AUTOEXEC.BAT and CONFIG.SYS files into the 911 directory too. Type the following and press Enter:

```
COPY AUTOEXEC.BAT C:\911
```

and

```
COPY CONFIG.SYS C:\911
```

Now use the DOS text editor to add the lines to the AUTOEXEC.BAT file that will automatically copy all the Windows .INI and .GRP files each time you exit Windows. Type the following and press Enter:

```
EDIT AUTOEXEC.BAT
```

At the very bottom of the AUTOEXEC.BAT file, add the following lines:

```
CD \WINDOWS
COPY *.INI C:\911
COPY *.GRP C:\911
CD \
```

Save the changes to the AUTOEXEC.BAT file by choosing File⇨Save. Sleep tight now. You always have a copy of your most recent Windows .INI and .GRP files in the 911 directory.

Starting Up

 Automatically launching Windows

When I turn on my computer, I have to type WIN to start Windows. When I used my friend's computer, it started Windows automatically. How can I make my computer act like her computer does?

You don't like typing WIN? It sounds so optimistic. It empowers me. Then again, I can't imagine a rough-and-tough writer like Hemingway typing in a chipper message like WIN to get into the down-and-dirty business of writing.

If you want Windows to start when your computer starts, you have to tell it. Inside the computer is an important file called the AUTOEXEC.BAT file. The name is short for *AUTOmatically EXECute this set of BATch commands.* The AUTOEXEC.BAT file tells the computer what to do every time it starts. You need to add a line to the bottom of the AUTOEXEC.BAT file to make Windows start automatically. Don't worry; it's easy.

First, make a copy of the AUTOEXEC.BAT file to a floppy disk. Because you're a Windows user, you can use the File Manager to make the copy. Highlight the AUTOEXEC.BAT file at the main, or *root,* drive C directory. Then use the File Manager's Copy command and drag the highlighted filename, AUTOEXEC.BAT, to the floppy drive where you want the copy. If you're a little leery about the drag action, choose File⇨Copy from the File Manager's menu bar.

Now change the AUTOEXEC.BAT file so the computer knows to start Windows when you turn it on. From the Windows Program Manager, choose File⇨Run. In the Run box, type the following and click OK:

```
SYSEDIT
```

The really important files that your computer needs to work are opened. (I know what you're thinking. Are there some not-so-important files?) Make sure that the *active window* (the window with the different colored title bar) says AUTOEXEC.BAT at the very top. You edit the file just as you edit any document. Make sure that the WINDOWS directory is in the PATH statement. Then use the arrow keys to go to the bottom of the AUTOEXEC.BAT file and type the following so it's the last line in the AUTOEXEC.BAT file:

```
WIN
```

Komando Klues

If you don't want to see the Windows welcome flag every time you start Windows, use the following line:

```
WIN :
```

Save the file (select File⇨Save) to save the changes you made to the AUTOEXEC.BAT file. Leave SYSEDIT by choosing File⇨Exit. The change won't take effect until the next time you start the computer.

Automatically launching application

I keep my little black book in Cardfile. How can I bring up the people in my Cardfile automatically when I start Windows?

Wow, you really need to get to those people quickly. Well, let me help. Many people like to have a particular application start when they enter Windows. You can have any application start automatically when Windows starts by placing a copy of the icon for that program in the StartUp group of the Program Manager.

Open the Program Manager. Then open both the StartUp group and the group that contains Cardfile. Holding down the Ctrl key, drag and drop the Cardfile icon from the Accessories window to the StartUp window. After you have released the mouse button, you can release the Ctrl key. Now, each time you start Windows, Cardfile will start automatically.

If you would like to open one of your Cardfile files along with Cardfile, you need to take a few more steps: Click on the Cardfile icon in the StartUp window and then press Alt+Enter. In the Command Line box, go to the end of the line and add a space and then the name of a file. For example, if you keep all your loved ones in Cardfile, the line may look like this:

```
C:\Windows\Cardfile.Exe Myloves
```

Automatically launching document

I'm writing my life story, so right now the only program I'm using is Microsoft Word. I'd like to save a few clicks and keystrokes by having Windows start with my manuscript on-screen automatically. I don't even need to see Program Manager.

Here's how you can dive right into your life every time you start Windows. The StartUp program group contains the programs that Windows launches when it starts. Makes sense, eh? First, you need to copy the Microsoft Word program icon into the StartUp group. To do so, open the Microsoft Word program group and then the StartUp program group. Highlight the Microsoft Word program icon so that it's selected. Now press and hold the Ctrl key and drag the Microsoft Word program icon into the StartUp program group.

Next, highlight the Microsoft Word program icon in the StartUp program group. From the Program Manager menu bar, choose File⇨Properties. In the Command Line box, go to the end of the line and add a space and then the manuscript's filename.

For example, the new command line should look something like the following one:

```
Msoffice\Winword\Winword.Exe C:\Book\Got2bme.Doc
```

You won't see Program Manager any more, at least not until you finish the book and remove the Microsoft Word program icon from the StartUp program group. Good luck on your book. You are going to put me in it, right? Why? I put you in mine.

Windows takes forever to load

I can take a shower in the time it takes Windows to load. How can I make Windows load faster? I have a 486 with 8MB of RAM.

Take shorter showers.

When you first installed Windows, it could carry all its applications in a little overnight bag. As time went by and you added a neat program here and a great-looking font there — and don't forget that awesome screen saver — the suitcase grew heavier and heavier. It's no wonder that Windows can barely drag itself to the screen. To speed it up, you need to lighten its load.

Install a new program du jour and odds are you also add icons, drivers, and possibly fonts to the WIN.INI file. It may be time to consider doing some housecleaning and deleting applications and other goodies.

Programs aren't the only things that weigh down the system. Fonts, screen savers, wallpapers, system events, and so on all pack on the pounds. Each of these items must be loaded every time you start Windows.

Note: Fonts are a big, big culprit. People tend to collect the little buggers the way they collect baseball cards. CorelDRAW! 5, for example, can install as many as 825 new fonts in your system. If you think the system is slow now, try loading that many fonts every time! I like to keep only 20 or so of my favorite fonts installed. You can easily delete the ones you don't need through the Control Panel (see Chapter 9).

While you're twiddling around in the Control Panel, you might consider scrapping the wallpaper or doing away with the long wave file that plays every time you open Windows. One guy I knew had the entire Star Trek theme play every time Windows started. His fellow employees wanted to stun him with their phasers. And he also asked me why Windows took so long to start. . . . It takes all kinds, I suppose.

Modes

Which mode am I in?

How can I tell whether Windows started in standard or enhanced mode?

From Program Manager, click Help and then About. Among other things, you'll see the mode in which Windows is running.

I want to run standard mode

I want to run my computer in Windows 3.1 standard mode, but Windows starts automatically in enhanced mode. Why?

The mode that Windows uses depends on the hardware and the amount of available random-access memory (RAM). Windows starts in standard mode if you have a slowpoke computer and barely passable memory or RAM. Technically speaking, Windows standard mode kicks in if you have a 286-based computer or above with at least 1MB of RAM that has 256K of free conventional memory and 192K of free extended memory. It also requires at least 6.5MB of free disk space (9MB is recommended) and at least one floppy disk drive. Windows also will run in standard mode on a 386-based computer that has less than 2MB of RAM.

To run Windows in enhanced mode, you need a 386-based computer or above with at least 2MB of RAM that has 256K of free conventional memory and at least 1MB of free extended memory. Enhanced mode also requires at least 8MB of free disk space (10.5MB recommended) and at least one floppy disk drive. Both modes require MS-DOS Version 3.1 or later.

If Windows sees that you have a computer with more get-go, it uses enhanced mode. To force the computer to use standard mode, type the following at the DOS prompt and press Enter:

```
WIN /S
```

I guess that you heard that standard mode was better. Betcha heard it from me. No? Hey, have you been seeing other computer advisers on the side? I feel cheated on.

Komando Klues

True, standard mode may be 20 percent faster than enhanced mode, but it has some drawbacks. In fact, it's not the mode of choice if you run more than one DOS program at a time or need to run DOS programs in a resizable window (standard mode won't work). And standard mode won't let you use the 386 enhanced mode virtual memory features that are swell if you're running low on memory.

P.S. If you read this answer because you were hoping for the command to run Windows in enhanced mode, type the following at the DOS prompt and press Enter:

```
WIN /3
```

I want to run enhanced mode

I want to run Windows 3.1 in enhanced mode, but it won't let me. My computer is a 486SX with 8MB of RAM. I use DOS 6.2, too.

Windows enhanced mode is very particular about the way memory is set up and how much is available. Although you have 8MB of memory in the machine, you may not have enough of the right kind of memory to run Windows in enhanced mode. Simply, Windows won't run in enhanced mode if the computer's memory is set up for expanded memory rather than extended memory.

The Bottom Line

To run Windows in enhanced mode, you need a 386-based computer or above and at least 2MB of RAM, including 256K of free conventional memory and at least 1MB of free extended memory.

You can try to force Windows into 386 enhanced mode by typing the following at the DOS prompt and pressing Enter:

```
WIN /3
```

If this command doesn't start Windows, your computer probably has less than the 1024K of extended memory that's required for Windows to run in 386 enhanced mode. To check the nitty-gritty details of where memory is being used in your computer, type the following at the DOS prompt and press Enter:

```
MEM/C/P
```

You'll get a blow-by-blow account of where all of the computer's memory is going. Verify that you are running an extended memory manager. HIMEM.SYS is the extended memory manager that comes with Windows 3.1, and it should be listed in the CONFIG.SYS file. To see the contents of the CONFIG.SYS file, type the following at the DOS prompt and press Enter:

```
TYPE CONFIG.SYS
```

If HIMEM.SYS isn't in the CONFIG.SYS file, make a backup copy of the CONFIG.SYS file because you are going to make some changes in CONFIG.SYS. Then type the following at the DOS prompt and press Enter:

```
EDIT CONFIG.SYS
```

Add the following line to the top of the file:

```
DEVICE=C:\WINDOWS\HIMEM.SYS
```

Select File⇨Save to save the changes. Select File⇨Exit to get back to the DOS prompt. Reboot the computer and try to start Windows in enhanced mode.

Komando Klues

If you still have no luck, you need to reconfigure the memory in the computer. Chapter 8 contains more information on configuring the computer's memory. Specifically, look in the index under *MEMMAKER*, which is DOS's handy-dandy memory manager.

Modes and general protection faults

Why do I receive *general protection fault* messages when running Windows in enhanced mode but not in standard mode?

Each mode utilizes memory in a different way. Standard mode doesn't take advantage of upper memory blocks (UMBs), for example, but 386 enhanced mode does. Upper memory is the memory above the conventional (640K) memory. If you have a memory conflict in the upper memory blocks, then there will be GPFs galore in enhanced mode while things are just peachy keen in standard mode.

Clearing up the conflict is actually pretty easy. You just need to do a little editing of the important configuration files that your computer uses. Don't forget to make backup copies of any files you edit just in case you make things worse. It happens.

The first file you want to change is the SYSTEM.INI file located in your WINDOWS directory. From Program Manager, select File↪Run. In the Command Line box, type the following and click OK:

```
SYSEDIT
```

I want you to be very careful using SYSEDIT. It shows you all the computer's configuration files.

Click the title bar for the window that has SYSTEM.INI in it. Or select Window from the menu bar and highlight, or select, SYSTEM.INI. Once inside the SYSTEM.INI file, scroll down to the [386enh] section and add the following line:

```
EMMExclude=A000-EFFF
```

Save your changes by choosing File↪Save.

If you're using an expanded memory manager, you'll also need to make a change to your CONFIG.SYS file. You need to either disable the memory manager or exclude the memory range shown previously with the appropriate EMM. If you don't, the memory manager's settings will be inherited by Windows. And those settings will override any entries in the SYSTEM.INI file.

So while you're still in SYSEDIT, highlight the CONFIG.SYS title bar so that it's the active window. Take a look at the line in which EMM386 is mentioned. Change the line so that it excludes the memory range with EMM386.EXE and looks like this:

```
DEVICE=C:\WINDOWS\EMM386.EXE NOEMS X=A000-EFFF
```

Save your changes to the CONFIG.SYS file by choosing File↪Save. Exit SYSEDIT. Then exit Windows and reboot your computer for the changes in the CONFIG.SYS and the SYSTEM.INI file to take effect.

If the general protection faults still haunt you, try starting Windows with the /D:V parameter. To do so, at the DOS prompt, type the following and press Enter:

```
WIN /3 /D:V
```

This command will turn on the virtual hard drive access, which occasionally gives some systems a headache (no, aspirin will not help). If this prevents the GPFs, it's time to make another change to the SYSTEM.INI file. Open the SYSTEM.INI file and add the following line to the [386enh] section of the SYSTEM.INI file:

```
VirtualHDIRQ=OFF
```

Save your changes to the SYSTEM.INI file. Exit Windows and restart Windows in enhanced mode. All should be well.

Missing WINA20.386 file

My computer tells me that the WINA20.386 file is missing. What is it and how do I get it back?

Have you tried flowers and candy?

Techies would tell you how WINA20.386 is the A20 handler and why Windows needs to have access to the A20 line. Let's move past all that stuff.

Just know that the file is needed for Windows 3.1 to run in enhanced mode. This file came with DOS 5.0 and later. The easiest way for you to restore this file on your hard drive is to reinstall the same version of DOS that you have on the computer.

And DOS

DOS vs. Windows

If I didn't know better, I'd think that the government made up DOS. I'm having a little trouble using Windows, though. How does the way I used the keyboard in DOS compare to the way I use a mouse in Windows?

Windows replaces the bizarre-looking DOS C:\> with something that's much cooler and easier to use. Windows has little pictures called *icons* that represent particular tasks. These icons are the reason why Windows is called a *graphical user interface (GUI)*.

Icons are everywhere. For example, they're on street signs (perhaps a stick figure to show where someone can cross the street), and they're in your car (maybe a miniature picture of a gas pump to indicate the gas gauge). Windows uses a paintbrush and palette to represent Paintbrush (a drawing program), and it uses a pen on a piece of paper to denote a word processor.

Usually, a *program group* window will contain different icons that have something in common. For example, the Games window contains the games that come free with Windows. If Windows were a restaurant menu, the appetizers, salads, and entrees would be group icons. The different types of food under the headings appetizers, salads, or entrees would be called program items. For example, shrimp cocktail is an appetizer, so it would be an item in the appetizer group.

When you double-click a group icon, its window opens. Since you're not using DOS, you no longer have to remember which directory on the computer contains which software program or, worse, memorize the commands that start the program. In Windows, you just find the icon that represents the program you want to use, place the mouse pointer over the program's icon, and double-click (quickly click the left mouse button twice). Double-clicking the icon starts the program.

The quickest way to get good at using a mouse is to play the card game Solitaire that's free with Windows. If your boss wants to yell at you for playing Solitaire on the computer, just say that you're learning how to use a mouse. I have an employee who has been learning how to use a mouse for eight months now.

Copying text from DOS to Windows

I love the cut-and-paste feature in Windows-based programs. It saves me a lot of work. I use some DOS programs from Windows. Can I cut and paste between a DOS program and a Windows program?

If you concentrate and click your heels three times . . . or try the following method. The DOS-to-Windows cut-and-paste process is very similar to the Windows feature you like. First, you need to have the DOS program in a window, instead of full-screen. If the DOS program is full-screen, press Alt+Enter to turn it into a window. After the program is in a window, you can copy text from it by clicking the box that has the minus sign in it (it's in the upper-left corner of the window). Then select Edit⇨Mark.

Now, use the mouse to highlight the text you want to copy from the DOS program. To do so, start in the upper-left corner of the text that you want to select and hold down the left mouse button. Continuing to hold down the mouse button, drag the mouse across the text until you have high-lighted the text that you want to copy. Release the mouse button and click the box with a minus sign in it. Choose Edit⇨Copy. You now can paste the text that you highlighted into a Windows program or into another DOS program.

Running DOS programs with Windows

I run DOS programs from Windows, but they are so darn slow. Can I do anything to speed them up a little?

Have you considered buying them some teensy-weensy Nikes?

When you run a DOS program under Windows, it has to share the CPU's attention with all the other programs that are currently running in Windows. Those programs are just like kids: they crave the spotlight, and having to share makes them pout and drag their feet. (It's too bad you can't reboot a kid. Or for that matter, turn them off for awhile.) You can control how fast your DOS programs run under Windows, however, by controlling what percent of the CPU's love and attention they get.

The next time you run a DOS session, press Alt+Enter to force DOS to run in a window like any other Windows program. You can then click the little box that has the minus sign in it, in the upper-left corner, to bring up a list of commands. Choose Settings to bring up a dialog box where you can adjust the amount of TLC that the CPU devotes to your DOS session; by increasing the Foreground and Background priority settings, you can give the DOS program more attention and speed up your sessions.

If you run your DOS programs from an icon, you can speed them up too. In the Main group is an icon called PIF Editor. PIF Editor enables you to change a program's PIF (*Program Information File*), which tells Windows what settings to use when it's running the program in question. To adjust the Foreground and Background priority settings, open PIF Editor and click the Advanced button. Don't forget to save the settings before closing the PIF Editor. *Note:* You especially need to change the DEFAULT.PIF file because Windows uses DEFAULT.PIF if a program doesn't have its own PIF file.

Program Manager

Retrieving Program Manager

My Program Manager is only partially visible. Worse, the menu bar is off the screen. How can I move the Program Manager back where it belongs?

I spy, with my little eye, a ProgMan way up in the sky! Sometimes, Program Manager's title bar and menus end up off the screen and beyond your reach. To get ProgMan back, do things the old-fashioned way and use the keyboard. Just press Ctrl+Esc to bring up the Task List and then highlight Program Manager.

But you may want to hide your mouse so it doesn't see that you really don't need it.

Closing annoying windows

I can't stand installing new software in Windows. Every time I do, up pops a new window that I have to close whenever I start Windows. How do I clean up Program Manager after loading new software so that these new windows stay closed?

Remember, nothing is permanent. Not the moon, or the sky, or the automatically opening windows.

Messy windows are a snap to fix. When most Windows-based programs are installed, they create their own group in the middle of the screen. Close the new program's window. Make sure that there is a check mark in front of Save Settings on Exit on the Options menu; if so, the new program's window will stay closed the next time you start Windows.

Turning off minimization

Whenever I go into File Manager and then exit it, my Program Manager icon is minimized. How do I turn this feature off?

From Program Manager, choose Options. Then take the check mark off the Minimize on Use option by clicking it once. This annoying little feature minimizes any running program when you start any other program. And as you noticed, it doesn't restore the previous Windows settings when you finish the program you started. I just leave this option turned off.

Standardizing interface

How do I make Program Manager look the same every time Windows starts? One day it looks one way, and another day it's completely different. It's more capricious than my girlfriend.

Really? Does she look different every day? Are you sure it's the same person? I've read in the *National Enquirer* about people who switch places with each other and about aliens who switch places with humans. And you know that the *Enquirer* always prints the truth.

From the Windows Program Manager, take a look at the menu bar. See the menu called Options? Click it and find the item that says Save Settings on Exit. If this option has a little check mark in front of it, click it to remove the check mark and tell Windows not to save settings on exit.

Note: The check mark made Windows save the way it looked when you exited Windows. It thought it was doing you a favor. Guess not.

Making Windows look the same every time it starts is easy. First, set up the Program Manager the way you want it to appear each time the computer starts. Open the windows you want open. Make them bigger if you want. Arrange the desktop.

After the screen is nice and tidy, you take a sort of computer snapshot of it. Windows uses this snapshot to remember how you want Program Manager to look each time Windows starts.

From the Program Manager menu bar, click File. Press and hold down the Shift key and, at the same time, click Exit Windows. You don't actually exit Windows; instead, you put that snapshot in a place where Windows can find it the next time you start the computer.

 Komando Klues If you change your mind and want your Windows desktop to look different later, don't worry. Just take another snapshot. If only plastic surgery were this simple.

 ## Standardizing desktop

I let my husband use the computer. While he was going through the Windows tutorial, I fell asleep. When I woke up, he had already turned off the computer. Now, every time I start Windows, I have to put all the icons back the way I had them. How can I make sure that this doesn't happen again?

Coffee, and lots of it. As for men, I swear they're just like kids — except kids can dress themselves in the morning.

Don't sweat it. He didn't really mess anything up. First, put everything back the way you want it on your Windows desktop. Afterward, hold down the Shift key and click on File⇨Exit. Don't worry, you won't exit as long as you keep the Shift key pressed down. This command makes Windows store a snapshot of the way the desktop should look whenever it starts, no matter what your husband does to the program groups and icons.

Now take a look at the Options menu and make sure that Save Settings on Exit does not have a check mark next to it. If you see a check mark, click it to remove it.

Changing desktop

When I make a program item for an application, such as WordPerfect 5.1, I initially can run the program from the icon. However, the program icon seems to vanish when I exit Windows. When I return, I see no new icon. This happens any time I try to make a new program item for any application. What's going on?

Well, it certainly isn't your WordPerfect 5.1. Get it? Going on? All right.

At some point, someone has added a little bit of security to the system and locked your Windows up tight. That person obviously didn't want anyone making changes to the desktop by adding or creating new icons.

The easiest way to prevent changes in the Program Manager is simply to make its initialization file, PROGMAN.INI, a read-only file. In this case, each time someone tries to make a new icon, the new icon seems to work on-screen. The catch is that the new icon can't be saved to the Program Manager's initialization file. To add a new program icon or group, you need to eliminate the read-only designation. To do so, first highlight the PROGMAN.INI file in File Manager. Next, choose File⇨Properties to see the Properties for PROGMAN.INI window. At the bottom of the window are four Attributes options. Take the X out of the box for the Read Only attribute. Now you can add the program icon for WordPerfect 5.1.

Another way to prevent changes to the Program Manager is to add Edit Level restrictions to the Program Manager's initialization file. To do so, use Windows Notepad to open the PROGMAN.INI and look for the heading [restrictions]. Then add one of the Edit Level commands listed in the following table to prevent other folks from making changes.

Edit Level Command	Effect
EditLevel=1	Prevents the creation, deletion, and renaming of program groups
EditLevel=2	Includes level 1 restrictions and prevents the creation and deletion of items in program groups
EditLevel=3	Includes level 2 restrictions and prevents changes in the command lines for program group items
EditLevel=4	Includes level 3 restrictions and prevents changes in the information for program groups items

If you find any of these restrictions in PROGMAN.INI, change the line to EditLevel=0 to gain full access to groups, icons, and all their properties. Make the changes to PROGMAN.INI and save the changes. You need to exit and restart Windows for the changes to take effect.

Reorganizing desktop

Some of my groups have grown so large that I can't get all the icons on-screen at one time. Is there a way to place the icons closer together so the kids won't have to scroll down the screen to find their favorite game?

Kids today have it soft. In my day, we had to scroll down for our favorite program, and we didn't complain about it. Of course, we didn't know any better.

You could just put their favorites at the top, but if they're like most kids, their favorites change on a daily basis. As a result, putting the icons closer together is probably your best bet. Open the Main program group and then the Control Panel. Open the Desktop and look for the icon spacing: it is in the lower-right half of the Desktop window. Click the upward- or downward-pointing arrow to increase or decrease the icon's spacing, respectively. Try 50 to 75; this setting seems to work best on my Windows desktop. Also put an X in the box for the Wrap Title option so the icons' titles don't overlap.

Changing the vertical spacing so that the rows are closer together is not so easy, but it's not impossible: you need to add a line to the WIN.INI file. To do so, make a backup copy of the WIN.INI file, use Windows Notepad to

open the file, and scroll down the file until you find the line
`ICONSPACING=`. Below that line, add the following line:

```
ICONVERTICALSPACING=(# of pixels you want between rows)
```

Save the changes and restart Windows to have the changes take effect.

Separate setups

My husband likes to change the screen saver and wallpaper every single darn time he uses Windows. I am sorry, but I just can't work with Cindy Crawford's body staring at me on my desktop. How can I make his and hers Windows setups?

I agree with you. Feeling guilt over not having typed anything for seven minutes is bad enough. Now Cindy is gloating over it. Besides, I kinda prefer a Mel Gibson screen saver myself.

Making separate setups is easy. The first thing you need to do is make sure that you have everything set up just the way you like it. Then make a copy of the SYSTEM.INI file and call it SYSTEM.HER. Do the same thing for the WIN.INI file and call it WIN.HER.

Now let your husband set up Windows the way he likes it, skimpily clad women and all. Open Windows Notepad and type the following lines:

```
CD\WIN
RENAME SYSTEM.INI SYSTEM.OLD
RENAME WIN.INI WIN.OLD
RENAME SYSTEM.HER SYSTEM.INI
RENAME WIN.HER WIN.INI
WIN
RENAME SYSTEM.INI SYSTEM.HER
RENAME WIN.INI WIN.HER
RENAME SYSTEM.OLD SYSTEM.INI
RENAME WIN.OLD WIN.INI
CD\
```

Save the file as WINHER.BAT. Now, when you want to start Windows with your setup, type **WINHER** at the DOS prompt. Your setup will appear on-screen. When you exit Windows, the setup is changed back to your husband's setup. When your husband wants to use Windows, he types **WIN** at the DOS prompt to see his friend Cindy.

Changing colors

I hate the Windows blue-and-white color scheme. How can I change it?

Windows has more color schemes than Zsa Zsa and Liz Taylor have exhusbands. You can personalize window borders, menus, text, the background, and more. From Program Manager, open the Main program group and then the Control Panel. The crayons are the Colors icon.

Open Colors and check out the Color Schemes. The Windows predefined color schemes are like a high-tech interior designer inside the computer. Click the downward-pointing arrow to see the list of options. Watch the sample desktop change colors accordingly as you highlight different options.

Pick the color scheme you like and click OK. Your Windows desktop has new colors.

Creating colors

I picked a color scheme in Windows, but I'd like to change the colors a bit. Can I make my own colors for my Windows desktop?

With me behind you, you can do anything. Open the Main program group and then the Control Panel. The crayons are the Colors icon. Open Colors and move down past the predefined color schemes. Toward the bottom of the window is a button for the Color Palette. Click the Color Palette to see a window that's full of different colors.

The sample window contains the elements of the Windows desktop: the active window, inactive window, title bars, borders, shadows, and more. Start at the top by clicking the Active Window title bar in the sample window. (Not sure you got it? Look in the Screen Element box, in the upper-right corner of the screen. It should say Active Title Bar.) The current color of the Active Title Bar is highlighted in the color palette (it has a black border around it). Now click any colored square to change the title bar's color. Then go back to the sample window and pick the next screen element that you want to change — perhaps the window's workspace, a button's face, text, or highlights. Keep clicking the sample elements and picking new colors.

Now is a good time to experiment with the Custom Color option, too, where you can make colors that are not in the color palette. After you click the Define Custom Colors button, another window pops open. To get a shade of some color, click the color in the color spectrum. On the right side of the color spectrum is a scroll bar. Slide the arrow up or down to increase or decrease color intensity. Then click Add Color, and the color appears in a box in the Custom Colors area. You can then use this color and assign it to an element in the sample window.

After you finish creating your new color scheme, click Save Scheme and type a name for it. Click OK, and you've got your new colors.

Where are my 16 million colors?

My monitor is set up for SVGA and will display 16 million colors. Maybe I'm looking in the wrong place, but the Colors icon shows a lot fewer color options. Did I get ripped off?

No, you didn't get ripped off. Windows has only 48 solid colors, which is plenty. Think about it. How many color schemes are there in your home? How many different colors do you wear a day? Although your computer may have the capability to display more than 48 colors, Windows can't display more than 48, so there's nothing you can do.

You should feel lucky that you can see even 48 colors. After all, there are starving children in China who can see only 16 to 20 colors, and most of those are red.

Where is the color in my life?

When I try to use the 256-color video display option under Windows Setup, no matter what I highlight within a Windows program, I "whiteout." When I go back to 16 colors, all is well. Why can't I add more color to my life?

Let me warn you, adding color to your computer will only temporarily add color to your life. If you want to add true and lasting color to your life, you need to look inside.

Komando Klues
Take a cooking class and meet new people.

Let me ask you a question. Are you sure your video card has the capability and sufficient memory to support 256 colors? Take a look in the documentation to see whether your card can handle that many colors, because not all cards can. Others include a driver for 256 colors but require a memory upgrade before it can be used. In most cases, you need at least 1 MB of RAM on the video card.

If you are absolutely sure the card has enough muscle to handle the task, then it's time to try a different video driver. If you're using the generic driver that came with Windows, install the drivers that came with your video card's software. It also may be to your advantage to contact the manufacturer for the latest version of their video drivers. You would be amazed how often video drivers are updated. I have seen new versions come out as often as a week apart.

Program groups/icons

Personalizing program groups

Am I stuck with the Windows program groups, or can I make my own?

Hey, good for you. Now that you've pasted your favorite "Far Side" to the monitor, you're getting the itch to personalize your computer's insides.

You can make your own program groups. From Program Manager, choose File⇨New. The New Program Object window will pop up, and you'll have to make a choice between a new program group and a new program item. Choose Program Group and click OK. In the Program Group Properties window, type a name in the Description box. Call it whatever you want: *Programs that Taunt Me*, *My Stuff*, or whatever. Click OK.

Hang out in Program Manager and open the program group you just made. Then open the program groups that contain the programs you want to add to the new program group. Instead of moving program icons from one program group to another, however, copy the icons. To copy a program icon, highlight it, hold down the Ctrl key, and drag the icon into the new group.

Because you now know how to create a custom program group, you're ready to set up your Windows desktop: Arrange the program groups the way you always want to see them when Windows starts. From the Windows Program Manager, click Options on the menu bar. If you see a check mark in front of the Save Settings on Exit choice, click it to get rid of the check mark (Windows thus will not save the settings when you exit).

From the Program Manager's menu bar, click the File option. Then hold down the Shift key and, at the same time, click Exit Windows. You won't exit Windows; instead, this command puts a snapshot of the way the desktop looks in a place where Windows can find it the next time you start the computer.

 Komando Klues
If you change your mind and want the Windows desktop to look different down the road, don't worry. Just take another snapshot of the desktop by using those secret combination keystrokes.

 ## Changing name of program group

I want to change the names of some windows, say from *Accessories* to *Worthless Stuff*. Do I have to re-create the program group again?

Use a program group title like that and Windows will know. Just press the Alt key and then double-click the program group whose name or description you want to change. The Program Group Properties window appears on-screen. In the Description box, type the new name for the program group. Double-click the close box (the little gray box in the window's upper-left corner) to close the window. Your changes are saved automatically.

 ## Changing icon of program group

I used a friend's computer, and she had a different icon for the DOS prompt. I asked her how she changed it, but she didn't remember. How do I change program icons?

Be careful if you do this. You may lose your memory. Well, your friend lost hers, didn't she?

You can dig up and change program icons easily in Windows. Here's how to change the icon for the DOS prompt. From Program Manager, open the Main program group and highlight the icon for the DOS prompt by clicking it once. From the Program Manager's menu bar, choose File⇨Properties. A new window pops open on-screen. Click the Change Icon button to see the different icons included with Windows.

If you have to call for help every time you use DOS, pick the yellow telephone for the new DOS prompt icon. You can find that icon by clicking the right arrow on the horizontal scroll bar. In addition to the telephone are icons for a camera, a safe, a typewriter, a newspaper, a chart, and more. Choose the new DOS icon by clicking the icon that you want to use. Click OK to close the icon viewer and then click OK to go back to the Main program group. All done. Now go tell your friend how she did it.

Finding new icons

I don't like how all my program group icons look the same. How do I assign different icons to Program Manager groups?

You're obviously a person who doesn't accept what's given to you. I bet you return Christmas gifts instead of throwing them in the closet. I bet you special-ordered your computer.

A long time ago, I too wanted to spruce up my desktop with something other than those boring boxes that Microsoft provides. Boy, was I disappointed to find out that the folks in Redmond had neglected my needs. Those techies just have no sense of style. Thank goodness, though, for third-party programs; some ingenious programmer is always waiting to pick up the slack and make neat options available.

Plug-In, shareware from Plannet Crafters, not only enables you to change the icons for program groups, it also provides custom cursors to make the Windows cursors bolder and easier to see; cursor wrap at screen edges; resource alerts that automatically track memory, system resources, and disk utilization; active title bar configuration options that include the date, time, resources, and a stopwatch, as well as features to change text color, background color, and fonts.

On the commercial software side, check with your local computer store or mail-order house for Icon Do-It from Moon Valley Software (800-473-5509). This program includes more than 200 icons, 25 of which are animated. You also get more than 50 mouse cursors, 10 of which are animated. Also, Icon Do-It includes four screen savers.

Moon Valley Software also makes Icon Hear It, which you can use to add sound effects, and Icon Make-It, which lets you create your own icons.

Changing icon text

I want to name Microsoft Word after me! How can I get my name under the Word program icon?

You may never see your name on the silver screen, but putting it on your computer screen is a snap. From Program Manager, click the Microsoft Word icon once. Then choose File⇨Properties. Type your name or whatever you want to appear below the icon in the Item Description. Click OK, and that's it.

But why stop there? Why not put the names of everyone in your family under the icons that remind you of them? For example, put your sister's name and a dollar sign below the icon for the modem to remind her that she has to pay for all the on-line time she uses.

Lost icon

I recently installed Excel for Windows and had no problem until I tried to use it yesterday. I *know* Excel is there, but I have lost the icon and can't get into the program! I use Windows 3.1 and DOS 6.2.

If an icon suddenly disappears, the cause is one of two things: you either need to do a little bit of housekeeping or maintenance on your hard drive, or someone is playing tricks on you and deleting icons.

Here's what you need to do. First, close Windows down and get back to the DOS prompt. Type the following at the DOS prompt and press Enter:

```
SCANDISK
```

If you're asked to convert lost clusters to files, just say no. Humans can rarely make heads or tails out of the information in those files anyway.

Next, run the DEFRAG program by typing the following at the DOS prompt and pressing Enter:

```
DEFRAG
```

DEFRAG will tidy up the files on the hard drive so that the computer can find things more quickly. The process takes a few minutes, so why not take the time to defrag your top desk drawer? Put all those disks in their boxes; put the pens together. And throw out that old Styx 45 of "Renegade." When you and DEFRAG have finished, reboot the computer and go back into Windows. Don't fret if the icon still isn't there; you haven't put it back yet.

From Program Manager, select the group that should have the Excel icon. Choose File⇨New. A little window pops up, asking whether you want to create a new group or a new item. Excel is a new item, not a group, so choose the button for a new item. Click OK, and in the Program Item Properties window that appears, click the Browse button. In the Browse window that appears, change to the drive and directory that Excel is in and then click the EXCEL.EXE filename in the list on the left side of the window. Click OK to return to the Program Item Properties window, where you should see EXCEL.EXE, the file that starts Excel, in the Command Line box. Type the name of the working directory (if you use one) and then click OK. Don't worry about the Change Icon option. Excel knows what icon to use from the filename in the Command Line box.

If you can't find the Excel directory or program, the hard disk may be messed up. If this is the case, you can restore the program from your backup disks or tape. If you don't have any backups, don't sweat it. You can reinstall the program from the original program disks; it takes only a few minutes.

Viewing icons

I recently downloaded a bunch of icons from an on-line service. Then I realized that I don't know how to display them! When I bring them up in Notepad, all I see is symbols.

You can get a variety of programs that will enable you to view those icons. But why waste your money? Unless you collect icons the way some people collect baseball cards, use the Windows Properties feature.

After you have unzipped the icons, their filenames usually have the .ICO file extension. Go into Program Manager, click on any icon, and hold the Alt+Enter keys down at the same time. In the Program Item Properties dialog box, click Change Icon. In the Change Icon window that appears, click the Browse button. Highlight the directory where the icons are located to see the icon(s) contained in that file. Be sure to click Cancel in each window if you don't want to change the icon of that application.

Automatically arranging icons

My kids love the computer, but they are not exactly great with the mouse yet. When they try to open programs, they often end up moving icons around accidentally. I must spend an hour a day putting things back where they belong. There has to be an easier way.

So your kids like to take the icons for a walk, do they? Are you sure that they are doing it by accident? (I bet you believed that the vase just fell on its own, too.)

With Program Manager on-screen, click the Options menu. Put a check mark next to Auto Arrange. Auto Arrange will make the icons snap into place automatically. Whenever a kid accidentally moves one of the icons, it will jump back where it belongs. The only problem is that after the kids notice what's happening, they'll start moving the icons on purpose just to make them dance. But hey, so will you. It's fun.

File Manager

Selecting multiple files

I'm a private investigator. I would like to copy all the files in one directory on my hard disk to a floppy disk. Sometimes I don't have time to piece-meal it. Is there a way to select a bunch of files in File Manager at once?

Somehow, I don't believe you. Anyway, Mr. Spy, there is a way.

Open File Manager and make sure that you have a formatted floppy disk in one of your computer's floppy disk drives. Near the top of the File Manager window, toward the left, you'll see little icons that represent the disk drives in your computer. On the right side, you'll see a branched listing of the directories in your hard drive. By using the mouse to select one of those directories on the right side of the workspace, you can open the directory and see the files in that directory.

If drive C isn't highlighted, click its icon. If the files are in one directory, highlight the first file in the directory by pointing and clicking on it. Now, press and hold the Shift key and highlight the last file in the directory. All the files should be highlighted or selected. Press the Ctrl key and click the mouse button on any of the highlighted files.

Komando Klues

Holding down the Ctrl key causes the files to be copied rather than moved. (If you're doing it right, a plus sign will appear on the document icons when dragged, too.)

Drag the files to the computer's floppy disk drive where you want them — that is, drive A or B. Windows will ask you to verify that you want to copy the files to diskette. Click the Yes button.

The same trick almost works for files that aren't in one directory: Highlight the first filename that you want to copy. Then press the Ctrl key and click all the files you want to copy. After you have highlighted these files, press the Ctrl key and drag the files to the icon that represents the drive where the files should be copied to.

Updating file display

If I view a disk in File Manager and then switch it for another, the same files still appear on-screen. Why doesn't File Manager realize I have changed floppies? How can I make it actually read the new disk?

It's kind of like changing your underwear. No one knows unless you tell them or you get into an accident and the folks in the emergency room find out. By the way, I can't resist passing on some advice from a park ranger. He said you can get four days out of a pair of underpants or briefs by wearing them frontwards and backwards and then turning them inside out and wearing them frontwards and backwards.

To speed things up, the Windows File Manager doesn't constantly monitor the floppy drives for changes. You have to tell File Manager that you changed disks. It's more of an inconvenience than a problem.

To update the file display after you change a floppy disk, click the drive icon once to force File Manager to read the disk again. If you do a great deal of disk swapping in File Manager, use the keyboard shortcut (Alt+W,R) or press the F5 key to refresh the file display.

To open a new window, double-click a drive icon. This technique comes in handy when you are copying files or moving files from a floppy disk to the hard disk.

Swap Files

Temporary vs. permanent swap files

In virtual memory, which is a better swap file, temporary or permanent?

If you can spare the hard disk space, a permanent swap file is the way to go. Windows uses the swap file as a kind of temporary storage space for data and files it's working with. What's that? You want to know why the swap file should be permanent if the storage is just temporary? Are you calling me an oxymoron?

755

When Windows wants to put information in storage with a temporary swap file, it first has to talk to the operating system and make it look around the hard drive for some spare disk space. Once a suitable location is found, the operating system reports the address to Windows, and Windows moves the information into that address.

The process is like turning a computer's processor chip into a real estate agent. "You say you're looking for a 3MB property with a view overlooking the Microsoft Word directories? Well, I have just the sector for you. It's a quiet little partition with plenty of room to grow as the information does."

I don't know about you, but I can think of better things for my operating system to be doing than showing Windows around the hard drive. By using a permanent swap file, you don't have to waste time looking for a place to rent. Windows gets a deed of trust to its own little 10MB spread (or whatever size you specify), and it always has a cluster to call home.

Creating swap files

How does Windows come up with the recommended size of a permanent swap file?

That's your most pressing computer question? Things are going well for you, I guess.

Windows figures out the size of a permanent swap file so that it fits in the largest area of contiguous space on a hard disk. That's why it's important to optimize your hard disk before creating a swap file. To do so, you don't even need to get your hands dirty. Exit Windows and, at the DOS prompt, use the DOS CHKDSK/F command if your DOS is Version 5 or lower; otherwise, use the DOS SCANDISK command and then the DOS DEFRAG command. Start Windows and create your swap file.

Swap files and repartitioned hard drives

I went to set up a Windows permanent swap file on my father-in-law's machine. He said I couldn't because of the way the hard drive is partitioned. I don't understand. There is only one partition and the drive has been defragmented.

I'm going to make a leap of faith here and assume that you're not trying to put that little old swap file on a compressed drive. Naturally, you already know that you just can't do that. Permanent swap files have temper tantrums when you try to move them to a stacked or a compressed drive. They prefer to take up residence on the host drive. But you already knew that, didn't you?

At some time, someone must have used a third-party software program to format Dad's hard drive. When a new drive is installed, it has to be formatted and partitioned for the operating system to be able to use it. If an operating system such as DR DOS or PC-DOS was used to format the drive and Dad has since switched to MS-DOS, you might run into this problem.

The first thing you need to do is back up everything on your father-in-law's computer (depending, that is, on how well he treated you at the wedding). This is just a precaution that, with luck, won't actually be needed. Next, use the FDISK /MBR command to create a new master boot record. You won't see anything happen at all after you type the command. You will just end up back at the DOS prompt, but you should then be able to create the swap file without a hitch.

If that doesn't do the trick, then it's time for those backup disks. You need to completely repartition the hard drive by using the FDISK command. This action will erase all the data on the drive, so it's a last resort. Be sure that you have everything backed up and a working boot disk on hand. The FDISK command is explained in more detail in Chapter 8.

Where is the swap file?

Windows can't find the file that contains the swap file. I receive the message that the swap file is corrupted. I have done everything possible to correct this problem.

Well, not everything, or you wouldn't have a problem.

Double your pleasure, double your fun. Double your hard drive and the fun's just begun. Drive-doubling programs are an inexpensive solution for those feeling the disk space pinch. The fun part starts when you try to put a permanent swap file on a compressed drive — you can't do it.

That's not to say that you can't compress your drive and use a permanent swap file. You just have to put that little old swap file on the uncompressed host drive.

If you already knew better than to put the swap file on a compressed drive, then you need to check for file corruption. The DOS command SCANDISK (use CHKDSK/F if your DOS is version 5 or lower) comes in real handy for this. It will mark any bad places on the hard drive as unusable and take care of any crosslinked files and files that don't have a home on the hard disk.

While you're doing routine maintenance, go ahead and use the DEFRAG command, too. It will take a fragmented drive and put all the files back together. I do this to my hard drive once a month! (If your drive is compressed, use the defragging program that came with the compression software rather than DEFRAG.)

Now that your hard disk is a picture of health, you can delete the corrupted swap file.

Open the Windows Main program group and then open the Control Panel. Double-click the 386 Enhanced icon. Once the menu screen comes up, select Virtual Memory. Windows will now present you with a screen displaying your current settings. The top section will detail your swap file settings, telling you where it is, its size, and its type (permanent or temporary). The bottom section tells you how the disk is utilizing the swap file (32-bit disk access on or off). Enable the Use the 32-Bit Disk Access option if your disk is Western Digital compatible and supports FastDisk. If you have Windows for Workgroups 3.11, you will also see a 32-Bit File Access option. If your PC has less than 8MB of memory, I don't recommend using this option, as it is a resource hog. Otherwise, enable it for increased system performance.

To get the swap file back, select Change; by default, Windows will place the cursor on the Size box. If Windows will let you, make your swap file larger than 10,240KB. Note that you must have more than 10MB of free space on your hard drive for this to even work. A permanent swap file larger than 10MB is best for most users.

Check the Type box and, if necessary, click the down arrow and select Permanent. Click OK and you will be prompted to restart Windows. Go ahead and do so. Windows will rebuild your swap file and your "corrupt" swap file messages should go away.

Using RAM drive for swap file

I want to use a RAM drive for my Windows swap file, but I don't know how to do it. Can I do it?

Yes, of course you can, but can your computer?

A swap file is hard disk space that Windows uses to simulate memory. That is, a swap file makes part of the disk drive look like RAM to the CPU. Thus, you should allow Windows to utilize as much extended memory as possible as is and cause it to use hard drive space for its swap file.

A RAM drive is basically using RAM memory to simulate hard disk space. Maybe it's just me, but it seems kind of silly to simulate RAM on a simulated hard disk that was RAM to begin with.

However, if you're dead set on using a RAM drive for your swap file (you folks know who you are), then you need to make sure the correct command is in your Windows SYSTEM.INI file in the [386enh] section. Do that by typing the following:

```
PagingDrive=n
```

where n is the letter of your particular RAM drive.

To edit the SYSTEM.INI file, use SYSEDIT, and for your sake, make sure that you have a backup of the file.

.INI Files

.INI files

What are .INI files? I have quite a few in my computer. Are they important, or can I delete them?

Whoa, there, cowpoke. I'm glad to see that you're clearing your hard disk of those mangy megabyte rustlers, but be sure that you're not sending any innocent files to Boot Hill. Before you get a little trigger-happy with that Delete key, maybe you should take a closer look at where you're aiming. Besides, you're going after the small potatoes. Look how small .INI files are. Would you want someone recklessly deleting you if you were that small? Pick on someone your own size.

759

The *.INI files* are the INItialization files that tell Windows and Windows-based applications how they should look when they start, where they should be on-screen, what volume to play, and much more.

The SYSTEM.INI file, for example, holds many settings that tell Windows about the computer's hardware. If you take a look inside this file, you'll notice that it is broken down into sections. Each section holds configuration information for a particular part of the system, such as the mouse, keyboard, video card, and monitor. Good luck getting Windows to start if you delete the SYSTEM.INI file. That deed may even get your face on a poster: *Wanted Dead or Alive — Murdered Innocent File*.

Deleting .INI files is not always disastrous. WINFILE.INI is the initialization file for the File Manager. If you delete it, WINFILE.INI is re-created the next time you use File Manager. The only harm done is that any customizing of File Manager options is lost and the options return to the default settings. No great catastrophe there, but you don't save any disk space.

Many Windows-based programs create .INI files that tell them what options you want to use. You can safely delete .INI files for any programs that you have removed from the hard drive, but leave the rest alone.

Komando Klues

If you don't have a backup of the .INI files and one of them becomes corrupted or damaged, reinstalling the program that created the .INI file is usually the best thing to do. It's quicker than trying to re-create the .INI file, and you don't have to worry about whether you included everything you needed to. In the case of the WIN.INI and SYSTEM.INI files, your best option is to reinstall Windows. This hassle is reason enough to keep current backups of the WIN.INI and SYSTEM.INI files.

Missing .INI files

My .INI files are missing in action. After deleting some programs, I now get exclamation boxes complaining about missing files in WIN.INI. How do I clean up this program residue?

First, write down the names of the files that Windows is nagging you about. Next, make a backup copy of your WIN.INI file and call it WIN.BAK or something.

Open the WIN.INI file in a text editor, such as Notepad or SYSEDIT. Use the Search command and find references to the offending files. Every time you find one, place a semicolon or the letters *REM* (not Beatles) and a space at the beginning of the line. The semicolon or REM causes the computer to ignore that line.

For example, if you erased the program Diet for Life from your Windows desktop, the .INI file for the program could be DIETLIFE.INI. In your Windows WIN.INI file, remark out the line(s) that reference the Diet for Life program. Save the changes and restart Windows.

Too bad we can't REM the boring insurance salesperson sitting next to you on the plane.

Cleaning up WIN.INI file

I am trying to clean up my WIN.INI file. There are a number of sound card categories in which most, if not all, the lines are preceded by a semicolon. Can these lines be safely deleted from the file?

Putting a semicolon in front of a line in an initialization file is similar to putting a REM (remark) statement in a batch file: your system looks at the line and then ignores it. This syntax can come in handy when you're not sure whether you should delete a line or not. You can remark out the line by putting the semicolon in front of it. If it turns out that you want the line, you simply delete the semicolon. If you run things for awhile and everything works great, feel free to go ahead and delete the entire line.

Deleting Programs and Files

Deleting sounds

Long-gone programs added sounds to my Control Panel Sounds icon. Since I no longer have the programs, I really don't need the sound events. How do I delete them?

Yes, the programs have moved on, but sometimes at night, when the air is calm, you can still hear the faint echoes of a tall ship that is being bombarded or a capitalistic carrier that is being sunk by lost revenues. Sorry . . . I slipped into my novelist mode for a second there.

Cleaning up those orphan sound events is easy, though. First, make a copy of the WIN.INI file and save it elsewhere on the system. Then, using Notepad or another text editor, open WIN.INI and scroll down to the [Sound] section. All you have to do is delete the sound events whose programs are no longer in the system. Save the file and pat yourself on the back. That was a job well done.

Deleting remnants of unwanted programs

I deleted a program icon, but the program is still on my computer's hard disk. Do I have a case of the program that won't die? It sounds like one of those B movies that my husband likes to watch.

Deleting a program icon doesn't erase a program from your computer. It merely wipes out the icon. You need to use File Manager to highlight the program's directories and then delete them. But a program's tentacles go way into Windows. There are DLL files (*Dynamic Link Library* files that enable Windows-based programs to exchange information with other Windows-based programs), drivers, and other references to the program on the computer's hard disk. Remnants left in the WIN.INI file cause Windows to take extra time to load the deleted program's references and also may cause error messages when Windows starts.

Pruning items from your hard disk and initialization files is no easy task. I don't recommend that you take on the big delete chore yourself. If you delete the wrong thing, Windows may not work properly, or it may even fail to start. Save yourself potential grief by investing in a software program that's designed to do the job.

Try UnInstaller2 from Microhelp (800-922-3383). It has a manufacturer's suggested retail price of $69.99. That means that you can find the program $10 or $20 cheaper in stores and in mail-order catalogs. When UnInstaller2 starts, all the programs that are located on the computer's hard disk appear in a list, along with their icons. You highlight the name of the program that you want to erase, and UnInstaller2 does the rest. It tracks down all the scraps left behind by unneeded applications and safely removes them for you. It has options for deleting unwanted fonts and video drivers, any duplicated files, and files left over from when you tried to uninstall a program yourself. (Imagine that. Did you ever think that there was money to be made from a program that deletes programs?) You'll recover a large amount of valuable disk space and keep your Windows spick-and-span.

So get your husband off that B-movie couch and send him out to get an uninstaller program.

Deleting special files

I paid for my Windows software, so how come I get the *Access Denied* message when I try to delete certain files? Is there some way, any way, to fix this at the DOS prompt?

Sounds as if they didn't invite you to their party. No biggie, you didn't want to go anyway.

Quite often, certain files are given special attributes to keep foolish people from doing something really stupid, such as deleting them. No names, but you know who you are. For example, DOS hides some system files, such as IO.SYS and MSDOS.SYS. That is not to say that they can't be deleted at all; you just need to be sure that you know what you are deleting first.

If you're bound and determined that the file must go, you can use the ATTRIB command in DOS to change the file's attributes. You want to remove any read-only, system, or hidden attributes. If, for example, a file is named TEST.FIL, then you simply type the following line at the DOS prompt and press Enter:

```
ATTRIB TEST.FIL -R -S -H
```

You will now have full access to the file.

Working with file properties is easier in Windows than in DOS: Open File Manager. Highlight the file's name and then choose File⇨Properties; all kinds of information appear about that particular file. Make sure that the boxes marked Read, Hidden, and System Only don't have any Xs, but leave an X in the Archive box.

Deleting duplicate .DLL files

I was Snoop Doggy Doggin' around in my computer and found something strange: duplicate DLL files. It seems that when a Windows program installs, it has many of the same files I already have in Windows, such as COMMDLG.DLL, VBRUN300.DLL, and so on. Can I just take the most recent version of these files and put them in my WINDOWS directory?

Good question, and a good idea, but you have to be Tu Poc Secure in what you're doing.

Files such as VBRUN300.DLL are "run-time libraries" for Visual Basic 3.0 programs. You may find that you have a VBRUN200.DLL with an older file date somewhere on your hard drive. This is the run-time library for Visual Basic 2.0 programs.

You would think that Version 2.0 programs could be run using something from Version 3.0, wouldn't you? Unfortunately, that's not the case; you need VBRUN200.DLL for Version 2.0 programs and VBRUN300.DLL for Version 3.0 programs. Other files may have the same type of restrictions. Even if the file has the same name, there is a chance that a newer version of a program won't run properly with an older version of a .DLL file.

If you have the time and are careful, you could try making a "junk" subdirectory and moving those files that appear to be duplicates into it. If you run your computer for a month or so without problems, you can then go back to this junk directory and clean things up; that is, delete it.

The bottom line is that it's probably best to let things stay the way they are. If you're really in need of more hard drive space, consider using DoubleSpace (if you have DOS 6.0 or 6.2) or Stacker 3.1 or later.

Deleting duplicate .GRP files

I have noticed several .GRP files in my Windows directory that appear to be duplicates (that is, MAIN.GRP, MAIN0.GRP, MAIN1.GRP). Are they? If so, which one is the one being used and which ones may I delete?

Is it possible? Could it be? Are your group files related to rabbits? They just keep multiplying and multiplying. They're having all the fun, and you're the one cleaning the cages.

Unless you actually have a Main group and a Main1 group, yes, these files are duplicates that were created during rebuilds and reinstalls. When Windows and the groups are accessed, the date is modified. If the .GRP doesn't have a current date, it's an old copy no longer in use.

Use Windows File Manager to search for all the files ending in .GRP. To do so, highlight the C:\WINDOWS directory and select File⇨Search. In the dialog box, type ***.GRP** and click OK. A listing of all the files ending in .GRP appears in a separate window. Check out the dates created and delete the older copies.

Deleting accessories

I am running a little short on hard drive space, so I would like to remove some of the things I don't use, such as wallpapers and certain accessories. Will it hurt if I delete these files, or is there an easier way?

It won't hurt a thing to delete these items. In fact, it might even boost your computer's performance a smidgen and give you more free system resources.

May I make one little suggestion? Manually deleting all those files is time consuming, and if you inadvertently delete the wrong file, you can really goof things up. Take the lazy way out and have Windows delete those items for you. To do so, look in the Main group under Windows Setup. If you click the Options menu, you will see an option to Add/Remove Windows Components. All you have to do is give it a click and select the items you want to trash.

Undeleting

 ## Undelete

How much time can you wait before using UNDELETE **to try to get a file back? I tried it, and it said nothing was found.**

It has nothing to do with time. It has to do with the number of files you saved on the hard disk before you tried to use the UNDELETE feature.

Just as a book is organized by different chapter numbers, hard disks have clusters full of files. DOS keeps the clusters organized and lists them in the hard disk's file allocation table (FAT).

Lately, fat has been under attack, but in this case FAT is good. The FAT is like a book's table of contents; it contains the locations of all of the files in the computer. When you erase a file from your computer, a flag goes up in the FAT table, making that particular cluster available for the next time you save something. The information or file is still there, however, until you save something. Larger files can take more than one cluster, making the recovery job tougher but not impossible.

The rule after you accidentally erase a file that you want back is to never save anything on the hard disk. The odds are much better of recovering the file by using UNDELETE or a third-party program, such as Norton Disk Utilities, if you haven't saved anything since you deleted the file. Now, go have a cupcake on me.

 ## What is Sentry?

Clear out of the blue one day, my File Manager decided to create a directory called *Sentry*. What is it?

I bet you're a hard person to keep a secret from. That directory is called Sentry for a good reason. It was created by the UNDELETE program, not Windows File Manager.

UNDELETE offers three different levels of protection (sounds like a deodorant ad). The most extensive level is the Delete Sentry mode. It stands guard 24 hours a day looking for deleted files. When it finds one of the little fellows, it immediately rounds it up and places it in that hidden directory you somehow managed to find.

Basically, Delete Sentry hangs onto anything you delete just in case you decide you didn't want to delete it after all. By the way, Delete Sentry will devote about 7 percent of your hard drive to storing those files. Eventually, if Delete Sentry runs out of space, it will get rid of the oldest files to make room for new ones.

Undelete has two other modes, Delete Tracker and Standard, which take up less space. You also can call up the UNDELETE screen from Windows and use it to purge your Delete Sentry files, just as you would delete anything else.

Komando Klues

Press F1 while the UNDELETE screen is displayed to get full information about UNDELETE.

Troubleshooting

Help and other troubleshooting tools

Colors

I just got a job at the IRS and the computers here are lousy. Can I change the color of the text in Windows Help? The green makes me want to throw up.

The short (form) answer: The colors for Help's text are held inside the WIN.INI file. Open the WIN.INI file, using SYSEDIT or Windows Notepad. Look for the section with the heading [Windows Help]. Try darkening the green to make it more readable by using the color code 0 150 0 for the PopUpColor and IFPopUpColor.

Now the long answer: Before I go any further, let me talk a little about color codes. Windows looks at colors as a series of three numbers set apart by spaces. The numbers represent the amount of red, green, and blue, respectively, that create a given color. For example, Windows gets a true red with the codes 255 0 0, and purple is shown as 128 0 128. (Purple is equal parts of red and blue.)

These color codes control the colors for the text in Help. You can have colors in five different areas in Help text files.

If the following lines are not in your [Windows Help] section of the WIN.INI file, you can just type them in:

```
[Windows Help]
JumpColor=r g b
IFJumpColor=r g b
PopUpColor=r g b
IFPopUpColor=r g b
MacroColor=r g b
```

JumpColor is the hypertext link between topics. IFJumpColor is for hypertext links between topics in the active help file and another file. PopUpColor is used with the dashed underline topics that link to the active help file. IFPopUpColor is for those topics that link to another file. MacroColor indicates the color code for embedded macros that you execute by clicking in the text.

Meanwhile,

r	Represents the amount of red
g	Represents the amount of green
b	Represents the amount of blue

Substitute the r, g, and b letters with numbers on a scale of 0 to 255, where 255 is the maximum color intensity. I already told you about red and purple; here are some other color codes:

White	255 255 255
Green	0 255 0
Blue	0 0 255
Yellow	255 255 0
Magenta	255 0 255
Cyan	0 255 255
Black	0 0 0

Bookmarks

Call me absentminded, but I am constantly looking up the same things in Help. Is there some kind of a shortcut for getting to the parts I use often?

OK, you're absentminded. The next time you're in Help, take a look at the menu bar. Find a menu called Bookmark. It allows you to mark a place in help so that you can move back to that section quickly. And you know what's even better? You can make bookmarks in any application that uses the Windows Help engine.

Marking your place is as simple as opening Help to a particular place and choosing Bookmark⇨Define. If you don't like the name Windows gives you for the bookmark, just type the new name before you save the marker. When you need to look up that section again, go to the Bookmark menu and pick which marker you want.

Because you're so absentminded, you may want to write that last detail down someplace. Don't forget where. You may want to make a note of where you wrote it down.

Annotate

Can I add things to the Windows Help files? I would like to add more information in certain areas; that is, the tricks I've found.

Tricks, huh? You don't suppose you'd be interested in writing a book with me, do you?

Annotate, a handy little command found in Help's Edit menu, allows you to electronically paper clip a note to any help file. It's really cool.

Next time you're using a Windows Help file to which you want to add an entry, select Edit; a dialog box will appear. Type your tricks and click Save. Now, scroll to the top of the help text and you'll see a green paper clip. Any time you want to see your annotations, click the paper clip; when you've finished reading, press Esc.

Komando
Klues

To erase an annotation, open the annotation and click the Delete button.

769

Finding SYSEDIT

Where can I find SYSEDIT? I can't recall how to invoke it.

Look in your sock drawer.

Open the Windows Main program group. Odds are you'll find the SYSEDIT icon. If it's not there, make one.

To do so, stay in the Windows Main program group or open the program group where you want the SYSEDIT icon. Choose File⇨New, and because SYSEDIT is a program item, select Program Item. Type **SYSEDIT** in the Description or perhaps in the Important Files. In the Command Line box, use the Browse button to select your C:\WINDOWS\SYSTEM directory and scroll through the list of files until you find SYSEDIT.EXE. Highlight it and click OK. The Command Line box should look like the following:

```
C:\WINDOWS\SYSTEM\SYSEDIT.EXE
```

You're all finished, so click OK to return to your Windows desktop.

Using SYSEDIT

I double-clicked the SYSEDIT icon. A bunch of windows came up, but now what? How does it work?

SYSEDIT is a great tool for making changes to your computer's start-up files, including the AUTOEXEC.BAT and CONFIG.SYS files, as well as your Windows SYSTEM.INI and WIN.INI files.

Be careful. These are the most important files that your computer needs to run Windows. Don't go changing things unless you know what you're doing or I said it was OK.

When you start SYSEDIT, your computer's start-up files and Windows configuration files automatically are seen in separate windows. SYSEDIT works a lot like Windows Notepad. If you're new at Windows, play around in Notepad before venturing into the SYSEDIT zone. A little practice will help prevent disasters, such as tossing the monitor out the window when it won't boot up.

To select the file you want to modify, highlight the file's window title bar. You'll see the filename on the title bar, which makes picking the right one easy. If you have messy windows in SYSEDIT, select Window from the menu bar and Tile or Cascade to put them back in order.

Once a file is selected, use the cursor keys to move around within the file. The Backspace, Delete, and Insert keys work in SYSEDIT as they do in any other text editing program. See why I wanted you to practice in Windows Notepad?

When you want to get rid of a line, don't delete the line unless you're 100 percent positive. Instead, use the REM (short for *remark*) statement, which tells the computer to ignore anything after the REM. For example, say that you want to remove the command to load the mouse driver in your AUTOEXEC.BAT file because Windows uses its own mouse driver. (*Note:* Remove this command only if your DOS programs don't use a mouse.) Select the AUTOEXEC.BAT window, use the cursor keys to move to the line, and type the letters **REM** and then a space. The line would look like the following:

```
REM SET MOUSE=C:\MSMOUSE
```

Be sure that there is a space after the letters REM. Save your changes to the file by selecting File⇨Save.

When you make changes to the AUTOEXEC.BAT or CONFIG.SYS files, you have to restart your computer for the changes to take effect. Accordingly, changes to the Windows configuration files and the SYSTEM.INI and WIN.INI files require that you exit Windows and restart Windows before the changes take effect.

Pay attention to this part. It's a lifesaver.

After editing the AUTOEXEC.BAT, CONFIG.SYS, WIN.INI, or SYSTEM.INI files, SYSEDIT creates a backup of the original files. The backups have an .SYD extension. For example, if you made a change to the AUTOEXEC.BAT file, SYSEDIT saves the original file as AUTOEXEC.SYD and the new file with the changes intact as AUTOEXEC.BAT. The same holds true with other files that you edit using SYSEDIT.

Komando Klues

I like to use the REM statement to remark a line. It's easy to see in a file. But you also can use the semicolon instead of the REM statement. In the example above, the statement would look as follows:

```
; SET MOUSE=C:\MSMOUSE
```

Where is Dr. Watson?

I think Dr. Watson went on a permanent vacation. I want to use him, but I checked in my DOS directory and he is nowhere to be found. Where is he, and what do I do with him when I find him?

I know, you have to be a regular Sherlock Holmes to find Dr. Watson. You will have much more luck locating the Doc if you look in the right place. Dr. Watson is a Windows-based program, not a DOS one, so look in the WINDOWS directory.

Dr. Watson is a diagnostic program that is used mostly by technical support people. When a program is causing general protection faults (GPFs), the techie dudes may ask you to run this program. It keeps a log of what is going on in the system when a GPF occurs. You also enter a comment in the log to record what you were doing at the time the GPF occurred. This information can be handy when you are trying to troubleshoot a renegade application.

To get the doctor on duty, go to Program Manger. Choose File⇨Run. In the Command Line box, type the following and click OK:

```
C:\WINDOWS\DRWATSON.EXE
```

This line creates a log that starts when you put Dr. Watson on duty.

Note: The log is a text file that you can open by using Windows Notepad or your word processor. The DRWATSON.LOG file is in the WINDOWS directory.

Generally, keep Dr. Watson going when you are having trouble with Windows or Windows-based programs. You really don't need to have it running otherwise. If you are getting GPFs, open the log and take a peek for clues. Or offer to send the log to the technical support team for the diseased software program so they can figure out what the problem is. Then erase the DRWATSON.LOG and restart Windows. The next time you use Dr. Watson, she'll open a new log for herself. In case you didn't know, and this is a real insider's secret, Dr. Watson is a woman.

Installing Windows

How much hard disk space do I need?

On the Windows 3.1 box, it says that you need about 6MB of free hard disk space to install the program. I have that much. When I ran the Windows SETUP **command, it told me that I didn't have enough hard disk space. What's going on here? Is Microsoft selling hard disks now too? I feel tricked again.**

No, as of this writing Microsoft is not in the hard disk business. But if it was, I have a feeling you would need much more hard disk space than you have now.

The Windows SETUP program that puts the operating system on your computer needs 6,144,000MB of free disk space for the minimum installation. OK, you can have this much hard disk space but still get an error message. The problem involves the cluster sizes of different hard disks, but who cares? You can't get Windows on your computer.

The bottom line is that you need to free up some more hard disk space (10MB would be good) before you can install Windows.

Will Windows work on XTs?

My son gave me his old computer. It has an *XT* on the front, and it's made by IBM. Can I use Windows 3.1?

No, Windows won't work on an XT. And I'm sorry to be the one to tell you, but that's probably why your son gave it to you. Nice son, huh?

Windows needs at least a 286-based computer to work — one technology level up from the XT. Of course, try Windows once on a 286 and you'll never do it again. Windows 3.1 running on a 286-based computer runs in two speeds: slow and stop. In other words, you really need a 386 or higher computer to use Windows.

Do what my mother does when she wants something from me: remind him about those hours you spent in labor and the long nights you spent nursing him through the flu. My mom's up to 468 hours of labor now. Oh, it's active labor, too, by the way. One more complaint and she'll be up to 486 hours of labor. That's as high as she'll go. There are no Pentium hours of labor!

Installation halts at disk 3

I followed the directions and ran the Windows SETUP**. It goes through disk 1. It goes through disk 2. When it gets to disk 3, the screen goes black. I've done this four times now. I've become an expert at putting disks 1 and 2 in the computer. Tell me there is more to computing than this horrible experience. I'm ready to haul my typewriter out of storage.**

Oh, yes, there is a lot more to computing. There are disks 3 through 7. Hanging up on disk 3 means one thing most of the time. You have some special hardware or memory-resident programs that are getting in the way of the Windows SETUP program.

You need to start your computer with a boot disk and try again. What's a boot disk? It's a special disk that contains just the essential files that your computer needs to start. Put a blank floppy disk in drive A and then type the following at the DOS prompt and press Enter:

```
FORMAT A: /S
```

When it's done, turn off the computer. Make sure that the disk you just made is in drive A and turn on the computer. When you see the A:\> prompt on-screen, insert Windows disk 1 and run the Windows SETUP program again. It should work.

Alas, it still doesn't work, you say? Time to open door number 2. Instead of typing **SETUP**, type the following at the DOS prompt and press Enter:

```
SETUP /I
```

The I part in the SETUP command tells Windows to ignore any funky hardware inside your computer that might be causing it trouble. While the Windows SETUP program is running, do some reading. Take a peek at the hardware compatibility list on the Windows box. If your computer is on the list, call Microsoft Windows technical support. You'll need some hand-holding through some special steps.

What is a clean install?

The techie dude at customer support said I needed to do a clean install of Windows. I didn't think to ask at the time, but what is a clean install?

That's easy. Get a bucket of warm soapy water and scrub your installation disks before you use them. And if you believe that, I have some swamp-land in Scottsdale to sell you.

Actually, a clean install is usually suggested when you have a file corruption problem that you just can't seem to get rid of. Rather than reinstall Windows over itself, Microsoft suggests that you install it to a completely new directory. Pretty easy, huh? Well, the fun has just begun.

You now have two copies of Windows on your hard drive, one that doesn't work and a new one that doesn't know where your applications are. What you have to do now is merge the two. This process can be a little confusing, so take your time. I am going to use the directory WIN as your new Windows installation and WINDOWS as the old one. *Note:* Be sure to substitute your directory names if they are different.

In the new copy of Windows, rename the .GRP files as .GRN, the .INI files as .INN, and the .FOT files (located in the WINDOWS\SYSTEM subdirectory) as .FOZ. Rename the REG.DAT file as REG.DAN. To do all this, quit Windows and type the following commands at the DOS prompt:

```
RENAME C:\WIN\*.GRP *.GRN
RENAME C:\WIN\*.INI *.INN
RENAME C:\WIN\REG.DAT REG.DAN
RENAME C:\WIN\SYSTEM\*.FOT *.FOZ
```

Now you need to remove the read-only attribute from any files in the C:\WINDOWS and C:\WINDOWS\SYSTEM directories. Copy all the files from the new installation into the original WINDOWS directory by typing the following at the DOS prompt:

```
ATTRIB -S -H C:\WINDOWS\*.* /S
ATTRIB -R C:\WINDOWS\*.* /S
XCOPY C:\WIN C:\WINDOWS /S
```

If Windows now runs from the original C:\WINDOWS directory, then pat yourself on the back for a job well done. You can go ahead and delete the directory C:\WIN and all its subdirectories and files. You also should delete any files with the extensions .INN, .GRN, and the file REG.DAN from your C:\WINDOWS directory, as well as any files with the extension .FOZ in the \SYSTEM subdirectory.

If Windows doesn't run, curse your machine, stomp around, scream and yell, and then sit back down because you have more work to do. Rename the original .INI files as .INO and rename the .INN files as .INI, as follows:

```
RENAME C:\WINDOWS\*.INI *.INO
RENAME C:\WINDOWS\*.INN *.INI
```

Edit the PROGMAN.INI file, changing all references to C:\WIN to C:\WINDOWS. Now get down on your knees and say a little prayer. Type those three little magical letters, **WIN**, and press Enter. If everything finally works right, then the problem is being caused by an improper setting in or corruption of one of the original .INI files. So back up any data files from all your Windows-based applications and then reinstall them. This action will ensure the correct WIN.INI, SYSTEM.INI, and directory settings for each application. It's rough, I know, but you gotta do what you gotta do. Oh yeah, you also have to re-create any customization you did to the Program Manager groups as well as desktop settings, such as color schemes and screen savers.

If Windows still does not run correctly, then you're having a really, really bad day. Start by renaming the .INN, .GRN, .FOZ, and REG.DAN files in the new copy of Windows as follows:

```
RENAME C:\WIN\*.INN *.INI
RENAME C:\WIN\*.GRN *.GRP
RENAME C:\WIN\REG.DAN REG.DAT
RENAME C:\WIN\SYSTEM\*.FOZ *.FOT
```

Now, back up all application data files and reinstall the programs under the new copy of Windows. You can go ahead and delete your old Windows directory and start using the new one.

Memory

Parity error

It's the strangest thing I've ever seen. How come I get a parity error in Windows but not in DOS?

Really? That's the strangest thing you've ever seen? You need to get away from your monitor for awhile. The world has changed a lot since you sat in front of it.

A *parity error* is a problem with the memory chips in the computer. Getting the parity error only in Windows is not that strange. DOS mainly uses just the first 640K of memory in the system. Windows, on the other hand, tends to use all of the available memory in the system. Many Windows-based programs, for example, use up all of the available memory and then some. You need to replace the bad chip or the entire SIMM, depending on what your computer uses.

Your best bet is to haul the computer into a service center. The hard part is finding out which SIMM is bad. A computer repair facility will test for bad chips and replace them.

Insufficient memory *message*

I've had it! No matter what I do, I keep receiving *insufficient memory* error messages at GDI.EXE. I have tried DOS MEMMAKER. I have over 600K of conventional memory. I have 16MB of RAM. Does this mean my memory is bad?

I forgot the question. Ah, yes. I'm going to wind up my propeller beanie for this one.

Almost everyone has at some point received that dreaded *insufficient memory* message. The root of the problem is that you're running out of system resources.

System resources refers to two 64K heaps of memory reserved for the exclusive use of two Windows housekeeping programs: USER.EXE and GDI.EXE.

USER.EXE's main job is to help Program Manager keep track of icons, icon positions, open Windows, and so on. GDI.EXE is an applications interface program that software developers use to create text, bitmap output, and more. Both programs need their own personal memory heaps to do their work. Once these heaps are full, you receive the *insufficient memory* error message. It's becoming clearer now. I see it in your eyes.

To make matters worse, you can still receive the error message after you close all running applications in Windows. You see, no matter how many applications you close, there are lots of things running in the background for Windows to track — screen savers, wallpapers, desktop color schemes, icons, sound, fonts, and, lest we forget, a terminate-and-stay program (TSR) or two.

Komando Klues

Program Manager is a resource hog. Every icon shown takes up about one percent of the system resources. You should keep unused groups closed, or minimized, and remove any icons that are simply taking up space.

Among the biggest culprits are Windows desktop replacement programs, or shell programs, such as PC Tools for Windows or Norton Desktop. These programs take over for the Program Manager in Windows and devour system resources.

Deleting complex wallpapers, never-used icons, and program groups may help and certainly won't hurt. You can use the Windows Setup icon in the Main Group to remove standard Windows applications.

Another culprit is programs that don't give back their system resources when they have finished running. The greedy little things have forgotten how to share. The only thing you can do to regain those resources is reboot Windows.

As you can see, there are times when you just have to try to work around the limitation on system resources. If it's any consolation, Windows 95 will manage system resources better than Windows 3.1, so perhaps this error message will be gone forever.

Uh oh, I think my propeller just . . . wound . . . down.

Speed

Speeding up a 386

My company has spent all it's going to spend, but Windows still runs like crap. I have a 386DX 33 with 8MB of RAM. What can I do to make this dog run faster?

You're going to be able to coax only so much oomph out of that old 386. And yet, I can understand why your company is not ready to put your computer to sleep. Your 386 will never be the fastest dog on the track, but with a little tweaking, you can get it to run a respectable race.

You can make a variety of changes to speed up the system. Bumping up to 8MB of RAM was a good start. Next, you need to use a disk cache of some kind. The SmartDrive program that came with the system is a good one. Without a disk cache, the system can appear to be very slow and sluggish, especially if you are accessing the disk frequently.

Switching from a temporary swap file to a permanent one also can help move things along a little faster. Just don't make the swap file too large, or the system will have to spend too much time searching for the information that is stored there. A 10–12MB swap file usually is sufficient if you can spare the hard drive space.

And yes, it's time to dig down deep. Do you really need all those fonts, screen savers, wallpapers, icons, and games? In other words, you need to delete all the fun, but doing so will help. Each of these items cuts into the available system resources.

I always recommend a regular schedule of hard drive maintenance to keep things in order. Over time, the hard drive can become badly fragmented as you add and delete files. Defragmentation can cause the drive to spend precious time searching for files that are scattered here and there across the disk. By running SCANDISK and DEFRAG once a month (weekly on some systems), you can keeps things moving at a nice pace.

If you don't have any applications that require 256 colors, run the 16-color driver in Windows. It may not be as pretty, but 256 colors can cause quite a performance drag for the system.

If your word processor has the option, run it in draft mode. The fonts may look ugly on-screen, but they will look just fine on your printout.

Last but not least, try not to run too many applications at the same time. When other programs are running in the background, they take away system resources and slow you down.

RAM drives

Are RAM drives as good as my friends say to speed up Windows?

It depends on your friends. Where did you meet them?

RAM drives are handy tools for speeding up some DOS programs, and they make wonderful temporary storage areas. However, when you use Windows, the memory you sacrifice to a RAM drive is wasted.

Windows craves memory. It eats it all up and then wants more. Whatever memory you devote to a RAM drive is lost to Windows. The only exception here is if you have a ton of RAM, say 16MB or more. If so, you can spare memory for a RAM drive. Even then, Windows would probably rather have all the memory for itself.

Slowing down Windows

When I try to run a DOS program, the screen says something about an error. I can't read it, though. The message just flashes and then disappears, and the computer goes back to Windows.

In a situation like this, three solutions come to mind:

➤ You can enroll in the nearest speed reading class.

➤ You can take a quick picture of the message (make doubles so that your computer can have a copy, too).

➤ You can put the brakes on Windows.

The speed reading could always come in handy, but it's a lot easier to just force Windows not to jump back in from that DOS session so quickly.

To take a good look at the error message so that you can figure out what to correct, you need to edit the .PIF file that controls the DOS application.

Take a look in the Windows Main program group and you will see an icon called the PIF Editor, which looks a lot like a luggage tag. By running the PIF Editor, you can change the way Windows handles the DOS program. You want to stop Windows from closing the DOS windows as soon as the application is finished running.

Any DOS program that runs in Windows uses a .PIF file — either its own or the DEFAULT.PIF included with Windows. You can modify a .PIF file by opening it in the PIF Editor. Once the file is open, disable the Close Windows on Exit option. This action leaves a DOS window open so that you can read any error message that may have been created. Rerun the problem program and take whatever steps are necessary to correct the problem.

When everything is working smoothly, reopen the .PIF file and enable Close Window on Exit. This way, when you are done using the DOS program, Windows comes back on-screen quicker.

General protection faults

What are general protection faults?

What are general protection faults, and are they my fault?

General protection faults, called GPFs for short, generally result from something happening that Windows didn't expect and doesn't know what to do about. Often, GPFs occur when an application or a Windows component reads or writes to a memory location that has not been allocated to it (memory that it does not "own"). A turf war breaks out when the application that owns that memory location notices the intruder; while the apps are duking it out, a *general protection fault* error message appears on-screen.

A GPF also may occur during the passing of information between applications and the Windows environment. A bad hand-off, such as incorrect parameters, can cause invalid instructions to be executed, resulting in the dreaded GPF. This problem usually arises when an application's internal program code sends data to Windows or a Windows-based application and the receiving end just doesn't know what to do with the info.

Normally, a quick call to the software program's publisher will ease the pain. When at all possible, write down the exact message and error number. This helps the technical support folks narrow down a solution.

On occasion, you will come across general protection faults that are nobody's fault. A bad installation or a corrupted file can cause these nasty little error messages to pop up. Reinstalling the problem app can clear things up.

What causes general protection faults?

***Application has violated system integrity.* Sounds like a political problem to me! How can I find out what caused a general protection fault?**

There's no way that could have been a political problem. Integrity has nothing to do with politics.

Tracking down the exact cause of a GPF is tricky at best. It's one of those things best left to techies who get paid for it. Even if I can manage to narrow it down to the application causing the problem, I tend to let the tech support gurus take it from there.

Figuring out just what program is making your life miserable requires a bit of detective work. It always pays to keep a pencil and some paper handy. If a GPF occurs, or any other error for that matter, jot down the exact error messages and note which programs were currently running. These are important clues and will help you crack the case.

For example, if I'm running an application and I receive a GPF caused by a file that has a name that sounds suspiciously like a video resolution (such as 256_1024.DRV), there is a good chance my video drivers are conflicting with the program I'm trying to run. Changing to a different resolution or updating the video drivers will probably clear this GPF up.

If the fault doesn't cause the application to close, it's a good idea to save your work and exit Windows. If you continue working and the fault reoccurs, you may lose everything you have done that session. Once you have exited Windows, use the DOS CHKDSK/F command (SCANDISK if you have DOS 6 or higher) to see whether a splattered file is the culprit. By running CHKDSK/F or SCANDISK, any lost allocation units or other file allocation table (FAT) errors are corrected. Afterward, take another few minutes and run the DOS program DEFRAG if you have DOS 6 or higher, to put the hard disk in tip-top shape. There's more information about these DOS commands in Chapter 8.

When a GPF occurs, you should always close and then restart Windows. Then, from Program Manager, select File⇨Run. In the Run command box, type the following and click OK:

```
C:\WINDOWS\DRWATSON.EXE
```

Dr. Watson is a Windows on-call program that tracks any errors in program executions. This handy little program runs in the background, monitoring system settings. It keeps a log of the activity and any errors that occur. The log (DRWATSON.LOG) file will be located in your C:\WINDOWS directory. Because it's a text file, you can open it in Windows Notepad or your word processing software.

If your Windows programs are back to normal but you can't leave well enough alone, you could try to re-create the GPF. Often, you'll find that you can't. The error may have been a one-time thing due to the combination of programs you had running.

If you can re-create the problem, then you want to start eliminating programs such as screen savers or fax managers that are running in the background. Keep eliminating applications until you have narrowed down to one specific program that is causing the trouble or to a combination of programs that don't play nicely together.

Armed with your knowledge and Dr. Watson log, call the technical support department of the program causing the GPF. Be in front of your computer when you call and have any notes on the error handy. Quite often, the software publisher has run into the problem before and knows just how to fix it. The publisher may send you a program update or patch if necessary.

Why can't I access File Manager?

When I try to access my File Manager in Windows, I receive the following message: *Application Error - WINFILE caused a General Protection Fault in module WINFILE.EXE at 0006:021D.* **Why can't I manage to get into the File Manager? I use Windows and DOS 6.22.**

Have you tried *open sesame* or *abracadabra* or *pretty please with a cherry on top*?

File Manager is like an old golf pro. It's pretty laid-back and rarely causes problems. Every once in a while, it does become a little cantankerous and tosses all its clubs in the water. Usually, this means its initialization file has somehow become corrupted.

First, do a little hard drive maintenance.

Exit Windows and, from the DOS prompt, run SCANDISK and then DEFRAG. These are really good programs to run every so often. Sometimes you develop bad spots on drives or crosslinked files, and these two DOS programs take care of them.

Hang out in DOS now. You're going to delete the WINFILE.INI file. Type the following at the DOS prompt and press Enter:

```
DEL C:\WINDOWS\WINFILE.INI
```

Don't worry, File Manager will re-create it. Each time you use the File Manager and then close it, it takes a picture of the way things are set up and writes these settings to the initialization file. Because you deleted File Manager's settings file, you'll have to customize File Manager again. If the initialization file contains corruption or invalid settings when you try to start File Manager, it becomes confused and, well, you've seen the results firsthand.

Other

 Windows security

What can I do to keep other people from using my Windows files?

A well-trained Rottweiler should do the trick. I tried motion sensors one time, but people complained when the alarms started ringing.

Windows has very little in the way of built-in security features. Letting someone else use your system calls for a great deal of trust on your part, especially when you have files named DIARY.DOC and LUVLIFE.DOC. Although you can't keep your files totally secure, you can put out a few stumbling blocks.

You can set some restrictions by editing the PROGMAN.INI file. The first thing you need to do is add the line [restrictions] to the PROGMAN.INI file. This line tells Windows that system restrictions will follow. By the way, any changes that you make to the lines in the PROGMAN.INI file won't take effect until the next time you run Windows.

The following table is a list of useful items you can add.

Edit	What It Does
NoRun=1	Disables the RUN command
NoClose=1	Disables the EXIT WINDOWS command
NoSaveSettings=1	Disables the SAVE SETTINGS ON EXIT command
NoFileMenu=1	Removes the File menu from Program Manager's main menu
EditLevel=0	Sets no restrictions on access to Program Manager
EditLevel=1	Prevents the creation, deletion, and renaming of program groups
EditLevel=2	Includes level 1 restrictions and prevents the creation and deletion of items in program groups
EditLevel=3	Includes level 2 restrictions and prevents changes in the command lines for program group items
EditLevel=4	Includes level 3 restrictions and prevents changes in the information for program group items

Or go buy a security program. PC Dynamics MenuWorks Advanced (800-888-1741) is one of the best around. Check it out.

Moving Windows to another drive

I moved Windows from drive C to drive D, and now it doesn't work.

Did your parents ever move one day and leave you no forwarding address? Similarly, Windows is feeling abandoned. When you copied your Windows files to drive D, it never really noticed the change. In other words, you haven't told Windows its new address.

Moving Windows from one drive to another drive is a huge escapade because of all the .INI files and the configuration files. Often, reinstalling Windows on the new drive is better and easier. Or you can save yourself a great deal of anxiety by simply imagining that you moved Windows from drive D to drive C. For those of you who are more adventurous, keep reading.

Many configuration settings are stored in the .INI files on your system. These files usually contain references to other files that are directories. If one of these references points to a file that you have moved from drive C to drive D, well, you could say that the mail gets Returned to Sender, Address Unknown. You need to use a text editor to check each .INI file (I do not recommend using your word processor because it will leave additional information in the file and Windows will not be able to use the file) and make any changes necessary. Your WINDOWS directory has a large number of .INI files, so this process could take a while.

The Bottom Line

Heck, just reinstall Windows on the new drive. Telling you how to check and double-check everything would take another book. Thanks for sticking with me, adventurous ones, but we must move on.

Hanging on exit

My IBM PS/2 just hangs there when I exit Windows. How do I fix this?

Big Blue is giving you the Big Blue Blues. The problem is inherent in some PS/2 models. They seem to hang on forever when you exit Windows before they finally return you to the DOS prompt. This problem is caused by the system's waiting to reinitialize the mouse port. Although this problem can be annoying, it isn't harmful to your machine (although I can't say the same thing for your productivity or your sanity).

Harmful or not, you don't need to settle for these little annoyances in life, and that's why you've written to li'l ole me. You can usually clear up the problem by adding a line to your SYSTEM.INI file. Make a backup copy of the SYSTEM.INI file. Then, using Notepad or another text editor, open the SYSTEM.INI file. Be careful. Scroll down to the [386enh] section of SYSTEM.INI and add the following line:

```
Init PS2MouseAtEXit=FALSE
```

Save the file, and the next time you exit Windows, hold on to your chair.

Missing screen saver

What's wrong? I can see all of my SCR files in the Windows directory and test and view them in Control Panel, but when I try to leave Control Panel with my changes, I get the message that Control Panel can't find the screen saver.

Step aside, let me handle this one. That sounds rather bogus, all right. It looks as if you have two or more CONTROL.INI files on the hard disk. The CONTROL.INI file contains the nitty-gritty details about the Windows screen saver information. Use the File Manager's Search feature to check out this possibility. Highlight the C: in the directory tree because you want to search all the files in all the directories on drive C. Then, in the search box, type the following and press Enter:

```
CONTROL.INI
```

The CONTROL.INI file should be listed only in the C:\WINDOWS directory. If you find one elsewhere on the hard disk, rename it by choosing File⇨Rename. Type a new filename, such as **CONTROL.OLD**. I bet the screen saver now works, or else my name's not Kim Komando.

Missing device driver

Microsoft Backup told me that I needed to add the line DEVICE=[ms-dos path]VFINTD.386 **into the [386 Enh] section of SYSTEM.INI file. I followed the directions, but now Windows can't find the device.**

Windows can't find the device? Maybe you backed up over it.

Windows is kind of funny about device drivers. For some strange reason, it wants to know exactly where the file is. I guess it's just easier that way. When you put the DEVICE line in your SYSTEM.INI file, did you by any chance type just as you did in your question?

Believe it or not, many people have made the same mistake. It's a natural thing to do. The error message may include *[ms-dos path]*, so you might think that you need to add that part into the device driver line. Not so.

When a book, error message, or anything else refers to *[ms-dos path]*, it's a shorter way of saying to include the drive and name of the directory where the file is located. The line you need to add to the SYSTEM.INI file should look like this:

```
DEVICE=C:\DOS\VFINTD.386
```

This line tells Windows where to find the VFINTD.386 driver and assumes that you have DOS installed on your drive C in a directory called DOS. Otherwise, you would add the [ms-dos] path information. If your computer's DOS is in a directory other than one named DOS (for example, DRDOS), then the line added to the SYSTEM.INI file would look like

```
DEVICE=C:\DRDOS\VFINTD.386
```

where DRDOS represents the name of your DOS directory.

Corrupted applications program group

My applications program group keeps getting corrupted in Windows. I have to re-create it every time. When I start, I receive an error message that says *Group File Error*. This seems to happen only with my applications group file.

Your Windows application group file has gone bad, corrupted, untoward, impure, sinister. . . . OK, maybe it's not that bad.

Time first for a little hard disk maintenance. Exit Windows and, at the DOS prompt, run the DOS program SCANDISK or if you have DOS version 5 or lower, use the DOS program CHKDSK/F. If you have DOS 6.0 or higher, run the DEFRAG utility, too.

Perhaps the applications group file was located on a part of the hard disk that had a little problem. You may have just fixed it, so try to start Windows again.

No luck? Delete the applications group and make a new one. Unfortunately, you may have to reinstall Windows. Before doing the reinstallation, save the files with the file extensions .INI and .GRP onto a floppy disk. (These are your Windows initialization files and group files.) After you reinstall Windows, you can move these files back from the floppy to the hard disk. But don't move the applications group file or else you'll be back where you started. You can make your own applications program group at this point.

Insufficient file handles

I have love handles, but apparently I don't have file handles. I receive an error message in Windows about *insufficient file handles*. How do I get rid of it?

The love handles or error message? You didn't make that clear.

You need to increase the number of files you can open simultaneously in Windows. Make sure that you have a backup copy of your CONFIG.SYS file because you need to make one little change.

From Program Manager, select File⇨Run. In the Command Line box, type **SYSEDIT** and click OK.

Highlight the CONFIG.SYS file window so that it's the active window. Look for a line that mentions FILES=(some number). Increase the number after the equals sign by 10 or 20. Usually, the number of files is between 30 and 50. If you don't have a FILES= statement in your CONFIG.SYS file for some strange reason, add the following line:

```
FILES=30
```

Select File⇨Save. Exit Windows and restart your computer for the changes to take effect. Start Windows again, and if you receive that annoying file handles error message, keep increasing the number in the FILES= statement by 10. Remember to save your changes and also remember that you need to restart your computer to see whether the new settings work.

Now, for your love handles, try going away from your computer for a while. Exercise and fresh air is good for you.

 VSafe

When I start my computer, I receive a VSafe Warning. This happens before the computer starts running Windows. Stop, update, or continue are my options. So far, I am continuing. Should I update?

I have always been curious. Why does someone run VSafe on their computer and then ignore it when it comes up with a warning message? Is it just stubbornness or the "It can't happen to me" syndrome?

VSafe is Microsoft's antiviral software that is used to warn you about viruses on your system. The first time you run the software, it makes calculations about each file in your system and stores these in a file called CHKLIST.MS in each directory. Whenever you attempt to access or run a file, it will take a little look-see at the file's size to see that it's the same as it was the last time it checked the file's size. A change could mean the file was edited for a legitimate reason. Or it could mean a virus has attached itself to the file.

When you receive this warning, you should think long and hard before just continuing. Have you done anything recently that would have changed the file? If you have, choose the Update to modify the checksum amount. If you are unsure about any possible changes, you should probably make a note of the filename and then choose the Delete option. Drastic, I know, but it is better than letting a virus infect other files. And, after all, you do have a backup of all your files, don't you? VSafe, VSmart, VSensible.

Q&A *Lost portion of repartitioned hard drive*

I've had to hand-write this letter because I recently repartitioned my hard drive. All my Windows applications were installed on my old drive E. Now Windows can't find them. How can I make Windows look to drive D?

Your letter had a lot of misspellings. You need Pencheck 3.1 for Papers.

You have to tell Windows to look on drive D to find the programs. To do so, highlight the Applications group icon in Windows Program Manager. Select File⇨Properties. These simple steps bring up the oh-so-wonderful Properties dialog box.

Komando Klues

Pressing Alt+Enter also brings up a program group's properties.

You will have to change the drive letter in the Command Line and Working Directory from E to D. You'll have to repeat these steps for each application that has changed from one drive to the other drive. Well, almost. If the Command Line displays a file with the .PIF file extension, the file is a Program Information File. Use the PIF Editor in the Main group to change any references from drive E to drive D.

This process will take a little time. However, it will take much less time than reinstalling all your programs. In fact, after accomplishing this, you still may have time to enjoy what's left of the weekend.

Chapter 21

Windows 95

What are the minimum hardware requirements?

I'm a little concerned about Windows 95. I checked the program's minimum requirements, and I barely have them. Just how will Windows 95 work on my machine?

Running Windows 95 on a computer that has just the minimum recommendations is like working for minimum wage. It's like driving a Porsche downhill with the engine off. It's like cooking without spices. It's like dining without utensils. It's like writing without adjectives. . . . Stop me when you get the point. Oh, OK.

Windows 95 is supposed to work as fast as Windows 3.1 on a 386-based computer with 4MB of memory. Fast is a relative term, but perhaps there is a history lesson here. Windows 3.1's minimum requirement was supposedly a 286-based computer. Well, Windows 3.1 ran on a 286-based computer, all right, but only in two speeds: slow and stop.

With Windows 3.1, users enjoyed the biggest performance boost after increasing the amount of the computer's RAM from 4MB to 8MB. Moving up from 8MB to 16MB of memory didn't give much raw performance increase, even though more memory is a good thing. Things are different with Windows 95; it keeps giving performance increases when more memory is added. In reality, Windows 95 will certainly perform better with a faster computer and more memory.

The Bottom Line

So what should you do with that 386 computer? Give Windows 95 a shot. If all you're doing is word processing and other basic tasks, it should run fine. Know, however, that a 486-based computer with 8MB of RAM is a typical minimum Windows 95 configuration. As is the case with most computer programs, the more computer you have, the better.

What's the Windows 95 dream machine?

I've always been my rich aunt's favorite. She offered me a graduation gift from college. All I have to do is tell her what I want. If I asked her to buy me the best computer to run Windows 95, what would the computer have inside?

A file in Microsoft Word that contains a thank-you note to your aunt is a good start.

As you enter the world, know the basics: You can never be too rich, too thin, or have too powerful of a computer. In other words, more is better. The bigger the hard drive, the more memory, and the more powerful the CPU is, the better Windows 95 (or any other operating system) will run.

Although Microsoft says that Windows 95 will run on a 386 computer with 4MB of memory, your aunt may as well give you a lump of coal. Here's my wish list: a Pentium computer with a 90MHz CPU, PCI bus motherboard, 32MB of memory, 1 gigabyte hard disk drive, 16-bit audio card, quad-speed CD-ROM drive, 64-bit PCI video card with 4MB of video memory, 17-inch SVGA monitor, a DAT tape backup drive, and a 28,800-bits-per-second modem.

Of course, time and technology never stand still. By the time you read this, there could be 150MHz Pentium-based computers and octo-spin CD-ROM drives. Actually, because books can last forever, you could have found this book at a 21st-century garage sale; if so, perhaps computers are obsolete and we all have chips in our brains. So substitute some items on my list with the latest and greatest hardware.

Now that I've answered your question, would you do me a favor? Drop me a note with your aunt's address. I think she'd like me, too.

What is Plug and Play?

What's this talk about Plug and Play with Windows 95? I'm not an engineer. I'm just a businessman who uses a computer.

Hey, you're not just a businessman. You're the capitalist wheels that keep this country moving, and don't you forget it.

Computers that support the new *Plug and Play* (PnP) standard will have special BIOS on the motherboard and other components that makes upgrading the computer easy. With PnP, adding a sound card, for example, won't require hours of hair-pulling configurations and prayers. You'll simply be able to open the computer case, insert card A in slot A, close the case, and restart the computer. It's kind of like opening the hood of your car, taking out the old distributor cap, and putting a new — wait, I forgot, you're not an engineer.

Windows 95 will sense that a new card has been added and automatically set itself up. Now, won't that be nice? The bad news is that the old motherboards and cards can't be changed to make them support PnP.

Will it be preinstalled?

When Windows 95 comes out, will it come preinstalled on new PCs as Windows 3.1 did?

Surely you don't think Microsoft would miss such a golden opportunity to include Windows 95 on new computers. Microsoft has signed, sealed, and delivered deals with most computer manufacturers to include Windows 95 on new systems. You should be able to buy a new computer with Windows 95 already installed on it a few days after Windows 95 ships. The only thing that's faster is Bill Gates rushing to the bank to cash your check.

How much drive space will it take?

How much hard disk real estate do I have to give up for Windows 95?

Before I tell you, I want you to guess. Now double it. You're still too low.

As programs become more powerful, they take more space to store on a hard disk drive. The good news is that as more people buy larger hard disk drives, the price goes down. I can remember the good old days when a huge 20MB hard disk drive cost several thousand dollars. Nowadays, hard disk space is under $50 per megabyte and becoming less expensive almost every day. You kids don't know how good you have it.

Windows 95 will take about 60MB of hard disk space. Don't get bug-eyed on me, now. Consider that Windows 95 includes both DOS and Windows. Windows 3.1 takes about 10MB. Or perhaps you currently use Windows for Workgroups 3.11, which consumes 20MB of hard disk space. Either way, you have MS-DOS, and the latest version, 6.22, uses about 5MB of space. Windows 95 includes DOS and a more powerful and easier-to-use flavor of Windows. So 60MB isn't too bad, is it? (OK, it is — but there's nothing you can do about it.)

Will the installation be torture?

I'm into time management, and I heard that Windows 95 is a huge program. The last time I installed a program, it took me four hours because of all the program disks. It ruined my day. How many disks will I have to feed to install Windows 95?

Where do you think Microsoft came up with the 95 in Windows 95? You don't think they named it after the year, do you?

Do you have a CD-ROM in your computer? If not, get one to avoid zapping your schedule or getting floppy disk anxiety. Windows 95 comes on floppy disks or on a CD-ROM. Allot at least one hour for the CD-ROM version to be installed; if you're stuck with the 20 floppy disks, count on two weeks. Just kidding, but it will take a few hours playing the floppy install game. Windows 95 is so fast, though, you'll make up the time in no time.

What if I don't like it?

I have bad luck. Something always seems to go wrong even when it's supposedly impossible. If I don't like Windows 95 or it doesn't work right, am I stuck with it on my computer?

Yes, I see what you mean by bad luck. Your letter was mutilated by the post office.

Software companies realize that people might want to change their minds about upgrading their operating systems. Since MS-DOS 5.0, Microsoft has given the user an option of uninstalling their programs. You can uninstall Windows 95 if you're unhappy. Click the uninstall option and in a few minutes, your Windows 3.1 desktop will be back. There are also options for system administrators of networks to customize the way Windows 95 will install and uninstall on networks.

I recommend making a full backup of your information on your hard disk before you install Windows 95. This way, in case you do want to go back to Windows 3.1, and something wrong does happen, it will make the job easier. You could restore your entire Windows 3.1 setup from the backup.

How will Windows 95 affect Windows 3.11?

Windows for Workgroups 3.11, not Windows 3.1, came on my computer. Will Windows for Workgroups be upgraded also, or will it be left out in the cold like a stray cat?

Windows 95 is the upgrade for Windows for Workgroups; it includes Windows 3.11's built-in network functionality. You can connect a Windows 95 computer to a Windows for Workgroups network, a Windows NT 3.5 network, and a Novell network. In fact, Windows 95 will work with a Novell network even better than Windows for Workgroups 3.1 because of Windows 95's increased performance features. There won't be a product called Windows 95 for Workgroups.

What if I'm the only one with Windows 95?

I'm a guy who likes to know what he's getting into before he jumps. Let's just assume that I take the leap and move to Windows 95. When will there be programs available that are native to the operating system? What if no one else has it and it never catches on? I'm afraid to commit to it.

Just like a typical male, afraid of commitment.

Step out of your shoes for a moment and pretend that you're the CEO of a software publishing company. Windows 95 offers you and your stockholders new revenue streams and profit centers. Sure, you'll need to spend some money in research and development. But new computers are shipping with Windows 95 preinstalled and folks who upgrade to Windows 95 will want to purchase programs that use the new interface and true multitasking features. Do you really have a choice not to release Windows 95 products? No, and neither do the other software publishers.

Windows 95-specific application development began as soon as the first test, or *alpha*, software was available. You're likely to find new versions of most major applications within 90 days of Windows 95 shipping. You'll be able to upgrade your favorite programs as they become available.

Does that mean that you won't be able to run your current Windows 3.1 and MS-DOS applications? Certainly not! Windows 95 will run virtually all of the current Windows 3.1 programs — and with better crash protection than Windows 3.1. MS-DOS programs, including most games, will run in Windows 95 without a problem, too.

Of course, Windows 95-specific programs will work better than Windows 3.1 programs. The new crop of programs — will take advantage of the multithreading and 32-bit aspects of Windows 95. *Note:* As a 32-bit operating system, Windows 95 will provide a way for Windows software programs to process more information and instructions much faster than their Windows 3.1 counterparts.

Will DOS still be there?

I've always hated DOS. It's stupid and hard to use. Do I still need to have DOS hanging around to use Windows 95?

Good question, and good news. Windows 95 is Windows without DOS; DOS is still included, but you don't see it. Good riddance. No longer will you have to boot DOS and type **WIN** at the DOS prompt to start Windows. You'll never even see the DOS prompt. Windows 95 takes you directly into a graphical environment full of pretty pictures.

Windows 95 will still let you run your DOS-based programs, though. There's an MS-DOS icon in Windows 95 that lets you go back to that old, comfortable DOS prompt. (Hey, some people find comfort in the thorny part of a rose.) Windows 95 includes versions of just about all the utilities that come with MS-DOS 6.*x*, too, including SCANDISK and BACKUP. The bad news? There isn't any. Good-bye and good luck.

What about configuration files?

I'm bummed. I spent a year fine-tuning my AUTOEXEC.BAT file and my CONFIG.SYS file. If Windows 95 doesn't have DOS, what happens to all my hard work?

I know how you feel. It's like tuning up, washing, and waxing your car just to sell it. But don't be too bummed. Think of how all that hard work has made you grow as a person. You're not the same person you were a year ago. You're a bit wiser, a bit . . . sorry, I was channeling Ann Landers for a second there.

Unlike DOS and Windows 3.1, Windows 95 doesn't need an AUTOEXEC.BAT file and a CONFIG.SYS file. Windows 95 figures out the computer's memory settings, device drivers, and system configuration automatically.

If Windows 95 finds an AUTOEXEC.BAT file and a CONFIG.SYS file on a computer, however, it will use some settings. For instance, if you set a PATH statement in your AUTOEXEC.BAT file, Windows 95 will use it. Some programs require settings in the AUTOEXEC.BAT file and/or the CONFIG.SYS file. Don't worry. Windows 95 will take settings from the files that certain programs need so that the programs work. Wow, it sure sounds as if Windows 95 is all things to all people.

Will installation be hard?

Windows 3.1 wasn't too tough to install. Because Windows 95 is so different, will I need to get an engineering degree or hire my local computer guru to set it up?

The thing I've found about computer gurus is that they love this kind of stuff. And they bore you to death about what they're doing when they're doing it. "And this is disk three. It's a high-density disk necessary to facilitate the operations. . . . " Zzzzzz.

Windows 95 is designed for easy installation by just about anyone. If you've been using Windows 3.1 for any time at all, you should not have trouble installing Windows 95. Heck, it's so easy that a five-year-old can do it. My nephew handled the job for me. Er, yes, Ms. Microsoft attorney, he was under nondisclosure at the time.

Windows 95 will examine your current Windows setup and convert it to the new setup. The installation program examines your computer hardware and sets Windows 95 up to work with the hardware. Wizards are used to step the user through adding or changing components of both hardware and software.

Think of installing Windows 95 as remodeling your house. Just as a good carpenter wouldn't start remodeling a house if the foundation is cracking, you shouldn't install Windows 95 on top of a shaky Windows 3.1 installation. In other works, before you change to Windows 95, clean out your hard disk. Get rid of all those programs that you swore you'd use some day, like those shoes that looked so good in the store but have found a home in the back of the closet. Afterward, use the DOS commands SCANDISK and then DEFRAG to put your hard disk in tip-top shape. A little bit of maintenance and planning will make installing Windows 95 even easier.

Remember, Windows 95 is a program, not magic. If your Windows 3.1 setup isn't working quite right, don't expect Windows 95 to be able to cure all your problems.

Will it be just like a Mac?

I hear Windows 95 is having a Big Mac attack. I've never used an Apple Macintosh computer, but I've always heard it was easier than Windows. Is it true that Microsoft stole the user interface off the Macintosh?

Contrary to popular belief, Apple didn't invent the graphical user interface (GUI) — it was invented at Xerox's research laboratories. A lot of money was spent on this issue as Apple battled Microsoft for patent infringement. Microsoft won, by the way, but the appeals continue. And as long as there are lawyers and tons of money from you and me, the appeals will continue.

True, Windows 95 looks a little bit more like a Macintosh than Windows 3.1, but in the way Democrats look like Republicans. In fact, Windows 95 also looks like OS/2, SunOS, and other GUIs, too.

The new Windows 95 user interface is a result of listening to people's complaints on the technical support line and conducting lots of research. Some of the research was, undoubtedly, looking at a "standard" GUI known as Motif. Most of the publishers of GUIs on the market have incorporated concepts from the Motif interface into their own product. Because the GUIs have been inspired by common designs, similarities in different GUIs are bound to happen. Think about it: How many different ways can you depict a computer's hard disk as a filing cabinet?

Standard GUIs are a good thing. Imagine if every different car maker put the gas pedal, speedometer, and radios in a radically different location. Although cars do have radios in different locations, you usually find the gas pedal to the right of the brake. Putting it somewhere else sure would make jumping into a rent-a-car an experience to remember. Standards help make learning different types of systems easier.

Please — no new tricks

At my age, I'm just not sure that I want to learn a whole new operating system. Is Windows 95 going to be a radical change or will this old dog feel at home?

If you're comfortable working in Windows 3.1 already, you'll have a pretty short learning curve.

Some familiar elements, such as Program Manager and File Manager, are gone. Instead, you'll get a Start button and an Explorer button. Although you'll have to unlearn a few old habits, you should find yourself working away in Windows 95 in no time. Much of Windows 95 is customizable, so you can change the look and feel of many of the interface's elements.

Some things, such as long filenames, will simplify your life. No longer will you have to come up with creative ways of abbreviating filenames, or worse, try to remember what the heck was in the file. For example, a Windows 3.1 filename could have been RPT2BOS.DOC, but in Windows 95, filenames can now be up to 255 characters long and include spaces. So the RPT2BOS.DOC file in Windows 95 could be called "Quarterly Sales Report to My Management Detailing How I Increased Sales Ten-Fold Since Being Hired, So Now I Deserve a Promotion, a Raise, a Company Car, New Office Furniture, a Private Phone Line, a Pentium, and a Secretary. I Hope It Works." And the file below it could be called "The Company Is in Trouble Because of a Recommendation I Made Two Quarters Ago. I'm Going to Be Fired, I'll Lose My House, and I Can't Even Afford to Pay for My Windows 95 Disks."

What if Windows 95 falls between the cracks?

I wonder whether Windows 95 will be too different to please steadfast Windows 3.1 users, but not enough of a program to attract the Mac and OS/2 users.

Have you ever met someone who drove a Chevy, only to find that his or her entire family drove Chevy cars? Operating systems inspire much the same loyalty. In fact, some operating systems create an almost religious conviction, pro and con. I know someone who hates Apple so much that she won't even eat the real ones.

It's an aspect of human nature to resist change. Once you've devoted the time to learn a program or an operating system, you're hesitant to jump ship for something new. Microsoft is aware of this and is working on making the transition from Windows 3.1 to Windows 95 as easy as possible. I've heard different estimates concerning the total number of users who will upgrade, but not even Microsoft is expecting every Windows 3.1 user to switch to Windows 95 in the first year.

Will Macintosh and OS/2 users switch to Windows 95? Undoubtedly some will; some people change their religions, too. If they choose wrong, the former could seem like hell, and the latter may actually take them there. In any case, there's no arguing that Windows is the most successful platform of any operating system in use on this planet.

Breaking the 640K barrier

Please, please make my day and tell me, will I finally be rid of that awful 640K barrier with Windows 95?

Believe it or not, the 640K barrier was designed when 64K was a lot of memory for a computer. In fact, back then, mainframe computers didn't even have 64K of memory.

Versions of MS-DOS 5.0 and later went a long way to make the best use of memory. Because Windows 95 works without MS-DOS, you can kiss the 640K barrier good-bye with one big *if*; that is, *if* you don't run any DOS programs. MS-DOS programs running under Windows 95 still have to deal with that old 640K memory limit. Device drivers for older equipment, such as certain CD-ROM drives and sound cards, will have to be run in regular old DOS memory, too. There's no way around this because DOS programs expect things to be a certain way. So the lesson here, kids, is that we can adapt better than DOS. Chalk one up for the humans.

Windows 95 programs and Windows 3.1 programs won't have to worry about that nasty old barrier any more. In fact, Windows 95 can deal with more memory in a better way than Windows 3.1.

Will my resource cup runneth over?

I am so tired of running on empty when it comes to system resources in Windows 3.1. My programs never have enough resources and give me *insufficient memory* error messages. Will Windows 95 put a little more gas in the tank?

Windows 95 has a much bigger gas tank and gets better mileage than Windows 3.1. Windows 3.1 had two 64K "heaps" of memory (don't you just love these technical terms) for use by all programs running. Keep in mind that Windows 3.1 was designed to run on an 80286 computer. The 80286-based computer could only work with 16 bits of information at a time.

Because Windows 95 is designed for an 80386 computer (or above) that can work with 32 bits of information at a time, the "heap" size has been increased. This means that there is more room for the resources to stretch their legs.

Even while running Windows 3.1 programs under Windows 95, you should see the system resources decline at a slower rate than before. Of course, programs designed for Windows 95 will be better able to take advantage of this new design.

Please don't take my DOS away

I've always liked DOS. My friends call me Crazy Charlie. Will I still get my DOS prompt after exiting Windows 95?

Why do you still *want* to get to your DOS prompt?

Windows 95 is Windows without DOS. When Windows 95 starts up, you go right into it without stopping so DOS can catch its breath. When you close down Windows 95, you don't exit back to DOS.

If you really have a desire to find your old friend, the DOS prompt, you can go from Windows 95 to a DOS session, sort of like you can with Windows 3.1. In this DOS session, you can use important DOS application programs (like your favorite DOS-based game).

Can Windows 95 hook me up to the Internet?

I heard that connecting to the Internet is part of Windows 95. Is this true?

Everybody wants to get on the Internet. It's cool to be able to connect to a computer on the other side of the world with just the click of a mouse button.

Windows 95 comes with all the *plumbing* to connect to the Internet. Networks, even the Internet, have to have a way to let the computers talk to each other. In addition to supporting Novell and other networks, Windows 95 talks the language of the Internet: TCP/IP. Like most all the other components of Windows 95, the TCP/IP uses 32-bit technology for improved speed and reliability.

Most people will connect to the Internet with their modems. To do this, you need what's known as a *SLIP* (*Serial Line Interface Protocol*) or a *PPP* (*Point to Point Protocol*) connection. PPP is newer than SLIP and is the preferable one to have. Windows 95 has built-in support for PPP dial-in to an Internet access provider. If your company is connected to the Internet, Windows 95's TCP/IP lets you connect to the Internet just as easily as it lets you connect to an in-house network.

Having TCP/IP and PPP built into Windows 95 is great. It's like buying a car that has a cassette deck and a CD player: you don't have to worry about getting someone else to install them for you later. Of course, that new cassette deck and CD player don't do anything unless you put a tape or a CD into it. Likewise, having the capability to connect to the Internet isn't that exciting unless you have programs like a World Wide Web browser that enable you to read information from the Internet.

Because IBM's answer to Windows, OS/2 Warp, includes all programs to let you read and transfer information and send electronic mail through the Internet, it's probably a good guess that Windows 95 will have similar programs when it's available. Windows 95 also supports a wide variety of public domain, shareware, and commercial programs written to a standard for communicating with the Internet.

What will Windows 95 do for mobile computing?

I just hit the air with my computer. How does Windows 95 make "mobile computing" easier?

Did you ever go to Disneyland and go on the ride where they play the song "It's a Small World after All" as you cruise through miniature towns from all over the world. You can't get that song out of your head for weeks.

Well, it is a small world. And it's getting smaller every day, thanks in part to computers and telephone lines. In fact, it's possible to *telecommute* to work a few days a week at some companies. Rather than drive to the office, some lucky workers can connect to their company's computer network by using their home computers and telephone lines. In Windows 95, this capability is called *Remote Access.*

Remote Access allows a computer to be hooked to a network even though it's just connected over a modem. Of course, the speed of the connection is limited by the modem you're using, but it's no different than having the computer connected to the network with a cable. (OK, there is one difference. When you're connected to a network with a cable, there's no chance that your son or daughter will pick up the phone to call his or her friends.)

Windows 95 even has dial-in security features on top of the regular network security features, so companies won't have to worry about hackers getting into their computer network. For even more security, Windows 95 will work with extra hardware security add-ons, or it can be set up to call back the person requesting access to the network at a specified number.

A couple of other features, such as briefcases and deferred printing, will make a mobile computer user's task easier.

Is Windows 95 accessible to the disabled?

I am physically challenged, and the computer has helped me tremendously. I'm fearful that Windows 95 will make computing more difficult for me. How, if at all, is Windows 95 handicapped accessible?

Computers can be great tools for helping people with disabilities become more productive. It's estimated that there are more than 30 million people in the U.S. alone who may have disabilities that limit their access to computers.

Windows 95 will improve on the accessibility features found in Windows 3.1:

➤ Parts of the visual display can be enlarged for easier viewing.

➤ The keyboard can emulate a mouse.

➤ The keyboard and mouse can be replaced by alternate input devices.

➤ The keyboard can be adjusted to compensate for difficulties in use.

➤ The keyboard can be set up for single-handed, single-finger, or mouth stick use.

➤ Hints come on-screen when errors are being made.

➤ Color settings improve visibility.

➤ Sound prompts help users with limited vision.

These features will be controlled through a special accessibility icon in the Control Panel.

Will my applications run faster?

With all the new features Windows 95 promises, can I expect to take a performance hit? What I mean is, will my current applications perform as well on Windows 95 as they do on Windows 3.1 today?

Here's the scoop. Windows 3.1 was designed to run on an 80286-based computer. OK, maybe *run* is the wrong word: if you've ever tried this, you'd call it something like walking or crawling instead.

I'd guess that there are very few copies of Windows 3.1 being used on an 80286 computer. The 80386 CPU has a lot more power than the lowly, old 80286. Windows 95 is designed to take advantage of the extra power of the 386-based computer. The 386-based computer can handle 32-bit computations; the 286-based computer could only handle 16-bit computations. Of course, the 80486- and Pentium-based computers can handle 32-bit computations just like the 80386-based computers, and they can do it a lot faster.

If you're like millions of people who have a 386-based computer with 4MB of memory, you wouldn't want to upgrade to Windows 95 if your computer would slow down. Microsoft has designed Windows 95 so that your Windows 3.1 programs will work just as fast, if not faster, with it.

Another thing that Windows 95 has going for it is that it uses memory much better. With Windows 3.1, the biggest performance increase you can experience is to upgrade from 4MB to 8MB of RAM. You continue to get better performance with more than 8MB of memory, but you don't see that dramatic performance increase you see when going from 4MB to 8MB. Windows 95's performance increases at a steady rate as more memory is added.

Windows 95 is a great step forward in computing, but it's not a magic cookie. If you're running Windows 3.1 programs that need more than 4MB of memory to work well now, you can't just put in Windows 95 and expect the program to run like it had 8MB of memory. It just doesn't work like that, folks.

Appendix A
Who Ya Gonna Call?

This appendix contains the telephone numbers (and, in many cases, the BBS numbers) of almost every software and hardware manufacturer you'll ever need. As of the writing of this book, these numbers are accurate, but nothing lasts forever. Remember: If the number doesn't start with 800, it's your dime.

#

3Com	Information	800-876-3266
3Com	BBS	408-980-8204
#9	Information	800-438-6463

A

Access	Information	800-800-4880
Access	BBS	801-364-7449
Acer Technologies Corp.	Information	800-637-7000
Acer Technologies Corp.	BBS	800-833-8241
Actix Systems	Information	800-927-5557
Adaptec	Information	800-959-7274
Adaptec	Technical Support	408-945-2550

Adaptec	BBS	408-945-7727
Adobe Systems	Mac Information	800-447-3577
Adobe Systems	Mac Technical Support	408-986-6500
Adobe Systems	Mac BBS	408-562-6839
Adobe Systems	PC Information	800-447-3577
Adobe Systems	PC Technical Support	408-986-6530
Adobe Systems	PC BBS	408-562-6839
Ahead Systems	Information	510-623-0900
Alpha Software Corp.	Information	800-451-1018
Altima	Information	800-356-9990
Altos Computer Systems	Information	800-258-6787
Always Technology	Information	818-597-1400
Always Technology	Technical Support	818-597-9595
Always Technology	BBS	818-597-0275
Amdek	Information	800-800-9973
Amdek	BBS	408-922-4400
Appian	Information	408-730-5400
Appian	Technical Support	800-422-7369
Apple Computer	Information	800-767-2775
Apple Computer	Technical Support	800-776-2333
APUG (PC User Groups)	Information	602-222-8511
APUG (PC User Groups)	BBS	408-439-9367
Archive Corp.	Information	714-641-0279
Artisoft	Information	800-846-9726
Artisoft	Technical Support	602-670-7000
Artisoft	BBS	602-884-8648
Ashton-Tate	Information	408-431-1000
AST Research	Information	800-876-4278
AST Research	Technical Support	800-727-1278
AST Research	BBS (>9600)	714-727-4132

Atari	Information	800-443-8020
AT&T	Information	800-222-7278
AT&T	BBS	908-769-6397
ATI Technologies	Information	800-955-5284
ATI Technologies	Technical Support	213-823-1129
ATI Technologies	BBS	416-764-9404
Award (BIOS)	Information/Technical Support	408-370-7979
Award (BIOS)	BBS	408-371-3139

B

Berkeley Systems Design	Information	800-877-5535
Berkeley Systems Design	Technical Support	510-540-5535
BoCA Research	Information	407-997-6227
BoCA Research	BBS	407-241-1601
Borland	Information	800-331-0877
Borland	Technical Support	408-461-9155
Borland	BBS	408-439-9096
Broderbund	Information	800-521-6263
Broderbund	Technical Support	415-382-4700
Broderbund	BBS	415-883-5889
Brother	Information	908-356-8880
BusLogic	Information	408-492-9090

C

Cabletron Systems	Technical Support	603-332-9400
CalComp	Information	800-225-2667
CalComp	Technical Support	800-541-7877
CalComp	BBS	714-236-3045

Canon	Technical Support	800-423-2366
Cardinal	Information	717-293-3049
Cardinal	BBS	717-293-3074
Cardinal	BBS (14.4 baud)	717-293-3124
Central Point Software	Information	800-445-4208
Central Point Software	Technical Support	503-690-8080
Central Point Software	BBS	503-690-6650
Centrum	Information	800-875-8912
Chicony	Technical Support	714-380-0928
Ciprico	Information	800-727-4669
Cirrus	Information	800-424-7787
Cirrus	BBS	408-943-4179
Citrix	Information	800-437-7503
Claris Corp.	Information	800-325-2747
Claris Corp.	Technical Support	408-727-9054
Claris Corp.	BBS	408-987-7421
CMS Enhancement Inc.	Technical Support	714-222-6000
Colorado Memory System	Information	800-346-9881
Colorado Memory System	Technical Support	303-635-1501
Colorado Memory System	BBS	303-635-0650
Commodore Business Machines	Technical Support	610-666-7950
Compaq	Technical Support	800-345-1518
Compaq	BBS	713-378-1418
Compton's New Media	Technical Support	619-929-2626
Compton's New Media	BBS	619-929-2597
CompuAdd	Information	800-925-3000
CompuAdd	Technical Support	800-925-0995
CompUSA	Information	800-266-7872
CompuServe Information Service	Information	800-848-8199

Computer Associates	Information	800-531-5236
Computer Associates	Technical Support	408-432-1764
Computer Peripherals Inc.	Information	800-854-7600
Computer Peripherals Inc.	Technical Support	714-454-2441
Computer Peripherals Inc.	BBS	805-499-9646
Computone Corp.	Information	800-241-3946
Computone Corp.	Technical Support	404-475-2725
Computone Corp.	BBS	404-343-9737
Connectix Corp.	Technical Support	800-950-5880
Conner International	BBS	408-456-4415
Conner Peripherals	Information	800-851-4200
Conner Peripherals	Technical Support	408-456-3388
Conner Peripherals	BBS	407-263-3502
Conner Peripherals	Fax Back	408-456-4903
Control Data Corp. (CDC)	Information	612-853-8100
Core International	Technical Support	407-997-6044
Core International	Technical Support	407-997-6033
Core International	BBS	407-241-2929
Corel	Information	800-772-6735
Corel	Technical Support	613-728-1990
Corel	BBS	613-728-4752
Cornerstone Technology	Information	800-562-2552
Cornerstone Technology	Technical Support	408-435-8900
Cornerstone Technology	BBS	408-435-8943
Creative Labs	Information	800-998-5227
Creative Labs	BBS	405-742-6660
Crosstalk Communications	Information	404-442-4000
Crosstalk Communications	BBS	404-740-8428
CTX International	Technical Support	800-282-2205

CTX International	BBS	909-594-8973
CYRIX	Information	800-462-9749
CYRIX	Technical Support	800-462-9749
CYRIX	BBS	214-680-3187

D

Data Technology Corp.	Technical Support	408-942-4000
Data Technology Corp.	BBS	408-942-4010
Datapoint	Technical Support	512-593-7000
Davidson	Information	800-545-7677
Davidson	Technical Support	310-793-0600
Dell Computer	Information	800-624-9896
Dell Computer	BBS	512-728-8528
DeLorme Mapping	Information	207-865-1234
Delrina Technology	Information	800-268-6082
Delrina Technology	Technical Support	800-268-6082
Describe	Information	800-448-1586
Describe	Technical Support	916-646-1111
Diamond	Technical Support	408-736-2000
Diamond	BBS	408-524-9301
Digiboard Inc.	Information	800-344-4273
Digiboard Inc.	Technical Support	612-943-9020
Digiboard Inc.	BBS	612-943-0812
Digital Research	Information	800-848-1498
Digital Research	BBS	408-429-7785
Distr. Process Technology	Technical Support	407-830-5522
Distr. Process Technology	BBS	407-831-6432
DTK Computer	Technical Support	818-810-8880
DTK Computer	BBS	818-333-6548

E

Eastman Kodak	Information	716-724-4000
Electronic Arts	Information	800-448-8822
Electronic Arts	Technical Support	415-572-2787
Emerald Systems	Information	800-767-2587
Emerald Systems	Technical Support	800-366-4349
Emerald Systems	BBS	619-673-4617
Epson	Information	800-289-3776
Epson	Technical Support	800-922-8911
Epson	BBS	310-782-4531
Everex Systems	Information	800-821-0806
Everex Systems	Technical Support	510-498-4411
Everex Systems	BBS	510-226-9694
Expert Software	Information	305-567-9990

F

Fifth Generation Systems	Information	800-766-7283
Fifth Generation Systems	Technical Support	800-873-4384
Fifth Generation Systems	BBS	504-295-3344
Fujitsu America	Technical Support	800-626-4686
Fujitsu America	BBS	408-944-9899
Future Domain	Information	714-253-0400
Future Domain	Technical Support	714-253-0440

G

Gateway 2000	Information	800-846-2000
Gateway 2000	BBS	605-232-2109
Gazelle Systems	Information	800-786-3278

Gazelle Systems	Technical Support	801-377-1289
Gazelle Systems	BBS	801-375-2548
Genoa	Technical Support	408-432-9090
Genoa	BBS	408-943-1231
Genovation	Information	714-833-3355
GeoWorks	Information	510-814-1660
GeoWorks	Technical Support	510-644-0883
GeoWorks	BBS	510-814-4262
Gibson Research	Information	800-736-0637
Gibson Research	Technical Support	714-362-8800
Gibson Research	BBS	714-362-8848
Goldstar	Technical Support	800-777-1192
Great Bear Technology	Information	510-631-1600
Grolier	Technical Support	800-356-5590
GT Interactive	Information	212-679-6850

H

HardDrives Intl.	Information	800-927-7848
Hayes	Technical Support	404-441-1617
Hayes On-Line	BBS	800-874-2937
Hercules Computer Tech	Information	800-532-0600
Hercules Computer Tech	Technical Support	510-623-6050
Hercules Computer Tech	BBS	510-623-7449
Hewlett-Packard Co.	Worldwide	415-968-5600
Hewlett-Packard Co.	Technical Support	800-544-9976
Hewlett-Packard Co.	BBS	208-344-1691
Hitachi	Information	800-448-2244
Hitachi	Technical Support	800-323-9712
Houston Instruments	Technical Support	800-444-3425

| Hyundai Electronics | Technical Support | 800-289-4986 |
| Hyundai Electronics | BBS | 800-955-5432 |

I

IBM	BBS NSC	919-517-0001
IBM	BBS (Canada)	905-316-4244
IBM	Customer Relations	201-930-3443
IBM	Educational Dept.	800-222-7257
IBM	Parts Order	303-924-4100
IBM	Personal Systems Help	800-772-2227
IBM	Product Info.	800-426-7699
IBM	Software Support/Serices	800-336-5430
IBM	Software Support	800-237-5511
IBM	Technical Support	800-426-7282
IBM	Technical Manuals	800-426-7282
Intel	Information	800-538-3373
Intel	Technical Support	503-629-7000
Intel	BBS	503-645-6275
Intel	Fax Back	800-525-3019
Interplay Productions	Information	800-969-4263
Interplay Productions	Technical Support	714-553-6678
Interplay Productions	BBS	714-252-2822
Intuit	Information	800-624-8742
Intuit	Technical Support	415-858-6010
Iomega	Technical Support	800-456-5522
Iomega	BBS	801-778-4400
Irwin	Technical Support	800-421-1879
Irwin	BBS	313-930-9380

K

Kensington Microware	Information	800-535-4242
Knowledge Adventure	Information	800-542-4240
Knowledge Adventure	Technical Support	818-542-4200
Knowledge Adventure	BBS	818-248-0166
Kodiak Technology	Information	510-226-7840
Kodiak Technology	BBS	510-659-0857
Kurta	Information	800-445-8782
Kurta	Technical Support	602-276-5533
Kurta	BBS	602-243-9440
Kyocera Unison Inc.	Information	908-560-3400
Kyocera Electronics Inc.	Information	619-576-2669

L

LAN (magazine)	Information	415-905-2200
Leading Edge	Customer Service	800-874-3340
Leading Edge	Technical Support	800-225-2283
Leading Edge	BBS	508-836-3971
Learning Company	Information	800-852-2255
Living Books	Information	800-776-4724
Logitech	Information	800-231-7717
Logitech	Technical Support	510-795-8100
Logitech	BBS	510-795-0408
Lotus	Information	800-345-1043
Lotus	Technical Support	404-399-5505
Lotus	BBS	617-693-7001
Lotus Word Processing	Information	800-831-9679
LucasArts	Information	415-721-3300
LucasArts	BBS	415-257-3070

M

Mace, Paul Software	Information	503-488-2322
Mace, Paul Software	BBS	503-482-7435
Macronix	Technical Support	408-453-8088
Magnavox	Information	615-521-4316
Magnavox	Technical Support	900-555-5500
Magnavox	BBS	310-532-6436
Maxis Software	Information	800-366-2947
Maxis Software	Technical Support	510-253-3755
Maxis Software	BBS	510-254-3869
Maxtor/Miniscribe	Information	303-651-6000
Maxtor/Miniscribe	Technical Support	800-356-5333
Maxtor/Miniscribe	BBS	303-678-2222
Maxtor/Miniscribe	Fax Back	303-678-2618
Maynard Electronics	Information	800-821-8782
Maynard Electronics	BBS	407-263-3502
McAfee Assoc.	Information	408-988-3832
McAfee Assoc.	BBS	408-988-5138
MECC	Information	800-685-6322
MECC	Technical Support	612-569-1678
Media Vision	Information	800-845-5870
Media Vision	Technical Support	800-638-2807
Media Vision	BBS	510-770-0968
Megahertz Corp.	Technical Support	800-527-8677
Metheus	Information	800-638-4387
Micro Help	BBS	404-516-1497
Micronet	Information	714-739-2244
Micronet	Information	714-453-6100
Micropolis Corp.	Information	818-709-3388

Micropolis Corp.	Technical Support	818-709-3325
Micropolis Corp.	BBS	818-709-3310
Micropose	Information	800-879-7529
Micropose	BBS	410-785-1841

Direct support for Microsoft products

Microsoft	Basic PDS	206-635-7053
Microsoft	C Compiler	206-635-7007
Microsoft	DOS 5	206-646-5104
Microsoft	Excel for Macintosh	206-635-7080
Microsoft	Excel for Windows & OS/2	206-635-7070
Microsoft	FORTRAN Compiler	206-635-7015
Microsoft	Macro Assembler	206-646-5109
Microsoft	Money for Windows	206-635-7131
Microsoft	PowerPoint for Windows & Mac	206-635-7145
Microsoft	Profiler	206-635-7015
Microsoft	Project for Windows & Mac	206-635-7155
Microsoft	Project for MS-DOS	206-635-7155
Microsoft	Publisher for Windows	206-635-7140
Microsoft	Quick Assembler	206-635-7010
Microsoft	QuickC Compiler	206-635-7010
Microsoft	Test Tools for Windows	206-635-7052
Microsoft	Visual Basic Start-up	206-646-5105
Microsoft	Word for Macintosh	206-635-7200
Microsoft	Word for MS-DOS	206-635-7210
Microsoft	Works for Macintosh	206-635-7160
Microsoft	Works for MS-DOS	206-635-7150

| Microsoft | Works for Windows | 206-635-7130 |
| Microsoft | All other products | 206-454-2030 |

Microsoft start-up and installation support

Microsoft MS-DOS 5.0 (first 90 days only)	206-646-5104
Microsoft QuickBASIC Start-up	206-646-5101
Microsoft Visual Basic Start-up	206-646-5105
Microsoft Windows Entertainment Pack	206-637-9308
Microsoft Windows Software Development Kit (SDK)	206-635-3329

Fast tips services

Microsoft Excel for Macintosh	206-635-7080
Microsoft Excel for Windows	206-635-7070
Microsoft MS-DOS 5.0	206-646-5104

Mindscape	Information	800-221-9884
Mitsubishi Inc.	Information	800-843-2515
Mitsubishi Inc.	Technical Support	800-344-6352
Mitsubishi Inc.	BBS	714-236-6286
Mitsumi	Information	214-550-7300
Mitsumi	Technical Support	408-970-9699
Monotype Typography	Technical Support	800-666-6897
Mountain Computer Inc.	Information	800-458-0300
Mountain Computer Inc.	Technical Support	408-438-7897
Mountain Computer Inc.	BBS	408-438-2665
Mouse Systems	Technical Support	510-656-1117
Mouse Systems	BBS	510-683-0617
Mylex	Information	800-776-9539
Mylex	Technical Support	510-796-6100
Mylex	BBS	510-793-3491

821

N

National Design	Information	800-253-8831
National Semiconductor	Information	408-721-5000
National Semiconductor	Technical Support	404-564-5699
National Semiconductor	BBS	408-245-0671
NCR	Technical Support	800-531-2222
NEC	Technical Support	800-388-8888
NEC	Fax Back	800-366-0467
NEC	BBS	508-635-4706
Nolo Press	Technical Support	800-992-6656
Novell	Information	800-638-9273
Novell	Technical Support	800-453-1267

O

Okidata	Information	800-654-3282
Okidata	Technical Support	609-273-0300
Okidata	BBS	609-234-5344
Olivetti	Information	408-996-3867
Olivetti Office USA	Information	201-526-8200
Ontrack Computer Systems	Sales	800-752-1333
Ontrack Computer Systems	Technical Support	612-937-2121
Ontrack Computer Systems	BBS	612-937-0860
Orange Micro	Technical Support	714-779-2772
Orchid Technology	Sales	800-767-2443
Orchid Technology	Technical Support	510-683-0323
Orchid Technology	BBS	510-683-0555
Origin	Information	512-328-5490
Origin	Technical Support	512-328-0282
Origin	BBS	512-328-8402

P

Pacific Data	Information	619-552-0880
Pacific Data	Technical Support	619-587-4690
Pacific Data	BBS	619-452-6329
Packard Bell	Information	818-865-1555
Packard Bell	Technical Support	800-733-4433
Packard Bell	BBS	818-313-8601
Panasonic	Information	800-742-8086
Panasonic	Technical Support	800-222-0584
Panasonic	BBS	201-863-7845
Paradise	Information	714-932-5000
Paradise	Technical Support	800-832-4778
Paradise	BBS	714-753-1234
Paramount	Information	415-812-8200
PC Power and Cooling	Information	800-722-6555
PC Power and Cooling	Technical Support	619-931-6988
PCubid (CPU fans)	Information	619-793-1328
Phoenix (BIOS)	Technical Support	617-551-4000
Phoenix	BBS	714-453-8619
PKWare (PKZip)	Information	414-354-8699
Plus Development	Information	800-624-5545
Plus Development	Technical Support	900-740-4433
Plus Development	BBS	408-434-1664
Practical Peripherals	Information	800-442-4774
Practical Peripherals	Technical Support	805-496-7707
Practical Peripherals	BBS	805-496-4445
Priam Systems	Technical Support	408-441-4180
Priam Systems	BBS	408-434-1646
Prime Solutions	Information	619-274-5000
Prime Solutions	Technical Support	619-272-4000

Prime Solutions	BBS	619-272-9240
Proteon	Information	800-666-4400
Proteon	Technical Support	508-898-3100
Proteon	BBS	508-366-7827
Pure Data	Technical Support	800-661-8210
Pure Data	BBS	214-242-3225

Q

Quantum	Information	800-345-3377
Quantum	Technical Support	800-826-8022
Quantum	BBS	408-894-3214
Quark	Information	303-894-8888
Quark	Technical Support	303-894-8899
Quarterdeck	Information	800-354-3260
Quarterdeck	BBS	310-314-3227
Quarterdeck	Technical Support	310-392-9701

R

Rancho Technology	Technical Support	714-987-3966
RC Electronics	Information	800-882-3475
Ricoh Corp.	Information	800-955-3453
Ricoh Corp.	Technical Support	714-566-3584
Rodime Inc.	Information	800-227-4144

S

S3	Information	408-980-5400
Samsung Info. Syst.	Technical Support	800-446-0262
Samsung Info. Syst.	BBS	201-691-6238
Santa Cruz Operation	Information	408-425-7222

Santa Cruz Operation	Technical Support	800-347-4381
Seagate Technology	Information	800-468-3472
Seagate Technology	Technical Support	408-438-8222
Seagate Technology	BBS	408-438-8771
Seagate Technology	Fax Back	408-438-2620
Seventh Level	Information	214-437-4858
Sharp	Technical Support	800-237-4277
Shugart	Technical Support	714-770-1100
Sierra On-Line	Information	800-757-7707
Sierra On-Line	Technical Support	209-683-8989
Sierra On-Line	BBS	209-683-4463
Silicon Valley Computers	Information	415-967-1100
Silicon Valley Computers	BBS	415-967-8081
Simon & Schuster Software	Information	800-624-0023
Simon & Schuster Software	Technical Support	212-373-8500
Sirius	Information	800-247-0307
SMC BB	Information	800-762-4968
Softlogic Solutions	Information	603-627-9900
Softlogic Solutions	Technical Support	603-644-5555
Softlogic Solutions	BBS	603-644-5556
SofNet	Information	800-343-2948
SofNet	Technical Support	404-984-9958
SofNet	BBS	404-984-9926
Softkey Software Productions	Information	404-426-0008
Softkey Software Prductions	Technical Support	404-428-0008
Softkey International	Technical Support	800-323-8088
Sony	Information	800-342-5721
Sony	Technical Support	408-894-0555
Sony	BBS	408-955-5107
Specialix Inc.	Information	800-423-5364

Spectrum Holobyte	Technical Support	510-522-1164
Spectrum Holobyte	BBS	510-522-8909
SPSS	Information	800-543-2185
Stac Electronics	Information	800-522-7822
Stac Electronics	Technical Support	619-431-6712
Stac Electronics	BBS	619-431-5956
STB Systems	Information	800-234-4334
STB Systems	BBS	214-437-9615
Storage Dimensions	Information	800-765-7895
Storage Dimensions	Technical Support	408-894-1325
Storage Dimensions	BBS	408-944-1220
Summagraphics	Technical Support	800-729-7866
Symantec	Information	800-441-7234
Symantec	Technical Support	408-252-5700
Symantec	BBS	408-973-9598
Syquest	Technical Support	510-226-4000
Syquest	BBS	510-656-0473
Sysgen	Technical Support	800-821-2151
Sysgen	BBS	408-946-5032

T

Tandy Corp.	Information	817-390-3700
Tatung Co. of America	Information	800-829-2850
Tatung Co. of America	Technical Support	800-827-2850
Teac AmeriInformation Inc.	Technical Support	213-726-0303
Tech Data	Technical Support	800-237-8931
Telebit Corp.	Technical Support	800-835-3248
Telebit Corp.	BBS	408-745-3861
Telix Support	Information	919-460-4556
Telix Support	BBS	919-481-9399

Texas Instruments	Information	800-232-3200
Texas Instruments	BBS	512-250-6112
TOPS Support	BBS	508-887-5915
Toshiba	Information	800-457-7777
Toshiba America	Technical Support	800-999-4273
Toshiba America	BBS	714-837-4408
Trantor	Information	408-945-8600
Trantor	BBS	408-945-7727
Travelling Software	Information	800-662-2652
Travelling Software	Technical Support	206-483-8088
Travelling Software	BBS	206-485-1736
Trident	Technical Support	415-691-9211
Trident	BBS	415-691-1016
Tripplite	Information	312-329-1777
Tripplite	Technical Support	312-329-1602

U

Ultrastor	Information	714-581-4100
Ultrastor	BBS	510-623-9091
Unicore	Information	800-800-2467
Unicore	Technical Support	508-686-2204

V

Video Seven	Information	800-238-0101
Video Seven	Technical Support	800-248-1850
Video Seven	BBS	510-656-0503
Virgin	Information	714-833-8710
Virgin	Technical Support	714-833-1999
Virgin	BBS	714-833-3305

W

Walnut Creek (CD-ROM)	Information	800-786-9907
Walnut Creek	Technical Support	510-674-0783
Wangtek	Technical Support	800-992-9916
Wangtek	BBS	805-582-3620
Weitek Corp.	Information	408-738-8400
Weitek Corp.	Technical Support	408-735-9348
Weitek Corp.	BBS	408-522-7517
Western Digital	Information	800-832-4778
Western Digital	BBS	717-753-1068
WordPerfect Corp.	Information	800-451-5151
WordPerfect Corp.	BBS	801-225-4414
Wyse Technology	Information	800-438-9973
Wyse Technology	Technical Support	800-800-9973
Wyse Technology	BBS	408-922-4400

X

Xerox	Information	800-832-6979

Y

Y-E Data	Information	404-446-8655

Z

Zenith Data Systems	Information	800-553-0331
Zenith Data Systems	BBS	708-808-2264
Zeos International	Information	800-255-4101
Zyxel Communications	BBS	714-693-0762

Installing the CD-ROM

Q&A

Wow, I Get a CD-ROM, Too!

Yes, this entire fact-filled and fun book of questions, answers, puns, and one-liners is contained on a CD-ROM. (In case you didn't notice, IDG packaged the CD-ROM in the back cover.) And this CD-ROM will make your life very easy: you can search for keywords or phrases, such as *mouse*, *COM port*, and *modem*. When you do such a search, the answers containing the search word or phrase appear on-screen faster than you can say *Komando*.

But, wait, that's not all. You also get a free, one-month trial membership (including ten free hours) with America Online, the nation's fastest growing on-line service. America Online, by the way, is home to my company's Komputer Klinic, where you can leave me a computer question, download shareware, and learn about the latest software specials and upgrades. And I give away free software every week!

Enclosed with this book (check the packet that held the CD-ROM) is a certificate that lists a temporary America Online screen name and password. Of course, the temporary sign-on screen names are pretty horrible. I mean, who wants to be called *Rsw-22-wiif* their entire on-line life? Don't worry: once you have signed on to America Online, you can devise your own screen name and password.

Installing *1,001 Komputer Answers from Kim Komando*

It's easy to use the CD-ROM version of this book. But first, you need to tell your computer how to use it:

1. Start Windows 3.1.

2. Remove the CD from this book's back inside cover.

   Sharp objects and CD-ROMs don't play together nicely, so forego your inclination to use a knife or can opener to get at the CD-ROM. Doing so might damage the disc. Instead, use your thumbnail to grab hold of the little flap that covers the disc and then pull the flap up and off.

3. Place the CD-ROM into your computer's CD-ROM drive.

4. From Windows Program Manager, select File⇨Run. In the Run dialog box, type the following and click OK:

   ```
   D:\INSTALL
   ```

   where D: represents the drive letter of your CD-ROM drive.

Follow the instructions on-screen and soon you'll have a Komando program group in your Windows desktop.

When you want to use the *1,001 Komputer Answers from Kim Komando* CD-ROM, place the CD-ROM in your computer's CD-ROM drive and double-click the Komando icon. In a few moments, every question and answer from the book will be a point and click away.

There are several ways to find the information contained on the CD-ROM. The Search box comes up immediately after you start the program. In this box, type the word or phrase you want to know about, then click Search. The Results box will give you a list of all places where your topic was found. Select the specific item that you want to read, then click Go To. When you arrive at your question and answer, you can minimize the Results box by pressing the down arrow in the upper-right corner of the box. In addition, across the top of the screen and underneath the menu bar is a toolbar with several buttons.

Komando Klues

When you are typing search phrases, you can use search operators such as *and*, *or*, *not*, *thru*, and *near* to further narrow your searches.

Installing America Online Software

On the CD-ROM that comes with this book is an America Online membership kit, good for a free one-month membership and ten free hours of usage time. To sign on to America Online for Windows, you need:

> ➤ A working, standard telephone line

> ➤ A Hayes or Hayes-compatible modem — America Online supports 1200, 2400, 9600, and (in most cities) 14.4 baud access

> ➤ Your registration certificate (it's in the pocket in the back cover where you found the CD-ROM), which contains your temporary screen name and password

> ➤ Windows 3.1

> ➤ A PC capable of running Windows 3.1 (in other words, you need at least a 386 with 4MB of RAM, a VGA monitor, and a mouse)

Becoming a member of America Online

1. Start Windows 3.1. Make sure all other applications are closed.

2. Remove the CD from this book's back inside cover.

   Sharp objects and CD-ROMs don't play together nicely, so forego your inclination to use a knife or can opener to get the CD-ROM out of the packet. Doing so might damage the disc. Instead, use your thumbnail to grab hold of the little flap that covers the disc and pull the flap up and then off.

3. Place the CD-ROM into your computer's CD-ROM drive.

4. From Windows Program Manager, select File⇨Run. In the Run dialog box, type the following and click OK:

   ```
   D:\SETUP
   ```

   where D: represents the drive letter of your CD-ROM drive.

When the installation is complete, click on the America Online icon. Then follow the on-screen instructions, which include a one-time registration process. You'll be asked to choose a screen name and password to use during future sessions on the service. You'll also be asked to enter your billing information, which will be used when your free trial membership ends.

When you see the Welcome window, your registration is complete, and you are on-line. Have fun. Oh, and be sure to drop me an e-mail note announcing your arrival; my e-mail screen name is KOMANDO.

International readers

To set up an account, readers outside the U.S. should call America Online customer service at 404-859-7700. International readers can "use" an address in the U.S., which they access via an international connection.

Future sign-ons

To sign on to America Online for Windows after your first session, double-click on the America Online icon. Type in your password when you reach the Sign-On window and then press Enter (or click the Sign-On button).

Keywords

Keywords are shortcuts that move you quickly between America Online areas. You can access keywords in any one of three ways:

➤ Select Go To⇨Keyword.

➤ Press Ctrl+K.

➤ Click on the Keyword icon on the toolbar.

After you access the keyword screen, simply type in a keyword and press Enter. Here are some keywords to help you get started:

Location	Keyword
Kim Komando's Komputer Klinic	KOMANDO
AOL overview	DISCOVER
Members' on-line support	SUPPORT
Directory of services	DIRECTORYOFSERVICES
Time magazine on-line	TIME
Omni magazine on-line	OMNI
Microsoft knowledge base	MICROSOFT
Search software libraries	FILESEARCH
News and finances	NEWS
Stock quotes/portfolio	STOCKS
Compton's encyclopedia	ENCYCLOPEDIA
People connection	PEOPLECONNECTION
Games and entertainment	ENTERTAINMENT
Travel and shopping	TRAVEL

For a complete list of keywords on America Online, select Go
To⇨Keyword and click on the Keyword List button.

Your trial membership offer

Your trial membership begins the day you first sign on to America Online;
it expires after 30 days. During this 30-day trial period, your membership
gives you

> ➤ Free sign-up
> ➤ Free first month's membership
> ➤ Ten free hours of connect time (these hours must be used within
>   30 days of your first sign-on)

After your trial time has ended, you don't need to do anything else to
become a member; you will be charged a monthly membership fee after
the first month ends.

When you go through the registration process, you select a billing option.
For example, you may ask America Online to automatically charge your
VISA, MasterCard, Discover Card, or American Express card. Or you may
have your charges deducted from your checking account. Checking
account customers are charged $2 per month to cover processing fees.

For information regarding how to cancel your membership, select Go
To⇨Keyword and type **Cancel** or call our toll-free number (800-827-
6364). You must cancel within 30 days of your initial connection to avoid
being charged your first monthly fee. Your membership will continue on a
month-to-month basis until you cancel.

Terms of Service

Your use of the America Online software constitutes your acceptance of
the America Online Terms of Service. The Terms of Service are available
on-line in the free Members' Online Support department. Please read them
to get important information and conditions of your membership. America
Online, Inc., reserves the right to change the Terms of Service, membership fees, and on-line charges at any time after giving notice to members.

Note: Use of America Online requires a major credit card or checking
account. Users outside the 48 contiguous United States pay a 20-cent-per-
minute surcharge at all times, including trial time. Additional phone
charges may apply. Limit, one free trial per household.

Index

Index

837

Index

839

Index

841

Index

Index

845

Index

847

Index

IDG BOOKS WORLDWIDE LICENSE AGREEMENT

4. Limited Warranty. IDG Warrants that the Software and disk(s) are free from defects in materials and workmanship for a period of sixty (60) days from the date of purchase of this Book. If IDG receives notification within the warranty period of defects in material or workmanship, IDG will replace the defective disk(s). IDG's entire liability and your exclusive remedy shall be limited to replacement of the Software, which is returned to IDG with a copy of your receipt. This Limited Warranty is void if failure of the Software has resulted from accident, abuse, or misapplication. Any replacement Software will be warranted for the remainder of the original warranty period or thirty (30) days, whichever is longer.

5. No Other Warranties. To the maximum extent permitted by applicable law, IDG and the author disclaim all other warranties, express or implied, including but not limited to implied warranties of merchantability and fitness for a particular purpose, with respect to the Software, the programs, the source code contained therein and/or the techniques described in this Book. This limited warranty gives you specific legal rights. You may have others which vary from state/jurisdiction to state/jurisdiction.

6. No Liability For Consequential Damages. To the extent permitted by applicable law, in no event shall IDG or the author be liable for any damages whatsoever (including without limitation, damages for loss of business profits, business interruption, loss of business information, or any other pecuniary loss) arising out of the use of or inability to use the Book or the Software, even if IDG has been advised of the possibility of such damages. Because some states/jurisdictions do not allow the exclusion or limitation of liability for consequential or incidental damages, the above limitation may not apply to you.

IDG BOOKS WORLDWIDE REGISTRATION CARD

RETURN THIS REGISTRATION CARD FOR FREE CATALOG

Title of this book: 1,001 Komputer Answers from Kim Komando

My overall rating of this book: ❑ Very good [1] ❑ Good [2] ❑ Satisfactory [3] ❑ Fair [4] ❑ Poor [5]

How I first heard about this book:

❑ Found in bookstore; name: [6] _____

❑ Book review: [7] _____

❑ Advertisement: [8] _____

❑ Catalog: [9] _____

❑ Word of mouth; heard about book from friend, co-worker, etc.: [10]

❑ Other: [11] _____

What I liked most about this book:

_____
_____
_____

What I would change, add, delete, etc., in future editions of this book:

_____
_____
_____

Other comments:

_____
_____

Number of computer books I purchase in a year: ❑ 1 [12] ❑ 2-5 [13] ❑ 6-10 [14] ❑ More than 10 [15]

I would characterize my computer skills as: ❑ Beginner [16] ❑ Intermediate [17] ❑ Advanced [18] ❑ Professional [19]

I use ❑ DOS [20] ❑ Windows [21] ❑ OS/2 [22] ❑ Unix [23] ❑ Macintosh [24] ❑ Other: [25] _____
(please specify)

I would be interested in new books on the following subjects:
(please check all that apply, and use the spaces provided to identify specific software)

❑ Word processing: [26] _____

❑ Spreadsheets: [27] _____

❑ Data bases: [28] _____

❑ Desktop publishing: [29] _____

❑ File Utilities: [30] _____

❑ Money management: [31] _____

❑ Networking: [32] _____

❑ Programming languages: [33] _____

❑ Other: [34] _____

I use a PC at (please check all that apply): ❑ home [35] ❑ work [36] ❑ school [37] ❑ other: [38] _____

The disks I prefer to use are ❑ 5.25 [39] ❑ 3.5 [40] ❑ other: [41] _____

I have a CD ROM: ❑ yes [42] ❑ no [43]

I plan to buy or upgrade computer hardware this year: ❑ yes [44] ❑ no [45]

I plan to buy or upgrade computer software this year: ❑ yes [46] ❑ no [47]

Name: _____ Business title: [48] _____ Type of Business: [49] _____

Address (❑ home [50] ❑ work [51] /Company name: _____)

Street/Suite# _____

City [52] /State [53] /Zipcode [54]: _____ Country [55] _____

❑ **I liked this book!** You may quote me by name in future IDG Books Worldwide promotional materials.

My daytime phone number is _____

IDG BOOKS

THE WORLD OF
COMPUTER
KNOWLEDGE

❏ **YES!**

Please keep me informed about IDG's World of Computer Knowledge.
Send me the latest IDG Books catalog.